T0340161

**THE COLLECTED PAPERS OF
FRANCO MODIGLIANI**

VOLUME 5
Saving, Deficits, Inflation, and Financial Theory

THE COLLECTED PAPERS OF
FRANCO MODIGLIANI

Edited by Simon Johnson

The MIT Press
Cambridge, Massachusetts, and London, England

See pages 461–463 for acknowledgments to publishers.

Library of Congress Cataloging-in-Publication Data

(Revised for vols. 4 & 5)

Modigliani, Franco.
 The collected papers of Franco Modigliani.

 Vol. 4– edited by Simon Johnson.
 Includes bibliographical references and indexes.
 Contents: v. 1. Essays in macroeconomics.—[etc.]—
 v. 4. Monetary theory and stabilization policies.—
 v. 5. Saving, deficits, inflation, and financial theory.
 1. Economics. I. Abel, Andrew B., 1952–
 II. Johnson, Simon. III. Title.
 HB171.M557   330   78-21041
 ISBN 978-0-262-13245-9 (v.5; hc.: alk. paper)—978-0-262-51933-5 (pb)

CONTENTS

Volume 5 Saving, Deficits, Inflation, and Financial Theory

Part III. Inflation: Causes and Real Effects

Part IV. Further Contributions to the Theory of Finance

INTRODUCTION

These two new volumes of collected papers, Volume 4 and Volume 5, assemble a selection of essays written mostly in the decade following the 1980 appearance of the first three volumes. They deal pretty much with the same broad areas that formed the core of the earlier collections—macroeconomic theory and policies—with principal focus on monetary theory, stabilization policies, and theory of corporate finance. The new volumes, however, pay far greater attention to phenomena that have moved to center stage in the past decade: inflation, fiscal and trade deficits, and the effectiveness of monetary controls. The papers are classified into six subjects, and within each subject they are arranged generally in chronological order, according to the date at which they were completed.

Volume 4 begins with contributions on the working of the monetary mechanism—that is, the mechanism through which the monetary authority, by controlling certain nominal variables, achieves (more or less) effective control over nominal income. The perceived view of this mechanism, whether embodied in the classical quantity theory of money or in the more recent Keynesian liquidity preference version, rested on the hypothesis of a predictable demand for the stock of money as traditionally conceived—to wit, the sum of all means of payments. The only difference is that in the Keynesian view, the predictable demand relationship depended not only on income but also on (nominal) interest rates, although this difference had important consequences, including a rather different paradigm to account for the stable demand relation. But both views concurred that income (and the price level) could only be controlled through the quantity of money.

These views, even the more refined Keynesian one, began to lose their appeal and relevance in the course of the 1970s. First, the relationship between income and traditional money (now called M1) has tended to become rather unstable. This phenomenon can be attributed to partly the turmoil produced by the oil cost push inflation interacting with financial regulation and partly financial innovations interacting with deregulation. Second, partly as a result of this development, the central banks of many countries have tended to replace or at least supplement M1 as the control variable with other aggregates, such as the sum of M1 and a variety of other close money substitutes, or with aggregates less directly associated with money and money substitutes, such as measures of total debt or credit.

These developments clearly called for reassessing the traditional views of the monetary mechanisms. The first three essays, the result of a close collaboration with Lucas Papademos, are devoted to this task. Specifically the essays aim at (1) demonstrating that the control of nominal income can be achieved in principle not only through M1 but also through any one of a wide variety of nominal aggregates of the monetary or credit type; (2) showing that the monetary mechanism corresponding to different aggregates is very different, calling for different paradigms; and (3) investigating which of the possible "intermediate" targets is the most effective in the sense of minimizing the possible deviations of realization from the final target.

The analysis is carried out through successive approximations. The first essay focuses on item 1, showing how nominal income can be controlled through bank credit, even though in this case M1 is entirely uncontrolled. This point is conveniently established relying on a stripped-down model with (short-run) rigid prices, no government debt, and a very simple financial structure in which all loans are made by banks. It is shown that a credit target works through a mechanism quite different from the traditional paradigms, namely, through the level of investment. From the point of view of comparative effectiveness, an interesting result (confirmed in later papers) is that credit is most efficacious under competitive markets, but becomes less effective in the presence of interest rate controls (reflecting regulation or collusion) and consequent credit rationing.

The second paper examines the effect of removing the simplifying assumptions of the first paper by taking into account a government sector and a richer financial structure, including equities as a source of corporate finance, and by allowing for varying degrees of price flexibility through an aggregate supply schedule. On the other hand we retain the assumption that all credit is supplied through bank intermediation. The analysis focuses on the effectiveness of an M1 target versus a broader aggregate or a credit target.

Among the main conclusions is that with price flexibility one must examine the effects not only of the traditional Keynesian "demand" shocks (to consumption, investment, and so on) but also of supply (or price) shocks. And similarly one needs to be concerned with the effectiveness of alternative instruments in stabilizing the *price level* versus stabilizing *output*. In the case of supply shocks, it turns out that if an instrument is more effective than another in stabilizing the price level, then it must necessarily be less effective in stabilizing output, and conversely no instrument can dominate another in both respects. It is shown that an M1 target tends to be more effective than an M2 target in containing the output effects of supply shock but consequently less effective in containing the price response. The difference can be traced to the demand for M1 being more interest elastic than that for M2.

In the case of demand shocks, by contrast, if an instrument dominates another in terms of reducing output variability, it will also dominate it in terms of reducing price variability.

The effectiveness of alternative intermediate targets with regard to demand shocks is examined most fully in the third paper, which differs from the second primarily by recognizing the possibility of ''disintermediation,'' that is, the practice of firms borrowing directly from the public (or a nonbank type of intermediary). The existence of substitutes for bank loans on the part of borrowers and for bank liabilities on the part of lenders would appear crucial, because one might conjecture that the effectiveness of bank credit targeting would become ineffective with the existence of close substitutes.

The main result of our analysis is that this conjecture is wrong. First, income can be controlled through an M2 or credit target even if for firms the substitution between bank and nonbank types of credit is perfect. Second, with respect to the traditional type of demand shocks, a bank credit target is most effective precisely when the substitution is perfect, although it remains superior to an M1 target even for smaller rates of substitution. It is inferior only in the presence of shifts between M2 and other assets. The reason is that perfect substitution between sources of borrowing for firms and of lending for households implies that spread between the return from lending to banks and direct lending must be a constant independent of the overall level of interest rates. This in turn ensures that demand for M2 (in contrast to that for M1) is independent of the overall level of interest rates. Thus if a demand disturbance occurs, say an upward shift in the investment schedule, interest rates will rise. If the control variable were M1, then the rise in interest rates, while containing aggregate demand, would also reduce the demand for M1, making it possible for income to depart from equilibrium. But if the target variable is M2, the demand for it is unaffected because the spread is unaffected by the rise in interest rates; hence in response to a demand disturbance, income cannot change and the interest rate must rise enough to just offset the impact of the disturbance. These seemingly paradoxical results may invite skepticism and a feeling that they must reflect some counterfactual assumption. This disbelief is promoted in our view by past experiences with large-scale disintermediation, making the control of bank assets, or liabilities, very ineffective. These experiences, however, have occurred in situations where the monetary authority was interfering with the competitive market process through interest rate ceilings and rationing. Under those conditions the demand for bank loans or liabilities will of course not be independent of the movement of market interest rates.

The last essay of Part I harks back to a theme that has been of great concern to me for a long time and was the subject of my presidential address to the American Economic Association; namely, the effectiveness of simple-minded rules versus discretion to stabilize the economy. (See "The Monetarist Controversy . . . " in Volume 1.) The events that have occurred since that paper (1976) have provided a rich source of new evidence that fully supports the propositions that "a private enterprise economy . . . needs to be stabilized, can be stabilized, and therefore should be stabilized" (p. 3).

The need for discretionary stabilization policies is confirmed by the wide swings in the M1 velocity of circulation since 1980. They imply that constant growth of money would have led to great instability of income.

The evidence that discretionary policies can successfully stabilize the economy is provided by the success of the Federal Reserve in the 1980s in maintaining a fairly steady path of income growth (except in 1982) consistent with a steady decline in inflation, despite the gyrations of velocity. This success was achieved by adjusting intermediate targets as seemed appropriate to track the final target—nominal income—even though that required a great variability in the annual growth rate of money—between 5 and 15 percent.

Monetarists have responded to the debacle of the policy they advocated by proposing some new rules that would mechanically adjust the constant growth for past changes in velocity. It is shown through simulations that these rules would have performed far more poorly than the "discretionary policy of the Fed."

Part II brings together a number of essays on economic stabilization. The first, coauthored with Lucas Papademos, is devoted to the most burning policy issue of the last two decades—how to bring to an end an inflationary spiral ignited by an exogenous disturbance, such as the oil shocks of 1973 and 1979. There is fairly general agreement that inflation can be reduced by enough economic slack. The paper endeavors to answer the following question: Given that both slack (unemployment) and inflation are socially costly, what is the optimum path of unemployment to return inflation to the long-run target, with a minimum social welfare cost? To this end we examine the nature of the trade-off between unemployment and inflation (the constraint) and propose a measure of the costs of unemployment and inflation in terms of a social welfare function. These constructs are used to derive the optimum unemployment path, which is shown to have characteristics akin to those implied a by so-called turnpike theorem: in response to an inflationary shock, unemployment should be promptly brought to an optimum level, largely independent of how large the slack is. It should then be kept close to that level—which essentially ensures the fastest decline of inflation per unit social cost—until inflation has been reduced to a level close to target, at which point unemployment can be returned to the long-run target.

These results are interesting in identifying basic characteristics of an optimal path—pointing, for example, to the suboptimality of raising unemployment to whatever level may be needed to bring inflation immediately back to target, or of maintaining a constant money growth. Unfortunately, from the point of view of policy applications, the usefulness of the results suffers from the sensitivity of the optimal path to alternative specifications and parameter estimates. Among other things there are reasons for doubting whether a Phillips curve, like the one we have used, has general validity outside the United States.

The next two papers represent elaborations and generalizations of my earlier contribution with Padoa-Schioppa ("The Management of an Open Economy with '100% Plus' Wage Indexation" in Volume 3). The first, written with an old collaborator, Jacques Drèze, deals with Belgium, which, like Italy, was characterized by a very high unemployment rate as well as capacity slack—a situation normally associated with overly restrictive aggregate demand policies. But as in the case of Italy, those demand policies were unavoidable to prevent a large deficit in the balance of payment, leading to depreciation of the exchange rate and inflation. We tried to measure how an increase in real wages would affect employment, allowing for its negative impact on net exports and the need to offset that effect by a decrease in imports through contractive domestic policy. We found that the short-run response is rather small (an elasticity of -0.2), which implies a substantial improvement in the income of workers as a whole, despite some losing their jobs. In the long run, however, firms reduce domestic production by scrapping (or transferring) their plant so that the response is very much larger—around -2—and total labor income is significantly reduced. The policy implication is that further increases in real wages must be avoided. To expand employment, because devaluation is not promising, given the widespread indexation of wages, we are led to the conclusion that the most promising course is work sharing, but at an essentially unchanged real hourly wage—though this solution is hardly to the liking of employed workers.

The next paper is a short comment of mostly historical interest. It was written early in the Reagan administration when a program of large fiscal incentives to investment and individual tax cuts was being pushed on the ground that it would greatly expand investment. In the comment I express serious reservations about the effectiveness of the program on the ground that what is required to expand investment is not just investment incentives but also an expansion of national saving. Now tax incentives to investment do not by and large lead to more saving—on the contrary they reduce national saving through a higher government deficit. Hence they lead to higher interest rates rather than more investment. Similarly cutting personal income taxes is not a promising way to increase individual saving. To be sure, it increases the net rate of return on assets. But the relevant effect on consumption is very uncertain because the tax reduction generates a substitution effect, making for postponing consumption, but also an income effect, making for more consumption and less national saving. Later experience confirmed these reservations: private saving did not rise, national saving declined sharply, (real) interest rates rose to unusual levels, and investment did not significantly increase. That interest rates did not rise higher and investment did not actually decline can be attributed to the conspicuous inflow of foreign capital attracted by the higher interest rates. But this inflow produced serious unfavorable effects through the deficit it generated in the trade balance.

The paper that follows, prepared in collaboration with Padoa-Schioppa and Rossi for a conference on unemployment, we assess the causes of the steady rise of unemployment in Italy since the beginning of the 1970s, which has culminated in a rate close to 12 percent in the most recent years. To that end a model is developed, and its parameters are estimated, and they are found on the whole to support the conclusions of the papers with Padoa-Schioppa and Drèze: excessive real wages in relation to productivity force on the policymakers an appropriately restrictive aggregate demand policy and high rate of unemployment to maintain equilibrium in the trade balance and hold out against mounting inflation. But we also find significant contribution to unemployment from wage-induced substitution of labor for capital and, for the more recent years, from the serious European stagnation. Thus substantial reabsorption of unemployment requires both wage restraint and an expansion of demand within the Common Market, resulting in an expansion of exports and making room for a substantial expansion of imports and employment.

European stagnation and how to end it is the subject of the next paper, issued by the Macroeconomic Policy Group of the Centre for European Policy Studies (CEPS), including Drèze, Giersch, and Layard, on the basis of a draft prepared by the two other members, myself and Mario Monti. The paper traces the extraordinary level of unemployment throughout the common market, caused partly by excessive real-wage growth during the 1970s and partly by the effect of inconsistent monetary and fiscal policy in Europe and in the United States. With current and prospective macro policies implying an annual growth of output of about 2½ percent, and given demographic and productivity trends, little reabsorption of unemployment can be anticipated in the foreseeable future. Accordingly more expansionary demand policies are required if the social scourge of unemployment—particularly youth unemployment—is to be cured. It is recognized that the problem cannot be solved by a massive dose of Keynesian-type demand policies because, despite the huge unemployment of labor, there is little excess capacity, and additions to capacity require time and savings. Accordingly the policy recommended is a moderate acceleration of demand—to around 5 percent—requiring an expansion of investment that could be financed from the rise in private and government savings resulting from the higher growth and from a reduced trade surplus. The expansion could not be undertaken by any one country acting alone, however, because of the large negative effect on its external balance, which could be avoided only by a simultaneous expansion.

The U.S. fiscal deficit and its foreign impact play an important role in the next paper, which assesses the effectiveness of Reagan's economic policies. The only important success of that policy is found to be the substantial reduction in the rate of inflation, but this reduction was not achieved painlessly, as promised, through the pursuit of monetarist and "supply" policies. The Federal Reserve was able to achieve a declining path for nominal GNP growth, but that involved a highly unstable growth of the money supply; the resulting disinflation was achieved not through supply side miracles but through the customary painful process of large and protracted unemployment, peaking at the highest level of the postwar period.

In the fiscal areas large tax cuts and a buildup of military expenditures were pushed through by the administration despite the evidence that the "Laffer curve" was not working and that other expenditures could not be cut significantly. The result was the largest peacetime fiscal deficits relative to GNP in U.S. history. These, together with the investment incentives (see page 2 of "Comment . . .," in Volume 4), resulted in high interest rates, currency appreciation, capital inflows, current account deficits, and rising indebtedness, thereby shifting the burden of the fiscal deficit on future generations. The large trade deficit in turn unleashed a vicious wave of protectionism, which the administration, to its credit, resisted firmly. Productivity growth was quite poor, and total output growth, though bolstered by a rapid expansion of the female labor force, was moderate in comparison with the postwar period, particularly the "Keynesian" Kennedy years. Real per capita disposable income performed somewhat better, but this was largely because of the reduction in taxes and the gains in terms of trade. But both sources of improvement may be expected to be transient and eventually reversed—the sooner the better.

The final paper draws on the analysis of all the preceding papers in this part to see which implications can be drawn on the nature of domestic and foreign constraints that are responsible for the extremely high rate of unemployment in Italy—the largest among the older industrialized countries and one of the largest in Europe—and on possible ways to relieve the problem. On the domestic side the major blame falls on the aggressive real-wage settlements imposed by the unions and enforced through extensive indexation and on the budget swing from a surplus position in the 1960s to a growing and large deficit during the 1970s and 1980s, reducing the availability of capital. On the international side stress is placed on the role of the U.S. fiscal deficit, leading to high world interest rates as an important cause of the European stagnation, which in turn is limiting Italy's ability to export. Many of these constraints have by now been relaxed or eliminated. It is suggested that the conditions are ripe for a concerted attack on unemployment. One constructive step would be a pause for real wages to help to increase Italy's competitiveness, until unemployment has returned to normal. The balance-of-payments constraint could be eased further by a concerted expansion of the other countries of the Common Market, ideally led by Germany, the country having the largest margin for such a maneuver.

Volume 5 brings together contributions to four different areas. Part I highlights my continuing interest in the life cycle hypothesis (LCH) as a useful framework to understand individual and national saving behavior. The first paper, written with Arlie Sterling, deals with an issue to which the life cycle hypothesis should provide a clear answer, namely, the effect of a compulsory public pension system, like Social Security, on private saving. The LCH would seem to imply that if participants pay a contribution in exchange for which they are guaranteed a retirement annuity, then they need to save less in personal accounts. Hence private saving should fall. But this conclusion has failed to receive clear empirical support. As was first shown by M. Feldstein and P. Munnell, a possible explanation for this failure is that in addition to the "substitution" effect, there is a "retirement effect," that is, making for more saving. This arises because Social Security tends to lengthen the duration of retirement (that in my earlier work had been assumed as given), and the life cycle model implies that a longer retirement gives rise to more saving.

We measure these two offsetting mechanisms, making use of a sample of countries that had rather different Social Security arrangements. The results of the analysis are rather interesting in that we find clear evidence, consistent with the LCH, that the private saving rate *declines* with the size of social pensions paid in relation to preretirement income, but tends to *rise* with the length of retirement. The results thus confirm the existence and importance of the two opposing effects of Social Security on saving. What is surprising is that these effects appear to very nearly offset each other. The result is that one can find no appreciable (simple) association between Social Security and saving. Yet the absence of association is seen not to be inconsistent with the life cycle hypothesis.

The second paper is the text of the Nobel Prize lecture given in Stockholm in 1985. It basically constitutes an update of "The Life Cycle Hypothesis of Saving Twenty Years Later" (in Volume 2) ten years later. It surveys the basic framework of the life cycle hypothesis—to wit, the Fisherian model of utility maximization over life—and how it leads to "life resources" (or

Friedman's "permanent income") as the major determinant of consumption. This construct in turn is shown to help in clarifying many puzzles in individual saving behavior. With respect to the aggregate private saving ratio, the most important implication is that saving depends on not income per capita (as once widely believed) but basically the rate of growth of income multiplied by the wealth-income ratio. Some of the factors that could affect that ratio are examined, in particular the possible role of bequests. Bequests imply that not all wealth is consumed within the life cycle as assumed in the elementary LCH. It is noted that the LCH framework can be generalized to include bequests without changing its aggregative implications other than to increase the wealth income ratio. That leads to the question of how large is the role of bequests compared with life cycle saving. Relying on the analysis developed in the immediately following paper, it is concluded that role is likely to be relatively modest.

That paper, the last of Part I, was prompted by a 1981 contribution of Kotlikoff and Summers, offering evidence that for the United States the life cycle (or the "hump" wealth) hypothesis might account for no more than one-fifth of total wealth, with the remaining four-fifths arising from bequests. This conclusion contrasts sharply with previous estimates suggesting a share of inherited wealth closer to one-fifth. The paper reviews the earlier investigations, based largely on survey data, and a number of more recent studies based on a variety of methods (estimating the flow of bequests from surveys of wealth and from probate statistics, as well as from time-series data). It finds that according to all of these empirical studies, the share of wealth received by bequests might be placed at 15 to 25 percent. The large difference between other estimates and those of Kotlikoff and Summers is traced in part to some errors by the authors but mostly to the use of definitions different from the customary ones. Relying on an alternative measure of importance, independent of definition, namely, the percentage change in wealth resulting from a 1-percent change in bequests, suggests a value of around 0.3. Even this number may appreciably overstate the importance of the bequest motive because some portion of bequests arises from a precautionary motive reflecting uncertainty about the length of life.

The six papers in Part II reflect the renewed interest in the economics of fiscal deficits arising from the widespread deficits of the 1970s and especially from the record ones under the Reagan administration. It was a subject with which I had dealt before as an application of the LCH (see "Long-run Implications of Alternative Fiscal Policies and the Burden of the National Debt" and "The Life Cycle Hypothesis of Saving, the Demand for Wealth and the Supply of Capital" in Volume 2).

The central paper in this section is the second, published in 1987, but actually written two years earlier. It first criticizes the widespread view that peacetime deficits are a cause of inflation—a view that has neither theoretical nor empirical support, except for the empirical association frequently observed between deficits and inflation. But this association is shown to be best accounted for by inverse causation, that is, inflation increasing deficits through the inflation-induced increase in interest rates and in government interest payments, but not the reverse. The other possible effect of a deficit is to shift the burden of current expenditure to future generations by crowding out private investment and thus reducing the stock of capital available to them. This view, which is shown to be consistent with LCH, has been the subject of repeated challenges (most lately by Barro) reviewed in the paper. A number of tests are presented using a variety of data for different countries and it is shown that they consistently support the hypothesis.

The first paper in Part II covers pretty much the same ground as the second paper, but in a somewhat abridged and more popularized version. The third paper, written jointly with Arlie Sterling, is a more extensive test of crowding out carried out for the United States in the postwar period. It is found that consumption is reduced by (permanent) taxes and not by government expenditure, which is consistent with crowding out and not with the Barro hypothesis.

The fifth paper, coauthored with Jappelli, is in the same spirit as the one preceding it, but is based on the experience of Italy, a country providing a valuable test case because of the large swings in fiscal deficits over the period of some 100 years for which the needed information can be pieced together. The results are quite similar to those for the United States in supporting the LCH in general and more specifically its implications with respect to the effect of alternative fiscal policies. In contrast to the United States, there is some evidence that consumption responds (negatively) not only to taxes but also to government expenditure; but the effect of expenditure is shown to be of an order of magnitude that is fully consistent with LCH and inconsistent with the hypothesis of no crowding out. The paper also attempts to throw light on the interesting question of whether consumption responds to the real interest payments by the government, as called for by informed rational behavior, or instead to the nominal payments. We cite rather convincing evidence that what matters is the real interest rate, which of course implies that in measuring the government deficit with regard to its effect on current and future aggregate demand, one should subtract from government outlays the real depreciation of the debt due to inflation.

The last paper develops another test of the crowding-out hypothesis based on the Italian experience, but this time relying on the relationship between the real interest rate and the deficit or the debt or both. When we control other variables affecting the interest rate (such as expectations of inflation, money supply, foreign interest rates and so forth) we find that the interest rate tends to increase very significantly with the size of the government *deficit*, which is what one would expect if, and only if, crowding out is important. There is instead very little evidence that the government *debt* has an effect on interest rates, which is consistent with a putty-clay investment function (see, for example, "On the Role of Expectations of Price and Technological Change in an Investment Function" in Volume 1).

The remaining paper, the fourth of this part, resulted from an urge to solve a seemingly fascinating puzzle. We know that President Kennedy was unable to secure passage of legislation to cut taxes to stimulate demand. This failure was attributed at the time to the fiscal conservatism of the American public, concerned with the deficit that would result from the tax cut. How then could it come to pass that less than twenty years later, President Reagan was successful in getting the country to accept a huge tax cut and to live with huge, persistent deficits? Had there been a sudden change in the public attitude toward deficits? Did it reflect the rise of the "now generation"? I was fortunate to elicit interest in the puzzle of my son, Andrea, a social psychologist with a standing interest in public opinion. The enjoyable and propitious collaboration produced what we believe is a solution to the puzzle. We found remarkably little change in basic public attitudes in the 1980s compared with the early 1960s. Indeed as far back as opinion polls are available, the public was overwhelmingly opposed to tax cuts that would result in a deficit; but we found that it was even more strongly opposed to increases in taxes to reduce an existing deficit. It favored instead a reduction in expenditure, although with wide disagreement as to what should be cut. The success of the administration in pushing through a tax cut despite these attitudes seems to be accounted for by its ability in persuading the public that the cut would *not* be a serious source of deficit because of its purported evasion-reducing and supply-stimulating effects predicted by the false prophets of the "Laffer curve." Eventually the monstrous deficit became apparent, but no effective action to eliminate it could be easily pieced together because of the traditional opposition to tax increases and irreconcilable disagreements within and between the public, Congress, and the administration as to what should be cut.

Part III brings together my main contributions to the economics of inflation—the hot subject of the last two decades. The opening paper was the result of a research project undertaken by a group of MIT faculty and graduate students, coordinated by myself and Donald Lessard out of concern with the devastating effects that inflation-swollen interest rates, together with interest ceilings, were having on the housing market, through both the supply and the demand for mortgage funds. The research was supported by HUD and the Federal Reserve Bank of Boston. We surveyed foreign experience and concluded that indexed loans (and possibly deposits) might provide a solution. But it was also apparent that in the U.S. this solution would run into insurmountable prejudices and opposition. We were able to come up with an alternative instrument which, like indexation, would ensure an annual payment rising at around the rate of inflation (and hence constant in real terms). This would eliminate the so-called front loading or tilt effect of inflation with conventional mortgages. Yet the contract woud be entirely stipulated in nominal terms; in particular the debtor would in each year be debited with interest on the outstanding balance at a nominal, reference, market rate plus service markup. Accordingly thrift institutions could have financed this type of mortgage by offering depositors the same reference rate.

We were all convinced that we had made a valuable practical contribution to a serious socioeconomic problem and were greatly disappointed that our solution was totally disregarded, at a time when the industry and the supervisory agencies were trying out an array of alternative solutions, all of them decidedly inferior to ours. To this date only a handful of institutions in the United States and abroad are using our approach and with success. To be sure, the problem itself has lost urgency with the worldwide abatement of inflation. At the same time our idea has found some application to the symmetrical and equally serious problem of pensions; that is, the annuitant is sometimes given the opportunity to opt for a stable life flow in real terms rather than in nominal terms, through an appropriate adjustment of the mechanism.

A popularized version of this paper, written in an effort to interest bankers and other institutions and potential borrowers in our MIT mortgage, is included as the last paper of this part.

The second paper, written midway between the first and second oil crises, contains a number of thoughts on the different causes of inflation, on whether a meaningful distinction can be made between demand pull and cost push, on the effects of alternative exchange regimes on inflation, on how inflation can be brought to an end, and so forth. More than ten years later, and a second oil crisis behind us, I still find these ideas pretty convincing as compared, for example, with the monetarist literature or with the notion then prevailing that inflation is caused primarily by government deficits even of moderate size. Some of these ideas have been developed more rigorously in later contributions (see, for example, "Optimal Demand Policies against Stagflation" in Volume 4 and the first two papers in Part II of Volume 5).

The next paper, the result of collaboration with my colleague and former student, Stanley Fischer, is an endeavor to understand the real effects and social costs of significant inflation. Public opinion tends to regard them as devastating, whereas the economic profession generally dismisses them as rather negligible. The dismissal rests on the broadly accepted view that money and the price level must be neutral in the long run, from which it is deduced that the change in money and prices must also be neutral. The only costs must come from the fact that inflation, by generating a negative real return on cash balances, leads to socially wasteful efforts to economize on cash holdings.

Our analysis uncovers many far more serious effects, even when the inflation is fully anticipated. They arise from the prevalence of nominal institutions—government taxation accounting practices, financial contracts such as mortgages and pensions, and by the failure of the public and government to understand that the cost could easily be relieved by appropriately modifying the institutions. Many further costly effects arise from unanticipated inflation. They include redistributional effects through existing nominal contracts, the effect of future uncertainty on the demand for assets and supply of liabilities, and on shortening financial contracts, which in turn influence real investment activity. Further consequences can be expected if in the presence of inflation the public and the government are unable to perform correct economic calculations, at least for a time. This possibility is illustrated in the two papers that follow with respect to the valuation of equities.

The first of these was prompted by a desire to clarify one of the many puzzles that arose in the decade of high inflation of the 1970s. Why had equities been progressively losing value (in real terms) in the course of the inflation, a phenomenon that was also observed at other times and in other countries? This valuation did not seem consistent with rational behavior given the behavior of profits (corrected for inflation) and real interest rates during the inflation. Our analysis instead pointed to the highly unorthodox conclusion that market behavior reflected two major inflation-induced errors committed by investors and portfolio managers: they fail to correct reported profits, depressed by the inflation-swollen interest rates, by subtracting from interest the real depreciation of the debt; and they tend to capitalize the equity earnings at a rate that reflects the nominal instead of the appropriate real rate. It is shown that this hypothesis is able to account for the widely observed inverse relation between inflation and market value and in particular for the behavior of share prices between 1953 and 1977. This hypothesis implied that as of 1977 the current market valuation could be put at 50 percent of the rational valuation. We also inferred from the model that the undervaluation would disappear when, and only when, high inflation and high interest rates disappeared. These inferences have turned out to be broadly consistent with the successive behavior of the market—the continuing weakness through 1982—the peak of interest rates—and the recovery through 1987 as nominal (but not necessarily real) rates declined.

In the next document, the text of a lecture given for the Industrial Liaison Program at MIT as a part of a symposium about the economy in the 1980s, I went further and suggested it was quite likely that if and when the fall in inflation would cause the market to recover toward rational valuation, the extra returns coming from the capital gains would tend to cause overshooting of the warranted level, pushing the market into a speculative boom and eventually collapse. This is pretty much the way I interpret the events surrounding October 1987.

The remaining paper, again coauthored with Cohn, summarizes in more popular language the earlier joint contribution, bringing it up to date, and adds the results of some tests based on a cross-section of individual stocks. These were designed to compare our undervaluation hypothesis against alternative hypotheses—in particular that the loss in value was due to an increase in risk premium or to a decline in profit expectations. It was found that the data strongly support our hypothesis, rejecting the other two.

The concluding Part IV brings together contributions to the area of finance, which continues to be one of my major interests.

The first paper, written jointly with one of my many outstanding former students, Robert Shiller, extends our earlier results on the structure of interest rates (compare "Inflation, Rational Expectations and the Term Structure of Interest Rates" in Volume 1), but this time focuses on the reasons for the yield spread between new issues and seasoned ones, an empirically significant phenomena. It is shown that the explanation lies in the favorable tax treatment of returns in the form of capital gains versus those in the form of coupon payment, which cause low coupon issues to sell at a premium. When interest rates rise, seasoned issues tend to have a coupon rate below the current market rate and therefore tend to sell at a premium. Thus their yield falls below the yield on new issues that firms are required (by the authority) to issue at par. A significant implication of this result is that in general the yield on new issues is better than the commonly used seasoned yield, as a measure of the long-term interest rates, especially when rates are unusually variable.

Since the publication of "Corporate Income Taxes and the Cost of Capital: A Correction" (in Volume 3), Merton Miller and I have become dissatisfied with the analysis and conclusions reached there and have pursued and proposed a more satisfactory answer. In both cases the revision was in part motivated by the recognition that what matters to the investor is the return net of all taxes, corporate as well as personal. Now interest, though receiving preferential tax treatment at the corporate level, is unfavorably taxed at the personal level, the more so the higher the recipient income. From these considerations and disregarding the role of portfolio diversification, Miller was led to conclude that leverage could in principle be worthless even in the presence of corporate taxes, and should actually be worthless under U.S. institutions (before the recent tax reform).

In the second paper in this section—my presidential address to the American Finance Association—I take issue with Miller and try to show that, taking into account optimal diversification, leverage must be valuable. In recognition of the fact (previously ignored in our analysis) that the tax savings are uncertain, however, I conclude that the gain from leverage per dollar of debt, although surely positive, is much lower than the corporate tax rate, as asserted in the original correction paper (in Volume 3). It is further shown that inflation, by increasing the tax advantage of debt, should tend to raise the relative value of levered firms and of incremental leverage. This latter conclusion unfortunately is not supported by observed behavior, possibly because of the valuation errors hypothesized in "Inflation, Rational Valuation and the Market" (in Volume 5).

The issues under debate with Miller are reviewed in more popular form in the last paper in this part, written for a symposium on the occasion of the thirtieth anniversary of the first Modigliani-Miller contributions (see Volume 3). It is shown in particular that the two alternative formulations have very different implications with respect to the effect that the Tax Reform Act of 1987 might be expected to have on the value of leverage. Miller expects that taxing capital gains at roughly the same rate as interest income will sharply increase the value of leverage toward the value estimated in the correction paper. By contrast it turns out that according to my analysis, the change in the value of leverage should be negligible. Thus the new tax legislation might provide the opportunity for a crucial experiment to discriminate between the two hypotheses, although I point to a number of reasons why the opportunity might never be realized.

The remaining contribution, the fourth in this part, is a survey of the literature dealing with the implications of inflation for financial management, including both investment in physical assets and the best way to finance them—retained earnings, debt of various maturities, and equity. In an ideal world of perfect markets and rational valuation, inflation would make some (but limited) difference (through the uncertainty of future inflation), provided the decision analysis is cast entirely in real or entirely in nominal terms. But serious errors may arise from mixing the two. In addition many complications arise through debt, taxes, and quite possibly through the market tendency to irrational valuation, discussed in "Inflation, Rational Valuation and the Market" (Volume 5). The paper deals with the implications of these complications, resulting from the nonneutrality of inflation, on corporate financial management.

PART I
Saving and Wealth

Determinants of Private Saving with Special Reference to the Role of Social Security—Cross-country Tests

Franco Modigliani
Arlie Sterling*

ABSTRACT

The aim of this paper is to develop and test hypotheses designed to explain international differences in saving behaviour. These hypotheses are derived from the life cycle hypothesis, which suggests that such differences may be explained by differences in the rate of growth of per capita income, length of retirement, demographic factors and the availability of social security retirement pensions. Attention is focused on the role played by social security. The life cycle hypothesis explains much of the international variation in saving behaviour, and although one can identify both savings replacement and induced retirement effects for social security they appear almost to offset each other.

I INTRODUCTION

This paper is concerned with developing and testing hypotheses to account for the great diversity in saving behaviour revealed by inter-

* The authors are Institute Professor and graduate student respectively, at the Massachusetts Institute of Technology. They would like to thank Stanley Fischer, Wolfgang Franz and Larry Summers for helpful comments.

24

national comparison. In formulating the hypotheses, we rely on the life cycle hypothesis (LCH), developed initially by Modigliani and Brumberg (1954) and generalised by Feldstein (1974).

It is shown that the LCH, with its emphasis on accumulation for retirement as the primary motivation for saving, implies that the major determinants of intercountry variation in the saving rate are differences in the rate of growth of per capita income, length of retirement, and demographic variables relating to the age structure of the population. Another important factor is the availability of support for older people through social security arrangements. Particular attention is devoted to understanding and testing the implications of the LCH with respect to the impact of social security systems on aggregate private saving behaviour.

In Section II of the paper we develop major implications of the LCH relevant to the analysis of cross-country variations. In Section III we discuss the data used and the approximations necessary to test those implications. In Section IV we report the empirical results.

The results suggest that the basic LCH framework developed here is capable of explaining a great deal of the international variation in savings behaviour. With respect to social security we find evidence for the two effects suggested by the extended life cycle model, namely, a saving reducing replacement effect and a saving augmenting retirement effect. Somewhat surprisingly, our estimates suggest that these two effects roughly offset each other.

II THEORETICAL FOUNDATIONS

There are several ways to analyse the determinants of private saving and wealth within a life cycle framework. One may start from the individual household decisions, or saving functions, and then aggregate over individuals. Alternatively, one may wish to focus on the determinants of individual and aggregate wealth. The second approach is most useful when studying steady-state implications. Indeed, with stable growth (or moderate fluctuations around a growth trend), the (private) saving rate, s, averaged over cyclical fluctuations, can be expressed as the product of the rate of growth income, p, times the (private) wealth-income ratio, a (cf. Modigliani, 1966):

$$s = \frac{S}{Y} = p\frac{A}{Y} \equiv pa \qquad (1)$$

Here S is aggregate private saving, Y is aggregate disposable income, and A is aggregate private wealth. We shall find it useful to rely on both approaches but will begin with the wealth ratio approach because we believe that it is most conducive to an understanding of the complex channels through which social security and (average) retirement age can affect saving and wealth.

1 SOCIAL SECURITY AND THE WEALTH–INCOME RATIO IN A STATIONARY SOCIETY

As is well known, and obvious from equation (1), in a stationary society ($p = 0$), s will be zero in steady states, independently of social security arrangements. But one can still inquire about the determinants of a in a stationary society.

The essential aspects of the problem can be adequately examined given assumptions of the elementary Modigliani – Brumberg model (1980). Specifically, we assume that: (i) income accrues at a constant rate e up to retirement; (ii) the rate of consumption during the W years of the working span, c, is a constant, while retired consumption during the R years of the retirement span is a constant fraction, λ, of the rate during the working span; (iii) no bequests are received or planned; (iv) assets have zero (real) returns; and (v) the government performs no function other than administering the social security system.

For a stationary population we can also make the convenient assumption of a zero mortality until terminal age L, and one household in each age cohort. Let y denote annual average disposable income, t the social security tax rate, and SST total social security benefits. In the absence of bequests, the individual's life budget constraint takes the form:

$$Ly = W(e - t) + SST = Wc + \lambda Rc \tag{2}$$

It follows that the rate of saving is a positive constant, e-t-c, up to retirement and then becomes a negative constant, $SST/R - \lambda c$ to age L. Thus, wealth rises linearly with age to a peak, $R\lambda c - SST$, representing the amount needed to finance that portion of retired consumption which is not covered by social security, and then declines linearly to zero over the R years of retirement.[1]

---

[1] This formulation relies on the simplifying assumption that social security benefits are received only upon retirement, which is frequently but not unequivocally the case. It is adopted because it greatly simplifies the exposition without any essential loss.

In view of the assumption of one household in each age cohort, aggregate private wealth is given by the area of a triangle of height $R\lambda c - SST$ and base $W + R = L$, or:

$$A = \tfrac{1}{2}(R\lambda c - SST)L$$

Since aggregate disposable income is $Y = Ly$, and making use of equation (2), the asset income ratio can be expressed as:

$$a \equiv \frac{A}{Y} = \left(1 - \frac{Z^*}{\lambda L}\sigma\right)a(0) \tag{3}$$

where $\sigma = SST/Ry$ is the 'social security replacement rate', $Z^* = W + \lambda R$, and $a(0) = R\lambda L/2Z^*$ is the wealth income ratio in the absence of social security ($\sigma = 0$). Note that if σ is zero and in addition $\lambda = 1$, then equation (3) reduces to $a = R/2$, which is the result obtained by Modigliani and Brumberg (1980) for this basic model.

It is seen from equation (3) that if social security had no impact on the length of retirement R, then its effect would be that of reducing the wealth income ratio at the proportional rate:

$$\frac{1}{a}\frac{\partial a}{\partial \sigma} = -\frac{1}{2}\frac{R}{a} \tag{4}$$

Saving and wealth are reduced even though consumption is unchanged – which it will be as long as social security contributions exactly offset benefits, leaving life disposable income unchanged – because of the rise in contributions, t, and consequent reduction in disposable income during the working span. This effect of social security on the pattern of accumulation, which Feldstein (1977) has labelled the wealth replacement effect, is shown graphically in the figures based on the standard graph from Modigliani (1966). It could be of substantial magnitude.

Thus, if λ were, say 0.8, $L = 50, R = 10$ and $W = 40$, one can deduce from equation (3) that an increase of σ from 0.2 to 0.3 would reduce a by roughly 16 per cent. But it should be recognised that a decline in the private wealth ratio need not imply an equal decline in the ratio of aggregate capital to income – that depends on the financing of government and, in turn, on the extent to which the liabilities of the social security system are funded. This point is stressed by Eisner (1980) and Hymans (1981).

In reality, equation (4) provides only a partial inference about the impact of social security on the wealth – income ratio, for it neglects possible effects on a through R which, as can be seen from equation (3), is a major determinant of a. Differentiating equation (3) with respect to

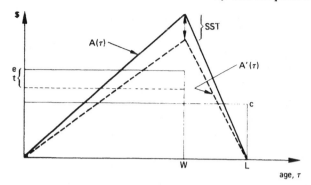

FIG. 2.1 The wealth replacement effect of social security

——— A(τ) = wealth at age τ in absence of social security
——— A'(τ) = wealth at age τ with social security benefits equal SST

σ, but recognising that R is also a function of σ, (and assuming λ independent of σ), one obtains:

$$\frac{da}{d\sigma} = -\frac{R}{2} + \frac{1}{2}\left[\frac{2a}{R} + \frac{\lambda(1-\lambda)RL}{(W+\lambda R)^2}\right]\frac{dR}{d\sigma} \tag{5}$$

The first term is again the private wealth (or saving) replacement effect and is necessarily negative. But there is an additional effect given by the second term of equation (5). It can be expected to be positive if, as we shall argue in the next section, a larger value of σ and associated higher contributions encourage earlier retirement so that $dR/d\sigma > 0$. This arises because basically a longer retirement span, R, requires the accumulation of a larger wealth to finance retired consumption, Rλc.

In view of these contrasting and offsetting responses, it is impossible to reach a definite conclusion, not only about the magnitude but even the sign of $da/d\sigma$, until we have considered the behaviour of $dR/d\sigma$ in a later section. For $da/d\sigma$ to be positive, however, requires that $dR/d\sigma$ be rather large, roughly between 6 (at $\sigma = 0$) and over 16 (at $\sigma = 0.3$).[2]

---

[2] In one potentially relevant case, however, the total effect would be exactly zero. It arises if a significant fraction of the population had no intention of retiring, and hence were not accumulating retirement wealth to begin with. The introduction of social security and forced 'accumulation' through contributions may be expected to induce early retirement but again no private saving.

It is also worth pointing out that there is a third channel through which the direct replacement effect is offset. That is, that σ may itself be a decreasing function of the retirement span, which arises when early retirement may only be taken at the cost of reduced benefits. Early retirement then reduces the replacement rate, and thus reduces the displacement of private saving.

2 EXTENSIONS TO NON-STATIONARY ECONOMY

In order to extend the analysis to a non-stationary economy, we rely on a fairly straight-forward generalisation of the approach pursued by Modigliani (1970). It uses the technique of summing up saving over all cohorts, taking into account the effect of productivity growth and of family size as well as of retirement. To this end, let w, r and $l = w + r$ stand for active, retired and total population. In addition, let D denote the average number of 'minor' years attached to a household over its life cycle, d the actual number of dependents, and λ_d the average yearly rate of consumption expenditure per minor relative to the rate of expenditure per active adult. Finally, define Z as $Z \equiv W + \lambda R + \lambda_d D$; it represents the length of life measured in terms of equivalent consumption years. One then arrives at the following expression for the saving ratio:

$$s \equiv \frac{S}{Y} \simeq \frac{S}{we} = \left(1 - \frac{Z}{\lambda L}\sigma\right)s(0) \tag{6}$$

where

$$s(0) = \left[1 - \frac{W}{Z}\left(1 + \lambda\frac{r}{w} + \lambda_d\frac{d}{w}\right) + \alpha_s\rho\right] \tag{6a}$$

is the saving rate in the absence of social security as derived in Modigliani (1970), equation (19) (except for obvious notational differences and for the last term approximating the effect of productivity growth, ρ, which is omitted in (19)). The first factor in equation (6) is very similar to that in equation (3). The only difference is that, in the coefficient of σ, Z^* is replaced by Z which allows for the effect of dependent population D. It follows that the replacement effect of social security is basically the same non-linear one in a stationary and non-stationary economy. It necessarily reduces saving (or wealth) though not linearly but rather by a *fraction* of what it would have been in the absence of social security, as given by s(0). The induced retirement effect will still tend to increase saving since the first and especially the second factor in equation (6) are increasing functions of R.

As shown in Modigliani (1970), s(0) in equation (6) can be expected to rise with productivity (i.e. $\alpha_s > 0$) because older generations are then richer and saving at a rate more than offsetting the dissaving of the retired. The second term of s(0), $\frac{W}{Z}\left(1 + \lambda\frac{r}{w} + \lambda_d\frac{d}{w}\right)$, shows the effects of population structure; clearly, saving will tend to decline in response to a rise in the proportion of retired population, r/w, or dependent population, d/w. A rise in population growth will tend to affect these two ratios in opposite directions, but should on balance increase saving since the effect of the smaller retired fraction should outweigh that of larger dependency ratio.

Equation (6) was derived assuming that the entire population is covered by social security and with the same replacement rate. To generalise to the case where one or both assumptions do not hold, let n_1 and n_0 be the fractions of covered and non-covered population. If the two groups are similar with respect to the mean value of other variables, so that s(0) is the same for both groups, then the national average saving ratio, being the weighted average of each groups' saving rate, will be given by equation (6) but with σ replaced by the 'effective' average replacement rate, $n_1\sigma$. If the two groups differ significantly in terms of some other arguments, modifications to equation (6) would be called for, though we shall ignore this complication.[3]

3 SOME QUALIFICATIONS

Before concluding this section, we must call attention to certain mechanisms which could cause the replacement effect to be less negative – possibly much less – than implied by equation (6).

One relates to the provision of retirement support through children. From the point of view of the accumulation of private wealth, what matters is λRc – (children support) – SST. This quantity may well remain unchanged as SST comes into being or rises, as this may be accompanied by a roughly equal decline in children support – implying no replacement effect. From the point of view of the working children, the lower support is offset by higher social security contributions, leaving accumulation unchanged.

Another effect, stressed by Dolde and Tobin (1980), works through the fact that saving is partly motivated by reasons other than retirement

[3] For example, if the recipients differ in terms of average income, then n_1 would have to be reinterpreted as the share of aggregate income rather than of population accounted for by participants. The assumption that participants have the same length of retirement as non-participants, may also be questionable since social security should tend to lengthen retirement. If this assumption is dropped, one would have to add to the right-hand side of equation (6) the term:

$$n_0 n_1 \sigma \left(\frac{R_0 - R_1}{\lambda L}\right)\left(1 + \lambda \frac{r}{w} + \lambda_d \frac{d}{w}\right)$$

where R_1 and R_0 are average expected retirement span of covered and non-covered households respectively.

– e.g. to acquire a house. Illiquid social security benefits cannot be used to satisfy these other purposes of saving while many types of private saving can. Hence, if the non-retirement use of saving is significant, the replacement effect will be diminished.

These considerations suggest that in equation (6) the coefficient of σ should be multiplied by a further factor smaller than unity – though how much smaller cannot be established *a priori*.[4]

III DERIVING A TESTABLE EQUATION AND THE DATA USED IN ESTIMATION

We endeavour to test the significance of the life cycle variables discussed above via estimation of an equation derived from equation (6) for a cross-section of countries, with individual variables generally measured as averages over the decade 1960–70. The sample consists of 21 OECD countries, for which time-series data for the period 1960–70 are available. By using averages and international cross-sectional data we hope to capture long-run relations across a broad range of social, economic and demographic conditions. This approach has been successfully applied by Houthakker (1965), Modigliani (1970), Feldstein (1977, 1979), Leff (1969), and Kopits and Gotur (1979), to mention but a few. A complete listing of the data by country is given in an appendix.

Implementation of equation (6) requires measurement of the savings ratio, rate of growth of productivity, population age distribution, length of retirement, and the fraction of annual lifetime average disposable income replaced by social security benefits. In this section we describe in some detail the approach taken in deriving approximations to the relevant variables and the data used in implementing these approximations.

1 SAVING AND INCOME

Our dependent variable is throughout the private savings ratio – the ratio of the sum of personal and corporate savings to private consumption plus private savings. We thus follow other authors in treating corporate savings as a perfect substitute for private savings.[5] Savings

---

[4] See also the considerations in note 2.

[5] We must report, however, that some partial tests raise questions as to whether this hypothesis is fully consistent with our sample, with the conclusion clouded by (presumably chance) collinearity of the corporate saving rate and the social security variables.

and consumption data are from the OECD (1973). The private savings ratio for each country is then the average of 11 observations from 1960 to 1970.

The relevant rate of growth of productivity is that of real per capita disposable income. It was estimated as the slope of b of the regression equation: $y_t = a + bt$ where y is the natural log of the income measure defined above, deflated by indices of population and price level from the OECD (1980). The fit of the income growth equations was uniformly excellent.

2 DEMOGRAPHIC CHARACTERISTICS

The age distribution variables, r/w and d/w, reflect differences in growth rates and variability in these rates over the relevant past, as well as retirement and family size preferences. A straightforward measure of the incidence of retirement is given by the ratio of aged people not working to the total working population. The trouble with this measure is that it treats as retired some people that have never been in the labour force, notably homemakers. One way around this problem is to confine the numerator and denominator to males only, though at the expense of excluding from the measure the effect of differential behavioural patterns of female participation in the (measured) labour force. In what follows we make use of three alternative measures of the proportion retired, namely: (i) all non-working people above the minimum age of retirement for social security purposes, relative to the population 20 and above; (ii) all non-working men above the age of 55 relative to the male labour force; and (iii) all non-working men above the age of 65, relative to the male labour force.

Measuring the fraction of young presents less serious difficulties. We use two measures: (i) all people below the age of 20 relative to the population 20 and above; and (ii) all children below the age of 15 relative to the male labour force. Population and labour force estimates are from the OECD (1979) and are averages of the 1960 and 1970 observations.

3 LENGTH OF WORKING LIFE

The expected length of working life, W, can be expressed as the difference between the expected length of active life, L, and the expected length of retirement, R, which can be measured as life expectancy at any given age weighted by the fraction of all retirees retiring at that age.

Consider a two-period two-generation world, in which people may retire at the end of the first period but, if they do not, work until death (at the end of the second period). As Reimers (1976) points out, if we may ignore net migration and temporary withdrawals, the number of retired can be expressed as:

$$\text{number retired} = (LFPR_1 - LFPR_2)P_2$$

where $LEPR_i$ is the labour force participation rate in cohort i, and P_i the population of cohort i. Now, if everyone retires at the end of period 1, the average length of retirement is simply LE_1, the life expectancy at the end of period 1. If, however, some people choose not to retire, the average length of retirement will be a weighted average of LE_1 and 0. Indeed, it will be precisely:

$$
\begin{aligned}
R &= LE_1 \frac{(LFPR_1 - LFPR_2)P_2}{LFPR_1 P_2} + 0\frac{LFPR_2 P_2}{LFPR_1 P_2} \\
&= LE_1 \frac{LFPR_1 - LFPR_2}{LFPR_1}
\end{aligned}
\tag{7}
$$

where R is the average length of retirement for those in the labour force.

Equation (7) suggests a simple way of approximating R in our sample. For the first age group we choose men aged 25–54, and for the second group men 65 and over. Using this approximation requires that we interpret LE_1 as the average life expectancy at retirement for all those who retire – not just those who retire at 65.[6]

We may now use equation (7) to calculate the approximate length of working life:

$$W \equiv L - R = A - B\Delta PR \tag{8}$$

where $A \simeq L$, $B \simeq LE$, the average expectation of life upon retirement, and ΔPR the ratio (Participation Rate 25–54 – Participation Rate 65 and over) / Participation Rate 25–54.

4 TEST EQUATION

In order to carry out estimations and tests we have to make the assumption that certain variables can be approximated as constant across

---

[6] The approximation abstracts from individuals who die before their planned age of retirement. The loss of these individuals reduces the population but not the labour force (since they would normally be retired) and thus increases the measured labour force participation rate of the older group, and biases downward our estimate of the expected length of retirement. Hopefully this bias may be roughly offset by individuals who live unexpectedly long after retirement.

countries to be estimated from the sample. Specifically, we will make
these assumptions for L and LE, and hence A and B in equation (8), as
well as for Z and the λs which have been defined earlier in connection
with equation (6). Then, using equation (8) to substitute for W in
equation (6), and taking into account the implication of incomplete
coverage, we can write:

$$
\frac{S}{Y} = (1 + \alpha_0 n_1 \sigma)\left[\alpha_1 + \alpha_2 \frac{d}{w} + \alpha_3 \frac{r}{w} + \alpha_4 \Delta PR + \alpha_5 \rho \right.
$$
$$
\left. + \alpha_6 (\Delta PR)\frac{d}{w} + \alpha_7 (\Delta PR)\frac{r}{w} \right]
$$

(9)

The coefficients $\alpha_0 \cdots \alpha_7$ are related to the underlying behavioural and
institutional parameters as follows:

$$
\alpha_0 = -\frac{Z}{\lambda L} \quad \alpha_1 = 1 - \frac{L}{Z} \quad \alpha_2 = -\frac{\lambda_d L}{Z} \quad \alpha_3 = -\frac{\lambda L}{Z}
$$

$$
\alpha_4 = \frac{LE}{Z} \quad \alpha_6 = \lambda_d \frac{LE}{Z} \quad \alpha_7 = \lambda \frac{LE}{Z}
$$

For the sake of getting some rough notion of the value of the above
coefficients consistent with the LCH, let us take $D = 20$, $W = 40$, and
$LE = R = 10$, and therefore $L = 50$. These values are consistent with
those implied by the age distribution variables in countries with little
population growth. We further guesstimate that λ, the retired rate of
consumption relative to the working year rate, can be placed at 0.8, and
λ_d, the rate of expenditure per minor year relative to the working rate, at
0.4. These values imply an estimate for Z of 56 and for L/Z of 0.89 –
estimates which are relatively robust to reasonable variations in the
above assumptions.[7] The implied values for the parameters of equation
(9) are given in Table 2.1. The productivity growth coefficient, α_5, has
been shown by Modigliani (1970) to be a function of the marginal
propensities to consume out of labour income and assets. Based on
reasonable values for these parameters we expect α_5 to be between two
and three.

In estimating equation (9) we will actually drop the last two product
terms since multicollinearity with the three variables involved in the
product makes it impossible to estimate reliably the coefficients α_6 and

[7] In particular, the ratio L/Z is invariant to equiproportional changes in L, D,
and R.

TABLE 2.1 *A PRIORI* ESTIMATES OF THE COEFFICIENTS
$$\alpha_0 \cdots \alpha_7$$

$\alpha_0 = -1.4$	$\alpha_1 = 0.11$
$\alpha_2 = -0.36\,(-0.31)$	$\alpha_3 = -0.72\,(-0.62)$
$\alpha_4 = 0.18\,(0.24)$	$\alpha_6 = 0.07$
$\alpha_7 = 0.16$	

α_7 which are, anyway, fairly small. This has the effect of 'biasing' the estimates of α_2, α_3, α_4, upward the last and downward the other two. The figures given in parentheses for α_2, α_3, and α_4 represent the estimated effect of the bias. Needless to say, the values we have assigned to λ and λ_d are little more than guesswork, and the interested reader may readily recompute the αs using other assumptions.

Equation (9) and the above estimates assume that the social security system is in steady state with respect to the relation between contributions and benefits current and prospective. This assumption is certainly questionable in view of the relatively recent formation and/or major revamping of the social security system of several countries in our sample. We have not attempted to deal with the behaviour of the saving rate during periods of transition because it depends intimately on the details of the transitional arrangements which are not readily available or quantifiable.[8]

5 SOCIAL SECURITY BENEFITS

The remaining problem in estimating equation (9) is the measurement of the effective social security replacement rate, $n_1\sigma$, which turns out to involve rather serious problems. One possible way to estimate this variable is to assume that σ may be approximated by the ratio of social security benefits (SS) per recipient to average income, y, and n_1 by the ratio of recipients to the number eligible, which could be identified as those retired above the minimum age required for retirement.[9] Thus:

---

[8] One fairly general implication of the LCH bearing on this problem is that the introduction, or a major revamping, resulting in higher benefits to people who had not expected them at the start of their life cycle, should lead to a transient reduction in saving, larger than the steady-state effect. Since the replacement rate of our sample countries was tending to rise, this transient effect may introduce an upward bias to our estimate of the replacement effect.

[9] To the extent that the retirement is not necessary to receive benefits, this measure is an underestimate of the eligible population. Since, however, not all non-workers are truly eligible, this should be a reasonable measure.

$$\sigma n_1 = \frac{SS}{Recipients} \bigg/ y \times \frac{Recipients}{Retired} = \frac{SS}{Retired} \bigg/ y$$

This measure can be computed for every country in the sample from information on total pension benefits from the ILO and on the number of retired from OECD (1979).

An alternative approach is to secure direct estimates of the replacement rate of the covered group, σ, and of the coverage rate, n_1. Olsen (1978) has estimated replacement rates for several countries, assuring comparability across countries by basing his estimate on a standardised situation. Specifically, he measures the ratio of social security benefits to average income in the relevant years preceding retirement for men in manufacturing. The replacement rate is computed both for single men and for couples. Unfortunately, his sample includes only twelve out of twenty-one countries.[10] Information on the coverage ratio is even more scanty: an estimate may be computed from data on recipients from OECD (1977, Table 2.1), but this estimate appears subject to considerable error and, in any event, is available only for nine countries of which but seven overlap with the twelve countries covered by Olsen. For these seven countries, we show in Table 2.2 the direct estimate of n_1 – column (1) – the Olsen estimates of the replacement rate for couples, σ – column (2) – their product representing the direct estimate, $n_1\sigma$ – column (3) – and finally the alternate measure of $n_1\sigma$, based on the ILO source – column (4).

Column (1) indicates that, not unexpectedly, coverage is quite similar for the seven countries and also quite high (with the United States somewhat of an exception). Accordingly, the estimate of the effective replacement rate is very similar to the replacement rate, though somewhat smaller. Unfortunately, this estimate of the effective replacement rate appears to bear little relation to the alternative ILO estimate. There are, to be sure, some conceptual differences between the estimates of columns (3) and (4), and some reason to think that the Olsen replacement rates may be downward biased.[11] But it is hard to account for a nearly total lack of correlation between the two estimates.

[10] Furthermore, we are able to use but one observation (for 1965) from Olsen's data.

[11] There are two considerations pointing in this direction: (i) replacement is measured relative to income just prior to retirement, at which time earnings should be at their peak; and (ii) social security systems are often redistributive so that (well-paid) men in manufacturing would have lower replacement rates relative to less-well-paid workers. On these grounds we would expect the estimates of column (3) to be somewhat smaller on average than those of column (4), an inference which is not supported by Table 2.2.

TABLE 2.2   A COMPARISON OF EFFECTIVE REPLACEMENT
RATE MEASURES

Country	(1) Coverage rate $(n_1)^a$	(2) Replacement rate (σ) Olsen	(3) Effective replacement rate $(n_1\sigma)$ (1) × (2)	(4) Effective replacement rate $(n_1\sigma)$ ILO
Canada	0.96	0.42	.40	0.25
Denmark	0.97	0.51	.49	0.35
Netherlands	0.86	0.50	.43	0.57
Norway[b]	0.84	0.38	.32	0.43
Sweden	0.90	0.44	.40	0.40
UK	0.99	0.36	.36	0.35
US	0.74	0.44	.33	0.27
mean	0.89	0.44	.39	0.37

[a] Average of 1960 and 1970.

[b] The minimum age of retirement in Norway was 70 for this period. The eligible reported here, however, are those over 65.

Clearly, if one is prepared to accept the Olsen estimate as a sound measure of the replacement rate, one is led to suspect that there may be a good deal of noise in the ILO estimate, perhaps because their estimate of benefits includes payments other than social security benefits.

On the whole, the comparisons of Table 2.2 strongly suggest that, for those countries for which they are available, estimates of the effective replacement rate based on the Olsen data may well be more reliable than those of the ILO. Furthermore, the high and stable coverage ratio of column (1) suggests that the 'effective replacement rate' available for only seven countries can be replaced with the replacement rate of column (2) which is available for twelve countries. Therefore, for the Olsen sample of twelve countries, one can use as a measure of social security benefits either the ILO adjusted replacement rate or the Olsen replacement rate, with the latter measure somewhat upward biased but probably a more reliable indicator of variations across countries.

For the full sample of twenty-one countries, one can also use the Olsen measure wherever available and the ILO measure otherwise, as well as the ILO measure alone. By mixing the concepts in the full sample, we are able to gain efficiency in the estimation of the non-social security parameters through a larger sample, but still utilise all the information available in the Olsen data.[12] To allow for differences in the relation

[12] Of course this procedure would not be efficient if the Olsen data contained no systematic information beyond that in the ILO data.

between the true social security measure and the two alternate approximations, we allow each of the two measures a different coefficient in the full sample.

IV THE EMPIRICAL RESULTS

Our tests of the LCH are primarily attempts to see if the lifetime budget constraint and planning period implicit in equation (2) are relevant for the representative individual. They are simultaneously tests of the validity of the approximations we imposed to generate a testable equation. These issues are addressed by the significance of the α coefficients and their magnitude relative to our *a priori* estimates, and the comparative fit of the non-linear versus linear specification. Also relevant is the sensitivity of our results to changes in specification and to any particular subset of data within the sample.

All the regressions reported below were estimated using a GLS technique to correct for heteroskedasticity. The variance of the residuals was

TABLE 2.3   SAVINGS RATIO EQUATIONS – VARIOUS
MEASURES OF SOCIAL SECURITY[a]

$$(T.3) \quad \frac{S}{Y} = (1 + \alpha_0 n_1 \sigma)\left(\alpha_1 + \alpha_2 \frac{d}{w} + \alpha_3 \frac{r}{w} + \alpha_4 \Delta PR + \alpha_5 \rho\right)$$

Equation	α_0 (ILO)	S_e	α_0 (Olsen)	α_0 (ILO)	S_e
I.1	−0.12 (0.56)	5.02	−0.20 (0.84)	−0.55 (1.36)	4.97
I.2	0.28 (1.18)	5.04	−0.31 (1.60)	−0.67 (1.81)	5.03
I.3	0.26 (1.22)	4.72	−0.30 (1.64)	−0.67 (1.95)	4.67
I.4			−0.43 (2.83)	−0.84 (2.53)	5.02
II.1	−0.23 (0.59)	4.54	−0.16 (0.31)		4.59
II.2	0.51 (2.01)	3.95	−0.50 (1.61)		5.0ᴈ
II.3	0.49 (2.11)	3.70	−0.50 (1.73)		4.82

[a] Equations I.1–I.4 are estimated for the full sample, II.1–II.3 over the Olsen sample of 12.

taken to be proportional to the sample variance of the savings ratio divided by the mean population in each country, which weights more heavily large countries with stable savings ratios. The United States has the highest weight (16 per cent of the total weight).[13] The weights are given in the Appendix.[14]

1 THE REPLACEMENT EFFECT

Initial results, not presented here, give us confidence that the life cycle variables other than social security have a significant and robust impact on the savings rate. In particular, the measure of retirement span, an innovation of this study, is quite significant. The direct effect of social security, however, proved more difficult to estimate. We thus proceed first to a discussion of the social security effect.

Rather than present the full set of coefficient estimates for each of the various samples and concepts discussed above, we will use an abbreviated format to get a broad overview. For each equation in Table 2.3, we report only the estimated coefficient on social security and its t-ratio, as well as the standard error of the equation. We rely on two samples. The top part of the table relates to the full sample of twenty-one

[13] The weighting by population corresponds to the variance reducing force of a larger sample size, while weighting by the variance of the savings ratio is suggested by our conjecture that measuring the steady-state savings ratio by the average ratio involves some error, the variance of which is greater if the actual savings rate is unstable. Though this weighting scheme is intuitively appealing, it has been pointed out to us that the two components are not independent. The variance component actually has limited influence on the estimates. On the whole, weighting by population alone tends to improve the results noticeably. Those results inconsistent with the LCH became less significant, while those consistent with it became even stronger.

[14] Though the determination of the savings rate and retirement habits are simultaneous endogenous decisions, it is unnecessary to use simultaneous equation estimation techniques (as Feldstein does) since the system of savings and retirement equations is recursive as long as there is no cross-equation correlation among the residuals. For a discussion of the retirement equation, see Section V.5.

One further problem may arise, however, in that the replacement rate might well be regarded as an endogenous variable, determined by the preferences of the country as expressed by the government. It is likely that interactions within the expanded system in which savings, retirement and social security benefits are simultaneously determined induce some correlation between the residual and the independent variables. Though we recognise that this problem may exist, we cannot forecast either its magnitude or direction, and have made no effort to correct for it.

countries and the lower part to the 'Olsen' sample of twelve countries. For each sample we show results for two alternative measures of social security replacement rate, $n_1\sigma$. Within each set, in equation (1), the retired fraction, r/w, is measured by the ratio of non-working people above the minimum age of retirement for social security purposes relative to population over 20, and the dependency rate, d/w, by people below the age of 20 to population over 20. In equation (2), the measure of d/w is the same, but r/w is the ratio of retired men above 55 to the male labour force. In equation (3), r/w is the same all male measure used in equation (2), but the dependency ratio is people below the age of 15 to male labour force.

Look first at the left-hand side, when the social security measure is the ratio of benefits per retired person from the ILO to per capita income. The results are rather discouraging. In no case is the coefficient of the expected order of magnitude or significantly negative. Indeed, in the preferred equations, the coefficient has the wrong sign and significantly so for the twelve-countries sample. Sensitivity analysis (along the lines of Belsley, Kuh and Welsch, 1980) shows that the results presented in the table are not swayed by any one particular country.

The estimates reported in the remainder of the table, however, present a considerably different picture. The lower right-hand portion reports the outcome of tests measuring social security benefits by the alternative measure available for twelve countries, namely the Olsen replacement rate. The remarkable result shown is that, for this sample, the two measures give diametrically opposite results. For the ILO measure, the results are pretty much the same as for the total sample. But when we use the Olsen measure: (i) the coefficient is always negative as expected; (ii) in equations (2) and (3) (which, however, do not give the lowest standard error for this sample), it has a reasonable order of magnitude; and (iii) in the last equation it approaches significance by the appropriate one-tail test. Sensitivity analysis shows that deletion of Switzerland appreciably increases both the point estimate and the significance of the coefficients of both the Olsen and ILO variables (thus pulling them further apart).

In the light of these contradictory results we proceed to re-estimate an equation for the full sample using a mixed measure of the replacement rate, namely the Olsen measures when available and the ILO measure for the nine countries for which it alone is available. To allow for different elasticities of the true variable with respect to the measured variables, we allow these two measures to have different coefficients, which are reported in the top right-hand side of Table 2.3. The results are rather suggestive. Looking first at the specifications I.1 to I.3, one finds that the coefficient of the Olsen variable is negative in every row, though in the first row it is somewhat on the small side. In addition, the coefficients of the ILO measure also become negative and significant at the 5 per cent level or better. The positive correlation between saving and the ILO measure of social security for the full sample is evidently due to a strong positive association with the twelve-country sample.

These encouraging results are further supported by the estimates presented in row I.4. They correspond to an alternative measure of the incidence of retirement, namely the ratio of non-active men over 65 (rather than 55) to active men. Though this specification results in a higher standard error than that for I.3, in many ways it seems the most appropriate way of measuring intended retirement in a life cycle context, especially since the apparent substantial differences in the incidence of non-active men in the 55 to 65 age group are perplexing. With this specification, the coefficients of both social security measures are significant at the 1 per cent level or thereabouts and, especially for the ILO, are of an order of magnitude which approaches consistency with the implications of the model.[15]

2 THE ROLE OF OTHER LIFE CYCLE VARIABLES

In the first two rows of Table 2.4, we report the full set of estimated coefficients for the mixed social security measure equations I.3 and I.4 of Table 2.3. It is apparent that these equations yield very similar estimates of the effect of all variables, except for the larger social security effect in equation I.4. Furthermore, comparison with Table 2.1 shows that, leaving aside again the social security variables, the coefficient estimates are remarkably close to the values suggested by the life cycle (allowing for the fact that the measurement of d/w in the empirical equation implies a coefficient, α_2, roughly half as large as suggested in Table 2.1), though α_4 is a bit high. These coefficients are, in addition, quite robust with respect to single country deletion.

Equation I.4 provides a test of one further specification, which was shown earlier to be a direct implication of the LCH, namely that the replacement rate should enter in a multiplicative rather than an additive fashion. This specification was imposed on all equations reported so far,

---

[15] To ensure that the mixed measure results are not due merely to separation of the sample into two groups, we added a dummy to the first component of (T.3). The dummy was completely insignificant, though it did sharply reduce the significance of the social security measures.

TABLE 2.4   SAVINGS RATIO EQUATIONS – COMPLETE COEFFICIENT ESTIMATES

$$\text{(T.4)} \quad \frac{S}{Y} = (1 + \alpha_0 n_1 \sigma)\left(\alpha_1 + \alpha_2 \frac{d}{w} + \alpha_3 \frac{r}{w} + \alpha_4 \Delta PR + \alpha_5 \rho\right)$$

Equation	α_0 Olsen	α_0 ILO	α_1	α_2	α_3	α_4	α_5	S_e	SSR
I.3	-0.30	-0.67	-0.01	-0.12	-0.65	0.37	3.00	4.67	305.6
	(1.64)	(.95)	(0.08)	(4.59)	(2.18)	(3.23)	(7.39)		
I.4	-0.43	-0.84	0.02	-0.14	-0.61	0.35	2.85	5.02	352.6
	(2.82)	(2.53)	(0.19)	(4.35)	(1.33)	(2.60)	(6.04)		
1.4[a]	-0.09	-0.16	0.05	-0.11	-0.48	0.27	2.33	5.31	394.3
	(1.99)	(1.87)	(0.86)	(3.97)	(1.22)	(2.69)	(7.59)		

[a] Social security enters linearly.

including I.4. Equation I.4ª differs from I.4 only in that the replacement rate is entered additively. It is seen that the linear specification yields estimates consistent with the non-linear one but results in a standard error some 6 per cent larger. Similar results were obtained for other specifications tested.[16]

3 ASSESSMENT OF TEST RESULTS

On the whole, it would seem that our results provide support for the LCH, quite strongly so for the role of the demographic variables and the growth rate, though rather weakly so in the case of the social security replacement rate. Our estimates of the replacement effect suffer from three weaknesses. First, the significance of the coefficients is uncomfortably sensitive to alternative measures of the demographic variables. Second, the point estimates are well below the *a priori* value of Table 2.1, namely I.4. Though, as we mentioned in Section II, there are a number of reasons why the replacement effect could fall short of the value derived from the simple LCH, the difference does appear rather large.

Last but not least, the social security coefficients for the full sample appear to be very sensitive to some extreme observations. In particular, eliminating Japan from the sample – an extreme country because of its very high saving ratio and low social security benefits – causes the coefficient of the ILO variable to lose any significance. Somewhat surprisingly, this happens to the coefficient of the Olsen variable as well, though Japan is not one of the Olsen countries. At the other extreme, if one drops Ireland, another of the nine countries, *both* coefficients rise by 20 per cent (becoming significant at the 1 per cent level or better for all specifications). Dropping both Ireland and Japan leads to estimates just a bit lower than those for the full sample.[17]

[16] One significant implication of the LCH, not stressed here, is that the savings ratio is independent of the level of income. This implication is easily tested by adding an income measure to the second component of (T.3). The income measure is described in detail in Section IV.5.

The results of such a test are clear. Income has no significant influence on the savings rate (the t-ratio is of the order of 0.1).

[17] Another source of uncertainty regarding the effect of social security arises in the partial tests of the responsiveness of private saving to variation in its corporate saving component mentioned in note 5. Though the hypothesis that corporate saving is a perfect substitute for household saving does not receive very strong support, the addition of a corporate savings variable – through its collinearity with the social security measures – has the effect of reducing somewhat the magnitude and significance of the social security coefficients.

TABLE 2.5   CONTRIBUTION, BY COMPONENT, TO THE SAVINGS
RATE

Component	Sample mean	Contribution to deviation from the mean US	Japan
(1) Constant	2.0	0.0	0.0
(2) d/w	− 12.7	− 2.8	− 0.2
(3) r/w	− 6.9	0.1	4.0
(4) ΔPR	24.5	0.2	− 8.6
(5) ρ	11.5	− 2.5	11.3
(1) + ··· + (5)	18.4	− 5.0	6.5
(6) Reduction due to social security (%)[a]	20.7	− 1.7	− 17.3
Saving rate (%)			
(7) (6)[a] (7)/100	14.6	− 3.8	9.4
(8) Actual	14.5	− 4.2	9.6

[a] For the sample mean, the social security effect is an average of the ILO and Olsen measures; for the US and Japan it is the Olsen and ILO measure respectively.

4 THE SOURCES OF INTERNATIONAL DIFFERENCES IN THE SAVING RATE

In Table 2.5, column (1), we show how the life cycle variables which we have examined and tested account for the sample mean saving rate. Each entry in the second column is the product of the mean value of the variable indicated in the first column by the coefficient as estimated in equation I.4. It is seen that the saving rate reflects a balance between two large negative factors – the dependency ratio and the proportion of population retired – and two even larger positive factors – length of retirement and productivity growth. Social security reduces the saving rate by an amount depending on the replacement rate. For our sample that reduction amounts, on the average, to some 20 per cent, nearly 400 basis points. (Note that the linear I.4[a] implies somewhat larger replacement effect.) Most of the variation in savings rates arises from income growth and length of retirement, while the two demographic variables vary less and tend systematically to offset each other (cf. data appendix).

The second and third columns of the table further show how our equation accounts for two well-known puzzles: the well-below-average saving rate of the US and the exceptionally high saving rate of Japan. The low savings rate in the US is accounted for by a below-average rate of growth of income and relatively high dependency ratio. The extremely high Japanese savings rate is largely due to a high rate of growth of income. Though the Japanese have a relatively short retirement span and thus lower planned saving, there are relatively few retired people currently dissaving. The effect of social security in the United States is roughly average, while in Japan the below-average replacement rate accounts for more than 400 basis points of the excess savings rate.

It should be emphasised that the reductions attributed to social security above refer to the direct or replacement effect alone. Estimates of the total effect of social security appear below.

5 RETIREMENT BEHAVIOUR

The results presented above confirm the empirically significant role of retirement in accounting for international differences in savings behaviour. In this section we try to explain observed variation in retirement behaviour with particular reference to the role of social security. This will complete our empirical analysis of the extended life cycle theory in which retirement behaviour as well as saving are endogenous.[18]

For a utility-maximising individual, and supposing that retirement is not inferior, the retirement span will be a decreasing function of the price of retirement, and an increasing function of the individual's initial wealth. The impact of a change in the wage rate is ambiguous as it generates both an income effect, tending to increase the length of retirement, and a substitution effect tending to reduce it.

The price of retirement is the amount of consumption that must be foregone to lengthen the retirement span. To find the change in lifetime consumption, C, required by an increase in the retirement span, we may differentiate the budget constraint and substitute for y to obtain:

$$\frac{1}{C}\frac{dC}{dR} = \frac{-L(1 - \sigma)}{(L - R)(L - \sigma R)} = \frac{(1 - \sigma)}{L\left(1 - \dfrac{R}{L}\right)\left(1 - \sigma\dfrac{R}{L}\right)}$$

where the reduction is expressed as a proportion of total consumption. It can be easily seen that the cost in terms of consumption is a decreasing function of σ, and is exactly zero at $\sigma = 1$. Since R/L is relatively small

---

[18] The informal discussion of this section is intended to motivate our retirement equation. More formal treatments may be found in Feldstein (1977) and Sheshinski (1978).

compared with unity, we will approximate the foregone consumption by a linear function of σ.

In deriving the cost of retirement, we assumed that individuals took σ as given. Actually, under most social security systems, it is possible for the individual to influence the replacement rate. Deferred retirement bonuses and/or means tests are two common mechanisms by which σ is partially endogenised. Unfortunately, it is a difficult empirical matter to summarise the relevant features of each country's social security system. The measure we were able to put together, which showed the influence of deferred retirement benefits and means tests on the replacement rate, had the expected effect on retirement when added to the equations of Table 2.6, but was rather insignificant.

We measure the wage rate by real GDP (in 1 000 US dollars) per worker, converted to constant US dollars by Summers, Kravis and Heston (1980), on the basis of detailed purchasing power parity information. We believe this measure of productivity is preferable to the more conventional per capita income, which as Eisner (1980) and Hu (1979) have stressed, is an endogenous variable, reflecting in particular the retirement choice. We have experimented with several specifications for the wage rate variable in an attempt to capture the possibility that the income effect is dominant at lower incomes, but becomes less so at higher incomes. While Feldstein endeavoured to model this effect by using both a linear and a reciprocal of income term, we have been most successful with the natural log of income.

Households face an additional influence not felt by the single individual, as the expenditures necessary to raise a family divert resources from consumption and retirement. Since children may in turn support their parents, this diversion of resources should be viewed as net of any back-bequest. Altogether, children presumably reduce the resources available for their parents' consumption and retirement, and thus shorten planned retirement. We measure the influence of family size on retirement by the fraction of the population under 15 relative to the male labour force.

Table 2.6 shows the estimated retirement equations, which were estimated using a GLS technique to correct for heteroskedasticity, on the assumption that the variance of the residuals is proportional to mean population. The first two rows indicate a surprisingly large effect of social security on retirement behaviour, whether measured by the ILO or by the mixed ILO–Olsen measure. The coefficients of (6.2) imply that $d\Delta PR/dn_1\sigma$ is roughly 0.65 and, given a life expectancy at retirement of roughly 10 years, suggests that $dR/d\sigma \simeq 6.5$. This result quantitatively

TABLE 2.6 THE RETIREMENT EQUATION ESTIMATES

$$(\text{T.6}) \quad \Delta PR = \beta_0 + \beta_1 n_1 \sigma + \beta_2 \ln(y) + \beta_3 \frac{d}{w}$$

Equation	β_0	β_1 Olsen	β_1 ILO	β_2	β_3	S_e	SSR
6.1	0.51 (13.26)		0.64 (5.09)			0.47	4.13
6.2	0.45 (12.19)	0.59 (7.08)	0.72 (2.74)			0.37	2.40
6.3	0.59 (6.49)	0.43 (5.20)	0.74 (3.46)	0.16 (3.14)	−0.41 (3.16)	0.29	1.39

is consistent with the findings of Pechman, Aaron and Taussig (1968, Appendix D), Feldstein (1977, 1979), Boskin (1977) and Boskin and Hurd (1978). Though it is difficult to compare our estimates with theirs, it appears that we estimate a stronger effect. The results of row 3 provide support for the hypothesis that a higher per capita income tends to lengthen retirement, while a larger incidence of dependents tends to shorten it.[19]

6 THE TOTAL IMPACT OF SOCIAL SECURITY

As we have seen in the first section, social security has two offsetting effects on saving: a direct negative 'replacement' effect, and an indirect positive effect, as a rise in the replacement rate lengthens retirement, which in turn raises the saving rate. Though one might suspect that the direct effect would be likely to dominate, leading to a negative overall effect, the issue cannot be settled *a priori*.

---

[19] A case can be made for adding a dummy to (6.3), taking the value one for the twelve Olsen countries and zero otherwise. The results turn out to be rather disturbing – the Olsen replacement variable as well as income coefficients become much smaller and insignificant. The reason seems to be that the Olsen countries have, on balance, a longer retirement and higher income, and apparently this effect can be caught by the dummy, with little additional information provided by income or social security.

However, since the dummy is totally insignificant, we feel there is ground for rejecting the hypothesis that the longer retirement of the Olsen countries is due to some nondescript common factor, in favour of the hypothesis that it is instead related to the variables in (6.3). Nonetheless, these results must be taken as a warning that the coefficients of (6.3) may overstate at least the role of income.

Feldstein (1977, 1979) has reported evidence that the net effect of social security is definitely to reduce saving. What inferences can be drawn from the estimates presented here?

Relying on specification (T.3) of Table 2.3, we can write:

$$\frac{d\frac{S}{Y}}{dn_1\sigma} = \alpha_0 S(0) + (1 + \alpha_0 n_1 \sigma) \frac{dS(0)}{d\Delta PR} \frac{d\Delta PR}{dn_1\sigma} \tag{10}$$

where $S(0) = \alpha_1 + \alpha_2 \dfrac{d}{w} + \alpha_3 \dfrac{r}{w} + \alpha_4 \Delta PR + \alpha_5 \rho$. Now $d\Delta PR/dn_1\sigma$ is the coefficient β_1 in equation (T.6), the estimate of which is found in Table 2.6, Row 3 (it has of course two values for the two measures of social security). The coefficient $dS(0)/d\Delta PR$ presents somewhat of a problem. Though, according to (T.4) the partial derivative of $S(0)$ with respect to ΔPR is given by α_4, the total derivative must take into account the effect of ΔPR on other variables, in particular, the retirement ratio r/w. This ratio is largely determined by two variables: the retirement habits measured by ΔPR and the age structure as measured by the proportion of people having reached retirement age – say 65 and over.

There are then two roughly equivalent ways of measuring the full impact of ΔPR on $S(0)$. One consists in actually regressing r/w on ΔPR and on the proportion of adult men 65 and over, M65. The result of this regression, with r defined as retired men over 65, is:

$$\frac{r}{w} = -0.08 + 0.109\Delta PR + 0.746M65 \tag{11}$$
$$\phantom{\frac{r}{w} =} (13.93) \quad (7.14) \qquad\quad (9.36)$$

The two independent variables are seen to account almost completely for r/w. Using equation (11) to substitute for r/w in (1.4), we find that the net coefficient of ΔPR in the savings equation becomes $[0.35 - 0.61(0.109)] = 0.28$.

The alternative consists in re-estimating (I.4), modifying its specification by replacing the retirement ratio by the population composition variable, M65. It can be shown that this specification represents an alternative linear approximation to the non-linear term $(W/Z.r/w)$ which appears in the right-hand side of the non-linear equation (6a). The result of this alternative specification is:

$$\frac{S}{Y} = [1 - 0.40\sigma(\text{Olsen}) - 0.81n_1\sigma(\text{ILO})][0.08 - 0.13\frac{d}{w}$$
$$(2.47) \qquad\qquad (2.37) \qquad\qquad (0.87) \quad (4.29)$$

$$- 0.50M65 + 0.26\Delta PR + 2.70\rho] \qquad S_e = 5.05$$
$$(1.27) \qquad\quad (2.54) \qquad\quad (5.24)$$

(1.4″)

It can be seen that in (I.4″) all the coefficients in common with (I.4) are very nearly the same except for that of ΔPR whose value (0.26) is appreciably smaller and is, instead, quite close to the value estimated above by substitution (0.28). One can thus estimate $dS(0)/d\Delta PR$ to be 0.26. Substituting in equation (10) this value and the values of α_0 from equation (I.4) and of β_1 from equation (6.3), we can estimate the total effects, direct and indirect, of social security.

The results of this calculation are rather surprising. Though the estimate varies from country to country (as the right-hand side of equation (10) depends on $S(0)$), it is not uniformly negative. On the contrary, it ranges from -0.05 (Greece) to $+0.08$ (Ireland), and is positive for over half the countries (including incidentally the US, 0.033). At the sample mean the effect is negligible (an increase of 0.1 in replacement rate would increase the saving rate by 10 basis points). This unexpected result (at least for us) is accounted for by the fact that the estimated replacement effect (α_0 in equation I.4) turned out lower than anticipated, while at the same time the estimated effects of retirement on saving (from I.4″)) and of social security or retirement (β_1 in (5.3)) appear rather large.

As a rough check on these results, we have re-estimated a reduced form obtained by replacing ΔPR in (I.4″) by the variables appearing on the right-hand side of equation (5.3). In practice that means dropping ΔPR and adding, instead, $\ln(y)$. Since social security then appears in both factors on the right-hand side, a linear specification is easier to interpret. We therefore rely on the linear approximation comparable with equation (I.4″). The result is:

$$\frac{S}{Y} = 0.016\sigma(\text{Olsen}) - 0.01n_1\sigma(\text{ILO}) + 0.22 - 0.16\frac{d}{w}$$
$$(0.20) \qquad\qquad (0.10) \qquad\qquad (2.64) \quad (2.79)$$

$$- 0.26M65 + 0.02\ln(y) + 2.14\rho \qquad S_e = 6.50$$
$$(0.64) \qquad (0.56) \qquad\quad (4.01)$$

(1.4″)

The coefficients of social security are seen to be of negligible magnitude and insignificant, providing striking confirmation that, on average, the direct and indirect effects of social security pretty much cancel each other out. This result is also consistent with the conclusion reached by others who have estimated 'reduced forms' analogous to (I.4″).[20]

V CONCLUSIONS

The results presented above provide strong support for the life cycle hypothesis. Estimates of the impact on the savings rate of income growth, demographic factors, and retirement span are quite close to those suggested by the LCH and are rather robust. The impact of social security, on the other hand, is harder to pin down. We have encountered difficulties in estimating reliably the replacement effect of social security; it is quite sensitive to specification of the non-social security variables and swayed by extreme observations in the sample. In addition, our best estimates of the direct replacement effect tend to be somewhat below our *a priori* expectations.

The indirect effect of social security on retirement, on the other hand, is unexpectedly large. The combination of the weak direct and strong indirect effects turns out to imply that, for most countries, the net impact of social security is close to zero, though possibly on the plus side. Thus, our results imply that there is little cause for concern that social security dramatically reduces the saving rate. On the other hand they do imply that the saving rate is maintained through a reduction of the working span and hence of income per capita, suggesting that a rise in social security may tend, after all, to reduce private per capita saving and wealth.[21]

[20] It is, in particular, consistent with the studies of Kopits and Gotur (1979) and Barro and MacDonald (1979), neither of whom took into account a measure of retirement span. It is not consistent with Feldstein (1977, 1979), who finds the total effect to be significantly negative. In general, Feldstein finds a much stronger replacement effect than we do. The difference apparently results from the difference in periods studied and his reliance solely on the Olsen data.

[21] Though our weak results with respect to the replacement effect of social security may be interpreted in support of Barro's (1974) 'Ricardian' hypothesis that saving for bequests offsets the government's social security programme, we believe there is strong evidence this is not the case. First, the significant positive coefficient on income growth strongly suggests that individuals' planning horizons are finite. Second, in preliminary empirical work to be presented in a forthcoming paper, we find that adding a measure of the surplus of the social security system does not have the negative impact on the savings rate expected under Barro's hypothesis.

Appendix A

In this appendix we list the data used in the savings and retirement equations. A key to the variable names is given below.

s/y	The private savings ratio
σ, Olsen	The Olsen replacement rates (not adjusted for coverage)
σ, ILO	Replacement rates calculated from ILO data
d/w(1)	Ratio of population below 20 to population 20 and above
d/w(2)	Ratio of children under 15 to the male labour force
r/w(1)	Ratio of retired population above the minimum age of retirement (for social security purposes) to population 20 and above
r/w(2)	Ratio of retired men 55 and above to male labour force
r/w(3)	Ratio of retired men 65 and above to male labour force
ΔPR	(Labour force participation rate 25–54 – Participation rate 65 and over)/Participation rate 25 through 54
ρ	Rate of growth (per year) of real per capita disposable income
ln (y)	Natural log of real GDP per worker ($1970 US)
W2NORM	The weights (normalised to sum to 1) assigned to each country by the GLS correlation for heteroskedasticity
M65	The ratio of men above 65 to male labour force

A more detailed description of the data, sources and approximation, may be found in the text.

Appendix B

	s/y	σ, Olsen	σ, ILO	d/w(1)
AUSTRALIA	0.1475	NA	0.263381	0.6043
AUSTRIA	0.1613	0.67	0.472441	0.4398
BELGIUM	0.1602	NA	0.209567	0.434
CANADA	0.1184	0.42	0.251799	0.6874
DENMARK	0.098	0.51	0.346535	0.476
FINLAND	0.1564	NA	0.39819	0.5695
FRANCE	0.1529	0.65	0.236842	0.4865
GERMANY	0.1704	0.48	0.582465	0.4128
GREECE	0.1359	NA	0.363575	0.4916
IRELAND	0.1347	NA	0.219325	0.6585
ITALY	0.1744	0.6	0.271493	0.4707
JAPAN	0.2413	NA	0.039841	0.574

LUXEMBOURG	0.1349	NA	0.426205	0.397
NETHERLANDS	0.1921	0.5	0.571429	0.5846
NORWAY	0.128	0.38	0.428669	0.4849
PORTUGAL	0.114	NA	0.083501	0.5986
SPAIN	0.1494	NA	0.134021	0.5505
SWEDEN	0.098	0.44	0.402613	0.4091
SWITZERLAND	0.1775	0.45	0.354389	0.4414
UNITED KINGDOM	0.1002	0.36	0.346439	0.4398
UNITED STATES	0.103	0.44	0.272346	0.6127

	$d/w(2)$	$r/w(1)$	$r/w(2)$	$r/w(3)$
AUSTRALIA	0.966	0.1177	0.1072	0.0891
AUSTRIA	0.8771	0.2032	0.2241	0.168
BELGIUM	0.8521	0.2195	0.2232	0.1753
CANADA	1.1899	0.1112	0.1214	0.0993
DENMARK	0.7914	0.1616	0.1408	0.1219
FINLAND	1.012	0.1105	0.1191	0.0843
FRANCE	0.9104	0.1938	0.1753	0.1282
GERMANY	0.7659	0.1631	0.1616	0.1287
GREECE	0.9013	0.1488	0.1294	0.0931
IRELAND	1.0832	0.1304	0.1097	0.0946
ITALY	0.8761	0.221	0.1754	0.1221
JAPAN	0.9225	0.0753	0.0646	0.0473
LUXEMBOURG	0.7474	0.1992	0.2158	0.1474
NETHERLANDS	1.0315	0.1386	0.1616	0.1313
NORWAY	0.8793	0.1458	0.1919	0.1687
PORTUGAL	0.9526	0.0994	0.0681	0.0475
SPAIN	0.9299	0.1067	0.0935	0.0737
SWEDEN	0.7168	0.1684	0.1727	0.1471
SWITZERLAND	0.6986	0.1219	0.0956	0.0837
UNITED KINGDOM	0.7792	0.1755	0.1315	0.1219
UNITED STATES	1.106	0.1432	0.1386	0.1112

	ΔPR	ρ	$\ln(y)$	W2NORM
AUSTRALIA	0.7428	0.03036	1.89664	0.036332
AUSTRIA	0.8726	0.03714	1.52181	0.034611
BELGIUM	0.9091	0.03857	1.94517	0.026139
CANADA	0.7184	0.03492	2.16387	0.045182
DENMARK	0.713	0.02793	1.84829	0.020016
FINLAND	0.7223	0.04196	1.58667	0.0205
FRANCE	0.7623	0.04689	1.87897	0.07586
GERMANY	0.7804	0.03779	1.81697	0.105145

GREECE	0.5876	0.06346	1.20791	0.024672
IRELAND	0.5018	0.03492	1.47254	0.02435
ITALY	0.7984	0.05238	1.58366	0.101239
JAPAN	0.4546	0.07997	1.36002	0.070892
LUXEMBOURG	0.8291	0.0203	2.15622	0.003649
NETHERLANDS	0.8335	0.04637	1.99009	0.051273
NORWAY	0.6684	0.0383	1.93442	0.015477
PORTUGAL	0.4003	0.06453	0.872588	0.012915
SPAIN	0.5344	0.05475	1.35913	0.061056
SWEDEN	0.7571	0.02289	1.96963	0.022896
SWITZERLAND	0.6229	0.0294	1.81125	0.027201
UNITED KINGDOM	0.7687	0.00974	1.7818	0.050571
UNITED STATES	0.7061	0.03168	2.36049	0.170027

	M65
AUSTRALIA	0.1189
AUSTRIA	0.1906
BELGIUM	0.1917
CANADA	0.1351
DENMARK	0.1683
FINLAND	0.1126
FRANCE	0.1644
GERMANY	0.1631
GREECE	0.1498
IRELAND	0.1718
ITALY	0.1499
JAPAN	0.0993
LUXEMBOURG	0.1737
NETHERLANDS	0.1564
NORWAY	0.1837
PORTUGAL	0.1117
SPAIN	0.126
SWEDEN	0.1905
SWITZERLAND	0.132
UNITED KINGDOM	0.1571
UNITED STATES	0.1545

REFERENCES

Belsley, D., Kuh, E. and Welsch, R. (1980), *Regression Diagnostics: Identifying Influential Data and Sources of Collinearity*, (New York: Wiley).

Barro, R. J. (1974), 'Are Government Bonds Net Worth?' *Journal of Political Economy*, 82, no. 6.

Boskin, M. J. (1977), 'Social Security and Retirement Decisions', *Economic Inquiry*, XV, no. 1, (January).

Boskin, M. J. and Hurd, M. D. (1978), 'The Effect of Social Security on Early Retirement', *Journal of Public Economics*, 10.

—— and MacDonald, G. M. (1979), 'Social Security and Consumer Spending in an International Cross-section', *Journal of Public Economics*, 11 (June).

Dolde, W. and Tobin, J. (1980), 'Mandatory Retirement Saving and Capital Formation', this volume.

Eisner, R. (1980), 'Social Security and Capital Accumulation', Northwestern University mimeo (December 1980).

Feldstein, M. (1974), 'Social Security, Induced Retirement, and Aggregate Accumulation', *Journal of Political Economy*, 82, no. 5 (September/October).

—— (1977), 'Social Security and Private Savings: International Evidence in an Extended Life-Cycle Model', in *The Economics of Public Services*, M. Feldstein and R. Inman (eds) (London: Dacmillan).

—— (1979), 'International Differences in Social Security and Saving', National Bureau of Economic Research Working Paper No. 335 (May).

Haanes-Olsen, L. (1978), 'Earnings Replacement Rate of Old Age Benefits, 1965–75, Selected Countries', *Social Security Bulletin* (January), 41, no. 1.

Houthakker, H. S. (1965), 'On Some Determinants of Saving in Developed and Underdeveloped countries', in E. A. G. Robinson (ed.), *Problems in Economic Development* (London: Macmillan).

Hu, S. C. (1974), 'Social Security, the Supply of Labor, and Capital Accumulation', *American Economic Review*, 69, no. 3 (June).

Hymans, S. (1981), 'Saving, Investment, and Social Security', (forthcoming) *National Tax Journal* (March), 34, no. 1.

International Labour Organisation. *Cost of Social Security*, Geneva, International Labour Organization (various issues).

Kopits, G. and Gotur, P. (1979), 'The Influence of Social Security on Household Savings: A Cross-Country Investigation', International Monetary Fund, Fiscal Affairs Department (August).

Leff, N. (1969), 'Dependency Rates and Saving Rates', *American Economic Review* (December).

Modigliani, Franco (1970), 'The Life Cycle Hypothesis of Saving and Intercountry Differences in the Saving Ratio', in *Induction, Growth and Trade*, Essays in Honour of Sir Roy Harrod, W. A. Eltis, M. Fg. Scott, and J. N. Wolfe (eds.), (Oxford: Clarendon Press).

—— (1966), 'The Life Cycle Hypothesis of Saving, the Demand for Wealth and the Supply of Capital', *Social Research*, 33, no. 2 (Summer).

—— and Brumberg, R. (1954), 'Utility Analysis and the Consumption Function: An Attempt at Integration', in *Post-Keynesian Economics*, Kenneth Kurihara (ed.) (Rutgers University Press).

—— and —— (1980), 'Utility Analysis and Aggregate Consumption Functions: An Attempt at Integration', in *The Collected Papers of Franco Modigliani*, Volume 2 (MIT Press).

Munnel, A. (1974), *The Effect of Social Security on Personal Saving* (Cambridge, Mass.: Ballinger).

OECD (1973, *National Accounts of OECD Countries, 1960–1971* (Paris).

—— (1975), *Labour Force Statistics 1962–1973*, (Paris).

—— (1977), *Old Age Pension Schemes* (Paris).

—— (1979), *Demographic Trends 1950–1990* (Paris).

—— (1980), *National Accounts of OECD Countries, 1950–1978*, Volume 1 (Paris).

Pechman, Aaron and Taussig, M. (1968), *Social Security, Perspectives for Reform* (Washington D. C: Brookings).

Reimers, C. (1976), 'Is the Average Age at Retirement Changing', *Journal of the American Statistical Association* (September), 71, no. 355.

Sheshinski, E. (1978), 'A Model of Social Security and Retirement Decisions', *Journal of Public Economics*, 10.

Summers, R., Kravis, I. B. and Heston, A. (1980), 'International Comparisons of Real Product and its Composition: 1950–1977', *The Review of Income and Wealth*, Series 26, no. 1 (March).

Barro, R. J., and MacDonald, G. M., (1979), "Social Security and Consumer Spending in an International Cross-Section", *Journal of Public Economics*, 11, pp. 275–289.

Errata

Page 25, 2 lines above equation (1): insert "of" in "rate of growth income."

Page 26, 2 lines below equation (2): the expression should have parentheses and read "(SST/R) − λc."

Page 26, end of last line: insert "(see Figure 2.1)."

Page 29, line 6: insert "adult" before "population."

Page 29, line 8: delete "actual number of dependents" and insert "ratio of dependents to adults."

Page 29, last paragraph, second line: "older" should read "younger."

Page 35, sixth line after Table 2.1: "αs" should read "α's."

Page 37, second paragraph, second to last line: delete "upward" and insert "possibly."

Page 37, footnote 12: insert "more" before "efficient."

Page 39, second to last line of first paragraph: "16" should read "17."

Page 41, third paragraph, seventh line: insert "hypothesis" after "life cycle."

Page 43, second paragraph, third line from end: "I.4" should read "1.4."

Page 44, first paragraph, fourth line: "by" should read "and."

Page 44, first paragraph, fourth line from end: "somewhat" should read "a somewhat."

Page 45: the extreme right-side expression should have a minus sign in front of it; the first L in the denominator should be deleted.

Page 48, third from last line: expression in parentheses should be "(W/Z) (r/w)."

Page 49: both equations should be numbered "(I.4 ′ ′)."

Page 49, second paragraph, second to last line: first set of parentheses should read "(from (I.4 ′ ′))."

Page 54, Hu reference: "1974" should be "1979."

LIFE CYCLE, INDIVIDUAL THRIFT AND THE WEALTH OF NATIONS

by

FRANCO MODIGLIANI

Sloan School of Management, Massachusetts Institute of Technology, Cambridge, MA

Introduction

This paper provides a review of the theory of the determinants of individual and national thrift that has come to be known as the Life Cycle Hypothesis (LCH) of saving. Applications to some current policy issues are also discussed.

Part I deals with the state of the art on the eve of the formulation of the LCH some 30 years ago. Part II sets forth the theoretical foundations of the model in its original formulation and later amendment, calling attention to various implications, distinctive to it and, sometimes, counter-intuitive. It also includes a review of a number of crucial empirical tests, both at the individual and the aggregate level. Part III reviews some applications of LCH to current policy issues, though only in sketchy fashion, as space constraints prevent fuller discussion.

I. *Antecedents*

(1) *The role of thrift and the Keynesian revolution*

The study of individual thrift and aggregate saving and wealth has long been central to economics because national saving is the source of the supply of capital, a major factor of production controlling the productivity of labor and its growth over time. It is because of this relation between saving and productive capital that thrift has traditionally been regarded as a virtuous, socially beneficial act.

Yet, there was a brief but influential interval in the course of which, under the impact of the Great Depression, and of the interpretation of this episode which Keynes suggested in the *General Theory* [1936], saving came to be seen with suspicion, as potentially disruptive to the economy and harmful to social welfare. The period in question goes from the mid '30s to the late '40s or early '50s. Thrift posed a potential threat, as it reduced one component of demand, consumption, without systematically and automatically giving rise to an offsetting expansion in investment. It might thus cause "inadequate" demand — and, hence, output and employment lower than the capacity of the economy. This failure was attributable to a variety of reasons including wage rigidity, liquidity preference, fixed capital coefficients in production and to investment controlled by animal spirits rather than by the cost of capital.

260

Not only was oversaving seen as having played a major role in the Great Depression, but, in addition, there was widespread fear that the problem might come back to haunt the post war era. These fears were fostered by a widely held conviction that, in the future, there would not be too much need for additional accumulation of capital while saving would rise even faster than income. This combination could be expected to result, sooner or later, in saving outstripping the "need" for capital. These concerns were at the base of the "stagnationist" school which was prominent in the 40s and early 50s.

(2) *Early Keynesian theories of the determinants of saving*

It is interesting and somewhat paradoxical that the present day interest and extensive research activity about saving behavior owes its beginnings to the central role assigned by Keynesian economics to the consumption function as a determinant of aggregate demand and to the concern with oversaving as a source of both cyclical fluctuations and long run stagnation. It is for this reason that the early endeavor to model individual and aggregate saving behavior was dominated by the views expressed on this subject by Keynes in the *General Theory*, and in particular by his well known "fundamental psychological [rather than 'economic'] law" [1936, p. 96] to the effect that an increase in income can be counted on to lead to a positive but smaller change in consumption. Even when the analysis followed the more traditional line of demand theory, it relied on a purely static framework in which saving was seen as one of the many "goods" on which the consumer could spend his income. Thus, income was seen as the main systematic determinant of both individual and national saving, and, in line with Keynes' "law", it was regarded as a superior commodity (i.e., one on which "expenditure" rises with income) and most likely a luxury, for which expenditure rises faster than income. Also, in contrast to other goods, the "expenditure" on saving could be negative — and, accordingly, dissaving was seen as typical of people or countries below some "break even" level of income. All these features could be formalized by expressing consumption as a linear function of income with a substantial positive intercept. This formulation appeared to be supported by the findings of numerous budget studies, and even by the newly developed National Income Accounts, spanning the period of the Great Depression, at the bottom of which saving turned small or even negative.

As is apparent, in this early phase the dominant approach could best be characterized as crudely empirical; little attention was given to why rational consumers would choose to "allocate" their income to saving. The prevailing source of substantial saving was presumably the desire of the rich to bequeath an estate (Keynes' "pride" motive, [1936, p. 108]). Accordingly, the main source of the existing capital *stock* could be traced to inheritance. Similarly, there was little evidence of concern with how, and how long, "poor" people, or countries, could dissave without having saved first or without exceeding their means.

3) *Three landmark empirical studies*

In the second half of the '40s, three important empirical contributions dealt a fatal blow to this extraordinarily simple view of the saving process. First, the

261

work of Kuznets [1946] and others provided clear evidence that the saving ratio had not changed much since the middle of the 19th century, despite the large rise in per capita income. Second, a path breaking contribution of Brady and Friedman [1947] provided a reconciliation of Kuznets' results with budget study evidence of a strong association between the saving rate and family income. They demonstrated that the consumption function implied by family data shifted up in time as mean income increased, in such a way that the saving rate was explained not by the *absolute* income of the family but rather by its income *relative* to overall mean income.

Ways of reconciling these findings with the standard linear consumption function were soon provided by Duesenberry [1949] and Modigliani [1949], though within the empirical tradition of the earlier period. Duesenberry's "relative income hypothesis" accounted for the Brady-Friedman results in terms of imitation of the upper classes. This is an appealing explanation, though it fails to come to grips with the budget constraint in the case of would-be dissavers below mean income. Similarly, the "Duesenberry-Modigliani" consumption function tried to reconcile the cyclical variations of the saving ratio with its long run stability by postulating that current consumption was determined not just by current income but also by its highest previous peak, resulting in a ratchet-like upward creep in the short run consumption function. In my own formulation, primary stress was placed on reasons why the savings rate should move procyclically and on the consideration that in an economy with stable long run growth, the ratio of the current to highest previous income could be taken as a good measure of cyclical conditions. Duesenberry, on the other hand, put more stress on consumers explicitly anchoring their consumption on the previous peak. This formulation was brought to its logical conclusion by Brown [1952] when he proposed that the highest previous income should be replaced by the highest previous consumption.

The third fundamental contribution was the highly imaginative analysis of Margaret Reid [not published] which pointed to a totally different explanation for the association between the saving ratio and relative income, namely that consumption was controlled by normal or 'permanent', rather than current, income.

This contribution was an important source of inspiration, both for the Life Cycle and for the roughly contemporaneous Permanent Income Hypothesis (PIH) of Milton Friedman [1957].

II. *The Life Cycle Hypothesis*

Between 1952 and 1954, Richard Brumberg and I wrote two essays, "Utility Analysis and the Consumption Function: an Interpretation of Cross Section Data" (Modigliani and Brumberg [1954]), and "Utility Analysis and the Aggregate Consumption Function: an attempt at Integration" (Modigliani and Brumberg [1979]) which provide the basis for the Life Cycle Hypothesis of Saving (LCH). They will be referred to hereafter as MB-C and MB-A respectively. Our purpose was to show that all the well-established empirical regular-

262

ities could be accounted for in terms of rational, utility maximizing, consumers, allocating optimally their resources to consumption over their life, in the spirit of Irving Fisher [1930]. (For an earlier and extensive, but strictly theoretical, application of utility maximization to the theory of saving by households, see Ricci [1926].)

(1) *Utility maximization and the role of Life Resources (Permanent Income)*

The hypothesis of utility maximization (and perfect markets) has, all by itself, one very powerful implication — the resources that a representative consumer allocates to consumption at any age, it, will depend only on his life resources (the present value of labor income plus bequests received, if any) and not at all on income accruing currently. When combined with the self evident proposition that the representative consumer will choose to consume at a reasonably stable rate, close to his anticipated average life consumption, we can reach one conclusion fundamental for an understanding of individual saving behavior, namely that the size of saving over short periods of time, like a year, will be swayed by the extent to which current income departs from average life resources.

This conclusion is common to LCH and to Friedman's PIH which differs from LCH primarily in that it models rational consumption and saving decisions under the "simplifying" assumption that life is indefinitely long. Accordingly, the notion of life resources is replaced by that of "permanent income", while the discrepancy between current and permanent income is labeled "transitory" income.

The notion that saving largely reflects transitory income has a number of implications which have been made familiar by the contributions of Friedman and by our own 1954 paper, and which have received ample empirical support, even with some occasional controversy. Among these implications, the best known and well established is that relating to the upward bias arising in estimating the slope of a saving-income relation from budget data, when, as is usual, the individual observations are classified by current income classes. Because of the correlation between transitory and current income (relative to mean income), the regression line tends to be steeper than the underlying true relation between the (permanent) saving rate and permanent income. Thus, the estimated saving function departs from the true one by being rotated counterclockwise around the mean, to an extent that is greater the greater the variability of transitory income, e.g., more for a sample of farmers than for one of government employees. It is this phenomenon that accounts for the finding of Brady-Friedman cited above, to the effect that the saving ratio, estimated from budget studies at different points of time, appears to depend on the income not in absolute terms but rather relative to overall mean income.

This same consideration provides an explanation for a famous counter intuitive empirical finding first observed in a large survey conducted in the USA in 1936, namely that black families appeared to save more (or dissave less) than white families at any level of income. The reason, of course, is that black families tend to have a much lower average level of permanent income, and, therefore, at any given level of *current* income the transitory component,

263

and hence saving, tended to be larger — see, e.g., Fisher and Brown [1958]).

The extent of bias in the cross-sectional saving function should tend to decline if the households are classified by some criterion less positively correlated with transitory income, and this prediction too has been extensively verified — see, e.g., Modigliani and Ando [1960]. However, we do not intend to pursue here any further the implications of the relation between saving and transitory income since, as already noted, these implications are basically the same for LCH as for PIH. We concentrate, instead, on those aspects that are specific to LCH.

(2) *LCH — The "stripped down" version*

By explicitly recognizing the finite life of households, the LCH could deal with variations in saving other than those resulting from the transitory deviations of income from life resources of PIH. In particular, it could focus on those systematic variations in income and in "needs" which occur over the life cycle, as a result of maturing and retiring, and of changes in family size — hence the name of Life Cycle Hypothesis. In addition, the LCH was in a position to take into account bequests and the bequest motive, which were not amenable to analysis within the approximation of infinite life.

In MB-C and in the first two parts of the MB-A, we made a number of simplifying, stylized, assumptions concerning the life cycle path of household opportunities and tastes, in order to draw out succinctly the essential implications of the LCH approach. These were: (1) opportunities: income constant until retirement, zero thereafter; zero interest rate; and (2) preferences: constant consumption over life, no bequests.

For this "basic" or "stripped down" model, the life cycle path of saving and wealth is described in the, by now familiar, graph of Figure 1. Because the retirement span follows the earning span, consumption smoothing leads to a humped-shaped age path of wealth holding, a shape that had been suggested earlier by Harrod [1948] under the label of hump saving (though "hump wealth" would seem like a more descriptive label).

In MB-A, it was shown that this basic model led to a number of implications which were at that time quite novel and surprising — almost counter intuitive. They included the following:

1. The saving rate of a country is entirely independent of its per capita income.
2. The national saving rate is not simply the result of differential thrift of its citizens, in the sense that different national saving rates are consistent with an identical individual (life cycle) behavior.
3. Between countries with identical individual behavior the aggregate saving rate will be higher the higher the long run growth rate of the economy. It will be zero for zero growth.
4. The wealth-income ratio is a decreasing function of the growth rate, thus being largest at zero growth.
5. An economy can accumulate a very substantial stock of wealth relative to income even if no wealth is passed on by bequests.
6. The main parameter that controls the wealth-income ratio and the saving rate for given growth is the prevailing length of retirement.

264

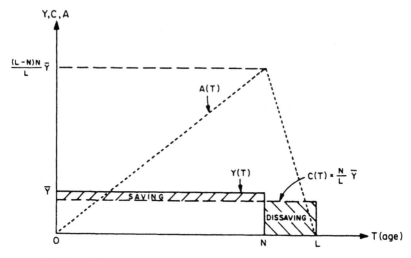

INCOME, CONSUMPTION, SAVING AND WEALTH AS A FUNCTION OF AGE

Figure 1

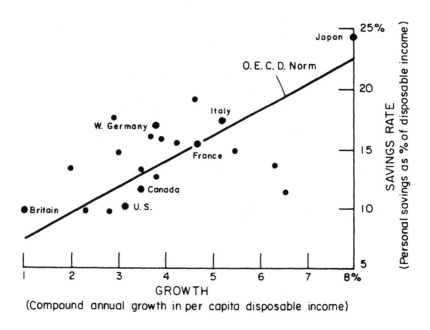

(Compound annual growth in per capita disposable income)

Figure 2

Source: "Determinants of Private Saving with Special Reference to the Role of Social Security —
Cross-country Tests" R. Hemming, ed., *The Determinants of National Saving and Wealth*, proceedings
of a Conference held by the International Economic Association at Bergamo, Italy, June 9–14,
1980, The Macmillan Press Ltd, London, 1983.

Title: The Relation Between Savings and Growth:
savings rate vs. growth for 21 OECD countries,   265
averages for 1960–1975.

6. The main parameter that controls the wealth-income ratio and the saving rate for given growth is the prevailing length of retirement.

To establish these propositions, we begin by considering the case of a stationary economy, and then that of steady growth.

i) *The case of a stationary economy.*

Suppose that there is neither productivity nor population growth, and assume, conveniently, that mortality rate is 1 at some age L and 0 before. Then, clearly, Figure 1 will represent the age distribution of wealth, saving, consumption, and income, up to a factor representing the (constant) number of people in each age bracket. Hence, the aggregate wealth-income ratio, W/Y, is given by the ratio of the sum of wealth held at each age — the area under the wealth path — to the area under the income path. This has a number of significant implications.

a) It is apparent from the graph that W/Y depends on a single parameter, the length of retirement, M — which establishes Proposition 6. The relation between M and W/Y turns out to be extremely simple, to wit:

$$W/Y = M/2 \tag{1}$$

(see MB-A, footnote 38).

b) In MB-A, for illustrative purposes, we conservatively took the average length of retirement as 10 years, implying a wealth-income ratio of 5. This result was an exciting one in that this value was close to the income ratio suggested by preliminary estimates of Goldsmith's [1956] monumental study of U.S. savings. It implied that one could come close to accounting for the entire wealth holding of the U.S. without any appeal to the bequest process — Proposition 5 — a quite radical departure from conventional wisdom.

c) With income and population stationary, aggregate wealth must remain constant in time and, therefore, the change in wealth or rate of saving must be zero, despite the large stock of wealth — Proposition 3. The explanation is that, in stationary state, the dissaving of the retired, from wealth accumulated earlier, just offsets the accumulation of the active population in view of retirement. Saving could occur only transiently if a shock pushed W away from $(M/2)\bar{Y}$, where $\bar{Y}$ is the stationary level of income; then, as long as Y remained at $\bar{Y}$, wealth would gradually return to the equilibrium level $(M/2)\bar{Y}$.

ii) *The case of a steadily growing economy*

In this case, the behavior of the saving rates can be inferred from that of aggregate private wealth, W, through the relation $S = \Delta W$, implying:

$$s \equiv \frac{S}{Y} = \frac{\Delta W}{W} \frac{W}{Y} = \rho w, \quad \frac{ds}{d\rho} = w + \rho \frac{dw}{d\rho} \tag{2}$$

where w is the wealth-income ratio and ρ is the rate of growth of the economy which in steady state equals the rate of growth of wealth, $\Delta W/W$. Since w is positive and is based on a level life cycle consumption and earning, which insures that it is independent of the *level* of income, we have established Propositions 1 and 2. If, in addition, the age profile of the wealth-income ratio

266

could be taken as independent of *growth*, then the saving rate would be proportional to growth with a proportionality factor equal to M/2, substantiating Proposition 3. Actually, the model implies that w is, generally, a declining function of ρ-Proposition 4-though with a small slope, so that the slope of the relation between s and ρ tends to flatten out as ρ grows.

When the source of growth is population, the mechanism behind positive saving may be labelled the Neisser effect (see his [1944]): younger households in their accumulation phase account for a larger share of population, and retired dissavers for a smaller share, than in the stationary society. However, w also falls with ρ because the younger people also are characterized by relatively lower levels of wealth holding. Thanks to the simplifying assumptions of the basic model, it was possible to calculate explicitly values for w and s: for ρ = 2 percent, w = 4, s = 8 percent; for ρ = 4 percent, w = 3 1/4, s = 13 percent.

When the growth is due to productivity, the mechanism at work may be called the Bentzel [1959] effect (who independently called attention to it). Productivity growth implies that younger cohorts have larger life time resources than older ones, and, therefore, their savings are larger than the dissaving of the poorer, retired cohorts. It was shown in MB-A that, if agents plan their consumption as though they did not anticipate the *future* growth of income, then w(ρ) and s(ρ) for productivity growth are just about the same as for population growth, for values of ρ in the relevant range.

It should be noted that this conclusion is diametrically opposite to that reached by Friedman [1957, p. 234], namely that productivity growth should tend to *depress* the saving ratio on the ground that a rise in income "expected to continue tends to raise permanent income relative to measured income and so to raise consumption relative to measured income". This difference in the implications of the two models — one of the very few of any significance — can be traced to the fact that, if life is infinite, there cannot be a Bentzel effect . To be sure, to the extent that agents anticipate fully future income, they will tend to shift consumption from the future to the present and this will tend to reduce the path of wealth and perhaps even generate negative net worth in early life (see e.g., Tobin [1967]). But this effect must be overshadowed by the Bentzel effect, at least for small values of ρ which, realistically, is what matters. (This follows from the continuity of ds/dρ in equation (2)).

The model also implies that the short run behavior of aggregate consumption could be described by a very simple aggregate consumption function, linear in aggregate (labor) income (YL), and wealth (W).

$$C = \alpha YL + \delta W \qquad (3)$$

An equation of this type had been proposed somewhat earlier by Ackley [1951], though both the functional form and the presumed stability of the coefficients rested on purely heuristic considerations. By contrast, it was shown in MB-A that, if income followed closely the steady growth path, then the parameters α and δ could be taken as constant in time and determined by the length of life (L), of retirement (M), and the rate of growth (MB-A, p. 135). For the

267

standard assumption L = 50, M = 10 and ϱ = .03, δ comes to .07 (See MB-A, p. 180). Furthermore, the parameters could be well approximated by the same constant even if income moved around the trend line, as long as the departures were not very long lasting and deep, except that YL should be interpreted as long run expected rather than current income. The short run equation (3) is, of course, consistent with the long run properties 1 to 6, as one can readily verify.

(iii) *Empirical verifications*

None of these long and short run implications of the basic model could be explicitly tested at the time they were established. There were no data on Private Net Worth to test equation (3), except for some indirect estimates pieced together by Hamburger [1951] and some preliminary Goldsmith figures for a few selected years. Similarly, information on Private National Saving were available only for a couple of countries. We could only take encouragement from the fact that the model seemed to fit the single observation available, namely the U.S. Both the wealth income ratio, 4 to 5, and the saving rate, S, "between 1/7 and 1/8" (Goldsmith [1956]) were broadly consistent with the prediction of the model, for a 3 percent growth rate, namely 4 1/3 for w and 13 percent for s.

But the availability of data improved dramatically in the next decade. For the U.S., an annual time series of Private Wealth was put together in the early 60s (Ando, Brown, Kareken and Solow [1963]), and equation (3) was tested (Ando and Modigliani [1963]). It was found to fit the data quite well, and with parameter estimates close to those predicted by the model. By now the consumption function (3) has become pretty much standard, having been estimated for many countries and periods. The coefficient of wealth is frequently lower than .07 quoted earlier but this can be accounted for, at least in part, by the fact that Y is typically defined as total rather than just labor income.

Similarly, by the early 60s, the United Nations had put together National Account statistics for a substantial number of countries, characterized by wide differences in the growth rate, and it became possible to test the relation between the national saving ratio and the growth rate. The early tests were again quite successful (Houthakker [1961 and 1965], Leff [1969] and Modigliani [1970]). The newly available data also revealed the puzzling and shocking fact that the saving ratio for the U.S., by far the richest country in the world, was rather low compared with other industrial countries (see, e.g., Figure 2). The LCII could account for the puzzle through a relatively modest growth rate. By now it is generally accepted that growth is a major source of cross country differences in the saving rate.

(3) *The effect of dropping the simplifying assumptions*

As was demonstrated in MB-A, most of the simplifying assumptions can be replaced by more "realistic" ones without changing the basic nature of the results, and, in particular, the validity of Propositions 1 to 5.

i) *Non Zero interest*

Allowing for a non zero interest rate, r, has two effects. One effect is on .ncome as we must distinguish between labor income, say YL, property income, YP, whose "permanent component" may be approximated by rW, and

268

total income, $Y = YL + YP = YL + rW$. If we continue to assume a constant labor income till retirement, then the graph of income in Figure 1 is unchanged However, the graph of consumption changes through an income and substitution effect: the addition of rW increases income, but at the same time r also affects the opportunity cost of current, in terms of future consumption. It is possible that the consumer would still choose a constant rate of consumption over life (if the elasticity of substitution were zero). In this case, in Figure 1, consumption will still be a horizontal straight line, but at a higher level because of the favorable "income effect" from rW. As for saving, it will be the difference between C and Y. The latter differs from the (piecewise) horizontal YL in the figure by rW, which is proportional to W. As a result, the path of W will depart somewhat from the "triangle" of Figure 1, and, in particular, the overall area under the path can be shown to decline with r. This means that W and, a fortiori, $w = W/Y$, will fall with r.

This result has interesting implications for the much debated issue of the effect of interest rates on saving. Turning back to equation (2), we see that: i) in the absence of growth, a change in r has *no* effect on saving (which remains zero), and ii) for any positive rate of growth, a higher interest rate means a lower saving rate. However, this conclusion depends on the special assumption of zero substitution. With positive substitution, consumption will start lower and will rise exponentially: this "postponement" of consumption, in turn, lifts saving and peak assets. If the substitution effect is strong enough, w will rise, and so will s, as long as ϱ is positive.

This same conclusion can be derived from (3) and the definition of Y. These can be shown to imply:

$$\frac{W}{Y} = \frac{1 - \alpha}{\rho + \delta - \alpha r} \tag{4}$$

Numerical calculations in MB-A suggest that α is not much affected by r, but δ is. In [1975] I hypothesized that the effect of r on δ might be expressed as $\delta = \delta^* + \mu r$ when μ is unity for 0 substitution, and declines with substitution (possibly to a negative value). Substituting for δ in (4), one can see that, when the interest rate rises, saving may fall or rise depending on whether μ is larger or smaller than α.

Which of these inequalities actually holds is an empirical matter? Unfortunately, despite a hot debate, no convincing general evidence either way has been produced, *which leads me to the provisional view that s is largely independent of the interest rate*. It should be noted in this connection that, insofar as saving is done through pension schemes aimed at providing a retirement income, the effect of r on s is likely to be zero (or even positive) in the short run but negative in the long run.

ii) *Allowing for the life cycle of earning and family size*
Far from being constant, average labor income typically exhibits a marked hump pattern which peaks somewhat past age 50, falls thereafter, partly because of the incidence of retirement, and does not go to zero at any age, though it falls sharply after 65. However, consumption also varies with age,

269

largely reflecting variations in family size, as one might expect if the consumer smooths consumption *per equivalent adult* (Modigliani and Ando [1957]). Now the life cycle of family size, at least in the U.S., has a very humped shape rather similar to that of income, though with a somewhat earlier peak. As a result, one might expect, and generally finds a fairly constant rate of saving in the central age group, but lower saving or even dissaving in the very young or old. Thus, as in our Figure 1, the wealth of a given cohort tends to rise to a peak around age 60 to 65 (see, e.g., Projector [1968], King and Dicks-Mireaux [1985], Avery, et.al. [1984], Ando and Kennickell [1985] and Diamond and Hausman [1985]).

It is also worth noting that available evidence supports the LCH prediction that the amount of net worth accumulated up to any given age in relation to life resources is a decreasing function of the number of children and that saving tends to fall with the number of children present in the household and to rise with the number of children no longer present (cf. Blinder, Gordon and Wise [1983], Ando and Kennickell [1985] and Hurd [1986]).

iii) *Length of working and retired life*

One can readily drop the assumption that the length of retired life is a given constant. As is apparent from Figure 1, a longer retirement shifts forward, and raises, the peak of wealth, increasing w and the saving rate. This does not affect the validity of Propositions 2 to 6, but could invalidate 1. It is possible, in fact, that, in an economy endowed with greater productivity (and, hence, greater per capita income), households might take advantage of this by choosing to work for fewer years. This, in turn, would result in a higher national saving rate. Note, however, that this scenario need not follow. The increase in productivity raises the opportunity cost of an extra year of retirement in terms of consumables, providing an incentive to *shorter retirement*. Thus the saving rate could, in principle, be affected by per capita income, but through an unconventional, life-cycle mechanism, and, furthermore, in a direction unpredictable *a-priori*. Empirical evidence suggests that the income effect tends to predominate but is not strong enough to produce a measurable effect on the saving rate (Modigliani and Sterling [1983]).

Aside from income, any other variable that affects the length of retirement could, through this channel, affect saving. One such variable, that has received attention lately, is Social Security. Several studies have found that the availability of Social Security, and terms thereof, can encourage earlier retirement (Feldstein [1974, 1977], Munnell [1974], Boskin and Hurd [1978], Modigliani and Sterling [1983] and Diamond and Hausman [1985]). To this extent, Social Security tends to encourage saving, though this effect may be offset, and even more than fully, by the fact that it also reduces the need for private accumulation to finance a given retirement.

iv) *Liquidity Constraint*

Imperfections in the credit markets as well as the uncertainty of future income prospects may, to some extent, prevent households from borrowing as much as would be required to carry out the unconstrained optimum consumption plan. Such a constraint will have the general effect of postponing consump-

270

tion and increase w as well as s. But, clearly, these are not essential modifications, at least with respect to the aggregate implications — on the contrary they contribute to insure that productivity growth will increase the saving rate. However, significant liquidity constraints could affect quantitatively certain specific conclusions, e.g., with respect to temporary tax changes (see III.1).

v) *Myopia*

LCH presupposes a substantial degree of rationality and self control to make preparations for retired consumption needs. It has been suggested — most recently by Shefrin and Thaler [1985] — that households, even if concerned in principle with consumption smoothing, may be too myopic to make adequate reserves. To the extent that this criticism is valid it should affect the wealth income ratio in the direction opposite to the liquidity constraint, though the effect of transitory changes in income from any source would go in the same direction. However, such myopia is not supported empirically. The assets held at the peak of the life cycle are found to represent a substantial multiple of average income (in the order of 5, at least for the U.S.) and an even larger multiple of permanent income which, in a growing economy, is less than current income. Such a multiple appears broadly consistent with the maintenance of consumption after retirement. This inference is confirmed by recent studies which have found very little evidence of myopic saving behavior. In particular, both Kotlikoff, Spivak and Summers [1982] and Blinder and Gordon [1983, especially figure 4.1], working with data on households close to retirement, find that for most families the resources available to provide for retired consumption appear to be quite adequate to support retired consumption at a rate consistent with life resources.

(4) *The Role of Bequests and the Bequest Motive*

i) *Evidence on the Bequest Process*

The basic version of the LCH that ignores the existence of bequests has proved quite helpful in understanding and predicting many aspects of individual and aggregate behavior. However, significant bequests do exist in market (and non market) economies, as can be inferred from two sets of observations. One observation relates to the behavior of saving and assets of elderly households, especially after retirement. The basic LCH implies that, with retirement, saving should become negative, and thus assets decline at a fairly constant rate, reaching zero at death. The empirical evidence seems to reveal a very different picture: dissaving in old age appears to be at best modest (e.g., see Fisher [1950], Lydall [1955], Mirer [1979] and Ando and Kennickell [1985]). According to Mirer, the wealth-income ratio actually continues to rise in retirement. (Note, however, that his estimate is biased as a result of including education in his regression. Given the steady historical rise in educational levels, there will be a strong association between age, educational attainment, and socio-economic status *relative* to one's cohort, if one holds constant the absolute level of education. Thus, his results could merely reflect the association between bequests, wealth, and relative income discussed below.)

Most other recent analysts have found that the wealth of a given cohort tends to decline after reaching its peak in the 60–65 age range (Shorrocks [1975],

271

King and Dicks-Mireaux [1982], Diamond and Hausman [1985], Avery, Ellhausen, Lenner and Gustavison [1984], Ando [1985]), though there are exceptions – e.g. Menchik and David [1983] discussed below. To be sure, the results depend on the concept of saving and wealth used. If one makes proper allowance for participation in pension funds, then the dissaving (or the decline in wealth) of the old tends to be more apparent, and it becomes quite pronounced if one includes an estimate of social security benefits. But, when the saving and wealth measures include only cash saving and marketable wealth, the dissaving and the decline appear weaker or even absent.

However, the latest US study by Hurd [1986] using a very large sample and relying on panel data finds that, at least for retired people, marketable wealth systematically declines, especially so if one leaves out the very illiquid asset represented by owner occupied houses.

The finding that decumulation, though present, is slow, may partly reflect the fact that survey data give an upward biased picture of the true behavior of wealth during old age, and for two reasons. First, as Shorrocks has argued [1975], one serious bias arises from the well-known positive association between longevity and (relative) income. This means that the average wealth of successively older age classes is the wealth of households with higher and higher life resources. Accordingly, the age profile of wealth is upward biased. Second, in a similar vein, Ando and Kennickell [1985] have found evidence that aged households which are poor tend to double up with younger households and disappear from the sampled population so that the wealth of those remaining independent is again an upward biased estimate of average wealth.

But even allowing for these biases, the decline in wealth – especially of the bequeathable type – is unquestionably less fast than one would expect under a pure life cycle with certain time of death.

This conclusion is confirmed by a very different set of observations coming from probate data. These data, discussed further below, confirm that there is a non negligible annual flow of bequests.

ii) How important is inherited wealth?

The next question is a factual one: just how important is the bequests process in accounting for the existing stock of wealth?

I recently [1985] reviewed a substantial body of information on inherited wealth based on direct surveys of households and on various sources of estimates on the flow of bequests. This review yields a fairly consistent picture suggesting that the proportion of existing wealth that has been inherited is around 20 percent, with a margin of something like 5 percentage points.

This conclusion has recently found support in an interesting calculation carried out by Ando and Kennickell (A&K) [1985]. Starting from estimates of national saving and allocating them by age, using the saving-age relation derived from a well-known budget study (the Bureau of Labor Statistics' Consumer Expenditure survey, 1972–73), they are able to estimate the aggregate amount of wealth accumulated through life saving by all the cohorts living in a given year. They then compare this with aggregate wealth to obtain an

272

estimate of the shares of wealth that are, respectively, self-accumulated and inherited.

Even though the age pattern of saving they use involves relatively little dissaving in old age, their estimate of the share of inherited wealth turns out to be rather small. For the years after 1974, it is around 25 percent, which agrees well with, and thus supports, the findings of my 1985 paper. For the years 1960 to 1973, the share they compute is somewhat larger, fluctuating between 30 and 40 percent. But this higher figure may, at least partly, reflect an upward bias in the A&K estimate of inherited wealth. The bias arises from the fact that the change in total wealth includes capital gains, while the change in the self-accumulated portion largely excludes them. In the period before 1974, capital gains were unquestionably significantly positive, and hence self-accumulation is underestimated and the share of bequests overestimated. In the years from 1973 to 1980, depressed conditions in the stock market reduce the significance of this effect, though this is partially offset by the boom in real estate values.

These estimates are conspicuously at odds with that presented in a provocative paper of Kotlikoff and Summers [1981] (herafter K&S). They endeavour to estimate the share of bequests by two alternative methods: 1) from an estimated flow of bequests, as above, and 2) by an approach methodologically quite similar to that of Ando and Kennickell except that instead of allocating aggregate saving to households by age, they allocate labor income and consumption to individuals 18 and over by age. Through this procedure, they estimate the life cycle wealth, accumulated by every cohort present in a year. Using the first method, K&S reach an estimate of inherited wealth of over one half, while using the second—which they regard as more reliable—their estimate rises even higher, to above four-fifths.

In the 1985 paper, I have shown that the difference between all other estimates, including Ando and Kennickell, and their much higher ones can be traced i) to some explicit errors of theirs, for example, their treatment of the purchase of durable goods, and ii) to unconventional definitions, both of inherited wealth and of life cycle saving. I have shown that when one corrects the error and uses the accepted definitions, one of the K&S measures—that based on bequest flows—coincides very closely with all other estimates. Their alternative measure remains somewhat higher, but it is shown to be subject to an appreciable upward bias which could easily account for the difference.

K&S have suggested an alternative operational criterion of "importance" which should be independent of definitional differences, namely: by what percentage would aggregate wealth decline if the flow of bequests declined by 1 percent? The suggestion is sound but is very hard to implement from available observations. However, a rough measure can be provided by considering the response of the representative household confronted with a larger bequest, but subject to the steady state conditions that he must, in turn, increase his bequest by even more (by a factor equal to the rate of growth of the economy times the average gap between inheriting and bequeathing). He may be better or worse off as a result. If we suppose that he is neither, then one shows that the "importance" of bequests is measured by total bequests received by those

273

currently living—capitalized from date of receipt to the present—divided by total wealth. This happens to. be the measure of the "share of bequests" advocated by K&S. But in reality, for realistic values of the return on wealth and of the growth of the economy one finds that the representative consumer can be expected to be notably better off. Under these conditions one finds that the relevant measure of importance is much closer to the standard measure of share (i.e., not capitalized) than to the K&S measure. Since the shares can be placed at below 1/4, one can conclude that, for the US, a 10 percent decrease in the flow of bequests would be unlikely to decrease wealth by more than 2.5 percent, and could well have an even smaller effect.

The only other country for which one can find some information seems to be the United Kingdom. The share of inherited wealth there appears to be, again, close to 1/5.

But how can one possibly reconcile the fact that the decumulation of wealth after retirement occurs rather slowly with the assertion that the share of inherited wealth is no more than 25 percent? Actually, this apparent puzzle can be readily clarified by means of two considerations. The first is to remember that one of the several ways by which we reached the above figure for the share relies precisely on estimating the flow of bequests from the observed holding of wealth by age: so, by construction, there cannot be any contradiction between the two observations.

The second and more fundamental substantive consideration is that, from the fact that bequeathed wealth is not much lower than the peak accumulation, one cannot conclude that most of the wealth ever accumulated is finally bequeathed. To see this, one need only realize that if one fixes the path of wealth from peak, around age 65, to death, there are still an infinity of possible paths from, say, age 20 to 65, and each of these paths implies a different amount of aggregate wealth. The quicker the average path approaches the peak value, the larger will be the wealth and hence the life cycle component. It can be shown that the observed path of wealth implies a much larger aggregate wealth than would correspond to the path chosen by a consumer scheduling to accumulate the observed average terminal amount of wealth while insuring for himself the highest feasible (constant growth) consumption path.

iii) *Sources of Bequeathed Wealth: the Precautionary Motive*

What accounts for the observed flow of bequests? One can distinguish two main motives which may also interact. The first is the precautionary motive arising from the uncertainty of the time of death. Indeed, in view of the practical impossibility of having negative net worth, people tend to die with some wealth, unless they can manage to put all their retirement reserves into life annuities. However, it is a well known fact that annuity contracts, other than in the form of group insurance through pension systems, are extremely rare. Why this should be so is a subject of considerable current interest and debate (see, e.g., Friedman and Warshawsky [1985a and b]). Undoubtedly, "adverse selection", causing an unfavorable payout, and the fact that some utility may be derived from bequests (Masson [1986])—see below—are an important part of the answer. In the absence of annuities, the wealth left

274

behind will reflect risk aversion and the cost of running out of wealth (besides the utility of bequests).

This point has been elaborated in particular by Davies [1981] (see also Hubbard [1984]) who has shown that, for plausible parameters of the utility function including a low intertemporal elasticity of substitution, the extent to which uncertainty of life depresses the propensity to consume increases with age. As a result "uncertain life time could provide the major element in a complete explanation of the slow decumulation of the retired" (relative to what would be implied by a standard LCH model).

Bequests originating from the precautionary motive fit quite naturally in the LCH framework since they are determined by the utility of consumption and furthermore the surviving wealth must tend, on the average, to be proportional to life resources.

iv) *The Bequest Motive in the LCH*

The second source of inherited wealth is the bequest motive. Contrary to a common perception, there is no intrinsic inconsistency between a significant amount of bequests induced by a bequest motive and the LCH view of the world—in particular, implications 1 to 5.

First, it is obvious that no inconsistency arises if planned bequests are, on average, proportional to life resources. However, this possibility is uninteresting. The most casual observation suggests that the planning and leaving of bequests is concentrated in the upper strata of the distribution of life resources, by which we now mean the sum of (discounted) life-time labor income and bequests received. This observation suggests the following hypothesis, first proposed in MB-A (pp. 173—4):

BI. The share of its resources that a household earmarks, on the average, for bequests is a (non-decreasing) stable function of the size of its life resource *relative* to the average level of resources of its age cohort.

We might expect the share to be close to zero until we reach the top percentiles of the distribution of resources, and then to rise rapidly with income.

One can readily demonstrate (cf. Modigliani [1975]), that this assumption assures that Propositions 1 to 5 will continue to hold at least as long as:

BII. The frequency distribution of the ratio of life resources to mean life resources for each age group is also stable in time.

Indeed, under these conditions, if income is constant, wealth will also tend to be constant and, therefore, saving to be zero, even in the presence of bequests. To see this, note first that BI insures that bequests left (BL) are a fraction, say γ, of life resources, $\hat{Y}$, $BL = \gamma(\hat{Y} + BR)$, where BR is bequests received. BII in turn insures that γ is constant in time (and presumably less than one). Next, note that life savings, LS, is given by:

$$LS = BL - BR = \gamma\hat{Y} - (1-\gamma)BR \qquad (5)$$

Thus, LS increases with Y and decreases with BR, and is zero if $BR = [\gamma/(1-\gamma)]\hat{Y}$. But this last condition must hold in long run-equilibrium since, if BR is

275

smaller, then there will be positive saving which will increase BR, and reduce LS toward zero; and vice versa if BR is larger.

This generalization of the basic model has a number of implications, a few of which may be noted here.

i) The age patterns of Figure 1 for a stationary society are modified, as bequests raise the average wealth path by a constant, equal to BR, beginning at the age at which bequests are received. The new path remains parallel to the old so that at death it has height BL = BR.

ii) If labor income is growing at some constant rate, then average BR will tend to grow at this same rate and so will BL, but BL will exceed BR by a factor $e^{\varrho T}$, where T is the average age gap between donor and recipient. Thus, with positive growth, and then only, the existence of bequests involves life-saving, on top of hump-saving. Alternatively, bequests result in a higher wealth-income ratio, depending on γ, and, hence, a higher saving ratio, to an extent that is proportional to ϱ.

iii) The share of life resources left as bequests could be an increasing function of the household's resources *relative* to the resources of his cohort. This, in turn, implies that at any age, the saving-income and wealth-income ratio for individual families could be an increasing function of *relative* (not absolute) income.

This last proposition, which is clearly inconsistent with PIH, is supported by a good deal of empirical evidence, from Brady and Friedman [1947] to Mayer [1972]. As for the first part of iii), and the underlying assumption BI, it receives strong support from a recent test by Menchik and David [1983]. In this imaginative contribution, the authors have assembled, from probate records, a large body of data on individual bequests which they have matched with income data from tax returns. Their sample covers persons born since 1880 (including a few before) and deceased between 1947 and 1978. They find striking evidence that a) bequests depend on the position of the household's life resources in the distribution of life resources of *its cohort*, b) that they are small for people whose estimated life resources fall below the 80th percentile in that distribution, but that c) beyond the 80th percentile, they rise rapidly with (permanent) income.

v) *The Quantitative Importance of the Bequest Motive*

It would be interesting to have some idea of how important is the role of the pure bequest motive—as distinguished from the precautionary one—in the accumulation of wealth. It should be apparent, in fact, that if one could conclude that it accounts for a very large fraction of total wealth, then the LCH and hump saving would lose considerable interest as an explanation of private accumulation. Unfortunately, at present, we know very little on this score and it is not even clear that we will even be able to acquire reliable knowledge. There is nonetheless a certain amount of evidence suggesting that the true bequest motive affects a rather small number of households mostly located in the highest income and wealth brackets.

The best known evidence is that coming from surveys conducted in the 1960s. In a 1962 survey (Projector and Weiss [1964]), only 3 percent of the respondents gave as a reason for saving, "To provide an estate for the family".

276

However, the proportion rises with wealth, reaching 1/3 for the top class (1/2 million 1963 dollars and over). Similar, though somewhat less extreme, results are reported for a Brookings study (Barlow, et.al. [1966]). Thus, the bequest motive seems to be limited to the highest economic classes.

This hypothesis is supported by the finding of Menchik and David that for (and only for) the top 20 percent, bequests rise proportionately faster than total resources, something which presumably cannot be explained by the precautionary motive. Actually, another very recent study (Hurd [1986]), yields results which are even more negative about the importance of bequests. It starts from the reasonable hypothesis that if the true bequest motive is an important source of terminal wealth, then retired households with living children should have more wealth and should save more (dissave less) than childless ones. It is found that in fact those with children have *less* wealth and, by and large, *dissave* the same fraction of wealth. The first result, as pointed out earlier, is fully consistent with the standard no-bequest LCH, because of the "cost" of children; but for this reason the rest may be biased. But the second result is indeed hard to reconcile with a significant bequest motive.

Considering that the overall share of inherited wealth can be placed below 1/5, we seem safe in concluding that the overwhelming proportion of wealth existing at a point in time is the result of life cycle accumulation, including in it a portion reflecting the bequest arising from the precautionary motive.

Aside from this quantitative evaluation, it is important to note that the model generalized to allow for bequests of all sources still satisfies Propositions (1) to (5). On the other hand, Proposition 6 must be generalized to allow for several forces, discussed in this section, that could affect the equilibrium wealth income ratio. These include the age structure not accounted for by steady-state population growth, rate of return on wealth, household access to credit, as well as the strength of the bequest motive. Another potentially important variable is Social Security, though its systematic effect on saving has so far proven elusive, a failure not convincingly accounted for by its having two offsetting effects on private saving (cf. section II.3, iii, above). Pursuing the above implications opens up a vast area of research that so far has been barely scratched.

III. *Policy Implications*

Limitations of space make it impossible to pursue a systematic analysis of policy issues for which the LCH has implications that are significantly different from those derivable by the standard Keynesian consumption function or refinements thereof. I will, however, list some of the major areas of applications with a brief statement of the LCH implications:

1. Short run stabilization policy

i) *The monetary mechanism:* The fact that wealth enters importantly in the short run consumption function means that monetary policy can affect aggregate demand not only through the traditional channel of investment but also through the market value of assets and consumption. (See Modigliani [1971]).

ii) *Transitory income taxes:* Attempts at restraining (or stimulating) demand

277

through transitory income taxes (or rebates) can be expected to have small effects on consumption and to lower (raise) saving because consumption depends on life resources which are little affected by a transitory tax change (empirically supported). (See the literature cited in Modigliani and Steindel [1977] and Modigliani and Sterling [1985]).

2. Long run propositions

i) *Consumption Taxes:* A progressive tax on consumption is more equitable than one on current income because it more nearly taxes permanent income (quite apart from its incentive effects on saving.)

ii) *Short and long run effects of deficit financing:* Expenditures financed by deficit tends to be paid by future generations; those financed by taxes are paid by the current generation. The conclusion rests on the proposition that private saving, being controlled by life cycle considerations, should be (nearly) independent of the government budget stance (Modigliani and Sterling [1985]), and therefore private wealth should be independent of the national debt (Modigliani [1984]). It follows that the national debt tends to crowd out an equal amount of private capital at a social cost equal to the return on the lost capital (which is also approximately equal to the government interest bill).

This conclusion stands in sharp contrast to that advocated by the socalled Ricardian Equivalence Proposition (Barro [1974]) which holds that whenever the government runs a deficit, the private sector will save more in order to offset the unfavorable effect of the deficit on future generations.

Of course, to the extent that the government deficit is used to finance productive investments, then future generations also receive the benefit of the expenditure, and letting them pay for it through deficit financing may be consistent with intergenerational equity.

In an open economy, the investment crowding out effect may be attenuated through the inflow of foreign capital, attracted by the higher interest that results from the smaller availability of investable funds. However, the burden on future generations is roughly unchanged because of the interest to be paid on the foreign debt.

Finally if there is slack in the economy, debt financed government expenditures may not crowd out investment, at least if accompanied by an accommodating monetary policy, but may, instead, raise income and saving. In this case, the deficit is beneficial, as was held by the early Keynesians; however, the debt will have a crowding out effect once the economy returns to full employment. LCH suggests that to avoid this outcome, a good case can be made for a so-called cyclically balanced budget.

278

REFERENCES

Ando, A., "The Savings of Japanese Households: A Micro Study Based on Data from the National Survey of Family Income and Expenditure, 1974 and 1979," Economic Planning Agency, Government of Japan, 1985.

—, E.G. Brown, J. Kareken and R.M. Solow, "Lags in Fiscal and Monetary Policy" in *Stabilization Policies*, prepared for the Commission on Money and Credit, Prentice Hall, 1963.

— and A. Kennickell, "How Much (or Little) Life Cycle is There in Micro Data? Cases of U.S. and Japan", paper presented at Istituto Bancario San Paolo di Torino Conference to Honor Franco Modigliani, in Martha's Vineyard, Massachusetts, September 19–21, 1985. Conference proceedings forthcoming.

Ackley. G. "The Wealth-Saving Relationship," *Journal of Political Economy*, April 1951.

Avery, R.B., G.E. Elliehausen, G.B. Canner and T.A. Gustafson, "Survey of Consumer Finances, 1983: A Second Report," *Federal Reserve Bulletin*, 70, 1984.

Barlow, R., H.E. Brazer and J.N. Morgan, *Economic Behavior of the Affluent*, Washington: The Brookings Institute, 1966.

Barro, R.J., "Are Government Bonds Net Wealth?" *Journal of Political Economy*, 82, 1974.

Bentzel, R., "Nagra Synpunkter pa Sparandets Dynamik," in *Festskrift Tillagnad Halvar Sundberg* (Uppsala Universitetes Arsskrift 1959:9) Uppsala, 1959.

Blinder, A., R. Gordon and D. Wise, "Social Security, Bequests and the Life Cycle Theory of Saving: Cross-sectional Tests," in F. Modigliani and R. Hemming, eds., *The Determinants of National Saving and Weath*, St. Martins Press, New York, 1983, pp. 89–122.

Boskin, M. and M. Hurd, "The Effect of Social Security on Early Retirement, *Journal of Public Economics, 10*, 1978

Brady, D.S. and R.D. Friedman, "Savings and the Income Distribution," *Studies in Income and Wealth, 9*, National Bureau of Economic Research, New York, 1947.

Brown, T.M., "Habit Persistence and Lags in Consumer Behavior," *Econometrica, 20*, 1952.

Davies, J.B., "Uncertain Lifetime, Consumption, and Dissaving in Retirement," *Journal of Political Economy, 89*, 1981.

Diamond, P.A. and J.A. Hausman, "Individual Retirement and Savings Behavior," *Journal of Public Economics, 23*, 1985.

Duesenberry, James S, *Income, Saving and the Theory of Consumer Behavior*, Harvard University Press, Cambridge, 1949.

Feldstein, M., "Social Security, Induced Retirement, and Aggregate Accumulation," *Journal of Political Economy, 82*, 1974.

—, "Social Security and Private Savings: International Evidence in an Extended Life-Cycle Model," in M. Feldstein and R. Inman, eds., The *Economics of Public Services*, Macmillan, London, 1977.

Fisher, F. and R. Brown, "Negro-white savings differentials and the Modigliani–Brumberg hypothesis," *Review of Economics and Statistics*, February 1958.

Fisher, I., *The Theory of Interest*, Macmillan, New York, 1930.

Fisher, J., "The Economics of an Aging Population, A Study in Income, Spending and Savings Patterns of Consumer Units in Different Age Groups, 1935–36, 1945 and 1949," Unpublished dissertation, Columbia University, New York, 1950.

Friedman, Benjamin M. and Mark Warshawsky, "The Cost of Annuities: Implications for Saving Behavior and Bequests", National Bureau of Economic Research Working Paper #1682, August 1985.

— and —, "Annuity Prices and Saving Behavior in the United States", National Bureau of Economic Research Working Paper #1683, June 1985.

Friedman, M., *A Theory of the Consumption Function*, Princeton University Press, Princeton, 1957.

Goldsmith, R.W., *A Study of Saving in the United States*, Princeton University Press, Princeton, 1956.

Hamburger, W., "Consumption and Wealth," Unpublished dissertation, University of Chicago, Chicago, 1951.

Harrod, R.F., *Towards a Dynamic Economics*, London, 1948.

Houthakker, H.S., "An International Comparison of Personal Saving," *Bulletin of the International Statistical Institute, 38*, 1961.

279

—, "On Some Determinants of Saving in Developed and Underdeveloped Countries," in *Problems in Economic Development*, E.A.G. Robinson, ed., Macmillan, London, 1965.

Hubbard, R. Glenn, "'Precautionary' Saving Revisited: Social Security, Individual Welfare, and the Capital Stock", National Bureau of Economic Research Working Paper #1430, August 1984.

Hurd, Michael D., "Savings and Bequests", National Bureau of Economic Research Working Paper #1826, January 1986.

Keynes, J.M., *General Theory of Employment, Interest and Money*, Harcourt, Brace, New York, 1936.

Kennickell, A., "An Investigation of Life Cycle Savings Behavior in the United States", Unpublished dissertation, University of Pennsylvania, Philadelphia, 1984.

King, M.A. and L-D. L. Dicks-Mireaux, "Asset Holdings and the Life-Cycle," *Economic Journal, 92*, 1982.

Kotlikoff, L.J., A. Spivak and L. Summers, "The Adequacy of Savings," *American Economic Review*, 72, 1982.

— and L. Summers, "The Role of Intergenerational Transfers in Aggregate Capital Accumulation," *Journal of Political Economy, 89*, 1981.

Kuznets, S., *National Income: A Summary of Findings*, National Bureau of Economic Research, New York, 1946.

Leff, N., "Dependency Rates and Saving Rates," *American Economic Review, 59*, 1969.

Lydall, H., "The Life Cycle in Income, Saving and Asset Ownership," *Econometrica, 23*, 1955.

Masson, Andre, "A Cohort analysis of wealth-age profiles generated by a simulation model in France (1949–1975)," *Economic Journal, 96*, 1986, March.

Mayer, T., *Permanent Income, Wealth and Consumption*, University of California Press, 1972.

Menchik, P.L. and David, M., "Income Distribution, Lifetime Savings, and Bequests," *American Economic Review, 73*, 1983.

Mirer, T.W., "The Wealth-Age Relationship among the Aged," *American Economic Review, 69*, 1979.

Modigliani, F., "Fluctuations in the Saving-Income Ratio: A Problem in Economic Forecasting," *Studies in Income and Wealth, 11*, National Bureau of Economic Research, New York, 1949.

—, "Monetary Policy and Consumption: Linkages via Interest Rate and Wealth Effects in the FMP Model," in *Consumer Spending and Monetary Policy: The Linkages*, Conference Series No. 5, Federal Reserve Bank of Boston, Boston, 1971.

—, "The Life Cycle Hypothesis of Saving Twenty Years Later," in M. Parkin, ed., *Contemporary Issues in Economics*, Manchester University Press, 1975.

—, "The Economics of Public Deficits," paper presented at Conference in memory of Abba Lerner. Tel Aviv University, Israel, May 28–31, 1984. Proceedings forthcoming.

—, "Measuring the Contribution of Intergenerational Transfers to Total Wealth: Conceptual Issues and Empirical Findings," paper presented at Modeling the Accumulation and Distribution of Personal Wealth seminar, Paris, France. September 10–11, 1985. Proceedings forthcoming.

—, and A. Ando, "Tests of the Life Cycle Hypothesis of Savings: Comments. —, and Suggestions," *Bulletin of the Oxford University Institute of Statistics*, 1957.

— and —, "The 'Permanent Income' and the 'Life Cycle' Hypothesis of Saving Behavior: Comparison and Tests" in *Consumption and Saving*, Vol. 2, Wharton School of Finance and Commerce, University of Pennsylvania, 1960.

— and —, "The 'Life Cycle' Hypothesis of Saving: Aggregate Implications and Tests," *American Economic Review, 53*, 1963.

— and R. Brumberg, "Utility Analysis and the Consumption Function: An Interpretation of Cross-Section Data," in K. Kurihara, ed., *PostKeynesian Economics*, Rutgers University Press, New Brunswick, 1954.

— and —, "Utility Analysis and Aggregate Consumption Functions: An Attempt at Integration," in A. Abel, ed., *Collected Papers of Franco Modigliani*, Vol. 2. MIT Press, Cambridge, 1979.

—, A. Mason and A. Sterling, "Effect of Fiscal Policy on Saving: Evidence from an International Cross-Section," paper in progress.

— and C. Steindel, "Is a Tax Rebate an Effective Tool for Stabilization Policy?" *Brookings Papers on Economics Activity*, 1977: 1.

280

- and A. Sterling, "Determinants of Private Saving with Special Reference to the Role of Social Security - Cross-country Tests," in F. Modigliani and R. Hemming, eds., *The Determinants of National Saving and Weath*, St. Martins Press, New York, 1983, pp. 24 – 55.

- and -, "Government Debt, Government Spending, and Private Sector Behavior: A Comment," 1985. Forthcoming in *American Economic Review*.

Munnell, A., *The Effect of Social Security on Personal Saving*, Ballinger Press, Cambridge, 1974.

Neisser, H.P. "The Economics of a Stationary Population," *Social Research*, 1944.

Projector, D., *Survey of Changes in Family Finances*, Board of Governors of the Federal Reserve System, Washington, 1968.

- and G. Weiss, *Survey of Financial Characteristics of Consumers*, The Board of Governors of the Federal Reserve, Washington, 1964.

Reid, M.G., "The relation of the within-group permanent component of income to the income elasticity of expenditure," Unpublished paper.

Ricci, U., "L'offerta del Risparmio," Part I, *Giornale degli Economisti*, 1926; Part II, *ibid*; 1926; "Ancora Sull'Offerta del Risparmio", *ibid*; 1927.

Royal Commission on the Distribution of Income and Wealth, *Report No. 5, Third Report on the Standing Reference*, HMSO, London, 1977.

Shefrin, H.M. and R. Thaler, "Life Cycle Vs. Self-Control Theories of Saving: A look at the evidence," Unpublished paper, 1985.

Shiba, Tsunemasa, "The Personal Savings Functions of Urban Worker Household in Japan," *Review of Economics and Statistics, 61*, 1979.

Shorrocks, A.F., "The Age-Wealth Relationship: a cross-section and cohort analysis," *Review of Economics and Statistics, 57*, 1975'

Tobin, James, "Life Cycle Saving and Balanced Growth," in Fellner, et al., *Ten Economic Studies in the Tradition of Irving Fisher*, J. Wiley, New York, 1967.

Modigliani, Franco, "The Life Cycle Hypothesis of Savings and Inter-Country Differences in the Saving Ratio" in W.A. Eltis et al., eds., <u>Induction, Growth and Trade</u>, Essays in Honor of Sir Roy Harrod, London: Claredon Press, 1970.

Errata

Page 261, second paragraph, line 15: "it" should read "saving."

Page 263, 2 lines from the end: "tend" should read "tended."

Page 265, source for Figure 2: insert "F. Modigliani and A. Sterling in F. Modigliani and" before "R. Hemming."

Page 266, point i, second line: insert "the" before "mortality."

Page 266, three lines below equation (2): delete "a."

Page 267, paragraph 3, second line: "who" should read "since he."

Page 268, point iii, line 5: "were" should read "was."

Page 268, point iii, line 8: "S" should read "s."

Page 269, first paragraph, line 10: insert a bar on top of Y in "YL."

Page 270, line 8: "[1985]" should read "[1982]."

Page 271, second paragraph, fifth from last line: "Blinder and Gordon" should read "Blinder et al."

Page 272, point ii, second paragraph, last line: insert "error of" after "margin of."

Page 273, 4 lines from the end of the third paragraph: delete the comma after "wealth."

Page 275, three lines above equation (5): "γ" should read "Y"; in the line below this equation, "Y" should have a hat.

281

Page 276, point iii, line 2: "his" should read "its."

Page 278, fourth line: replace "(empirically supported)" with "(this is empirically supported)."

Page 278, point 2 (ii), second line: "tends" should read "tend."

The Role of Intergenerational Transfers and Life Cycle Saving in the Accumulation of Wealth

Franco Modigliani

T he purpose of this paper is to review what economists know at present about the following question: How large a portion of the existing wealth is the result of a bequest motive, that is, of accumulation for the specific purpose of leaving bequests? I will also endeavor to clarify why an answer to this question is of interest.

In the early Keynesian period when the study of national saving first attracted wide interest, relatively little attention was paid to what led people to save, though it was generally understood that the main systematic reason was to leave bequests. J. M. Keynes, in the famous chapter 9 of the *General Theory of Employment, Interest and Money* (1936), had listed seven distinct motives for saving besides the leaving of bequests. But five of these, which include "to increase one's future income," or "to insure one's independence and power," implied that all, or nearly all, the accumulation would finally wind up as bequeathed wealth. This, in turn, meant that most private wealth originated through bequests—that is, it either had been received through bequests or was destined to be bequeathed. And, indeed, how else could society accumulate wealth?

However, Keynes (1936, p. 107) also mentioned two further motives: "Precaution," that is, "to build up a reserve against unforeseen contingencies;" and "Foresight," that is, "to provide for an anticipated future relation between the income and the needs of the individual or his family different from that which exists in the present, as, for example, in relation to old age, family education, or the maintenance of dependents." These motives, in contrast to most of the previous ones, have the

■ *Franco Modigliani is Institute Professor and Professor of Economics and Finance, Sloan School of Management, Massachusetts Institute of Technology, Cambridge, Massachusetts and the 1985 Nobel Laureate in Economic Sciences.*

characteristic that the current saving is motivated by and destined to pay for future consumption through later dissaving.

But Keynes himself did not dwell on the implications or importance of this source of saving and wealth. This task was first partially undertaken by Harrod (1948) who referred to the transitory accumulation as "hump saving," although it would be more correct to call it "hump wealth." The Life Cycle Model (Modigliani and Brumberg, 1954; 1980) can be seen as an endeavor to study the magnitude and implications of transitory saving and hump wealth by relating it to the classical theory of consumer choice and more particularly to the hypothesis of optimal allocation over time, elaborated by Irving Fisher (1930). According to this hypothesis, the planned consumption path reflects the allocation of life resources to consumption over the life span. At least in the absence of bequests, this implies that there will tend to be saving resulting in transitory accumulation of wealth when current income is above, and/or current consumption below, average. There will be dissaving, financed from the transitory accumulation, in the opposite case.

One of the most significant early results of the Life Cycle Hypothesis was to establish that, even in the absence of bequests, the mere fact that income dries up with retirement could generate, for the entire economy, an amount of (hump) wealth quite large relative to income. Specifically, assuming a stylized life cycle of income and consumption—to wit, level consumption through life, income constant up to retirement and a stationary economy—it was shown that the ratio of wealth to income would be equal to one-half the length of retirement which (at the time) could be taken as of the order of 5. The wealth estimate of Goldsmith, which became available around that time, showed that for the United States the ratio of private net worth to disposable income was of that magnitude, or, if anything, a little lower. It was thus at least conceivable that the bulk of wealth might be acquired not by intergenerational transfers but instead be accumulated from scratch by each generation, to be consumed eventually by the end of life.

Still, the existence of some role for bequeathed wealth, especially among those in the upper strata of the distribution of wealth (human and nonhuman), was self-evident. For this reason, in the second of the two papers laying the foundation of the LCH (Modigliani and Brumberg, 1980) and several later ones (for example, Modigliani and Ando, 1957; Modigliani, 1975), the question of inheritance was dealt with explicitly. It was shown that bequests could be readily incorporated in the model without changing its basic implications, provided the leaving of bequests satisfied two reasonable assumptions.

First, the share of its resources that a household earmarks, on the average, for bequests is a (non-decreasing) stable function of the size of its life resources *relative* to the average level of resources of its age cohort.

Second, the frequency distribution of the ratio of life resources to mean life resources for each age group is also stable in time.

While the second assumption is hard to test, the first has recently received strong support from a study by Menchik and David (1983) described below. If the bequest motive satisfies these assumptions then one can readily establish that the ratio of inherited wealth to income will tend to be constant and independent of per capita income (Modigliani, 1975). But in turn, this means that a generalized life cycle model including both hump and inherited wealth will continue to exhibit all the basic macro properties of the elementary model, including 1) the saving rate is independent of per capita income, but rises with its rate of growth, and, 2) aggregate saving is not merely a reflection of individual thriftiness in the sense that a country with higher growth will save more than another, even though individuals in each country have identical life cycle saving behavior.

But acknowledging that aggregate wealth could arise from both transitory hump wealth and from the transfer of wealth through bequests from one generation to the next conveys nothing about the importance of each of these processes in accounting for existing wealth. In particular, is the bequest motive the main source of existing wealth, as supposed by the traditional view, or is it swamped by hump saving?

This question has attracted attention at least since the early 1960s when a number of investigations (reviewed below) were undertaken. The interest was spurred, in part, by scientific curiosity. But the question also has relevance for the design of economic policies because the two sources of wealth may be expected to respond to very different stimuli. According to the Life Cycle Hypothesis, hump wealth should respond to variables or institutions like length of retirement, family size, liquidity constraints, uncertainty of income (at least from labor), private and public pension arrangements, and health insurance. Most of these variables would likely have little effect on bequests, though, admittedly, economists know rather little as to what, other than estate and gift taxation, would have a significant impact on bequests.

Thus, knowledge of the relative contributions is important to assess the effectiveness of measures designed to affect saving and wealth as well as the effects on wealth of measures intended to achieve other goals, such as estate taxation designed to reduce economic inequalities.

Estimates of the Share of Inherited Wealth

From the early studies of the 1960s and until the recent contribution of Kotlikoff and Summers, it has been generally accepted that the importance of the contribution of the bequest process to total wealth could be measured by the ratio of wealth received through inheritance and major gifts by those living to total private (nonhuman) wealth. Though this ratio may not be an altogether appropriate measure of the importance of the bequest motive (as discussed below), I will start by reviewing available estimates of the share, both because most of the existing information relates directly to this variable and because this measure provides a useful building block for alternative measures.

Several methods have been utilized to estimate the share of private wealth accounted for by bequeathed wealth: 1) asking people directly through a survey; 2) estimating the annual flow of bequests and then using an appropriate "blow up" factor to infer the *stock* of inherited wealth; and 3) inferring inherited wealth indirectly by first estimating life cycle wealth and then subtracting it from an independent estimate of private wealth.

The Survey Method

This was the first method used, in connection with three U.S. studies carried out in the 1960s. In the study by Morgan et al. (1962), respondents were asked "about your own personal reasons for saving," with twelve answers offered. Only 3 percent mentioned "to provide an estate for family"! All the reasons most frequently mentioned are consistent with hump saving, such as "old age" (41 percent), "emergencies" (32 percent), and "children's education" (29 percent). The proportion of people referring to the bequest motive does increase, as one might expect, with wealth, but even in the top wealth class (half a million 1963 dollars and over), only one-third of the respondents mention it. Very similar results were found in the 1964 Brookings Study (Barlow et al., 1966).

The results of the three early surveys are summarized in the first four rows of Table 1. The estimates of the share of presently held wealth resulting from bequests (and possible major gifts) is reported in the last column. In view of the nature of the studies, these estimates are neither very precise, nor entirely comparable; for example, the study in Row 2 covered only people in the top 10 percent of the income distribution. Yet the small scatter of results appears to support the view of a fairly modest ratio of inherited to total wealth, between one-tenth and one-fifth (Modigliani, 1975). All the studies report that the share rises with the income and wealth of the recipient.

However, these figures may incur some suspicion because the respondents' replies were largely undocumented and could suffer from serious recall biases. For instance, it is not inconceivable that respondents would tend to underestimate, systematically and significantly, the extent to which their wealth was bestowed on them by others, rather than representing the fruits of their own efforts. It is therefore useful to compare these direct estimates with those obtained through alternative methods.

The Flow of Bequest Approach

This method starts from an estimate of the flow of bequests, which is then translated into a stock of inherited wealth. Three alternative methods have been employed to estimate this flow.

Estimates Based on Age-Specific Wealth Holding and Mortality. This method, first applied by Kotlikoff and Summers (1981), infers the flow of bequests from the distribution of wealth by age and age-specific mortality rates. They apply this method for the year 1962, relying on the distribution of wealth by age provided in Projector and Weiss (1964). From this source they arrive at an estimate of the transfer flow of $11.9 billion. To this, however, one must add bequests received through life insurance

Table 1

Estimates of the Share of Wealth Resulting from Transfers

Source	Nature of data	Nature of transfers included	Valuation	Share of wealth from transfers (%)
Morgan et al., (1962)	response to survey question on size of transfer received	all(?)	at time of receipt(?)	less than 10
Projector & Weiss (1964)	response to survey question on share of wealth from transfer	inheritance and large gifts from outside family	at time of receipt	[16][a]
Burlow et al., (1966)	response to survey question on fraction of wealth transfers. Limited to income $10,000 and over	inheritance and gifts	at time of receipt	one-seventh
same	same	same	at time of receipt, plus capital appreciation to present	less than one-fifth
Kotlikoff & Summers (1981)	estimated from wealth of those dying: age gap: 25–30 years	intergenerational bequests	at time of receipt, corrected for price level changes	17
Projector & Weiss (1964)	response to question on transfer received during year; age gap: 25–30 years	inheritance and gifts from outside family	same	$15\frac{1}{2}$
Menchik and David (1983)	Probate records; age gap: 25 years	all bequests other than intraspousal	same	$18\frac{1}{2}$

[a]Wealth-weighted average of respondents answering that inherited assets were a "substantial portion" of total assets.

death benefits and newly established trusts (since neither of these items is included in the data), which raises the estimated intergenerational flow to $16 billion.

To transform the flow into a stock of wealth, Kotlikoff and Summers rely on the assumption that beneficiaries, on average, receive a constant fraction of their life labor income in the form of bequests, and that the average gap between the age of the bequeathers and that of the beneficiaries is a constant, say g years. These assumptions insure that, in steady growth, the ratio of inherited to total wealth tends to a constant. Denote by B the current flow of bequests left (and received). Then, if the economy were stationary, one can readily infer that the aggregate amount of bequests received by those currently living, say T, would come to B for each of g years, or $T = gB$. However, if population and/or productivity increase at a stable rate, say n, then the flow of transfers made and received t years earlier would be smaller than B, amounting to Be^{-nt}. One can then infer that the stock of inherited wealth will be

$$(1) \qquad T = \frac{\left(1 - e^{-ng}\right)}{n} B.$$

(Note that this equation is not the one used by Kotlikoff and Summers. The reasons are discussed below.) To arrive at an estimate of the aggregate transfer T received by all those living, one still needs values for the growth rate n and the age gap g. For the growth rate n, one can use the estimate used by Kotlikoff and Summers (1980), namely 3.5 percent. For the age gap, on the other hand, there is very little solid information to rely on. I will follow their choice of 30 years, though 25 years might be a more reasonable guess (as suggested by data for the United Kingdom assembled by the Royal Commission on the Distribution of Income and Wealth).

With these parameters, the stock of inherited wealth T implied by equation (1) is 18.6 times the flow (as compared with 30, in the absence of growth). With the annual flow of bequests B estimated at $16 billion per year, the stock of inherited wealth T comes to just below $300 billion. Now, in 1962 the stock of household net worth, as estimated by the Federal Reserve Board (1981), came to $1.75 trillion. Thus, the flow of bequests is somewhat short of 1 percent of wealth, and the estimated shares of wealth resulting from bequests can be placed at 17 percent (as reported in Table 1, Row 5). This figure is broadly consistent with the various estimates based on the direct survey method summarized in Table 1 (though it should be recognized that the Kotlikoff and Summers measure of transfers is probably somewhat less inclusive than that used in the surveys, since they purport to estimate "distant in age" intergenerational transfers).

Estimates Based on Survey Information. In the Projector (1968) follow-up study, respondents were asked: "During 1963 did you ... receive any gifts or inheritances from persons outside the family?" The answer to this question should provide an alternative estimate of the flow of gifts and bequests. A recent unpublished tabulation of this data yields an estimate of the average reported amount received of $205 per household, or a total of $11.6 billion,[1] compared to the Kotlikoff and Summers estimate of $12 billion before corrections. After correcting for trusts, one arrives at a share of inherited wealth for the bench mark year 1962 of some $15\frac{1}{2}$ percent (Table 1, row 6), again well within the range of the earlier estimates.

Estimates Based on Probate Statistics. The third approach, which is potentially the most promising in terms of the objectivity and quality of the information, is becoming feasible at present through the painstaking efforts of Menchik and David. Their 1983

[1]I wish to express my gratitude to Kim Kowalewski of the Federal Reserve Bank of Cleveland for computing these averages from an edited version of the tape of the "Survey of Changes in Consumer Finances" (Projector, 1968).

paper relying on probate records of people who died in Wisconsin between 1947 and 1978 provides information from which one can estimate that the mean bequest (including life insurance proceeds and reported inter vivos transfers) for all male decedents is $20,000 (in 1967 dollars).[2] Accepting this figure as representative of both sexes (though probably upward-biased), and multiplying by the 1.5 million adults deceased in 1962, the (upper) estimate of the total flow of bequests in that year would be 29\frac{1}{2}$ billion (in 1967 dollars). But one should subtract transfers between husband and wife from this figure.

On the basis of estimates of interspousal transfers provided by David and Menchik (1982, Table 5) and vital statistics, I have concluded that the amount of such transfers can be placed at just above $8 billion (Modigliani, 1984) yielding an estimate for the overall non-intraspousal transfer flow of 19\frac{1}{2}$ billion, in 1962 prices. This estimate is substantially above that of $16 billion arrived at by Kotlikoff and Summers, but this result can be explained at least partly by the consideration that their measure is meant to include only intergenerational transfers.

Data presented by David and Menchik (1982) suggest that intergenerational transfers may account for around 60 percent of the total transfers. If so, the Kotlikoff and Summers estimate of intergenerational transfers would appear larger than that implied by the probate statistics, though the difference does not appear worrisome in view of the many guesses involved in each estimate.

In converting the estimate of the annual flow of total non-intraspousal transfer of 19\frac{1}{2}$ billion into a share of wealth, one must remember that the average age gap between bequeather and beneficiary must presumably be appreciably lower for this flow than for purely intergenerational transfers, though it is hard to say by how much. If the age gap is, say, 15 years, for the roughly one-third of bequests that are not intergenerational, while the average for the remaining two-thirds that are intergenerational stays at 30 years, then the average gap would be 25 years, implying a "blow up" factor of 16.7 and an inherited share of wealth of some 18$\frac{1}{2}$ percent (see Table 1, Row 8).

In summary, direct estimates of the annual flow of bequests based on three different approaches appear broadly consistent, especially if one allows for some differences in the definition of the flow being measured. They all imply a rather small annual *flow compared with total wealth*, around 1 percent, more or less. It is this modest annual flow that insures that the total stock of bequeathed wealth (the sum of the annual flow over the transfer gap, adjusted for the effect of growth), is itself modest, between 15$\frac{1}{2}$ and 18$\frac{1}{2}$ percent, the latter measure corresponding to the broadest definition of the bequest flow. These estimates are clearly not inconsistent with the figures suggested by the three direct surveys.

---

[2] This figure, as well as all averages cited below, represents the mean for all persons dying in the course of the three decades spanning the years 1947 to 1978. Presumably, in the course of this span of time, bequests have tended to rise with the rise in per capita income. However, since this discussion is using 1962 as a benchmark, a year which is right in the middle of the period covered, it is reasonable to assume that the mean for the entire period is a fair approximation to the mean for the years of the early 1960s.

Indirect Estimates Based on Life Cycle Saving and Wealth

The essence of this approach is that it endeavors to estimate hump saving and wealth directly, and then derives transfer wealth as a residual. Following this method, Ando and Kennickell (1985) have set out to estimate life cycle wealth by starting from available annual estimates of national saving. For each year, they allocate the aggregate wealth over the age groups present, using the savings-age profiles derived from survey data (in their case, the Bureau of Labor Statistics' Consumer Expenditure Survey for 1972 and 1973) to obtain estimates of saving for individual age group cohorts in any given year. By summing up the saving of any given cohort up to any given year, they can estimate the self-accumulated, or non-inherited, wealth of that cohort in that year (except for capital gains and losses, discussed below). Finally, they arrive at national non-bequeathed wealth in any given year by summing over the cohorts present in that year. The result of this calculation, using both the 1972 and the 1973 age profiles, is reported for every year from 1960 to 1980, and then compared with the actual value of household net worth for the last quarter of each year (Federal Reserve Board, 1984).

The shares of self-accumulated wealth implied by the two profiles are very similar except that the one for 1973 is consistently five percentage points higher. Based on the 1973 profile, one finds that from 1974 to the end of the series in 1980, the share of self-accumulated wealth falls between 80 and 85 percent, a finding remarkably consistent with the consensus of the studies already described. For the earlier years, the share of self-accumulated wealth is smaller, around 60 percent until 1968, then drifting up to over 70 percent by 1973. But the lower figure for the early years may, at least partly, reflect a downward bias in the Ando and Kennickell estimate arising from the fact that their estimate of self-accumulated wealth omits change in real wealth arising from capital gains or losses. In the period before 1974, capital gains were unquestionably significantly positive, and hence self-accumulated wealth is under-estimated. On the other hand, from 1974 to 1980, this effect was, presumably, undone by the depressed state of the stock market, even though this may have been partly offset by rising real estate values.

Thus, this alternative and totally independent method yields results which for the last decade are broadly similar to those produced by all other methods of Table 1.

Estimates from Other Countries

It would be interesting to compare these findings with estimates for other times and countries. The only relevant information of which I am presently aware relates to the United Kingdom and is the result of the work of the above-mentioned Royal Commission on the Distribution of Income and Wealth. Their method relies on an estimate of the age pattern of recipients of bequests left by decedents of different age and sex, and on information on the flow of bequests for a long stretch of years terminating in 1973. From this information, they obtain an estimate of the 1973 stock of inherited wealth. Combining this data with total wealth in that year (based on the estate duty method) they arrive at an estimate that inherited wealth is 20.3 percent of total wealth, a share which rises to 24.7 percent when gifts ("all forms of transmitted wealth") are included (Report No. 5, Chapt. 9, tables 90 and 91). This figure is of the same order as those found for the United States, but it includes interspousal transfers. Considering that interspousal transfers in the United States seem to represent somewhat over one-fourth of the total, the share of total wealth that was inherited in the United Kingdom appears to be, if anything, a little smaller than suggested by U.S. data.

Evidence Suggesting a Major Role for Bequests

The evidence presented in the previous section suggests that the bequest process plays an important, but quantitatively modest, role in the process of accumulation of national wealth. However, this conclusion has been seriously criticized and challenged on the basis of variety of evidence seemingly inconsistent with this conclusion.

The Behavior of Wealth in Old Age

In the stylized, pure life cycle model, wealth must be clearly declining after retirement, and at a sufficiently fast pace to reach exhaustion at the end of life. The actual behavior of wealth by age seems quite different, especially after correcting for the fact that successively older households belong to cohorts which typically enjoyed a smaller life income. Several studies find that dissaving in old age is small at best (Fisher, 1950; Lydall, 1955; Menchik and David, 1983). Some studies (for example, Mirer, 1979) even find that wealth actually continues to rise in retirement. Such a finding, if valid, would certainly be inconsistent with significant smoothing of consumption over life; it would mean that as income dries up with retirement, the reduction is entirely absorbed by consumption and accumulation can continue. Thus, even with a bequest motive, smoothing implies that wealth must decline after retirement unless retired consumption can be entirely financed by the return on accumulated wealth (Hurd, 1986), an outcome which would require a ratio of wealth at retirement to per capita consumption far larger than the ratios typically observed.

Actually, most recent analysts have concluded that the wealth of a given cohort tends to decline after reaching its peak in the age range 60–65 or somewhat beyond it, and in any event after retirement, though the extent of the decline depends on the concept of saving and wealth used (Shorrocks, 1975; King and Dicks-Mireaux, 1982; Avery, Elliehausen, Canner and Gustafson, 1984; Bernheim, 1984; Diamond and Hausman, 1985; Ando, 1985; Ando and Kennickell, 1985; Hubbard, 1986; Hurd, 1986). If one makes appropriate allowance for participation in pension funds, then the dissaving (or the decline in wealth) of the old tends to be more apparent, and it becomes quite pronounced if one includes an estimate of social security benefits and wealth,[3] and if one focuses on retired households. Hurd (1986), relying on a large

---

[3] Bernheim (1984) finds that including pension and Social Security does not increase the dissaving of the old, but this is only because of his unconventional and questionable valuation of annuities. Given that saving — or income minus consumption — is the change in wealth, the consumption of a pension must reduce wealth.

sample of panel data of retired people over a ten-year span, found that even market wealth declines at appreciable rates of about $1\frac{1}{2}$ percent per year for all marketable wealth, and nearly 3 percent if owner-occupied houses are excluded.[4]

Also, several factors tend to bias the age profile of wealth upward. One source of bias, to which Shorrocks has called attention, arises from the well-known positive association between longevity and (relative) income. This effect means that the average wealth of successively older age classes is the wealth of households with higher and higher life resources, hence the age profile of wealth is upward-biased. In a similar vein, Ando and Kennickell (1985) have found evidence that aged households which are poor tend to double up with younger households and disappear from the sampled population so that the wealth of those remaining independent is again an upward biased estimate of average wealth.

But even allowing for these biases, the rate at which marketable wealth is being drawn down during retirement does not appear consistent with the elementary no-bequest form of the life cycle model. However, this result is not very revealing since the issue is not whether bequests exist, but rather their level of quantitative importance. The evidence on behavior of wealth in old age cannot answer that question. To be sure, the post-retirement (past 65) path, particularly at advanced ages, does tell something about the flow of bequests left. However, the *share* of bequest received in total wealth depends on total wealth and hence also on the path of wealth before retirement. If one fixes the path of per capita wealth from its peak, there will still exist an infinity of possible paths from, say, age 20 to 65, and each of these paths implies a different amount of aggregate wealth. The earlier the average path approaches the peak value, the larger will be aggregate wealth and hence the hump wealth component. So, a slow decline from peak is not inconsistent with inherited wealth being a modest share of total wealth.

Actually, there are good grounds for holding that the observed slowly decreasing path of wealth for the United States is fully consistent with the estimate of a bequest share of roughly one-fifth of total wealth. One of the methods of estimation which yielded the one-fifth figure consisted in using the flow of bequests estimated by Kotlikoff and Summers from age specific wealth holdings and mortality. The wealth holdings by age were those reported by the 1962 Federal Reserve Survey of Consumers' Finances, and that data also exhibits the characteristic of slow decline of wealth in old age. Clearly the one-fifth estimate of the share of wealth from bequests, being derived from such a slowly declining path of wealth, must be fully consistent with that path.

---

[4] Bernheim (1984) relies on the same basic data but breaks the period into two five-year periods, 1969–1975, and 1975–1979. He finds that dissaving is fairly sizable for all groups except couples in the second period. But Hurd's data suggest that this result may not be reliable as it reflects an entirely improbable rise of 23 percent between 1977 and 1979 in the wealth of couples. This rise is most unlikely to reflect voluntary accumulation and must be supposed to arise either from noise in the data and/or from unusual capital gains.

Temporal Changes in Retirement Habits and the Saving Rate

Another piece of evidence that has been adduced against a relatively important role for life cycle accumulation is the fact that since the 1930s retirement ages have fallen and life expectancy has risen, spelling a longer average retirement span. This lengthening should have increased the need for accumulation to finance retirement and thus resulted in a higher saving rate. In fact, there is no evidence of a rise in saving. However, the lengthening of retirement was accompanied by another large scale phenomenon: the Social Security revolution. Social Security should tend to reduce saving, offsetting the rise that should result from a longer retirement span induced, at least in part, by the Social Security (Feldstein, 1977; Modigliani & Sterling, 1983). However, the issue of the interaction between Social Security, retirement and saving is a complex one, beyond the scope of this paper.

In addition, the argument of the previous section applies here as well. The importance of inherited wealth cannot be settled by focusing exclusively on retirement behavior, since the rapidity with which hump wealth accumulates during a lifetime is motivated also by considerations other than length of retirement.

Simulation Studies

One method sometimes used to assess the importance of life cycle saving is to rely on simulation techniques: one assumes values for the preference parameters and for the opportunity set and derives life paths of saving and wealth, which are then aggregated to obtain national totals. In fact, this method was used by Modigliani and Brumberg (1954, 1980) to study properties of the life cycle model. But this technique, while useful to suggest possible ranges of outcomes and the responses to changing parameters, cannot settle the empirical issue of the relative importance of hump wealth and bequeathed wealth, because the outcomes are greatly affected by the choice of certain critical parameters which are largely arbitrary. Evans (1984) has demonstrated this point strikingly in his criticism of a frequently cited paper by White (1978). To illustrate, he shows that under plausible assumptions about the economy's growth rate (3.5 percent) and the rate of return (4 percent) by varying the assumed preference parameters, namely the elasticity of temporal substitution and the rate of time preference, between .25 and .5 and 0 and 1 percent respectively, one obtains simulated values of the life cycle rate of saving varying between 2 and up to 11 percent, which is consistent with a lot of room for bequests at one end or very little at the other.

The Kotlikoff and Summers Estimates

In their 1981 paper cited earlier, Kotlikoff and Summers have also reached the conclusion that the share of inheritance and gifts in total nonhuman wealth in the United States is far higher than the one-fifth share indicated by Table 1. In fact, they argue the share may be as high as four-fifths.

This conclusion rests on two alternative estimates of the share of wealth bequeathed or transferred by gifts. The first is based on a variant of the indirect method later employed in the Ando and Kennickell (1985) study discussed earlier. The difference is that instead of allocating saving among groups of households defined by the age of the household head, they impute to each cohort of each sex, in every year since 1900, an income *from labor only* and a consumption. The difference is labelled the cohort's "life cycle" saving which is capitalized and cumulated in order to arrive at an estimate of the "life cycle" wealth of each age and sex cohort and, finally, of aggregate life cycle wealth in a given year. Aggregate inherited (transfer) wealth is obtained by subtracting this estimate from aggregate wealth.

Although they present and discuss several variants of life cycle wealth based on alternative measures of interest rates and treatment of interspousal transfers, I will concentrate on their figure of $733 billion (from their Table 2, LCW2, series 2). This figure is conceptually the most relevant, as it correctly includes the life cycle accumulation of a deceased spouse into the life cycle accumulation of the survivor, instead of including it in inherited wealth. Also, this variant is the one they tend to stress. That figure implies that life cycle wealth is only about 19 percent of total wealth, and that therefore the share of transfer wealth comes to 81 percent!

Their second approach consists in measuring the stock of bequeathed wealth by the method (described earlier) of "blowing up" an estimate of the annual flow of bequests obtained from age specific wealth and mortality rates. Even though they rely on the same method and basic sources, they arrive at an estimate which, though less extreme than 81 percent, is still a good deal larger than ours, namely 46 percent.[5] Why the large discrepancies? I propose to show that they arise primarily from differences between the definitions of "inherited" and "self-accumulated" wealth used by Kotlikoff and Summers and the definitions underlying the estimates reported in Table 1.

Superficially, their definitions do not seem to differ from the usual ones. In fact, they coincide with them in the elementary kind of Modigliani-Brumberg (1980) streamlined model in which the return on capital is zero, all people begin earning at the same constant rate until retirement and there are no bequests. But once these simplifying assumptions are dropped, significant differences came to light.

According to the definition used in Table 1, self-accumulated wealth for an individual household is the summation of saving from the formation of the household to the present, where saving is defined as income (inclusive of capital gains) minus consumption. In turn, aggregate self-accumulated wealth is the sum of self-accumulated wealth over all households present (families and single individuals). Correspondingly, transfer wealth is the sum over all households of bequests (and major gifts) received (in constant prices). This definition differs from that of Kotlikoff and Summers in two ways: the treatment of return on inheritance and the definition of the transfer flow.

---

[5] In their 1981 paper, the figure was actually given as 52 percent, but that was due to an algebraic error in the blow up formula (Modigliani, 1984) which they have since corrected.

First, Kotlikoff and Summers deduct from income and the saving flow, as defined above, the return on inherited wealth, which they add to the flow of bequests. As a result, their inherited wealth is not just the cumulation of bequests received but is instead augmented by the inclusion of the capitalized value of the earnings since receipt of the inheritance. With an average age gap between bequeathers and beneficiary on the order of 25–30 years, this definition adds a great deal to the measure of Table 1.

The second important difference in measuring self-accumulated wealth is that instead of using the household as the basic economic unit responsible for the consumption-saving allocation, Kotlikoff and Summers artificially split the household into individual males and females, to each of whom they impute income and consumption on the basis of their age and family composition. Because of this choice, they are unable to use the formation of the household as the point from which accumulation begins, and are forced instead to pick, more or less arbitrarily, a critical age above which saving is imputed to all members of a cohort, including those still dependent, through an imputation of labor income and consumption. They choose a critical age of 18 for both men and women. This procedure has the implication that the (imputed) consumption of all persons that are above 18 but are still dependent, and hence have no income, is treated implicitly as though it represented a life cycle dissaving; accordingly, it is *subtracted from life cycle saving* and *added to inherited wealth* as those terms were defined in Table 1.

Table 2 provides estimates of the quantitative impact of these definitional differences. I start from the Kotlikoff and Summers measure and show how altering the definitions reduces their estimate until it coincides with the estimates of Table 1.

Effect on the Share Based on the Flow of Bequests. Part A of Table 2 deals with the measure of transfer wealth based on the flow-of-inheritance approach. As already described, their estimate of the share of total wealth that is inherited in this case is 46 percent (see row 1) and mine is 17 percent (see row 4). The adjustment in row 2, amounting to 5 percentage points, is the only one that reflects differences of assumption rather than of definition. Specifically, in reporting the correction for an error in the original "blow up" formula, Kotlikoff (1987) indicates assuming that, on the average, bequests are left by people aged 65, 10 years before death. I believe it is more reasonable to assume that bequests are left at death.

The next adjustment (row 3) subtracts from the stock of inherited wealth as defined by Kotlikoff and Summers that part which represents the capitalized consumption imputed to all dependent persons over 18 years of age. Actually, Kotlikoff and Summers do not have an estimate of that flow but have tried a partial remedy by adding to the estimated flow of inheritance at least one portion of that missing flow that happens to be substantial and is possible to estimate: the flow of expenditure for college education estimated at $4.6 billion (in 1962 dollars) per year. Eliminating this addition, the share of bequests is reduced by another 9 percentage points.

Row 4 corrects for the different treatment of the return on bequests. If the stock of inherited wealth is defined as the sum of inheritances received, then the relation

Table 2

Reconciliation of Kotlikoff and Summers with other estimates

	A. *Estimates based on flow of bequests*	
	Correction (percentage points) (1)	*Corrected share of wealth (%)* (2)
Kotlikoff & Summers estimate		46
Assuming transfer at death	− 4.8	41.2
Elimination of educational expenses	− 9.2	32
Elimination of capitalization of inheritance	− 15	17

	B. *Estimates based on cumulation of life cycle saving*	
	Correction (percentage points) (1)	*Corrected share of wealth (%)* (2)
Kotlikoff & Summers estimate		81
Error in treatment of durable goods expenditure	− 14	67
Elimination of capitalization of inheritances	− 31.5	35.5
Correction for expenditure on dependent over 18 and other unspecified sources	− 15.5	20

between the flow and the stock of inherited wealth was shown to be given by equation (1); but when it is defined as the sum of the capitalized value of inheritance received, then the appropriate formula becomes:

$$(2) \qquad T^* = \frac{e^{(r-n)g} - 1}{r - n} B$$

where T^* is their definition of inherited wealth. For their estimated age gap g of 30 years and interest rate of 4.5 percent, equation (2) yields a "blow-up" factor of 35, very nearly twice as large as the value of 18.6 implied by equation (1). Accordingly, when their measure of the share is recomputed using the definition underlying Table 1, the estimate drops dramatically, by 15 percentage points, to the point when it coincides with the 17 percent figure described earlier and presented in row 5 of Table 1.

Estimates Based on Capitalized Life Cycle Saving. Table 2B presents a similar reconciliation for their alternative procedure in which the share of transfer wealth is derived by cumulating capitalized "life cycle" saving of each cohort present in 1974.

Row 1 reports the share of 81 percent corresponding to their preferred estimate of life cycle wealth of 19 percent. The first correction in row 2 arises from an error in their calculation of consumption and saving. In the figures they present, they measured consumption as inclusive of the purchase of durable goods, instead of treating such goods as a depreciable investment including only current year estimated depreciation in consumption and the excess of purchases over depreciation as a saving to be cumulated into a stock. Their calculations could, therefore, be expected to produce a large downward bias in the estimate of life cycle wealth, especially since in the United States younger age groups will tend to be significant investors in durables, while older people tend to disinvest.

I have tried to estimate the magnitude of this error, as Kotlikoff and Summers have kindly made available their basic data and helped in carrying out the necessary, fairly extensive computations. The correction was found to increase the estimates of life-cycle wealth, as expected, but by an amount so large—26 percentage points—as to raise questions about its plausibility. However, the fact that such a wild estimate could be generated using Kotlikoff and Summers's method and a set of assumptions which they regarded as reasonable in the context of their approach does raise some question about the reliability of their capitalized life cycle saving method.

Kotlikoff and Summers (1986) have subsequently suggested a different correction for the error in the numerator of their share—which arises from omitting the net accumulation of durables—by making the same error in the denominator, that is, not including durables as wealth. With durables representing some 14 percent of the stock of wealth, they arrive at a correction of a mere 3 percentage points. But their suggestion that two wrongs make one right has little merit. Indeed, most of the wealth that is being taken out of the denominator should instead be added to the numerator. In the limit, if all durables belonged in life cycle wealth, the correction would come to an increase in life cycle wealth and corresponding decrease in the inherited share of 14 percentage points. Lacking a more solid base, row 2 reports the correction based on this alternative.

The third row of Table 2B shows the effect of eliminating from their estimate of inheritance the capitalized earnings from bequests. As was shown above, the exclusion of these earnings reduces the value of transfer wealth by 47 percent. Accordingly, in row 3, the share of inherited wealth is reduced to only $35\frac{1}{2}$ percent. As can be seen from row 4, this is still some 16 percent higher than my preferred estimate of the share of inheritance—around 20 percent—based on probate statistics.

The bulk of this difference is probably accounted for by Kotlikoff and Summers' inclusion of the imputed capitalized consumption of all dependent persons 18 years of age and over. There is, unfortunately, no way of estimating directly how much this inclusion adds to the conventional measure of inherited wealth, but several considerations suggest that the addition must be appreciable. To begin with, a large portion of those between 18 and 24 are still dependent, especially at the younger end of that spectrum. For instance, in 1970 about two-fifths of those aged 18–19 and one-third of those aged 18 to 24 were not in the labor force; the fraction of dependent persons would, presumably, be substantially higher. Another suggestive item is provided by the Kotlikoff and Summers estimate that expenditures for college education, which could hardly be a major component of all expenditure on dependents aged over 18, represents just over 20 percent of the total flow of bequests. In terms of Table 2B, this college adjustment alone would reduce the estimate in row 3 by 7.8 points. The large role of dependent consumption is also supported by two Figures (1 and 2) provided in K & S (1981) which show, for selected cohorts, the life path of income and consumption. According to these graphs, the cohort of 1910 is estimated to have life cycle dissaving for the first 50 years of its life, while the cohort of 1940 saved nothing over a similar span. Similar results are reported for other cohorts in the paper cited.

These results, which provide the foundations for the negligible accumulation of life cycle wealth, are inconsistent with information from many other sources using the household as the basic unit, and the conventional definition of saving. First, available information from many surveys indicates that households have, on average, substantial saving and net worth at least after age 25 (for example, Ando & Kennickell, 1985, Table II.1). Second, such saving is consistent with the fact that wealth rises fairly smoothly between age 25 and age 45 (according to Projector and Weiss, 1964, wealth rose in 1962 by roughly one thousand dollars per year of age; see also Ando & Kennickell, 1985). This rise in wealth cannot be attributed to inheritance to any significant extent, since, as one would expect, the receipt of important inheritance is rare before age 45 (Projector and Weiss, 1964, Table A32). For the same reason, the saving of these younger age groups cannot be reasonably attributed to the return on inherited wealth.

The residual of row 4 and the inconsistencies noted above may, of course, also reflect the entirely different data as well as methodology employed by Kotlikoff and Summers, for it is obvious that each method is affected by the many somewhat arbitrary auxiliary assumptions that need to be made. This problem particularly affects the Kotlikoff and Summers study, considering the large number of imputations and assumptions it involves, from age profiles, to return on capital, to the treatment of interspousal transfers. Their results are particularly sensitive to errors and assumptions affecting saving in the early years, for a difference in early saving affects wealth at every later age, and increasingly so, as the saving gets capitalized. This conjecture is supported by tests on the sensitivity of their results to variations in the auxiliary assumptions, which they report in their 1981 paper.

These considerations lend support to the claim that the bulk of the discrepancy between their estimate of 80 percent and the earlier consensus figure of around 20 percent is attributable to differences in the definitions, with the remainder accounted for by the unavoidable imprecision of all estimates. This inference receives further support from the estimates of Ando and Kennickell (1985) cited earlier. Using the same methodology of estimation as Kotlikoff and Summers but relying on the conventional definition of self-accumulated wealth as household actual income minus consumption, they arrive at a life cycle share much lower than Kotlikoff and Summers and broadly similar to the figures reported in Table 1.

Assessing the Merits and Shortcomings of Alternative Definitions.   There are two basic definitional differences: how to define life cycle (hump) accumulation, and how to treat the return on inherited wealth. With respect to the first issue, the Kotlikoff and Summers redefinition was shown to have the effect of subtracting from the standard measure of hump wealth the capitalized value of all expenditure imputed to dependents age 18 and over (as well as all minor gifts and contributions in support of another household).

This redefinition has little merit, at least when the focus is on the effect of inheritance and gifts on the stock of (nonhuman) wealth. First, the supposed transfers (and contributions) are not in the nature of either bequests or major gifts. Second, they go to pay for current consumption and do not represent an addition to the assets of the recipient or society. Third, the downward adjustment implied by the Kotlikoff and Summers procedure depends on the choice of the critical age of independence, and as a result their share of life cycle wealth in total wealth can be made to rise or shrink by the fairly arbitrary choice of the critical age. Finally, these imputed transfers are quite different in nature from bequests and major gifts because, unlike these transfers, they would be hard to modify through policy actions, and, even if modifications were attainable, the effect on wealth could be very different.

One consideration that may lend some attractiveness to the Kotlikoff and Summers definition is that the expenditure on dependents that they treat as transfers includes the outlays for college education. One may feel that these large outlays are bequests of a sort, since they take the form of an investment in "human capital." But this consideration would be relevant mainly for other issues, such as the hereditary transmission of economic inequality or the contribution of transfers to total capital—nonhuman and human. But in this case the denominator of the ratio should include human capital, too. Furthermore, the numerator should include many other expenditures on human capital, not necessarily only on behalf of dependents 18 years old and over—like all private schooling. And why should the line be drawn at schooling and not include all expenditure on children? But clearly that would be an entirely different story. To answer the question this paper began by posing, I submit that no customary expenditure on dependents should be treated as a transfer.

The next question is whether inherited wealth should be defined to include the capitalized earnings thereon over the lifetime of the recipient. I have chosen to exclude it on two grounds. First, treating earnings on bequests as income conforms to the generally accepted definition of saving as income minus consumption. It also conforms to the usual definition of life accumulation as bequests left, minus bequests received (adjusted for inflation). By contrast, under Kotlikoff and Summers's definition, a person leaving as much as he received would, if the real rate of return were positive, be counted as a dissaver to an extent depending on the rate of return. The second reason is that one can measure directly what bequests have been received, but there is no direct way of telling whether some years later the wealth of the recipient will be larger by the capitalized value of the bequests, or whether instead the recipient will have consumed some or all of the return or even some of the principal.

Kotlikoff and Summers might object to this definition in that life cycle income as I am defining it includes the income from bequests, which makes life cycle saving depend on bequests received. The measure of life cycle saving they advocate (labor income minus consumption) is, instead, independent of bequests. In addition, this measure, since it requires subtracting the return on bequests from earnings and saving, provides a justification for adding capitalized returns to the stock of bequests received.

At first sight, this may seem like a persuasive argument; yet it suffers from a major flaw. While it is true that the measure I am supporting will generally vary with the size of bequests, theirs is also not independent of bequests received as long as these have effects on consumption (or labor supply). Their measure would be appropriate only in the limiting case in which consumption is absolutely unaffected by bequests received—that is, if all returns were saved. But consider the polar case in which all the returns are consumed; then it is the measure of bequests and hump saving I am advocating that is the appropriate one.

The Contribution of the Bequest Process to Total Wealth

What lesson can be drawn from the above considerations? They clearly suggest that the share of inherited wealth, whether capitalized or not, does not provide a valid answer to the question: *how much does the bequest motive contribute to society's total wealth?* Kotlikoff and Summers have correctly pointed out that this issue is the really interesting one. They have further proposed measuring the impact of bequests on total wealth by the elasticity of total wealth with respect to flow of bequests: that is, by the percentage change in total wealth resulting from a 1 percent change in the bequests' flow. This elasticity, which may be labelled the "true measure of importance of bequests," can be written as

$$(3) \qquad \eta = \frac{\Delta W}{\Delta B} \frac{B}{W} = \frac{\Delta W}{\Delta T} \frac{T}{W}.$$

Here, the second equality follows from the consideration that the stock of inherited wealth T is proportional to the annual flow of bequests B (though the proportionality factor depends on the definition). The first equality, on the other hand, shows that (given the flow of bequests) the true measure of importance is independent of how one chooses to define the share, as must be the case since the elasticity is, in principle, an observable fact. The second equality brings to light a simple relation between the "true" measure of importance and the measures of the share of bequests with which we have been concerned so far. Specifically, let T^j stand for any stated measure of aggregate wealth, such as T^*, the definition used by Kotlikoff and Summers, or T, the definition I am advocating. Then the corresponding measure of the share, T^j/W, will be an upward biased measure of importance if $\Delta W/\Delta T^j$ is less than one; it will be downward biased in the opposite case.

No measure of the aggregate inherited wealth presented thus far is likely to measure the desired elasticity correctly for several reasons. In the first place, when the economy is growing, the share of wealth received by bequests must tend to under-estimate the contribution of bequests to total wealth by not allowing for the effect of accumulation earmarked for future bequests. Some simulations carried out by Kennickell (1984) suggest that the shortfall of the inherited share as a measure of importance rises quite rapidly as growth increases. Second, there is reason to believe that $\Delta W/\Delta T$ is not unity, however it is defined, simply because beneficiaries of bequests will probably change their consumption by an amount positive, but less than the full return on bequests.

Measuring the Elasticity

Consider first the case where the stock of inherited wealth is T^*, defined in accordance with Kotlikoff and Summers. These authors have endeavored to estimate the value of $\Delta W/\Delta T^*$. Their calculations are based on some very special and rather arbitrary assumptions about preferences (namely that the utility is additive, separable in consumption and leisure and logarithmic) and on the even more questionable assumption that all transfers—be they inheritances or major gifts or family expenditure in support of members over 18—have identical effects on wealth. Nonetheless, the results should provide a general indication of magnitude.

They find that $\Delta W/\Delta T^*$ depends almost exclusively on the difference between the interest rate and the growth rate $(r - n)$, decreasing as that figure increases for reasons that will be discussed presently. For a value of $(r - n)$ consistent with their estimates of r and n, namely .01, they find that $\Delta W/\Delta T^* = .7$. This result, together with equation (3), means that the share of bequeathed wealth, measured according to Kotlikoff and Summers definition, T^*/W, greatly *overstates* η, the true effect of bequests on total wealth, to wit, by $1/.7$, or over 40 percent.

I have endeavored also to estimate $\Delta W/\Delta T$, but by an alternative procedure which is less dependent on specific assumptions about preferences, and was initially inspired by Darby (1979). He proposed identifying the "true" life cycle component of wealth as the amount of wealth that would be in existence in society if households accumulated just enough assets to enable them to finance their observed (average) retirement consumption --- with accumulation up to retirement, and decumulation thereafter, occurring at a constant rate.

Darby has applied this method to U.S. data around 1966. The rate of consumption to be financed during retirement was estimated using data from the 1967 Survey of Economic Opportunities and the portion of this to be financed through "life cycle accumulation" was obtained by subtracting, from consumption other sources of income, such as labor income and Social Security. The retirement fund was assumed to earn the rate of return of 4.5 percent which was adopted in our previous calculations. This method estimates the share of "life cycle wealth" at only 23 percent, implying that over three-fourths of wealth is bequest-related.

But Darby's approach, for all its ingenuity, cannot provide much useful information because of the entirely arbitrary nature of the underlying assumptions. His assumption that accumulation for retirement occurs smoothly while accumulation for bequests is the jagged residual (see Darby's figure 12, p. 37) is a caricature of consumption smoothing based on life cycle utility maximization, which implicitly treats most hump wealth as bequest-related wealth.

This consideration suggests modifying his approach by replacing the ad hoc assumption that consumers smooth the accumulation of retirement provisions with the "rational" assumption of consumption smoothing. Specifically, given the amount to be bequeathed, how would that amount be accumulated by a person choosing an optimal life consumption path, subject to the constraint imposed by available lifetime resources? For the representative household, these resources consist of lifetime earnings plus bequests received, less the amount the household intends to bequeath. Steady state considerations imply that, on the average, bequests left will exceed those received by the growth factor e^{ng}, where n is the rate of growth and g the age gap between donor and recipient. Wealth holding due to bequests can then be computed as the difference between the path of wealth with and without bequests.

As long as the optimal consumption follows a smooth path (a constant rate of growth) which is consistent with commonly assumed additive utility functions, one can readily show that accumulated wealth due to bequests will rise smoothly to an amount equal to the difference between the bequests left at death and those received, capitalized from the date of receipts.

If the preferred consumption path grows at the rate c, the annual increment to wealth due to bequests in the year τ can be shown to be:

$$(4) \qquad \Delta s_{\tau} = \frac{A e^{c\tau}(r - c)}{1 - e^{-(r-c)L}}$$

where L is length of life and A is the present value, at the beginning of life, of the difference between the bequest received and left. The path of wealth is the cumulant of Δs_{τ} plus the amount of the bequests once received (capitalized).

Equation 4 describes the path for a single household. To obtain the aggregate amount of bequests-related wealth at a given point of time, we must sum over the wealth of each cohort present, allowing for the fact that, because of growth, the cohorts of age τ can expect to receive and leave bequests which are larger than those left by the one currently deceased by the factor $e^{(L-\tau)n}$. National wealth is the summation of wealth over the cohorts adjusted for mortality. Finally, taking into account that the steady state bequests must grow at the rate n, bequests received will be Be^{-ng}. This formulation permits us to derive an expression for aggregate bequests-related wealth, ΔW, in terms of the current flow of bequests left, B, and the parameters c, n, r, g, p_t and L, where p_t is the force of mortality at age t. Taking as an illustration the case in which mortality is zero until age L and 1 at L, the result can be written as

$$(5) \qquad \Delta W = \Delta T^*(1 - D)$$

where T^* is the stock of bequeathed wealth according to K & S's definition as given by equation (2), and D takes the somewhat lengthy expression:

(6)
$$D = \frac{e^{-(r-n)L}}{1 - e^{-(r-c)L}}\left[e^{(r-n)L} - 1 - (1 - e^{-(n-c)L})\frac{r-n}{n-c}\right].$$

Equations (5) and (6) have a number of plausible and interesting implications. Consider first the case where the economy is stationary: r is zero and so is n. In this case, since bequests are passed on unchanged, they have no effect on income, consumption, or life cycle earnings. Thus, $T^* = T$, and $D = 0$, and by (5), $\Delta W/\Delta T^* = \Delta W/\Delta T = 1$. In this case, the two definitions of the share of inherited wealth coincide and correctly measure "importance."

Consider next the case of a stationary economy, but in which $r > 0$. Here the receipt of inheritance has, on average, a favorable income effect, as it earns interest but requires no additional accumulation; one can show that, for this reason, my definition of the share, T/W, has an upward bias in measuring η, but using Kotlikoff and Summers' measure, the upward bias is clearly even greater. On the other hand, a positive growth tends, through the "accumulation" effect, to impart a downward bias to either measure of the share. Thus, r and n work in opposite and, in fact, offsetting ways, as is apparent from the fact that in equation (6), r and n often appear in the form $(r - n)$. So, the Kotlikoff and Summers measure of the share is upward biased as long as $r - n > 0$, and their parameter choices imply that $r - n$ is 0.01. This is sufficient to impart a strong upward bias to T^*/W as a measure of η. Indeed, assuming again for g and L the values of 25 and 55 respectively, one finds from (6) that $D = 0.3$, and hence, from (5), $\Delta W/\Delta T^* = 1 - D = 0.7$. (Note that this corresponds with the estimate of dW/dT^* reported by Kotlikoff and Summers.) Then, from (3)

(7a)
$$\eta = .7\frac{T^*}{W}$$

confirming that the Kotlikoff and Summers share overestimates the true measure of importance by over 40 percent. On the other hand, for the alternative measure of the importance of inherited wealth that I am advocating, equation (5) implies

$$\frac{\Delta W}{\Delta T} = \frac{\Delta W}{\Delta T^*}\frac{\Delta T^*}{\Delta T} = \frac{\Delta W}{\Delta T^*}\frac{T^*}{T} = (.7)(1.7) = 1.19$$

where T is computed from equation (1) and T^* from (2). Hence:

(7b)
$$\eta = 1.19\frac{T}{W}.$$

Thus, as expected our share underestimates "importance" (because it neglects the accumulation effect due to growth), but the bias is fairly small (in the relevant range of parameters).[6]

---

[6] The calculations reported above assume a zero value for the rate of growth of consumption c. But the value of $\Delta W/\Delta T^*$ is not significantly affected by variations in c in the relevant range. Thus, for $c = .02$, $\Delta W/\Delta T^* = .723$, and $\Delta W/\Delta T = .723 \times 1.7 = 1.23$.

Estimates of the Elasticity. As for the actual value of the elasticity η, it can be computed either starting from our definition of the share T/W and using (7b) or from Kotlikoff and Summers T^*/W and using (7a)—and the result should coincide, at least as long as the shares are based on the same definition of bequests. As shown in Table 2A, my estimate of T/W is 17 percent (line 4) implying $\eta = .17 \times 1.19 = 20$ percent. The Kotlikoff and Summers estimate of T^*/W is .46 percent (Table 2A, line 1) which, however, falls by 41 percent if one accepts the hypothesis that bequests are typically left at death. Using (7a), this would imply an elasticity of .29. However, the estimates are still comparable because Kotlikoff and Summers are including in their flow of bequests and gifts the imputed consumption of dependents over 18 years of age.

As argued earlier, this expenditure should not be included in the bequest flow. With respect to the present problem, there is one further reason for exclusion, namely that no allowance was made for such flows in our (or as far as I can see, in Kotlikoff and Summers's) calculation of $\Delta W/\Delta T$.

If we accordingly eliminate from T^*/W the component of line 3, which reflects this expenditure, the share falls to 32 percent, implying η around .22, pretty close to our .2. But both estimates may tend to underestimate η because the Kotlikoff and Summers measure of the flow of bequests, which ignores nonintergenerational transfers, is presumably too narrow. Probate data and the results of Ando and Kennickell (1985) suggest a larger value for T/W, say between $1/5$ and $1/4$. Using (7b), this would imply an elasticity of between .25 and .30.

There remains to consider Kotlikoff and Summers's alternative estimate of T^*/W, based on the capitalization of life cycle saving, which is analyzed in Table 2B. If we correct as well as we can for the treatment of durable goods, as described earlier, line 2 shows that T^*/W would come to .67, which, together with (7a), implies $\eta = .47$. But, the above value of T^*/W is greatly biased upward by the inclusion of the consumption of family members over 18. Unfortunately, there is no way to measure that bias at present. Correcting for only a portion of the above expenditure—namely expenditure on college education—would lower T^*/W from .67 to .57 (cf. Table 2A) and bring η down to .4. One can conjecture that the full correction would bring η pretty close to the upper range of .3.

We can, therefore, conclude that when we focus on the "importance" of bequests as measured by the elasticity, all results point to a value of η of up to 30 percent, give or take a few points.

The Precautionary Motive and the Importance of Bequested Motivated Wealth

However, this value of .3 overestimates the contribution to wealth of inheritances and gifts related to the bequest motive because a substantial portion of the observed bequest flow undoubtedly reflects the precautionary motive arising from the uncertainty of the time of death. Indeed, in view of the institutional obstacles of dying with negative net worth, people tend to die with some wealth, unless they can manage to put all their retirement reserves into life annuities. In the absence of annuities, the wealth left behind will reflect risk aversion and the cost of running out of wealth (besides the possible utility of bequests).

This point has been elaborated in particular by Davies (1981) (see also Hubbard, 1984) who has shown that, for plausible parameters of the utility function including a low intertemporal elasticity of substitution, the extent to which uncertainty of life depresses the propensity to consume increases with age. As a result "uncertain life time could provide the major element in a complete explanation of the slow decumulation of the retired," relative to what would be implied by a standard Life Cycle Hypothesis model.

Clearly, bequests originating from the precautionary motive are quite different by nature from those dictated by the bequest motive. Indeed, they belong with pure life cycle accumulation since they are determined by the utility of consumption, and furthermore, the surviving wealth must tend, on the average, to be proportional to life resources.

However, using the precautionary motive as an explanation for life cycle wealth does run into some problems. If the purpose of the wealth accumulated at retirement was really to support consumption, then given uncertainty of life, risk aversion and the availability of annuity contracts, why don't more households use most of their wealth to buy annuities?

This criticism is important, but a number of counterarguments have been proposed. First, a fair amount of consumer wealth at retirement is, in fact, in the form of annuities: namely, all that is accumulated in the form of claims on pension funds and Social Security. Indeed, one might turn the above question around and ask: if households accumulate primarily to leave bequests, why have pensions and Social Security met with so much success and growth? Second, as has been pointed out in particular by Friedman and Warshawsky (1985a, 1985b), one important factor discouraging the purchases of annuities is the very unfavorable rates which are currently offered on such contracts (estimated by these authors at 4 to 6 percent below market rates of return). Of this "load," only one portion (around 1.5 percent) can be attributed to adverse selection (the fact that those who chose to buy annuities tend to have above average life).

Friedman and Warshawsky have shown that this unfavorable load factor is probably not large enough to lead a person to choose self-insurance if that person derived no utility whatever from bequest. However, the actual situation is different since, as a rule, households do derive some utility also from bequests (Masson, 1986). Friedman and Warshawsky have shown that, in this case, under plausible assumptions, the extra load factor can account for the rarity of private annuities. They also report that under the same conditions, the household would tend to leave an amount of bequest relative to terminal consumption that appears broadly consistent with the observed behavior of wealth as a function of age, indictating that this behavior might be accounted for even in the absence of a pure bequest motive.

The Importance of the Pure Bequest Motive

It would be interesting to obtain some estimate of the importance of purely bequest-motivated transfers. A certain amount of evidence suggests that the pure bequest motive—the accumulation of wealth entirely for the purpose of being distributed to heirs and not be used for own consumption—affects a rather small number of households, mostly located in the highest income and wealth brackets.

First, the recent study of Hurd (1986) supports the hypothesis that the bequest motive is not important for a broad cross section of households. He starts from the reasonable hypothesis that if the true bequest motive is an important source of terminal wealth, then retired households with living children should have more wealth and should save more (dissave less) than childless ones. It is found that, in fact, those with children have less wealth and, by and large, dissave the same fraction of (marketable) wealth. The first result is fully consistent with the standard no-bequest life cycle consumption smoothing because for given life resources the "cost" of raising children reduces the retired consumption of parents. But the second result is indeed hard to reconcile with a significant pure bequest motive. It is, however, consistent with the finding of Projector and Weiss (1964) that only 3 percent indicated they were saving "to provide an estate for the family." At the same time, the proportion rose with wealth, reaching one-third for the top class (over half a million 1963 dollars). Thus, the bequest motive seems to be concentrated in the highest economic classes.

This hypothesis is supported by the finding of Menchik and David that for (and only for) the top 20 percent of the distribution of estimated life resources bequests rise proportionately faster than total resources.

This result suggests that the share of bequests due to the pure bequest motive is likely to be well below one, even allowing for the fact that the wealth of those with pure bequest motives may be a sizable part of the total. Recalling that our estimate of elasticity of wealth with respect to the entire flow of bequests came to somewhere around .3, it would seem safe to conclude that the importance of pure bequest motivated transfers, as measured by the elasticity of wealth with respect to that flow, is very unlikely to exceed one-fifth or so.

Summary and Conclusions

Clearly, part of the private wealth held at any time reflects hump or life cycle wealth and part reflects wealth transmitted through inheritances and major gifts. The interesting question is: how large is each component? The available evidence, reported in seven studies largely relying on independent methods but using broadly similar, customary definitions, consistently indicates that the share of wealth received by transfer does not exceed one-fourth. One recent contribution, that of Kotlikoff and Summers (1981), based on different definitions and partly on a different methodology, has arrived at a much larger share of 45 to 80 percent.

It has been shown that the differences between these and the other estimates reflect mainly definitional differences which have the effect of substantially increasing K & S's measure of the share. These differences consist in adding to the bequests and major gifts received: 1) the capitalized value of the earning on the inheritance since the time of receipt, and 2) the capitalized value of the expenditure on family members over 18 years in age.

But these definitional differences lose relevance when we focus on the elasticity of wealth with respect to the flow of bequests. It is first argued that, with respect to this issue, Kotlikoff and Summers's treatment of expenditures on family members over 18 years of age as bequests is not appropriate. Once that component is eliminated, the two measures of the share are shown to give rise to roughly similar values of the elasticity; a 10 percent decline in the flow of bequests might result in a decline in wealth of the order of 3 percent, more or less.

Even this figure overestimates the role of bequest motivated transfers, which seem to play an important role only in the very highest income and wealth brackets. Some portion of bequests, especially in lower income brackets, is not due to a pure bequest motive but rather to a precautionary motive reflecting uncertainty about the length of life, although it is not possible at present to pinpoint the size of this component.

References

Ando, Albert, "The Savings of Japanese Households: A Micro Study Based on Data from the National Survey of Family Income and Expenditure, 1974 and 1979," Economic Planning Agency, Government of Japan, 1985.

Ando, Albert, and A. Kennickell, "How Much (or Little) Life Cycle is There in Micro Data? Cases of U.S. and Japan," paper presented at Istituto Bancario San Paolo di Torino Conference to Honor Franco Modigliani, in Martha's Vineyard, Massachusetts, September 19–21, 1985. Conference proceedings forthcoming.

Avery, R. B., G. E. Elliehausen, G. B. Canner, and T. A. Gustafson, "Survey of Consumer Finances, 1983: A Second Report," *Federal Reserve Bulletin*, December 1984, *70*, 857–68.

Barlow, Robin, H. E. Brazer, and J. N. Morgan, *Economic Behavior of the Affluent*. Washington, D.C.: The Brookings Institution, 1966.

Bernheim, B. Douglas, "Dissaving after Retirement: Testing the Pure Life Cycle Hypothesis," NBER Working Paper #1409, July 1984.

Board of Governors of the Federal Reserve System Flow of Funds Section, Division of Quarterly Statistics, *Balance Sheets of the U.S. Economy 1945–1980*, October 1981.

Darby, Michael R., *The Effects of Social Security on Income and the Capital Stock*. Washington, D.C. The American Enterprise Institute, 1979.

David, Martin, and P. Menchik, "Distribution of Estate and Its Relationships to Intergenerational Transfers," In Department of the Treasury, Internal Revenue Service, Statistics of Income Division, *Statistics of Income and Related Administration Record Research: 1982*, October 1982.

Davies, J., "Uncertain Life Time, Consumption and Dissaving in Retirement," *Journal of Political Economy*, June 1981, *89*, 561–77.

Diamond, Peter A., and J. A. Hausman, "Individual Retirement and Savings Behavior," *Journal of Public Economics*, February–March 1985, *23*, 81–114.

Evans, O. J., *The Life Cycle Inheritance: Theoretical and Empirical Essays on the Life Cycle Hypothesis of Saving*. Unpublished Ph.D. dissertation, University of Pennsylvania, 1981.

Evans, O. J., "Empirical Tests of the Life Cycle Hypothesis: Comment," *American Economic Review*, March 1984, *74*, 254–257.

Federal Reserve Board, Flow of Funds Section, Division of Research and Statistics, *Balance Sheets for the U.S. Economy, 1945–80*, 1984.

Feldstein, Martin, "Social Security and Private Savings: International Evidence in an Extended Life-Cycle Model." In Feldstein, M., and R. Inman, eds., *The Economics of Public Services*. London: Macmillan, 1977.

Fisher, Irving, *The Theory of Interest*. New York: Macmillan, 1930.

Fisher, J., "The Economics of an Aging Population, A Study in Income, Spending and Savings Patterns of Consumer Units in Different Age

Groups, 1935–36, 1945–1949." Unpublished dissertation, Columbia University, New York, 1950.

Friedman, Benjamin M., and M. Warshawsky, "The Cost of Annuities: Implications for Saving Behavior and Bequests," National Bureau of Economic Research Working Paper #1682, August 1985a.

Friedman, Benjamin M., and M. Warshawsky, "Annuity Prices and Saving Behavior in the United States," National Bureau of Economic Research Working Paper #1683, June 1985b.

Harrod, R. F., *Towards a Dynamic Economics.* London: Macmillan, 1948.

Hubbard, Glenn R., "'Precautionary' Saving Revisited: Social Security, Individual Welfare, and the Capital Stock," National Bureau of Economic Research Working Paper #1430, August 1984.

Hubbard, Glenn R., "Pension Wealth and Individual Saving: Some New Evidence," *Journal of Money, Credit and Banking,* May 1986, *XVIII(2),* 167–78.

Hurd, Michael D., "Savings and Bequests," National Bureau of Economic Research Working Paper #1826, January 1986.

Keynes, J. M., *General Theory of Employment, Interest and Money.* New York: Harcourt, Brace, 1936.

Kennickell, A., "An Investigation of Life Cycle Savings Behavior in the United States," unpublished doctoral dissertation, University of Pennsylvania, Philadelphia, 1984.

King, M. A., and L-D. L. Dicks-Mireaux, "Asset Holdings and the Life-Cycle," *Economic Journal,* June 1982, *92,* 247–67.

Kotlikoff, L. T., and L. H. Summers, "The Role of Intergenerational Transfers in Aggregate Capital Accumulation," *Journal of Political Economy,* August 1981, *89,* 706–32.

Kotlikoff, L. T., and L. H. Summers, "The Contribution of Intergenerational Transfers to Total Wealth: A Reply," National Bureau of Economic Research Working Paper #1827, 1986.

Long, Clarence D., "The Labor Force Under Changing Income and Employment," National Bureau of Economic Research, General Series 65, Princeton University Press, 1958.

Lydall, Harold, "The Life Cycle in Income, Saving and Asset Ownership," *Econometrica,* April 1955, *23,* 131–50.

Masson, Andre, "Cohort Analysis of Wealth-Age Profiles Generated by a Simulation Model in France (1949–1975)," *Economic Journal,* March 1986, *96.*

Menchik, Paul, and M. David, "Income Distribution, Life Time Saving and Bequests," *American Economic Review,* September 1983, *73,* 672–90.

Mirer, T. W., "The Wealth-Age Relationship among the Aged," *American Economic Review,* June 1979, *69,* 435–43.

Modigliani, Franco, "The Life Cycle Hypothesis of Saving, Twenty Years Later." In Parkin, M., ed., *Contemporary Issues in Economics.* Manchester: Manchester University Press, 1975, pp. 2–36.

Modigliani, Franco, "Measuring the Contribution of Intergenerational Transfers to Total Wealth: Conceptual Issues and Empirical Findings," Paper presented at a seminar on Modeling the Accumulation and Distribution of Personal Wealth, in Paris, France, September 1984.

Modigliani, Franco, and Albert Ando, "Tests of the Life Cycle Hypothesis of Savings: Comments and Suggestions," *Bulletin of the Oxford University Institute of Statistics,* 1957, 99–124.

Modigliani, Franco, and Richard Brumberg, "Utility Analysis and Aggregate Consumption Functions: An Attempt at Integration." In Abel, A., ed., *The Collected Papers of Franco Modigliani.* Cambridge, MA: The MIT Press, 1980.

Modigliani, Franco, and Richard Brumberg, "Utility Analysis and the Consumption Function: An Interpretation of Cross-Section Data." In Kurihara, K. K., ed., *Post-Keynesian Economics,* New Brunswick: Rutgers University Press, 1954, pp. 388–436.

Modigliani, Franco, and Arlie Sterling, "Determinants of Private Saving with Special Reference to the Role of Social Security Cross-Country Tests," In Modigliani, F., and R. Hemming, eds., *The Determinants of National Saving and Wealth.* New York: St. Martins Press, 1983, pp. 24–55.

Morgan, J. N., M. H. David, W. J. Cohen, H. E. Brazer, *Income and Welfare in the United States.* New York: McGraw-Hill Book Company, Inc., 1962.

Projector, Dorothy, *Survey of Changes in Family Finances.* Washington, D.C.: The Board of Governors of the Federal Reserve System, 1968.

Projector, Dorothy, and Weiss, Gertrude S., *Survey of Financial Characteristics of Consumers.* Washington, D.C.: The Board of Governors of the Federal Reserve System, 1964.

Royal Commission on the Distribution of Income and Wealth, Report No. 5, Third Report on the Standing Reference.

Shorrocks, A. F., "The Age-Wealth Relationship: A Cross-Section and Cohort Analysis," *Review of Economics and Statistics,* May 1975, *57,* 155–63.

White, Betsy Buttrill, "On the Rationality of Observed Saving: A Critique of the Life Cycle Hypothesis and Aggregate Household Saving," *American Economic Review,* September 1978, *68,* 547–60.

Government deficits, inflation, and future generations

Franco Modigliani*

I have three main points to make in this paper. The first is that current deficits are not a major cause of inflation; on the contrary, I shall argue that inflation is a major cause of deficits. The causation goes from stagflation to deficit, not the other way around.

Next, I want to argue that deficits are, nonetheless, a bad thing. They may not be bad in the short run, under some circumstances, but if they continue in the long run, they have serious consequences.

Finally, I propose to establish that deficits are not the cause of our current trouble, despite the fact that they are bad, for the simple reason that there are scarcely any deficits. That is, in terms of that deficit which is harmful, there are very few deficits of any significance at this time.

Let me begin by making it clear why we are so concerned with deficits. Figure 1 shows the behaviour of deficits in the United States. The top line shows the U.S. national debt for 1946 alone, and then the rapid and finally precipitous rise in that debt from 1969 on. It shows how, as Mr. Reagan was taking office, the national debt was just crossing the $1 trillion line. Mr. Reagan told us that if the debt were stacked in dollar bills it would reach the moon, or some such gruesome thing. Of course, since then, his administration has proceeded to bigger and bigger deficits, and one can see from the projections for the future, shown by the broken lines, that the stack is really going beyond the moon, towards Mars. The top line of Figure 2 (I will come back to the rest of the figure later) shows roughly the same thing, but in terms of the flow of deficits rather than the stock of debt. One can see how the current deficit took off

* Professor, Department of Economics, Sloan School of Industrial Management, Massachusetts Institute of Technology.

55

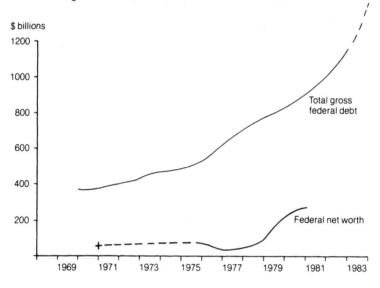

Figure 1
U.S. federal government debt and net worth

somewhere in the late seventies and, like the national debt, is also going through the ceiling. These huge deficits have been connected, in many minds, with our current deep economic problems - with the problem of stagflation. Figure 3 may help to explain why. The top panel again shows the deficits, but this time by five year periods. It shows that we had small deficits right after the Second World War, but that beginning in the late sixties deficits got bigger and bigger. As this happened, the next panel shows, we went from little inflation to more and more inflation. At the same time, as the last panel shows, productivity growth, which had been high, became small, zero, and finally negative.

Figure 4 draws a similar picture from the experience of nine major OECD countries. The height of the first column in the upper panel shows the annual average deficit (if above the horizontal line) or surplus (if below) for each country during the 1960s. The second column relates to the period 1975-80. It is apparent from the columns that in the sixties there were surpluses almost everywhere. Then came the seventies, and almost everywhere deficits replaced surpluses. The columns in the bottom panel represent inflation in the same periods. It is apparent that, as

56

Figure 2
U.S. Government deficits with adjustments

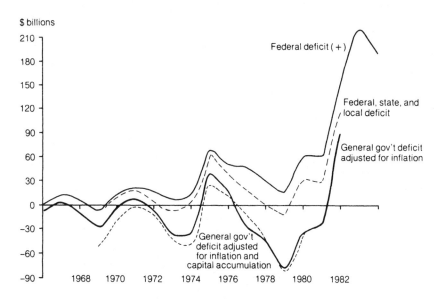

$ billions

deficits grew everywhere, so did inflation. Furthermore, the growth of inflation was greatest in Italy, where the deficit went way up, and in the U.K., where the budget went from a large surplus to a substantial deficit. Again, it seems as though deficit goes with inflation. The connection looks impressive, and it may have inspired the story that Reagan told the American people when he took over. The problem we have, according to Reagan, is that the government spends too much. As it spends more and more, it finds that it cannot increase taxes any further, because people cannot take it. Consequently, it starts running a deficit - it resorts to the printing press. The printing press creates inflation, and inflation creates disruption, depression, and low productivity. That is the mechanism. In my view, this argument is almost entirely fallacious.

The first thing that I want to examine is the relation between deficit and inflation. There is absolutely no reason to think there is association between the two, at least in the sense that deficit implies recourse to the printing press which, in turn, means inflation. We have to remember that in all reasonably developed countries the government finances its deficits by selling bonds, not by printing money it cannot print. Money is printed

57

Figure 3
Federal deficits, inflation, and productivity growth in the United States
(5-year intervals)

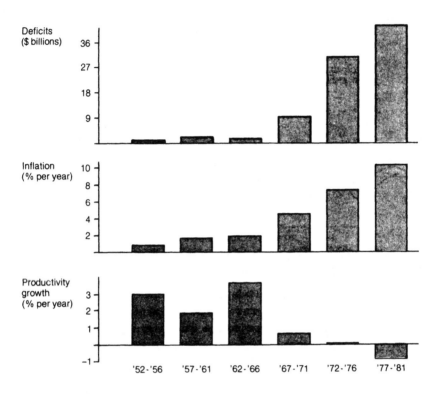

by the central bank, which decides how much government debt and other assets it wants to buy with it. There is no mechanical connection between running a deficit and creating money supply, and we have countless illustrations of the lack of such a connection. Just think, for example, of what happened in the United States in 1982. The deficit was enormous; it was well over $100 billion. Yet the central bank expanded its monetary base by only about $10 billion. Furthermore, this increase was less than it had been in years when the government deficit was smaller. Of course, in an underdeveloped country, one that has no financial markets, the government may sometimes have no way to sell bonds except to the central bank. Even when this does occur, one suspects that there is a will to

58

Figure 4

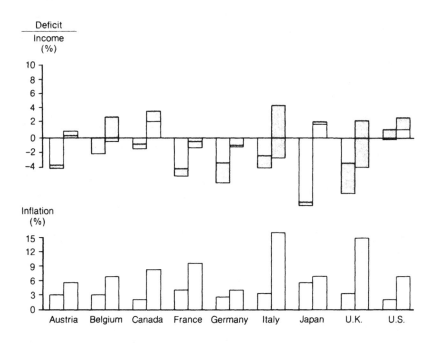

finance the deficit by inflation. But we are not concerned with primitive countries. In general, in developed countries there is no simple connection between deficits and money creation.

If the deficit is not a cause of inflation, is the deficit otherwise so bad? The issue of whether the deficit is bad, the issue sometimes referred to as crowding-out, is one of the classic issues that economists have enjoyed debating for several centuries. Many reputations have been made and destroyed in the course of that debate. There are essentially four views relating to the question of whether a government deficit is a burden on anybody, particularly whether it is a burden on future generations. These can be labelled (i) the 'naive' view that there is a burden, (ii) the 'naive' view that there is no burden, (iii) the 'sophisticated' view that there is a burden, and (iv) the 'super-sophisticated' view that there is no burden after all. Let me go over these four views quickly.

The naive view that there is a burden is the view of the man in the

59

TABLE 1
Data used in Figure 4

Country	Central government saving ratio[a] 1960-9	1975-9	Inflation[b] 1960-9	1975-9	Correction to the reported deficit[c] 1960-9	1975-9
Australia	0.050465	0.013353	0.024045	0.117895	0.011089	0.027738
Austria	0.037609	-0.010345	0.033976	0.057454	0.003478	0.008099
Belgium	-0.001391	-0.029698	0.031556	0.070521	0.021515	0.034553
Canada	0.003766	-0.037943	0.022407	0.084385	0.011234	0.016414
Denmark	0.073913	-0.01	0.054386	0.092829	0.009158	-0.014876
Finland	0.078771	0.054062	0.046312	0.115629	0.004886	0.002821
France	0.041526	0.004055	0.041855	0.09777	0.010221	0.009494
Germany	0.03152	0.005045	0.027447	0.041678	0.003097	0.00045
Greece	0.016939	-0.021731	0.023773	0.13601	0.001757	0.004615
Ireland	0.009101	-0.04746	0.043744	0.148322	0.036695	0.068093
Italy	0.024045	-0.04557	0.037764	0.163895	0.017369	0.073298
Japan	0.090176	-0.022078	0.055875	0.071025	0.003517	0.001854
Netherlands	0.050697	0.013545	0.040377	0.069184	0.01856	0.017083
Norway	0.07443	0.068906	0.037337	0.085353	0.010968	0.028107
Portugal	0.008798	-0.02356	0.025933	0.218809	0.003291	0.027861
Spain	0.036677	0.021976	0.058174	0.184303	0.014329	-0.002334
Sweden	0.051581	-0.006825	0.037589	0.101621	0.012383	0.030878
Switzerland	0.020921	0.016528	0.037852	0.029977	0.004876	0.002818
United Kingdom	0.035459	-0.023902	0.037146	0.152347	0.04289	0.06449
United States	-0.010934	-0.028794	0.022621	0.070369	0.012292	0.01777

a Shown in upper graph of Figure 4; b Shown in lower graph of Figure 4; c Shown by distance between the upper and lower limits of the shaded bars in the upper graph of Figure 4.

street. It rests on the notion that the debt of a government is just like the debt of a family - in the future you will have to pay the interest on it and to repay the principal, and that will curtail your future ability to consume. The same must be true of the government too: a government debt is, therefore, bad in the sense that it 'mortgages' the resources of future generations.

The naive no-burden view claims that the first view is all nonsense because the debt of the family is a debt due outside the family, but the debt of the government is due inside the country - we owe it to ourselves. Certainly, future generations will have to pay interest on the debt, but future generations will also receive that interest. All that takes place is a transfer from one group to another. According to the eighteenth-century French economist, le Chevalier de Melun, the public debt is like the debt of the left hand to the right hand, which in no way weakens the body. In other words, what matters is disposable income, or income produced minus taxes paid, plus interest received. When you raise the taxes and pay the interest, these two flows cancel out, and disposable income will not be affected.

One other way of supporting the no-burden argument is to say that it is impossible for this generation to eat the wheat of future generations. We can only eat the wheat we produce. Thus, we cannot shift the burden from the present to the future.

Next comes the sophisticated view that there is a burden. In essence, this view says that we can, indeed, affect future output. We can affect it by the amount of capital we bequeath to the future. Whenever the government runs a deficit, it finances that deficit by tapping current saving that would otherwise have gone into investment. Therefore, investment is reduced. Investment is a source of income for the future, and that income has been lost. The disposable income argument is false, for while it is true that when we have a deficit one hand pays the other, if we did not have the deficit one hand would receive not from the other but from the capital that produces income. Therefore we have lost the income that the capital would have produced.

This argument is sound, except that one may wonder whether the deficit's effect on investment might not be made up later. How do we know that the loss is permanent? It is useful at this point, I think, to fall back on another way of looking at the issue, which I refer to as a life-cycle perspective.

61

The life-cycle hypothesis (LCH) is, essentially, a model of the determinants of aggregate wealth. There used to be a view that the wealth we see around us was something we had inherited from the past - that was how the wealth came to be here. About thirty or forty years ago, the work I did on the life cycle pointed out that there was no need of bequests to explain all the wealth that is in existence, for it could easily be generated by 'hump saving' - that is, people saving currently for later expenditure and for retirement. All that happens is that the same physical assets change hands from the old who are selling them to consume to the young who are accumulating; you do not need transfers by bequest at all.

In a more general formulation, one may expect that wealth is generated in part by bequests and in part by life-cycle saving. In any event, this model tells us that the amount of wealth that exists in society is determined basically by society's income. That income determines both how much we allocate to the future and how much may be bequeathed. Wealth may also be influenced by forces such as income growth and population structure, but what is important is that one can rule out the proposition that the amount of wealth that society wishes to hold is systematically related to the size of government deficit. This means that a debt occupies a portion of the wealth that people would wish to hold, and thereby reduces the portion of wealth available to finance capital. So if people were to hold in wealth, say, four times income, and if there were no debt, then capital would be four times income. But if there were debt equal to one times income, then the available capital would be only three times income. Essentially, then, what we have here is another way of looking at the crowding-out phenomenon. The government deficit crowds out capital because the desire for wealth is satisfied by the government debt instead of being satisfied by productive physical capital.

This way of looking at things has many convenient aspects - for instance, it provides a measure of the overall burden of the national debt. Suppose a country has a deficit of $1 trillion. What is the burden, in terms of diminished capital, that this deficit imposes on future generations? It is equal to the return on the amount of capital it displaces. Now, according to LCH, $1 trillion of government debt should tend to displace $1 trillion of capital. If the interest rate is, say, 5 per cent per year, then the loss is essentially 5 per cent of $1 trillion, or $50 billion a year. In other words, to a good approximation, the flow of the burden can be

62

measured by the annual interest paid on the national debt.

The basic argument also suggests its limitations and qualifications. First of all, the interest may not be a good measure of the burden, because the capital may produce more than the interest rate on account of the tax wedge. With a corporate tax of 50 per cent, if the return to capital were 10 per cent, it would reduce to 5 per cent after tax, which also equals the interest rate. That is, when the government displaces $1 billion of capital, there is not only a loss of $50 million in income to the holders, but also a loss of $50 million in tax revenue to the government. So the loss is not just the interest bill, but the interest bill plus the tax bill thereon.

Again, the burden exists because the deficit displaces capital; but if the debt is used to finance government capital, then there will be a return from it that makes up for the private capital displaced. In principle, what matters is not the deficit but the deficit minus the value of income-earning assets, financial or physical, that the government may hold, with the return being calculated not necessarily in terms of cash return but in terms of social return.

Two other points are, I think, relevant to the current discussion. One is that the argument I have developed about the burden of the debt is clearly valid when resources are fully utilized, so that the government deficit does, in fact, displace investment. If there is slack in the economy, then the government deficit need not displace investment (and may actually increase it). Therefore, there need not be any burden, at least in the short run. One has to be careful here, because whether or not the deficit does displace other things is not just a function of the availability of resources, but also a function of the monetary policy being pursued at the same time. If we have slack resources and would like to use them, then there should be a monetary policy that permits investment and government deficit to go on together, preventing the crowding-out.

On the other hand, it may be that we have slack but do not want to use it. In many places, such as the United States, policymakers feel that the slack is needed at present to reduce inflation. In situations where the slack is wanted, the government deficit may again displace investment. But this applies only in situations like the current one where the slack must be maintained because of other services it performs. Let me remark in this connection that when I am asked by people whether we are going through a repetition of the Great Depression, I say that there is a great

63

difference between then and now: then we did not know how to control unemployment; now we do, reasonably well. We have been using the knowledge, particularly in the United States, to create a lot of unemployment as a way to fight inflation. Whether that is a good way or not is a separate issue. At least it has worked, though with a lot of pain.

Finally, there is the question of debt in the family - or outside the family. Suppose that instead of borrowing domestically, we borrow abroad. Does that make any difference to the burden argument? Even those who maintain that there is no burden from an internal debt must acknowledge that an external debt does cause a burden, since we have to pay the interest outside. My argument implies that, if we are using resources fully, it is immaterial, at least to a first approximation, whether the borrowing is inside or outside. If we borrow inside, we displace investment and lose the income from those investments. If we borrow outside, we continue to have those investments, but we have to pay the income to outsiders and, therefore, our society loses the same amount. The net result is the same, except for second-order refinements that depend on taxation and so on.

It remains to consider the 'super-sophisticated' no-burden argument. This is an argument that probably has not gone much beyond sophisticated economists. It is sometimes traced way back to Ricardo, although I do not think this is a correct way of putting it. My opinion is that Ricardo did suggest the possibility but thought it was not practically relevant. The basis for the argument is as follows. Suppose we assume that life is infinite, as economists not infrequently do, and that all taxes are strictly proportional to income. Suppose further that the government intends to spend $100 and has a choice of either collecting a tax for $100 now or floating a loan for $100 and then raising taxes to pay the interest from now on. Whatever choice the government makes, everybody will be in exactly the same position. Paying $100 now and paying $5 forever have exactly the same present value, and the taxpayer really shouldn't care a bit which is chosen. So, tax financing and debt financing are equivalent. The burden is in the use of resources, not in the way their acquisition is financed.

This argument, resting on infinite life, has recently been extended by Barro (1974) and others to the case in which life is finite, through the mechanism of inheritance. Suppose that you, at present, are making decisions for yourself and your heirs as to how you and your heirs will

64

allocate your resources to consumption over time - so much to you, so much to the heirs. Now along comes the government and says, 'We are going to reduce your taxes by $100 by raising a loan whose interest will be paid by future generations.' If you are a rational man you will say, 'Why should I let the government decide that I should be better off - and my heirs worse off - than I originally decided? I've made a certain decision and I am going to stick by it. To do this, I have only to use the tax rebate to buy the $100 worth of bonds that the government offers and pass them on to my heirs, so that when the collector comes around for $5 a year they can simply pay him with the $5 they receive from the bonds. They will be as well off as before, and I will be as well off as before.' Again, in this kind of world, it is immaterial whether the government taxes or uses deficit financing.

The only trouble with this argument is that it has nothing - or almost nothing - to do with the real world. Why is that so? There are many reasons, and let me quickly point out some. To begin with, just consider the simple case in which people are not identical: I happen to have no children and you happen to have twenty. In this case, the choice between taxing and borrowing can make an enormous difference. I, who have no children, would much rather see the tax put on children; you, who have twenty, would much rather have the tax paid now. It is clear that alternative methods of financing are not neutral and that the differential effects on current consumption are not necessarily going to cancel out.

A more serious shortcoming of the argument results from 'asymmetry'. Suppose I decide that the optimum allocation calls for my children to consume less and for me to consume more than our respective life incomes. If I could, I would elect for a negative bequest, or a transfer from my children to me. But I can't; the closest to optimum is to plan no bequests. If an additional tax is put on me to retire debt, I would like to shift it to the future, which I could do only by reducing bequests. But with zero initial bequests, all I can do is stay where I am. So, in general, whenever the actual planned bequest is zero and the optimal is negative - calling for a transfer from children to parents - the choice of financing is relevant. Replacing taxes with deficits will transfer from the future to the current generation. In fact, it is precisely for this reason that the choice of financing may be a way for the current generation to achieve a desired outcome not achievable through private transfers. For example, if we finance a major war by debt, then the generation of the

65

war will come out of the war with debt that it can sell to support a higher consumption. It will, thereby, reduce the net saving of society in the future, since the new generation's saving will go into buying existing bonds instead of adding to the stock of capital. Thus, we can, by our choice of financing, control how the burden is distributed between the present and the future.

In general, the empirical relevance of Barro's paradigm depends on the quantitative role of bequests as an intergenerational bridge. This is a very big issue, and I do not have time to discuss it fully here. It is closely related to the importance of bequests as a determinant of national wealth, which is currently hotly debated. Some people have recently claimed that most wealth is, in fact, the result of bequests. I have done some fresh work in this area, and my results suggest very strongly that, at least in the United States in this century, bequests are a modest portion of wealth between 15 and 20 per cent of the total. This estimate is derived from many different sources, from inquiries made through surveys to analysis of wills. They all point clearly in the direction of a relatively modest amount of transfers, it being understood that the transfers relevant here exclude those between husband and wife. These appear in wills as bequests but, of course, really occur inside the household. If they are taken out, and they are very substantial, the remaining bequests are relatively unimportant.

Consequently, I would not expect bequests to significantly offset public financing decisions, and accordingly I see the national debt having an unfavourable effect on the stock of capital in terms of crowding out tangible capital.

This conclusion is supported by some empirical work I have done in this area. We have estimates for the United States of private national wealth, or the wealth of households, going back to the beginning of the century, mostly due to the work of Goldsmith (1963). Since the beginning of the post-war period, we have official estimates from the Federal Reserve Flow of Funds series. We also have data on the amount of government debt - federal, state, and local - so we can ask the following question: Is there any evidence to support Barro's hypothesis, as against the LCH? How would we tell the two apart?

If Barro is right, whenever the government borrows, people will decide to accumulate more so that they can offset the debt burden on their children. In other words, they want to pass on to their children addi-

66

tional wealth equal to the debt the government has floated, so that the future generations will be no worse off. Hence, one would expect wealth to rise, dollar for dollar, as the debt rises. This is the same as saying that the amount of wealth minus debt - call it private tangible capital - is independent of the amount of debt. That would be evidence that there is no burden, no crowding-out. On the other hand, there is evidence of crowding-out if wealth does not rise with debt and, hence, tangible capital declines with debt.

An earlier study of mine (1966) examined the United States' evidence for the period 1900 to 1958, and found that the private wealth/income ratio is absolutely independent of the government debt/income ratio. In fact, the coefficient of the debt/income ratio, instead of being 1, as implied by Barro, is -.04, and statistically totally insignificant. I have recently rerun this test with alternative formulations and found approximately the same results. I have also extended the tests to the period 1900-80, and again the general result is that there is no evidence of the debt having an effect on wealth. Or, equivalently, private tangible wealth decreases roughly dollar for dollar with the debt.

Barro has suggested to me that the test was unsatisfactory because, if people are truly rational, they will look not at the debt, but at the debt minus the assets the government holds. They know that whenever the government has one more dollar of debt they need to leave one dollar more of bequest, while when the government increases its assets by a dollar they need, on balance, to leave one dollar less. What really matters, then, is the net worth of the government. I have, therefore, run the same regressions using not the debt but the net worth of the government, and the results are exactly the same. There is no evidence that the net worth of the government has any effect. Interestingly enough, if you look separately at the effect of assets and liabilities, the assets have a slightly negative effect, consistent with Barro, but the liabilities also have a slightly negative effect - and both effects are very small and very insignificant. On the whole, then, the data for the U.S. appear to reject Barro's hypothesis and to support the view that government debt crowds out private tangible wealth.

Tests have also been carried out relying on a cross-section of countries and looking for evidence that, where the deficit is large, saving is large. For, if Barro is right, where the government deficit on current account is large, savings should be large. Preliminary results show no

67

positive association between the private saving rate and the current account deficit. Indeed, the association appears slightly negative - where the deficit is large, saving is small and vice versa - but not significant. Again, there is absolutely no evidence in favour of the Barro hypothesis, and a strong presumption in favour of the hypothesis that debt crowds out capital.

The conclusion that deficits have an unfavourable effect on the economy, in particular through crowding-out of investment, raises the question of whether the recent exceptionally large, and widespread, cash deficits, of which we saw evidence at the start, could be a source of our present difficulties - high inflation, high unemployment, low productivity growth.

I am going to suggest that the answer is very clearly negative, and the reason - somewhat paradoxically - is that there really are no significant 'crowding-out' deficits anywhere. This proposition might seem totally inconsistent with the figures discussed earlier. But there is no contradiction, because the figures show the cash deficit, whereas the deficit that creates crowding-out is the rise in the real debt. The change in the real debt differs from the change in nominal debt, or cash deficit, because of the loss of real value of the debt due to inflation. When an adjustment is made for the depreciation of the debt, which is the same as computing the interest bill using the real, rather than the nominal, interest rate, one finds that this has a large impact on the deficit.

Take as an example the United States, where the debt is around $1.2 trillion. If inflation is, say, 10 per cent, it implies a $120 billion correction. In 1982, the U.S. deficit, though exceptionally huge, is, in fact, of a very similar magnitude. Thus, after subtracting a correction for $120 billion, one is left with roughly zero. This somewhat exaggerates the correction, because it should be applied not to the gross, but to the net, debt (i.e., net of financial claims). Still, if one does the correct calculation for past years, one will find that, in fact, the correction exceeds the cash deficit itself. This is shown in Figure 2. The top curve is the unadjusted federal deficit, and the second, dotted line is the consolidated deficit of all governments - federal, state, and local. The consolidation already makes quite a bit of difference, because it happened that, while the federal government was running a deficit, the state and local governments were running surpluses. The lower solid curve is corrected for inflation, and the broken line that follows it is corrected for inflation and for investment so that it represents deficit on current account.

68

One can see that by the time all the adjustments are made, there are essentially no deficits up to 1982. The modest exception occurs in 1975, but this deficit is largely of a cyclical nature. I pointed out earlier that it is all right to have a deficit when there is a depression and that, in fact, a sound fiscal structure should lead to counter-cyclical deficits, as tax receipts should vary cyclically and expenditure should move counter-cyclically. If Figure 2 were adjusted for the cyclical deficit, as John Bossons and Peter Dungan have done for Canada in a paper (1983) that I understand is being debated these days, it would be clear that there really is no significant deficit anywhere in the United States.

What we have just found for the United States holds roughly for other OECD countries and, in particular, for the nine shown in Figure 4. This exhibits a correction of the cash deficit for the depreciation of the debt due to inflation. The correction is represented by the shaded area subtracted from the column representing the cash deficit. Thus, the lower boundary of the shaded area represents the inflation-corrected deficit (if above the horizontal line) or surplus (if below). One can see, for instance, that for Austria, in the first period, there was very little inflation and hence a slight correction for inflation. In the second period, there was a larger cash deficit; corrected for inflation, however, the deficit becomes zero. Similar results hold for most other countries: correction for the effect of inflation generally wipes out the deficit and even turns it into a surplus. Indeed, it is apparent that, after correction for inflation, there were hardly any deficits on current accounts in the late seventies, except in Japan and, I am afraid, in Canada. Note that Japan, which has a slight deficit, is one of the countries with the lowest inflation rate. One can clearly see, from Figure 4, that there are no grounds for holding that the stagflation was produced by an outburst of uncontrolled deficits.

On the contrary, one can argue just the opposite: that stagflation is the cause of deficits. Why? The main link comes from the fact that inflation means high interest rates, and high interest rates mean a large interest payment. It would be rational and consistent with sound fiscal policies to meet this enhanced interest bill by borrowing rather than by raising tax rates - unless one is bent on a policy of actually reducing the real national debt. The reason, of course, is that the higher interest reflects the inflation premium, which itself is equivalent to a repayment of the (real) debt. Thus, unless one intends to reduce the real debt, funds required to pay the inflation premium should come from borrowing, not

69

from taxes. As a result, a high rate of inflation could be expected to produce deficits of a magnitude related to the inflation correction. Similarly, high unemployment tends to cause high cyclical deficits.

An examination of Figure 4 suggests that, in most countries, policymakers have been willing to accept, in part, the higher cash deficits implied by stagflation under constant tax rates. In part, however, they have tended to contain the higher cash deficits through higher tax rates (partly the result of the so called 'bracket creep' effect of progressive taxation), with the outcome that, on balance, correctly measured deficits have been lower, not higher, in the more recent period. It is these considerations that lead me to reject the popular view that stagflation has been the result of irresponsible fiscal policies and to suggest, instead, that the observed association of deficits and stagflation reflects the causal link from stagflation to deficits, when tax rates and real expenditures on goods and services are held constant.

That seems to be the essential story for the past. There has been no problem coming from deficits, though deficits can pose a serious problem, because there have been no significant deficits. What about the future? Here it may be useful to go back to the United States' chart (Figure 1) for it suggests that Mr. Reagan is trying very hard to make a non-problem into a problem. For a man who came to power telling us that deficit was the worst thing in the world, the huge deficits he is proposing for the coming years are quite a change and quite a puzzle. If they come at a time when inflation has largely abated and unemployment has largely disappeared, they will be truly of the crowding-out variety. There is no warranted correction that can make them shrink. Therefore, they will represent a serious problem.

Of course, the implications of the large deficit for the U.S. are serious in many ways for the rest of the world as well. The displacement of investment will, presumably, mean a continuation of high interest rates, which, given the size of the country, will tend to mean damagingly high interest rates for the rest of the world. However, one should separate the past from the future. In the past, deficits have not represented a major problem. In countries such as Canada, which are not facing a huge armaments build-up, I suspect that the future does not look too bleak. For the United States, the deficits do look quite disturbing, and they have ominous implications for the rest of the world. But one must hope that something will be done before things get serious.

70

REFERENCES

Barro, R.J. (1974) 'Are government bonds net wealth?' Journal of Poltical Economy 82:6, 1095-1117.

Bossons, J. and P. Dungan (1983) 'Government deficits: too high or too low?' Canadian Tax Journal 31:1, 1-29.

Goldsmith, R. and R.E. Lipsey (1963) Studies in the National Balance Sheet of the United States' (Princeton, N.J.: Princeton University Press, National Bureau of Economic Research. Studies in Capital Formation and Financing, 11).

Modigliani, F. (1966) 'The life cycle hypothesis of savings, the demand for wealth and the supply of capital,' Social Research 33:2, 160-217.

Errata

Page 56: put "x" on vertical axis of Figure 1, with expression "1946 = 271."

Page 56, second paragraph, fourth line: after period insert "(For a full explanation of this figure, see page 69)."

Page 57, five lines from the end: insert "an" before "association."

Page 60, Table 1: insert "*Sources:* Economic Report of the President (various issues) and Robert Eisner, *How Real is the Federal Deficit?* New York, The Free Press, 1986."

Page 62, second paragraph, line 9: "a" should read "government."

Page 62, second paragraph, 6 lines from the end: delete "one times."

Page 63, second paragraph, fourth line: insert "rate" after "corporate tax."

Page 63, third paragraph, second line: insert "formation" after "capital."

Page 65, third paragraph, fifth line: insert "an" before "optimum."

Page 65, 7 lines from the end: insert "bequest" after "optimal."

Page 66, second paragraph, 6 lines from the end: "analysis" should read "analyses."

Page 66, second to last paragraph: insert "and Lipsey" after "Goldsmith."

Page 68, top line: insert "government's" before "current account."

Page 68, bottom line: insert "a" before "deficit."

Page 69, first paragraph: delete last line and replace with "was no significant structural deficit in the post-war U.S."

Page 69, third line from end: insert "payment" before "reflects."

Page 70, third paragraph, seventh line: insert "a" before "deficit."

The Economics of Public Deficits[1]

Franco Modigliani

INTRODUCTION

There are three basic issues connected with the economic consequences of the flow of deficits and the resulting stock of public debt.

1. Does the deficit contribute to the creation of aggregate demand and thus to output (with or without effect on prices), or does it, instead, crowd out other components, leaving the total unchanged? This issue is reviewed in Section I.

2. Are deficits *the* major, or at least *a* major source of inflation, either through the effect on demand and/or through the way they are financed? This is the question that is examined in Section II.

3. In so far as the crowding out occurs, what is crowded out, consumption or national saving and investment? And who bears the burden (the cost) of the resources absorbed by government purchases under alternative ways of financing them? The answers to these questions, in turn, are essential for an understanding of the inter-generational effect of expenditure and financing, and the choice of tax versus debt financing. Section III confronts these questions at the theoretical level, while Section IV brings to bear a variety of empirical evidence.

I SHORT RUN EFFECTS OF DEFICITS: INCREASED OUTPUT VERSUS CROWDING OUT, PARTICULARLY OF INVESTMENT

This is an old issue which was at the core of the debate between the Keynesian and the classical view, but deserves a brief review to allow for the role of monetary policy. One must distinguish several possibilities.

3

Slack and Accommodating Monetary Policy – The Pure Keynesian Multiplier Case

According to the standard Keynesian analysis, a rise in deficit not only does not crowd out investment but, instead, it increases – or crowds in – output by the additional demand directly produced by the fiscal action, amplified by the multiplier. The extent and composition of the increase depends on the source of change in deficit and can be inferred from the standard national income identity and aggregate demand equation:

$$Y = C + I + G; \qquad C = c(Y - T); \qquad Def = G - T \qquad (1)$$

where Y, C, I, G, Def, and T are respectively income produced, consumption, investment, government expenditure, deficit and taxes net of transfers. Consumption is assumed, conventionally, to depend on disposable income, thus abstracting from the Barro-type hypothesis, discussed later, that it might also be affected, directly, by government consumption. From these relations, one can infer that a rise in Def due entirely to a reduction, ΔT, in taxes, 'crowds in' consumption and output by $(c/1 - c)\Delta Def$ (a direct effect of $c\Delta T$, magnified by the multiplier $(1/(1 - c))$). If Def rises because of a rise in G, T constant, then to the above effect one must add the rise in output needed to meet the government demand, ΔG. This result is the standard investment multiplier:

$$\left(1 + \frac{c}{1-c}\right) \Delta Def = \left(\frac{1}{1-c}\right) \Delta Def$$

Finally, if the rise in G is accompanied by an equal rise in T, leaving Def unchanged, then the consumption effect is cut off and what is left is only the direct effect of 1 (balanced budget multiplier). In addition, there can be a rise of investment through accelerator effects, increasing the impact on output.

But these results are subject to some important qualifications. First, they represent short-run effects – i.e., while the slack persists. In the long run, there may still be crowding out effects, as discussed below. Second, for those results to hold, even in the short run, two crucial conditions must be satisfied: there must be enough slack in the economy for the additional demand to be satisfied without pressure on prices, and, even when there is enough slack, there must be an accommodating monetary policy that permits the expansion of output, with stable prices, without putting pressure on interest rates and credit market.

Slack and Non-accommodating Monetary Policy – the Intermediate Case

Suppose there is adequate slack in the economy, but monetary policy is not fully accommodating in the sense of providing enough liquidity to keep interest rates and credit markets from tightening in the face of a rise in output such as would correspond to the fiscal action and the multiplier. Then the rise in interest rates will crowd out investment, reducing demand directly, and through the multiplier and thus enforcing the containment of Y. The extent of the crowding out will depend on monetary policy as well as the type of fiscal expansion. Specifically, from (1) one can derive:

$$\Delta I = (1 - c)\Delta \bar{Y} - \Delta G + c\Delta T \tag{2}$$

It is seen that a rise in deficit due to G, T constant, will crowd out Investment, dollar per dollar, less, however, $(1 - c)\Delta \bar{Y}$, the rise in saving due to the rise in income $\Delta \bar{Y}$ allowed by Central Bank policy. But, as long as monetary policy is not fully accommodating, and thus the rise in income is constrained to fall short of the full multiplier response, the rise in saving must be insufficient to prevent crowding out from occurring. In the limiting case where income is prevented from rising at all, the additional deficit crowds out I fully, as government absorption replaces investment, while consumption remains constant.

If the deficit rises through a fall in taxes, then I gets crowded out by a rise in consumption. But, the crowding out is less than dollar per dollar. In the first place, consumption rises, and investment is reduced, only by cdT, while $(1 - c)$ of the tax cut is saved, reducing the crowding out effect of the rise in deficit. In addition, to the extent that monetary policy allows Y to rise, the resulting rise in saving reduces the crowding out further, though again not to the point of eliminating it.

Finally, if G rises with a balanced budget, and hence with an equal rise in T, most of G is accommodated by a fall in consumption by cdG, due to the higher taxes, while the crowding out of investment is limited to the fall in saving, $(1 - c)\Delta G$, less, again, the rise in saving resulting from the rise in income and saving.

It appears therefore that, as long as the money supply is not accommodating enough to permit the rise of income by the full multiplier, an expansionary fiscal policy – i.e. a rise in deficit or even a rise in expenditure covered by taxes – will create some crowding out of private investment, even if there is excess capacity and wasting resources.

Note that when monetary policy forces a *de facto* crowding out in the presence of idle capacity, this may be due to errors in the design or execution of policy, but it may also be due, as was the case recently, to a target Y below feasible full employment, in order to help the winding down of inflation.

No Slack: the Classical Case

When there is no slack, the effect of deficit can be inferred from (2) above by putting $dY = 0$: the deficit will necessarily crowd out investment, dollar for dollar, when due to G, and by $(1 - c)$ dollar per dollar when due to tax reduction. This conclusion holds as long as consumption does not directly respond to expenditure, for given taxes. The implication of that assumption, as well as its empirical relevance, are taken up in Sections III and IV below.

It must be recognised that even when the fiscal expansion occurs in an economy at full employment, if the money supply is unchanged, there will tend to be some upward pressure on prices and some temporary rise in output. To this extent, the crowding out may be less than indicated above, but only transiently. Similarly, the inflation should also be transient, resulting in a higher price level but not in an inflationary process (see Section II below).

II DEFICITS AS THE CAUSE OF INFLATION

The 'Conventional Wisdom'

The view that budget deficits cause inflation, or, in the extreme view, that they are its main cause, is a popular one. Apparently it has its origin in the view that when the government spends more than it collects, it pays for the differences by the 'printing press', and that the printing of money is inflationary. This perception is reinforced by memories of major war deficits, being accompanied by monetary expansions, and by major inflationary episodes. There is also a strand of Keynesian origin that holds that deficits can cause inflation by increasing demand. Most recently these views have been reinforced by the experience of the 1970s after the oil crisis. In many, indeed most, countries there were fairly severe bouts of inflation, accompanied by significant deficits or, at the very least, appreciable deterioration in the government account.

This view that deficits cause inflation was at the core of the Reagan economic platform through the early part of his administration. In fact, he suggested that deficits were the cause of the widespread stagflation of the time, as the inflation produced economic turmoil, which, in turn, led to unemployment.

Deficits and Money Creation

The basic fallacy in the argument is the proposition that government deficits have to be financed by creation of money. This is patently false in economies with a reasonably well developed financial system. There, the government does not create money and pays for deficits by issuing appropriate non-money IOU's. Money is created, instead, by the Central Bank when it buys government debt or other assets, or by the banking system buying assets with monetary liabilities, within limits set by Central Bank.

The task of the Central Bank is to stabilise output and prices through its control of M. Hence, there is no reason why it should expand or contract money and credit according to the size of deficit. The only limited exception is when a deficit accompanies a cyclical slack, either through built-in stabilisers or through *ad hoc* budget policy. In this case, the growing deficit (surplus) should be accompanied by an appropriately expansionary (contractionary) monetary policy. But, in these circumstances, there should be no cause for inflation.

There are, however, some special circumstances in which the deficit is accompanied, more or less unavoidably, by monetary expansion, and thus inflation. One is the case of major war, referred to earlier. In such cases, the government may need to acquire more resources than can be secured through taxation and absorption of government liabilities on the part of the public, both voluntary and compulsory –

account being taken of the disincentive effects of taxation and forced saving. In that case, the government may have to fill the gap by selling part of the debt to the Central Bank and the banking system, who pay by creating money for the government to spend.

A second case is that of primitive financial structure when there are no mechanisms for the government to sell its debt to the public (or private banks). It must therefore sell it to Central Banks, expanding the money stock. This mechanism seems to be important in some Latin American type inflation.

A third circumstance in which deficits might lead to inflation is the one described by Sargent and Wallace (1981) in which, essentially, the debt grows so large that the interest cannot be paid by tapping current private saving. Hence, at least a part of the deficit has to be paid by money creation (or, equivalently, through the inflation tax). But this extreme case would seem to be of very limited empirical relevance.

One fourth and final mechanism arises from the circumstance described earlier about the impact of deficit under conditions of near full employment. The crowding out of investment may not occur promptly unless interest rates are allowed to rise through a stable (or in fact appropriately reduced) money supply. However, the Central Bank might endeavour to prevent interest rates from rising, either by mistake or because of subservience to a Government that does not wish to see an unpopular rise in interest. This policy tends to lead to an expanding M and continuing inflation, as long as it persists. Here the expansion of M and accompanying inflation might be directly associated to the deficit. Yet what feeds the inflation is not printing of money to finance the deficit, as in the naive version, but the endeavour to hold the line on interest rates, in the face of the more expansionary fiscal policy. Indeed, in this case, the growth of money is related to a more expansionary fiscal policy, regardless of whether such a policy leads to a deficit or merely to a smaller surplus. Little is known as to whether this particular mechanism of inflation is empirically important. But, at least for the United States, empirical studies do not generally seem to find that it is (see, e.g., Blinder (1983), and the references cited therein).

Can Deficits Explain the Recent Inflation?

If the recent inflation were due to the deficits that developed more or less simultaneously, it would have to be through one of the four mechanisms examined above. Yet the first three are clearly inapplicable in the relevant period, at least for the developed countries. As for the last mechanism, whatever one's assessment about its empirical relevance in general, one can rule out the possibility that the recent inflation was due to it for one quite compelling reason, namely that there were no significant 'true' deficits through most of the period. This statement is fully consistent with the above-mentioned observation of rising deficits reported in most countries, because the reported deficit represents the growth in *nominal* deficit. To measure the deficit correctly, one must calculate the change in the real debt; that change is equal to the nominal deficit less the loss of purchasing power of the outstanding debt, GD, in the course of the year, due to the inflation, $\dot{P}$, i.e., less $\dot{P}GD$. This is equivalent to saying that the true interest actually paid and received on the government debt should be computed as $RD - \dot{P}D = rD$, when the first term in the left side is the actual interest paid, and $r = R - \dot{P}$ is the real rate. The correction term $\dot{P}D$, can be quite large when inflation gets high. It is therefore not surprising that, once corrected for inflation, in general, the deficits as a percentage of income do not appear to have risen significantly over the recent period, and may even have declined in some cases.

Thus, Cukierman and Mortensen (1983) in a study of five major Common Market countries found that, according to official statistics, in all countries but one (France), there were substantial reported deficits by the end of the 1970s, and they were generally strikingly larger than a decade earlier. However, once the official figures are corrected for inflation, they find that the deficit increased significantly for only one country, Belgium, where inflation was not particularly serious, and very moderately for Germany, a low inflation country. For the remaining high inflation countries, the deficit has been steady or has even declined as in France and Italy, while in the UK there were mostly surpluses, though declining in the course of the 1970s.

An alternative way of minimising the effect of the inflation bias in the official statistics is to look at the behaviour of the ratio of government debt to nominal GNP, which provides a good measure of whether there has actually been an increase in the burden of the debt. Siegel and Protopapadakis (1984) have studied the behaviour of this ratio in recent years for seven major industrial countries, including in the debt the entire public sector. They find that since the early 1970s this ratio has risen appreciably only in three countries, Germany, Japan and Italy, of which the first two had relatively moderate inflation and also had very low debt at the beginning. For the remaining countries, including high inflation ones, like the UK and France, but also the US and Switzerland, the ratio has been roughly constant.

What Accounts for the Recent Association Between Reported Deficits and Inflation?

We suggest that a major, if not *the* major answer is to be found in 'inverse causation': it was the relatively high and widespread rate of inflation (generated primarily by the successive oil shocks – see below) that caused a rise in nominal deficit, and not vice versa. Inflation contributed to nominal deficits both by increasing outlays and by decreasing revenues.

Outlays rose for two reasons. First, the inflation tended to be reflected in higher nominal interest rates (as suggested by Fisher's law), and hence interest expenses. This effect can be quite substantial. Thus, if we suppose a debt income ratio of 30 per cent, (not far from the average for OECD countries), and a real rate of 3 per cent, then a rise in inflation from zero to 10 per cent will increase the interest bill more than fourfold, from 0.09 to 3.9 per cent of income. Second, the effort at stopping and reducing the inflation through a non-accommodating monetary policy resulted, at least for a time, in a fall in employment and output, which in turn reduced revenues and increased expenditure for transfers, such as unemployment compensation. This is the standard cyclical reaction of the budget in the presence of automatic stabilizers. The only partial offset to these mechanisms has tended to come through the so-called 'bracket creep' – the effect of inflation of pushing tax payers with an unchanged real income into higher tax brackets, thus raising real taxes and revenues. But, the magnitude of this effect, which in any event depends on specific tax institutions, was frequently reduced by adjustments of the brackets, whether automatic or discretionary.

Of course, the budget deficit could have been controlled by raising taxes, but this course was not followed on a significant scale, either because governments knew that the increase of the deficit was partly fictitious and partly the result of built-in stabilisers, or because they were disinclined to raise taxes in an already depressed economy.

But if inflation was not caused by deficits but rather caused them, then what caused inflation? As already indicated, the major cause in the 1970s and early 1980s were supply shocks, basically oil shocks. They sparked a wage price spiral, made possible by partial monetary accommodation. But the accommodation was, or at any rate, eventually became, sufficiently limited to generate substantial cyclical unemployment and thus stagflation.

We conclude therefore that deficits can be the cause of inflation only under rather special circumstances. These circumstances were, in particular, not present during the widespread inflationary episodes of the 1970s. Those episodes were, instead, largely the results of huge supply shocks, which produced stagflation and hence government deficit.

III WHAT IS CROWDED OUT BY DEFICITS AND DEBT – AND WHAT DIFFERENCE DOES IT MAKE?

A Review of the Traditional Debate

The classic issue relating to the public deficit is generally posed as: are there any costs in using deficit financing in place of taxes? What are they? Who bears them? What is implied with respect to using it? Going back in the centuries, one finds a variety of sharply contradictory major views, with countless variants.

1. There is, first, the timeless view held by the concerned man of the street that the public deficits are essentially like a family's debt. They are a burden on the family's future by 'mortgaging' future resources for the payment of interests and the repayment of principal. It was last heard with great vigour by Keynesian supporters of the New Deal deficit spending and during the battle over the Kennedy tax cut, in the early 1960s.

2. There is next the sophisticated rebuttal of that view set forth by 'economists' since a couple of centuries ago, arguing that the analogy with private debt is false because we owe it to ourselves: the future generations pay the interest and principle, but future generations get it. It is but a transfer; disposable income is unaffected. This argument is reinforced by the proposition that the deficit cannot be a burden on future generations because we cannot consume their resources of the future which have not yet been produced. It also follows from this reasoning that an exception must be made for public debt contracted outside the family, i.e., abroad; that, and only that, will impose a future burden, analogous to private debt.

3. Next comes the yet more sophisticated rebuttal of the sophisticated rebuttal, also going back a long time, according to which the man in the street is pretty much right after all, even if, largely, for the wrong reason. This view rests on three basic considerations.

(a) Deficit financing is a burden on future generations to the advantage of the current generation because it reduces the tax burden of the current generation, allowing it to consume more, and the larger consumption crowds out investment, as saving is diverted from financing investment to financing the government deficit.

(b) It is through this crowding out process that the current generation can, in effect, succeed in consuming more at the expense of a reduction in the future availability of means of production and thus, finally, of future output.

(c) The interest on the debt is not a transfer: in the absence of deficit, the payment received by holders of the claim would have come *not* from taxing others but from the additional output made possible by the investment; thus, the higher taxes paid are, indeed, a measure of the output lost and of the burden borne by the future.

(d) The intergenerational effects of Deficit financing in (a) and (b) hold independently of whether the government borrows domestically or abroad. In the latter case, there need not be a crowding out of domestic capital formation or stock of capital. However, that capital will not produce income for the domestic population but, instead, for the foreign lender. This conclusion holds well if the government borrows domestically, but the higher domestic interest rates attract foreign capital, which is tapped by the private sector. This is, broadly speaking, the mechanism that has prevailed in the course of the current US deficits binge.

Some variant of this crowding out effect represents the prevailing (but not uncontrasted) view at present.

Crowding Out in an LCH Framework

Basic formulation

The above argument runs in terms of flows – the deficit crowds out investment. It suffers from failure to demonstrate that the initial loss of investment will not be made up later. This issue can be investigated by carrying out the analysis in terms of stocks – where one can also, usefully, bring to bear the Life Cycle Hypothesis (LCH) framework.

One can start from the identity that non-human net wealth (net worth), W, held by the private sector and representing the aggregate market value of net asset of individual households, is the sum of two components: (i) the market value of tangible assets and equity claims to tangible assets, K, and, (ii) the market value of all Government Debt, GD. Thus, $W = K + GD$. It follows that $K = W - GD$, so that an increase in GD must reduce K by an equal amount, *provided only the aggregate amount of wealth the private sector wishes to hold is not significantly influenced by the size of the public debt*. This condition is referred to hereafter as 'Wealth Independent of National Debt', or WIND. A sufficient condition for WIND is that private saving is not affected by the extent of government deficit current or past. But this is, at least to a first approximation, what is implied by the LCH where accumulation in relation to income is controlled by retirement and other hump saving requirements which can be fulfilled by any existing asset. (Some reasons why WIND may not hold exactly are considered below.)

Under WIND then, the government debt displaces, or crowds out, an amount of private capital, ΔK, equal to the market value of debt held by the public – that is, the relation between flows holds equally between stocks. The (annual) burden of the debt can then be measured as the income lost because of the debt. That is equal to the amount of capital crowded out, ΔK, times the productivity of capital; the former is $\Delta K = -GD$, and the latter can be approximated by (no less) than r. Thus, to a first approximation, the (annual) burden of the debt is rGD, or the interest service. In terms of flows, the current deficit reduces capital formation by $\Delta I = Def$, and the loss of investment leads to a permanent reduction in the capital stock, which makes future generations poorer, by $rDef$.

Some qualifications and limitations

The above formulation helps to call attention to a number of limitations of the proposition (cf. Modigliani, 1961).

(i) To the extent that the government debt is offset by government capital, KG, whose real return is commensurate with the private return, r, then the loss of income, rGD, is compensated by the higher income, rGK. To that extent, there is no net burden on future generations (though there may still be redistribution within generations). Thus, the burden is more precisely $r(GD - GK)$, or, the service on the so-called deadweight debt. In flow terms what matters is the deadweight deficit. Needless to say, the task of measuring net government investments, including (net) expenditures producing future flows of income, is a formidable one. The National Income Account measures are but a rough approximation.

(ii) The rate paid by the Government on GD is likely to be a substantial underestimate of the true productivity of Capital. The main reason is profit taxes, introducing a wedge between productivity and the market rate, r. In other words, when the government issues debt, it must not only collect rD, but, in addition, it loses the tax revenue on the income generated by the displaced project. Another reason is that the government may grant special privileges and/or impose constraints with respect to holding its debt: for instance, require financial institutions to hold debt at low interest rates, or grant tax exemptions. Thus, the interest bill tends to underestimate the true burden.

(iii) A third reason why r may differ from the marginal productivity of capital is the risk premium required by the market, which causes a wedge between the riskless rate r and the (expected) return on risky capital – though a very good case can be made that this correction of r is unwarranted.

(iv) The crowding out is accompanied by, indeed occurs through, a rise in r. But this may cause GD to affect the optimum life path of accumulation and thus, indirectly, aggregate wealth. Unfortunately, it is impossible to say in what direction, though available information suggests the effect is unlikely to be large.

(v) The stock of tangible capital consists of two components: reproducible tangible capital, RTW, and non-reproducible, tangible $NRTW$ – like land and other natural resources. Since we can take the latter as fixed in quantity, what is relevant is the effect of GD on RTW. Now the market value of $NRTW$ can be expected to depend inversely on r. Thus, as GD rises, raising r, the value of $NRTW$ will tend to decline: if W is unaffected, then a rise in G will actually reduce RTW by less than one-for-one. The importance of the 'offset' mechanism depends on the size of $NRTW$ relative to W and GD (for the US, in recent years, $NRTW$ (basically private land) is estimated at about 20 per cent of private net worth (cf. Board of Governors of the Federal Reserve System, 1981)).

(vi) There is finally one potentially important mechanism through which G or Def could affect W and hence modify the one-for-one crowding out. At the time the Def occurs, the future generations that suffer from the reduction in K, or future payment of $rDef$, consist of all those living beyond the time of the crowding out. Obviously, that includes members of the current generations, as long as they survive. This has two implications: (i) part of the burden of the deficit falls on the current generation – basically the present value (*PV*) of the taxes to pay the interest, which will be levied on the current generation. Still, because of mortality (finite life), the taxes paid by the current generation must be a declining fraction of the taxes collected to pay interest in successive years. Therefore, the *PV* of those taxes must, necessarily, be less than the taxes the current generation has saved itself through the deficit; (ii) the deficit may have some transitory effects on the accumulation and the stock of privately held wealth, to the extent that the private sector is a highly rational calculator and a smoother of consumption.

To see this, suppose *Def* arises from a rise in *G*, tax (and net of tax income) remaining constant, and it is expected to continue indefinitely, or at least for a while. Then, the debt must rise in time, and the rational consumer will anticipate paying rising taxes to cover the interest bill: *t* years later total interest will have grown to *rtDef*. The cost to the representative household is the *PV* of the stream, adjusted for mortality. If he is a consumption smoother he will cut the consumption over his remaining *T* years of life, by an annuity whose *PV* is the *PV* of the loss. Because *C* is, thus, reduced by a step, while net of tax income falls gradually as the debt grows, the current generation might be expected to respond to the deficit by saving more for a number of years, which grows with the length of the remaining life (*T*). In the limiting case where *T* is infinite, and only in that case, the cut in *C* and rise in *S* is, initially, precisely equal to *Def* and remains such thereafter. Accordingly, the government debt has the effect of increasing wealth by an equal amount thereby failing to cause crowding out of private capital. But this result occurs only with inifite life. When life is finite, the wealth will rise, but the rise is less than the debt – and is transitory. Thus, there will be some initial crowding out of *K*. How much depends on both the average length of life and on the rate of discount, both as shown by Sterling (1984). For reasonable values of these parameters the difference between the growth in wealth and debt is substantial. And the effect on wealth is transitory in the sense that, if and when the debt stops growing, eventually the crowding out will become complete.

Similarly, suppose the *Def* is due to a *one time* cut in taxes. A rational smoothing consumer would increase consumption less than the cut in taxes in order to avoid the need to reduce *C* later, to meet the rising taxes. Instead, he would determine the extent of maintainable rise in C by taking the difference between the tax rebate and the PV of new taxes, and spreading it into an annuity of T years. With T finite, the result is again some temporary saving and a temporary bulge in W partly offsetting Def and GD.

The same general approach and conclusion holds if the cut in taxes relative to government expenditure is *permanent* and rGD rises over time: consumption will rise by a step, but less than the cut in taxes, initially producing saving, which eventually, as the taxes levied grow larger, turn to dissaving, completing the crowding out.

Non-crowding-out in the Barro Hypothesis

Barro's hypothesis

Quite recently, the issue of who bears the burden of deficit financed government expenditure has been reopened by a school arguing that the view that the man in the street is right, is, after all, really wrong: there are no intergenerational effects, or shifting of the burden to the future, resulting from debt as such. This argument is today commonly associated with the name of Barro (1974), though it was first set forth – and rejected – by Ricardo (Sraffa, 1962, p. 887) two centuries ago.

The basic contention of this new line is that there is a burden on the current, and possibly future, generations when the government uses resources for current consumption (as distinguished from investment yielding a social return, comparable to that of private investment); but that the way the acquisition of resources is financed – taxes or deficit – is of no consequence to anyone. Taxes and deficit are equivalent (tax neutrality).

Though at first surprising, this conclusion is really a straightforward implication of the perfect rationality, perfect markets, LCH, for the limiting case of life approaching infinity. As was just shown, in that limiting case, the deficit arising, e.g., from a reduction in taxes, results in an equal rise in W, or additional S, matching Def and leaving I and K unchanged.

The most obvious objection to the Barro model is that life *is* finite, and that this circumstance is sufficient to establish the intergenerational effects of deficits.

However, Barro has demonstrated that infinite life is sufficient (under perfection of markets and rationality) but not necessary to establish the tax neutrality proposition. Finite life can lead to the same implications, if one supposes that, through the bequest mechanism, the members of the current generation allocate optimally their resources over the current generation and their heirs; the allocation being optimal in the sense that any other allocation within the feasible set would make the *current* generation worse off. It is then obvious that, if the government rebates taxes, thus financing a part of G by deficit, and if the current generation increased its consumption accordingly, leaving its bequests unchanged, it would accept a redistribution of resources away from the initial allocation, in its favour and against future generations. But the initial allocation is still available since the fiscal reshuffling does not change the budget constraint. In fact, that allocation can be easily secured by not consuming the rebate and using it to buy the debt. This incremental investment in government securities is first used to pay the new tax, as long as the initial agents survive, and then left as a bequest to be used by the heirs to pay their new taxes, without changing consumption. And this course will actually be followed since, by assumption, the initial allocation was optimal.

This imaginative reasoning relies on a large number of explicit and implicit assumptions, whose failure will invalidate his conclusions, at least in part.

Shortcomings within Barro's bequests framework

Let us for a moment grant Barro his assumption that every household is bent on making optimal allocations of his resources over the family tree. His conclusions will still fail to the extent that:

(i) Significant *market imperfections*, plus uncertainty, create liquidity constraints and make government borrowing cheaper than private. To this extent, government surplus and deficits may be an effective device to reshuffle consumption over time;

(ii) Not all agents are *super rational* in the sense of being able to figure out precisely the implications of the government's fiscal actions and how to remedy them; in particular, they may suffer from myopia about effects of deficit on future generations.

(iii) *A tax rebate* accompanied by later taxes is *not readily predictable* nor is it *neutral* in terms of distributional effects between different *stirpe* (lineage), as is implied by relying on 'the representative household'. Such a failure is especially evident with progressive taxes which make it essentially impossible to foresee what share of the burden will fall on one's heir. But even under the simplifying assumption that all pay the same per capita tax at any given date, it is obvious that the deficit will enrich *stirpes* with no, or less than average, children (and descendants) and impoverishes those with many descendants.

One might think that Barro's proposition could still be salvaged in the aggregate; for while those who are better off will increase their consumption, those worse off will reduce theirs; and why should the two effects not cancel? But in fact that is most unlikely: the increase in consumption of those with less children, who are made better off, will tend to exceed the decline of those who cut back. This can be illustrated in the convenient case in which the change in resources is allocated evenly over the current and next generation. One can then write an expression for the change in C of the current generation which shows that the change in consumption as a function of the number of children is convex from above. It follows that, if with two children per family, ΔC is zero, if the same children are redistributed, creating some childless families and some numerous families, the former will increase their C more than the large families will reduce theirs.

(iv) *Bequests are constrained to be non-negative.* With existing institutions, an individual's ability to secure the optimal allocation between generations is constrained by the fact that he cannot enforce a *negative* transfer. Suppose the optimal solution calls for that – and it may well be a common event, given that, these days, our children, on the average, are substantially richer than we are. Then, the non-negativity constraint prevents enforcement, and we end with a corner solution of no bequests, where the person's welfare would be increased if he could arrange to transfer resources from future generations to himself. If then taxes are raised, expenditure constant, unconstrained households would choose to reduce their bequests; but with the bequest already at zero, they have no choice but to reduce consumption, raising national saving and investment. Conversely, when taxes are reduced (or fail to rise to meet higher expenditure), this provides an opportunity to improve allocation by raising current consumption through the transfer of resources from the future. In short, non-negativity may lead even Barro type agents to behave as though they had no concern for their heirs, destroying tax neutrality.

But, if this is so, why do we not observe more deficit financing? One may suspect that, under normal conditions, people will be bound by a self-imposed constraint, calling for them not to go out of their way to encroach on their children. But deficits might be relied upon (and seem to be) in cases when exogenous circumstances make the current generation poorer than surrounding ones, e.g., major war.

Critique of bequest framework

(i) *How important are bequests?* For the Barro hypothesis to be empirically relevant it would have to be the case that all households generally plan to, and actually do, leave substantial bequests to their heirs. Yet there is a good deal of evidence that inheritance accounts for a relatively small fraction of private wealth, though this proposition is, at present, rather controversial.

Before the development of the LCH, it was widely understood that the major reason for saving was to leave bequests, and that, accordingly, the existing stock of wealth was, primarily, the result of transfers from earlier generations. The LCH, or more generally hump saving, provided an alternative explanation for the origin of wealth; in particular, it was shown (cf. Modigliani and Brumberg, 1979) that, relying on some stylised assumptions about the length of life and retirement, the LCH could account, all by itself, for the amount of wealth, relative to income, held by the private sector in the United States (and in other countries as well when data became available).

Clearly, bequests and major gifts also contribute to wealth: just how large a share is an interesting empirical issue. A number of empirical studies, many carried out in the mid-1960s and reviewed in Modigliani (1984), arrived at several interesting conclusions: (i) a remarkably small fraction of households say that they save for the purpose of leaving bequests, even among relatively well-to-do families, while the overwhelming proportion give reasons consistent with hump saving; (ii) from the answers to a question asked by several surveys about what fraction of the respondent wealth was received by inheritance, one arrives at an estimate of the overall share of inherited wealth (excluding intramarital transfers) of 15–20 per cent; (iii) estimating this share from the annual flow of bequests derived from a variety of sources (survey, probate statistics, wealth of deceased), one arrives at a broadly similar figure – but ranging up to 25 per cent; (iv) estimates for Great Britain, the only other country for which some information seems available, suggests a share comparable to the United States, if anything a little lower.

These estimates have recently been subjected to a number of

criticisms, in particular by Kotlikoff and Summers (1981). These authors endeavour to estimate directly the share of life cycle wealth, from which they derive the share of transfer wealth as a residual. Their basic procedure is to calculate the LC wealth held by each age (and sex) group by capitalising and cumulating the difference between an estimate of labour income and of consumption, at each earlier age. They find that the share of life cycle wealth in total wealth is quite low, probably as low as 15 per cent, implying that the share of wealth received by transfer could be put at 85 per cent. It has been shown by Modigliani (1984) that the huge difference between this estimate and that of around 20–25 per cent, arrived at by directly measuring bequests and major gifts, can be accounted for by three specific factors, rather than by that to which K & S hint, namely huge unreported flows of *intra vivos* transfers.

One cause of discrepancy arises from a conceptual error, which affects their estimates and is, numerically, quite sizeable; it concerns the treatment of consumers' durables which were, in effect, regarded as consumption instead of an investment. A second source arises from their way of measuring LC saving and wealth which is at odds with, and greatly understates, what is usually meant by LC saving (wealth). There are two major discrepancies. The first is their definition of income which is quite different from the standard one in that it excludes one part of property income, namely the part that represents the return on transfers received plus accumulated interest thereon (but includes the return on wealth transferred, plus accumulation thereon!): This definition implies that the return on inherited wealth is not income but a further inheritance. It, clearly, results in a substantial understatement of LC income and hence saving and wealth, while correspondingly overestimating the flow of transfers and the stock of transferred wealth.

The second difference originates in their decision to depart from the standard practice of taking the household as the basic decision unit and holder of wealth and to rely, instead, on individual males and females to which they have to assign (labour) income and consumption by an elaborate imputation procedure. With this formulation they cannot rely on household formation as an objective criterion for deciding whether a person has entered the life cycle accumulation process. They, thus, decide, quite arbitrarily, that the criterion is eighteen years of age, regardless of whether the person is self-supporting or is, instead, primarily supported by another household and thus part of *its* consumption. Those aged eighteen and over, not yet working, are thus assigned appropriate positive consumption and a *zero* labour income. This results in large, negative, LC savings at the beginning of life, that cumulate into a large, *negative*, LC wealth until the person begins working.

When one makes allowance for these errors and conceptual differences, one finds that one can account pretty closely for the entire difference between the 85 per cent transfer of wealth claimed by K & S and the estimate of 20–25 per cent for the share of wealth actually received by inheritance and major bequests.

We may thus conclude that according to presently available evidence, the process of bequests and other transfers is not of a dimension sufficient to support the intergenerational links implied by the Barro hypothesis.

(ii) *Non-Barro motivated bequests.* The estimate of 20–25 per cent for the share of wealth received through transfers is likely to overstate appreciably the importance of bequests that might respond to the motivation postulated by Barro. As examples of alternative motivations, one might suggest a utility function whose arguments are life consumption and bequests, independently of the utility or endowment of one's heirs. An even more important motivation is uncertainty of life together with limited annuity markets. A third and very different mechanism has been suggested by Bernheim *et al.* (1985).

IV SOME EMPIRICAL TESTS OF CROWDING OUT

Criticism of Barro's hypothesis suggests that his no-crowding out theorem is likely to have limited emirical relevance at best. However, there should be no need to speculate on this issue since the proposition is in principle testable. This section presents a number of such tests.

It has been shown that the controversy about crowding out can be reduced to the following: whether, and to what extent, the amount of wealth held at any point depends on the stock of government debt, properly measured. Equivalently, in terms of flows, the issue is whether the private sector's saving depends on the (properly measured) deficit of the government. The LCH model suggests that there should be some dependence, but modest and partly transient. The Barro (and partly the US Treasury (1983)) tax neutrality hypothesis, in its pure form implies, instead, that the effect should be dollar for dollar, and permanent: each dollar of public debt would increase wealth by a dollar – or each dollar of deficit should increase saving by a dollar, except possibly for some short run slippage.

These contrasting hypotheses can, in principle, be tested, and a number of such are reported in the rest of this section.

Tests Based on Stocks – US 1900–83

A number of tests, focusing on the stock aspect, were carried out for the US nearly twenty years ago, well before Barro's hypothesis (see Modigliani, 1966). The test relies on the LCH hypothesis of accumulation which implies that, with a relatively stable rate of growth, and in the absence of government debt, private net worth, W, should be proportional to (permanent) disposable income, $D\hat{Y}$, up to stochastic disturbances. Allowing for debt, the test equation can be formulated as:

$$\hat{W} = aD\hat{Y} + bGD \qquad 0 < b < < 1 \qquad (3)$$

where $\hat{W}$ is the equilibrium wealth (which now includes the public debt), $D\hat{Y}$ anticipated permanent private disposable income, and b should be unity for Barro and positive but relatively small under the standard view. For testing purposes $\hat{W}$ was replaced by $W + e$, e being an error term, and W an estimate of private net worth based on Goldsmith's information. $D\hat{Y}$ was approximated by an estimate of private income after net taxes, and GD by an estimate of net public sector debt. To minimise the problem of heteroscedasticity, the equation was estimated in ratio form, scaled by Y, for the years then available, 1900 to 1955. The estimate of a came to 4.7, very much in line with the implications of simple life cycle models, while that of b is essentially zero (slightly negative) with a standard error of 0.1 (the standard error of 0.22 given in the original article is incorrect). If one adds the post-war years, and replaces the estimates for the years 1946 to 1958 by later estimates, the results are strikingly similar: a is 4.6, and b is slightly negative with a standard error of 0.16.

These results, however, suffer from one serious shortcoming, which passed unnoticed at the time of writing because of the then state of the arts, namely that the residuals are highly serially correlated, as evidenced by a DW statistic of 0.66 for the first period, and 0.55 for the entire period. Such a high serial correlation is, of course, very much to be expected: for when any shock (e.g., a boom in the stock market) pushes the wealth income ratio away from its equilibrium value, it will take considerable time before saving (and capital gains) gradually restore the equilibrium. This consideration suggests reformulating the hypothesis in stock adjustment form:

$$\Delta W = \gamma[\hat{W} - W(-1)]$$

Substituting for $\hat{W}$ from (1) yields:

$$\Delta W = \alpha \hat{D} Y + \beta D - \gamma W(-1) \qquad \alpha = a\gamma, \ \beta = b\gamma \tag{4}$$

This equation was estimated using $W(-1)$ as the scale factor. (Some estimates were also done with Y as the deflator, but the results were always quite close.) Another desirable improvement would be to measure permanent income, $\hat{Y}$, by consumption, rather than current income. Unfortunately, an estimate of consumption (as distinguished from consumer expenditure) is available only for the post-war period.

A summary of results is provided in Table 1.1. For each period and subperiod we give two estimates. The first is based on (4) above, while the second is obtained from an equation in which we have added to (4) the percentage change in an index of the stock market. The reason is that, in the short run, such changes can be taken as largely exogenous to the process of accumulation and yet account for a substantial fraction of the short run movements in wealth. By controlling for this important but erratic source of capital gains, we are able to analyse more effectively the determinants of other sources of accumulation and, in particular, saving.

It appears from the table that the gradual adjustment hypothesis is well supported by the evidence. Indeed, the speed of adjustment is rather low, mostly between 20 and 30 per cent per year, and falls further to the 10–20 per cent range, when one controls for those swings in wealth that are associated with the stock market. Understandably, the estimated speed does become larger when the target wealth is related to the more stable measure of permanent income, represented by consumption, a formulation which, as expected, also leads to a closer fit (cf. col (5) of rows 5 to 8). The estimate of the equilibrium wealth–income ratio (a in col (3)) is quite stable, especially when the stock market variable is included: 5.7 for the entire 80-year period (row 2), versus 5.8 for the original period (row 4)

Table 1.1 Tests of crowding out – for the US stock from 1900–1980*

		(1) β	(2) γ	(3) a	(4) b	(5) SE
1. 1900–50	$\hat{y} = y$	−0.01 0.1	0.20 0.05	5.3	−0.05	0.058
2. Same + Stock Market	(SM)	−0.06 0.08	0.12 0.04	5.7	−0.5	0.042
3. 1900–58	$\hat{y} = y$	−0.07 0.13	0.21 0.06	5.5	−0.3	0.063
4. Same	+ SM	−0.07 0.1	0.12 0.05	5.8	−0.62	0.047
5. 1947–80	$\hat{y} = y$	0.02 0.14	0.27 0.14	4.7	0.06	0.045
6. Same	+ SM	−0.12 0.1	0.16 0.09	5.4	−0.8	0.03
7. 1948–80	$\hat{y} = dCon$	0.17 0.14	0.35 0.16	5.1	0.5	0.039
8. Same	+ SM	−0.06 0.11	0.27 0.11	5.7	−0.2	0.028
9. Replace Gov. Debt by Eisner's Net Worth	+ SM	0.06 0.09	0.27 0.11	5.4	0.22	0.028

*The entries below the parameter estimates are standard errors.

and 5.4 for the post-war period (row 6). These figures are somewhat higher than the observed mean of the ratio, but this is to be expected in a growing system, in the presence of a rather slow adjustment.

From the point of view of testing Barro versus the standard view, the crucial parameter is, of course, the coefficient of debt, b, and the associated estimate of β. It is seen that in the equations without the stock market, b is sometimes positive and sometimes negative, but always insignificant and negligibly small, except possibly for the post-war period regression in which permanent income was approximated by consumption (row 7). However, when the stock market variable is added (with a substantial reduction in the standard error), then the b coefficient is found to be uniformly negative, though still insignificantly different from zero. This applies also to the equation of row 9, where the net government debt has been replaced by a variable which, as indicated earlier, is theoretically more appropriate, namely an estimate of the 'dead weight debt' or difference between the debt and the capital held by the government (see Eisner and Pieper, 1984). Actually, in row 9 we use the government net worth, which is the negative of deadweight debt; accordingly, for Barro this coefficient should be close to -1. Instead, the estimate is positive, though, again, not significant.

The conclusion from this battery of tests seems unequivocal: using the LCH, it is possible to account rather closely for the behaviour of wealth in the United States over nearly a century, but there is no evidence that accumulated wealth grows or declines significantly in response to movements in the national debt, or in government net worth.

Tests Based on Saving Flows

Operational formulation

The Barro and the standard hypothesis also have different, testable implications for the determinants of consumption (and hence saving). According to the traditional view, private consumption, C, responds to: (i) long term expectations of before tax income, $\hat{Y}$, less, (ii) the taxes (net of transfers including interest) expected to be levied against that income (both measured as rates per unit of time); and (iii) private net worth, W, consisting of the market value of tangible assets plus net claims on the public sector (plus, in an open economy, net claims on the rest of the world). Thus:

$$C = c(\hat{Y} - \hat{T}) + dW \tag{5}$$

According to Barro, instead, taxes, as such, have no effect on consumption, and the same is true of that component of private net worth which consists of claims in the public sector. What influences consumption, instead, is the current (and anticipated) government purchase of goods and services for consumption, $\hat{G}C$, which results in a loss of resources available to the private sector, no matter how they are financed. Again, this hypothesis can be formulated operationally as:

$$C = c(\hat{Y} - \hat{G}C) + d(W - GD) \tag{6}$$

Clearly, these hypotheses are not mutually exclusive. Certainly the LCH version of the standard view suggests that, within modest limits, some of the people some of the time might behave in a way consistent with (6). Conversely, we have seen that, even if one accepts Barro's assumption of super-rational behaviour and concern for heirs, there might still be a non-negligible response to taxes and government debt. For test purposes, then, we can formulate a general hypothesis by taking a linear combination of (5) and (6) with positive weights, w_1 and w_2, adding up to one:

$$C = c[w_1(\hat{Y} - \hat{T}) + w_2(\hat{Y} - \hat{G}C)] + d[w_1 W + w_2(W - GD)] \qquad (7)$$
$$= c(\hat{Y} - \hat{T}) + dW - cw_2(\hat{G}C - \hat{T}) - dw_2 GD$$

Thus, if we regress C on the four right-hand side variables of (7), the coefficient of the first variable – 'disposable income' – provides an estimate of the marginal propensity to consume, c, that of the third – the government deficit – divided by c, yields an estimate of the weight w_2; it is seen that if Barro's limiting hypothesis held exactly, or $w_2 = 1$, then, for given disposable income, a dollar of deficit would reduce C by c (or increase private saving by c). The second and the last coefficient measures, respectively, the propensity to consume with respect to wealth, and the same multiplied by w_2.

From (7) we can infer the following expression for the national saving function:

$$S = Y - C - GC = s(\hat{Y} - \hat{T}) - (1 - cw_2)(\hat{G}C - \hat{T}) - dW + dw_2 GD$$

$$= sD\hat{Y} - (1 - cw_2)(\hat{D}ef) - dW + dw_2 GD + TDY - TDef$$

Here, $D\hat{Y}$ and $\hat{D}ef$ are 'permanent' disposable income, and government deficit respectively, while $TDY = (Y - T) - (\hat{Y} - \hat{T})$ is transitory disposable income and $TDef$ the transitory budget deficit. Thus, under the standard hypothesis ($w_2 = 0$) for given disposable income, a permanent deficit reduces national saving (and national investment in a closed economy) by a dollar per dollar, whereas for the extreme Barro hypothesis the reduction is only $(1 - c) = s$ dollars per dollar.

Equation (7) embodies the basic test with which we are concerned, namely how closely consumption (and saving) behaviour can be accounted for by this hypothesis, and how large is w_2: relatively close to zero as called for by the LCH, or close to unity, as implied by Barro's model?

There are, however, some auxiliary issues, revolving around the deficit and its measurement which we also propose to test. The most serious one concerns the measurement of T which we have defined as taxes net of all transfers, including the interest on the national debt. the national income accounts of the US (and other countries as well) measure that interest as the amount actually paid by the government, say RGD, where R is the nominal interest rate, without making any allowance for the fact that inflation, $\dot{P}$, erodes the purchasing power of the debt by the rate of inflation or by $\dot{P}GD$. As noted earlier, when account is taken of this loss, the income effectively earned by the holders, as well as the effective cost to the government becomes:

$$RGD - \dot{P}GD = rGD$$

where $r = R - \dot{P}$ is the so-called effective 'real rate of interest'. We shall accordingly measure T as $T^* - \dot{P}GD$, where T^* is net taxes, as reported in the government budget and National Income Accounts; note that T appears both in the calculation of net of tax income and of the deficit.

This procedure, however, raises another issue, namely the possibility that the private sector may suffer from some inflation illusion (as the public sector budget seem to suffer) and actually base its consumption, at least partially, on nominal rather than real interest. We can test this hypothesis by adding to (7) a term $f\dot{P}GD$. If there were complete money illusion, f would be equal to the coefficient of the interest variable, which is implicitly constrained to equal $c(1 - w_2)$. Less than full illusion would imply a lower value.

There remains one further problem. By calculating T as described above, we are implicitly assuming that rational consumers respond to the current real return on debt, r. In reality, we should expect them to respond to the 'permanent' return, say $\hat{r}$ (both with respect to income and with respect to the perceived deficit in Barro's formulation). Now, in periods of high and volatile inflation, the *ex post* real rate, r, is likely to be a very poor approximation to $\hat{r}$. Unfortunately, $\hat{r}$ is unobservable and difficult to measure. Yet, in view of the experience of the post-war period, which constitutes our sample, we propose as a reasonable approximation, to treat $\hat{r}$ as constant, say $\bar{r}$. This suggests adding to (7) one further term of the form $g(r - \bar{r})GD$. Noting that rGD is a constant, (7) finally reduces to:

$$C = cDY + dW - cw_2 Def - (dw_2 + g\bar{r})GD + f\dot{P}GD + grGD \qquad (8)$$

The coefficient g should be negative, if, in forming expectation about the future real return on government debt, the market gives relatively more weight to $\bar{r}$ and little weight to the current rate r; in the limit it could be as small as $-c(1-w_2)$. However, these inferences are uncertain because, at least according to LCH, the coefficient of property income, given wealth, could be quite different from that of labour income and hence from c (cf. Modigliani, 1975). However, whatever the value of g, to test money illusion, the coefficient f should be compared with $c(1-w_2)+g$, which measures the total effect of government interest income.

Equation (8) – or as close an approximation to it as was permitted by the availability of data – was used to test the alternative hypothesis, with three distinct sets of data as follows:

(i) Quarterly data for the US for the period from 1952 to 1983. The US was chosen because of its obvious importance as well as because of the availability – and presumably quality – of the data.

(ii) Time series of annual data for Italy, from 1952 to 1982. Italy provides an unusually interesting case because of the extreme variations that have characterised many of the crucial variables. Thus, the debt income ratio ranged from a low of less than 40 per cent up to 71 per cent, and inflation has also been quite variable reaching at times close to 20 per cent. As a result, variables such as the ratio of government interest payments to nominal income have been as low as just over 1 per cent up to very nearly 10 per cent. Unfortunately, only annual data are available at this time and some of the series, such as private wealth, could only be estimated in a somewhat crude way.

(iii) A sample covering some 33 countries for five selected years in the interval between 1960 and 1980. The sample covers all the countries included in the *UN Yearbook of National Account Statistics* for which the required data were available for a sufficient number of years (at least three).

United States

Several tests of the Barro tax neutrality propositions, based on the effects of fiscal variables on consumption, have been carried out for the US (and Canada) besides those reported below. However, none has used the specifications of equation (8) which we regard as the warranted ones. Several of the previous tests, especially those using specifications closer to ours, have reported results which, like ours, tend to reject the Barro hypothesis. These include Yawitz and Meyer

(1976), Barro (1978), Tanner (1979), Seater (1982), Carmichael and Hawtrey (1981) and Feldstein (1982). A few others, however, have reached opposite conclusions, some on the basis of very inadequate specification, e.g., Tanner (1970), and Kochin (1974). The one puzzling case is that of Kormendi (1983) whose specifications are, at first sight, not so terribly different from our own and yet reports diametrically opposite results in almost all respects. That case will be discussed in a forthcoming note. A few other papers reach essentially inconclusive results.

Table 1.2 reports the results of a test of equation (8) for the US in the post-war period. The first row shows the standard consumption function including only net-of-tax income and wealth. Expected income was approximated by a first degree polynomial distributed lag including the current and 19 lagged quarters. (A few tests were made allowing for separating disposable income into before-tax income and net taxes, and allowing the coefficients of these two components in the distributed lag to be different – cf. Modigliani and Steindel (1977). Since the coefficients of the two variables turned out to have a fairly similar shape, and no other estimates seem to be appreciably different, these results are not reported here.) There was strong evidence that lagged value of wealth contributed significantly to the explanation of consumption and, accordingly, all tests include a first order polynomial distributed lag including four quarters. The residuals exhibited high serial correlation (see column (8)), and, therefore, all the results reported are based on the autoregressive transformation.

The only slight surprise in the first row is the relatively high value of the income and low value of the wealth coefficients, both of which appear to be the result of the autoregressive correction. The second row tests Barro's tax neutrality proposition by adding two fiscal variables, the national debt and the annual deficit. The estimated coefficient of debt is positive – that is, *larger* than that of other wealth. This result rejects the Barro hypothesis according to which the contribution of Debt should be smaller – around zero – implying a negative coefficient in col (4) of the magnitude of that of wealth; it is, instead, consistent with the LCH. At the same time it must be acknowledged that, in view of the larger standard error, this conclusion cannot be regarded as very robust. The coefficient of Deficit is negative, as expected under either Barro or LCH; but the implied value of w_2 – a measure of the empirical relevance of the Barro hypothesis – is close to zero, and with a relatively small error of estimate – on this score, the rejection of Barro is quite robust.

Table 1.2 US flow tests, 1952–82, quarterly

ID no.	Const.	Income	Wealth	National Debt	Deficit	Inflation loss	Govt. interest	ρ	SE
1	−0.21	0.91	0.022					0.82	0.0110
	0.04	0.03	0.008						
2	−0.30	0.92	0.022	0.047	−0.002			0.83	0.0110
	0.09	0.03	0.008	0.042	0.029				
3	−0.30	0.93	0.020	0.046	−0.022	−0.45		0.83	0.0111
	−0.09	0.034	0.008	0.043	0.032	0.43			
4	−0.20	0.91	0.019	0.011	−0.021	0.47	0.51	0.83	0.0992
	0.11	0.03	0.008	0.046	0.032	0.33	0.32		
5	−0.22	0.92	0.022		−0.014	−0.47		0.83	0.0111
	0.04	0.03	0.008		0.031	0.51			
6	−0.17	0.90	0.019		−0.019	0.51	0.56	0.82	0.0109
	0.05	0.03	0.008		0.031	0.29	0.28		

The next row, 3, tests the inflation illusion hypothesis and appears to reject it, as the estimate of the coefficient of col (6) is actually negative, though the difference from zero is not very significant. Row 4 probes further into inflation illusion by dropping the maintained hypothesis that government interest has the same effect on consumption as any other income (on top of the effect of debt as part of net worth). As pointed out, the effect could be larger or smaller, and it is the total effect that is relevant in assessing the coefficient of inflation. Accordingly, in row 4 we add the government interest (which is already included in net taxes and thus in income and deficit). The effect of this addition turns out to be rather unexpected. From column (7) it appears that the estimated effect of government interest on consumption is positive rather than negative, and fairly large. It implies an overall effect in the order of 1.4 dollars of additional consumption per dollar of government real interest. What is even more puzzling is that the estimates of col (6) imply an appreciable inflation illusion effect. The point estimates suggest that the public treats about one-third of the compensation for the inflation loss (0.47/1.4) as though it were true income. The other difference in row 4 is that the coefficient of debt becomes smaller, but it still remains positive.

Because the three variables, Debt, Interest and Inflation (GD, PGD and rGD) all involve the variable, GD, they might suffer from multicollinearity problems which could contribute to the surprising results of row 4. Accordingly, in rows 5 and 6, we drop the insignificant variable GD. But this turns out to throw little light on the puzzle. In row 5, which includes only inflation, the results are very close to row 3; in particular, inflation has a very similar negative coefficient. But, when interest is added back in row 6, its coefficient, as well as that of inflation, are even a bit larger and more significant than in row 4.

One puzzling aspect of these results is why inflation appears to have little, or even negative, effect before interest appears in the equation, and then turns around so strongly. One possible clue may be provided by a very strong negative correlation between the inflation and real interest variables (-0.87), reflecting in part the effect of unanticipated inflation. Suppose that real interest truly has an appreciably stronger effect on consumption than other sources of income, but that its effect is forced to be the same as other income, as in rows 3 and 5. Then a high inflation will, on the average, be accompanied by a low real rate, which will make for a lower consumption than accounted for by those equations. As a result, the error term will be negatively correlated with inflation which would make for a negative, or at least a downward biased, inflation coefficient. Under this interpretation, the negative values of rows 3 and 5 would reflect downward bias, while the positive ones of rows 4 and 6 could be relatively unbiased.

A second question is whether the very high estimate of the effect of government interest on consumption should be believed or, instead, be attributed to some type of bias. We shall postpone facing this issue until we have examined the outcome of remaining tests.

Italy

A set of results for Italy is reported in Table 1.3. They are taken from a forthcoming joint paper by the author together with Marco Pagano and Tullio Jappelli (1984). The tests in Table 1.3 are laid out pretty much along the same lines as in Table 1.2, and the results are, in many ways, surprisingly similar, though in Table 1.3 we can provide only results for annual observations.

The basic consumption function of Row 1 is based only on *current* income and taxes, since, in contrast to the US, there was no indication of any significant role for lagged values of the variables. The other major differences with the US are: (i) the much lower propensity to consume, 0.6 versus 0.9, offset by an appreciably higher wealth coefficient. (The differences may be partly spurious because of the constant terms appearing in each equation with opposite signs, accounting for somewhat less than 1 per cent of mean consumption of the US but nearly 5 per cent for Italy. These constants should really be zero, and the non-zero estimate may reflect some missing variables which could bias the estimate of c and d; (ii) the appreciably poorer fit – the error is about 3 per cent of the mean as against just over one-half of 1 per cent. These differences suggest that the hypothesis is not as effective in explaining consumption behaviour in Italy as it is for the US, but it is hard to say how much of the difference might be traced to the quality of the data.

Row 2 tests the role of the fiscal variables with results qualitatively similar to the US. The coefficient of Debt is again positive, though a bit smaller; that of Deficit is negative, as expected, but substantially higher. Still it implies a value of w_2 which is only 30 per cent as high as that hypothesised by Barro.

Row 3 tests inflation illusion by adding an estimate of the inflation loss on the national debt; its coefficient should be between zero (no money illusion) and a positive value, possibly as high as the coeffi-

Table 1.3 Italy. Consumption function and fiscal variables – 1952–82 annual. Dependent variable: aggregate consumer expenditure

ID no.	Method of estimation	Const.	YD NI-Tax	Wealth	Coefficient of National debt	Deficit	Govt. interest	Inflation loss	ρ	SE
1	AR	0.040	0.60	0.045					0.67	0.79–0.02
		0.012	0.032	0.006						
2	AR	0.037	0.59	0.046	0.029	−0.22			0.69	0.79–0.02
		0.012	0.032	0.007	0.043	0.071				
3	AR	0.043	0.61	0.040	0.007	−0.18		0.19	0.68	0.80–0.02
		0.019	0.022	0.013	0.070	0.12		0.48		
4	AR	0.041	0.60	0.042	0.026	−0.16	−0.11	0.06	0.68	0.82–0.02
		0.014	0.031	0.005	0.030	0.13	0.33	0.6		
5	AR	0.042	0.61	0.040		−0.16	−0.05	0.20	0.69	0.84–0.02
		0.016	0.033	0.012		0.13	0.23	0.30		
6	INS	0.043	0.59	0.043	0.044	−0.092	−0.22	−0.01	0.70	0.83–0.02
		0.021	0.063	0.017	0.096	0.15	0.36	1.0		
7	INS	0.041	0.63	0.036		−0.16	−0.05	0.25	0.65	0.80–0.02
		0.016	0.035	0.013		0.16	0.19	0.31		

cient of government interest, which is $c(1 - w_2)$, or around 0.4, in the present case. The point estimate turns out to lie just about midway between the two polar cases. At the same time it is seen that the estimate has a large standard error and that the variable does not contribute significantly to explaining consumption.

The next row, 4, probes further into inflation illusion by adding the (real) government interest, rGD. The result is far more reasonable than for the US, as the coefficient of interest is slightly negative. Surprisingly, the inflation coefficients also falls near zero. The other coefficients do not change appreciably. Dropping the insignificant, and possibly collinear debt variable, makes the interest coefficient yet closer to zero, while raising again the inflation estimate to 0.20.

The final two rows present an alternative set of estimates of the coefficients of the previous two rows, 4 and 5, using an instrumental variable approach to minimise the danger of simultaneity bias that could affect, in particular, the income and the deficit coefficients. It is seen that these estimates are generally close to those of the corresponding rows 4 and 5. In 5, the coefficient of debt is a bit higher and that of interest noticeably lower, but both are rather insignificant, and so is inflation. Row 7 is just about the same as 5 – except for a little large inflation effect, still, however, lower than its standard error.

To summarise, the Italian evidence agrees with that for the US in decidedly rejecting the implications of tax neutrality – the coefficient of debt is generally positive and higher than that of other wealth, and the effect of deficit, though larger than for the US, is still much smaller than required by Barro's hypothesis. The large effect of government interest is not supported by the Italian evidence, and as for inflation illusion, the hypothesis fails to receive a strong backing because of high standards errors, presumably reflecting collinearity.[2]

Evidence from a cross-section of countries

Table 1.4 reports the results of some cross-country tests carried out in a forthcoming joint paper by Modigliani, Mason and Sterling (1984). A test based on a cross-section of countries is appealing for two main reasons. First, one would expect to find more variations across countries, than for a single country over time, in variables such as the Government debt–income ratio, the deficit rate, and the rate of inflation, which are crucial for testing the two sets of hypotheses with which we are concerned. Second, by taking as the unit of observation for each country an average of several years, one can come close to measuring long run effects, thus eliminating the additional large variations in the saving or consumption–income ratio, that come from short run cyclical and other disturbances. Furthermore, an average of past values is likely to provide a better measure of long run expectations, which should govern behaviour.

However, the cross-section approach also involves some costs and difficult trade-offs. The trade-off is between the sample size and the quality of the data. Obviously, one would prefer a sample as large and diversified as possible. But this preference conflicts with the requirement that the data for each country be, as nearly as possible, comparable conceptually, of high quality, and available for a span of time long enough to permit the desired averaging.

To ensure the comparability, we limited the sample to those countries whose national income accounts are included in the *UN Yearbook of National Income Statistics* and which also report in the *UN Demographic Yearbook*. Table 1.4(a) gives a list of the 33 countries which satisfied this criterion, as well as the time span criterion discussed further below.

The 'cost' of cross-sectional tests is twofold. In the first place, our basic hypothesis (8) calls for two variables that are not part of the National Accounts framework, namely Wealth and Government Debt. Unfortunately, estimates of Wealth are available only for a handful of countries, and, frequently, only for selected years. Information on National Debt, appropriately measured (net, domestic, privately held), is also very limited. Accordingly, these two variables had to be dropped from the test.

The second 'cost' of the cross-sectional approach is that, especially in the absence of wealth information, one cannot presuppose a stable marginal (and average) propensity to consume, c, for different countries, as is the case for different years for a single country. Indeed, there are wide variations in the private saving rates across countries, ranging from near zero, or even negative, to over 20 per cent in a few cases. Hence, in a cross-section, one has not only to model the (expected) income flow which determines consumption, as in Tables 1.2 and 1.3, but also what accounts for the variation of c. The research that has been done on this issue points to two major forces responsible for cross-country differences, namely: (i) the rate of growth of income, and (ii) demographic composition in terms of the share of the non-working age population.

With these considerations in mind, we propose to rely on the following cross-sectional variant of equation (8):

Table 1.4(a) Countries and years included in cross-section sample

Country	1960	1965	1970	1975	1980
Algeria			×	×	×
Australia	×	×	×	×	×
Austria	×	×	×	×	×
Belgium	×	×	×	×	×
Canada	×	×	×	×	×
Denmark	×	×	×	×	×
Finland	×	×	×	×	×
France	×	×	×	×	×
Germany	×	×	×	×	×
Greece	×	×	×	×	×
India	×	×	×	×	×
Ireland	×	×	×	×	×
Italy	×	×	×	×	×
Japan	×	×	×	×	×
Korea, Republic of	×	×	×	×	×
Madagascar		×	×	×	
Netherlands	×	×	×	×	×
Norway	×	×	×	×	×
Papua New Guinea	×	×	×	×	×
Peru	×	×	×	×	×
Portugal	×	×	×	×	×
Spain	×	×	×	×	×
Sudan		×	×	×	
Sweden	×	×	×	×	×
Switzerland	×	×	×	×	×
Taiwan			×	×	×
Thailand	×	×	×	×	×
Tunisia	×	×	×	×	×
United Kingdom	×	×	×	×	×
United States	×	×	×	×	×
Venezuela	×	×	×	×	×
Zambia		×	×	×	×

$$C = [c_0 + c_1 g + c_2 gd][(NY - T) + a_1(G - T) + a_2 PD + a_3 RD \qquad (9)$$

The first square brackets replaces c in equation (8) with a function of g, the rate of growth of permanent income, and d a measure of the effects of demographic factors, summarised by the 'dependency ratio' or ratio of population under 15 to population over 15. This variable is multiplied by g, on the general ground that the effect of growth is multiplicative; with zero growth, saving should be zero (or, $c = 1$).

The second bracket models the effect of the expected income flow, net of taxes. As in (8), it includes income measured by National (NY), less direct taxes, the deficit, the inflation loss, and the interest bill. However, it omits the two stock variables, Debt and Net Worth, which are not available.

For each country, the data for each variable in the second square bracket were obtained from the *UN Yearbook* for as many of the five years 1960, 1965, 1970, 1975, and 1980 as were available. For each country, 'decadal' observations were computed when possible by averaging three consecutive observations, spanning a ten-year interval. As shown in Table 1.4(a), some of the required annual observations are missing at the beginning or at the end. In such cases, the country is included in the sample, provided at least three consecutive data points were available, but the number of observations for that country was cut down to two (e.g., Turkey) or one (e.g., Taiwan). For this reason, and also because of other occasional missing data, the total number of observations used in the regression is reduced to 80 (compared with a potential maximum of 99).

As for the variables in the first bracket, *g* (the growth rate of permanent income), is measured by the percentage growth of (real) consumption between the two end points of each decade. The dependency ratio, *d* (a very slowly changing variable), is calculated from the *UN Demographic Yearbook* for the single year 1970. Finally, in the regression, all the national income data for each included year were scaled by national income (before averaging), thus avoiding both the problem of converting them in equivalent real units and the problem of heteroscedasticity produced by the large variability, across countries of variables like real income or consumption, whether aggregate or per capita.

Some problems are encountered in measuring government interest, *rGD*, and the inflation loss, *ṖGD*. The *nominal* interest, *RGD*, can be obtained from the National Income data. However, lacking information on the net government debt, *GD*, we are unable to obtain a direct measure of either *ṖGD* or the *real* interest, *rGD*. Accordingly, in computing taxes net of transfers less government interest, we subtract the nominal interest (*RGD*) rather than the appropriate *rGD*. As for the inflation loss, we have endeavoured to arrive at a rough estimate by relying on information on the rate of inflation and on *nominal* interest. To this end, we first note the identity for each country, *j*, and decade, *t*,:

$$(\dot{P}GD)_{jt} = \frac{(RGD)_{jt}}{r_{jt}\dot{P}_{jt}} \, \dot{P}_{jt} \tag{10}$$

which follows from the definition of the real rate. We next make the rather heroic assumption that the difference in the ten-year average real rate across countries, and 'decades', is sufficiently small so that r_{jt} can be approximated by a constant $\bar{r}$. We have tried to estimate $\bar{r}$ by scanning over values from 0 to 0.07 to find the value minimising the residual variance, for several of the equations reported in Table 1.4(b). It was found that in some form of the equation the error variance decreased slightly as $\bar{r}$ rose, while in others it declined slightly, but in every case it was quite insensitive to the value assigned to $\bar{r}$. It was therefore decided that one could save computations and the multiplication of variants of the test, by assigning to r a reasonable value, which was finally chosen to be 3 per cent. Replacing this value for r_{jt} in (10) yields the estimate of $(PGD)_{jt}$ which was used in all relevant tests of Table 1.4(b). It should be recognised that, as long as we use the nominal interest in computing net taxes, if the private sector has no, or limited, inflation illusion, the equation could be misspecified, unless it includes the variable PGD, which, in principle, can provide an offset to RGD.

The outcome of the tests is summarised in Table 1.4(b). The first row reports the results of estimating the scaled version of equation (9) reproduced at the top of the table. The two variables designed to

Table 1.4(b)   Cross-section of 33 countries, 1960–80

Hypothesis tested:
$$\frac{C}{NY}=\left[\,c_0+c_1g+c_2d\,\right]\left[1-\frac{T}{NY}+a_1\left(\frac{G-T}{NY}\right)+a_2\frac{PGD}{NY}+a_3\frac{RGD}{NY}\right]$$
Specification

Weighting	Taxes (T)	c_0	c_1	c_2	a_1	a_2	a_3
Unweighted	NT–RD	0.88	−1.56	1.46	0.27	0.17	
		0.019	0.42	0.46	0.12	0.54	
Unweighted	NT	0.88	−1.57	1.49	−0.27		0.78
		0.019	0.33	0.42	0.12		0.32
Unweighted	NT	0.88	−1.64	1.58	−0.24	−1.82	2.24
		0.19	0.43	0.49	0.13	2.19	1.61
Weighted	NT–RD	0.89	−2.48	2.85	−0.22	0.64	
		0.12	0.30	0.53	0.18	0.52	
Weighted	NT	0.89	−2.54	2.88	−0.24		1.19
		0.012	0.31	0.52	0.17		0.31
Weighted	NT	0.88	−2.68	3.28	−0.15	−5.6	5.47
		0.012	0.29	0.52	0.17	2.7	1.52

account for propensity to consume, c, namely, growth, g, and dependency ratio, d, are both quite significant, with t-ratios above 3. Assigning to the dependency ratio a typical value of one-third, the effect of income growth, g, is just over one, implying that an increase of one percentage point in the consumption–income ratio and hence to an equal rise in the saving rate; similarly, for a growth rate of 5 per cent, roughly the mean for the sample, a rise of 0.10 in the dependency ratio decrease the saving rate by about two-thirds of one percentage point.

Proceeding to the test of fiscal policy, the estimated coefficient of deficit, a_1, is negative, as expected, and fairly significant; however, its size is only about one-fourth as large as predicted by the Barro hypothesis, whereas it is quite consistent with LCH. Finally, the effect of inflation, a_2, is rather close to zero; however, because we are subtracting from net taxes the *nominal* interest, in the absence of inflation illusion, the coefficient of $\dot{P}D$ should have been equal to $(1 - a_1)$, or -0.73. The estimate of 0.17 is some 0.9 higher, supporting the hypothesis even though the standard error is large.

In the estimate of row 1, all the observations are weighted equally. But since the countries in the sample vary greatly in size, a good case can be made for appropriately weighting the observations. Several weighting schemes have been proposed and used in this type of analysis; one scheme that has been used repeatedly is to weight the observations in proportion to the square root of population. (Cf. Houthakker, 1965; Modigliani, 1961.)

The results of the weighted regression are given in the last three rows, each of which matches the specifications of each of the first three rows. They are broadly similar to the corresponding unweighted ones but do present some interesting differences. First, the estimated effect of growth on the saving rate is appreciably higher; e.g., in row 4, for a dependency ratio of one-third it comes to $1\frac{1}{2}$ percentage points per one percentage point change in g, which agrees more closely with some earlier results (cf. Modigliani, 1961; Modigliani and Sterling, 1983). Similarly, the effect of d is also larger: at a 5 per cent growth, a rise in dependency by 0.10, decreases saving by nearly $1\frac{1}{2}$ percentage points. The estimated effect of deficit is marginally lower and less significant. With respect to inflation effects, row 4 shows a rather surprisingly large coefficient, a_2, even allowing for a large standard error; indeed, even with inflation illusion, the coefficient should not exceed zero.

Once again one may wonder whether this result might be related to having constrained the interest coefficient to be the same as that of other components of income. To throw light on this question in rows 2 and 5, we have taken the nominal interest, RGD, out of net taxes and added it as a separate variable. In row 2, the estimate of the interest coefficient a_3, (0.78), turns out quite close to the constrained value $(1 + a_1)$, or 0.73, while the weighted regression, 5, is somewhat high, but not significantly so, when allowing for the standard error.

The last step in our test is again to enter both interest and inflation. Here we should again expect little change in the estimate of a_3, while a_2 should be between zero (full illusion) and $-a_3$. Unfortunately, the result of this specification is, again, disconcerting. In the first place, not unlike the case of the US, the coefficient of interest rises to a surprising extent. In equation (5), it is threefold larger than in (4), and it is quite significant. At the same time, the inflation coefficient turns quite negative; it approaches $-a_3$ in (5). In (8), the rise of a_3 is even more conspicuous and alarming, and so is that of a_2. As a result, the 'no illusion' hypothesis, $a_2 = -a_3$, could clearly not be rejected.

We conclude that the results of the international cross-section confirm the role of income growth and dependency as major determinants of the consumption (or saving) income ratio; they also confirm that deficits tend to reduce consumption and encourage saving, but to a relatively modest extent, which is consistent with the LCH but amounts to only one-sixth to one-fifth of the full Barro effect. Finally, the results with respect to inflation illusion are largely inconclusive. As long as the coefficient of interest is forced to be equal to that of all other pre-tax income, the evidence, notably from the more reliable weighted regression, suggests a rather strong inflation illusion effect, though subject to a non-negligible error. However, when we drop that constraint, the coefficient of interest rate becomes large, while the inflation illusion effect largely vanishes. It is entirely possible that this inconclusiveness reflects the rather crude approximation to inflation on which we were forced to rely.

CONCLUSIONS

This chapter is concerned with analysing the impact of government expenditure and tax policies on the stock of capital in the economy and, thereby, on future generations. The issue is examined both in the presence of economic slack and when resources are fully utilised, a condition that may be associated with the long run.

It is argued that the conventional Keynesian multiplier, according to which an increase in deficits – or an increase in expenditure matched by an equal rise in taxes – will not 'crowd out' investment but will instead 'crowd in' output, requires for its validity not only enough economic slack but also a suitable monetary policy. Crowding out of investment will occur despite the slack, if monetary policy fails to accommodate fully the expansion of output that would be called for by the multiplier.

Concerning the long-run effects, various theories are reviewed and, in particular: (i) the currently prevailing one, according to which a dollar of National Debt displaces, permanently, a dollar of private tangible capital – or close to a dollar in the Life Cycle version – and, (ii) the newly fashionable one that claims, instead, that deficits cause an equal permanent increase in private wealth with the result that the path of private capital is unaffected and tax policy is 'neutral'.

The differential observable implications of the two theories are brought out and made the basis of a number of empirical tests. A test based on US data finds that, for a period of nearly a century, there is absolutely no evidence that private wealth has responded to the size of the national debt. The other test, based on post-war data for the US and Italy, pursues two central implications of tax neutrality: (1) that the government *debt*, unlike other private wealth, does not affect consumption, and (2) that, given after-tax income, government *deficit* displaces consumption by a roughly equal amount. The evidence rejects squarely these implications of tax neutrality; the estimated effect of debt on consumption is even greater than that of other wealth, and the effect of deficit, though of the right sign, is much too small to come even near to support tax neutrality. These results are, instead, fully consistent with the LCH version and very large tax effects. One final test was based on a cross-section of 33 countries. Though this test could not provide information on the effect of the debt, because of lack of data, it does fully confirm the modest magnitude of the effect of deficit.

The tests also provided the opportunity for investigating the distinct, but related, question of inflation illusion; given that consumption responds to taxes less government interest, does it seem to respond to the real interest, as it should? Or does the private sector suffer from inflation illusion so that consumption responds, at least in part, to nominal interest? The results of the tests show some evidence of inflation illusion, but far from conclusive, as the estimates for each sample are sensitive to small changes in specifications, and they further vary across samples in an apparently unsystematic fashion.

Notes

1. I wish to express my appreciation to Arlie Sterling who provided valuable advice and assistance, in particular for the US and cross-section tests reported below, and to Marco Pagano and James Poterba for reading the manuscript and making helpful suggestions.
2. A recent paper of Lecaldano *et al.* (1984) has explored similar issues. The results, though hard to compare because of differences in the period covered, in data, in frequency (they use quarterly data versus annual), and in emphasis, appear to be broadly consistent with ours, both with respect to the fiscal variables and to inflation illusion. Some of their tests suggest a more pronounced inflation illusion.

REFERENCES

Barro, R. (1974). 'Are Government Bonds Net Wealth?', *Journal of Political Economy*, vol. 82, no. 6.

Barro, R. (1978). *The Impact of Social Security on Private Savings – Evidence from U.S. Time Series.* American Enterprise Institute, Washington, DC.

Bernheim, B., Shleifer, A. and Summers, L. (1985). 'The Strategic Bequest Motive', *Journal of Political Economy*, 93, no. 6 (December), pp. 1045–76.

Blinder, A. S. (1983). 'On the Monetization of Debt', in *The Economic Consequences of Government Deficits*, Laurence H. Meyer (ed.) (Boston: Kluwer-Nijhoff Publishing).

Board of Governors of the Federal Reserve System (1981). Flow of Funds Section, Division of Quarterly Statics, *Balance Sheets of the U.S. Economy 1945–1980*, October.

Carmichael, J. and K. Hawtrey (1981). 'Social Security, Government Finance, and Savings', *Economic Record*, vol. 57, no. 159, pp. 332–43.

Cukierman, A. and J. Mortensen (1983). 'Monetary Assets and Inflation Induced Distortions of the National Accounts – Conceptual Issues and Corrections of Sectoral Income Flows in 5 EEC Countries', Commission of the European Communities – Directorate General for Economic and Financial Affairs.

Eisner, R. and Paul Pieper (1984). 'A New View of the Federal Debt and Budget Deficits', *American Economic Review*, vol. 74, no. 1, pp. 11–29.

Feldstein, M. A. (1982). 'Government Deficits and Aggregate Demand', *Journal of Monetary Economics*, 9.

Houthakker, H. W. (1965). 'On Some Determinants of Saving in Developed and Underdeveloped Countries', in E. A. G. Robinson (ed.), *Problems of Economic Development* (London: Macmillan) ch. 10.

Kochin, L. (1974). 'Are Future Taxes Discounted by Consumers', *Journal of Money, Credit and Banking*, 6 (August) pp. 385–94.

Kormendi, R. (1983). 'Government Debt, Government Spending and Private Sector Behaviour', *American Economic Review*, vol. 75, no. 5 (December) pp. 994–1010.

Kotlikoff, L. T. and L. H. Summers (1981). 'The Role of Intergenerational Transfers in Aggregate Capital Accumulation', *Journal of Political Economy*, vol. 89, no. 3.

Lecaldano, E., S. La Terza, G. Marotta and R. S. Masera (1984). 'Consumo, Risparmio e Fasso di Interesse: la Correzione per l'Inflazione', in *Moneta ed Economia Nazionale* (Cassa di Risparmio di Torino).

Leff, N. H. (1969). 'Dependency Rates and Savings Rate', *American Economic Review*, LIX (December) 886–95.

Modigliani, F. (1961). 'Long-Run Implications of Alternative Fiscal Policies and the Burden of the National Debt', *Economic Journal*, vol. 71 (December).

Modigliani, F. (1966). 'The Life Cycle Hypothesis of Saving, the Demand for Wealth, and the Supply of Capital', *Social Research*, 33 (Summer) pp. 160–217.

Modigliani, F. (1975). 'The Life Cycle Hypothesis of Saving Twenty Years Later', in M. Parkin (ed.), *Contemporary Economic Issues* (Manchester University Press).

Modigliani, F. (1983). 'Government Deficits, Inflation and Future Generations', in D. W. Conlkin and T. J. Courchene (eds), *Deficits: How Big and How Bad*, Ontario Economic Council Special Research Project.

Modigliani, F. (1984). 'Measuring the Contribution of Intergenerational Transfers to Total Wealth.' *Proceedings of Conference on Modeling the Accumulation and Distribution of Personal Wealth, Paris, France*, September 1984, forthcoming.

Modigliani, F. and R. Brumberg (1980). 'Utility Analysis and Aggregate Consumption Functions: An Attempt at Integration', in Andrew Abel (ed.), *The Collected Papers of Franco Modigliani: The Life Cycle Hypothesis of Saving*, vol. 2 (Cambridge, MA, The MIT Press).

Modigliani, F. and C. Steindel (1977). 'Is a Tax Rebate an Effective Tool for Stabilization Policy', *Brookings Papers on Economic Activity*, 1.

Modigliani, F. and A. Sterling (1983). 'Determinants of Private Saving with Special Reference to the Role of Social Security-Cross Country Tests', in F. Modigliani and R. Hemming (eds), *The Determinants of National Saving and Wealth*, London: Macmillan Press, pp. 24–55.

Modigliani, F., Tullio Jappelli and Marco Pagano (1985). 'The Impact of Fiscal Policy on National Saving: the Italian Case', *Banca Nazionale del Lavoro Quarterly Review*, no. 153, June 1985, pp. 91–126.

Modigliani, F., A. Mason and A. G. Sterling (1984). 'Effects of Fiscal Policy on Saving: Evidence from an International Cross-Section', unpublished manuscript, MIT, Sloan School.

Sargent, T. and N. Wallace (1981). 'Some Unpleasant Monetarist Arithmetic', *Federal Reserve Bank of Minneapolis Quarterly Review*, vol. 5 (Fall).

Seater, J. J. (1982). 'Are Future Taxes Discounted', *Journal of Money, Credit, and Banking*, vol. 14, no. 3 (August) pp. 376–89.

Siegel, J. J. and A. Protopadakis (1983). 'An Overview of Trends in Government Debt and National Income in Seven Industrialized Countries'. Presented at the Conference on Economic Policy and National Accounting in Inflationary Conditions, Dorga, Italy.

Sraffa, P. (ed.) (1962). *The Works and Correspondence of David Ricardo*, Vol. IV, *Pamphlets and Papers, 1815-1823* (Cambridge).

Sterling, A. G. (1984). *Public Debt and Private Wealth: The Role of Anticipated Taxes*, Doctoral dissertation, Dept. of Applied Economics, MIT, preliminary.

Tanner, J. E. (1970). 'Empirical Evidence on the Short-Run Real Balance Effect in Canada', *Journal of Money, Credit, and Banking*, vol. 2 (November) pp. 473-85.

Tanner, J. E. (1979). 'An Empirical Investigation of Tax Discounting', *Journal of Money, Credit, and Banking*, vol. 11, no. 2 (May) pp. 214-18.

Tobin, J. and W. Buiter (1980). 'Fiscal and Monetary Policies, Capital Formation, and Economic Activity', in G. M. von Furstenberg (ed.), *The Government and Capital Formation* (Cambridge, MA: Ballinger).

US Treasury Department (1983). 'Government Deficit Spending and its Effects on Prices of Financial Assets', Office of the Assistant Secretary for Economic Policy, May.

Yawitz, J. B. and L. H. Meyer (1976). 'An Empirical Investigation of the Extent of Tax Discounting', *Journal of Money, Credit, and Banking*, vol. 8 (May) pp. 247-54.

Errata

Page 6, second line: delete "and saving."

Page 6, fourth paragraph, "$(1 - c)$" should read "c."

Page 6, fourth paragraph, fifth line: insert "government" before "expenditure."

Page 8, second paragraph, last line: "inflation" should read "inflations."

Page 8, fourth paragraph, eighth line: insert "rates" after "interest."

Page 9, five lines from end: "(1984)" should read "(1983)."

Page 10, third paragraph, five lines from end: delete "of" before "pushing."

Page 12, point (c), first line: insert "a" after "of."

Page 12, point (d), first line: "Deficit" should read "deficit."

Page 15, paragraph two, line 17: "inifite" should read "infinite."

Page 17, point (i), line 3: "surplus" should read 'surpluses."

Page 19, third paragraph, sixth line: the reference is to "Modigliani and Brumberg, 1980."

Page 20, second paragraph, fourth line: "source" should read "error."

Page 20, four lines from bottom: delete the commas before and after "thus."

Page 22, ninth line after equation (3): Y should read "$D\hat{Y}$."

Page 23, the line immediately preceeding equation (4): "(1)" should read "(3)."

Page 24, lines 5 and 9: "b" should read β."

Page 25, three lines below (5): "in" should read "on."

Page 26, paragraph below equation (7), second to last line: "measures" should read "measure."

Page 26: the first line of the second equation should include "$+ TDY - TDef$."

Page 27, second paragraph, third line: "seem" should read "seems."

Page 28, top line: "expectation" should read "expectations."

Page 31, second paragraph, second to last line: "are" should read "is."

Page 32, third line in "Italy" section: "(1984)" should read "(1985)."

Page 32, fourth paragraph, line 9: insert ")" after the period.

Page 34, second paragraph, fourth line: "coefficients" should read "coefficient."

Page 34, third paragraph, last line: "large" should read "larger."

Page 34, fourth paragraph, last line: "standards" should read "standard."

Page 36, equation (9): insert "]" at end.

Page 41, last paragraph, fourth line: insert "rate" after "interest."

Page 43: in Modigliani (1983), "Conlkin" should read "Conklin."

Government Debt, Government Spending and Private Sector Behavior: Comment

By Franco Modigliani and Arlie Sterling*

Roger Kormendi (1983) presents apparently strong evidence that, in contrast to the standard view, consumption *is not* reduced by taxes but *is* reduced by government expenditure. He interprets his results as supporting a "consolidated" approach to private sector behavior in which consumers effectively internalize the government budget constraint. Specifically, he claims that consumers regard government spending as the true measure of the government's claim on private resources, and so do not respond to changes in taxes, given spending. This is basically the approach advocated by Robert Barro (1974) and known also as the Ricardian Equivalence Proposition (hereafter REP).

Kormendi's results appears to contradict other empirical work based on the Life Cycle Hypothesis (for example, Martin Feldstein, 1982; Modigliani 1984a; Sterling, 1985) although results similar to his have been reported (see David Aschauer, 1985; John Seater and Roberto Mariano, 1985 and the references in Kormendi). In our view, Kormendi's analysis is seriously flawed. His heuristic derivation of the consumption function leads him to a specification of the aggregate consumption function, which is not consistent with the Life Cycle Hypothesis (LCH) or with REP, and to questionable methods of estimation. Once his conceptual and methodological errors are corrected, his formulation and, more generally, the REP hypothesis are found to receive little empirical support.

In the next section we rely on the LCH to derive an aggregate consumption function

which shows explicitly how government expenditure and taxes should effect private consumption. This derivation helps to bring out the observable implications of REP, which are shown to be equivalent to a limiting form of the LCH in which the planning horizon is infinite. It also serves to clarify the appropriate specification of the variables appearing in the consumption function. Next, Section II reports our empirical estimates and tests. Section III compares our results with Kormendi's. Finally, Section IV reports the results of endeavors to improve the specification of fiscal variables, notably by distinguishing between permanent and transitory tax changes.

I. Government Spending and Taxes in the Aggregate Consumption Function

We begin with the standard model of aggregate consumption, in which consumption, C_t, is proportional to the sum of beginning-of-period aggregate nonhuman wealth, A_t, and aggregate human wealth:

(1)

$$C_t = c \left[A_t + \sum_{i=1}^{R} m_i (Y_{t+i} - T_{t+i})(1 + \mu)^{-i} \right],$$

where $\sum_{i=1}^{R} m_i (Y_{t+i} - T_{t+i})(1 + \mu)^{-i}$ equals the weighted present value of anticipated after-tax labor income and R is the length of life. The m_i weights equal the proportion of consumers present at time t who are expected to be alive at time $t + i$; Y_{t+i} represents before-tax labor income and T_{t+i} taxes on labor income. After-tax income is discounted at the rate μ, and c is the propensity to consume. The specification (1) is derived in Sterling. It can be shown to hold even if one allows for the presence of a bequest motive. Olivier Blanchard (1985) analyzes a

*Sloan School of Management, Massachusetts Institute of Technology, 50 Memorial Drive, Cambridge, MA 02139, and Marsoft Incorporated, One Kendall Square, Cambridge, MA 02139, respectively. James Meehan provided capable research assistance.

similar model in a general equilibrium setting.

Equation (1) seems to support the standard view that consumption depends only on taxes. But the relevant taxes are *future* as well as current ones. As a result, one can readily show, by taking into account the intertemporal government budget constraint that, in general, C will depend on both taxes and government expenditure. The government budget constraint can be written as

$$(2) \qquad T_t = E_t + rG_{t-1} - D_t,$$

where E_t represents government expenditures on goods and services, rG_{t-1} interest payments on beginning-of-period government debt, and D_t the current deficit. Using (2), the present value of weighted discounted taxes can be expressed in terms of government expenditures on goods and services and the deficit:

$$(3) \qquad \sum_{i=1}^{R} m_i T_{t+i} (1+\mu)^{-i}$$

$$= \sum_{i=1}^{R} m_i E_{t+i} (1+\mu)^{-i}$$

$$+ rG_t \sum_{i=1}^{R} m_i (1+\mu)^{-i}$$

$$+ r \sum_{i=1}^{R} \sum_{j=1}^{i-1} D_{t+j} m_i (1+\mu)^{-i}$$

$$- \sum_{i=1}^{R} m_i D_{t+i} (1+\mu)^{-i}$$

$$= \sum_{i=1}^{R} m_i E_{t+i} (1+\mu)^{-i} + s_1 G_t$$

$$- \sum_{i=1}^{R} m_i (1 - b_i) D_{t+i} (1+\mu)^{-i}$$

where we have used the identity $G_{t+i} = G_{t-1} + \sum_{j=1}^{i} D_{t+j}$ and define

$$(4) \qquad s_i = r \sum_{j=i}^{R} m_j (1+\mu)^{-j};$$

$$b_i = s_{i+1} / m_i (1+\mu)^{-i}.$$

The coefficients s_i measure the present value to those living at time t of the stream of interest paid by a dollar of debt, where the present value is calculated at the personal discount rate μ and the mortality rate is accounted for by the m_i factors. The b_i coefficients measure the same present value, but for those alive at the time the debt is issued.

Substituting for taxes in the consumption function yields

$$(5) \quad C_t = c \left[A_t - s_1 G_t + \sum_{i=1}^{R} m_i Y_{t+i} (1+\mu)^{-i} \right.$$

$$- \sum_{i=1}^{R} m_i E_{t+i} (1+\mu)^{-i}$$

$$\left. + \sum_{i=1}^{R} m_i (1 - b_i) D_{t+i} (1+\mu)^{-i} \right].$$

Or, using (2) and letting T_t^* denote taxes net of all transfers, including interest (i.e., $T^* = E_t - D_t$), one finally obtains

$$(6) \quad C_t = c \left[A_t - s_1 G_t + \sum_{i=1}^{R} m_i [Y_{t+i} - E_{t+i} \right.$$

$$\left. + (1 - b_i)(E_{t+i} - T_{t+i}^*)](1+\mu)^{-i} \right]$$

$$= c \left[A_t - s_1 G_t + \sum_{i=1}^{R} m_i [Y_{t+i} \right.$$

$$\left. - (1 - b_i) T_{t+i}^* - b_i E_{t+1})](1+\mu)^{-i} \right].$$

Taxes net of interest appear in (6) because, as noted above, the coefficients s_i and

b_i reflect the anticipated taxes due to an issue of debt. Thus, that component of taxes that is due to interest payments must not be included in the explicit tax term, as it is already incorporated in the effect of the debt.

Equation (6) shows that consumption depends, in general, on a weighted average of net taxes and government expenditure on goods and services, where the weights $(1 - b_i$ and b_i, respectively) sum to one—and that it should respond only partially to wealth in the form of government debt. There is only one limiting case in which only expenditure matters while taxes and debt matter not at all, namely, *if μ were equal to r, and the planning horizon R were infinite*. In this case, in fact, $m_i = 1$ for all i, and, as can be seen from (4), s_1 and the b_i would all be unity. In that special case, the consumption function reduces to

$$(7) \quad C_t = c \left[A_t - G_t \right.$$
$$\left. + \sum_{i=1}^{\infty} (Y_{t+i} - E_{t+i})(1 + r)^{-i} \right].$$

It will be recognized that (7), the limiting form of LCH for an infinite planning horizon, embodies the relevant implications of REP; consumption depends on: (i) a measure of private net worth which excludes all government debt, and (ii) on government spending on goods and services, but is unaffected by the way that expenditure is financed, whether by taxes or by selling debt. Nor is this surprising since, in effect to derive REP, Barro postulates an infinite planning horizon for all economic agents, through the intermediation of an infinite chain of intergenerational bequests.

However, there are many considerations that suggest rejecting the Barro hypothesis of an infinite horizon and recognizing that that representative household will behave as though R is very much finite and not much larger, if at all, than the length of life, as suggested by the standard "life horizon" Life Cycle Hypothesis (LH-LCH). The relevant considerations have been elaborated at length by many authors (see, for example, Modig-

liani, 1984a, b, and James Tobin, 1980, ch. III). Similarly, there are grounds for hypothesizing that μ may tend to exceed r (Fumio Hayashi, 1982).

These considerations suggest that the coefficient of debt, s_1, and that of expenditure, b_i, in the consumption function should fall well below unity, while that of taxes should not be far from unity. Sterling has shown that, when the population age distribution is approximated by an exponential, s_i, varies between 0.6 (for $r = \mu = 0.02$) and 0.2 (for $r = 0.02$, $\mu = 0.08$) for $i = 1$ and that it declines monotonically with i, as the stream of interest, of which s_i is the weighted present value, gets shorter. These results imply that, under the LH-LCH, the liability for future interest may offset the value of government debt held in private portfolios, but to a modest extent at best. Similarly, for given taxes, an increased deficit, and hence government expenditure, may dampen consumption because of anticipated future taxes to pay interest, but, again, quite moderately at best.

Our conclusions with respect to the role of fiscal variables in the consumption function can now be summarized as follows: (i) consumption should respond negatively to a weighted average of taxes and expenditure; (ii) the coefficient of the weighted average should equal minus that of income (or, equivalently, the coefficients of the income and that of the weighted average should add up to zero) reflecting the fact that, whether consumption depends on taxes or on government expenditure, it must respond dollar per dollar to the combination of the two; (iii) the weight of taxes should be not far from unity, and that of government consumption much less than unity, whereas REP's infinite planning horizon hypothesis would imply the reverse; (iv) the coefficient of government debt, given private net worth, should be close to zero (and might even be somewhat positive,[1] whereas, according to REP, it should equal minus that of wealth.

---

[1] If (i) government real interest included in T^* is subject to great variability, as typically happens during period of high and variable inflation; (ii) consumption

II. Estimates of the Aggregate Consumption Function

The consumption function (6) cannot be estimated directly since it is in terms of unobservable expectations of future income, taxes and expenditure (or deficits). We assume that the expectations can be modeled as a distributed lag of past values of these variables. Accordingly, the basic equation estimated and used in testing alternative hypothesis takes the form

$$(8) \quad C_t = a + b_0 A_t + b_1 G_t$$

$$+ \sum_{i=1}^{L} c_i (Y_{t-i} - T_{t-i}) + \sum_{i=1}^{L} d_i D_{t-i}.$$

The last two terms of (8) are based on a regrouping of the expression in the square bracket in the summation term of (6):

$$Y_{t+1} - (1 - b_i) T_{t+i}^* - b_i E_{t+i}$$

$$= Y_{t+i} - T_{t+i}^* - b_i D_{t+i},$$

where D_{t+i} denotes the budget deficit, $E_{t+1} - T_{t+1}^*$.

This formulation has the desirable property of insuring that the constraint that the tax and expenditure coefficients add up to minus the income coefficient, as dictated by (6). Since the coefficients d_i in (8) correspond to $-b_i$ in (6), while b_1 in (8) corresponds to s_1 in (6), according to the conventional LCH formulation, both coefficients should be close to zero, whereas according to the REP/Kormendi hypothesis, the Σd_i should be close to $-\Sigma c_i$, while b_1 should be close to $-b_0$.

The explanatory variables appearing in (8) have slightly different definitions from the analogous variables appearing in (6). The changes are necessary to accommodate the expectations formation mechanism and data limitations. Specifically, income and net taxes include income from and taxes on capital, and are measured, respectively, by net national product and all government taxes (net of transfers including government net domestic interest payments). The deficit equals the difference between government expenditures on goods and services and net taxes. Net interest payments to the domestic sector equal the *ex post* real payments, calculated by subtracting the product of the actual rate of inflation and the stock of net government debt from net interest payments.[2,3] In order to insure comparability with Kormendi, all tests reported here are based on annual data.

The c_i and d_i, $i = 1, \ldots, L$ distributed lag coefficients in (8) reflect both the expectations formation mechanism and behavioral parameters. Sterling has shown how the behavioral coefficients can be estimated directly in such a formulation. For the purposes of this comment we shall interpret them as behavioral parameters. In all results reported below, the distributed lag coefficients are constrained to lie on a first-degree polynomial with five lags (including the contemporaneous term). Only the sum of the current and lagged coefficients is reported.

Column 1 of Table 1 reports the results of estimating (8) over the 33 postwar years 1952–84. The results are seen to provide solid support for the LCH and unequivocal rejection of Kormendi/REP, especially in the light of the very close fit (the standard error is 0.47 percent of the mean). First, for REP the sum of the d_i coefficients should be negative and equal in magnitude to the sum of the income coefficients; for LCH it should be close to zero. The actual estimate is not very significantly different from zero and

---

depends positively on the permanent real rate and not current rate (as is true for the LCH); (*iii*) the permanent real rate is approximately constant, say ρ, then (6) might contain an additional term proportional to ρG so that the coefficient of G is the sum of a positive and a negative term, whose sign is uncertain.

[2] See the Data Appendix for a more detailed description of the data.

[3] This approximation is justified by the consideration that for the United States in the postwar period, inflation appears to be fairly well forecastable—see Robert Barsky (1985).

TABLE 1—ESTIMATES OF THE AGGREGATE CONSUMPTION FUNCTION, 1952–84[a,b]

Independent Variables		(1)[c]	(2)[c]	(3)[c]	(4)
Constant	a	−0.38	−0.45	−0.436	−0.436
		(0.06)	(0.12)	(0.052)	(0.061)
Net Worth (A)	b_0	0.023	0.027	0.022	0.022
		(0.005)	(0.005)	(0.004)	(0.005)
Government Debt	b_1	0.073	0.106	0.096	0.096
(G)		(0.024)	(0.033)	(0.021)	(0.031)
Net National	Σc_{1i}	0.922	0.901	0.928	0.931
Product (Y)		(0.020)	(0.041)	(0.017)	(0.070)
Net Taxes (T)	Σc_{2i}	−0.922	−0.901	−0.928	−1.081
		(0.020)	(0.041)	(0.017)	(0.151)
Deficit (D)	Σd_i	0.171	0.115	0.187	–
		(0.082)	(0.086)	(0.069)	
Government	Σd_i^*	–	–	–	0.146
Expenditure (E)					(0.136)
Transfers (TR)	Σt_i	–	0.005	–	–
			(0.102)		
Transitory	Σh_i	–	–	0.633	0.645
Taxes (T^*)				(0.182)	(0.339)
SE		0.015	0.014	0.012	0.013
Log Likelihood		96.33	98.50	103.44	103.88
D-W		1.43	1.73	1.92	1.90

[a] Dependent variable: Consumption per capita; shown in thousands of 1972 dollars. Standard errors are shown in parentheses.
[b] The mean of the dependent variable is 3.21 and its standard deviation is 0.73.
[c] In these equations, the coefficients of taxes, Σc_{2i}, are constrained to equal the negative of the income coefficients, $-\Sigma c_{1i}$.

actually positive. Second, the estimate of b_1, far from being close to $-b_0$, as implied by REP, is seen to be positive, which is not inconsistent with LCH. The point estimate is somewhat high, but the estimate is not very precise.

III. Comparison with Kormendi's Analysis

The results presented in column 1 of Table 1 are drastically different—in fact, just about diametrically opposite—to those reported by Kormendi in his various tests. This difference is clearly brought out by a comparison of the results of column 1 with those reported below, which rely on Kormendi's definition and measurement of variables (as nearly as we could match it) and on his precise specifications, including in particular the use of first differences. The only difference consists in the omitting of the years previous to 1952 (for which several of the series used in col. 1 are not readily

available). The results of the replication are

$$(9) \quad C^* = 0.02 + 0.27Y_t^* + 0.02Y_{t-1}^* + 0.01A_t^*$$
$$(0.01) \quad (0.07) \quad (0.04) \quad (0.01)$$

$$- 0.09G_t^* - 0.22E_t^* + 0.16T_t^* + 0.86TR_t^*$$
$$(0.05) \quad (0.10) \quad (0.12) \quad (0.40)$$

$$R^2 = 0.72; \ SE = 0.02; \ D\text{-}W = 1.7;$$

Log Likelihood = 68.08, Sample: 1952–76.

(The asterisks indicate that Kormendi's data definitions are used.)

It is readily apparent from a comparison of (9) with Kormendi's Table 5, that the results for the postwar period are substantially the same as those obtained by Kormendi for the longer period 1931–76 —the only significant exception being private wealth, which is substantially more important in his original period. In particular, with respect to the variables crucial for our

TABLE 2—ESTIMATES OF THE AGGREGATE CONSUMPTION FUNCTION, 1952–76[a,b]

Independent Variables		$(1)^c$	$(2)^c$	$(3)^c$	(4)	(5)
Constant	a	−0.394	−0.148	−0.238	−0.167	−0.121
		(0.152)	(0.222)	(0.114)	(0.127)	(0.141)
Net Worth (A)	b_0	0.031	0.030	0.031	0.030	0.032
Government Debt	b_1	0.073	0.106	0.096	0.096	
(G)		(0.058)	(0.063)	(0.042)	(0.046)	(0.051)
Net National	Σc_{1i}	0.896	0.835	0.876	0.882	0.763
Product (Y)		(0.028)	(0.055)	(0.021)	(0.076)	(0.046)
Net Taxes (T)	Σc_{2i}	−0.896	−0.835	−0.876	−0.840	−0.438
		(0.028)	(0.055)	(0.021)	(0.221)	(0.165)
Deficit (D)	Σd_i	0.016	−0.100	0.109	–	–
		(0.012)	(0.132)	(0.086)		
Government	Σd_i^*	–	–	–	−0.070	−0.062
Expenditure (E)					(0.154)	(0.132)
Transfers (TR)	Σt_i	–	0.013	–	–	–
			(0.118)			
Transitory	Σh_i	–	–	0.864	0.848	–
Taxes (T^*)				(0.200)	(0.367)	
SE		0.015	0.014	0.010	0.010	0.011
Log Likelihood		74.18	76.44	84.42	86.52	81.95
$D\text{-}W$		1.50	1.46	2.26	2.33	2.08

[a] See Table 1.
[b] The mean of the dependent variable is 2.89 and its standard deviation is 0.50.
[c] See Table 1.

tests, one finds that (i) the coefficient of taxes, instead of being strongly negative as in column 1, is positive (though insignificantly so); (ii) government expenditure, insignificant in column 1, is negative and rather significantly so; (iii) finally, since in (9) wealth (A^*) excludes government debt, the coefficient of that variable should be positive for LCH and zero for REP; it is actually negative and large—though it is rather imprecisely estimated. All of these results are, at least qualitatively, consistent with the "consolidated" REP hypothesis and inconsistent with LCH.

But a closer examination of (9) raises some serious questions as to the reliability of the results and their consistency with REP. To begin with, all the income and wealth variables have preposterously low coefficients—the long-run marginal propensity to consume with respect to income is less than .3(!), compared with an average propensity of over .9 and a customary estimate of the marginal propensity .7 to .9. Similarly, the wealth effect is but a fraction of the usual estimates and not even significant. Since none of the remaining fiscal variables are particu-

larly significant, it is not surprising to find that the equation has quite a large standard error as compared with that of column 1 (or to others reported in Table 2 for the same period as (9)).

Looking more specifically at the fiscal variables, the first highly disquieting feature of (9) is that the coefficients completely fail to meet the consistency requirement that the sum of the coefficients of taxes and expenditure approximately match in magnitude that of income. Indeed, Kormendi's T and E coefficients add up to but −.06 compared with an already very low income coefficient of .29. Thus, according to (9), consumption weakly responds to income, and, in addition, responds even less to the loss of resources through a balanced-budget increase in taxes and government use of resources. Hence, an increased government use of resources would have to result in a large loss of net capital formation—clearly not what the REP model implies.

But what is most incongruous about equation (9) and other Kormendi results is the huge and even quite significant coefficient of transfer payments, TR^*. Clearly, transfer payments are part of net taxes, and by the REP hypothesis net taxes must have a near zero coefficient. Kormendi's explanation in terms of people hit by positive taxes not responding at all to the resulting loss of income (or even responding positively according to (9)), while people hit by negative taxes respond by a huge rise in consumption, is not only totally unconvincing but in addition, if true, would be as anti-REP a finding as one may conceive: it implies that those who receive a deficit-financed rise in transfer consume it merrily, thinking nothing of the effect on future generations, while all the rest equally fail to respond by cutting their consumption—with the result that the fall in net taxes would result in a rise in consumption, even though government expenditure were constant.

What accounts for the striking differences between the results of Kormendi and those reported in column 1? We can first investigate one obvious possibility, namely the difference in periods. Indeed, column 1 includes 8 years in addition to the 25 used in (9), and these years were characterized by extreme values of the deficit, not to mention variables like interest rates or inflation that could affect results. However, in Table 2, column 1 shows that estimating the basic equation (8) for the shorter period 1952–76, yields results very close to those of Table 1. None of the coefficients change significantly and, in particular, the coefficient of the deficit remains insignificantly different from zero.

We propose to show that the differences between (9) and the estimates of Table 1 are traceable in part to several errors in Kormendi's construction of the data and, to a much greater extent, to serious misspecifications of his equations.

There are three major flaws in Kormendi's data construction. First, he incorrectly deflates government expenditures, taxes, and transfers by a price index based on goods purchased by the government (in the case of government expenditures) or by the implicit price deflator for net national product. The correct price index, which gives the value of government spending, taxes, and transfers in terms of consumption goods, should be based on an appropriate consumption basket. Sec-

ond, Kormendi creates his own measure of the service-flow measure of consumption, but does not use the analogous price index. (We use the service-flow measure of consumption developed by the Federal Reserve to support their quarterly econometric model.) Third, Kormendi uses an incorrect measure of real government interest payments. The correct measure should be based on the product of the real interest rate and the stock of debt; Kormendi instead deflates the reported nominal interest payments by the net national product price index. His procedure does not correct for change in real debt due to inflation (which corresponds also to the inflation premium built into the government's interest payments when Fisher's Law holds). The relevance of this correction for accounting purposes is pointed out by Stanley Fischer and Modigliani (1978); Modigliani, Tullio Jappelli, and Marco Pagano (1985) analyze its behavioral significance. (Our correction to the government's interest payments is based on the *ex post* interest rate.)

The role of these measurement errors can be assessed by comparing our (Kormendi's) equation (9) with the equation below which uses corrected data, but is identical to (9) in terms of specifications and sample period.

$$(9')\quad \Delta C = 0.02 + 0.24 Y_t + 0.11 Y_{t-1} + 0.01 A_t$$
$$(0.01)\ (0.08)\quad (0.05)\quad\ (0.01)$$

$$+\ 0.05 G_t - 0.04 E_t - 0.00 T + 0.77 TR_t$$
$$(0.09)\quad (0.14)\quad (0.11)\quad (0.27)$$

$$R^2 = 0.74;\ SE = 0.019;$$
$$D\text{-}W = 2.06;\ \text{Log Likelihood} = 66.2.$$

(Note: A includes government debt.)

Equation (9') shares with (9) the characteristic of little credibility—in particular, the coefficient of wealth and that of income remain unbelievably low, and the standard error is hardly smaller. However, with respect to the fiscal variables, even the limited support for REP that (9) appears to provide vanishes: the coefficient of debt becomes positive, though even less reliably estimated, and the coefficient of expenditure is essentially zero.

The remaining drastic difference between (9') and Table 2, column 1, must clearly result from the unsatisfactory specification underlying Kormendi's tests. In the first place, once it is realized that the flow variables appearing on the right-hand side of (8) represent basically very long-run expectations, it becomes clear that it is entirely unsatisfactory to approximate these expectations just by the current value (or, at most, for income, current and lagged once); what is needed, at the very least, are reasonably long distributed lags. This conjecture is fully confirmed by the empirical evidence which also suggested five years as an adequate approximation.

A second shortcoming of Kormendi's specification is that he fails to impose the consistency condition requiring that the coefficients of taxes expenditure and income add up to zero. A final and more consequential shortcoming is that he chooses to estimate coefficients in the first difference form, a rather arbitrary procedure since, when he estimated an autoregression coefficient, its value, though fairly high (as Kormendi reports in his Table 1), is significantly below unity. But, in addition, the high autoregression coefficient he obtains is largely a predictable consequence of his failure to allow for sufficiently long distributed lags. With a five-year distributed lag, we find uniformly that D-W statistics are above the critical level; accordingly, all equations reported in Tables 1 and 2 have been estimated in level form by ordinary least squares (OLS).[4] These estimates were also checked using an instrumental variables procedure, but the results were not noticeably different from the OLS estimates and are therefore not reported separately.[5]

Replacing Kormendi's specification with ours not only reduces drastically the serial correlation of the errors, but, in addition, produces a substantial improvement in fit —the standard error of Kormendi's (9) is about $1/3$ larger that those of Tables 1 and

2. Note that the improvement occurs even though Kormendi's equation includes, and ours excludes, the questionable variable transfer payments which is seen to contribute to his fit more than any other variable. But, as can be seen from columns 2 in Tables 1 and 2, our qualms about the role of this variable were justified: indeed, when transfer payments are added to the properly specified equations of both columns 1, the contribution of this variable, measured by the sum of the lagged coefficients, is essentially zero, implying that the effect of transfer payments on consumption is the same as that of any other component of net taxes. Finally, the coefficients of the traditional variables are reasonable and credible. We suggest, therefore, that Kormendi's results, and conclusions based thereon, can be dismissed without further ado.[6]

IV. Suggested Improvements in the Specification of Fiscal Variables

We would like to suggest some possible improvements in the specification of our equations of columns 1, Tables 1 and 2. That

---

[4] In every case where the D-W statistic approached the critical level we reestimated the equation using an autoregressive transformation; the autoregression coefficient was never significantly different from zero even at the 5 percent level, and the estimated coefficients were not appreciably different from those reported in the table.

[5] Lagged income and government expenditures were used as instruments for income and the deficit, while wealth and debt were treated as exogenous.

[6] Barro has pointed out (in private communication) that, in some cases, the coefficients on taxes in the consumption function may reflect their predictive power for future government spending. This would be the case if, as Barro has postulated (1979, 1984, 1985), the government attempts to smooth tax rates to reflect long-term government spending rather than transitory expenditures. If taxes are indeed better predictors of government spending then are past spending, the REP implies they should be negatively correlated with consumption. (Note that, as Modigliani, 1984b, points out, tax smoothing is not an implication unique to the REP.) This "tax smoothing" effect appears to play no significant role in our analysis. We tested the predictive power of lagged taxes for government expenditure by estimating a regression of government expenditure on goods and services on lagged (four years) expenditures and various measures of net taxes (taxes net of transfers, taxes net of transfers and government real interest payments, permanent net taxes and permanent taxes net of transfers and real interest). In no case did the tax measure contribute significantly to the explanatory power of the regression. The largest value of the test statistic for the restriction that taxes played no role in the forecasting equation was 4.63; the critical value at the 5 percent confidence level is 9.49. Lagged expenditure alone "explains" more than 98 percent of the variation in government expenditures on goods and services over the 1953–84 period.

specification imposes the constraint that the sum of the coefficients of taxes expenditure and income be equal to zero at each of the five lags. This is unnecessarily restrictive; indeed, the shape of the distributed lags are intended to reflect the expectation formation mechanism, and there is no reason why this mechanism should be identical across different variables. This consideration is especially relevant with respect to taxes, since, as pointed out by Modigliani and Charles Steindel (1977), changes in the tax rate component of tax receipts are, typically, of a permanent nature. The above constraint can be readily eliminated by estimating separate distributed lags for income and each of the two fiscal variables. This procedure will, of course, also eliminate the valid "consistency" restriction that the overall sum of the coefficients, over all variables and lags, be close to zero. But, precisely for this reason, unconstrained estimation provides an opportunity to test whether the "consistency specification" is supported by the data.

A second shortcoming of the specification relates to the measurement of taxes. It is apparent from equation (6) that the income, tax, and expenditure terms in (8) are all meant to measure the average value (weighted for time and survival rates) of these variables expected by those currently living. This poses a problem when current and past values cannot be taken as representative of the future. A clear instance of nonrepresentativeness is the well-known case of tax changes which are announced, and presumably believed, to be but transitory. In the period covered by our sample there have been two important cases of transitory tax changes—one is the surtax of 1968–70, and the other the 1975 rebates. One can also conceive of significant transitory government expenditures (for example, major wars), but no important instance appears to have occurred during our sample period.

Since transitory tax changes should add relatively little to the present value of the weighted future tax liabilities, their effect on consumption should be much closer to zero than the permanent tax effect. To test this hypothesis, and hopefully reduce the unexplained error, one can continue to use the total tax variables of columns 1 and 2 in Table 1, but add the transitory tax component as a separate variable: the coefficient of this variable (h_t) will then measure the differential effect on consumption of transitory vs. permanent taxes.

The role of transitory taxes is tested for the entire period in columns 3 and 4 of Table 1, using the approach described above. In column 3, in order to focus on transitory taxes, we maintain the constraint on the sum of income, expenditures, and (permanent) tax coefficients. It is seen that the effect on consumption of temporary taxes is much less negative than that of permanent taxes—the estimated difference is 63¢ per dollar of taxes, and it is highly significant, resulting also in a striking improvement in fit and reduction in serial correlation of the residuals. This estimate implies a marginal effect of temporary taxes on consumption of only −.48 (with a standard error .2), and even this figure probably overestimates the negative effect, given that the point estimate of the effect of permanent taxes appears upward biassed (larger than −1). In column 4, we have, in addition, eliminated the "consistency" restriction, estimating separately coefficients for before tax income (Σc_{1i}), net taxes (Σc_{2i}), and government expenditure (Σd_i), as well as for transitory taxes (Σh_i).

It is apparent that the unrestricted coefficients of column 4 of Table 1 come very close to satisfying the consistency requirement, as the sum of the (permanent) tax and expenditure coefficients offset about exactly that of before tax income. Accordingly, as shown by a comparison of the likelihood statistic for columns 3 and 4, the restriction imposed in column 3 cannot be rejected at any reasonable level of significance. The only problem with the results of column 4 is that, in common with those of columns 1 through 3, they tend to give an unreasonably high point estimate of the effect of permanent taxes, matched by an equally questionable positive effect of government expenditure on consumption. However, this may be accounted for by imprecision of the estimates, as measured by their standard error. In particular, the tax coefficient differs from the income coefficient by but one standard error and the same is true of the difference of the expenditure coefficient from zero.

For the sake of completeness, the test of columns 3 and 4 of Table 1 are reported for the shorter period in Table 2. The estimate of the temporary tax effect for this period must be regarded as less reliable because only a portion of the experience of the 1975 tax rebate is reflected in the data. Nonetheless, the estimates are seen to confirm that the effect of transitory taxes on consumption is a great deal smaller than that of permanent taxes. Furthermore, the difference (even greater than in cols. 3 and 4) is highly significant, resulting, again, in a considerable improvement in fit. In Table 2, column 4 confirms again that the constraint imposed on column 3 is not rejected by the data—indeed, the coefficients of column 3 are all very similar to those of column 2. It is also encouraging that the permanent tax coefficient is of very reasonable magnitude both absolutely and relative to that of income, and that the coefficient of expenditure has the expected negative sign, though small, as implied by LCH.

Column 5 of Table 2 reports one more result which we find instructive. The coefficients in this column are estimated without constraint but also omitting the temporary taxes. It appears that failing to allow for the much smaller impact of transitory taxes, seriously biases up (i.e., towards zero) the coefficient of the tax variable. As a result, the sum of the coefficients of taxes and expenditure is but $-.5$, compared with an income coefficient of .76. It is not unlikely that failure to allow for transitory taxes may be one of the reasons why Kormendi could not find a negative effect of taxes on consumption and obtained coefficients which completely fail to meet the consistency test.

There is one more empirical result that we feel compelled to report. It was shown in Tables 1 and 2, columns 2, that transfer payments, when added as an additional variable, receive a coefficient near zero. Yet, when transfer payments are added to column 3 of Table 1—which separates transitory from permanent taxes—the effect is truly devastating: the coefficient of transfers is .54 with t-ratio of 5(!); since this variable

is already included in income minus net taxes (coefficient .77) and the deficit (coefficient .23), the total implied effect of transfers comes to 1.54. For the short period, the results are about as incredible, as the total effect of transfers is 1.36 with a t-ratio of 2.5. In addition, the estimated differential effect on consumption of transitory vs. permanent taxes rises in Table 1, column 3, from .63 to 1.4; since the effect of permanent taxes implicit in the coefficient of income and deficit is 1.0 (already rather unreasonably large), the effect on consumption of temporary taxes would be 0.4; that is, a dollar of temporary taxes would *increase* consumption by 40¢. One further surprise is that the residuals exhibit a marked negative serial correlation, a rather suspicious finding for these kind of time-series regressions.

One explanation for the significance of transfers in the consumption function is that they may provide a reliable signal of one component of permanent income. In particular, Social Security and other transfers to the elderly may be more certain than labor income, which may be reduced or eliminated by unexpected retirement. That informational role may be enhanced in economic downturns, which could account for the peculiar interaction with temporary taxes. Nevertheless, we found no substantial improvement in the results when transfers were replaced by social security payments.

On the whole, these results appear so preposterous that, in our view, they should be disregarded—although they also appear so unlikely to reflect pure chance that they deserve to be filed under agenda for the future.

V. Conclusions

We have derived an aggregate consumption function based on the life cycle paradigm and have shown that it implies that consumption should be affected both by taxes and by government expenditure and by private claims on the government as well as the wealth. It was shown that the relative significance of taxes and government expenditure in the consumption function reflects mortality rates, the length of life, and both the personal discount rate and interest

TABLE 3—DATA USED IN THE REGRESSIONS[a]

Year	C	A	G	Y	TR	T	E	D	T*
1949	2.09830	10.24789	2.54671	2.94840	0.14645	0.48932	0.47835	−0.01097	0.00000
1950	2.16033	10.31647	2.56432	3.13978	0.17216	0.72363	0.45953	−0.26410	0.00000
1951	2.20120	10.45613	2.26725	3.31530	0.12779	0.89179	0.65505	−0.23674	0.00000
1952	2.24048	10.88833	2.12983	3.31906	0.12572	0.82212	0.78714	−0.03498	0.00000
1953	2.27847	10.94125	2.12317	3.37896	0.13028	0.81541	0.83085	0.01544	0.00000
1954	2.29297	10.94416	2.15840	3.25165	0.14768	0.70030	0.73847	0.03817	0.00000
1955	2.36421	11.54037	2.15594	3.44293	0.15272	0.79534	0.70773	−0.08761	0.00000
1956	2.42094	12.16621	2.08327	3.47656	0.15750	0.84806	0.72193	−0.12613	0.00000
1957	2.44090	12.25389	1.98322	3.48123	0.17389	0.83292	0.75576	−0.07716	0.00000
1958	2.45015	12.09346	1.95084	3.39446	0.20396	0.73773	0.79536	0.05764	0.00000
1959	2.50200	12.98754	2.00864	3.56677	0.20311	0.84357	0.78826	−0.05531	0.00000
1960	2.53064	13.33399	1.96582	3.56636	0.20892	0.87105	0.77912	−0.09193	0.00000
1961	2.55696	13.22858	1.93199	3.57854	0.23107	0.82274	0.81353	−0.00921	0.00000
1962	2.60643	13.93548	1.95742	3.76567	0.23059	0.89504	0.86360	−0.03144	0.00000
1963	2.65242	13.59904	1.94225	3.86097	0.23651	0.93752	0.87738	−0.06014	0.00000
1964	2.74833	14.24857	1.90374	4.02640	0.23926	0.92876	0.89661	−0.03215	0.00000
1965	2.84715	15.05566	1.89709	4.23856	0.25113	1.00115	0.92685	−0.07431	0.00000
1966	2.95633	15.37331	1.85059	4.43978	0.26568	1.10352	1.01637	−0.08716	0.00000
1967	3.03115	14.80681	1.81809	4.51820	0.30450	1.09996	1.11343	0.01347	0.00000
1968	3.14352	15.45900	1.84912	4.70265	0.33124	1.23030	1.17176	−0.05854	0.05166
1969	3.24328	16.28678	1.81697	4.80729	0.34923	1.33364	1.16609	−0.16755	0.06845
1970	3.31416	15.64229	1.74252	4.75079	0.39903	1.21346	1.16140	−0.05206	0.04359
1971	3.36932	15.80857	1.79200	4.90640	0.45008	1.17574	1.18371	0.00797	0.00000
1972	3.49398	16.42354	1.86056	5.14208	0.47539	1.29634	1.21862	−0.07772	0.00000
1973	3.59773	17.64463	1.82951	5.38611	0.50738	1.41186	1.22128	−0.19058	0.00000
1974	3.61446	17.10263	1.67637	5.21342	0.54295	1.40182	1.23742	−0.16441	0.00000
1975	3.67342	16.26371	1.64065	5.16574	0.63499	1.15164	1.28036	0.12872	−0.06880
1976	3.80017	17.63173	1.86191	5.44617	0.65774	1.24486	1.29434	0.04948	0.00000
1977	3.92910	18.68652	1.94918	5.72281	0.66191	1.38205	1.32615	−0.05590	0.00000
1978	4.05878	18.82615	1.97971	5.93879	9.65673	1.52707	1.34803	−0.17904	0.00000
1979	4.15649	19.90689	1.85136	5.97227	0.66265	1.55996	1.34092	−0.21904	0.00000
1980	4.19528	19.94764	1.72724	5.77520	0.70522	1.45075	1.35888	−0.09187	0.00000
1981	4.23351	20.73876	1.71721	5.87696	0.72533	1.40111	1.37129	−0.02981	0.00000
1982	4.26121	20.65688	1.77052	5.66342	0.75579	1.21792	1.44791	0.23000	0.00000
1983	4.36233	21.23510	2.06152	5.83235	0.77590	1.22102	1.45229	0.23127	0.00000
1984	4.49736	21.91946	2.29538	6.15170	0.75358	1.31457	1.44690	0.13233	0.00000

[a]All data are in real thousands of 1972 dollars per capita terms.

rate, but that as long as the representative planning horizon does not extend significantly beyond life, the role of taxes could be expected to be substantially larger than that of expenditure and the role of debt close to that of other wealth.

We have endeavored to show that Kormendi's contrary empirical findings—that consumption does not respond to taxes but only to government expenditure—are the result of errors in the measurement of variables and, to a greater extent, the consequence of serious misspecifications of his test equations. Specifically, Kormendi fails

to allow for the relatively long lags required to approximate permanent income, or to distinguish between permanent and temporary tax effects and relies on an inefficient method of estimation.

We have provided evidence that, once Kormendi's measurement errors and misspecifications are corrected, the data for the United States in the postwar period are strikingly and unmistakenly consistent with a "Life Horizon"-Life Cycle approach to consumption behavior and equally inconsistent with the infinite horizon-REP formulation.

DATA APPENDIX

The data used in this paper are from the Federal Reserve data bank. A detailed specification of the data is available in documentation accompanying the Federal Reserve data tapes. All data are per capita and expressed in thousands of 1972 dollars.

Consumption: The sum of expenditures on nondurable goods and services plus a fraction of expenditures or durables and a measure of the flow of services from the stock of consumer durables.

Price Index: A consumer price index based on prices of nondurables, services and durable goods weighted according to their proportions of consumption.

Income: Net national product.

Taxes: Total federal plus state and local taxes (including employer's contribution to social security), net of transfers and real interest payments. Real interest payments are calculated by subtracting the product of the rate of inflation and the beginning-of-period government debt from actual total government (including the Federal Reserve) net interest payments. Our estimate of temporary taxes is taken from the Economic Reports to the President of 1969 and 1975.

Government Expenditures: Federal and state and local expenditures on goods and services.

Wealth: Net worth of households.

Debt: The sum of federal and state and local net financial liabilities.

The data used in the regressions are reported in Table 3.

REFERENCES

Aschauer, David Alan, "Fiscal Policy and Aggregate Demand," *American Economic Review*, March 1985, *75*, 117–27.

Barro, Robert J., "Are Government Bonds Net Wealth?," *Journal of Political Economy*, November/December 1974, *82*, 1094–117.

_____, "On the Determination of the Public Debt," *Journal of Political Economy*, October 1979, *87*, 940–71.

_____, "U.S. Deficits Since World War I," paper presented at Conference on Growth and Distribution: Intergenerational Problems, Uppsala Sweden, June 1984; *Proceedings* forthcoming.

_____, "Government Spending, Interest Rates, Prices and Budget Deficits in the United Kingdom, 1730–1918," Working Paper No 1, University of Rochester, March 1985.

Barsky, Robert, "Three Interest Rate Paradoxes," unpublished doctoral dissertation, MIT, 1985.

Blanchard, Olivier J., "Debt, Deficits and Finite Horizons," *Journal of Political Economy*, April 1985, *93*, 223–47.

Feldstein, Martin S., "Government Deficits and Aggregate Demand," *Journal of Monetary Economics*, January 1982, *9*, 1–20.

Fischer, Stanley and Modigliani, Franco, "Towards an Understanding of the Real Effects and Costs of Inflation" *Weltwirtschafliches archiv* (*Review of World Economics*), No. 4, 1978, *114*, 736–81.

Hayashi, Fumio, "The Permanent Income Hypothesis: Estimation and Testing by Instrumental Variables," *Journal of Political Economy*, October 1982, *90*, 895–916.

Kormendi, Roger C., "Government Debt, Government Spending and Private Sector Behavior," *American Economic Review*, December 1983, *73*, 994–1011.

Modigliani, Franco, (1984a) "The Economics of Public Deficits," in *Economic Policy in Theory and Practice* (*Proceedings* of 1984 Pinhas Sapir Conference on Development in Memory of Abba P. Lerner, May 28–30, 1984, Tel-Aviv University), New York: McMillan, forthcoming.

_____, (1984b), "Comment on 'U.S. Deficits Since World War I' by R. J. Barro," presented at Conference on Growth and Distribution: Intergenerational Problems, Uppsala Sweden, June 1984; *Proceedings* forthcoming.

_____ and Steindel, Charles, "Is a Tax Rebate an Effective Tool for Stabilization Policy?," *Brookings Papers on Economic Activity*, 1 : 1977, 175–209.

_____, Jappelli, Tullio and Pagano, Marco, "The Impact of Fiscal Policy and Inflation on National Saving: The Italian Case," *Banca Nazionale del Lavoro Quarterly Review*, June 1985, No. 153, 91–126.

Seater, John J. and Mariano, Roberto S., "New Tests of the Life Cycle and Tax Discounting Hypotheses," *Journal of Monetary Economics*, March 1985, *15*, 195–215.

Sterling, Arlie, "Public Debt and Private Wealth: The Role of Anticipated Taxes," unpublished doctoral dissertation, MIT Sloan School of Management, April 1985.

Tobin, James, *Asset Accumulation and Economic Activity* (Yrjo Jahnssen Lectures), Chicago: University of Chicago Press, 1980.

Errata

Page 1168, equation (1), and all subsequent equations: the summation should run from $i = 0$ to R.

Page 1168, second line in second column: "effect" should read "affect."

Page 1169, equation (2), and the line above equation (4): "G_{t-1}" should be replaced by "G_t."

Page 1169, fourth line of equation (3): the "i-1" upper bound in the double summation should be replaced by "i." The lower bound should read "$j = 0$."

Page 1169: the "s_1" multiplying "G_t" in (3), (5), and (6) should be replaced by "s_0."

Page 1169, equation (4): in the definition of b_i, s_{i+1}" should read "s_i."

Page 1170, eighth line in second paragraph of second column: delete comma following "s_i."

Page 1170: insert close parenthesis on last line of second column.

Page 1171, last line before equation (8): "hypothesis" should read "hypotheses."

Page 1171, second equation: subscript on first term on left side should read "$t+i$" not "$t+1$."

Page 1175, fourth line of the second paragraph in the first column: insert a comma before and after "expenditure."

Page 1175, footnote 6, line 9: "then" should read "than."

Page 1176, fifth line of the first column: "are" should read "is."

Page 1177, seventh line of section V: delete "the" before "wealth."

Page 1179, second line in "consumption" category: replace "or" with "on."

THE GROWTH OF THE FEDERAL DEFICIT AND THE ROLE OF PUBLIC ATTITUDES

ANDRE MODIGLIANI AND
FRANCO MODIGLIANI

Abstract How can the recent explosion in the fiscal deficit of the United States be reconciled with the well-known support of the American public for fiscal conservatism? It is first shown that the reputation for fiscal conservatism is fully supported by public opinion polls dating back over a period of four decades. Solid majorities have consistently opposed tax reductions that might produce an unbalanced budget. Recently, however, the public has also shown strong opposition to increases in taxes to close the fiscal gap, which might appear to imply a new acquiescence to the deficit. But this opposition, too, is shown to have persisted for a long time and to be not logically inconsistent with rejecting tax cuts resulting in deficit. Another fashionable explanation for the deficit holds that the budget process in a democratic society is biased toward deficit because the cost of higher taxes is immediate while the cost of deficit is delayed. But it is inconsistent with the fiscal history of the United States over the last 100 years, which reveals no systematic bias toward deficits, at least until recent years. The major explanation that emerges is that the administration succeeded in misleading the public (and perhaps even itself) into believing that the tax cut would not result in deficit thanks to "supply" and "Laffer curve" effects.

The Issues

Since President Reagan's phased tax-reduction program first began to take effect in 1982, the United States has been incurring federal deficits approaching 5% of the gross national product. It is widely recognized that this wholesale abandonment of orthodox balanced budget policies is building up to one of the most serious economic issues facing the

ANDRE MODIGLIANI is Associate Professor of Sociology at the University of Michigan. FRANCO MODIGLIANI is Institute Professor and Professor of Economics and Finance at the Massachusetts Institute of Technology.

United States. When receipts do not cover current expenditures and the government is forced to tap private saving to make up the difference, the bill is passed on to future generations who will enjoy a smaller after-tax income because of the taxes they will have to pay to service the debt or, equivalently, because of the smaller stock of capital at their disposal. In addition, the deficit has immediate adverse effects by raising interest rates, thereby also causing an appreciation of the exchange rate, which in turn results in a foreign trade deficit.

Actually, the deficits seem to antedate Reagan. According to official statistics, the budget has been in the red every single year since 1970, and in 11 of these 17 years it has exceeded 2% of GNP. This phenomenon is a very surprising one, considering that the American public has long been reputed to be very conservative in fiscal matters and might be expected to elect like-minded representatives (Cantril and Free, 1968; Gallup, 1978:75).

There are two issues that seem worth investigating. First, how well-founded is the public's reputation for fiscal conservatism in the light of evidence provided by public opinion polls. Second, if it is confirmed, then how could such a reckless fiscal policy come into existence and be so passively tolerated for so long.

Evidence of Public Opposition to Deficits

With respect to the issue of fiscal conservatism, one of the striking episodes supporting this proposition goes back to the early presidency of John Kennedy, some 25 years ago. It was during the economic showdown of 1962 that Kennedy, despite some current deficit, proposed a reduction of taxes to stimulate the economy and help restore full employment (Kennedy, 1962). Congressional reaction was far from enthusiastic and, in the end, the president was unable to get his proposal through Congress. It was widely held that this performance reflected the opposition of the public. This is confirmed by the result of a Gallup poll conducted in June 1962. Confronted with the question "Would you favor or oppose a cut in federal income taxes at this time, if a cut meant the government would go further into debt?" fully 72% of those polled were opposed, with only 19% in favor (Gallup, 1972 [Q13][1]).[2]

---

1. All opinion items referred to in the text are listed in the Appendix in chronological order, numbered Q1 to Q28. Both exact wording and marginal distribution are shown.
2. The lopsided opposition to tax cuts seen here is not found on items phrased so as to omit any suggestion that a tax reduction might further unbalance the budget. In September 1963, for example, when Gallup asked simply, "Do you favor or oppose a cut in income taxes now?" 60% indicated they were in favor (Gallup, 1972 [Q16]). Similarly

But the evidence of opposition to tax cuts financed by deficit is by no means limited to the Kennedy episode, as can be inferred from the reply to questions similar to the above which were posed on several occasions prior to 1962. Thus, in August 1946, in connection with the winding down of the war effort, respondents were asked "Which do you think is more important to do in the coming year—balance the budget or cut income taxes?" Seventy-one percent thought it was more important to balance the budget, with only 20% giving priority to the tax cut (Gallup, 1972 [Q1]). The issue was posed again in a pair of 1953 surveys. In the first (January), respondents were asked "If the new Congress finds that it cannot balance the budget for this year and at the same time reduce income taxes, which do you think it should try to do first?" Again, 67% wanted the budget to be balanced first, with only 26% giving priority to a tax cut (Gallup, 1972 [Q8]). In the second survey (July), the question was worded in a somewhat different and more complex fashion, and although there was once again a substantial majority against a tax cut, it was less lopsided—52% opposed and 36% in favor (Gallup, 1972 [Q10]). Thus, at least as far back as 1946 the public showed a consistent, strong opposition to voting itself a tax cut financed by deficit, with the opposition running typically around 70%.

A further indication of opposition to deficit spending is to be found in the public's strong support of a constitutional amendment to balance the federal budget. In a series of surveys conducted between March 1976 and July 1985, the percent in favor of such an amendment was typically between 65% and 81% (Gallup, 1978, 1979; Gallup International, 1980, 1981, 1985 [Q17, Q19, Q20, Q27]). In an analysis of some of these surveys, Blinder and Holtz-Eakin (1984) confirm that support for the amendment is substantially rooted in fiscal conservatism.

Perhaps even more striking evidence of such conservatism comes from responses to three surveys conducted between 1946 and 1956 in which respondents were asked what to do with an actual or potential budget surplus—should it be used to cut taxes or to reduce the national debt? The percentage who favored reducing the debt rather than taxes is amazingly high; it actually represents a plurality in two of the sur-

worded items posed by Katona and his colleagues, between August 1962 and August 1963, produced similar levels of support for a tax cut (Katona et al., 1964:201 [Q14, Q15]). Evidently, alternative wordings that omit reference to potential budget deficits tend to shift the issue from one of *national* well-being to one of *personal* well-being. As Katona notes in a recent review of the 1962–63 period, ". . . the majority of Americans agreed it would be best for *them* to pay lower taxes, but bad for the country. 'I'd like to pay lower taxes' and 'the government can't afford it' were two frequent responses" (Katona, 1981:7). Since in the present paper we are primarily concerned with people's assessment of the national implications of tax cuts rather than with their perception of its purely proximate consequences, and since many people evidently can have both levels in mind, items making explicit reference to potential deficits clearly provide the better indicator.

veys (53% versus 38% in April 1947 and 49% versus 43% in January 1956) and close to half in the other (44% versus 48% in November 1946) (Gallup, 1972 [Q2, Q3, Q11]).

We can conclude, then, that evidence of public opposition to tax cuts leading to deficits is overwhelming. This makes the question of why deficits have recently been so high a very perplexing one.

Are Democratic Governments Deficit-Prone?

Not surprisingly, this question has elicited the interest of several authors and has led to a number of theories. One widely held view is that a bias toward budget deficit is built into our system of budget making and can only be eliminated by adoption of some form of constitutional amendment. The best known advocate of this view, James Buchanan, has asserted, "Fiscal prudence simply cannot be made to pay off in democracy" (Buchanan, 1985:217). The reason is that "deficits allow politicians to increase spending without having directly and forthrightly to raise taxes. There is little obstacle to such a policy. Surpluses, on the other hand, require government to raise taxes without increasing spending—a program far more capable of generating political opposition than budget deficits" (Buchanan and Wagner, 1978:4–5). Furthermore, according to Buchanan the tendency to deficits has greatly increased in the postwar era because of the Keynesian revolution. This is not because Keynes favored deficits, but rather because he overthrew the previous "Victorian fiscal morality" embodied "in the long standing rules for fiscal–monetary prudence . . . [that] were required to hold the tribal instinct in check" (Buchanan, 1985:192).

Unfortunately, these bold hypotheses do not find much support in the historical record of the federal budget. Figure 1 illustrates this point by exhibiting the fiscal deficit or surplus in percent of GNP for the last 100 years (1887 to 1986). It includes every year except major wars (1917–1919 and 1941–1945) and the Great Depression (1931–1940)— leaving a total of 82 years of observations. It is apparent that at least up to 1970, a period of 65 years, there is no evidence whatever of an inherent bias toward deficits. If we call a budget in balance as long as the surplus relative to GNP is within, say, plus or minus one-half of one percent, one finds that in over half of these years—33 out of 65—the budget shows no significant departure from balance. The remaining years include 10 significant deficits, but these are more than offset by no less than 22 years of significant surplus. Clearly, Congress and the administration succeeded pretty well in steering away from deficits. This was in the absence of any constitutional requirement—simply a result of good government and, presumably, of public opinion pressure.

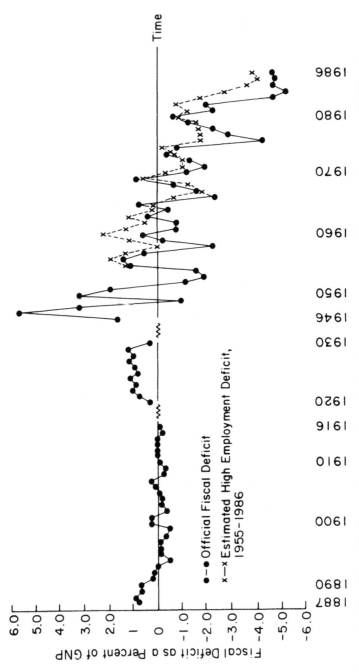

Figure 1. The Fiscal Deficit or Surplus of the United States over the Last Century (Percent of GNP). Sources: *Official Fiscal Deficit: 1887–1954*, U.S. Bureau of the Census, 1971:224 (table, series F1-5), 1104–1105 (table, series Y335–342); *1955–1984*, Eisner 1986:196, table B11; *1985*, Economic Report of the President, 1986, table B78; *1986*, Ibid., estimated from fiscal year deficit. *Estimated High Employment Deficit: 1955–1975*, Eisner, 1986:87, table 8.3, col. 2; *1976–1986*, Holloway, 1986:17, table 6, col. 7.

This story, however, is incomplete in one sense. An examination of the graph will reveal that the frequency of deficits tended to increase in time. Thus, in the 41 years preceding the Great Depression, from 1887 to 1930 (but excluding 1917–1919), there were 27 years of no significant imbalance, or over two-thirds; moreover, there was but one barely significant deficit, while there were 13 years of significant surpluses. Thus, in this initial period there was a definite bias, but in favor of surplus, suggesting an extremely conservative approach to the budget. Between 1946 and 1969 the fiscal stance appears to take a less conservative turn, as there are only 6 years in which the imbalance is less than 1/2 percent and as many as 9 years of deficits in excess of that limit. This would seem consistent with the Buchanan (1985) hypothesis. However, this appearance is misleading because it reflects, at least in part, the striking increase in the variability of the fiscal balance since the end of World War II. But this greater variability, in turn, is but the expected outcome of the enormous growth in the size of the government budget relative to GNP. At the beginning of the period, in 1887, expenditures represented less than 2.5% of GNP, and by 1930 it had grown only to less than 3%. But by 1946 it had jumped to nearly 17.5%. The rise has continued even beyond 1946 but at a modest pace, reaching not quite 25% by the end of the period. The growth implies that the same relative short fall of receipts as compared with outlays would result in a much larger deficit, relative to GNP, in the period after 1946 than before. Thus, to make the pre- and post–World War II figures more nearly comparable, one should broaden the range outside of which an imbalance is regarded as significant. If, accordingly, we raise the limits for a significant imbalance to plus or minus 1%—which corresponds roughly to an imbalance in excess of 5% of expenditure— then one finds that also between 1946 and 1969, 13 years, or more than half, do not show significant imbalances; furthermore, the number of years of significant deficits is down to 5 and is more than balanced by 6 years of significant surplus. In addition, most of the 5 deficits have special causes, as explained below.

However, when we come to the last 16 years, we find a remarkably different story. Even using the 1% standard, significant deficits occur in all but 3 years, without a single year of significant surplus to offset them.

The 1970 Break—A Shift in Public Opinion?

How can one account for this rather abrupt major change? Could it be that a significant shift has occurred between the 1960s and the 1970s in public attitudes in the form of reduced qualms about budget deficits and a concomitant greater willingness to shift the current cost of government to future generations? There is certainly some prima facie support for this hypothesis. A particularly striking piece of evidence is the overwhelming opposition expressed by the public in recent years to higher taxes as a means for reducing the deficit. Thus, as early as November 1981, Gallup confronted respondents with a forecast of a 1982 deficit of $80 to $100 billion and asked them "Do you think there should or should not be an increase Federal Income Taxes to help reduce the deficit?" The reply was an overwhelming rejection of tax increases—70% against versus 19% in favor. Similarly worded questions were asked seven times between January 1983 and January 1986 with rather similar results: the proportion opposing tax increases ranged between 79% and 67%, while that approving was between 14% and 29% (Gallup International, 1983, 1985, 1986 [Q22, Q24, Q28]).

One could readily find a variety of explanations for this recent seeming shift in public attitudes. One appealing explanation could be based on the growth of a social and psychological malaise that Christopher Lasch (1978) has called the "new narcissism." According to this view of the recent evolution of American society, increasing parental ineptitude at raising children has combined with the overwhelming social problems of our contemporary society to breed a new sense of helplessness which, in turn, has produced a compensatory, narcissistic drive oriented to obtaining quick, personal gratification. "We become disinclined to settle for anything less than everything—all at once and at this very moment" (Coles, 1979:104). In the present context, it is the selfish, wholly inconsiderate aspect of narcissism that is of relevance. If this form of social and psychological disturbance has been on the increase, it is clear that those who are under its sway would not be inclined to renounce current gratification even if at the expense of future generations. Attention has also been directed to the recent spread of credit cards that has spawned an enjoy-now–pay-later philosophy.

While these explanations for the change in attitude are ingenious and appealing, we suggest that they can be rejected on one basic ground: as we shall presently show, there is no evidence of significant change in public attitudes toward deficit spending, at least from the early postwar period to the present.

In support of this thesis, we may first note that it would be a mistake to infer, from the recent opposition to tax increases, that the public is not much concerned with the deficit. Between December 1984 and November 1985, when respondents were asked four times whether they felt that the federal budget deficit was a problem for the country, around 80% indicated they regarded it either as very serious (58%) or at least as fairly serious (22%) (Gallup International, 1984, 1985 [Q26]). In

September 1983, and again in May 1984, a similar question asked respondents how great a threat to the economy they felt the deficit was, and again it was found that 76% to 81% felt that it was either a great threat (46%), or at least somewhat of a threat (Gallup International, 1983, 1984 [Q25]).

More direct support for our contention of little change in attitude comes from evidence that the recent overwhelming opposition to higher taxes as the proper way of responding to a deficit (so apparently inconsistent with fiscal conservatism) is not a new phenomenon. As early as October 1949, Gallup asked a question fairly similar to that posed between 1981 and 1984, namely, "President Truman says the United States Government is spending more money than it is taking in and, therefore, federal income taxes must be raised next year. What is your opinion about raising federal income taxes next year?" Only 14% approved the proposal, with 76% rejecting it (Gallup, 1972 [Q5]). Earlier that same year, respondents were asked a basically similar question: Given that the government is now running a deficit and is expected to run an even bigger one next year, "which one of these three things do you think the government should do: (1) increase taxes; (2) cut down on expenses; (3) borrow whatever is necessary. . . ." Only 10% favored increasing taxes. (But interestingly enough, even fewer (9%) chose "borrow"—the overwhelming preference (71%) was "cut expenses" (Gallup, 1972 [Q4]).) A related question was asked some 10 years later in January 1959: "If the time should come when government income cannot pay for all the things in the budget, which would you favor—cutting back on certain things or increasing taxes?" Again, the proportion opting for tax increases was quite low—15%—with 72% favoring reduced expenditures (Gallup, 1972 [Q12]). Thus, the opposition to the use of taxes to close the deficit gap is not at all a novel feature of the last few years. When the question was posed some 30 and 40 years ago, the proportion favoring higher taxes was only between 10% and 15%, even lower than the recent one of 14% to 25%.

Correspondingly, there is evidence that the opposition to tax cuts when they result in a deficit is not limited to the Kennedy era and earlier. Although economic conditions were such that there was little occasion for polling the public on that issue, there is one item, asked in January of 1978, that has the requisite wording: "It has been said that tax cuts would lead to a bigger deficit in the federal budget and make it very difficult for the president to fulfill his promise to balance the budget by 1981. Do you think it is more important to work toward balancing the budget or to cut taxes at this time?" Those opposing cutting taxes again outweighed those favoring it (53% to 39%), although the margin is not quite as overwhelming as in the 1950s and 1960s (Gallup, 1979 [Q18]).

Thus, the evidence seems to point very clearly in the direction of no significant change in the attitude of the public toward public deficits and how to deal with them. Respondents have steadily regarded public deficits as serious and threatening to the future of the economy. They have steadfastly indicated a readiness to forego tax cuts that would result in deficits (sometimes even rejecting tax cuts when the budget was in surplus), *but* they have also overwhelmingly rejected tax increases as a recourse for reducing an existing deficit. But one may ask, "Are not these three sets of declared preferences mutually inconsistent?" It would seem, in particular, that foregoing tax cuts implies that one is willing to sacrifice current income to avoid deficits, while rejecting tax increases means that one is not.

In reality these replies need not be contradictory, and for two reasons. In the first place, those rejecting tax increases need not necessarily prefer a deficit to the loss of income—they might prefer the other possible way of closing the gap, namely, reduce expenditure. And, as was shown above, whenever respondents are given an opportunity to choose this alternative, a very large fraction does so. Furthermore, when the public is confronted with expenditures that are regarded as nonreducible, such as military expenditure for a popularly supported war, then an increase in income taxes tends to receive substantial support. Thus, when in October 1950 respondents were told that "To pay the costs of the Korean war . . . income taxes will have to be raised . . . or the government will have to borrow money and go deeper into debt," 51% thought the government should increase taxes and only 26% thought it should borrow (Gallup, 1972 [Q6]). A similar question asked in February 1951 finds 48% favoring higher taxes versus 24% favoring borrowing (Gallup, 1972 [Q7]).

In the second place, even if rejecting the tax increase meant choosing the deficit, this choice need not be inconsistent with rejecting a tax cut. Indeed, these choices simply imply that most of the public assesses the cost of foregoing a tax cut as being smaller than that of incurring a deficit, which in turn is assessed to be smaller than that of paying more taxes. This ranking is not inconsistent given a set of preferences that attach a high value to the status quo: giving up something one does not now enjoy may be less painful than giving up something one presently enjoys. If so, continuing to shoulder old taxes is less unbearable than shouldering new ones. Facing a deficit presumably lies in between.

These considerations, however, appear to point to a new puzzle. For if the budget-making process does not suffer from an *inherent* bias toward deficits and the public attitude toward deficits has not changed appreciably for many decades, why did the country shift more and more into deficits beginning with the turn of the 1960s?

The Role of Cyclical Factors and Inflation in the 1970–1980 Period

To solve the apparent puzzle, we suggest, to begin with, that despite appearances there really is no significant mystery for the years immediately preceding the Reagan administration, 1970–1980. There are two considerations supporting this assertion. The first is that the official budget figures are not always an accurate indicator of the fiscal stance, especially in the postwar period. Indeed, the difference between receipts and expenditures reflects not only the tax and transfer rates and other expenditures set by Congress, but also the ups and downs of business activity. These determine what receipts and expenditures actually materialize with the given rates. In general, it is known that the instability of the economy will be minimized if tax and transfer rates are not varied to counter the effect of business fluctuations on receipts, thus allowing the budget to go into deficit (or smaller surplus) when there is a contraction. This type of fiscal structure, which acts as a "built-in stabilizer" by causing deficits to rise when activity turns down, has been universally applied in the postwar period. Under these conditions, the most meaningful way to measure the fiscal stance of the government has proved to be the so-called full employment (or structural) surplus, i.e., the amount of surplus (or deficit) that would be generated by the existing tax, transfer, and expenditure structure at a level of income that corresponds roughly to full employment. As it happens, the 1970s, especially after the oil crisis of 1974, were a period of relatively high unemployment leading to substantial cyclical deficit. Correcting for this by replacing the actual deficit in a year with an estimated full employment deficit makes a substantial difference, up to 2½ percentage points in some years.

   This can be seen from Figure 1, in which we represent by x's joined by a dotted line the "full employment" surplus or deficit, beginning with 1955—the first year for which the information is available. It is seen that in terms of this measure in the period 1955–1970, there were but 3 deficits of which only 2 are significant, 1967 and 1968, and these 2 in turn are largely the consequence of war financing in connection with the Vietnam War. By contrast, there still are 7 significant surpluses. This indicates that the Buchanan hypothesis of a post-Keynesian tolerance for fiscal imprudence is rejected by the evidence.

   As for the period 1970–1980, there were deficits in the first five years, but once they are cyclically adjusted, they are insignificant—within the 1% range.

   In the remaining years, however, even the cyclically corrected figures show a deficit that is significant in 5 years out of 6. But there are good reasons why even these deficits might have failed to cause concern. The most important one is the role of inflation. Inflation tends to raise interest rates more or less by the rate of inflation. This, in turn, raises the total interest payment so that, taxes constant, the deficit appears to swell. But in reality the rise in interest rates merely offsets the inflation-induced loss of purchasing power of the debt—which is a loss for the creditor but a gain for the government. Thus, to measure the true interest cost of the government debt, one must subtract from total interest, and hence from the deficit itself, an adjustment equal to the product of the rate of inflation times the (net) debt outstanding. Between 1974 and 1981, inflation was appreciable in this country, running between 6% and 11% per year. Since the federal debt in that period was around one-quarter of GNP, the inflation correction is quite substantial: between 1½ and nearly 3 percentage points. With this correction, the deficit falls within the 1% margin in 10 years out of 11, while the remaining one shows a significant surplus!

We must conclude that up to 1980 the government continued to pursue, by and large, the conservative budget policy which prevailed since last century. This is confirmed by the fact that two common measures of the burden of the national debt, namely the ratio of (gross) debt to GNP and the (net) debt per capita in constant dollars, which began declining at the end of the war, continued their decline from 1970 to 1980, and in the latter year were at or close to their lowest value since the end of the war (Eisner, 1986).

It may be objected that while the public could be expected to have a rough understanding that deficits (and surpluses) of a purely cyclical character can be discounted, it is most doubtful that it would also understand, or know how to estimate, the appropriate correction for inflation. But this is not essential, for even if we confine ourselves to the cyclically adjusted series shown in the chart, it is easy to understand why the deficits even between 1975 and 1980 might not rate as a serious source of public concern: (1) the cyclically adjusted deficits were not very large—at most 2%, (2) some were the result of special measures intended to foster the recovery of the economy, (3) they were consistently decreasing in time so that by 1979 the amount was no longer significant, and (4) the public was occupied with much more serious concerns such as the high rate of unemployment and high inflation. Thus, when the public was asked by the Gallup Poll to indicate which was the most serious problem facing the country between 1970 and 1980, inflation and unemployment were typically mentioned by over 50% of the respondents, while government deficit or debt hardly gets mentioned (never more than 3%) (Gallup, 1980, 1981).

The Reagan Period—How the Explosion Came About

We thus arrive at the most recent years of the Reagan administration, 1981 to 1986. Here the picture is quite different: (1) the unadjusted figures show 6 huge deficits, (2) even the cyclically adjusted figures show 5 significant deficits out of 6, (3) beginning with 1983 the adjusted deficits are larger than any recorded in peacetime years, and (4) they show no sign of abating. The deficit adjusted for inflation, though a bit smaller, shows the same pattern, which is to be expected because inflation abated rapidly after 1981. We see all the indications of a sharp break with the conservative fiscal tradition.

How did such a sudden break come about, without any apparent change in public attitude and under a president whose major election campaign theme had been a crusade against the scourge of public deficits (which, ironically, were not really there, as the chart shows)?

To account for this baffling development, one must unravel two issues: (1) How did the administration and Congress manage, first, to slip into the deficit and then live with it for several years? and (2) Why did the public not rise up and demand an end to policies running counter to its own fiscal conservatism?

The key to the first puzzle seems to be the failure of the administration to realize the magnitude of the fiscal gap implied by the combination of both much lower tax rates and an increase in military expenditures—a failure convincingly depicted by Stockman (1986b) in *The Triumph of Politics*. Nor did it appreciate the difficulties associated with carrying out the cuts in expenditure that would be needed to prevent a further growth of the inherited deficit, especially after major items such as Social Security and interest payments were acknowledged as exempt from cuts. No doubt part of the delay in recognizing the problems came from the Laffer curve delusion: that cutting of taxes would have such a powerful effect on reducing tax evasion, on increasing work incentives, on encouraging both savings and investment, and ultimately on spurring economic expansion, that tax revenue might not fall much or might even increase. In fact, the growth rate turned out to be half as high as predicted, the tax revenue fell pretty much in line with the cut in rates, and, if anything, the saving rate fell. With the rising deficit cutting deeply into national savings, investment was at best maintained, and then only because it was financed by foreign capital, with traumatic consequences for the balance of trade.

Stockman himself gradually began to appreciate the impossibility of balancing the budget, while at the same time holding on to the tax cut. But the White House was not listening to his message, for there was no real willingness to face such unpleasant facts. Indeed, the tax reduction was so ideologically important and so popular that one could not jeopardize it by acknowledging and broadcasting its implications for massive deficits or deep expenditure cuts. As Stockman puts it: "I underestimated how determined [the president] was to stand pat on the tax cut he had originally enacted that was too big" (Stockman, 1986a), and "the truth had been buried . . . deliberately, in order to win the tax battle" (Stockman, 1986b:332). And if in the end the unavoidable big deficit would eventually turn up, it "would become a powerful battering ram forcing Congress to shrink the welfare state" (Stockman, 1986c:59).

By the beginning of 1982 the Council of Economic Advisers, despite its overoptimistic forecasts, had to acknowledge that the administration's tax and expenditure plan was going to create a huge deficit in 1982, almost unmatched in peacetime, and that it would be a long-lasting one, but the Council tried to reassure the public that this deficit would shrink to just over 1% by 1987. To this end, the president was prepared to cut some nondefense expenditure, but he failed to reckon with the fact that this was precisely what Congress was not willing to do—it would rather have raised taxes, unpopular as that might be. But failing that, it would rather put up with a deficit than accept deep cuts in nondefense expenditure. Since taxes could not be raised or defense expenditures cut over the opposition of the president, and nondefense outlays could not be appreciably reduced over the opposition of Congress, living with a deficit became the only feasible compromise—until the situation became unsustainable.

In light of the opinion polls, the public's initial acceptance of a policy of tax reduction after years of official budget deficits is presumably explainable by its trust in a newly elected, conservative leader who had won in a landslide. The administration's argument that the tax cut, through the Laffer curve, would produce a vast improvement in the economy after the sluggish years of the oil crisis, may also have come to be accepted by many. Certainly the public was unaware that the tax reductions would generate enormous deficits, and it did not have any reason to suspect this because the policy was being recommended by a man who projected an image of unswerving opposition to government deficits.

This explains why the tax cut was supported even though, on the basis of opinion polls, the public could be expected to reject a cut avowedly to be financed out of deficits. Once the tax law had been put over and the huge deficits began to make their appearance, the initial failure to push for remedial action can be understood in terms of the asymmetric attitude of the public toward the use of tax reductions and tax increases as ways of warding off deficits. As on previous occasions, the public was just not willing to close the fiscal gap by paying higher taxes. It was this confluence of White House and public opposition that prevented using the most natural remedy to an overdose of tax reductions—namely, reversing the cut.

There are indications that by rejecting a tax increase the public did not mean to endorse the deficit but rather to support cutting of government expenditure. But it is questionable whether there was enough consensus on which expenditures should be slashed and on whether they could be cut deeply enough to close the gap.[3] It is suggestive that when in May 1981 Gallup asked for a reaction to the cuts in spending proposed in the administration's budget—which were of course utterly inadequate to eliminate the deficit—only 12% of those polled thought they were too low as against 34% who labeled them as too high and 46% who viewed them as about right (Gallup International, 1981 [Q21]). In any event, the only program for which cuts have been repeatedly approved by a substantial majority has been National Defense (66% to 57% in favor versus 28% to 36% opposed), which happened to be the president's other sacred cow (Gallup International, 1983, 1985, 1986 [Q22]).

This lack of coherence, both within and between actors, that was needed to repair the harm done by the tax reform of 1981 would seem to explain the paralysis on remedial action that prevailed until 1985. One further cause of the acquiescence is most likely related to the public's failure to comprehend the true damage wrought by the deficit. To be sure, the deficit did produce the expected negative results. Interest rates skyrocketed and the balance of trade showed a massive deterioration, but the public was not led to connect these developments with the burgeoning deficit. Similarly, although the interest paid on the government debt rose substantially, the administration hid this from popular view by not increasing taxes and instead raising the needed revenue by more borrowing, thus further deepening the deficit. While remaining relatively unaware of these negative consequences, the public probably tended to assess the effects of the deficit by using the two indicators most commonly utilized in recent years to judge the performance of the economy: inflation and unemployment. In other words, they assumed that if the deficit was really bad for the economy, both these indicators should increase. Thus, in Gallup polls conducted

3. Recent studies of public attitudes on government spending and taxation fail to provide a coherent picture of the public's willingness to accept budget reductions commensurate with its desire to maintain or decrease levels of taxation. In reviewing a large body of national poll data, Ladd (1979) suggests that there are some major contradictions: "Public attitudes vis-a-vis . . . State . . . taxing and spending are splendidly ambivalent. Specifically, there is real resistance to taxation and real support for the services which taxation provides" (p. 132). On the other hand, Welch (1985), based on a specifically designed study conducted in one Midwestern state, finds that only a small proportion of her respondents favored a "free lunch"—an increase in government services coupled with neither budget reallocation nor an increase in taxes.

in September 1983 and May 1984, some 80% of respondents indicated that they regarded the deficit as a threat to continued economic recovery (Gallup International, 1983, 1984). This inference was, of course, quite wrong—deficits normally have little relation to inflation and should tend, if anything, to raise employment. Thus, when both inflation and unemployment continued to abate after the spurt in deficit spending, this came as no surprise to many economists but did not fit well with the public's stereotype. In addition, the tax reduction contributed to a sense of improved well-being, though this only reflected the "enjoy now, pay later" character of the public deficit. Taken together these factors might be expected to nurture a feeling that the deficit did not, after all, require such urgent mending.

The paralysis was finally broken only by the Gramm-Rudman bill which made the deficit reduction the government's fixed and unchangeable responsibility, to which all other priorities had to be subordinated. One may criticize many aspects of the specific bill, but that concept seems essential to getting out of the fiscal morass.

Summary and Implications

To summarize, the great deficits that began in 1982 are something altogether unparalleled in the fiscal history of the United States, except during major wars and depressions. They therefore cannot be attributed to any failure inherent in our budget-making process that could be overcome only by a balanced budget amendment. Nor can they be attributed to any fundamental change in the attitudes of the public; despite appearances, the opposition to government deficits has remained steadfast and stable as far back as public opinion polls are available. At the same time, though, this opposition does not rank as high as the antagonism to raising taxes as a way of reducing deficits (except in national emergencies).

The way the great leap into the red occurred nonetheless is through the large tax cut of 1981. The public accepted it on the belief, nourished by very persuasive administration arguments, that the tax reform would not be a serious source of deficit because of its powerful evasion-reducing and supply-stimulating effects, and because of generic forthcoming cuts in expenditure. It is somewhat of an open question whether the administration was entirely candid in making these claims or whether, instead, it felt justified in sacrificing candor to the higher goal of cutting taxes. Once the tax cut was enacted and followed by a hefty rise in defense expenditures, the deficit became evident, but no effective action to eliminate it could be pieced together because of the resistance to tax increases, the profound divisions about what expenditures could and could not be cut, and the failure of the public to understand properly the costs of the deficit.[4]

Is there a lesson for the American people in this experience? One might suggest two. First, the American public should learn to mistrust extravagant claims about being able to have one's cake and eat it too, such as have been pushed by the administration and other prophets of the Laffer curve. Second, it should be leery of tax cuts until there is a surplus to be distributed, or until one is clearly in the making, through policies which have ample consensus.

References

Blinder, Alan S., and Douglas Holtz-Eakin (1984)
  "Public opinion and the balanced budget." American Economic Review Papers and Proceedings, May, pp. 144–149.
Buchanan, James M. (1985)
  Liberty, Market and State. New York: New York University Press.
Buchanan, James M., and Richard E. Wagner (1978)
  Fiscal Responsibility in Constitutional Democracy. Studies in Public Choice, Vol. 1. Boston: Martinus Nijhoff Social Sciences Division, Leiden.
Cantril, Hadley, and Lloyd A. Free (1968)
  The Political Beliefs of Americans. New York: Simon and Schuster.
Coles, Robert (1979)
  "Unreflecting egotism." The New Yorker 55 (August 27): 98ff.
Economic Report of the President (1986).
Eisner, Robert (1986)
  How Real Is the Federal Deficit? New York: The Free Press.
Gallup, George F. (1972)
  The Gallup Poll: Public Opinion 1935–1971. New York: Random House.
———— (1978)
  The Gallup Poll: Public Opinion 1972–1977. Wilmington, DE: Scholarly Resources.
———— (1979–1982)
  The Gallup Poll. (One volume per year.) Wilmington, DE: Scholarly Resources.
Gallup International (1965–)
  Gallup Opinion Index/Gallup Political Index/Gallup Report. (Monthly, June 1965–.) Princeton: American Institute of Public Opinion.
Holloway, Thomas M. (1986)
  "Cyclically adjusted federal budget and federal debt: Revised and updated estimates." Survey of Current Business 66 (March):11–17.
Katona, George (1981)
  "The lessons of the 1964 tax cut: Will they apply today?" Public Opinion 4:7–9.
Katona, George, Charles A. Lininger, and Eva Mueller (1964)
  1963 Survey of Consumer Finances. Ann Arbor, MI: Survey Research Center, Institute for Social Research.
Kennedy, John F. (1962)
  Economic Report of the President. Washington: U.S. Government Printing Office.

4. Paul E. Peterson (1985) concurs with our conclusion that the great leap in deficit financing must be laid on the shoulders of the administration rather than on any chronic shortcoming of the system. However, his conclusion rests more on the fact that "Congress seems to defer to the President on fiscal policy" than on the administration's success in misleading the public (and perhaps itself).

Ladd, Everett (1979)
    "The polls: Taxing and spending." Public Opinion Quarterly 43:126–135.
Lasch, Christopher (1978)
    The Culture of Narcissism: American Life in an Age of Diminishing Expectations.
    New York: Norton.
Peterson, Paul E. (1985)
    "The new politics of deficits." Political Science Quarterly 100:575–600.
U.S. Bureau of the Census (1971)
    Statistical History of the United States. New York: Basic Books.
Stockman, David (1986a)
    As interviewed on Larry King Live! CNN, April 24.
——— (1986b)
    The Triumph of Politics. New York: Harper & Row.
——— (1986c)
    "The triumph of politics." Newsweek 107 (April 21): 40ff.
Welch, Susan (1985)
    "The 'more for less' paradox: Public attitudes on taxing and spending." Public
    Opinion Quarterly 49:310–316.

Appendix: Opinion Items Referred to in the Text

(From Gallup Polls Unless Otherwise Noted)

Q1 (8/46): Will you tell me what is meant by "balancing the federal budget"?

Generally correct answer	49%
Incorrect answer	51

(Asked of those giving generally correct answers) Some people say that if we're going to balance the federal budget we've got to keep income taxes at the present rates. Others say it is more important to cut income taxes than to balance the budget. Which do you think is more important to do in the coming year—balance the budget or cut income taxes?

Balance budget	71%
Cut income taxes	20
No opinion	9

Q2 (11/46): Do you think the new Congress should reduce income taxes in 1947, or should this wait until some of the national debt has been paid off?

Wait	44%
Cut taxes	48
No opinion	8

Q3 (4/47): The United States to-day has a billion dollar surplus in its running expenses. Should this money be used to reduce income taxes, or should it be used to reduce the national debt?

Reduce debt	53%
Cut taxes	38
No opinion	9

Q4 (5/49): As you know, the government in Washington is now spending more money than it is taking in. The outlook for next year is that still more money will be spent than is taken in. In view of this, which one of these three things [on card] do you think the government should do: (1) increase taxes; (2) cut down on expenses; (3) borrow whatever is necessary—that is, increase the national debt?

Increase taxes	10%
Cut expenses	71
Borrow	9
No opinion	10

Q5 (10/49): President Truman says the United States Government is spending more money than it is taking in and, therefore, federal income taxes must be raised next year. What is your opinion about raising federal income taxes next year?

Against it, don't like it, opposed	46%
Taxes already too high	22
Cut government expenses instead	8
General approval: if needed, Truman probably right	14
Miscellaneous	6
No opinion	7

Q6 (10/50): Congress voted recently to increase taxes for all taxpayers. To pay the costs of the Korean War and our defense program, income taxes will have to be raised even more or the government will have to borrow money and go deeper into debt. Which do you think the government should do—increase income taxes still more, or borrow more money?

Borrow	26%
Increase taxes	51
Other answers	9
No opinion	14

Q7 (2/51): Our government in Washington plans to spend this coming year about $25 billion more than was spent last year for national defense. How do you, yourself, think this additional money for defense should be raised—mostly by an increase in personal income taxes, or mostly by borrowing money to be paid back later?

Borrowing	24%
Increasing taxes	48
Other	14
No opinion	14

Q8 (1/53): If the new Congress finds that it cannot balance the budget for this year and at the same time reduce income taxes, which do you think it should try to do first?

Balance the budget	67%
Reduce taxes	26
No opinion	7

Q9 (2/53): Some members of Congress argue that federal income tax should be cut ten percent beginning this July 1. Others argue that income taxes should not be cut until the budget is balanced. With which side do you agree?

Balance budget first	69%
Cut taxes first	25
No opinion	6

Q10 (7/53): The Republicans have said they will cut personal income taxes and business taxes next January. Some people say that if this is done, the budget could not be balanced. If this is the case, should taxes be cut in January or not?

Should not be cut	52%
Should be	36
No opinion	12

Q11 (1/56): If the government has any money left over after paying expenses, should this money be used to reduce the national debt or to reduce income taxes?

Reduce debt	49%
Reduce taxes	43
No opinion	8

Q12 (1/59): If the time should come when government income cannot pay for all the things in the budget, which would you favor—cutting back on certain things or increasing taxes?

Favor cutting back	72%
Favor increased taxes	15
No opinion	13

Q13 (6/62): Would you favor or oppose a cut in federal income taxes at this time, if a cut meant the government would go further into debt?

Oppose tax cut	72%
Favor	19
No opinion	9

Q14 (8/62): [Survey Research Center, Survey of Consumer Finances] President Kennedy proposed that income taxes should be reduced next year; what do you think of this proposal?

Good idea	65%
Bad idea	19
Depends	7
Don't know	9

Q15 (5/63): [Survey Research Center, Survey of Consumer Finances] Our government is considering a proposal to reduce income taxes next year; what do you think of this proposal?

	5/63	*8/63*
Good idea	65%	68%
Bad idea	17	11
Depends	4	7
Don't know	14	14

Q16 (9/63): Have you read or heard about the Kennedy proposal to reduce income taxes?

Yes	52%
No	48

(Asked of those who had read or heard about the proposal) How do you, yourself, feel? Do you favor or oppose a cut in income taxes now?

Favor	60%
Oppose	29
No opinion	11

Q17 (3/76): Would you favor or oppose a constitutional amendment that would require Congress to balance the federal budget each year, that is, keep taxes and expenditures in balance?

	3/76	6/78	2/79
Favor	78%	81%	78%
Oppose	13	11	12
No opinion	9	8	10

Q18 (1/78): It has been said that tax cuts would lead to a bigger deficit in the federal budget and make it very difficult for the president to fulfill his promise to balance the budget by 1981. Do you think it is more important to work toward balancing the budget or to cut taxes at this time?

Work toward balancing budget	53%
Cut taxes	39
Don't know	8

Q19 (3/80): A proposed amendment to the constitution would require Congress to approve a balanced federal budget each year. Government spending would have to be limited to no more than expected revenues, unless a three-fifths majority of Congress voted to spend more than expected revenue. Would you favor or oppose this amendment to the constitution?

Favor	67%
Oppose	13
Don't know	20

Q20 (4/81): Have you read or heard about the proposal for a constitutional amendment which would require the federal government to balance the national budget each year? A proposed amendment to the constitution would require Congress to approve a balanced federal budget each year. Government spending would have to be limited to no more than expected revenues unless a three-fifths majority of Congress voted to spend more than expected revenue. Would you favor or oppose this amendment to the constitution?

	4/81	9/81
Favor	65%	67%
Oppose	21	19
No opinion	14	14

Q21 (5/81): The Reagan Administration has called for cuts in the federal budget in a number of areas. Do you feel that the total amount of spending cuts that the Reagan Administration wants to make is too high, too low, or about the right amount?

Too high	34%
Too low	12
About right	46

Q22 (4/85): At present the federal budget deficit is running at the rate of over 200 billion dollars per year. Basically, there are only a few ways this deficit can be reduced. Please tell me whether you approve of each of the following ways to reduce the deficit. Cut defense spending? Cut spending for social programs? Raise income taxes? Cut entitlement programs?

	1/83			
	Cut Defense	Cut Soc. Prog.	Raise Taxes	Cut Entit. Prog.
Approve	57%	41%	18%	12%
Disapprove	36	52	77	83
No opinion	7	7	5	5
	12/84			
Approve	61%	41%	23%	11%
Disapprove	32	52	72	84
No opinion	7	7	5	5
	4/85			
Approve	66%	39%	18%	9%
Disapprove	28	55	76	87
No opinion	6	6	6	4
	1/86			
Approve	59%	42%	22%	9%
Disapprove	33	51	73	88
No opinion	8	7	5	3

Q23 (11/81): Economists are now predicting that there will be an 80 to 100 billion dollar deficit in the Federal budget for fiscal 1982. Do you think there should or should not be an increase in Federal income taxes to help reduce this deficit?

Should not be an increase in taxes	70%
Should be	19
No opinion	11

Q24 (9/83): It is estimated that the Federal government's budget deficit for fiscal 1984 will be as much as $200 billion—that is, it will spend more than it takes in—unless some steps are taken to reduce the size of the deficit. Do you approve or disapprove of raising income taxes as a way of reducing the deficit?

Disapprove of raising taxes	79%
Approve	14
No opinion	7

Q25 (9/83): For each item on this list, please tell me whether you think it will be a great threat, somewhat of a threat, or not much of a threat to continued recovery of the economy. The federal government's budget deficit?

	9/83	*5/84*
Great threat	42%	50%
Somewhat	34	31
Not much	13	10
No opinion	11	9

Q26 (12/84): In your opinion, is the current Federal budget deficit a very serious problem for the country, a fairly serious problem, not a serious problem, or is this something you haven't thought much about?

	12/84	*4/85*	*8/85*	*11/85*
Very serious	57%	58%	57%	61%
Fairly serious	21	23	21	23
Not serious	2	5	2	3
Haven't thought about	20	12	20	12

Q27 (8/85): Under a proposed constitutional amendment, any federal budget passed by Congress would have projected tax revenues that are equal to projected government spending unless a three-fifths majority of Congress voted not to do so. Would you favor or oppose this amendment to the constitution?

Favor	49%
Oppose	27
No opinion	24

Q28 (8/85): Would you approve or disapprove of raising personal income taxes to reduce the federal budget deficit?

	8/85	*11/85*
Disapprove	68%	67%
Approve	25	29
No opinion	7	4

Fiscal Policy and Saving in Italy since 1860

FRANCO MODIGLIANI AND TULLIO JAPPELLI

I INTRODUCTION

In this chapter we use more than a century of Italian data to study the determinants of consumption and saving and, in particular, the extent to which they are affected by fiscal policy. More than ten years ago, Barro (1974) set forth the proposition – referred to hereafter as the Ricardian equivalence proposition (REP) – that the choice of financing a deficit by borrowing instead of by taxation is of no practical importance, since agents can be expected to incorporate in their budget equation the present value of all future tax liabilities implied by current deficits and therefore private saving will rise by exactly the same amount as the increase in deficit. As a consequence, national saving and the rate of capital accumulation are unaffected.

Completely different implications for the behaviour of national saving can be derived within the framework of the life cycle hypothesis (LCH), according to which consumption will in general respond to the way a given level of government consumption is financed. In particular, an increase in government deficit due to a switch from taxation to borrowing will reduce national saving because consumption will in general increase in response to a tax cut, so that private saving will not increase enough to compensate for the decrease in government saving.

Another related issue is whether crowding out of national saving can result also through inflation illusion – because the public regards as income some portion of government interest payments which represent an inflation premium, i.e. a compensation for the inflation erosion of the outstanding stock of government debt. Since government interest enters the private sector budget equation only as a component of net taxes, and since, under REP, net taxes have no effect whatever on consumption, it follows that inflation could also not affect saving, at least through this channel. But under the LCH, where net taxes have a major influence on consumption – given before tax income – if the inflation premium is regarded as part of perceived government interest income, and, accordingly, nominal interest transfers result in a fall in perceived net taxes, the outcome may very well be a significant rise in consumption and crowding out of capital formation at least for a while in the short run. Hence, testing for possible effects on consumption of the inflation premium component of nominal rates is of major interest both as a test of the relevance of REP and for an understanding of the consequences of inflation. Note that an effect of the inflation premium on consumption is sufficient to reject REP, but a lack of this effect requires only absence of inflation illusion, and hence is not inconsistent with the LCH.

While in this study we focus primarily on the determinants of saving, our empirical tests are based on a consumption function because consumption, as opposed to saving, can be measured independently from the definition of income, and thus permits testing for the effect of inflation.

In recent years a number of empirical tests have been performed to investigate these issues, mainly using US data. Although some (notably Kormendi, 1983;[1] Seater and Mariano, 1985) have found support for the neutrality proposition, most of the recent empirical analysis (for example Feldstein, 1982; Modigliani, 1984; Modigliani and Sterling, 1985) have rejected it and found evidence in favour of the LCH. In a recent study (Modigliani et al., 1985) we have used Italian postwar yearly data to test whether substituting debt for taxes has any effect on national saving and whether private consumption responds to the nominal portion of government interest payments. We found that the response of consumption to deficit has been fairly small in the Italian postwar experience; we also estimated that when one corrects for the effect of inflation and for government investment, the rise in deficit in recent years is small if compared to the change in the commonly quoted unadjusted deficit. However, due to multicollinearity of the data, we had to leave the issue of inflation illusion open for further research.

In this chapter we propose to carry out a similar test, but using a much larger data set that covers more than 100 years of Italian history which include wide variations in the rate of saving. Although the data that we have used before 1950 are undoubtedly less reliable, we hope that they constitute at least an approximation to the behaviour of the most important Italian economic variables, and that they can help to shed some light on the issues under investigation. We also feel that the present analysis of the consumption function, using an unusual set of data, can be of value in putting today's economic problems in a historical perspective.

The chapter is organized as follows: in section II we lay out the specification of the model to be estimated. Section III describes the data used in the estimation, sections IV and V report parameter estimates and tests of hypotheses. Finally, section VI utilizes the estimates to account for the historical behaviour of national saving.

II A GENERAL FORMULATION OF THE CONSUMPTION FUNCTON

In the standard model of intertemporal utility maximization, the problem of a consumer choosing a consumption plan that maximizes utility subject to a lifetime budget constraint, will lead to the following first order conditions:

$$C = a(H + W) \tag{6.1}$$

where H and W are human and non-human wealth respectively, and a depends on the rate of time preference, age, the rate of interest and the form of the utility function. Using the notion that human wealth can be expressed as the present discounted value of labour income net of the present discounted value of net taxes over the lifetime of the consumer, Sterling (1985) and Modigliani and Sterling (1985) have derived the following specification of the consumption function, in which expectational variables are expressed in terms of present and past values of observable variables:

$$
\begin{aligned}
C &= \sum_{i=0}^{-n} a_i (\mathrm{NNP}_i - T_i) + bW + cD + \sum_{i=0}^{-n} d_i G_i \\
&= \sum_{i=0}^{-n} a_i \mathrm{NNP}_i - \sum_{i=0}^{-n} (a_i + d_i) T_i + \sum_{i=0}^{-n} d_i E_i + bW + cD
\end{aligned} \tag{6.2}
$$

Here NNP is net national product, T is taxes net of all transfers (including government interest payments corrected for actual inflation), W is the stock of private wealth (inclusive of government debt D), G is the current account government deficit, and E is government expenditure. The second equality follows from the identity $G = E - T$.

The parameters

$$c \quad \text{and} \quad \sum_{i=0}^{-n} d_i$$

depend on the age structure of the population, on the length of the planning horizon and on the personal discount and interest rates (see Sterling, 1985). One limiting case of equation 6.2 corresponds to the case when the planning horizon of the individual is infinite. In this case the coefficients

$$\sum_{i=0}^{-n} d_i$$

can be shown to be equal to the negative of the coefficient of income

$$\sum_{i=1}^{-n} a_i$$

and the coefficient of debt to equal the negative of that of wealth. As a result, the tax variable disappears, and equation 6.2 reduces to

$$C = \Sigma a_i (\mathrm{NNP}_i - E_i) + b(W - D) \qquad (6.3)$$

But this limiting case is basically the one that underlies Barro's derivation of REP. He effectively assumes that individuals have an infinite planning horizon because in his model generations are connected by an infinite chain of intergenerational bequests. It is therefore not coincidence that equation 6.3 exhibits the basic characteristics of the REP: private consumption (a) depends on the physical product of the society net of the portion used up by the government; and (b) is independent of how E is financed. For the same reason that deficits do not affect consumption, government debt is not part of net wealth, since the infinite lived consumer correctly anticipates the future taxes that the government will raise in order to repay the principal and the interest on its obligations.

On the other hand, consider the case of a myopic consumer, whose planning horizon is effectively zero, and who therefore does not take into account the future taxes implied by current deficits; in this particular case, the coefficient of deficit (Σd_i) will be zero, as well as the coefficient c of government debt, so that the general model equation 6.2 reduces to

$$C = \Sigma a_i(\mathrm{NNP}_i - T_i) + bW \qquad (6.4)$$

which is the standard specification of the consumption function.

It should by now be apparent that from the LCH perspective in which individuals are recognized to have a life planning horizon, Σd_i should fall between Σd_i and 0, i.e. consumption should depend on net taxes as well as on government consumption. In assessing the size of the deficit coefficient (Σa_i), the following considerations are paramount:

- the planning horizon of the individual is not likely to exceed greatly the average length of life, and it is possible that it is much shorter; this is true even allowing for bequests, as long as they are of limited importance, and the utility of the donor is not generally determined by that of the beneficiary (Modigliani, 1984);
- if some individuals are liquidity constrained, they will respond by increasing consumption one for one in response to a tax cut, and this will lead consumption, in the aggregate, to respond to deficit and taxes;
- in the presence of imperfect capital markets, and when the rate at which individuals can borrow exceeds the rate at which they can lend, the government can effectively change the budget constraint faced by individuals, by opening (or by rendering more favourable) the possibility of trading current for future consumption; in this case one should expect a tax cut financed by borrowing to increase current consumption and not only saving.

For these reasons, we expect that, although in principle consumption should respond negatively to the government deficit for a given level of taxes (or, equivalently, to government consumption as well as taxes), the coefficient Σd_i should be rather small in absolute value, and far from the negative of the coefficient of income implied by the infinite horizon REP. Similarly, the coefficient of government debt – once wealth is defined to include debt – might be negative, in that consumers probably respond at least partially to the future liabilities implied by the current outstanding debt, but well below the coefficient of wealth in absolute value.

To summarize, both the REP and the 'limited horizon' for inflation (LH–LCH) belong to the same LCH family and imply the same form of consumption function, namely equation 6.2. Both models imply that consumption should be reduced by a deficit, given taxes ($\Sigma d_i < 0$), or, equivalently, by taxes and government consumption. The difference lies in the relation between the coefficients of the variables that are assumed to affect consumption: REP implies that Σd_i should come close to minus the income coefficient Σa_i, while LH–LCH suggests a value much closer to zero so that taxes matter most. Similarly, REP implies that the coefficient of debt should equal minus that of wealth, while for LCH this coefficient should be around zero (or possibly somewhat positive, see below).

So far, we have neglected the second issue that we propose to investigate, namely the question of whether consumers suffer from inflation illusion or are instead capable of distinguishing that part of interest income (and deficit) that is purely a compensation for the inflation losses (gains) suffered in periods of inflation (deflation). This is because we have lumped in the definition of net taxes, T, all transfers (and therefore both the positive transfers represented by nominal interest payments (RD) and the negative transfers represented by the inflation loss on government obligations (pD)). Therefore, our definition of disposable income ($NNP - T$) and current account deficit have been both adjusted for inflation and do not correspond to the conventional measures of national accounts. This formulation implies that consumers are rational and therefore consumption responds to *real* interest payments, and that, in principle, the response is the same as to any other component of taxes and transfers. That response is given by the sum of the coefficients of income and deficit ($\Sigma a_i + \Sigma d_i$). However, since in periods of high and volatile inflation, consumers cannot instantly adjust for the current inflation rate which cannot be directly observed or reliably gauged, consumption might be expected to respond to some measure of expected inflation, or equivalently, to the expected real rate, rather than to the actual one. Moreover, one can think of the expected real rate as the sum of two components, the permanent rate, that should reflect very long-run expectations and be rather stable, and the transitory deviations of the expected real rate from the permanent one; it is for this reason that the propensity to consume out of current expected real interest payments may well be different (lower) than the propensity to consume out of other forms of (net) transfers and that debt might have a positive coefficient reflecting the 'permanent' real rate (cf. Modigliani et al., 1985, section 1). In addition, one should allow for the possibility that consumers suffer from inflation illusion and thus base their consumption decisions on the *nominal* interest earned on the national debt, largely disregarding the loss of principal due to inflation.

In order to assess the actual effect of inflation on consumption, we define net taxes ($T^* = T + (R - p)D = T - rD$) as the sum of direct and indirect taxes minus all transfers except interest, and denote by $r^eD = (R - p^e)D$ the expected real interest payments on government debt. We can then rewrite equation 6.2 as

$$C = \Sigma a_i(NNP_i - T_i^*) + bW + cD + \Sigma d_i G_i^* + fRD + hp^eD \quad (6.5)$$

where $G^* = E - T^*$. We therefore propose to test for the presence of inflation illusion by decomposing the expected real interest bill in nominal interest payments and expected depreciation of the stock of public debt. Full rationality requires $f = -h$, while in the case of complete inflation illusion $h = 0$. Any significant value of h between zero and $-f$ would imply that all consumers suffer from *some* inflation illusion (or that some proportion is affected by complete inflation illusion while others still act rationally).

If, in addition, the response of consumption to the expected real interest income $(r^c D)$ is the same as all other forms of income and taxes, then f could reach a value of $(\Sigma a_i + \Sigma d_i)$; as noted before, due to the variability of inflation, f may well be lower than $(\Sigma a_i + \Sigma d_i)$ and, in principle, even be negative if the substitution effect prevails over the income effect.

There are some straightforward implications that can be derived from the consumption function equation 6.5 for the behaviour of national saving; since the latter is defined as $S_T = \text{NNP} - C - E$, using the identity $E = G^* + T^*$ and turning equation 6.5 in an aggregate saving function, we obtain

$$S_T = [(\text{NNP} - T^*) - \Sigma a_i(\text{NNP}_i - T^*)] - (G_i^* + \Sigma d_i G_i^*) \qquad (6.6)$$
$$- bW - cD - fRD - hp^c D$$

From equation 6.6 it can be seen that under the REP hypothesis $\Sigma a_i = -\Sigma d_i$, $f = 0$, $c = -b$ and, presumably, $h = 0$, so that equation 6.6 reduces to

$$S_T = [(NNP - E) - \Sigma a_i(NNP_i - E_i)] - b(W - D) \qquad (6.7)$$

and neither taxes, debt nor inflation are seen to affect the behaviour of the national saving rate which, accordingly, depends only on government consumption and on wealth other than government debt.

On the other hand, in the LH–LCH model one expects the sum of coefficients Σd_i to be negative, but fairly small, so that the effect of an increase in government deficit, given income net of taxes, is to crowd out saving by close to a dollar per dollar. If, in addition, there is complete rationality, $h = -f$ and the last two terms of equation 6.6 collapse in $-fr^c D$; if, instead, there is complete inflation illusion, $h = 0$ and S_T depends only on the nominal rate, fRD. Thus, the LH–LCH recognizes a significant role for each of these variables, deficit, government debt, government interest, and possibly, for inflation.

As mentioned above, in our previous paper, because of the collinearity of data and the limited number of observations, we were not able to establish conclusively whether the observed behaviour reflected rational consumers' response to the fluctuations of real interest rates or the irrational response of consumers suffering from inflation illusion. The present study, in which we make use of a much larger data set, was intended in part to provide more reliable evidence and more precise estimates of the parameters of interest.

III PRESENTATION OF THE DATA

As operational definitions, income $Y^*(= NNP - T^*)$ is defined as private disposable income net of real interest payments, deficit $G^*(= E - T^*)$ is the current account deficit net of real interest payments, consumption includes expenditure on durables, beginning of period net wealth includes the stock of government debt, interest payments do not include payments to foreigners.

The Appendix contains a detailed explanation of the definition and sources of the variables used in the estimation for the period 1862–1950 (except for wealth, available only after 1882); afterwards we have used the same data set as used by Modigliani et al. (1985), with the only exception of government debt, for which a newly published series, elaborated by Spaventa et al. (1984), has been used.

Although we have tried to preserve consistency among the different series and definitions, in many cases the variables are not strictly comparable; in fact, the major differences between them are:

- wealth is defined as the sum of the stock of capital and government debt from 1882 to 1950, whereas afterwards it includes also currency in circulation;[2]
- government debt, which ideally should result from the consolidated balance sheets of the central and local governments, before 1950 only includes the debt of the central government (net of government claims), but does not take into account – unless reflected in the balance sheet of the central government – the debt of local institutions, government agencies, social security funds and public enterprises (included in the series elaborated by Spaventa);
- similarly, government deficit, for which we have relied on the work of Repaci (1962) because it was consistent with the definition of disposable income provided by Ercolani (1969), only includes the deficit of the central government. However, a portion of these expenditures, such as those that financed investment of government enterprises, cannot be considered as current expenses. The issue is relevant because, according to REP, it is only current consumption expenditure (as opposed to capital investment) that reduces private consumption. Since it is not easy to assess the magnitude of these expenses, we rely on two definitions of deficit, the one measured by Repaci and another that excludes most capital expenses (G_1) from the government budget, but may exclude also some items that are truly government consumption.[3]

To summarize, it can be seen that the fiscal variables are all biased in the same direction (namely, they only consider the central government in the years preceding 1950). However, considering that local institutions and government agencies have grown in importance mostly within the last decades, we hope that our measures will not be seriously distorted.

In table 6.1 we present average values for the entire period and selected subperiods of a number of variables expressed as a percentage of private income as conventionally measured ($Y^* + RD$). Column (1) reports consumption; (2) wealth; (3) debt; (4) current account government deficit; (5) government investment; (6) nominal interest payments; and (7) inflation losses on government debt. In column (8) we also report the national saving rate (relative to NNP), and in columns (9) and (10) the consumption and the deficit to income ratio corrected for actual inflation loss (pD). Finally, in columns (11) and (12) we report the average inflation rate (measured as the rate of depreciation of the deflator of private consumption) and the average rate of growth of real NNP.

The swings of many of the variables (even though averaged over many years) are very remarkable, reflecting the length of the period of observations, the presence of two major wars and the succession of different regimes and economic and political institutions. The period that runs from 1862 until the turn of the century is essentially characterized by economic stagnation (with the exception of a period of moderate growth in the 1880s, followed by a deep depression). At the same time, there were government deficits (including public investments). The combined effect of these deficits, fuelled in part by high interest rates, plus the inheritance by the new Italian State of the old obligations of the pre-existing States, caused the burden of the public debt to increase enormously until the end of the century, by which time it had doubled since the beginning of the 1880s.

The years between 1897 and 1907 represented, in all respects, the period of most rapid growth that the Italian economy had experienced; following the growth in income, private saving increased for the first time above the average of 3.3 per cent of the previous period to an average of 10.2 per cent of disposable income in the first decade of the century.

The combination of balanced budgets at the beginning of the century, some inflation and income growth, in turn resulted in a substantial decline of the national debt to income ratio during the period immediately preceding the First World War (1908–14), a period which is similar in many respects to the previous decade of rapid growth and high propensities to save on the part of the private sector.

Table 6.1

Periods	C (1)	W (2)	D (3)	G*+RD (4)	G_i (5)	RD (6)	pD (7)	S_T/NNP (8)	C/Y (9)	G/Y (10)	Inflation (11)	NNP Growth (12)
1864–1896	96.4	—	1.03	0.1	1.8	4.8	0.8	3.3	96.7	-0.1	0.6	-0.1
1897–1907	91.4	14.0	1.12	-2.4	2.1	4.8	0.8	10.2	92.3	-3.3	0.9	2.4
1908–1914	89.7	3.6	0.80	-1.9	2.7	2.8	1.4	11.2	91.0	-3.3	1.9	1.3
1915–1918	80.7	2.7	0.58	22.5	1.5	2.3	12.8	-3.1	92.8	11.3	31.2	1.5
1919–1923	88.8	3.4	0.81	16.2	2.5	3.5	6.1	-4.7	95.3	10.2	11.6	0.0
1924–1939	91.4	4.1	0.93	2.8	3.1	4.5	0.2	5.2	91.8	2.3	0.9	0.1
1940–1945	90.7	3.6	0.76	28.1	1.7	3.6	24.8	-17.7	121.7	4.1	68.1	11.4
1946–1950	89.8	3.1	0.25	2.0	9.3	1.2	3.9	7.5	93.4	-2.0	24.0	11.0
1951–1963	84.0	3.1	0.22	-2.5	—	1.6	0.7	16.0	84.6	-3.2	3.4	6.5
1964–1982	78.9	3.2	0.35	3.8	—	3.7	3.7	15.0	82.0	0.2	10.9	3.5
1981–1982	79.1	3.7	0.51	10.2	—	8.9	7.7	9.5	85.7	2.7	17.8	1.0
1864–1950	93.2	2.9	0.92	1.4	2.7	4.2	0.8	5.0	94.2	0.4	2.9	0.6
1950–1982	81.3	3.1	0.30	1.4	—	2.8	2.4	15.2	83.0	-1.0	7.7	4.6
1864–1982	89.6	3.0	0.75	1.3	—	3.8	1.3	8.2	90.9	-0.2	4.4	1.7

Period average of: the propensity to consume (1), wealth (2), debt (3), deficit (4), government investment (5), nominal interest payments (6), and inflation losses on government debt (7) relative to income as conventionally measured in the national accounts (Y*+RD). National saving ratio as a percentage of NNP (8), propensity to consume (9) and deficit income ratio (10) corrected for actual inflation (pD), average inflation (11) and average rate of growth of real per-capita NNP (12). The periods 1864–1950 and 1864–1982 exclude the war years.

At first glance it seems that the propensity to consume falls also in the years immediately following, corresponding to the First World War, characterized by huge deficits (column (4)) and high inflation (almost 300 per cent in the years 1916–20). But if one corrects income for *ex-post* inflation, the average propensity to consume actually rose moderately during the First World War and the period 1919–23. The inflation resulted in very large negative real rates which in turn contributed greatly to reducing the huge nominal deficits of column (4) – see column (10) – and to contain the fall in national saving (column (8)) and to reduce substantially the debt ratio (column (3)).

During the fascist period, and up to the Second World War, the propensity to consume continues to average around 90 per cent of disposable income, but because of huge government deficits – especially at the end of the 1930s in preparation for the Second World War – government debt climbs back to historically high levels, national saving falls back to the low levels of the previous century, while growth also shrinks to zero. With the Second World War, there is a large decline in output while the high inflation rate reduces drastically the debt to income ratio by about 75 per cent.

The 1950s and early 1960s are characterized by unprecedentedly rapid growth, accompanied by a high propensity to save, a decline in the wealth to income ratio, government surpluses and a stable (and low, from an historical point of view) relation of debt to income.

In the last period, beginning in the mid 1960s, the propensity to consume appears to decrease further and very substantially (to an average of 78.9 per cent), but if one looks at column (9) where consumption is divided by income corrected for the *ex-post* inflation loss, it appears that the reduction is really not striking, and that by the 1980s we actually observe an increase in the corrected propensity to consume. At the same time, the debt to income ratio started to rise again at the end of the 1960s and reached, at the beginning of the 1980s, a value more than twice as high as it was in the 1950s and at the beginning of the 1960s. Spaventa et al. (1984) have estimated that it has reached a value as high as 66.5 per cent of GNP in 1984 and could be as high as 80 per cent by 1988.

In some circumstances, the government was able to reduce the burden of the public debt by relying on the inflation tax through negative interest rates (as in the two postwar periods); in others, as at the beginning of the century, the debt to income ratio diminished because the economy was experiencing a period of fast and steady growth. Today the prospect of a rate of growth of the economy higher than the real interest rate is particularly uncertain. In addition to this fact, it seems that the government has lost its ability to obtain credit at substantially negative real rates.

This can best be seen by looking at figure 6.1(a) and (b), where we have plotted the nominal interest rate on government bonds together with the rate of inflation. What is particularly striking is the apparent stickiness of the nominal rate and its lack of responsiveness to the volatile inflation rates, up to the early 1970s. Indeed, throughout this period the nominal interest on government obligations remained close to the 5–6 per cent range, and seemed to be completely unaffected by the rate of inflation. Even during the two hyperinflations, the nominal rate did not move from its usual values. (Note that the hyperinflation periods are not drawn on the same scale.[4]) It was 5.39 in 1915, it then fell slightly to 4.87 in 1917, after which it rose again until 1920, but only to 5.68. During the second hyperinflation, prices started to increase in 1940, but the inflation was particularly high in the years 1944–46. The nominal interest rate on government debt was 5.66 in 1940, reached a peak of 8.22 in 1943, and then actually declined to 6.59 in 1944, 5.95 in 1945 and 5.85 in 1946.

As can be seen from figure 6.1(b), it is only in the last decade that nominal interest rates have started to increase, seemingly to compensate for inflation. But even this late behaviour might be rationalized as partly the result of significant recent innovations in the Italian financial markets. Thus, one might be led to conclude that some degree of inflation illusion, if not complete inflation illusion, must have characterized the behaviour of Italian consumers and investors in fixed assets, at least until the most recent period, when the persistence of substantial inflation initiated a learning process through which the Italian consumers have finally begun to shed their inflation illusion. This interpretation would, in practice, validate Fisher's law only in the latest period of our sample, and interpret the behaviour of the Italian economy as characterized by complete inflation illusion throughout the major part of its history.

However, as will be shown in section V, a quite different explanation is possible for the observed behaviour which is not inconsistent with Fisher's law and rational behaviour of consumers and investors throughout the period. We will also indicate why, in our view, this alternative provides a better and more credible explanation of the facts.

IV TEST OF THE BASIC MODEL

In table 6.2 we test the specification of the LCH model presented in section I. The variables used in the estimation are per caput and

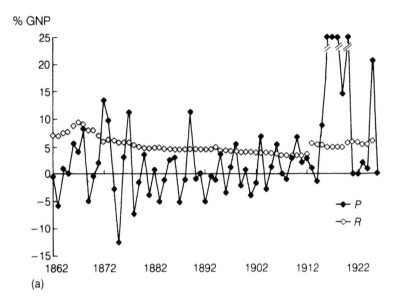

(a)

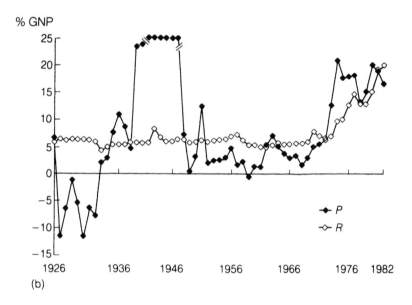

(b)

Figure 6.1 (a) Inflation rate (*P*) and nominal interest rate on Government bonds (*R*), 1862–1924 (b) inflation rate (*P*) and nominal interest rate on Government bonds (*R*), 1924–82.

expressed in thousands of 1970 lire through deflation by the implicit deflator of private consumption; they are described in the Appendix. Except for the net stock of capital available from 1882 to 1982, and an estimate of the value of land available from 1882 to 1950, all other variables are available from 1862 to 1982. To account for long-run expectations, we relied on current and lagged values of the income variable appearing in equation 6.2. It may be desirable to consider a higher number of lags on both income and the deficit; however, by adding a lag to the deficit, a second lag to all variables, or by using Almon polynomial lags, the sum of the coefficients of income and of the deficit was always very close to the sum of current and lagged coefficients of the income variable and of the current deficit, so that we feel that not much is lost by the specification that we have adopted.

Our strategy will be to present first in table 6.2 estimates of the basic model represented by equation 6.2 without taking into account the effect of real interest payments on public debt. This is fully justified if one is interested in testing the REP model against the LH–LCH, since, according to the REP, the coefficient of the deficit should offset that of net income. Consequently, interest, as well as all other taxes and transfers, should not affect consumption. In tables 6.3 and 6.4 we then proceed to analyse the effect of debt and interest on debt and try to assess the effect, if any, of inflation on consumption (equation 6.5).

In table 6.2 we begin by showing estimates for the postwar period (1950–82) for which the information is deemed to be substantially more reliable, and the results of previous studies, including our own (Modigliani et al., 1985) are available. We next give results for the earlier period beginning not later than 1882 but in some tests as early as 1862. Finally, results are given for the two periods pooled, including tests of homogeneity. All results omit the years of the First and Second World Wars (1915–18 and 1940–45, respectively), unless otherwise stated.

Regression (2.1) presents an estimate of the basic equation 6.2. We use the formulation of the first equality of equation 6.2 to insure the constraint that the effect of taxes and government consumption should add up to the income coefficient. The fit of the regression is quite good as the standard error is only about 2.0 per cent of the mean (2.3 per cent of the smallest value) of the dependent variable. The constant term is positive which is not strictly consistent with the predictions of both models that consumption should be independent of the absolute level of income, but fairly small (around 6 per cent of the mean of consumption over the period 1950–82) and not very significant.

The wealth coefficient is close to expectations and subject to small error. We note also that the coefficient of the deficit is only about one-

Table 6.2 Estimates of the basic LCH model

ID	Period	C (1)	Y* (2)	Y*_{-1} (3)	W (4)	G* (5)	RHO (6)	SE (7)
2.1	1950–1982	34.0 (1.7)	0.48 (9.3)	0.20 (3.0)	0.029 (3.6)	−0.17 (−1.6)	0.77 (6.8)	7.54
2.2	1950–1982		0.45 (8.2)	0.28 (5.7)	0.032 (3.5)	−0.33 (−2.3)	0.77 (6.8)	0.01196
2.3	1882–1950 (W includes land)	15.2 (0.5)	0.50 (14.7)	0.20 (6.2)	0.027 (1.2)	−0.30 (−5.4)	0.85 (12.3)	4.03
2.4	1882–1950 (W includes land)		0.51 (16.6)	0.20 (6.1)	0.035 (6.5)	−0.34 (−5.0)	0.77 (9.3)	0.02165
2.5	1882–1950	30.6 (2.4)	0.51 (15.6)	0.19 (5.4)	0.028 (1.7)	−0.29 (−5.2)	0.80 (10.2)	4.02
2.6	1864–1950	34.7 (3.8)	0.49 (15.7)	0.21 (6.7)	0.020 (.1.7)	−0.28 (−5.4)	0.79 (11.4)	3.91

2.7	1864–1950 (G* includes G_i)	31.1 (3.2)	0.52 (14.7)	0.22 (6.4)	0.019 (1.5)	−0.22 (−4.0)	0.77 (10.4)	4.20
2.8	1864–1982	33.1 (8.2)	0.48 (21.7)	0.20 (7.5)	0.028 (6.3)	−0.23 (−4.6)	0.76 (12.3)	5.08
2.9	1882–1982 (W includes land until 1950)	5.2 (0.7)	0.49 (20.3)	0.22 (8.3)	0.035 (5.7)	−0.27 (−5.2)	0.82 (13.9)	5.32
2.10	1882–1982 (W includes land until 1950)		0.51 (22.1)	0.22 (8.5)	0.033 (9.8)	−0.33 (−6.0)	0.78 (11.9)	0.0177
2.11	1864–1982 (includes wars)	31.6 (8.8)	0.49 (21.9)	0.21 (7.5)	0.025 (5.5)	−0.23 (−5.7)	0.78 (13.7)	5.33

t-statistics in parentheses. The mean of the dependent variable (in 1970 thousand lire) in the regressions estimated in level forms is 594 in the period 1950–1982, 204 in 1882–1950, 197 in 1864–1950, and 313 in 1864–1982 (always excluding the war years). Income (Y*) and deficit (G*) are net of real interest transfers. Regressions (2.2), (2.4) and (2.10) are estimated in ratio form. In regression (2.7) G* includes government investment (G_i). Regression (2.11) includes the war years (1915–1918 and 1940–1945). Wealth excludes land unless otherwise stated.

quarter of that of income (Σa_i), and that the difference between the two coefficients is significantly different from zero beyond any reasonable level but broadly consistent with the predictions of the LH–LCH.

Regression (2.1) uses the linear specification. For an economy growing rapidly, such a specification might be questioned for lack of homoskedasticity. For this reason, regression (2.2) is estimated in ratio form; it can be seen that the estimates are not greatly affected except for the coefficient of the deficit which rises to 0.3 but remains broadly consistent with the LH–LCH and not with the REP. We are inclined to believe, however, that the results reported in row (2.2) are biased by the omission of the constant term, which, as explained below, may be proxying the value of land which is excluded from our definition of wealth.

Regressions (2.3) through (2.8) report the results for the earlier portion of our sample. The main features distinguishing this period from the one considered above are:

1. the rate of development of the economy, very slow to moderate in the period 1864–1950, and exceptionally vigorous during most of the later period, especially in the years of the 'miracle', though less so towards the end; and
2. the reliability of the data, which is unavoidably less in the earlier period.

In row (2.3) we present an estimate for the period 1882–1950, the only one for which we have available an estimate of the value of land to include in wealth. The results for the seven decades preceding the Second World War are remarkably similar to those for the postwar period considering the institutional developments, the large difference in the rate of growth and the enormous associated variation in the personal saving rate (or C/Y^*). This can be seen by comparing (2.3) with (2.1) in linear form where the only difference of any account is in the coefficient of the deficit; but even this difference disappears in comparing the ratio estimations (2.2) and (2.4). The only difference is then that the fit is considerably closer in the later period – the standard error is 1.2 per cent in (2.2) versus 2.2 per cent in (2.4) – which could readily be accounted for by the quality of the data. At the same time, the similarity of the two estimates justifies confidence also in the previous data.

The comparability is somewhat marred by the fact that land is included in the estimates of wealth for the prewar, but not for the postwar, years. To secure full comparability, in row (2.5) we have re-estimated (2.3) omitting the value of land from the definition of wealth. It is seen that the only appreciable difference is a rise in the value (and significance) of the constant term. This is understandable, since the constant term is presumably proxying the omitted value of agricultural land, which was, in fact, nearly constant – or moving very slowly – throughout this period. At the beginning of the 1880s, it was around one-half of the value of total wealth (inclusive of debt and land), but then declined to less than 30 per cent of the value of wealth at the beginning of the 1950s.

As noted before, our suspicion is that a similar mechanism could have been operating in the latest period of the sample (1950–82) – namely, that during the period of rapid industrialization the relative importance of land kept shrinking, making its omission less serious, but producing a moderately positive constant term.

In regressions (2.3) through (2.5), the estimates are for the period 1882–1950, because the wealth series was only available over this period. However, since the other variables are available over the entire period 1864–1982, we have extrapolated backward the value of the wealth series – excluding the value of land – by simply assuming that its behaviour could be described by the average rate of growth of real income in the period 1864–82. To test whether this rough approximation was at least unbiased, we have re-estimated regression (2.5) starting in 1864 and added a multiplicative dummy on wealth in the first period of estimation (1864–82). It was found that the dummy on wealth was rather small and completely insignificantly different from zero. On the basis of these results we have felt it worthwhile rerunning our basic equation for the entire period 1864–1950, dropping the dummy, with the results reported in regression (2.6).

It is apparent that the estimated coefficients in row (2.6) are nearly identical to those provided by row (2.5). However, one can also note, much as one would expect, (a) a further rise in the constant term (to 18 per cent of the mean of the dependent variable) since land is again omitted, and also (b) a reduction in the value of the coefficient of wealth, consistent with the poorer measurement of this variable.

We do not report a ratio estimate corresponding to (2.6) since we feel that the suppression of the constant is no longer justifiable, but that the comparison of (2.3) and (2.4) convincingly establishes that heteroskedasticity is not a problem in this period of very limited growth.

Regression (2.7) is similar to (2.6) but tests an alternative measure that adds government investment (G_I) to government consumption in computing the deficit. It is seen that this measure, that we regard as less appropriate, produces in fact a somewhat poorer fit and a lower and less significant coefficient of deficit.

The remaining four equations of table 6.2 are based on the pooled sample (1864–1982 or 1882–1982). Since in this case the problem of heteroskedasticity might be even more serious than in the two separate subperiods, a number of tests were conducted, but none found that the size of the squared errors was directly related to any of the independent variables, and particularly to the income variable.[5] The reason is that in the first part of the sample the change in real income – more appropriate than the actual level, since we always obtain high serial correlation of the errors – is characterized by a standard deviation about six times the mean, while in the second half of the sample the standard deviation is only about 1.7 of the mean. It would appear that the period of stability that characterized the 1950s and 1960s, as well as the presence in the postwar years of more effective stabilization policies, played an important role in explaining the absence of heteroskedasticity in the residuals of our equations.

It is seen that the pattern of the coefficients of (2.8) comes very close to those estimated in both the first part of the sample (row (2.6)) and the second one (row 2.1)). It is thus not surprising that a Chow test for structural break yields an F statistic of only 0.3, and one cannot reject the null hypothesis that the structure of the economy has remained stable over the entire period.

One troublesome aspect of (2.8) is that the constant term is highly significant. However, if we re-estimate (2.8) starting from 1882 instead of from 1864 and include land in the wealth variable, we obtain very similar coefficients and a fairly small and insignificant constant term (2.9).[6] A further test of heteroskedasticity can be made by estimating (2.9) in ratio form (row 2.10), where the results clearly show no appreciable change in the coefficients with respect to (2.9).

So far, all our estimates have excluded the two World Wars because these wars were of catastrophic proportions and involved huge government expenditure and deficits and quite high rates of inflation. In addition, the Second World War also resulted in large-scale destruction of private and public capital. These periods involve both extreme observations and may be non-representative of normal behaviour because of the unusual circumstances, including the role of patriotism in the First World War and that of price and related controls. It seems, none the less, of some interest to see how sensitive the estimates are to the inclusion of the wars. As can be seen by comparing (2.11) with (2.8), the change in the coefficient estimates is very small, although the standard error is increased by some 5 per cent, indicating, not surprisingly, larger shocks during war years.

We can summarize the results presented in table 6.2 by noting that the estimates of the basic model are remarkably stable over various sample periods, and lead to the conclusion that the main prediction of the REP, that private saving will completely offset any change in government deficit, is not supported by the data; the point estimate of G^* is in fact negative, as predicted by both models, but in absolute value is relatively modest – especially in the most recent period – as predicted by the LH–LCH.

V   TESTS OF THE EFFECT OF INTEREST INCOME, DEBT AND INFLATION ON CONSUMPTION

In this section we turn to the second set of our tests, namely the effect of debt, interests on debt and inflation on consumption, that is, to tests of the specification of equation 6.5. Table 6.3 reports the results for each of the two subperiods, while table 6.4 presents estimates for the two periods combined. We begin again with the postwar period.

Regression (3.1) adds first the national debt D to the variables of row (2.1) in table 6.2. According to the REP, its coefficient should be the negative of that of wealth; according to LH–LCH, the coefficient should be zero, or possibly a small positive number, reflecting the effect of the long-run expected real rate. It is seen that the coefficient of debt is positive and very significant (the standard error of the regression is reduced from 7.6 to 6.7). This result points towards a clear rejection of the REP. To be sure, the coefficient of D is somewhat high even for LCH, but this could reflect the role of the interest, given a fairly constant long-term expected real rate. Indeed, when in (3.2) we further add nominal interest payments, the coefficient of D becomes small and insignificant. At the same time, the RD coefficient points to a clear-cut rejection of the REP, that transfers in the form of interest have no effect on consumption because it is seen to be highly significant, and to imply an effect on consumption that is quite close to that estimated for all other taxes and transfers, namely, 0.5 (the sum of the coefficients of columns (2), (3) and (5)) which is consistent with LH–LCH.

Row (3.3) reports a test of whether consumption responds to nominal or to real interest payments, i.e. to payments adjusted for the inflation-induced loss of purchasing power on claims against the government. To this end we should add to (3.2) a variable measuring this loss in purchasing power. However, as mentioned in section II, it must be recognized that the perceived loss cannot be identified with the *ex-post* loss due to actual inflation; rather it should properly be identified with the anticipated loss because the actual, simultaneous inflation loss cannot be fully known or reacted to instantaneously. We considered several alternative ways of estimating the unobservable expected inflation and tested a few. We report here the results of the approach

Table 6.3 Test of the effect of interest, debt and inflation, 1950–1982 and 1864–1950

ID	Period	C (1)	Y* (2)	Y*_{-1} (3)	W (4)	G* (5)	RD (6)	P^eD (7)	D (8)	RHO (9)	SE (10)	LL (11)
3.1	1950–1982	56.2 (3.8)	0.43 (8.3)	0.22 (3.5)	0.018 (2.3)	−0.20 (−2.0)			0.12 (2.9)	0.68 (5.2)	6.74	106.4
3.2	1950–1982	45.5 (3.6)	0.45 (9.0)	0.26 (4.3)	0.009 (1.1)	−0.22 (−2.4)	0.50 (2.2)		0.027 (0.5)	0.62 (4.5)	6.31	104.4
3.3	1950–1982	40.2 (3.9)	0.44 (9.3)	0.27 (4.5)	0.015 (1.7)	−0.22 (−2.4)	0.70 (4.1)	−0.30 (−1.4)		0.63 (4.6)	6.13	103.4
3.4	1950–1982	40.2 (3.4)	0.44 (9.1)	0.22 (4.2)	0.03	−0.20 (−2.2)	0.63 (3.6)	−0.46 (−2.3)		0.66 (5.0)	6.32	104.4
3.5	1950–1982	35.5 (3.4)	0.43 (8.6)	0.24 (4.0)	0.030 (5.1)	−0.19 (−2.0)	0.59 (3.4)			0.61 (4.4)	6.38	104.7
3.5	1950–1982	46.5 (3.2)	0.42 (7.9)	0.22 (4.1)	0.03	−0.20 (−2.2)	0.51 (2.1)	−0.47 (−2.3)	0.043 (0.8)	0.68 (5.2)	6.37	104.7
3.7	1882–1950 (W includes land)		0.47 (14.1)	0.17 (4.8)	0.040 (7.3)	−0.32 (−5.1)	0.28 (2.8)		0.031 (1.4)	0.78 (9.6)	0.0189	150.4
3.8	1882–1950 (W includes land)		0.47 (13.9)	0.17 (4.8)	0.040 (16.6)	−0.32 (−4.6)	0.28 (2.7)	0.01 (0.1)	0.030 (1.4)	0.78 (9.6)	0.0191	149.9
3.9	1864–1950	31.8 (4.1)	0.48 (14.9)	0.21 (6.7)	0.038 (2.9)	−0.29 (−5.5)	0.92 (1.7)		−0.07 (−3.0)	0.75 (9.9)	3.74	210.7

t-statistics in parentheses. The periods 1864–1950 and 1882–1950 exclude wars. In regression (3.5) the variable RD is replaced with $(RD - p^eD)$. Regressions (3.7) and (3.8) are estimated in ratio form. W excludes land unless otherwise stated. Column (11) reports the log of the likelihood function.

that appeared most satisfactory. It consists of obtaining estimates of expected inflation, p^c, by means of a rolling regression of the actual inflation on lagged inflation rates and using the estimated coefficients for each year to forecast that year's inflation. This approach is supported by a number of considerations. First, it is evident that in this period the nominal interest rate reflects inflation along the lines of Fisher's hypothesis since it is highly correlated with inflation; a regression of R^7 on p yields, in fact, a coefficient of p of 0.69 (with a t ratio of 7.4 and an R^2 of 0.64). Second, inflation was generated by a very persistent – and therefore predictable – process; indeed, our measure of expected inflation predicts actual p^c quite closely since the correlation between p and p^c is 0.86. One further test consists in regressing R on p^c and $(p - p^c)$. If p^c is a good approximation to expected inflation, it should be able to account for R, while $(p - p^c)$, representing unexpected inflation, should not contribute significantly to the explanation of R (under Fisher's hypothesis). It is found that p^c has a coefficient of 0.65 and highly significant t-ratio of 8.0. On the other hand, the coefficient of $(p - p^c)$, although it has a positive point estimate (0.3), has a standard error so large (0.16) that one cannot reject the hypothesis that the coefficient is zero, at the 5 per cent level of significance. Furthermore, a good portion of the positive effect of $(p - p^c)$ can be traced to the highly transitory Korean war inflation of 1951 which was, *per se*, unforecastable and generated no inflationary expectations as is apparent from the behaviour of R.

Thus, in (3.3) we add $p^c D$ to (3.2); as a measure of the expected loss of purchasing, the results of the test, reported in row (3.3), cannot reject the null hypothesis of inflation illusion ($h = 0$), since the coefficient of $p^c D$, though negative, is not significantly different from zero. However, (3.3) and (3.2), as well as (3.1), run into another problem, namely, that the coefficient of wealth is unreasonably small compared with the results of table 6.2 (and also those of other investigations) which hover around 0.03 and reach as high as 0.04. In (3.1) and (3.3) the coefficient is half as high (and in (3.2) even less) although the difference is hardly significant in view of the very large standard error. This consideration suggests a strong likelihood of the presence of collinearity between W, RD, D and $p^c D$, making for large standard errors and erratic estimates. To test this hypothesis in row (3.4), we have constrained the coefficient of wealth to take the reasonable value of 0.03 and dropped the insignificant debt variable. The results are striking because: (a) the constraint imposed on the coefficient hardly reduces the fit and could not be rejected even at the 5 per cent level and higher, (b) the coefficient of $p^c D$ becomes significant so that one can reject the hypothesis of complete inflation illusion, and (c) it is not very different from that of RD, as one would expect under full rationality (and supposing that p^c is a good approximation to perceived inflation).

We have actually carried out a formal test of 'rationality' by re-estimating (3.4) constraining the coefficients to be the same (that is, entering $RD - p^c D$ instead of RD and $p^c D$ separately). The result given in (3.5) indicates that the hypothesis of complete rationality cannot be rejected either comparing the unrestricted (3.3) with (3.5), or (3.4) with (3.5) since the difference in the likelihood ratio test is 2.6 and 0.6 respectively, well below any customary level of significance. We also note that the coefficient of wealth turns out to be again of an order of magnitude consistent with our expectations and is also very significant.

The last regression that we report for the period 1950–82 (3.6) adds back to (3.4) the national debt D. To control for multicollinearity, we again constrain the coefficient of W to be 0.03. The coefficients of the other variables are hardly changed except that those of RD and $p^c D$ move even closer. The coefficient of D is again positive, but is again so imprecisely estimated that one cannot meaningfully make any reliable inferences. The difficulty of assessing the effect of debt (which will be further taken up) derives from the fact that the coefficient of wealth is itself very small, so we are looking for small effects, and from the fact that, not surprisingly, there appears to be strong multicollinearity among wealth, debt D, nominal interest bill RD, and expected depreciation of the stock of public debt $p^c D$.

Proceeding next to the earlier subperiod, results are reported in the last three rows of table 6.3. In (3.7) the period of estimation is 1882–1950 and wealth includes the value of land. This regression should be compared with (2.4) and is estimated in ratio form on the grounds that the constant term can be dropped when wealth includes land. In (3.7) the coefficient of RD is significant and makes for a substantial reduction in the standard error (from 2.2 per cent in (2.4) to 1.9 per cent). As in the postwar period, the coefficient D is positive but imprecisely estimated.

In (3.8), we test for the effect of $p^c D$, having computed p^c by the same rolling regression method used in the second part of the sample. It is seen that this variable has no effect on consumption. One might interpret this result as providing evidence of inflation illusion in the prewar period. There is, however, an alternative and more subtle explanation which is suggested by the imaginative contribution of Barsky (1985). Relying on American and English historical data, he concludes that 'inflation evolved from essentially a white noise process in the pre-World War I years to a highly persistent, nonstationary ARIMA process in the post-1960 period' (p. 78). It turns out that the Italian experience mirrors quite closely his findings, as is readily apparent from figures 6.1(a) and (b).

During the period 1864–1914 inflation appears more or less as a white noise process and, indeed, a regression of p on p_{-1} yields a coefficient of zero (if also p_{-2} is included, inflation shows some moderate negative correlation). The period that follows the First World War (1919–39) shows some evidence of moderate positive correlation (a coefficient of p_{-1} of 0.4 with a t-statistic of 2.4). It follows that in the prewar period, to a first approximation, inflation was, by and large, unexpected, and the best predictor of inflation is a constant. This conclusion is consistent with the fact that in this period the nominal rate is independent of inflation, as can be verified from figures 6.1(a) and (b) and is confirmed by a zero correlation between R and p. Obviously, under these conditions, the *nominal* rate can be taken as a valid approximation of the *expected* real rate and the irrelevance of $p^c D$ in (3.8) is consistent with rational behaviour.

Row (3.9) extends the period of estimation to 1864–1950 and drops land from the wealth variable. The result is a notable 'deterioration' of the estimates, as (a) the coefficient of RD is 0.9 – too high even from the LH–LCH perspective – and estimated with a large standard error, and (b) the coefficient of D turns out to be much too negative even for the REP. In view of the limitation of the data for the 18 added years, these results must be regarded as not very reliable.

In table 6.4 we present results for the whole period 1864–1982 and try to pin down the value of the critical coefficients (RD and $p^c D$) by relying on a greater number of observations. Regression (4.1) is one step in this direction, since the coefficient of RD is high and very significant. A Chow test comparing the subperiod regressions (3.2) and (3.9) with the restricted counterpart (4.1) yields an estimated F of 0.94 and indicates that the hypothesis that the structure is the same throughout the period cannot be rejected at the 5 per cent level of significance.

However, we have reason to believe that different subperiods differ considerably with respect to the role of p^c because, as we have seen, until the postwar period the nominal rate was unaffected by actual inflation, suggesting that inflation was largely unexpected; at least up to the First World War this hypothesis is supported by the fact that current inflation appears to be statistically independent of previous inflation. Accordingly, the overall $p^c D$ was introduced with two multiplicative dummies, one for the years 1864–1914 and one for 1919–50. The result reported in (4.2) – where, as in table 6.3, we constrain the coefficient of W to control for multi-collinearity – confirms that the

Table 6.4 Test of the effect of interest, debt and inflation, 1864–1982

ID	C (1)	Y* (2)	Y*₋₁ (3)	W (4)	G* (5)	RD (6)	$p^e D_1$ (7)	$p^e D_2$ (8)	$p^e D$ (9)	D (10)	RHO (11)	SE (12)	LL (13)
4.1	38.8 (14.9)	0.49 (24.0)	0.23 (9.2)	0.014 (2.8)	−0.25 (−5.5)	0.64 (5.0)				−0.02 (1.6)	0.74 11.4	4.57	320.4
4.2	29.5 (8.8)	0.47 (22.3)	0.21 (9.1)	0.03	−0.26 (−5.4)	0.56 (4.4)	0.36 (2.0)	0.46 (3.0)	−0.37 (−2.8)		0.75 (11.7)	4.69	323.3
4.3	30.1 (8.9)	0.47 (22.6)	0.20 (9.0)	0.03	−0.25 (−5.4)	0.56 (4.4)			−0.37 (−2.8)		0.75 (12.0)	4.68	322.9
4.4	28.0 (9.5)	0.478 (21.8)	0.22 (8.5)	0.029 (7.4)	−0.24 (−5.0)	0.48 (4.0)					0.72 (10.8)	4.75	324.6
4.5	30.3 (9.6)	0.48 (11.8)	0.20 (4.9)	0.028 (6.9)	−0.09 (−1.3)	0.45 (3.5)					0.71 (10.5)	4.97	329.5
4.6	29.0 (9.2)	0.46 (21.5)	0.22 (8.4)	0.031 (.6)	−0.23 (−5.0)	0.53 (4.0)				−0.01 (−0.8)	0.70 (10.4)	4.76	324.8
4.7	31.3 (8.2)	0.48 (21.6)	0.21 (7.6)	0.026 (5.2)	−0.23 (−4.6)					0.02 (0.9)	0.76 (12.1)	5.08	331.9

t-statistics in parentheses. The period of estimation excludes wars. In regressions (4.4), (4.5) and (4.6) the coefficient of $p^e D$ is constrained to be the opposite of that of RD. Regression (4.5) is estimated by instrumental variables.

Saving, Deficits, Inflation, and Financial Theory

'expected inflation' effect is important and close to the right magnitude for the postwar period, but is just about zero in the remaining two subperiods.[8] On this basis, we introduce in (4.3) a new measure of 'effective expected inflation' which is zero up to 1950 and p^c as defined earlier thereafter. The results are strongly supportive of the LH–LCH and contrary to the REP. This is true not only with respect to the deficit coefficient, but also in that interest income is very important, and so is the correction for effective expected inflation.

If, however, (4.3) is re-estimated without imposing the constraint on wealth, the coefficient of $p^c D$ becomes smaller in absolute value and is estimated with larger error – a pattern of results similar to that observed in the postwar period – (cf. (3.3) and (3.4)). In view of our previous results (table 6.2) and the fact that the coefficient of wealth rises when we replace RD and $p^c D$ with $r^c D$ (cf. (3.5) and, below, (4.4)) we feel that the restriction is not inconsistent with the data, and that we can, on the basis of (4.3), reject the null hypothesis of inflation illusion ($h = 0$) in the entire sample.

To be sure, the coefficient of $p^c D$ is a little smaller than that of RD, but as is shown by (4.4) – where RD is replaced by $r^c D$ – the full rationality hypothesis calling for equal and opposite coefficients cannot be rejected even at the 5 per cent level. Note also that the results (4.4) are completely consistent with the constraint that the wealth coefficient be 0.03, as the unconstrained coefficient in (4.4) is almost the same (0.029 with a t-ratio of 7.4).

Finally we want to mention that our estimates could be criticized on the ground that they might be affected by simultaneity bias arising from the potential endogeneity of income and deficit. As shown by Feldstein (1982) and Seater and Mariano (1985) the problem is important and has to be carefully handled. Moreover, the potential bias of the deficit coefficient works in favour of the REP and against the LH–LCH, since, over the business cycle, lower income would lead to lower consumption and taxes and increase the deficit, thus inducing an upward bias in the deficit coefficient. When we tried to correct for the endogeneity of income and the deficit using instrumental variables, the results did not differ much from those presented. For this reason we only report the results that one obtains if (4.4) – the regression that we will use in the next section to account for the forces that have driven the national saving rate – is re-estimated by an instrumental variable procedure. In row (4.5) the instruments chosen are exports and government expenditure.[9] The differences from (4.4) are very small, with the exception that, as expected, the coefficient of the deficit comes closer to zero and is estimated with a larger error.

In the two final regressions of table 6.4 we try to come to grips with the separate effect of the stock of government debt. It is clear that we do not succeed. The point estimates are consistent with the LCH in both (4.6) and (4.7) where, fearing correlation between D and r^cD we have dropped the r^cD variable. But they are subject to such margin of errors relative to the reference wealth coefficient that no reliable conclusion would be justified.

VI   THE EFFECT OF GROWTH AND FISCAL POLICY ON THE NATIONAL
SAVING RATE

The empirical test of the model laid down in section II has shown that:

- the response of consumption to government deficits is negative, in accordance with the LCH, but rather small, as predicted by the LH–LCH;
- in constrast with the prediction of the REP, interest transfers have strong positive effects on consumption – roughly equal to that of all other forms of transfers; also, the evidence is not inconsistent with the hypothesis that consumers have taken into account expected real, rather than actual, nominal interest transfers, as called for by rational behaviour, although only in the latest years can we reject the null hypothesis of inflation illusion.

These behavioural characteristics can be used to account for the forces that have driven the national saving rate in the last century. For this purpose, we propose to rely on regression (4.4) of table 6.4 in which consumption responds to the expected real (rather than to the nominal) rate measured by the difference between nominal payments and expected inflation. Recalling equation 6.6 in section II, we can thus write:

$$S_T = [(NNP - T^*) - \Sigma a_i(NNP_i - T_i^*) - bW - cD \qquad (6.8)$$

$$- [(E - T^*) + \Sigma d_i(E_i - T_i^*)] - fr^cD$$

For the special case of regression (4.4) in which the maximum lag on income is one, there is no lag on the deficit, $\Sigma a_i + d = f$ and $c = 0$, we can rearrange the terms of equation 6.8 and divide by NNP to derive the following decomposition of the national saving rate:

$$\frac{S_T}{NNP} = (1 - a) + a_2\frac{\Delta NNP}{NNP} - a\,\frac{E}{NNP} \qquad (6.9)$$

$$- (\Sigma a_i + d_i)\frac{(G_i^* + r^cD_i)}{NNP} - \frac{bw}{NNP} - a_2\frac{\Delta E}{NNP} - \frac{k}{NNP}$$

$$= 0.31 + 0.22 \frac{\Delta NNP}{NNP} - 0.69 \frac{E}{NNP} - 0.23 \frac{G^* + r^c D}{NNP}$$

$$- 0.22 \frac{G^*_{-1} + r^c D_{-1}}{NNP} - 0.029 \frac{W}{NNP} - 0.22 \frac{\Delta E}{NNP} - \frac{28}{NNP}$$

where $a = a_1 + a_2$ is the marginal propensity to consume, $d_2 = 0$ and k is the constant term in regression (4.4).

From equation 6.9 it appears that the national saving rate:

- increases with the rate of growth of income;
- increases when the wealth to income ratio declines, and consumers reduce consumption in order to restore its long-run equilibrium value. The wealth to income ratio in turn should tend to decline with the rate of growth of income (Modigliani, 1975), providing one further reason for the association of growth and saving;
- decreases when there is a rise in government expenditure for a *given* deficit, that is, when there is a rise in tax financed expenditure. This is because the rise in taxes lowers disposable income and hence private saving by about 0.3 per dollar;
- decreases when there is a rise in the deficit expenditure held constant, that is when there is a fall in taxes, because of the resulting rise in disposable income and consumption; the effect is less than that via disposable income (Σa_i) to the extent that consumption decreases when there is a rise in deficit (d) and according to (4.4) the net effect is (0.69 − 0.24), or 0.45.

Since we find that consumers' behaviour is consistent with rationality and that the response to $r^c D$ is similar to that of T^*, the same applies whenever expected real interest payments increase.

From equation 6.9 it can also be seen that fully anticipated inflation does not affect the national saving rate except in so far as it is systematically associated with the real rate itself. Otherwise inflation results in offsetting changes in R and p^c which leave r^c unaffected. If, however, inflation turns out to exceed the expectation, our results suggest that the private sector still consumes on the basis of the expected real rate and hence more than would be justified by the *ex-post* real rate. None the less, according to our results, unexpected inflation does not affect national saving, because, as is apparent from equation 6.9, the only way saving could be affected by inflation is through the deficit term − but this tends to depend on the perceived real rate and not on the *ex-post* realized one. Stated differently, both private consumption and, of course, public consumption E depend on r^e and not on actual inflation.

To summarize, our model predicts that the national saving rate depends on two factors: (a) a growth factor, that includes the effect of ΔNNP, of the wealth income ratio and of the constant term, to the extent that it is proxying for growth; and (b) a fiscal factor, that includes the effect of the rate of government consumption and of deficit financing.

In figures 6.2(a), (b) and (c), we have plotted the national saving rate and the forces that have been driving it.[10] The construction of these figures is most easily explained with reference to figure 6.2(c)

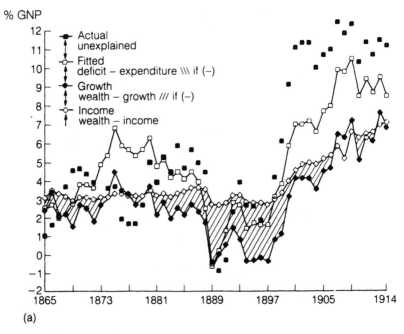

(a)

Figure 6.2 (a) National saving rate and its major determinants, 1864–1914
Note: Actual net saving rate relative to NNP (actual). The other variables are divided by NNP multiplied by the coefficient in regression (4.4) according to the decomposition (9) and subtracted from their mean (last row of table 6.5). Line *income* is the reciprocal term of (9). Line *growth* adds to income the growth factors (the variables W and ΔNNP multiplied by their coefficients in (9)). Line *fitted* adds to growth the fiscal factors (the variables E and $(G^* + r^c D)$ multiplied by their coefficients in (9)), and represents our fitted values. Each variable has been smoothed with a three-year moving average. The shaded area between fitted and growth indicates the negative contribution of fiscal policies to the fitted saving rate. The shaded area between growth and income is the negative contribution of the growth factor to the saving rate. The difference between fitted and actual is the *unexplained* residual, that includes also the autocorrelated component of the error term

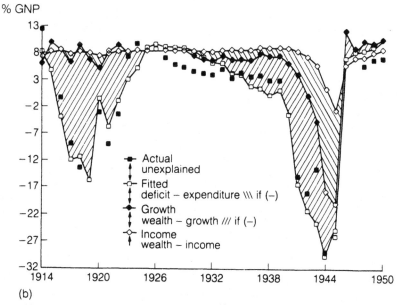

Figure 6.2 (b) National saving rate and its major determinants, 1914–50
Note: see note to (a). The variables for the war years, excluded in estimating (4.4), are actual values and are not based on moving averages

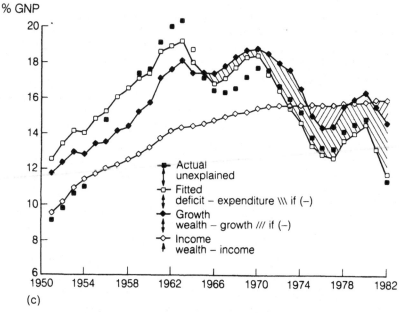

Figure 6.2 (c) National saving rate and its major determinants, 1950–82
Note: see note to (a)

and looking at the years around 1960. Three broken lines are identified; looking at the side, the point labelled 'Income' represents the constant term times the reciprocal of income. The second line, labelled 'Growth', is the sum of the income and the growth effect which consists of two components: the wealth income ratio and the rate of change of income, each multiplied by its coefficient. The growth effect itself is, of course, the distance between the income and the growth lines. It indicates a positive effect on saving to the extent that the growth line exceeds the income line, and a negative effect when it falls below. The third broken line labelled 'Fitted' represents the rate of national saving as computed from our empirically fitted equation. The area between it and the growth line is the remaining component of equation 6.4, the fiscal factor consisting of the expenditure and the deficit, both multiplied by their coefficients. To pinpoint the thrust of fiscal policy and growth on national saving, we have shaded the areas between Growth and Fitted, and between Growth and Income so that one can readily locate the year in which fiscal policy and/or growth make a negative contribution to the saving rate. Finally, the dots not joined by a line 'Actual' represent the actual value of saving so that the vertical distance from the fitted line measures the residual error. It should be noted that we regard as 'unexplained residual' not only the white-noise residual that we obtain from regression (4.4), but also the autocorrelated component of the error. Since we are interested primarily in the long-run behaviour of the national saving rate, rather than in its cyclical variations, the graphs in figures 6.2(a) (1865–1914), 6.2(b) (1914–50) and 6.2(c) (1950–82) are based on a three-year moving average of all the relevant variables. In figure 6.2(b), however, and only for the war years, we present the *actual* saving rate (as well as the actual values of the explanatory variables) and not the average because we are interested in learning how our equation (fitted *excluding* the war periods 1915–18 and 1940–45) actually performs in those brief episodes.

Table 6.5 provides an overview of the information in figures 6.2(a), (b) and (c) by giving, for each of nine selected subperiods, the mean of the national saving rate and the mean of the 'causal' variables, all in deviations from the overall mean, and multiplied by the coefficients in regression (4.4). In table 6.5 we have separately reported each of the components of equation 6.9 so that the fiscal effect in figure 6.2 is the sum of columns (3) and (4) of the table, the growth effect is the sum of (2) and (5), while the 'absolute income' effect is reported in column (6). Column (7) of the table reports the average of the difference between the Actual and the Fitted line over the selected periods. In choosing the benchmarks, we have tried to follow the swings of the saving rate, as well as to account for some of the

Table 6.5 Breakdown of the national saving rate (S_T)

Periods	Actual (1)	W (2)	G*+r°D (3)	E (4)	NNP_{-1} (5)	I (6)	Unexplained (7)
1865–1881	−4.8	0.1	0.2	1.5	−0.7	−4.8	1.1
1882–1897	−5.1	−1.6	0.4	1.0	−0.7	−4.9	−0.7
1900–1914	3.2	−0.1	1.2	1.6	−0.2	−2.0	−2.7
1924–1929	−0.9	0.3	0.7	0.3	−0.4	−0.5	−2.3
1936–1939	−5.3	−1.4	−3.2	−3.1	−0.4	1.1	1.7
1948–1950	−1.0	0.8	0.4	−0.5	1.1	−0.8	−2.0
1961–1964	11.3	2.7	1.9	−1.1	1.1	6.1	−0.6
1976–1978	5.5	−0.5	0.3	−1.8	−0.4	7.6	0.3
1980–1982	3.2	−0.9	—	−3.0	−0.4	7.9	−0.4
1983	0.2	−2.1	−0.3	−4.0	−0.8	7.9	−0.5
1984	0.2	−1.6	0.5	−3.8	−0.2	7.9	−2.6
Mean 1865–1982	8.2	−10.1	−0.5	−3.2	0.5	−10.0	—

All variables are multiplied by their coefficient in regression (4.4) of table 6.4, subtracted from their mean (last row of the table) and divided by NNP. The period over which we have computed the mean (1865–1982) excludes the two war periods. The sum of the last row of the table is 8.2 (the average saving rate) up to the constant term $(1 − a)$, where a equals $a_1 + a_2 = 31.5$. In the years 1983 and 1984 we have used regression (4.4) to forecast the value of the net national saving rate; for these years column (7) thus represents the forecast error.

major events that have characterized the Italian economic history: the long period of stagnation until the end of the century, the ensuing first take-off until the First World War, the slowdown of economic activity and the war finance during the fascist regime, the economic boom of the 1950s and (after 1964) the beginning of a period of more moderate growth followed by the shocks of the 1970s.

The first two rows of table 6.5 and figure 6.2(a) show that in the first period (1865–97) the saving rate, after rising somewhat at the beginning of the 1880s (by some considered the first Italian industrial revolution), at the end of the century was back to levels similar to those prevailing at the beginning of the period. But it is important to note that its composition was substantially different: the government was in fact running balanced budgets at the beginning of the period, and surpluses by the end of the century, and, since these were only partially compensated by an increase in expenditure financed by taxes, gave a positive contribution to national saving in the 1890s. At the same time, the growth of the economy was so slow that the net saving of the private sector was very low throughout the period (around 3 per cent). One should also note that the fit of our equation yields large errors from 1865 to 1881 (first row of table 6.5) but improves somewhat from 1882 to 1897 (second row of table 6.5), due, presumably, to the better quality of data available since 1882.

It is at the turn of the century, in connection with a period of sustained and high growth, comparable with the 'miracle' of the 1950s, that the saving rate exhibited a very substantial increase (not fully accounted for by our equation) and remained high, reaching an average of 11.4 per cent of NNP in the period 1900–14 (second row of table 6.5). In fact, after the peak reached in 1907, the saving rate stabilized until the beginning of the First World War, mainly because of a reduction in government surpluses (reflected in a shrinking of the shaded area in figure 6.2(a)) and a slowdown of economic activity. It can be seen that during the period as a whole the fiscal variables contributed partly to the high saving as both the deficit and tax financed expenditure were distinctly below average. However, a significant factor accounting for the rise in saving rate of 8.1 percentage points turns out to be (unfortunately) the constant term (the Income line) that rises from an average of −4.9 to an average of −2.0, thus contributing 2.9 percentage points to the explanation; this result was to be expected in view of the large constant term and rapid growth, though as we have suggested, this effect could reflect at least partly the wealth effect of land omitted from wealth (see section IV).

In figure 6.2(b), we have plotted our variables for the period 1914–50. Note that the war periods were not included in our sample and that they are not smoothed with a moving average. After the First World War (discussed below) the saving rate reached, in the mid 1920s, levels not much lower than in the immediate prewar period, but by 1936–39 it had fallen by 5 per cent of NNP because of a very negative fiscal policy effect during the fascist period reflecting government expenditure and deficit (especially after 1934) to finance the Ethiopian war and to prepare for the Second World War. The distinctive feature of this period is in fact that the combined effect of expenditure and deficit contributes to substantially lowering the saving rate, as opposed to what we have observed in the pre-World War period.

It is immediately apparent from figure 6.2(b) how the movements in the saving rate during the two World Wars are entirely dominated by those of government expenditure and the extent of reliance on deficit financing. We have estimated that, contrary to the REP, government deficit crowds out national saving by roughly one-half and that expenditure reduces it by roughly 0.70. Clearly, these estimates, even though obtained by omitting the war years, explain the developments during the wars remarkably well. From figure 6.2(b) we also note that in the First World War the saving rate did not become negative until 1917, that it reached its lowest value in 1919, and that it only fully recovered to the prewar level in 1923. The reason is that both expenditure and deficits remained very large, due to the enormous burden of military outlays, until at least 1922.

The situation was somewhat different during the Second World War. In 1940 the saving rate was already substantially negative, and it declined further until the end of the war. But in the year immediately following the war, the economy recovered quickly as the deficit was brought nearly under control. Thus by 1946 the saving rate was already higher than in 1939, and in 1950 it was as high as it was in 1924.

In figure 6.2(c) it can be seen that in the period that followed (1951–63), characterized by unprecedented growth and economic stability, the saving rate continued to rise and reached a historical peak in 1963 (more than 20 per cent of NNP). The characteristics of this period (as well as the performance of our equation), are similar to the ones of the first decade of growth at the turn of the century. In both periods the impact of fiscal policy on national saving was positive but limited, in both the growth effect contributed substantially to national saving, but, in addition, the constant term effect also contributed appreciably to the rise in computed saving rate (Income line).

Finally, the last two decades (1963–82) have seen a decline in the saving rate (interrupted by modest improvement corresponding to the economic recoveries of the late 1960s and late 1970s) by about 9 per cent of NNP from the peak of 1963 to 1982. From figure 6.2(c) one can see that the performance of our equation is quite good in this period; from table 6.5 it appears also that all of our variables contribute to explain this decline. In particular, the combined effect of the fiscal variables is very strong, since they account for some 3.8 points of the decline of the saving rate; by observing the difference between Fitted line and Growth line, it can also be seen that the substantial positive fiscal effect of the early 1960s has turned to a negative one since the mid 1970s. The residual and important part of the change in the saving rate can be attributed to the sharp slowdown in the rate of growth of the economy. This slowdown is reflected in the difference between the Growth and Income lines, which is positive and growing until 1970 and declines rapidly afterwards, becoming small and even negative after the mid 1970s. This slowdown is reflected in a rise in the wealth to income ratio which contributes more than $3\frac{1}{2}$ percentage points to the fall in the saving rate (cf. column (2) in table 6.5) and to a rate of change effect (column (5)) which contributes another $1\frac{1}{2}$ points. The slowdown begins with the transitory episode of 1964 and ensuing monetary stringency but then resumes on a larger and more persistent scale with a series of real shocks. These include the second wage explosion of 1969 (the '*autunno caldo*') and subsequent years, the growing labour immobility, the oil crisis and the subsequent slowdown in world demand.

The last two rows of table 6.5 show that the decline in net national saving rate continues for the years 1983 and 1984 which are not included in our sample. They also show how well our equation performs when extrapolated to these years. The outcome is quite close in 1983 when the computed value is 8.9. The decline from the 11.4 value of the previous period is explained both by the continued slowdown and by both components of fiscal policy. The forecast for 1984 is appreciably worse, as it wrongly predicts a recovery of the saving rate by 2 percentage points as a result of improvements in both growth and fiscal stance not now visible in the data. But it should be noted that the error is still well within our standard error.

In discussing the postwar period we have mentioned that fiscal policy contributed significantly to the reduction in the national saving rate after 1970. This conclusion does not appear particularly novel and, indeed, is widely accepted by both experts and public opinion. It must be noted, however, that our analysis offers a rather different assessment of the magnitude and mechanism at work. The general perception is that the harm came from the rise of the total borrowing requirement (and, consequently, of the outstanding public debt) of the public sector, which reached the enormous level of some 15 per cent of NNP by the early 1980s and which, it was feared, would reduce national saving by a commensurate amount. The behaviour of this variable is depicted by the top line (B in the graph) of figure 6.3. However, our estimate of the effect of the deficit on national saving is only -0.5 (last row of table 6.5) in the early 1980s. There are three reasons that account for the fact that we obtain so small an estimate of the recent impact of the deficit on saving:

1 The first is that in this study we are concerned with the determinants of net national saving, and therefore we must subtract from the total borrowing requirement that part of the deficit that finances productive investment. We have thus concentrated on the current account deficit (line $G^* + RD$ in figure 6.3) on the assumption that national income accounts' distinction between public consumption and public investment is a meaningful one.

2 However, the line ($G^* + RD$) measures the nominal deficit. In the presence of inflation one has also to take into account the depreciation of the stock of public debt. Conventionally, the deficit is corrected by subtracting pD (the *ex-post* inflation

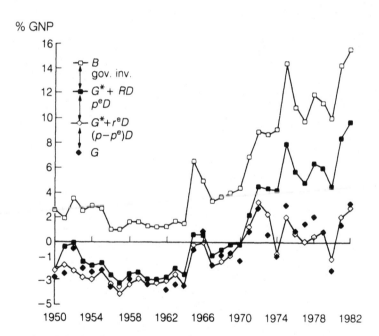

Figure 6.3 Four measures of government deficit, 1950–82
Note: Total government borrowing relative to NNP (B), government deficit as conventionally measured ($G^* + RD$), corrected for expected inflation ($G + r^cD$) and for actual inflation (G)

loss) from nominal interest transfers. This measure of the deficit is shown by the dots G in figure 6.3. But we have argued that, from the point of view of crowding out, what matters is the nominal deficit corrected for the *expected* depreciation of the debt – or p^cD (line $G^* + r^cD$ in figure 6.3). Since the difference between actual and expected inflation is modest and not systematic in the postwar period, the latter two measures of the deficit do not differ much from each other.

3   Finally, we have shown that deficits do not crowd out national saving one for one in that we estimate that the effect is roughly 0.5 $(\Sigma a_i + d)$, given, of course, the level of expenditure.

The main implication of these findings is that, contrary to the commonly held view, the deficit was not a major problem until the early 1980s, at least as far as national saving is concerned. Of course it is also true that the 'true' measure of deficit $(G^* + r^cD)$ has increased very substantially since the 1950s and 1960s but mainly because substantial surpluses have turned into moderate deficits (from an averge of -3 per cent of NNP to 1 per cent of NNP in the early 1980s). Somewhat surprisingly, according to our calculations, the effect of the deficit is of the same order of magnitude of that represented by the rise in government expenditure (2 points of NNP) and described at the beginning of this section. Note also that in equation 6.9 expenditure reduces national saving via disposable income by a larger amount than the deficit (0.67 versus 0.45) and thus expenditure has increased by only about $\frac{2}{3}$ of the deficit in the last two decades.

In figure 6.4 the graph shows three measures of the saving rate. The first is the net national saving of figure 6.2 (S_T).[11] The second is the conventional measure of private saving (SPN $= Y^* + RD - C$). The third is the 'corrected' measure in which income includes expected real interest (SPC $= Y^* + r^cD - C$). To obtain S_T one can alternatively subtract from SPC the corrected measure of the deficit $(G^* + r^cD$ in figure 6.3) or from SPN the conventional measure $(G + RD$ in figure 6.3). It can be observed that until the early 1970s, the two measures of private saving do not differ much from each other. However, in times of inflation, the difference can be very substantial, as can be noted by the divergent paths of SPC and SPN since the turn of the 1960s. The reason is that SPN is *not* independent of inflation; on the contrary, it is positively correlated with inflation, while SPC and S_T are, as we have shown, independent of inflation provided the private sector does not suffer from inflation illusion and the expected real rate is independent of inflation. The high rate of inflation of the last decade

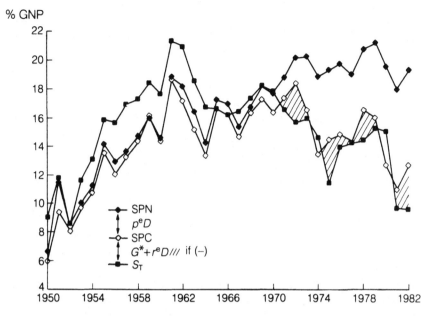

Figure 6.4 National and private saving rate, 1950–82
Note: private saving rate as conventionally measured (SPN = Y^* + RD − C), corrected for expected inflation (SPC = Y^* + $r^c D$ − C) and net national saving rate (S_T). The shaded area between S_T and SPC indicates government deficits corrected for expected inflation

has swollen SPN, creating the false impression that Italy was continuing to enjoy uncommonly high private saving as during the golden period of the late 1950s and 1960s. In reality, saving, properly corrected, has declined rather dramatically, as a consequence of the severe slowdown of the economy.

VII CONCLUSIONS

In this chapter we have analysed the behaviour of the private consumption and national saving over the entire history of the Italian State, a period covering some 120 years. This experience is of notable interest as it covers a wide variety of circumstances, including persistent stagnation, moderate growth and unusually fast development, periods of stable prices and rapid inflation, orthodox fiscal policies and seemingly huge government deficits, especially in connection with two major wars, one of them catastrophic. This varied experience is reflected in the behaviour of the national saving rate. Previously available statistics on aggregate saving ratios, based mostly on developed countries, had created the impression that the ratio is a relatively stable number, at least within a given country; but in the case of Italy, net national saving has exhibited wild fluctuations, with extended periods of very little saving – as low as 3 per cent of NNP – while in other periods the rate hovered in the 17 to 20 per cent range.

Our analysis suggests that all of this varied experience can be explained, to a very large extent, by a life cycle type of consumption function and that, furthermore, the hypothesis that the coefficients of this function have *remained stable* throughout the period of well over a century cannot be rejected on the basis of standard statistical tests.

The consumption function we have used differs from earlier formulations in that it endeavours to take explicitly into account the role of fiscal variables. Once it is recognized that consumption depends on *expected* net-of-tax income, and account is taken of the intertemporal government budget equation, one finds that consumption is reduced not only by current taxes as in the conventional view, but also by expected taxes and government expenditure. Equivalently it responds positively to expected net income and negatively to government deficits. The quantitative effect of deficits turns out to depend on the length of the average planning horizon. If the horizon is infinite, as is effectively postulated by the proposers of the REP, then taxes matter not at all, while the response of consumption to government expenditure (or equivalently to deficit, given net income) would coincide with the propensity to consume. This of course implies that budget deficits have *no* effect on national saving, and the same would be true of any transfer, including payment of interest on national debt. These implications are the well-known essence of the Barro/RE proposition. By contrast, if the planning horizon is of the order of the length of remaining life, as postulated by the standard version of the LCH, then the coefficient of expenditure and deficit should be appreciably lower than the propensity to consume. It thus follows that the effect of deficits (including interest) on national saving will be large, not much lower than the propensity to consume.

The consumption function estimated for Italy appears to reject convincingly the REP and to be fully consistent with the life horizon LCH; specifically, we find: (a) that the estimated effect of the deficit on consumption is generally between $\frac{1}{3}$ and $\frac{2}{3}$ of the propensity to consume, and this seems to hold even in war periods, when the deficits are huge and hence their contribution can be estimated more reliably; and (b) that consumption responds to interest payment on national debt much as it responds to any other transfer, provided the interest payments are adjusted for the perceived loss of real principal due to expected inflation. One further possible test is, however, totally inconclusive – namely that relating to the effect on consumption of that component of private wealth that consists of government debt. Since our measure of wealth includes debt, and its coefficient is around 0.03, we can infer that, if debt is added to the equation, its coefficient should be around -0.03 for the REP and, say, between zero and around -0.01 for the LH–LCH. In fact, the coefficient estimated for the entire period is found to be precisely -0.01, but it is so poorly estimated (standard error -0.012) that no definite conclusion would be justified. For sub-periods, the results are equally inconclusive – for the postwar period as well as for the period 1882–1950, the coefficient is typically positive but again very imprecisely estimated. However, if one adds to the prewar period the 18 years 1864–81 for which the data are incomplete, then the coefficient becomes negative but too much so to be accounted for by the REP hypothesis. We conclude that the tests on the whole support LCH but by no means conclusively, and that a test of these implications does not look like a promising route for testing REP versus LH–LCH.

One significant result of our analysis is that while fiscal policy and, in particular, the deficit are important determinants of national saving (thereby playing an important role in domestic investment), their impact cannot be gauged from the behaviour of the current account deficit as conventionally measured. In the conventional measure the deficit includes the nominal service of the debt. We find instead that what affects consumption, and hence the deficit relevant to the estimation of the crowding out effect, is the *expected real* interest payment. This measure can be very much different from the nominal one under conditions of persistent, readily predictable inflation. Such conditions have prevailed since the early 1970s – though, apparently, not in earlier times.

Summing up, our empirical results indicate that the long swings in the saving ratio reflect primarily two forces – fiscal policies via expenditure and deficits, and variations in the growth rate of the economy, which manifest themselves in variations of the wealth to income ratio, in the rate of change of income effect and, presumably, in part, in the constant term. To illustrate, between 1936–39 and 1961–64, the national saving ratio increased $16\frac{1}{2}$ percentage points – from 3 to $19\frac{1}{2}$. The change explained by our equation is a little larger, $17\frac{1}{2}$. Of that change 7 points are attributable to fiscal policy – 5 of which are due to the swing in the budget from large deficit to a substantial surplus. Another $5\frac{1}{2}$ is attributable to the combined wealth and rate of change effect as the overall growth rate rose from zero to 6.5 per cent. The remaining

5 points are due to the constant term and presumably reflect in part a further wealth effect (via land) and possibly some absolute income effect.

As for the recent decline from the early 1960s to the early 1980s of some 8 percentage points (of which 7 are accounted for by the equation), we find that, contrary to a widely held perception, the major cause of decline is not the seemingly huge and highly visible deficit. Indeed, when the deficit is correctly measured it appears rather small even in the 1980s. Accordingly, fiscal policy accounts for less than half of the decline, and only half of that is due to the deficit. Furthermore the effect is not due to a substantial deficit *now* but, rather, to a substantial surplus *then*. The more important component of the decline in savings is related instead to the sharp drop in the growth of the economy, from 6.5 per cent to 1 per cent.

Finally, our analysis suggests that the observed variations in saving cannot be attributed to a systematic, direct effect of inflation. Indeed, that variable does not appear explicitly in our final equation, though it was tested on various occasions. This does not exclude the possibility of an indirect effect if, for example, (a) inflation had a systematic effect on the expected real rate (i.e. Fisher's law systematically fails to hold), and/or (b) taxation were, as a rule, adjusted to keep in balance the *nominal* budget. There is, however, little evidence that either of these two phenomena has played an important role in recent Italian history.

The LCH model suggests that other variables, in principle, should affect savings. These include in particular the demographic structure of the population and the social security system. While these variables are, by their nature, slowly changing, they could be important over the long span covered by our analysis. We have not so far found any satisfactory way to test for the presence of these effects but we do regard them as important topics for future research.

APPENDIX: SOURCES OF DATA

The sources of the data for the period 1950–82 (except for the series on government debt, that has been revised) can be found in the Data Appendix of Modigliani et al. (1985). From 1862 to 1950 we had to rely on a number of sources, of different quality and not always entirely consistent. Below we describe how each series has been constructed.

Private Consumption

Source: Ercolani (1969, p. 422, table 4.1.A). This variable, as well as consumption after 1950, includes expenditure on durables.

Disposable Income

Ercolani (1969, p. 427, table 4.4) provides an estimate of disposable income (gross of depreciation); we have computed the net disposable income of the private sector by subtracting depreciation. (Source: ISTAT, 1957.)

Wealth

Ercolani (1969, p. 418, table 3.3), provides an estimate of the stock of capital and of the value of agricultural land from 1882 to 1952. From 1861 to 1882 we have extrapolated this series backward, assuming the change in the stock of capital to be the same as the average rate of growth of disposable income. Finally, wealth is defined as the sum of the net stock of capital and government debt.

Government Debt

It is the only variable that has been revised from the one used by Modigliani et al. (1985), because a new series provided by Spaventa et al. (1984) was available at the time we started working on this paper. Essentially, Spaventa et al. (1984) have computed a series of the net debt of the public sector from 1960 to 1982, and improve upon previous available statistics because they subtract from the stock of debt of the public sector the amount of deposits of Central and Local Government to the banking sector. To preserve consistency, in the period 1950–60 we have rescaled the series on debt provided by Spaventa et al., assuming that the growth pattern of the public sector debt (unobservable from 1950 to 1960) could be approximated by the series on Central Government debt.

For the period 1864–1950 we relied on the following sources: from 1861 to 1900, Romani (1976, p. 268, table 12); from 1901 to 1935, ISTAT (1957, p. 173); from 1935 onward, United Nations, (1955, p. 89). The series from 1862 to 1950 excludes foreign debt but does not include the debt of local governments and public agencies, so that it is not readily comparable with the series provided by Spaventa et al., although one might argue that the importance of the debt of local governments and agencies has been growing in importance only in recent years.

Government Deficit

There are two estimates of government deficit over the period 1861–1950, the official one provided by ISTAT (1957) and another by Repaci (1962). Since the estimate of disposable income relies, among other sources, on the estimates done by Repaci, we have used the latter estimate of government deficit. It must also be noted that, as in the case of government debt, the deficit only refers to the Central Government.

Government Investment

Source: Ercolani (1969), series 'Servizi Economici' (p. 435, table 4.10). This series includes a number of different items, but generally refers to government investment for public services (electricity, railroads, etc.) and financing of public enterprises. The series is not entirely consistent with the definition of deficit elaborated by Repaci because it is based on the official statistics of the Central Government balance sheets.

Taxes

The sum of direct and indirect taxes. Source: Repaci (1962).

Nominal Interest Payments

Defined as interest paid by the Central Government to residents. From 1862 to 1900 the source is Romani (1978), from 1901 to 1935 ISTAT (1957) and from 1937 onward, United Nations (1955).

Inflation Loss on Government Debt

Defined as:

$$pD = (D/\text{defl}) (\text{Defl} - \text{Defl}_{-1})$$

where p is the actual inflation rate, D is the beginning of period debt outstanding and Defl is the end of period deflator or private consumption.

Deflator of Private Consumption

Source: Ercolani (1969, p. 424, table 4.1.B).

Population

Source: Ercolani, p. 412, table 2.1.

Nominal Interest Rate on Government Obligations

(Used in figure 6.1) for the period 1862–1912, Romani (1976, p. 101, table 16); for the period 1926–50, Ercolani (1969, p. 456, table 5.2); for the period 1951–82, IMF, row 61b. For the period 1913–25 we had to rely on Spinelli (1979), who provides a series on the commercial paper rate.

NOTES

1 For a critique of Kormendi's approach, see Modigliani and Sterling (1985).
2 The way the variable is constructed also greatly differs among the two periods (see the Data Appendix in Modigliani et al. (1985), also Ercolani (1969)).
3 To give a feeling of the magnitude involved in the correction of government deficit for capital expenses, the item that we subtract from government deficit is about 10 per cent to 15 per cent of government expenses (except for the years following the Second World War, in which it reaches a peak of 46 per cent of government expenses). In terms of disposable income,

government investment usually is in the range of 2 per cent to 3 per cent, except for the postwar period in which it reaches a peak of 7.3 per cent of disposable income.

4 The actual rates of inflation in those years were 43 in 1916, 44 in 1917, 29 in 1918, 15 in 1919 and 41 in 1920. During the Second World War, inflation was 38.5 in 1942, 61 in 1943, 145 in 1944, 118 in 1945, 36 in 1946 and 73 in 1947.

5 We have conducted a Goldfeld test – assuming that the size of the errors was an increasing function of income – and the more general Park–Gleiser test; in no case did the errors appear to be heteroskedastic.

6 Regressions (2.9) and (2.10) have been estimated with multiplicative dummies on wealth and on the constant term, to account for the fact that wealth includes land until 1950 and that the constant term in (2.1) appears to be higher than in (2.3). Since the coefficients of the dummies were very small and never significant, we have dropped them and obtained the results reported in the table.

7 In the regression, we have used the market interest rate on medium-term government bonds. This measure of R is not entirely consistent with the RD variable, since RD is *not* the product of R and D, but is taken from the national account statistics. Thus, the implied R of our variable RD reflects the maturity structure of the public debt. It is, therefore, moving slower and is more serially correlated than the market rate. Since Fisher's law relates expected inflation to the market rate, we have used this latter variable in computing correlations among R, p and p^c.

8 A dummy on $p^c D$ was introduced also in (3.7) to allow for a different coefficient in the period 1864–1914 and 1919–39. Since the dummy, as well as the coefficient of $p^c D$, was zero, we have not reported this regression.

9 To obtain consistent estimates in the presence of auto-correlated residuals, we have also added to the list of instruments the lagged dependent variable, the exogenous variables and all variables lagged once.

10 In plotting the variables as well as in computing the averages presented in table 6.5, we have been careful in carrying on the calculations based on the values of the coefficients of regression (4.4). Therefore, the coefficient of $r^c D$ (0.53) is not assumed to be equal to $(\Sigma a_i + d)$. Equation 6.9 is for illustrative purposes only, although the differences with the actual values are negligible.

11 Note that S_T in figure 6.4 differs from S_T in figure 6.2 because the latter is smoothed with a three-year moving average.

REFERENCES

Barro, R. 1974: Are government bonds net wealth? *Journal of Political Economy*, 82, 1094–1117.

Barsky, R. 1985: Three interest rate paradoxes, MIT, Ph.D. Thesis.

Ercolani, P. 1969: Documentazione Statistica di Base. In Giorgio Fua (ed.) *Lo Sviluppo Economico in Italia*, Fronco Angeli Edibone, Milano, pp. 380–455.

Feldstein, M. 1982: Government deficit and aggregate demand, *Journal of Monetary Economics*, 9, 1–20.

ISTAT 1957: Indagine Statistica sullo Sviluppo del Reddito Nazionale dell'Italia dal 1861 al 1956, Rome.

Kormendi, R. 1983: Government debt, government spending and private sector behavior, *American Economic Review*, December, 73, 994–1010.

Modigliani, F. 1975: The life cycle hypothesis of saving twenty years later. In M. Parkin (ed.) *Contemporary Issues in Economics*, Manchester University Press, Manchester.

Modigliani, F. 1984: The Economics of Public Deficits, *Proceedings of the Conference on Economic Policy in Theory and Practices*, Israel, May.

Modigliani, F. and Sterling, A. 1985: Government debt, government spending and private sector behaviour: a comment (forthcoming in *American Economic Review*).

Modigliani, F., Jappelli, T. and Pagano, M. 1985: The impact of fiscal policy and inflation on national saving: the Italian case, *Banca Nazionale del Lavoro Quarterly Review*, June, 91–126.

Repaci, F.A. 1962: *La Finanza Pubblica in Italia nel Secolo 1861–1960*, Zanichelli, Bologna.

Romani, M. 1976: *Storia Economica d'Italia nel Secolo XIX, 1815–1914*, Vol. 2, Giuffre, Milano.

Seater, J. and Mariano, R. 1985: New tests of the life cycle and discounting hypothesis, *Journal of Monetary Economics*, 15, 195–215.

Spaventa, L., Artoni, R., Morcaldo, G. and Zanchi, P. 1984: *L'Indebitamento Pubblico in Italia: Evoluzione, Prospettive e Problemi*, Report prepared for the V Commission of the Chamber of Deputies, Rome, September.

Sterling, A. 1985: Public debt and private wealth: the role of anticipated taxes, MIT Sloan School of Management, April, Ph.D. Thesis.

IMF, *International Financial Statistics*, various issues. United Nations, Department of Economic Affairs, 1948. Public Debt 1914–1946. New York, Lake Success.

Spinelli, 1980: The demand for money in the Italian economy, *Journal of Monetary Economics*, 6, 83–104.

Errata

Page 129, third to last line: replace Σd_i" with Σa_i."

Page 130, second indented section, last line: "deficit" should read "deficits."

Page 130, second to last paragraph, second to last line: insert "LH-" in front of "LCH."

Page 131, equation in second line of last paragraph: the plus sign should be a minus sign.

Page 131, third line from end: "in" should read "into."

Page 132, two lines above equation (6.6): "in" should read "into."

Page 135, table 6.1, column (2): "14.0" should read "4.0." In the text for table 6.1, the second line should read "(7), all relative." Insert after this sentence, "all columns except (2) and (3) are in percentage terms."

Page 136, first paragraph, last two lines: "contain" should read "containing," and "reduce" should read "reducing."

Page 136, fifth line from end: insert "real" between "negative" and "interest rates."

Page 138, Figure 6.1: in both diagrams the vertical axis should be labeled "%" not "% GNP."

Page 141: add to text for table 6.2, "C here stands for the constant term; SE is the standard error of the regression; RHO is the autocorrelation coefficient."

Page 142, second paragraph, third line: before semicolon insert "using Y^{**}."

Page 145, second line in section V: "interests" should read "interest payments."

Page 146: second regression numbered "3.5" should be "3.6." The coefficient "0.59," presently lying between columns (6) and (7), should be wholly in column (6); in column (7) there should be a coefficient of "-0.59."

Page 147, first paragraph, line 8: delete "7" which is superscript on R, and put it as a superscript at end of sentence; in line 11 "p^e should read "p.

Page 147, second paragraph, second line: insert "power" after "purchasing."

Page 150, line 4.4, column 2: the coefficient is not "0.478" but "0.47." In column (9) add the following coefficients for lines 4.4, 4.5, 4.6 respectively: -0.48, -0.45, -0.53. At end of notes for table insert "SE is the standard error of the regression; LL is the log likelihood ratio. Variables D_1 and D_2 are defined in the last four lines of p. 145. The 'expected inflation' effect for each of the two subperiods is calculated by adding the subperiod dummy (column (7) or (8)) and the coefficient in column (9.)."

Page 152, second line: insert a comma after r^eD.

Page 152, third and fourth lines: "margin of errors" should read "margins of error."

Page 152: equation (6.8): the first set of square brackets closes after the second set of "parentheses."

Page 152: equation (6.9) should read

$$\frac{S_T}{NNP} = (1 - a) + a_2 \frac{\Delta NNP}{NNP} - (1 - a)\frac{E}{NNP} - (a_i + d_i)\frac{(G^* + r^eD)}{NNP}$$

$$- a_2 \frac{(G^*_{-1} + r^eD_{-1})}{NNP} - \frac{bw}{NNP} - a_2 \frac{\Delta E}{NNP} - \frac{k}{NNP}.$$

Page 153, first line of equation at top of page: third coefficient is not "-0.69" but "-0.31."

Page 153, second indented point, fourth line: replace "with the rate of growth of income" by "as the rate of growth of income increases."

Page 153, fourth indented point: insert a comma in the first line, after "deficit." Last line, delete ", or 0.45" and insert "from 4.4 and alternatively $(0.22 + 0.23)$ from equation (6.9)."

Page 153: the three-line paragraph that follows the fourth indented point should actually be part of that paragraph.

Page 156, line 12: "6.4" should read "6.9."

Page 157: insert at end of notes for table, "I is the constant term divided by net national product."

Page 158, top line: delete "the."

Page 159, second paragraph, fourth line: insert "the" before "government"; in the sixth line, "0.7" should read "0.3."

Page 160, second paragraph, second to last line: delete "not now visible in the data."

Page 162, first main paragraph, sixth line: "averge" should read "average"; in the third line from the end, "larger" should read "smaller," "0.67" should read "0.31"; in the second to last line, "2/3" should read "3/2."

Page 162, first main paragraph, ninth line: "magnitude of" should read "magnitude as."

Page 162, second paragraph, fifth line: insert "payments" after "interest."

Page 163, first line of section VII: delete "the" before "private."

Page 164, third paragraph, eight lines from the end: insert "the" before "national."

Page 165, first paragraph, line 10: -0.012" should read "0.013"; in the last sentence "tests" should read "test," and "support" should read "supports."

Page 167, "Wealth" section, second line: "1952" should read "1950."

Page 167, "Government Debt" section, first paragraph, line 7: "to the banking" should read "with the banking"; in the second paragraph, fourth line, delete "excludes foreign debt"; in the last line delete "in importance."

Page 168, "Nominal Interest Payments" section, second line: "1978" should read "1976."

Page 168, last line of the "Inflation Loss on Government Debt" section: "or" should read "for."

Page 169, note 5: "Gleiser" should read "Glejser."

Page 169, note 10, second line: "carrying on" should read "carrying out."

THE DETERMINANTS OF INTEREST RATES IN THE ITALIAN ECONOMY*

Franco Modigliani and Tullio Jappelli

1. Introduction

The economic effects of fiscal policy have been recently the subject of much controversy. The debate has centered on the relation between the government deficit, saving, interest rates, and capital accumulation. The purpose of the present study is to contribute to this debate by providing new empirical evidence on the link between fiscal policy and interest rates, and, more generally, to study the fundamental determinants of interest rates in the context of the Italian economy.

Recently a number of papers have investigated similar issues in relation to the United States experience. A common concern of many of these studies is to test whether the government deficits increase interest rates, thereby reducing the rate of capital accumulation. The prevailing view is that an increase in the government deficit should reduce the supply of national saving, inducing a rise in interest rates and a reduction in the demand for investment. We will refer to this view as the "conventional" view as opposed to that held by those economists who believe that the government deficits are matched by a parallel shift in private saving. Since the supply of national saving is unaffected, the equilibrium levels of interest rates and of capital accumulation are left unchanged. We refer to this hypothesis as the Ricardian equivalence proposition. To help clarify these issues in the present study we estimate a reduced form of the nominal interest rate. Although we cannot

* An acknowledgement is due to Marco Pagano and Luigi Guiso for useful discussions on a preliminary version of this paper. Errors are the authors' responsibility. Financial support from CNR (grant n. 87.01618.53) is gratefully acknowledged.

9

identify all structural parameters of the model, the estimated coefficients make it possible to discriminate between the conventional model and the Ricardian proposition.

Besides providing new evidence on the relation between fiscal policy and interest rates, this paper aims at improving on most of the previous analyses in one or more of the following aspects:

i) the estimated equation is explicitly derived within the framework of the Life-Cycle Hypothesis (LCH), which includes the Ricardian equivalence proposition as a limiting case, and is best suited for studying the issue of crowding-out of capital formation.

ii) Most published tests presented in the literature do not separate the effect of cutting taxes from that of increasing government expenditure. This distinction is important when testing the Ricardian proposition; the failure to consider it may introduce serious bias in the estimated coefficients and in their interpretation.

iii) We take into account the potentially different effects on interest rates of the *flow* of the government deficit and of the accumulated *stock* of government debt. If the capital-labor ratio of installed capital can be freely modified ex-post (the putty-putty hypothesis), the interest rate depends negatively on the stock of capital, and hence must increase with the stock of government debt. If, however, factor proportions can only be altered ex-ante (the putty-clay hypothesis), the interest rate is related to current investment and therefore to the current deficit, but is independent of the stock of capital and of the accumulated stock of government debt.

iv) Finally, we use a definition of the deficit which subtracts from the conventional government budget (as measured by the national accounts) the inflation-induced depreciation of the stock of government debt owned by the private sector. The correction is particularly significant when one estimates reduced forms of nominal interest rates that include expected inflation and deficits (or net taxes, which include nominal interest transfers) among the regressors. If consumers and investors are able to correct nominal rates for the rate of expected inflation they should also be able to correct nominal interest transfers for the inflation-induced depreciation of the stock of public debt. Lack of either of these two

10

effects would undermine the hypothesis of rational and consistent behavior on the part of the private sector.

The paper is organized as follows: Section 2 briefly reviews the existing literature and the data. Section 3 presents the model to be estimated in Section 4. Section 5 concludes our study and outlines some policy issues.

2. Motivation of the Study

There are two circumstances in which there should be no relation between deficits and interest rates:

ii) in a small open economy, with perfect capital markets, interest rates are exogenously given. Thus, a decline in national saving caused either by a decline in private saving or by an increase in the government deficits would be completely offset by an increased flow of capital from abroad. In this case, domestic interest rates and domestic investment would be unchanged.

ii) According to the Ricardian proposition private saving rises with the deficits, because consumers, fully discounting the future tax liabilities implied by the current deficits, offset that liability by increasing private saving. As a consequence, national saving is unchanged, and interest rates do not rise.[1]

The top panel of Table 1 displays the means of the net national saving rate and of its major uses and sources (in percentages of full employment gross national product) for selected subperiods of the sample, which covers the years 1958-85. One of the most striking facts of the Italian economy emerging from this table is that over the last thirty years net national saving — S_T in column (1) — declined by almost 10 percentage points from the beginning of the 1960s to the mid 1980s.

The breakdown of national saving into net private investment, net government investment, and outflows of domestic capital is reported in columns (2), (3), and (4) respectively. The current account, which turned from surplus into substantial deficit after

---

[1] See Barro [1974] for a theoretical discussion, and Kormendi [1983] for an application with United States data.

11

Table 1*

BREAKDOWN OF THE NET NATIONAL SAVING
BY USES AND SOURCES, 1958-1985

Period	Uses				Sources			
	S_T (1)	I_P (2)	I_G (3)	NX (4)	S_P (5)	S_G (6)	$S_P - p^e D_{-1}$ (7)	$S_G + p^e D_{-1}$ (8)
1958-1963*	17.3	13.3	3.0	1.0	14.3	3.0	13.9	3.4
1964-1969*	15.5	10.2	2.6	2.7	14.8	0.7	14.1	1.4
1970-1974*	14.4	12.0	2.8	−0.4	17.1	−2.7	16.0	−1.6
1975-1979*	11.9	8.2	3.0	0.7	17.4	−5.5	12.5	−0.6
1980-1985*	8.8	6.6	3.6	−1.4	15.7	−6.9	8.7	0.1
1985*	7.6	5.2	3.6	−1.2	15.7	−8.1	9.0	−1.4
1958-1985*	13.6	10.1	3.0	0.5	15.7	−2.1	13.0	0.6

* Based on the old national accounts, unavailable before 1980. Saving and investment exclude depreciation. Each variable is divided by full employment GNP. Definitions and sources of variables can be found in the Appendix. The sum of the values of columns (2), (3), and (4), of columns (5) and (6) and of columns (7) and (8) is identical to the value reported in column (1). The last two columns correct private and public saving by the expected inflation-induced depreciation of the stock of public debt.

1980, only partially offset the decline in national saving. Since government investment (I_G) has stayed constant — or increased slightly over the sample period, private investment (I_p) declined dramatically, bearing the bulk of the adjustment. The behavior of I_p and NX casts therefore serious doubts on the validity of proposition (i), that capital inflows fully offset movements in the national rate of saving, leaving investment unchanged.

Columns (5) and (6) display the two sources of national saving e.g. private (S_p) and government saving (S_G). At first glance one may conclude that private saving stayed high (except for some cyclical swings) over most of the three last decades, and that the crowding-out of national saving has to be attributed almost entirely to government dissaving. However, both S_p and S_G include the nominal interest bill, and are not corrected for the inflation induced depreciation of the stock of public debt. In times of inflation the effect of the correction is to reduce S_p and increase S_G by the amount of the inflation tax (see columns (7) and (8)). In two recent papers (Modigliani, Jappelli and Pagano, 1985, and Modigliani and Jappelli, 1987) it was shown that, if one takes into account this correction, the decline in S_T can be explained by two major factors.

12

Increased deficit financing (corrected for inflation) and increased government expenditure are responsible for the decline in net national saving of about 4 percentage points, while the slowdown of economic growth accounts for the remaining reduction in S_T by other 6 percentage points. From the finding that S_T depends on the government deficits, we concluded that the Ricardian proposition was not supported by the data, and thus rejected proposition (ii) above.

In this paper we provide new evidence consistent with our previous findings, and in favor of the hypothesis that increased government expenditure and reliance on deficit financing have increased interest rates, thereby — other things equal — reducing private investment. We do so by estimating a reduced form for interest rates. Although reduced forms of interest rates have no direct behavioral interpretation, we are able to impose testable restrictions on some estimated parameters which enable us to distinguish between competing hypothesis.

Much empirical literature has dealt with issues similar to the ones that we address in this paper. Bernheim [1987] provides an exhaustive survey of the available tests of the Ricardian proposition using reduced forms for interest rates. The evidence is related mainly to the United States economy, where the recent huge rise of budget deficits has stimulated research in this area. As with other controversial issues, the empirical evidence is very mixed.

Two papers supportive of the Ricardian proposition are Plosser [1982] and Evans [1987]. The first paper tests one implication of the capital market efficiency hypothesis, namely that only innovations in fiscal variables should affect the term structure of interest rates. Plosser finds no effect of debt innovations on interest rates, and interprets his results as evidence in favor of the Ricardian view.

Evans [1987], using monthly data from June 1908 to March 1984, finds no positive association between budget deficits and current interest rates. He further tests the hypothesis that expected budget deficits increase current interest rates. If future taxes are correctly anticipated by consumers and investors, the residuals of the interest rate equation should tend to be positive before tax cuts

13

and negative before tax hikes. However, the residuals of the regression do not behave in this way, and Evans concludes in favor of the Ricardian proposition.

Feldstein [1986] finds no evidence of a positive association between interest rates and *current* full employment deficits over the period 1960-84, but the results are reversed when he replaces the current deficits with a measure of the expected *future* deficits. When this measure of the deficit is used in the estimation, Feldstein also finds the coefficient of government debt to be insignificantly different from zero, and interprets this result as supportive of investment models embodying substantial costs of changing the capital-labor ratio of installed capital.

Although Feldstein repeatedly stresses the importance of international capital movements, a measure of world interest rates is never included in any of his estimated equations. Furthermore, he claims to reject the Ricardian proposition, but fails to test, as he should, for the separate effect of government expenditure and to correct deficits and taxes for the inflation-induced depreciation of public debt (see (ii) and (iv) in Section 1).

One common problem of these studies is that in the post-war period the U.S. economy has experienced little variation in the long-term interest rate and in the government deficits, except for the episode of the 1980s. In the Italian economy, on the other hand, over the past thirty years the swings of key variables have been remarkable. From the late 1950s to the mid 1980s the nominal interest rate has risen by almost 12 percentage points, the ratio of the deficit corrected for inflation relative to GNP by 5 points (and the unadjusted deficit by 11 points), and the ratio of government debt to GNP is three times as large as it was in the late 1950s. Thus, Italian data provide an ideal opportunity to investigate the relationship between fiscal policy and interest rate because in principle the data should allow one to discriminate sharply between the competing hypotheses.

3. A Model of Interest Rates

In this section we present a simple structural model of the

14

economy, to test for the main determinants of nominal interest rates. We will first consider the case of a closed economy, which we model as follows:

(1) $C_t = a(Y_t^P - T_t^P) - bG_t^P + cW_{t-1} - dD_{t-1} + u_{1t}$

(2.1) $I_t = f_1 CAP_t - g_1(R_t - p_t^e) + u_{21t}$

(2.2) $K_t = I_t + K_{t-1} = f_2 Y_t - g_2(R_t - p_t^e) + u_{22t}$

(3) $M_t = mY_t - hR_t + u_{3t}$

(4) $I_t = S_{Tt} = Y_t - C_t - E_t$

The variables consumption C_t, income Y_t, government deficit G_t, government expenditure E_t, net taxes T_t, capital stock K_t, wealth W_t, government debt D_t, net national saving S_{Tt}, private investment I_t, and money stock M_t are measured in current liras and "deflated" by current liras full employment gross national product (Y_T^F). The 'P' superscript indicates "permanent" variables. Permanent income, net taxes and the deficit are defined to include the inflation-induced expected depreciation of the stock of debt, i.e. the product of expected inflation and the stock of debt at the beginning of the period ($p^e D_{t-1}$).

The variable R_t is the long-term nominal interest rate, p_t^e is expected inflation, and CAP_t the capacity utilization rate. The parameters of the model are all positive. The terms u_{1t}, u_{21t}, u_{22t}, and u_{3t} represent, respectively, the error components of the consumption function (1), of the two versions of the investment function (2.1) and (2.2), and of the money demand function (3). For notational simplicity, the "t" subscript will be dropped in the remainder of the paper.

The first equation is a very general consumption function, derived by Modigliani and Sterling [1986]. Private consumption (C) depends on permanent income net of permanent taxes ($Y^P - T^P$), where T^P are permanent taxes net of transfers, permanent government deficit ($G^P = E^P - T^P$), beginning of period wealth inclusive of government debt (W_{-1}), and government debt (D_{-1}). Equation (1) reduces to the standard specification of the consumption function if b=d=0. If individuals regard a tax cut as equivalent

15

to a future tax liability, a=b and c=d and equation (1) reduces to

$$C = a(Y^P - E^P) + c(W_{-1} - D_{-1}) + u_1,$$

a formulation consistent with the Ricardian equivalence proposition.

When we estimated equation (1) for the Italian economy, we found very strong evidence pointing to a value of b=0.2 (or lower), a=0.70, c=0.03, and d=0: on these grounds, we rejected the Ricardian proposition (see Modigliani and Jappelli, 1987). We also found that the impact of the deficit cannot be gauged by the behavior of the current account deficit as conventionally measured. What affects consumption, and hence the deficit relevant to the estimation of the crowding-out effect are the expected real interest payments rather than the nominal interest bill. We concluded that government deficits have some impact on consumption and private saving, but a rather modest one, consistent with a formulation of the LCH with finite horizons. Alternatively, by substituting (1) into (4), we showed that a reduction in taxes (T^P), for a given level of government expenditure (E^P), reduces national saving by (a−b), which, in the case of the Italian economy, we estimated at approximately 0.5.

Equations (2.1) and (2.2) are two alternative formulations of the demand for investment. The first formulation, shown in equation (2.1), is a linear approximation of the putty-clay (P−C) model of investment, according to which current investment has a capital-labor ratio fixed through its life, because factor proportions cannot be changed once the capital has been installed. Accordingly, new investment is proportional to the change in desired capacity, with the factor of proportionality a function of the cost of capital. The arguments of this function include, among other variables, the expected real rate (see for example Modigliani et al. [1974]). In equation (2.1) we take a linear approximation of the P−C model, with the current rate of utilization (CAP) proxying for desired addition to capacity, and the expected real rate (R−p^e) proxying for the cost of capital.

Equation (2.2) is an alternative formulation of the investment

16

equation, and is derived from the putty-putty (P—P) model, according to which factor proportions can be changed ex-post, as well as ex-ante. By assuming a Cobb-Douglas production function and perfectly competitive markets, it is readily established that, for a cost minimizing firm, the desired stock of capital (K) is linearly related to the level of current output (Y), with the coefficient of proportionality depending on the cost of capital. In equation (2.2) we take a linear approximation of the P-P model, and proxy the cost of capital with the expected real rate.

Solving equations (2.1) and (2.2) for $(R-p^e)$, assigning weights w and $(1-w)$ to the P—C model and to the P—P model, and assuming that the behavior of K can be approximated by the difference between the stock of total net wealth (W) and government debt (D), i.e. $K=W-D$, the following expression for the expected real rate may be obtained:

(5) $R - p^e = - [(w/g_1 + (1-w)/g_2] I + [(1-w)f_2/g_2] Y - [(1-w)/g_2] W_{-1}$
$+ [(1-w)/g_2] D_{-1} + (wf_1/g_1) CAP + (w/g_1) u_{21} + [(1-w)/g_2] u_{22}$

The expression above reduces to (2.1) if $w=1$, and to (2.2) if $w=0$. Equation (5) highlights the role of government debt and of the stock of wealth in affecting the expected real rate. In fact, only under the P—P hypothesis $(w=0)$ is there a strong relation of the real rate to the stock of capital and hence to the government debt, given wealth. It should be further noted that, according to both models, $(R-p^e)$ depends on the rate of investment, and, thus, on permanent income, taxes, and expenditure, as can be seen by equations (1) and (4). The importance of these variables in affecting interest rates is however greater if $w=1$, because the interest rate elasticity of investment is smaller in the P—C model $(g_1<g_2)$. According to this model a new level of desired capital stock can be achieved only by modifying *new* investments, and thus the adjustment to the desired level of capital stock implied by a different cost of capital takes much longer if the capital-labor ratio of installed capital is fixed.

Equation (3) is a linear approximation to a standard LM func-

17

tion. In the empirical implementation of the model, it is assumed that real money, deflated by full employment GNP, is exogenous. Accordingly, R is a function of the real money supply, holding the price level as a constant, and of the level of current income relative to full employment GNP.

Net national saving is identical to the difference between current income and private and government consumption (equation 4). Furthermore, in equilibrium, in a closed economy the supply of saving is also equal to the demand for investment. Equations (1), (3), (4) and (5) represent a model of four equations in C, I, Y and R. We solve it for the nominal interest rate R:

$$(6) \quad R = \alpha_1 p^e + \alpha_2 M + \alpha_3 Y^P + \alpha_4 G^P + \alpha_5 E^P + \alpha_6 W_{-1} + \alpha_7 D_{-1} + \alpha_8 CAP + v$$

where v is a composite error term. The relation of the reduced form coefficients to the structural parameters of the model is provided in Table 2. Columns (2) and (3) indicate, respectively, the reduced form and the structural coefficients of equation (6). Column (4) reports the values of the structural coefficients for the case of w=1, and column (5) the values for the case w=0. Each coefficient in Table 2 is divided by Δ, whose value is reported in the last row of the table for the general model, and for the P−C and the P−P models.

As can be seen by comparing columns (4) and (5), the form of the investment equation has far reaching implications for the behavior of interest rates. In particular, under the P−C hypothesis (w=1) the interest rate is only slightly affected by the stocks of total private wealth and public debt and strongly influenced by addition to capacity.

As far as the role of other variables, equation (6) predicts that the response of the nominal interest rate to expected inflation is positive ($\alpha_1 > 0$) but not necessarily equal to one, as Fisher's law would suggest for a world of perfectly flexible prices and continuous full employment. The reason that the nominal rate cannot rise as much as expectations is that the rise in the nominal rate rises velocity (hence Y, since M is held constant), which must be accom-

18

Table 2[*]

RELATION OF REDUCED FORM COEFFICIENTS
TO STRUCTURAL FORM COEFFICIENTS
OF EQUATION (6)

Variable (1)	Coefficient (2)	Structural Form Coefficient (3)	P-C: w=1 (4)	P-P: w=0 (5)
p^e	α_1	$wg_1 + (1-w)g_2$	$g_1>0$	$g_2>0$
M	α_2	$-[(w/m) - (1-w)(1-f_2)/m]$	$-(1/m)<0$	$-(1-f_2)/m<0$
Y^P	α_3	a	$a>0$	$a>0$
G^P	α_4	$(a - b)$	$(a-b)>0$	$(a-b)>0$
E^P	α_5	$(1-a)$	$(1-a)>0$	$(1-a)>0$
W_{-1}	α_6	$-(1 - w - c)$	$c>0$	$-(1 - c)<0$
D_{-1}	α_7	$(1 - w - d)$	$-d<0$	$(1 - d)>0$
CAP	α_8	$w f_1$	$f_1>0$	0
v		$u_1 + (u_3/m) + wu_{21} +$ $+ (1-w)[u_{22}-(u_3 f_2)/m]$	$u_1+u_{21}+u_3/m$	$u_1 + u_{22} +$ $+ [(1-f_2)/m]u_3$
Δ		$(h/m) + wg_1 +$ $+ (1-w)[g_2-(hf_2/m)]$	$g_1+(h/m)>0$	$g_2 + [h(1-f_2)/m]>0$

[*] The reduced form coefficients in column (3) are all divided by Δ. The expression for Δ is given in the last row of the Table. The term v is the composite error term of equation (6). The variables M, Y^P, G^P, E^P, W_{-1} and D_{-1} are divided by Y^F.

panied by more investment and a lower real rate. In the P-C case, for example, the coefficient of expected inflation would be smaller than one unless

$$g_1/[g_1 + (h/m)] = 1$$

e.g. under the implausible assumptions of a zero elasticity of money demand to interest rates (h=0), or an infinite interest sensitivity of investment ($g_1 \to \infty$)

Under both the P−C model (w=1) and the P−P model (w=0) an increase in the money supply shifts the LM curve to the right, increasing income and decreasing the interest rate ($\alpha_2>0$). It is notable, however, that under the P−P model the effect is smaller — in absolute value and as long as $f_2<0$ — because the increase in M raises the desired level of capital stock and increases investment (as well as saving), so that equilibrium can be achieved at a new level of interest rate which is higher (closer to the initial equilibrium) than in the P−C case.

19

Under both models, an increase of permanent income *relative* to full employment income, current income constant, increases private consumption at the expense of saving, thereby lowering the supply of funds and increasing the interest rate ($\alpha_3 > 0$). The effect is not identical in the P−C and in the P−P models, because the coefficient of Y^P — as well as all other coefficients — differs in each case for the different combination of parameter Δ by which it is divided. It can be seen that Δ_{P-C} is smaller than Δ_{P-P} as long as

$$g_1 + (hf_2/m) < g_2$$

Since the ratio in the expression for Δ (hg_2/m) is presumably a small number, the condition is respected if $g_1 < g_2$. The coefficient of Y^P is expected to be larger in the P−C model, confirming that movements in the variables affecting the national saving rate have a more powerful effect on interest rates when the desired capital stock cannot be adjusted instantly.

Similarly, the deficit and government expenditure, being a major determinant of national saving, have a smaller effect on R if $w = 0$. An increase in the deficit, perceived to be permanent (or a tax cut, expenditure constant), is thus expected to always increase R, except when $a = b$ (the Ricardian case) while a rise in expenditure unambiguously increases R ($\alpha_4 > 0$, $\alpha_5 > 0$).

It follows that a crucial test of the LCH versus the Ricardian proposition is $\alpha_4 > 0$. Although the coefficients "a" and "b" cannot be separately identified in equation (6) the coefficients α_4 and α_5 give useful information on the implied values of the two structural coefficients. If $b = a$, as in the Ricardian model, then $\alpha_4 = 0$; α_4 should be positive and significant under the LCH, which predicts a value of "b" well below the value of "a". In view of our estimates of the parameters of the consumption function ($a = 0.70$ and $b = 0.20$), we expect the ratio of the coefficient of the deficit to the coefficient of expenditure, $(a-b)/(1-a)$ in Table 2 to be around 1.7 or possibly higher. As an upper limit for this ratio one can take the value of 4, resulting from a combination of $a = 0.8$ and $b = 0$. Note, however, that *any* positive and significant value of α_4 is sufficient to reject the Ricardian proposition.

20

As mentioned above, the effect of the stock of wealth, which is defined to include public debt, and of public debt itself depends on whether w, the weight attached to the P−C model, is close to one or not. If w=0, the coefficient of wealth (α_6) should be negative and significant. If w=1, α_6 should be positive, but fairly small, given that the propensity to consume out of total wealth (c) is a small number. Under the P−C model, the coefficient of D_{-1} reduces to $-d/\Delta$. Since our previous studies have indicated that "d" — the extent to which the private sector regards debt as a future liability — is very close to zero, we expect α_7 to be small and insignificantly different from zero if w=1. On the other hand, a high and significant value of α_7 would point toward a low value of w, thus rejecting the P−C model.

We conclude that: i) a priori the effect of wealth could be either positive or negative, depending on the value of w; ii) the coefficient of D_{-1}, instead, should be non-negative, but could be negligible if the P−C is a good approximation of reality; and iii) in the P−P case most movements of the nominal interest rates should be explained by movements of government debt and wealth, for given expected inflation. It follows that a crucial test of the P−C versus the P−P model lies in the magnitude and significance of the coefficient of government debt.

One important further test of the two investment models is provided by the coefficient α_8 of the capacity utilization rate (CAP), used to proxy for changes in desired capacity. This coefficient should be zero under the P−P, but significantly positive according to the P−C.

Up until now, we have neglected the effect of international financial markets on interest rates. In an open economy the equilibrium condition $I = S_T$ should be changed to include the current account balance (NX), e.g. $S_T = I + NX$. In a small economy, the net outflow of capital from home to abroad can be specified as an increasing function of the differential between the world and the domestic interest rate, corrected for the expected depreciation of the exchange rate of the home country (R^f). A common assumption in the literature is the expression of the

21

current account as a linear function of the interest rate differential, or:

(7) $NX = -q(R-R^f)$

with $q > 0$. With high capital mobility, one expects q to be high. On the other hand, with capital controls or if home assets are not good substitutes for foreign assets, q should be fairly small. If one adds (7) to the system (1), (3), (4) and (5) and solves again for R, one finds that a new term, $\alpha_9 R^f$, must be added to the reduced form (6) with $\alpha_9 = q/\Delta^*$, where Δ^* replaces Δ from which it differs in that $\Delta^* = q + \Delta$. Clearly, when domestic and foreign assets are perfect substitutes, q tends to infinity, α_9 tends to one and all the other coefficients tend to zero. This establishes that within this framework it is impossible to distinguish between the Ricardian proposition and the hypothesis of perfect capital mobility.

To summarize, although we have resorted to a number of simplifying assumptions, the model that we have presented is sufficiently rich to discriminate between competing hypotheses. In particular, we can address the following issues:

i) the neutrality of deficit financing. As we have shown, a crucial test of this hypothesis lies in the coefficient of the deficit (α_4), which should be zero if agents fully discount future tax liabilities (a=b), and positive and significant if the relevant consumption model is the LCH with a finite lifetime horizon.

ii) The empirical relevance of the P−P model of investment, according to which stocks should have a more powerful effect on interest rates than the corresponding flows. Supports for this hypothesis (w=0) would show up in a negative coefficient of the wealth variable ($\alpha_6 < 0$), in a positive coefficient of government debt ($\alpha_7 > 0$) and in an insignificant coefficient of the capacity utilization rate ($\alpha_8 = 0$). The direction of the effect of the deficit and of government expenditure is the same under both the models of investment, but, since $g_1 < g_2$, the magnitude of these effects should be smaller under the P−P.

iii) The hypothesis of a high degree of capital mobility would

22

be supported by a coefficient of world interest rates close to unity ($\alpha_9 = 1$), together with the coefficients of the other variables close to zero.

4. Empirical Results

From the discussion of the previous section it appears that R is a function of several variables, among which expected inflation, money supply, the government deficit and, possibly, the stocks of wealth and debt, capacity utilization and world interest rates should have primary importance.

In the estimation we use annual data from over the period 1958-1985 because the series of actual and potential capacity are available only over this period. Sources and definitions of all variables used in the estimation can be found in the Appendix. All variables are deflated by full employment gross national product (Y^F). Such series is not available in Italy, and we have computed it from the predicted values of a regression of real Y on its lagged value and a time trend.

The reduced form (6) calls for the introduction of permanent income (Y^P), expenditure (E^P) and the deficit (G^P) relative to Y^F. It is not easy to measure Y^P, or to distinguish it empirically from our measure of Y^F. Furthermore, when Y is continuously growing as in the first half of the sample, the measure of Y^F is also a reasonable approximation of Y^P. With the recession of 1974 and the subsequent economic slowdown, it is likely that our measure of Y^F overestimates Y^P. It is also likely, however, that, given the way in which we have measured Y^F, the ratio of the two does not deviate much from unity. Thus, the contribution of permanent income should be captured by the constant term of (6). Accordingly, we have excluded this variable from the set of regressors.[2]

It is also clear that only the permanent deficit relative to Y^F

---

[2] In 1985 the gross national product was revised. The new series, which is available only after 1980, shows that Italian GNP had been previously underestimated by about 15 percent. To check the robustness of our results, we have replicated the regressions using an estimate of the revised GNP series. Before 1980 we simply assume that GNP is 15 percent lower than the old series. The results of this experiment do not differ from the one presented in the text.

23

should affect interest rates. In what follows we assume that actual expenditure E is a good proxy for E^P. Econometrically, what is important is the assumption that E is uncorrelated with the composite error term v in equation (6). However, the variable T^P in equation (1) may differ from actual taxes (T) for two reasons: i) because of the cyclical behavior of taxes, and ii) because of unexpected and transitory tax levies. Thus, it is likely that during the business cycle the error terms of the investment equations — u_{21} and u_{22} in equations (2.1) and (2.2) — are correlated with the deficit variable, so that $cov(u_{21}G)<0$ and $cov(u_{22}G)<0$, inducing a downward bias in the coefficient of the deficit. This bias works against the LCH, and in favor of the Ricardian proposition, because it makes it harder to reject the null hypothesis that $\alpha_4=0$.

Contrary to what is commonly observed in other countries, the deficits are not very cyclical in the Italian economy until the tax reform of 1974.[3] Thereafter, however, they show a more pronounced cyclical component. Furthermore, unexpected taxes have been levied repeatedly on Italian consumers after the 1973 oil shock. To try to take into account the possible endogeneity of the deficit, most regressions are estimated by an instrumental variables procedures.

The results are organized as follows. Table 3 presents the basic specification of the interest rate equation and tests for the separate effect of the stocks of public debt and private wealth. The G variable in Table 3 subtracts from the conventional measure of the deficit the expected depreciation of the stock of public debt in the course of the period (p^eD_{-1}). In Table 4 we attempt to carry on the decomposition of G into expenditure minus taxes (the so-called primary deficit), and the real interest component of the deficit. Since the Durbin-Watson statistic indicates the presence of substantial serial correlation of the errors, the majority of the regressions are estimated by the Cochrane-Orcutt method. As will be seen, the correction for autocorrelation does not alter our main results.

---

[3] This is partly because until 1974 taxes were not collected in the same year in which taxable income was reported, but with a lag of at least one year.

24

Table 3*
TEST OF THE EFFECT OF THE DEFICIT, CAPACITY,
MONEY SUPPLY, WORLD INTEREST RATES
AND OF THE STOCKS OF DEBT AND WEALTH

Notes**	ID	C (1)	p^e (2)	M (3)	G (4)	D_{-1} (5)	W_{-1} (6)	CAP (7)	R^f (8)	RHO (9)	DW (10)	SE (11)	LL (12)
OLS	3.1	4.2 (6.7)	0.68 (11.4)								1.14	2.06	−59.0
OLS	3.2	18.4 (4.4)	0.59 (10.4)	−0.12 (−2.8)	0.70 (3.1)			0.40 (3.8)	0.07 (2.7)		1.04	1.38	−45.4
AR-IV	3.3	19.1 (3.3)	0.57 (7.9)	−0.12 (−2.0)	0.97 (2.9)			0.44 (3.7)	0.07 (3.0)	0.50 (3.0)	1.24		−40.8
AR-IV	3.4	15.9 (1.9)	0.54 (6.2)	−0.10 (−1.3)	0.79 (1.6)	0.03 (0.5)		0.39 (2.5)	0.07 (3.2)	0.51 (3.1)	1.19		−39.0
AR-IV	3.5	19.2 (1.8)	0.57 (5.6)	−0.12 (−1.7)	0.98 (2.3)		−0.01 (−0.1)	0.44 (3.1)	0.07 (2.8)	0.50	1.28		−40.9
AR-IV ΔD	3.6	9.9 (2.5)	0.68 (8.7)	−0.04 (−0.8)	0.49 (3.1)			0.46 (3.9)	0.02 (0.5)	0.45 (2.6)	1.27		−41.5

* t-statistics are in parentheses. The mean of the nominal interest rate over the 1958-85 period is 9.62 percent. The variables M, G, D_{-1}, and W_{-1} are ratios to full employment GNP. The variable CAP is measured as the difference of actual from potential capacity relative to potential capacity.
** OLS: Ordinary Least Squares. IV: Instrumental Variables. The instruments used are one lag on taxes and expenditure, and a time trend. AR: autoregressive transformation. ΔD: the deficit is measured as the change in the stock of debt, and includes government investment.

Regression 3.1 in Table 3 tests the simplest version of Fisher's hypothesis, namely that nominal rates only respond to expected inflation, and real rates are forever constant, up to a random term reflecting all other effects. The nominal interest rate is the average yield on government bonds with a maximum of nine years to maturity.[4] Expected inflation is computed from a rolling AR(2) forecast of actual inflation, a procedure which has the advantage of using only information available to consumers and investors at the time of the forecast. The coefficient of p^e in column (2) is high (0.68), and it is significantly different from unity at the 1 percent level: this indicates that expected inflation has reduced real rates over the sample period.

Regression 3.2 adds the variables money supply, current deficit G, the capacity utilization rate CAP, and a measure of world

---

[4] Results using a longer term interest rate (up to twenty years to maturity) did not change the results appreciably.

25

interest rates R^f. The latter has been proxied by the nominal interest rate of United States government bonds corrected for the expected devaluation of the exchange rate between the lira and the dollar. Before 1970 it has been assumed that the expected devaluation of the dollar is zero. Afterwards, we have computed it by means of a rolling forecast of a regression of the exchange rate on two lags of the exchange rate, and one lag each of inflation and money supply growth.[5]

The standard error of 3.2 represents very substantial improvement with respet to 3.1, and all coefficients are significant and have signs consistent with the model presented in Section 3. The coefficient of G is positive, highly significant and indicates that an increase of the deficit (corrected for expected inflation) of 1 percent relative to full employment GNP has increased nominal rates by 0.7 percent during the estimation period. The result provides very strong evidence against the Ricardian proposition, and in favor of the LCH.

The coefficient of the variable CAP is positive and very significant, a fact which is consistent with the $P-C$ but not with the $P-P$ model. The coefficient of R^f is also positive and significant, but much smaller than what might be expected under the hypothesis of high capital mobility. This result can be explained by the widespread controls of capital movements which have been used in Italy, even if in varying degree.

At first sight, one disturbing result of 3.2 is that the coefficient of p^e drops to 0.59, a value which is somewhat lower than 0.68, the coefficient of p^e in 3.1. One explanation is that the correlation between p^e and R^f is relatively high (0.58), since past inflation rates (reflected in our measure of p^e) are likely to be correlated with the expected depreciation of the exchange rate included in the measure of R^f.

The second explanation for the generally low coefficients of p^e in 3.1 and 3.2 is that investors use other variables, besides past

[5] The typical rolling regression shows that the exchange rate between the dollar and the lira is strongly positively correlated with its lagged value and with the lagged inflation rate, while the growth of the stock of money has a very unstable coefficient, which varies in size and significance across the sample.

26

inflation, to forecast future inflation. Current deficits, to the extent that part of the deficit leads to future monetization, may convey information about future monetary policy. The variable R^f, which includes expectations about the future evolution of the exchange rate, may also be correlated with current expectations of inflation. Thus, the coefficient of p^e in 3.1 and 3.2 captures only the effect of *past inflation* on expected inflation. To some extent, the effect of further forces affecting expectations — such as monetary policy, the deficit and the expected depreciation of the exchange rate — on expected inflation may be reflected in the coefficients of other variables of the regression.

Because in 3.2 the DW statistic is low, the other regressions of Table 3 are corrected for serial correlation. In these regressions we also take into account the cyclical behavior of deficits, which may cause the error term of the equation (v) to be negatively correlated with the error of the investment equation $[wu_{21} + (1-w)u_{22}]$, and induce a downward bias in the estimated coefficient of the deficit. Ideally, we should use a measure of the permanent deficit, which may be proxied by a measure of full employment deficit. Unfortunately, no such measure is available in Italian statistics, and we resort to an instrumental variables procedure. It is seen that in regression 3.3 the coefficient of the deficit is substantially higher than in 3.2 (0.97 against 0.70), and that the other coefficients are only marginally affected.

Regression 3.4 adds to the set of regressors the beginning of period stock of government debt (D_{-1}) which, according to the $P-P$ model should have a high and positive impact on R. The introduction of D_{-1} is seen to reduce the size and significance of the coefficient of government deficit. Yet, the coefficient of D_{-1}, though positive as expected, is fairly small and hardly significant; in fact, the standard error and the likelihood of regression 3.4 improve only marginally with respect to regression 3.3.

In regression 3.5 we test for the separate effect of the stock of net private wealth, W_{-1}, and the coefficient turns out to be insignificant. Overall, the results of 3.4 and 3.5 provide very strong evidence in favor of the $P-C$ formulation.

27

In the last regression of Table 3 we measure the government deficit by the change in government debt, in place of the difference between current expenditures and taxes. In Italy these two measures differ substantially, because the change in debt includes government investment and some financial items excluded from the current account of the public sector.[6] According to both the LCH and the Ricardian proposition, only current expenses should crowd-out investment and increase interest rates, while government investment — to the extent that it represents addition to the capital stock of the economy — merely substitutes for private investment. This idea receives some support from the results of regression 3.6, which exhibits a slightly larger standard error than the corresponding regression 3.3 (1.27 versus 1.24).

The first regression presented in Table 4 adds to the set of regressors of 3.3 the variable E, which measures government expenditure. It is seen that in 4.1 the t-ratios of the coefficients of G and M decline with respect to 3.3, and that the coefficient of E turns out to be positive, as expected, but small and insignificant. The ratio of the coefficient of G to that of E is 4, a value which is too high to be consistent with our previous estimates of the parameters of the consumption function "a" and "b" (see Section 3), but a fortiori inconsistent with the Ricardian proposition. However, given that the coefficient of E is estimated with a large standard error, the values of $a=0.7$ and $b=0.2$ fall well within customary confidence intervals.

In the last two regressions of Table 4 we endeavor to test for the separate effect of the expected real interest rate bil. Thus, we decompose G into primary deficit and real interest payments. The latters result from the difference between the nominal interest bill (IN) and the inflation–induced depreciation of the debt ($p^e D_{-1}$). It is worth noting that IN is taken from the public sector accounts, while $p^e D_{-1}$ is computed as the product of p^e and D_{-1}. Testing for the separate effect of expected real interest payments is important

---

[6] Modigliani et al [1985] discuss the distinction between total debt and deadweight debt, and of the appropriate measure of government expenditure when testing the Ricardian proposition versus the LCH (see especially Section 4).

28

Table 4*

TEST OF THE SEPARATE EFFECT OF EXPENDITURE AND INTEREST TRANSFERS

Notes**	ID	C (1)	p^e (2)	M (3)	G (4)	E (5)	IN (6)	$p^e D_{-1}$ (7)	CAP (8)	R^f (9)	RHO (10)	SE (11)	LL (12)
AR-IV	4.1	13.7	0.54	−0.10	0.80	0.18			0.39	0.07	0.49	1.18	−38.6
		(1.5)	(7.1)	(−1.5)	(2.0)	(0.7)			(2.9)	(3.2)	(3.0)		
AR-IV	4.2	15.3	0.85	−0.12	0.81***	0.10	1.83	−2.29	0.40	0.05	0.52	1.15	−36.6
		(1.7)	(2.7)	(−1.5)	(1.8)	(0.4)	(2.4)	(−1.7)	(2.7)	(2.1)	(3.2)		
AR-IV	4.3	13.5	0.66	−0.09	0.66***	0.04	1.49	−1.49	0.35	0.06	0.51	1.06	−35.1
		(1.7)	(6.7)	(−1.5)	(1.9)	(0.2)	(2.8)		(3.0)	(2.8)	(3.1)		

* t-statistics are in parentheses. The mean of the nominal interest rate over the 1958-85 period is 9.62 percent.

** *IV*: instrumental variables. The instrument used are one lag on taxes and expenditure, and a time trend. *AR*: autoregressive transformation.

*** In regressions 4.2 and 4.3 the current government deficit is replaced by the primary deficit, and the nominal interest transfers (IN) and the expected depreciation of the stock of debt ($p^e D_{-1}$) are entered as separate regressors. In regression 4.3 the coefficient of $p^e D_{-1}$ is constrained to equal the negative of the coefficient of IN.

in this context, since one should expect that if consumers and investors are able to distinguish nominal from real interest rates, they should be able to distinguish nominal interest transfers (IN) from real interest transfers (IN-$p^e D_{-1}$).

If consumers and investors are rational, the coefficient of $p^e D_{-1}$ should be the opposite of that of IN (see Modigliani and Jappelli, 1987, Section 2). In addition, if interest transfers are regarded by consumers as every other transfer, the magnitude of the coefficients of the two variables should be similar to that of the coefficient of G which in our equations measures the effect of taxes on interest rates, expenditure constant. In regression 4.2 the coefficients are less precisely estimated than in 4.1, while the overall standard error of the regression improves only slightly over that of 4.1. The coefficients of IN and $p^e D_{-1}$ have the expected signs, though the magnitude of these coefficients is unplausibly high. The regression indicates the presence of collinearity among the regressors, which is likely to be high especially among the p^e, $p^e D_{-1}$ and IN variables.

The results improve somewhat in regression 4.3, where we constrain the coefficient of IN and that of $p^e D_{-1}$ to have opposite

29

signs, as warranted by the hypothesis of rational behavior. Since the likelihood and the standard error of 4.3 improve substantially over the corresponding values of 4.2, it is apparent that the constraint is not rejected by the data. The results support also the correction of the deficits for $p^e D_{-1}$, which was imposed in the regression of Table 3. However, the magnitude of the coefficient of the real interest bill $(IN-p^e D_{-1})$ is too high to be consistent with the LCH, and, in particular, much higher than the coefficient of G.

Overall, we must regard the results of Table 4 as rather disappointing, because the attempt to investigate the separate contribution of government expenditure, primary deficit (e.g. taxes, given E), and interest rate bill is made difficult by multicollinearity problems and unreliable point estimates. Nevertheless, the general picture supports the traditional view that interest rates respond to taxes, and not to government expenditure, and that consumption responds to the real rather than to the nominal interest rate.

5. Conclusions

In this paper we have estimated a reduced form equation of the nominal interest rate. Our findings support the conventional view that nominal interest rates can be accurately explained by the movements of expected inflation, money supply, the permanent component of the current deficit, by a measure of utilization of capacity, and by the movements of foreign nominal interest rates adjusted for the expected devaluation of the exchange rate.

To illustrate our results, we report in Table 5, for selected subsample periods, the averages of the variables that, according to our model, have contributed to the movements of the nominal interest rate. The table is based on regression 3.3, which is estimated by instrumental variables and corrected for serial correlation. In Table 5 each variable is subtracted from its mean and multiplied by its coefficient in regression 3.3. The means for the period as a whole, multiplied by the coefficients, are reported in the last row of the table. In column (8) we also report the unexplained residuals — in deviations from the mean —, e.g. the

30

differences between the deviations of the actual values of the nominal interest rate displayed in column (1) and the sum of columns (2) to (7), which represents our fitted values.

One implication of our estimates is that, for a given real deficit, money stock and foreign rates, expected inflation has been accompanied by a reduced real rate of interest because the adjustment of nominal rates to expected inflation is substantially less than unity. On the other hand, the deficit and foreign rates have contributed to increase real rates considerably.

Table 5*

DECOMPOSITION OF THE NOMINAL INTEREST RATE
BY SOURCES OF VARIATION

Period	Actual (1)	α_0 (2)	$\alpha_1 p^e$ (3)	$\alpha_2 M$ (4)	$\alpha_4 G$ (5)	$\alpha_8 CAP$ (6)	$\alpha_9 R^f$ (7)	Unexplained (8)
1958-1963	−4.27	0.0	−3.22	1.57	−2.70	0.09	−0.46	0.45
1964-1969	−4.02	0.0	−2.92	0.42	−0.68	−0.10	−0.34	−0.40
1969-1974	−2.05	0.0	−2.31	−1.48	2.31	0.33	−0.40	−0.50
1975-1979	3.08	0.0	4.56	−1.49	−0.01	−0.79	0.15	0.66
1980-1985	7.45	0.0	4.30	0.50	0.67	0.40	1.00	0.58
Mean 1958-1985	9.62	19.10	4.56	−9.81	−0.60	−3.90	0.70	−0.43

* In column (1) we report the actual values of the nominal interest rate, in deviation from its mean. The other variables are subtracted from their means and multiplied by their coefficient in regression 3.3. The means — multiplied by the coefficients — are reported in the last row of the table. The last column displays the unexplained residual (in deviations from its mean), obtained by subtracting from R (column 1) the sum of the values of column (2) to (7). The residuals include the autocorrelated component of regression 3.3. The sum of the number of the last row of the table (except column 1) is 9.62, which is the average nominal interest rate over the period 1958-85.

From Table 5 it appears that the increase in interest rates of 11.7 percentage points from the 1958-63 period to the 1980-85 period (7.45– –4.27) is explained for 7.5 percentage points by a rise in inflation expectations. The increase in the current government deficit accounts for 3.3 points, and the increase in foreign interest rates for 1.5 percentage points. Finally, the money stock has reduced R by more than 1 percentage point over the period.

In conclusion, the major findings of this paper may be summarized as follows:

31

i) the Ricardian proposition, which predicts no relation between the deficits and interest rates is not supported by the data; on the contrary, in the context of the Italian economy, the deficits have played a quite significant role in increasing interest rates.

ii) The putty-putty model of investment, which calls for a strong effect of the stocks of wealth and debt on interest rates, is soundly rejected by the results of regressions 3.5 and 3.6 of Table 3. This result implies that the interest rate is influenced much more by the current deficits than by the stock of accumulated debt.

iii) The effect of the world market rate on domestic rates is unmistakably confirmed. However, in the case of Italy it appears rather small, confirming the broadly held view that in the period in question the free movement of capital was impaired by regulation, institutions and habits.

iv) We have attempted to separate the effects of expenditure and deficit (or taxes, for given expenditure) from that of the interest rate component of the deficit. The results of Table 4, and particularly those of regressions 4.2 and 4.3 support the hypothesis that investors and consumers treat nominal interest payments as a positive transfer, and the inflation-induced depreciation of the stock of debt as a negative transfer. However, these regressions yield point estimates which are numerically somewhat implausible, limiting the ability to come to reliable conclusions.

32

Appendix: Definition and Sources of Variables

R: average yield of government securities with a maximum of nine years to maturity (IMF, line 61b).

p: change in the deflator of private consumption (OECD National Accounts, vol. 1 - Main Aggregates, 1987 ed. until 1980, and 1987 Report of the Bank of Italy thereafter). From 1980 to 1985 we have used the recently revised deflator of private consumption.

p^e: expected inflation, computed with an AR2 forecast of the change in the deflator of private consumption. At each point in time, the forecast uses only information available at that time.

Y: gross national product (OECD National Accounts, vol. 1-Main Aggregates, 1987 ed.). The proxy for full employment income is the fitted values of a regression of real per-capita Y on a time trend.

M: sum of currency outside banks, demand deposits, time, savings and foreign currency deposits of residents (M2) (IMF, sum of lines 34 and 35).

G: current account deficit of the public sector (Spaventa et al. [1984], Table 1.2.2., until 1980, and 1987 Report of the Bank of Italy, Table aC2, thereafter). In the estimation G is corrected for the expected inflation-induced depreciation of the stock of government debt ($p^e D_{-1}$).

E: government expenditure of the public sector (Spaventa et al. [1984], Table 1.2.2 until 1980, and 1987 Report of the Bank of Italy, Table aC2, thereafter).

IN: nominal interest payments, net of interest income (Spaventa et al. [1984], Table 1.2.2 until 1980, and 1987 Report of the Bank of Italy, Table aC2, thereafter).

W: end of period stock of net wealth (including government debt) of the private sector (Modigliani, Jappelli, Pagano, 1985).

D: end of period stock of public sector debt, net of holdings of the Central Bank, of foreign debt, and of the deposits of the banking sector (Spaventa et al. [1984], Table 3).

CAP: capacity utilization rate of the manufacturing sector. Up until 1976 the series has been kindly provided by Mr. Bodo of the Research Staff of the Bank of Italy; thereafter the source is the 1987 Report of the Bank of Italy, Table aB22 (Indice Generale).

R^f: medium term interest rate of U.S. government securities (IMF, line 61b), corrected for the expected devaluation of the exchange rate between the lira and the dollar (e^e). We assume that e^e is zero until 1970. After 1970, e^e is the forecasts of a rolling regression of the exchange rate on two lags of the exchange rate, one lag of inflation and one lag of money supply growth.

I_P, I_G: private and government investment, net of depreciation (OECD, National Accounts, vol. 1 - Main Aggregates, 1987 ed.). The source for depreciation is OECD, National Accounts, vol. 2 - Detailed Statistics, Tables 2 and 6, 1986 ed.

NX = net capital inflows (OECD, National Accounts, vol. 1 - Main Aggregates, 1987 ed.).

33

BIBLIOGRAPHY

Barro, R., "Are Government Bonds Net Wealth?" *Journal of Political Economy*, November 1974.

Bernheim, D., "Ricardian Equivalence: an Evaluation of Theory and Evidence," *1987 NBER Macroeconomic Annual*, Cambridge University Press.

Evans, P., "Interest Rates and Expected Future Budget Deficits in the United States," *Journal of Political Economy*, February 1987.

Feldstein, M., "Budget Deficits, Tax Rules and Real Interest Rates," *NBER Working Paper*, No. 1970, July 1986.

Kormendi, R., "Government Debt, Government Spending and Private Sector Behavior," *American Economic Review*, December 1983.

Modigliani, F., A. Ando, R. Rasche, and S. Turnowsky, "On the Role of Expectations of Price and Technology Change in an Investment Function," *International Economic Review*, June 1974.

——, T. Jappelli, and M. Pagano, "The Impact of Fiscal Policy and Inflation on National Saving: the Italian Case," *Banca Nazionale del Lavoro Quarterly Review*, June 1985.

——, and A. Sterling, "Government Debt, Government Spending and Private Sector Behavior: a Comment," *American Economic Review*, December 1986.

——, and T. Jappelli, "Fiscal Policy and Saving in Italy Since 1860," in *Private Saving and Public Debt*, M. Boskin, J. Flemming and S. Gorini Eds., Basil Blackwell, London 1987.

Plosser, C., "Government Spending and Assets Returns," *Journal of Monetary Economics*, May 1982.

Spaventa, L., R. Artoni, G. Morcaldo, and P. Zanchi, "L'Indebitamento Pubblico in Italia: Evoluzione, Prospettive e Problemi," Report prepared for the V Commission of the Chamber of Deputies, Roma 1984.

34

PART III
Inflation: Causes and Real Effects

Inflation and the Housing Market: Problems and Potential Solutions*

Donald Lessard, Massachusetts Institute of Technology
Franco Modigliani, Massachusetts Institute of Technology

The rising and variable rate of inflation over the past ten years has seriously destabilized the housing sector. The standard mortgage appears to be a major culprit given its limitations as a financing instrument in such periods of inflation. This article provides a review of the M.I.T. mortgage study sponsored by the U.S. Department of Housing and Urban Development and the Federal Home Loan Bank Board. The authors explain the shortcomings of the standard mortgage, describe five viable, alternative mortgage designs and propose a provocative package of recommendations. *Ed.*

Introduction

The increased rates of inflation accompanied by high and volatile interest rates experienced in recent years have affected the entire economy. The most drastic effect of these factors, however, has been on housing as shown by wide swings both in construction activity and in turnover of existing housing. There is a growing feeling that adequate housing is beyond the reach of an increasingly large number of households. The conclusions of the M.I.T. mortgage study are that (1) these effects can largely be attributed to the standard mortgage, and that (2) this instrument, in many ways therefore obsolete, should be supplemented by alternative mortgage designs.

The Shortcomings of the Standard Mortgage

The recurrent crises which have plagued the housing industry in the last decade can largely be traced to the interaction of a rising and variable rate of inflation with two major institutional features which have characterized the financing of housing in the U.S. These are (1) almost exclusive reliance on the traditional fully-amortized, level-payment mortgage as the vehicle

* This article is adapted from the introductory chapter in *New Mortgage Designs for Stable Housing in an Inflationary Environment* edited by Franco Modigliani and Donald Lessard, forthcoming in the Federal Reserve Bank of Boston Conference Series. It draws on the research of all members of the mortgage study which, in addition to the authors who were coordinators, included Richard Cohn—Sloan School at M.I.T., Stanley Fischer—Economics Dept. of M.I.T., Daniel Holland—Sloan School at M.I.T., Dwight Jaffee—Economics Dept. of Princeton, James Kearl—Economics Dept. of Brigham Young University, Ken Rosen—M.I.T. Harvard Joint Center, and Craig Swan—Economics Dept. of the University of Minnesota.

19

for financing the purchase of single family houses, and (2) overwhelming dependence for mortgage funds on thrift institutions which secure the bulk of their funds through relatively short-term deposits. This framework functioned satisfactorily in the period of relative price stability that prevailed until 1965. However, in the period of rising and fluctuating inflation since then, these same characteristics have had a devastating effect on both the demand for housing and the supply of mortgage funds.[1]

The Effects of Inflation on the Demand for Housing

At first glance, it would appear that inflation should have little impact on the ability of households to acquire housing. The cost of owning and using a house for a predetermined period consists of the outlays to acquire the house less the value of the house when sold. Clearly, financing costs will rise because a given increase in the anticipated rate of inflation tends to raise long-term interest rates by an inflation "premium" needed to compensate the lender for the anticipated erosion in the purchasing power of his claim. However, as long as the value of the house changes with the general price level, the inflation "premium" paid to finance the house will be recaptured through an eventual capital gain. In fact, taking into account the asymmetric tax treatment of interest charges and capital gains on a primary residence, inflation should actually *lower* the real cost of ownership.

Nevertheless, inflation has an adverse effect on the demand for houses financed through mortgages, because the rise in the mortgage rate results in a distortion of the time pattern of real mortgage payments, that is, payments expressed in dollars of constant purchasing power. In a world with inflation, real mortgage payments are much higher in early years and much lower in later years than they would be in a world with no inflation. The reason for this distortion in real payments is that payments are spread over a long period of time. Since the essence of the standard mortgage is that payments are level in current dollar terms, i.e., with no adjustment for changes in purchasing power, they must be set at a very high level, relative to what they would be in the absence of inflation, to offset the decrease in their real value over time. The tilting effect of a rising inflation rate on the stream of annual payments expressed in constant purchasing power is shown vividly in Figure 1, which is a graph of the real payment required in *each* year on a $20,000, thirty-year mortgage with zero inflation, 4 percent inflation, and 8 percent inflation.

To the extent that households are constrained in the amount of housing they can afford by the size of the monthly payment relative to their income in the first few years of the contract, this distortion will depress the demand for housing and result in financial hardship. For example, for a household with a real income of $10,000 throughout the term of the

---

[1] Most studies of inflation and housing have focused on supply effects. See Poole [2] and Tucker [3] for discussions of demand effects.

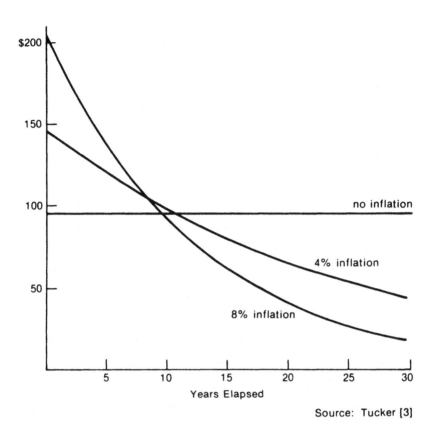

Source: Tucker [3]

Figure 1   Real Value of Monthly Payments

mortgage and with zero inflation, $85 or roughly 10 percent of the household's $853 monthly income would be necessary to cover the payments in all years. With a 4 percent rate of inflation, over 15 percent of income is required in the first year, but this would fall to less than 3 percent by the final year. Finally, with an 8 percent inflation rate, over 20 percent of income is required in the first year, but this would decrease to less than 2 percent in the final year. As one would expect, a higher rate of inflation also results in a more rapid decline in the outstanding debt. Correspondingly, the owner's equity builds up more rapidly if the real value of the house remains the same. In reality, this distortion is even greater than indicated by the example since household real incomes tend to rise over time.

In a world of perfect markets and infinite ingenuity, this distortion of the relationship between the time-stream of mortgage payments and household income might not affect the demand for housing. Borrowers would raise the funds needed for the high initial payments through second mortgages or unsecured personal loans. But borrowers may be reluctant to enter into such arrangements and, in any event, current lending practices tend to limit borrowing to the amount that the household can cover in the initial years with level payments, ignoring the decrease in the real value of these payments over time.

Another shortcoming, though admittedly of secondary importance, is apparent in periods of significant uncertainty about the future rate of inflation. At such times the standard mortgage, as a fixed long-term contract, becomes a risk for the borrower as well as the lender. The risk to the borrower is mitigated to some extent by the prevailing early repayment provisions on mortgages, mandated by law in many states. However, this protection is not without cost since the rational financial intermediary recognizes this asymmetry by exacting an appropriate premium for this option.

Many countries including the U.S. have tried to relieve the demand problem with various schemes, such as controlling interest rates with ceilings and providing interest rate or housing subsidies. Other countries, particularly Brazil but also Finland and Israel, have adopted mortgage designs which provide streams of payment which are stable in terms of purchasing power. Only a few countries, notably Sweden, have experimented with a combination of subsidies and financial innovation and government guarantees. It is our view that subsidies are an unnecessary and wasteful approach. Since higher interest rates arising from inflation do not change the overall real cost of the house, inflation per se should not be a ground for subsidies. If our analysis is correct, the real demand problem arises from the idiosyncrasies of the standard mortgage, which requires borrowers to repay the debt at an unreasonably fast pace and, therefore, the solution lies in the redesign of the mortgage instrument.

The true solution to this demand effect must therefore lie in devising instruments such that the repayment of the loan (measured in terms of purchasing power) will be independent of the rate of inflation. This solution would amount to an elimination of the tilting effect of the standard mortgage.

The Effects of Inflation on Housing through the Supply of Mortgage Funds

Supply effects arise not from the rate of inflation as such, but rather from its variations and from its interaction with interest rate ceilings. Both are intimately related to the unique structure through which the bulk of funds to finance mortgages has been raised in the U.S. in recent decades.

By far the largest share of private mortgage funds, especially those financing owner-occupied housing, has come from the thrift institutions—savings and loan associations and mutual savings banks—and to some extent from commercial banks and life insurance companies.[2] These institutions in turn have obtained the funds almost entirely from deposits through much of the postwar period. These deposits were mostly short-term and highly liquid and regarded as demand liabilities.

As a result of these practices, thrift institutions acquired an extremely unbalanced or mismatched financial structure, consisting of very long-term assets and very short-term liabilities. Such an unbalanced portfolio imposes risks of failure on these institutions.

Portfolio imbalance did not create any difficulty during the period of relative price stability which lasted until the mid-1960s. But the weaknesses in such a structure became apparent in the era of rising and variable inflation which followed. Rising interest rates, during periods of monetary stringency, made it difficult to attract depositors at the rates of the earlier period. If institutions competed to retain deposits, they would have had to offer rates which would have resulted in severe losses and ultimate collapse. To prevent this outcome, regulatory authorities imposed ceilings on all deposit intermediaries often well below short-term market rates.

Because of these ceilings, thrift institutions' liabilities lost their attractiveness. The unfavorable response of depositors became more pronounced at successive "crunches." These periods of famine were typically followed by periods of heavy inflows. The wide swings in deposit inflows resulted in similar swings in the supply of mortgage funds causing wide fluctuations in construction activity and housing markets.

Obviously, institutions financing housing should not continue to lend through traditional mortgages, which are long-term instruments, while relying on very short-term liabilities as a source of funds. Rather they must have a financing instrument which allows them to earn a return commensurate with changing short-term market rates. The basic principle that prudent financial structure requires matching the characteristics of assets and liabilities is a tenet recognized by the institutions which finance housing in other countries. Some examples of foreign remedies to mismatching pitfalls are the following.

1. Conventional mortgages are typically financed by mortgage bonds (Sweden and many other countries).
2. Interest rates of mortgages financed by short-term deposits are subject to change (U.K.).
3. When mortgages are financed by liabilities of intermediate-term, the balance still due at the end of that term is refinanced at the then prevailing rate (Canada).

In the next section a number of alternative mortgage designs are reviewed. Each alternative is assessed in terms of how well it fits matching requirements of the lending institution's portfolio and suits borrowers'

---

[2] Government funds, in particular mortgages by the FNMA, have played an increasingly important role in mortgage financing in recent years.

interests as well as how effectively it eliminates or reduces the demand effect of inflation-induced changes in interest rates and consequent instability in construction activity resulting from such changes.

Alternative Mortgage Designs

A mortgage is simply a loan contract which specifies a rule for (1) determining the interest rate applying in any year to the debit balance then outstanding, called hereafter the debiting rate, and (2) calculating the periodic payments through which the debtor is to pay the interest and amortize the principal over the life of the contract. The traditional mortgage can thus be viewed as a special case of a much broader class, and a large number of alternative designs can be constructed by varying the various parameters characterizing the instrument. The designs discussed are only those which are presently at least being promoted here or abroad and which provide a viable solution to the problems enumerated in the previous section.

The Variable Rate Mortgage (VRM)

The alternative to the traditional mortgage that has received by far the greatest attention is the variable rate mortgage. Already adopted in some parts of the country, VRM is being promoted primarily by lending intermediary interests.

The essential characteristic of the VRM is that the rate charged on the borrower's outstanding balance, i.e., the *debiting* rate, is not fixed at the outset but is allowed to float up or down, being tied to some agreed "reference rate." This specification is consistent with a variety of designs in terms of (1) choice of specific reference rates such as a short, intermediate or long-term market rate, or the deposit rate of the intermediary originating the loan; (2) frequency with which the debiting rate is changed; (3) limitations, if any, on the maximum permissible change at revision points or over the life of the contract; and (4) methods for computing the periodic payments.

Two major alternative designs fall within the VRM classification. In one design, which has been adopted in the U.K. and elsewhere, the periodic payment is fixed at the beginning of the contract as in the traditional mortgage. Because a discrepancy between the debiting rate and the rate used to compute the payment at the outset leads to a corresponding discrepancy between the amount *available* for the amortization of principal and the amount *scheduled* for that purpose, the payments do not necessarily terminate at the original scheduled maturity, but only when the principal has been fully amortized. Thus, the instrument is of variable maturity. In the other design, the maturity is fixed but the periodic payments change with the debiting rate.

The adoption of the VRM could be expected to alleviate, if not solve, the intermediaries' mismatching problem and, hopefully, the supply aspect of swings in housing markets. In terms of its effect on the borrower, however, the VRM appears to offer little relief to the housing problems and, in fact, is likely to make matters worse. This shortcoming is primarily due to the VRM's failure to come to grips with what we have labeled the demand effect of inflation. Since payments depend on a market rate of interest, the effect of inflation on these rates will cause higher initial payment to income ratios. Further, wider variations in short-term interest rates are likely to exacerbate swings in demand due to changes in initial periodic payments, although the generally lower level of these rates, relative to long-term rates, may stimulate demand over the long term.

A more common criticism of the VRM advanced by consumer advocates has been that making the interest rate variable increases the borrower's risk. This conclusion is open to question if one recalls that some of the risk of the VRM is offset by the long-term positive association between the borrower's money liability and his money income. However, it is true that with the fixed-maturity version of the VRM the borrower does face some additional risk. Although variations in the periodic payment are broadly associated with those in the rate of inflation and money income, in the short run the association is not close, partly because of the jerky nature of payment changes. As a result, the ratio of payment to income could vary substantially over the mortgage term. For example, if the rate of inflation rises from 3 to 5 percent, the scheduled payment under VRM rises by 24 percent, whereas the effect on the average homeowner's nominal income would be more like 2 percent. The reason for this much higher percentage change is that the higher inflation, by raising the nominal rate used in computing the constant payment for the rest of the contract, implies a further tilting of the real repayment schedule. For similar reasons, an absolute decline in inflation produces a much larger percentage decline in the scheduled payment.

The potentially large fluctuations in payments over time with the fixed-maturity VRM could be relieved by a variety of modifications. One modification is the fixed-payment variable-maturity version of VRM. But this version can afford only limited relief when the maturity is long, as is the case in the early years of the contract, and when most of the periodic payment consists of interest. Even small upward revisions in the debiting rate produce large changes in the scheduled maturity, and the point is soon reached where a fixed payment proves insufficient to ever amortize the debt. Thus the variable-maturity VRM is capable of "smoothing" minor fluctuations in the interest rate, but not major shifts such as those observed in recent years.

Various other modifications to improve the borrower's lot have been proposed for the variable-payment VRM. But conversely, these modifications reduce the benefits of the VRM to the lender and hence also its effectiveness in solving the supply problem. Indeed, any of these proposals increase the probability that the market value of the mortgages will vary relative to their par value and thus deviate from the value of intermediaries' liabilities.

All of these proposals relate directly or indirectly to a basic dilemma in VRM design. From the perspective of the lender who obtains a significant proportion of funds with short-term liabilities, a short-term debiting rate is desirable, while from the borrower's perspective a longer-term rate is desirable because of its lower volatility. This dilemma, and the extent to which the various proposed modifications of the basic VRM instrument resolve it, can be best understood by considering the dual-rate VRM, a novel variant of the VRM which emerged during the course of our study.

The Dual-Rate VRM and Other Approaches to the VRM Dilemma

The dual-rate VRM endeavors to resolve the above dilemma by using two distinct interest rates. One, the debiting rate, is used to compute the interest on the outstanding balance; the other, which we term the payment factor, is used to compute the periodic payment. For the debiting rate, one would use as reference a short-term rate or preferably the deposit rate. The periodic payment, on the other hand, is recomputed at fixed intervals by applying to the principal then outstanding the standard annuity formula using some longer-term rate. This effectively reduces the magnitude and possibly the frequency of changes in payment.[3]

If the debiting rate differs from the payment factor, the actual amortization of the debt may differ from that implied by the payment factor. Thus, when a new periodic payment is computed, it could differ from the previous payment because of the discrepancy in principal and because of a change in the reference rate for the payment factor. Nonetheless, the variations could be expected to be appreciably smaller than for a standard VRM which used the same debiting rate. There are three reasons why this is so. First, the discrepancy in principal should not be large since the average debiting rates—short-term rates—should not differ markedly from the longer-term rate which is, after all, a forecast of the average short-term rates. Second, the discrepancy, if any, is spread over the remaining life of the contract and thus will not have a major impact on the payment. Finally, the payment rate, a longer-term rate, should be smoother than the debiting rate.

Thus a dual-rate VRM, with appropriately chosen reference rates and frequency of adjustment, can both enable the lending intermediary to earn a rate adequate to keep its deposit rate competitive with other short-term market instruments and still result in a smooth path of periodic payments in money terms. Its primary drawback, however, is its complexity.

Another approach to the dilemma is simply to use a longer-term rate

---

[3] The mechanics of this design are discussed in detail by Cohn and Fischer in "Alternative Mortgage Designs," in *New Mortgage Designs for Stable Housing in an Inflationary Environment, op. cit.*

for debiting as well as computing the payment. Insofar as its liabilities are of shorter term, this approach, as noted earlier, exposes the intermediary either to the danger of its revenue not keeping up with the rate it must pay on its liabilities or equivalently to the risk that the market value of its assets will fall short of that of its liabilities. Ideally, this risk would be avoided if the liabilities were term deposits with maturities matching that of the debiting rate.

To summarize, the VRM would be helpful to lenders and with in-genuity might not impose too great a burden on borrowers as compared with the standard mortgage. The dual-rate VRM appears to go furthest in mitigating the disadvantages to the borrower for a given gain to the lender by using a short-term debiting rate such as the deposit rate, while eliminat-ing much of the inconvenience and risk placed on the borrower through large, sudden changes in the periodic payment. However, the VRM in any form still fails to resolve, and at least to some extent worsens, what we have called the demand effects of inflation, namely the capricious changes in initial level of payments due to inflation-swollen interest rates.

A quite different foreseeable shortcoming that might result from widespread adoption of the fixed-maturity VRM is of a macroeconomic character. A change in the debiting rate would result in an increase of the periodic payments for millions of homeowners. If the reference rate is a market rate, there would be public pressure on the central bank to hold down that rate when stabilization considerations would, on the contrary, call for higher rates (reflecting, e.g., inflationary expectations). This sort of pressure, which even now interferes with appropriate policy, would certainly be greatly magnified under the VRM. If the debiting rate for the VRM were the deposit rate, the same pressures would be directed toward holding that rate down in the face of rising market rates. If successful this pressure would, much like the imposition of ceilings, cause the inter-mediaries' deposits to lose attractiveness, thus recreating the very supply effect that the VRM was designed to solve. The recent experience of the U.K. provides an enlightening illustration of this scenario.

The Graduated-Payment Mortgage (GP)

Since a major impact of inflation on the homebuyer is the tilting of the time-stream of payments, one obvious solution to this problem is a mortgage which involves relatively lower money payments in early years. Clearly, unless such a mortgage is subsidized or of longer maturity, it must involve relatively higher money payments in later years in order to fully amortize the loan and provide the required return to the lender. Graduated-payment mortgages, with contractually rising payment streams, have been advocated in the U.S. and have been implemented in some other countries including the U.K. and Germany.

In a world with a steady rate of inflation, a graduated-payment mortgage, with payments which increase over time at a rate equal to the rate of inflation, would eliminate the tilt effect in terms of constant purchasing power dollars and restore the basic feature of the traditional mortgage in a noninflationary environment—level payments over the life of the mortgage. Under normal circumstances, this would imply the same ratio of mortgage payments to household incomes and the same equity buildup as the traditional mortgage instrument.

One feature of the graduated-payment mortgage which might generate resistance on the part of both borrowers and lenders is that the outstanding principal in the early years of the contract would actually increase. The rising payments would eventually exceed interest charges and fully amortize the principal by the end of the contract period. While this situation raises some interesting tax questions, it should not be a cause for alarm on the part of either the borrower or the lender. The value of the house, and hence of the borrower's equity and the lender's collateral, can be expected to rise with the loan buildup.

Any resistance, then, would be the result of a failure to take into account the changing value of the dollar due to inflation. This is not to say that this "money illusion" will not be present or hard to overcome; hopefully it should be possible to overcome through information and education.

Unfortunately, the GP mortgage suffers from several serious shortcomings. First, with uncertainty about future rates of inflation, a contract calling for payments rising at the *expected* rate of inflation would be extremely risky for both the borrower and the lender. Additionally, a graduated-payment mortgage with a fixed interest rate over its entire life, being a long-term instrument, would do nothing to solve the supply problem stemming from the thrift institutions' reliance on short-term deposits as a source of funds. In fact, it would exacerbate the problem since it would lengthen the duration of the mortgage.

We must conclude that neither the VRM nor the GP is an attractive solution to the distortions in mortgage financing brought about by inflation and the accompanying high and uncertain interest rates. Each is a partial solution that benefits either the lender or the borrower, but at the expense of the other party.

In contrast to these partial solutions, one mortgage design which, in the abstract at least, has the potential of satisfying these requirements is the price-level adjusted mortgage (often referred to as a price-level indexed or index-linked mortgage).

The Price-Level Adjusted Mortgage (PLAM)

The basic mechanics of the PLAM involve a contractual interest rate which abstracts from inflationary anticipations, and a periodic revaluation of the outstanding principal in accordance with the change in the price-level index to which it is tied. In effect, the debiting rate on the PLAM is a *real* rate of interest, differing from the current money rate by the exclusion of the inflation premium, which reflects the anticipated change in the price-level over the period of the contract. Payments are recomputed whenever the principal is revised, using the contract rate as the payment factor. As a result, the PLAM payment stream changes exactly in line with the reference price level.

To illustrate, assume that the rate of inflation is 6 percent, the current short-term interest rate is 9 percent, and thus, the real rate of interest (the rate of interest in dollars of constant purchasing power) is 3 percent.[4] For a $20,000, thirty-year PLAM, the payment at the end of the first year based on this 3 percent rate would be $1,020.[5] At the end of the year, the payment is subtracted from the adjusted principal—the beginning principal plus interest plus revaluation of the principal for inflation. Specifically:

Beginning principal	$20,000
Add: Interest (3%)	600
Add: Revaluation of principal for inflation (6%)	1,200
Subtract: Payment	1,020
Ending principal	$20,780

Thus, the lender has earned 9 percent (the 3 percent real rate plus the rate of inflation) and the principal is $780 higher at the end of the year than at the outset. The next payment is computed by applying the annuity formula to the $20,780 for the remaining twenty-nine years with a 3 percent interest rate. The resulting $1,083 is almost exactly 6 percent higher than the first payment. This process continues in each year and ensures that payments change in line with the price level.

PLAM has a number of advantages for borrowers. First and foremost, it completely eliminates the tilting effect of inflation on the stream of payments in purchasing power terms which results from the traditional mortgage (or the VRM); under PLAM the stream of real payments is constant over the life of the contract and is, in fact, equal to the payment required by a traditional mortgage in the absence of inflation. Second, a constant stream of payments in real terms, in contrast to one decreasing at a rate capriciously determined by the happenchance of the rate of inflation, could be expected to suit the bulk of potential homeowners. A third important property of PLAM is that, by contractually establishing the total payment in terms of purchasing power, it eliminates the risk to borrowers associated with unanticipated variations in the price level.

To summarize then, PLAM (in contrast to VRM or GP) does appear to offer a more complete solution to the range of problems which we have labeled the demand effects of inflation. It does so through a contract which, in effect, produces the same real consequence for the borrower (and the lender) as would the traditional mortgage in the absence of inflation—

---

[4] This is only an approximate result but is adequate for purposes of illustration.
[5] For simplicity we assume a single annual payment at the end of each year.

and does so no matter what the rate of inflation either anticipated or realized.

While some form of PLAM has actually been adopted in several countries (Brazil, Israel, Finland, Colombia and Chile), its novelty presents a drawback in the U.S. Borrowers and lenders are used to contracting in money terms with nominal rather than "real" rates. Rates of inflation have not been so high and persistent in the U.S. as to make people fully aware of the pitfalls of money illusion. Thus, fixing the payments in real terms with the actual payment depending on inflation may be regarded by many as increasing rather than decreasing risk. This hurdle could presumably be surmounted with an educational effort. To the extent that consumers are acquainted with wage escalators and other such price-level-indexed contracts, this task will be made somewhat easier.

There is however one further, and in the short run, more serious difficulty. Reaping the full benefits from PLAM would require substantial changes in the type of liabilities issued by financial intermediaries and possibly some changes in existing laws. Specifically, if thrift institutions are to be encouraged to offer PLAMs, they should be enabled to hedge this asset by a price-level adjusted deposit—or PLAD—that is, a deposit whose principal would be revalued periodically on the basis of the reference price-index, and which accordingly would pay a real rate.

In our view, the addition of PLADs to the menu of presently existing assets would be highly desirable in the presence of substantial and uncertain inflation, as it would make it possible for savers to hedge against the risk of price level changes. Such an opportunity is not presently available, especially where *small* savers are concerned. One further advantage of empowering thrift institutions to offer PLADs is that it would go a long way toward also solving the supply problem, assuming of course that supervisory authority would refrain from placing ceilings on PLAD rates. Indeed, there are sound reasons for supposing that PLADs could effectively compete with other instruments even in periods of interest rates swollen by inflationary expectations.

As for the straightforward solution involving PLAMs hedged by PLADs, despite its great attractiveness in principle, we fear that its introduction and acceptance would face serious obstacles and resistance, at least in the near future. First, as already indicated, this solution would require substantial changes in the thinking of both borrowers and lenders, as well as substantial changes in regulations affecting thrift institutions. Second, authoritative financial circles have frequently expressed strong opposition to the introduction of price-level adjusted deposits, fearing that this would disrupt the market for other instruments and/or force widespread adoption of price-level adjusted securities. They further argue (though wrongly in our view) that any reform that would reduce the pains of inflation should be opposed, as it would sap the will to fight inflation. Finally, the adoption of PLAMs and PLADs might well require some changes or reinterpretation of the tax laws.

For all of these reasons, we believe that a more promising solution to the problem may be found in the adoption of a somewhat different instrument which we label the "constant-payment-factor VRM." This instrument combines most of the advantages of the PLAM-PLAD approach, while requiring a minimum of institutional changes.

The Constant-Payment-Factor Variable Rate Mortgage

This instrument may be thought of as either a variant of the dual-rate VRM outlined earlier or as a hybrid of the variable rate and the graduated payment mortgage.[6] Just like the dual-rate mortgage, the constant-payment-factor VRM makes use of two separate rates: a debiting factor which is charged on the outstanding balance and a payment factor which is used to recompute the periodic payment at regular intervals by applying to the then outstanding principal the standard annuity formula. As in all VRMs, the debiting rate varies in accordance with an appropriate reference rate reflecting market conditions. There is some room about the choice of this reference rate, but ideally it should be chosen with reference both to the frequency with which the rate is adjusted and to the term of the instrument with which the mortgage is financed.

The basic difference with respect to the dual-rate VRM, and also the essential ingredient of the instrument, is the choice of the payment factor. This factor would be chosen to *approximate the "real" rate and would be kept fixed for the duration of the contract.* If there is inflation, the debiting rate will exceed the payment factor, and the payment will be insufficient to cover the interest and the "scheduled" amortization implicit in the annuity computation. If inflation is very high, the payment will not even cover the interest. In any case, when the payment is next recomputed, it will rise even though the payment factor is not changed.

For the sake of illustration, suppose that a homebuyer takes out a $20,000, thirty-year mortgage with an initial variable debiting rate of 9 percent. The annual payment on a 9 percent level-payment mortgage would be $1,947.[7] With the constant-payment-factor VRM the payment would be $1,020, based on a 3 percent rate. With the debiting rate of 9 percent, however, the total payments made in the first year would fall short of the interest charge by $780. At the end of the year, this "shortfall" would be added to the loan principal. Specifically:

Beginning principal	$20,000
Add: Interest (9%)	1,800
Subtract: Payment	1,020
Ending principal	$20,780

[6] Tucker [3] advocates a graduated-payment VRM with either a fixed schedule of graduation or a schedule which varies with changes in the reference interest rate. Cohn and Fischer, *op. cit.*, show that the latter version, which calls for recomputing the entire stream of payments whenever the reference rate changes, is identical to the constant-payment-factor VRM.

[7] Again, we assume a single annual payment to simplify the illustration.

The new annual payment would be computed so as to amortize this new balance over the remaining twenty-nine years. This would give a new figure of $1,083, an increase of 6 percent, which is equal to the difference between the debiting and payment factors. This process would continue over time, provided that the real rate is reasonably stable, or equivalently, that the debiting rate less the rate of inflation does not deviate widely or systematically from the payment factor. The annual payment in current dollars would tend to change over time at roughly the rate of inflation or, equivalently, the payment in constant purchasing power would remain unchanged over the life of the contract.[8]

Further analysis revealed that moderate "errors" in the choice of the payment factor would not produce serious consequences for either the lender or the borrower. This conclusion, when combined with the evidence that the real rate is quite stable, has one implication of considerable practical importance: an institution that chose to offer a constant-payment-factor VRM could afford to post a payment rate that changed at very infrequent intervals if at all.

If the lender were anxious to avoid the risk of too slow a rate of repayment and/or the borrower were anxious to avoid the risk of his payment stream rising in time, one could readily reduce the risk to any desired extent by choosing for the payment rate an upward-biased estimate of the real rate. This would of course imply a higher initial payment, and on the average a correspondingly declining real payment stream. Further, this option would be greatly preferable to the traditional mortgage in which both the initial payment and the anticipated rate of decline are determined by the happenchance of inflationary expectations.

It is apparent that with this instrument thrift institutions could offer an array of short-term and longer-term deposits, matching their asset maturity structure, and could always afford to pay rates competitive with the market. This is because the debiting rate, which is the rate they earn on their assets, would be based on the rate which they need to pay to attract deposits. The scheme is thus fully consistent with the intermediaries performing the function for which they were designed, while eliminating the supply effects of inflation.

To summarize, the constant-payment-factor VRM relies on two basic ingredients: a payment factor related to the "real" rate and hence independent of the rate of inflation, and a variable debiting rate tied to an appropriate market rate, with maturity related to the frequency of rate revisions. By combining these ingredients in different ways one can readily put together a wide variety of specific contracts capable of suiting the needs and preferences of both borrowers and lenders, providing thereby a solution to many of the present problems of housing and of the thrift institu-

---

[8] If these conditions hold, the time pattern of payments and outstanding principal of a PLAM and a constant-payment-factor VRM with a payment factor equivalent to the real rate used in the PLAM will be identical.

tions. The instrument achieves this result because it combines the desirable features of a VRM from the viewpoint of the lending intermediaries and the main positive aspects of the PLAM from the viewpoint of the borrowers.

Transition Problems

The adoption of either the PLAM or the constant-payment-factor VRM (or any other VRM for that matter) would allow lenders to better match asset and liability maturities, thus reducing the periodic profit squeezes and related problems that have contributed to interruptions in mortgage supply. However, supply difficulties will be resolved fully only if deposit rates paid by institutions are competitive. If rate ceilings continue or if rates are repressed in any other fashion, fluctuations in supply will continue.

A major obstacle to competitive deposit rates is that most thrift institutions still have large proportions of their assets tied up in low yielding fixed-interest rate mortgages. Therefore, an immediate shift to fully competitive, and presumably on the average higher, deposit rates would worsen their profit position and would threaten the solvency of many of them.

It seems clear to us, at least, that the entire burden of this adjustment should not be imposed on the thrift institutions. While part of the current problem no doubt can be blamed on their shortsightedness, it is quite clear that it resulted primarily from behavior patterns forced on them by government regulation as well as major changes in the economic environment over which they had no control.

To achieve a rapid phasing out of rate ceilings would require not only the adoption of new types of mortgages along the lines presented in the previous section, but also some form of one-time government transfers to compensate institutions for the losses they would incur in the short run and thus maintain their solvency. While such a subsidy program might appear to be expensive, its cost would be modest when measured against that of wild gyrations in construction and the fact that an increasing proportion of Americans cannot acquire adequate housing. In addition, this once and for all subsidy should make it possible to eliminate many of the costly housing subsidy programs which have come into being in an effort to counteract these difficulties.

Obviously, there are many issues to be dealt with in the transition to new mortgage lending patterns. Inasmuch as these transition issues were not part of the study, we do not pretend to present a complete set of recommendations. However, it is clear that they must be dealt with in relation to any potential changes in patterns of mortgage lending.

Conclusions and Recommendations

The analyses summarized in this article support the conclusion that the standard mortgage has been a major contributor to the problems which have plagued housing during the recent inflationary period. Further, they provide the basis for the hopeful conclusion that innovations in mortgage financing could substantially alleviate these problems, eliminating the need for further resort to housing subsidies or to greater direct government intervention.

Alternative mortgage designs were analyzed along two dimensions: (1) the extent to which they resolve the demand problem by eliminating inflation-related distortions in the time pattern of real payments and (2) the extent to which they resolve the supply problem by allowing closer asset liability matching. The position of each instrument along these dimensions

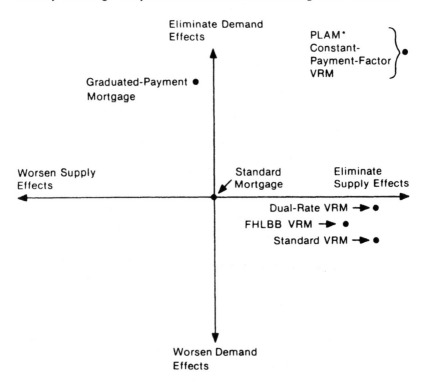

* If price-level adjusted deposits are issued.

Figure 2   Classification of Mortgage Designs by the Extent to Which They Eliminate Supply and Demand Effects of Inflation

is shown in Figure 2. Of all the mortgage innovations studied, only the price-level adjusted mortgage and the class of variable rate mortgages with smoothed real payment streams (of which the constant-payment-factor VRM appears to be best) rate well on both dimensions.

Based on these analyses, we offer the following four recommendations which should be considered as a package.

1. Price-level adjusted mortgages and/or variable rate mortgages with constant-payment-factors should be offered to the public. Federal and state regulations, as well as institutional practices, should be changed where necessary to allow for these instruments.
2. Thrift institutions should maintain a much closer balance between asset and liability maturities by both shortening effective asset maturities through PLAMs or VRMs (hopefully with constant-payment-factors), and lengthening liability maturities through more extensive use of term deposits and mortgage bonds.
3. Regulation Q ceilings should be abandoned as quickly as possible in order to restore the allocative mechanism of financial markets and reduce fluctuations in the supply of funds through traditional mortgage lenders.
4. Some form of once and for all subsidy (or other form of public intervention) should be granted to thrift institutions which will erase past mistakes and will not penalize housing and depositors of these institutions for past errors of financial policy.

References

[1] Modigliani, F. "Some Economic Implications of the Indexing of Financial Assets with Special Reference to Mortgages," Proceedings of the Conference on the New Inflation, Milano, Italy, June 1974, forthcoming.

[2] Poole, W. "Housing Finance under Inflationary Conditions." In *Ways to Moderate Fluctuations in Housing Construction*, Board of Governors, Federal Reserve System, 1972.

[3] Tucker, D. "The Variable-Rate Graduated Payment Mortgage." *Real Estate Review*, Spring 1975, pp. 71-80.

SOME CURRENTLY SUGGESTED EXPLANATIONS AND CURES
FOR INFLATION:
A COMMENT

Franco Modigliani
Massachusetts Institute of Technology

Somewhat to my present surprise, I found Professor Haberler's analysis of inflation - - the great problem of the day - - not very different from my own. I was especially relieved that he too does not believe that the problem can be quickly dismissed by pointing the finger at an excessive growth of the money supply. But, more generally. I find that the areas of agreement far exceed those of disagreement. Thus, my remaining comments largely deal with details and even questions of semantics.

One such question is whether one can usefully distinguish between demand pull and cost push inflation and if so, how. I tend to differ somewhat from the author in that I have concluded that the behavior of wages and prices can be most usefully approached with the help of the so-called search theory (particularly in the form elaborated by C. C. Holt), and an oligopolist mark-up model: aggregate demand determines the available jobs, which together with the labor force, determine vacancies and unemployment and hence wages and finally prices. In terms of this model (almost) every increase in the prices of domestic output is cost push, because it reflects increased wages and other costs; but at the same time, a faster rate of growth of prices can always be traced back to demand pull, in the sense that every increase in demand causes a faster rate of growth of wages. Yet I believe that a distinction between the two types of inflation is useful in so far as they call for different remedies. Accordingly I suggest labeling demand pull a situation in which monetary and fiscal policies create a level of aggregate real demand (job openings) and a related level of vacancies and unemployment larger than is consistent, in the medium run, with an "acceptable" rate of inflation. Note that, in view of the delayed response of wages to unemployment, of prices to wages, and finally of wages to prices and so on, when demand pull first occurs, the rate of inflation may, initially, remain below the acceptable level. Furthermore, it need not be true that prices stay ahead of non-profit incomes, unless capacity utilization is also significantly strained.

When demand pull in the above sense prevails, the appropriate remedy is clearly to change the monetary-fiscal mix so as to reduce aggregate demand. To be sure, the above criterion of classification is somewhat vague both because what is "acceptable" is a value judgment and because the implied warranted level of unemployment will change over time with the composition of the labor

179

force and is, in any event, somewhat uncertain at any point of time. In particular, one may, or not, be prepared to accept as relevant the notion of a vertical Phillips curve, in which case the warranted rate would be unique, though still uncertain. But I am afraid that this vagueness and room for divergent views is a fact that should not be hidden either to ourselves or to the laymen. Furthermore, the "vagueness" is not too great. I suspect that most economists would agree that demand pull prevailed at least in '66, '68-'69 and again in '73 - - with the problem in the latter year compounded by the fact that, as the critical zone was being approached, demand was rising much too fast.

By contrast, I would label as cost push a situation in which aggregate demand (unemployment) is at or below (above) the warranted rate, and yet wages and prices rise faster than the target rate. A most common case of cost push is as an aftermath of demand pull; because of the long and complex lags referred to earlier, the process of inflation, once put into motion, will go on for some time, feeding, as it were, on itself.

The appropriate remedy in such a situation is unfortunately much less obvious, and therefore the area of disagreement, understandably, much wider. My own prescription is that, once aggregate real demand has been brought back to the warranted level, estimated rather conservatively, one should just wait for the inflationary process to die down gradually. This implies avoiding the temptation of speeding up the process either with a "right" maneuver of breaking sharply and letting the unemployment rate go much above the warranted level, unnecessarily punishing ourselves for past sins, or with a "left" manuever of wage price controls, which are likely to create more harm than good, except possibly under very special circumstances. Note that if the above prescription is followed, then the required rate of expansion of the money supply is likely to stay for a while above the norm, given roughly by the sum of the target rate of change of prices and real rate of growth of the economy. But it would be wrong to say that this abnormal rate of growth is the cause of inflation and more accurate to characterize it as the effect.

The above discussion of demand pull, subsequent cost push, and proper remedies may perhaps be clarified by an analogy. Consider a car driven by a hurried driver, on a flat road subject to a speed limit. Clearly he should aim to keep the car at the speed limit. There is some position of the gas pedal which will result in this speed. If by error, the driver pushes the pedal beyond this "warranted" position, the car will exceed the speed limit - - the analogue of my demand pull - - and the correct response is to reduce the pressure on the pedal at least back to the warranted position. However, when this is done, the car will continue for a while to exceed the speed limit - - the analogue of cost push - - though it will eventually get back on course. Finally, to see the parallel

180

with the money supply behavior, note that since the wheels are connected with the motor, while the car is slowing down, the motor will be running too fast; but it is the wheels that push the motor, not the motor that pushes the wheels.

The duration of a cost push situation depends on price-wage rigidities - - the speed with which they respond to an easy or tight market. I would agree, with Haberler, partly on the basis of some still unpublished empirical work, that unions contribute significantly to such rigidities - - while they tend to slow down the response to excess demand, they slow down the return to equilibrium, once the excessive demand stimulus has been eliminated. However, there are indications that rigidities have increased substantially over recent decades while, as Haberler acknowledges, the importance of unions has not changed appreciably in the U.S. In this sense, it seems hard to attribute to unions a significant portion of post-war inflationary tendencies. On the other hand, one factor that may have contributed significantly is minimum wage legislation, which he does not mention explicitly in this paper, though he has done so on many previous occasions. The above mentioned empirical study indicates that attempts at narrowing wage differentials by pushing up the lower end of the scale, and pegging it, tend to be followed by a reappearance of the differential at a higher overall level.

While demand pull is the most common, it is not the only possible cause of cost push. One other cause is that of "inconsistent claims of the various groups on national product," to which Haberler refers. I doubt that this mechanism has been important in the U.S. except quite recently (see below). Trade unions may be important contributors to this mechanism in other countries in which they cover a much greater fraction of the labor force and play a pace-setting role. The dilemma for policy makers may be especially unpleasant in this case, for, in order to redimension wage demands to realisitc levels, as is necessary to stop inflation, there may well be no alternative but to increase, at least temporarily, the target level of unemployment.

The U.S. inflation of 1974 is clearly of the cost push variety, by my definition, since prices are rising at two digit rates while unemployment has already reached the area of 6%, which is widely agreed to exceed, at least moderately, the warranted rate. Yet it cannot be fully accounted for either by previous excess demand nor by inconsistent claims - - though both factors play some role. One must also take into account a set of "special factors" - - oil, poor crops, devaluation - - whose essence according to Haberler, "is that they imply a reduction - - in aggregate domestic supply of goods and services." This is an interesting way of looking at the problem for it calls attention to the connection, which in my view also is very important, between the current inflation and the painful process of adjusting to a loss of real income. I fear, however,

181

that Haberler pushes his approach too far when he suggests that the direct price impact of the special factors can be measured by his "mental experiment." Indeed, it can be verified that his proposed measure reduces to the change in a price index in which prices are weighted by current quantities (Paasche index), on the assumption that (i) all quantities other than the "special" goods are constant and (ii) the total value of the basket is the same before and after the reduction of some supplies. For the case in which only the quantity of the commodity s is curtailed by ΔQ_s, Haberler's measure of direct impact reduces to:

$$(1) \qquad \Delta P^* = \frac{P_s^0 \, \Delta Q_s}{Y_0} \equiv H$$

where P_s^0 and Y_0 denote respectively the price of s and the value of the commodity basket (aggregate supply) before the reduction. Thus Haberler's measure, H, is simply the value of the reduction in supply at pre-reduction prices, relative to total supply. By this measure, he concludes correctly that the direct impact is fairly negligible even if we add together oil, crops, and devaluation. The trouble with his measure is that it does not take properly into account the "importance" of the commodity for the economy: (i) by assuming all other outputs constant, it fails to allow for reductions in output of complementary commodities; (ii) by relying on the initial price, it misses the full impact on the consumers as measured by the loss of consumers surplus or, more operationally, by the elasticity of demand (η). Indeed, H would have the same value whether the reduction of 1% in volume is due to a failure of the strawberries crop or to the oil embargo!

It is easy to show that if one repeats Haberler's mental experiment but then chooses to measure the direct impact by a conventional Laspreyre index, one finds

$$(2) \qquad \Delta P^* = H(1 + \frac{\Delta P_s}{P_s}) = H(1 - \frac{1}{\eta} \frac{\Delta Q_s}{Q_s})$$

which is necessarily larger than (1) especially if in ΔQ, we now include the secondary loss of output. But even (2) still assumes, like (1), that all prices are perfectly flexible, and on the whole, adjust promptly downward - - as they must if expenditure is to remain constant and the demand for the special commodity is inelastic. If one measures the impact effect on the assumption that all other prices are constant, the Laspeyre measure is

182

$$(3) \qquad \Delta P^* = H \frac{1}{\eta}$$

which is even larger than (2) if $\eta < 1$. And even (3) underestimates the full effect since it neglects the likely rise in prices of close substitutes.

I would thus conclude that the "direct impact" of the special factors of '73-'74 is a good deal larger than suggested by Haberler's mental experiment. Still I am inclined to agree that the most serious effect of the "special factors" may well come from the general endeavor to resist the unavoidable loss of real income through wage escalation, which raises prices, and so on. This adds an element of "inconsistent claims" to the direct effects and to the cost push process already in course as a result of the demand pull of '73. One interesting implication of this situation is that the public is by now thoroughly convinced that it is worse off because of the inflation, whereas it is more nearly true that the high rate of inflation is a consequence of their being worse off, the result of a fruitless endeavor to avoid the unavoidable loss of real income. Educating the public on this point, which no official has tried to do, might concievably help to cut short the cost push process without plunging the economy into deep recession.

Haberler devotes one section to the great debate about the relation between inflation and alternative exchange rate systems. I will refrain from extensive comments since, in my view, the debate is getting sterile. It all comes down to the simple proposition that flexible exchange rates (i) provide the opportunity for insulating the country from outside inflation but also (ii) permit the country to pursue or not resist inflationary tendencies free of the potential restraint imposed by the balance of payment, under fixed rates. Each side of the debate chooses to emphasize one of these two implications. I doubt, however, that one can establish a universally valid ranking since clearly neither alternative totally dominates the other.

On the issue of recycling. I would like to take exception to Haberler's assertion that "there is no economic justification for treating oil and nonoil deficits differently." To the contrary, I would argue that, at least to a first approximation, for the major developed countries, the target deficit on trade account should be commensurate to their oil deficit. The basis for this proposition is straightforward: there is at the moment extreme uncertainty as to how the current dislocation in balance of trade will eventually find a "permanent" solution, e.g., by a substantial reduction in oil countries' surplus, whether due to a lower price or to a shift in output away from the countries with the highest propensity to run a surplus; or by increased commodity imports; or by massive investments in the LDC's, and so on. Until this uncertainty is resolved, and a

183

new permanent pattern of trade develops, it would be wasteful for countries to engage in large scale re-allocation of resources merely for the purpose of temporarily reshuffling the deficit among them. If this reasoning is accepted, I would go on to suggest that the exchange rate pattern appropriate to the above balance of trade targets is almost certain to require extensive intervention by central banks, financed, one would hope, from a cooperatively established oil facility.

Coming finally to touch briefly on policies to deal with the current inflation, my recommendation, as already indicated, is to aim for a conservative target rate of unemployment - - somewhere between 5 1/2 and 6% - - and stick to it until the inflation has abated (or the approach has clearly proved a failure). Simulation with the MPS model suggests that this policy would require a significantly larger rate of growth of M_1. It would also require other measures such as raising the ceilings on deposit rates at thrift institutions to revive housing, and some fiscal stimulus. Like Haberler, I can see little point in a public employment program aimed at re-absorbing those pushed out of private employment by our own deflationary policy. I would rather favor a reduction in payroll taxes which would have beneficial effects on prices - - much like a cost push in reverse. Finally, I would favor measures designed to reduce the greatest discomfort of a protracted period of inflation. These might include a reform of the mortgage instrument and possibly of savings deposits through indexation or other equivalent devices which would help home buyers, the housing industry, and the small savers. (To fully accomplish this task, some form of subsidization of the thrift institution may be necessary to take care of their seasoned portfolio.)

If one holds that these remedies are too slow in reducing inflation, then, rather than pursuing what seems to be the present policy of stern deflation with the result of a serious depression, one should try a new round of incomes policy - - say a ceiling on wage increases with the commitment that if the rate of change of prices exceeds some limit, then there will be some reduction in taxes. This should be accompanied by an educational campaign to persuade the public that a fall in real income is unavoidable and the only choice is between getting there through a wage freeze or through a painful depression.

Errata

Page 179: the full reference for the C. C. Holt work cited is: Holt, Charles C., "Job Search, Phillips' Wage Relation, and Union Influence: Theory and Evidence," in E. S. Phelps, editor, *Microeconomic Foundations of Employment and Inflation Theory,* Norton, 1970.

Page 181, third paragraph, third line from end: "realisitc" should read "realistic."

Page 183, third paragraph, fourth line from end: "payment" should read "payments"; the comma should be deleted.

184

Towards an Understanding of the Real Effects and Costs of Inflation

Stanley Fischer and Franco Modigliani

Contents: I. The Indexed Economy. — II. Real Effects of Nominal Government Institutions. — III. Real Effects of Nominal Private Institutions. — IV. Real Effects of Unanticipated Inflation through Existing Nominal Contracts. — V. Real Effects of Uncertainty of Future Inflation. — VI. Real Effects of Government Attempts to Suppress Symptoms of Inflation. — VII. Concluding Comments.

There is no convincing account of the economic costs of inflation that justifies the typical belief — of the economist and the layman — that inflation poses a serious economic problem, relative to unemployment. In this paper we present a systematic account of the real effects of inflation that we hope will contribute to understanding of and continuing research on the costs of inflation.

It will become clear that the effects of inflation can vary enormously depending on two major factors: first, the institutional structure of the economy; and second the extent to which inflation is or is not fully anticipated. Because the institutional structure of the economy adapts to ongoing inflation, the real effects (and costs) of inflation can be expected to vary, not only among different economies, but also in the same economy at different periods.

The organization of the paper is simple. We start by examining the real effects of anticipated inflation in an economy that has fully adapted to inflation. In particular, in this economy: (i) public institutions are fully attuned to inflation (or inflation proof), (ii) the same is true of private institutions, (iii) current and future inflation is fully reflected in inherited contracts, and (iv) future inflation is fully reflected in contracts for the future. After we have discussed the effects of anticipated inflation in this environment, we examine the real effects of inflation that arise as the assumptions (i) to (iv) are dropped one after the other. The effects cumulate in the sense that those present in the economy that has fully

Remark: This is a substantially revised version of the paper presented at the Baden conference. We are indebted to Pekka Ahtiala, Rudi Dornbusch, John Flemming, Jacob Frenkel, Lucas Papademos, Kari Puumanen and James Tobin for comments. Research support to Fischer was provided by the National Science Foundation.

Table 1 — *The Real Effects of Inflation*

Source of effect	Nature of effect	
	direct	indirect (general equilibrium)
I. Fully Indexed Economy		
No interest paid on currency, a government (outside) liability	1. Increase in government revenue (inflation tax)	G1 Reduction in other taxes or increases in government spending
	2. Economizing on currency	G2 Diversion of resources to transactions (shoe-leather costs)
Need to change prices more frequently	3. Reduction in private net wealth	
	4. Resource costs of price change ("menu costs")	G3 Offsetting increase in capital stock, lowering real interest rate
II. Real Effects of Nominal Government Institutions		
Progressive taxation of nominal income	5. Increased real income tax bill	G5 See G1 above
Nominal tax base	6. Reduction of net of tax real return on lending relative to pre-tax real rate	G6—10 Potential effects on cost of capital to corporations and individuals, with resultant effects on capital accumulation; changes in patterns of financing
(a) taxation of nominal interest income received by persons		
(b) deductability of nominal interest paid by persons	7. Reduction of net real cost of borrowing relative to pre-tax real rate	
	8. Return to equity holders in levered corporations rises given constant debt-equity ratios, constant real pre-tax interest rate on bonds, and constant marginal product of capital	G9 See also G1
(c) deductability of nominal interest paid by corporations	9. Changes in government tax recepts; net effect depends on induced changes in pre-tax real interest rate on bonds, differences in tax rates between debtors (including corporations) and creditors	
(d) depreciation at original cost	10. Return to equity-holders declines	G10—11 See also G1 Combined effects vary among firms, depending on nature of assets; likely shift away from use of long-lived assets; shift in inventory accounting methods from FIFO to LIFO
(e) cost of goods sold measured at original cost	11. Tax revenue increases	
(f) taxation of nominal capital gains	12. Post-tax return to equity owners on realized gains declines if pre-tax return remains constant	
	13. Lock in effects	
Nominal accounting methods used by government	14. Distortions in interpretations of economic situation, e.g., nominal interest share in GNP rises, savings rate misinterpreted since both income and savings measured incorrectly; overstatement of government deficit	
III. Real Effects of Nominal Private Institutions and Habits		
Continued reliance on nominal annuity contracts, mortgages	15. Declining real repayment streams relative to nominal streams	G15 Possible effects on real interest rates, and therefore investment
Nominal accounting methods	16. Distortion of reports of profits; other money illusions based on confusion between real and nominal interest rates possible	G16 Effects on stock market valuation of firms; investment decisions

continued

continued

Source of effect	Nature of effect	
	direct	indirect (general equilibrium)

IV. Real Effects of Unanticipated Inflation through Existing Nominal Contracts

Existing contracts for goods or services fixed in money terms or otherwise sticky	17. Redistribution between buyer and seller if quantity of services fixed by contract	G17—19 Effects on level of economic activity (Phillips curve)
	18. Effects on quantity of services provided	Short-run functional income redistributions by income size
	19. Distortions of relative prices fixed at different times	G19 Misallocations of resources arising particularly from need to search for relative price information
Existing debt contracts fixed in nominal terms	20. Redistribution from private to public sector	
	21. Redistributions between private debtors and creditors	G20 Ultimately intergenerational transfers

V. Real Effects of Uncertainty of Future Inflation

| Need to make decisions without knowledge of future prices | 22. Reluctance to make future commitments without knowledge of prices; absence of safe asset | G22 Changes in patterns of asset accumulation |
| | 23. Shortening of nominal contracts | G23 Increased transaction costs of making frequent contracts, and loss of planning ability |

VI. Real Effects of Government Endeavors to Suppress Symptoms of Inflation

| Public dissatisfaction over inflation, and government reactions | 24. Wage and price controls | G24 Shortages, possibly pervasive; misallocations of resources |
| Government concern over potential bankruptcies and other financial losses resulting from a rise in interest rates | 25. Control of interest rates, intervention in bond markets | G25 Instability of financial flows, with possible effects on direction and level of investment activity |

Note: The real effects cumulate. For instance, the effects described in Section I are present also under the assumptions of Section II.

adapted to inflation are also present in economies with non-inflation proof institutions, and so on.

The organization of the paper enables us to provide a coherent listing of the major real effects of inflation[1]. The list is long and surprisingly pervasive, and is contained in its essentials in Table 1. The remainder of the paper may be regarded as a commentary on Table 1, which will also be useful as a guide to the subsequent discussion. We should note that the space devoted in this paper to the items on the list is not necessarily a judgment on their relative importance, but in part reflects what is known about the particular effect. For instance, we have much to

---

[1] The listing is probably incomplete, and the emphasis possibly not to everyone's liking. We have been struck by reactions to this paper of the nature: "Of course, you omitted (or failed to emphasize) the most important item, X," where X varies widely. Such reactions of course reflect the lack of quantitative knowledge of the effects of inflation.

say about the wealth redistributions associated with unanticipated inflation but relatively little about the misallocations that result from increased uncertainty that typically accompanies inflation. The latter effect may well be extremely important, but very little systematic is known about it.

We have one other disclaimer to enter before we begin the substantive part of the paper. Although the measurement of the social and private costs of inflation is one eventual goal of research in this area, we do not attempt here to cost systematically individual effects of inflation and hence to provide a quantitative appraisal of the overall cost of inflation[1]. Any measures would be almost totally speculative at this stage; our listing of the real effects of inflation will show that considerable detailed work is necessary before it will be possible to provide serious answers to the key question of the real costs (and benefits) of those effects. We do, however, provide numerical estimates of the magnitudes of some of the important effects, and in any event, we believe that the systematic listing and discussion of the real effects or inflation that is provided in this paper is a necessary step toward estimating the costs of inflation.

I. The Indexed Economy

The starting point for analysis is a fully indexed economy. All debt instruments are indexed, except currency, on which no interest is paid (because there is no convenient way to do so); wage and salary contracts are indexed; the exchange rate is freely flexible; tax brackets, fines, and other payments fixed by law are indexed; real rather than nominal returns on assets are taxed; there are no nominal interest rate ceilings; and so on. Demand side disturbances in this economy, arising for example from a change in the nominal stock of high powered money, would have temporary real effects, depending on the frequency with which index adjustments are made. Similarly, changes in the general price level might be the result of real supply side disturbances, such as a change in the terms of trade. In discussing the effects of inflation in such an economy, we abstract from the frictional real effects of demand disturbances, and from the effects of real disturbances other than those on the general price level.

In this section we discuss the effects of anticipated inflation, noting in passing, however, that in a fully indexed economy unanticipated inflation has very minor real effects, consisting essentially of a redistri-

---

[1] Surveys of the costs of inflation are contained in Phelps [1972], Foster [1972], Laidler and Parkin [1975], and Flemming [1976]. — Laidler [1975], Okun [1975], and Solow [1975] contain useful non-survey discussions of the costs of inflation. The present paper has benefited considerably from the stimulus of a paper by Tobin [1976].

52*

bution between the private and public sectors. Such redistributions are discussed in more detail in Section IV.

The real effects and costs of anticipated inflation in a fully indexed economy would result from the absence of interest payments on currency, and from the "menu costs" of changing prices and wages. First we examine the effects arising from the non-payment of interest on currency, assumed initially to be a government liability, which is outside wealth for the private sector. Anticipated inflation represents a tax on real currency holding, since it reduces the real return earned by currency holders. The other side of the tax analysis is that the government obtains tax receipts through the issue of new currency, if the inflation is caused by the growth of high-powered money.

There are two potential routes for the anticipated inflation to affect real variables. First, the demand for real currency should be expected to fall as a result of the increased cost of holding it, producing the well-known shoe-leather costs of inflation, the welfare cost of which is measured by the size of the triangle under the demand for currency function[1]. As the optimal inflation tax literature has emphasized, the optimal rate of inflation is not necessarily either zero or negative[2]. The costs of inflation have to be calculated relative to that rate of inflation that, as part of the overall pattern of taxation, minimizes the social costs of raising government revenue. From this viewpoint, there are welfare costs from inflation that is below the optimum rate, as well as from inflation above the optimum rate.

The costs of inflation arising from the reduced demand for currency have the distinction of being the only costs that have been carefully measured. An estimate, for the United States, can be constructed based on an assumed stock of currency of about $ 100 billion, and a very generous estimate of the interest elasticity of demand for currency of one-half. The annual cost of an increase of the inflation rate from, say, 5 percent to 6 percent, would then be under $ 0.5 billion — and this is a relatively high estimate because the elasticity assumption is upward biased[3].

The second potential route through which fully anticipated inflation could have real effects in the fully indexed economy is through the relationships among inflation, saving, and capital accumulation. Capital

---

[1] This cost has the dimension of a flow, $/time. For some purposes one may be interested in the capital value of this flow, through suitable discounting. A recent paper by Martin Feldstein [1977] raises some difficulties about the discounting procedure.

[2] See, for instance, Phelps [1973].

[3] Even if we assumed the inflation tax applied to M_1, the annual welfare cost of the tax would be under $ 2 billion. But in the fully indexed economy, demand deposits would pay interest at least equal to the rate of inflation.

accumulation, through life cycle savings effects, results from the reduction in outside wealth caused by the reduced value of high-powered money. Further, capital accumulation may be encouraged as a result of the fall in the anticipated rate of return on an asset alternative to capital, namely currency. Calculation will show that the reduction in wealth caused by the anticipated inflation is small; given that fact and also the fact that currency holdings are very small relative to those of capital, the effects of the induced changes on the capital stock would probably also be small. Nonetheless, such changes would tend to offset the reduction in welfare caused by the loss of liquidity[1].

So far we have been considering the costs of a perfectly anticipated inflation in an indexed economy where high-powered money is an outside asset. If currency were inside money, then an increase in the inflation rate would still produce a deadweight loss as the anticipated inflation reduced real currency holding. However, with the right to issue currency now being assigned to the banking system, an increased real bank revenue due to inflation would increase the value of bank stocks and thus wealth, perhaps leading to a decline in capital accumulation; the effects of a reduced return on currency on the demand for capital would tend to work in the opposite direction.

The other source of the effects of inflation in a fully indexed economy is the "menu costs" of changing prices. In principle, most prices in the indexed economy could be quoted in the unit of account, the cost of a commodity basket. In that case, the costs of changing nominal prices would be largely the costs of calculating the nominal amount to be handed over in each transaction, based on the stated indexed price of goods. There would be no need to change marked prices in an indexed economy more often than in a non-inflationary environment.

At low rates of inflation it would probably be most convenient (cheapest) to fix prices for many commodities in nominal terms. We have to distinguish here between auction markets, in which prices are set to clear markets more or less continually, and in which the costs of changing prices would not be affected by the rate of inflation, and "custom" markets in which prices are set and usually held for some time[2]. The menu costs of inflation arise in the custom markets, which include those for labor, manufactures, much of wholesale and retail trade, trans-

---

[1] The effects of anticipated inflation on capital accumulation have been at the center of a long controversy. Such effects do arise in the context of life-cycle utility-maximizing individuals or families with finite horizons, but in some models they do not occur in steady state if the family effectively has an infinite horizon [Sidrauski 1967; Fischer 1979].

[2] The distinction is Okun's [1975]; it is related to some Hicksian distinctions.

portation, and such obvious examples as pay telephones, vending machines, and parking meters.

If we assume nominal pricing would be used at some low rates of inflation, and that there is a fixed cost of changing a given nominal price in the custom sector, then we should expect the frequency of price changes to increase with the rate of inflation — though we should, of course, recall that relative prices change even in the absence of inflation. However, as the inflation rate rose, prices would probably be adjusted *relatively* less frequently, so that the variability of relative prices might increase as the frequency of absolute price changes increased[1]. If the system continued using nominal pricing, the menu costs of inflation could become dramatic at high rates of inflation. Before such costs were incurred, however, the system would probably switch over to the use of indexed pricing. Tokens would be used for telephones and other vending machines, and parking cards could be used in place of parking meters. The new real monies would compete with the depreciating money, be a nuisance to carry, and likely reduce the government's seignorage. The transitional costs of moving to such a system would also be large.

Thus we should expect menu costs to rise with the (anticipated) inflation rate up to some fairly high rate of inflation, at which time the system would start switching over to another unit of account, and for some purpose, to stores of value that substitute for currency. The costs of changing nominal prices thereafter would be largely the costs of calculating nominal prices from stated real prices.

Overall, the non-payment of interest on currency and the menu costs of changing prices do not generate substantial real effects of moderate rates of inflation[2]. Additional real effects of inflation come into play when we recognize the existence of nominal government institutions, to be discussed next in Section II.

II. Real Effects of Nominal Government Institutions

The way in which anticipated inflation interacts with nominal government institutions to produce real effects on the economy depends on the particular institutional structure of the economy. Our discussion in this section relates primarily to the United States; while similar conclusions may apply in other economies, the details are surely not identical.

The major source of the real effects of inflation that occur as a result of "nominal" government institutions is the tax system. The tax system

---

[1] The "might" is included since the variability of relative prices would depend on both the correlation of the timing of price changes and the frequency of such changes.

[2] Increased variability of relative prices might absorb resources as individuals search for information on prices; this point is taken up in more detail in Section IV.

in the United States was clearly intended for non-inflationary times, but it has been little amended in response to the inflation of the last ten years. It is significant that although indexation, particularly in regard to taxation of capital gains, was discussed in the debates over the tax "reforms" to be introduced in 1979, such measures were not included in the bill finally passed.

Perhaps the best known tax effect occurs as a result of the non-indexation of tax brackets in progressive income tax schedules. As nominal incomes rise, and nominal tax brackets are not adjusted, the proportion of income that is taken by the personal income tax rises. However, this effect is quite small: Sunley and Pechman [1976] estimate an elasticity of real income taxes with respect to the price level of 1/2. In 1977, personal taxes were of the order of $ 150 billion; a 1 percent increase in the price level would increase taxes by about $ 0.75 billion. Even this small effect could be removed by the simple step of indexation of brackets, a change that has been introduced in Canada and other countries. It is also emphasized in Aaron [1976] that in fact the Congress has made discretionary income tax changes that have kept average personal income tax rates at about the same levels as in the fifties, despite the intervening inflation.

The effects of taxes on corporations and asset holders are potentially more important than those arising from non-indexation of brackets. Taxes are levied on the total nominal interest income received by individuals. Thus, if the pre-tax real rate of return on an asset remains constant as the inflation rate increases, the after-tax real rate to the asset holder will fall. The magnitude of this effect at the individual level is quite dramatic. Consider an individual for whom the tax rate is 25 percent, and who is earning pre-tax and pre-inflation, 5 percent nominal and real on his bonds. His after-tax real return is 3.75 percent. Now, let the inflation rate rise to 5 percent, and the interest rate to 10 percent. Then the nominal after-tax interest rate is 7.5 percent, and the after-tax real rate received by the asset holder is 2.5 percent. The 5 percent inflation reduces the net of tax real return by one third.

The other side of this coin, from the viewpoint of the individual, is that nominal interest *paid* on personal debts is deductible from income on which taxes are levied. Thus, insofar as nominal rates adjust fully so as to leave the real rate unchanged, preventing a redistribution from creditors to debtors in pretax income, there would still be a redistribution of after-tax income between creditors and debtors. This redistribution in taxes may have further social implications which will be examined later in connection with redistribution of wealth effects. In addition, there would tend to be overall effects for net government tax take. Since the household sector is, on balance, a creditor, net taxes should tend to rise, but this effect could be more or less fully offset by the fact that debtors appear to be on the average richer, and hence in higher tax brackets, than creditors (see below).

Corporations too are allowed to deduct nominal interest from their profits before the corporate tax liability is calculated. As of a given debt-equity ratio, and given a constant real interest rate and marginal product of capital, the real return to stockholders would tend to increase. Whether the owners of the firm, including bondholders, would have a greater or smaller real after-tax return, depends on the relation between the corporate and individual income tax rates. If we start with the strong and unrealistic assumption that the tax rate paid by all individuals is the same, and also assume the pre-tax real interest rate on bonds and marginal product of capital constant, the firm's owners could have exactly the same real return independent of the rate of inflation if corporations and individuals paid the same tax rates. If the corporate tax rate is higher than the individual rate, an increase in the inflation rate would reduce total taxes paid by the firm's owners and government tax collection, and vice versa.

As long as we consider only the treatment of interest by the tax system, the effects of inflation on total post-tax real returns of the owners of corporate firms appear likely to be small; and after-tax real returns would not necessarily be adversely affected by inflation. Subsidiary effects would arise if there were changes in the relative post-tax real returns of bond and equity holders, which induced a change in the debt-equity ratio and perhaps a change in the cost of capital.

The next two elements in Table 1 that relate to the nominal tax system tend to increase the taxes paid by corporations as the inflation rate rises. First, depreciation is charged off at historical cost; the present discounted value of the depreciation deduction from taxes falls as the inflation rate rises, given any particular depreciation schedule. This unambiguously raises the cost of capital to a corporation, as of given real interest rates. The second element — the measurement of the cost of goods sold at original cost, and the consequent overstatement of profits — is not required by the tax laws. Firms have the choice of using LIFO rather than FIFO inventory accounting methods, and the former will prevent the overstatement of profits that FIFO produces in an inflationary environment. Firms did growingly switch to LIFO as the inflation rate increased in the 1970s.

The more general effects of original cost depreciation depend on the nature of firms' assets. There is in general a rise in the cost of capital as the inflation rate rises, with the effect being greatest for firms using the longest lived capital. There would presumably be both a fall in the rate of investment, and a shift to shorter-lived capital, as the inflation rate increased. It should be noted that the effects of inflation that work through the tax treatment of depreciation are not present in countries that allow 100 percent write-off of investment expenses in the first year.

The presumption from the various effects of inflation on tax revenues that we have discussed so far is that government revenue would rise with inflation, mainly through a fall in the real value of the depreciation deductions. Davidson and Weil [1976] find an elasticity of about three for the corporate income tax with respect to inflation, based on a sample of large firms, and omitting capital gains on outstanding debt. With corporate income taxes of about $ 40 billion in 1976, the effect of a one percent increase in the price level is to increase corporate income taxes by $ 1.2 billion. Allowing for tax exemption of interest payments, the inflation premium included in interest is likely to offset this effect to a very large extent[1], but there remains a net effect through higher taxes on personal interest received. Any increases in government revenue would make it possible to reduce other taxes or increase government spending, given the deficit[2].

The taxation of nominal capital gains results in the after-tax real return to equity and other asset holders being reduced by inflation, if the pre-tax real return remains constant. It leads also to lock-in effects, given the principle of taxation only on realization of the gains. The first effect tends to reduce the return to equity holders, and would therefore likely lead to an increase in the cost of capital for firms, and reduced investment. The allocative effects of lock-ins are difficult to establish a priori; there is a general case to be made that they inhibit the efficient operation of the capital markets by encouraging some asset holders not to register their expectations in the market place by buying and selling assets.

The tax effects reviewed are clearly complicated and many. The net directions of those effects are not all obvious, and the overall impact of the tax system on the sensitivity of the post-tax rates of return received by asset holders and the cost of capital to the rate of inflation is uncertain[3].

---

[1] This conclusion is suggested by a comparison of the magnitude of the overstatement of equity returns due to inventory and nominal depreciation with the magnitude of the understatement due to real capital gains or debt. See, e.g., the study of Shoven and Bulow [1975; 1976] and Davidson and Weil [1976].

[2] It is estimated by Fellner, *et al.* [1975] that taxes in 1974 were $ 17 billion higher than they would have been had the tax system been indexed. The inflation rate in that year was about 10 percent and tax receipts $ 265 billion.

[3] The effects discussed in this section have been studied recently by Feldstein and others; see, for example, Feldstein and Summers [1978].

But it appears that on balance increases in the inflation rate will tend to increase the cost of capital and reduce the after-tax real rate of return to wealthholders, given the marginal product of capital and the pre-tax real interest rate.

Finally, in our consideration of nominal governmental institutions, we turn to the inflation illusion that is present in economic statistics. It is clear first that inflation increases the reported share of interest in GNP, since interest is reported as nominal and not real. It would be preferable to present real interest earnings by deducting the capital losses on outstanding bonds from interest, and adding them to profits or whatever other category they should enter.

In particular, insofar as net interest is paid by the government, the inflation premium portion should be treated as a repayment of principal to the debt holders and thus deducted from government expenditure. Failure to do so leads to an overstatement of the current government deficit which can be quite large when inflation is significant. Thus, a recomputation of the deficit to reflect the fall in the real value of government liabilities — or repayment of real debt through the inflation premium — would involve a major change in the perspective on the last few years deficits in the U.S.; for instance, in 1978, government liabilities to the public will fall in real value by about $ 45 billion, or approximately the size of the deficit.

Similarly, the nominal treatment of private and government interest payments leads to an overstatement of both personal and disposable income as well as saving, since it treats as income and saving respectively what should be correctly treated as a return of capital and the reinvestment thereof. It might be argued that with respect to the government, the nominal deficit is still the relevant measure since it is the amount that needs to be financed with resulting crowding out effects. But in reality that portion of interest payments that represents a repayment of principal should give rise to matching "saving" available for reimbursement by the public. To be sure, to the extent that the public is fooled into treating as income what is not, there may be some net reduction in real saving with final effects analogous to crowding out. But there is clearly no reason why these effects would be captured by using a wrong measure of interest earned and paid.

The accounting errors referred to in the previous two paragraphs are not widely recognized, and may even influence policy. Thus, the overstatement of the government deficit creates at least the potential for errors in fiscal management. At any rate, it is hard to believe that intelligent policy making is systematically aided by the use of inappropriate measurement.

III. Real Effects of Nominal Private Institutions

The private sector as well as the government has continued to use nominal institutions and practices in the face of ongoing inflation. At the same time, there have been financial innovations in the past decade that mitigate the effects of inflation on the private sector — one important illustration is the introduction of floating rate debt instruments. In this section we concentrate on the effects arising from the continued use of nominal annuity contracts and mortgages, and from the reliance on nominal accounting methods, while still maintaining the assumption that inflation is *anticipated*.

Reliance on the level payment nominal mortgage as the major vehicle for financing residential housing means that the time pattern of real repayments on a mortgage is tilted by inflation. Since the nominal payment is the same in each month on a level payment mortgage, the real value of the payment falls over time if there is inflation; the tilt is greater the higher the inflation rate. If the real interest rate remains constant, initial real repayments, for a mortgage of given real value at the time of purchase, will rise with the inflation rate. Similar statements can be made in the case of nominal annuities, purchased by constant nominal payment streams; the real value of the payments by the purchaser of the annuity will fall over time; then after the annuity starts paying out to the purchaser, the real value of the receipts fall over time[1].

The consequences of the tilting of the repayment stream on mortgages are thoroughly explored in Modigliani and Lessard [1975]. The use of nominal mortgages means that inflation substantially increases the real burden of financing in the early years of home ownership, and on those grounds reduces the demand for housing (of course, the demand for housing may rise because it is an inflation hedge; see below).

The continued use of constant nominal repayment mortgages poses problems also for the financial intermediaries that issue them. We discuss these difficulties in Section VI, though they fit in also in Section IV.

The continued use of nominal accounting methods in the private sector leads to distortions of reported profits and other accounting magnitudes. Evidence by Shoven and Bulow [1975; 1976] and Davidson and Weil [1976] indicates that these distortions are substantial as between firms in a given period. Such distortions create potential misallocations of resources, partly because internal firm data may be misinterpreted, and partly because markets may incorrectly assess the relative desirability

---

[1] In principle, the tilting of the payments stream could be offset by anyone with access to the capital markets, by borrowing to make the early payments. Loans for such smoothing purposes do not appear to be readily available.

of investment by different firms, and provide capital at an inappropriate cost. It is possible to argue that such errors would ultimately be self-eliminating, but we find it difficult to know how the stock market and the capital markets in general are to divine "true" profits of corporations if the firms themselves do not know the profits[1].

Accounting reforms have been proposed by committees in a number of countries, but have not been adopted. The failure to change accounting methods stems both from the inertia arising from the need to convince and educate the accounting profession and from the intellectual difficulties of problems such as the appropriate treatment of inflation-induced gains to firms from the reduction in the real value of their outstanding debt. Nor is it clear that firms whose accounting profits would change with the reform would be uniformly enthusiastic about changes in accounting systems.

The use of nominal accounting methods is one example of the type of money illusion that may remain in the economic system despite continuing inflation; this illusion results from the convenience of using money as a unit of account, rather than the medium of exchange function. On a priori grounds we are reluctant to believe such illusions can remain in the system over long periods, but there does appear to be some evidence of their continued existence. They are familiar in everyday discussion; it also appears that even the supposedly sophisticated capital markets may be using nominal interest rates to capitalize real profits [Modigliani and Cohn, 1979]. All such illusions must ultimately be self-destructive, but the surprise is that they still persist.

IV. Real Effects of Unanticipated Inflation through Existing Nominal Contracts

We now consider the real effects of unanticipated inflation that occur through the existence of nominal contracts for goods and services, and for debts. The primary effects that have received major attention are the redistributions of income and wealth associated with unanticipated inflation; there are in addition possible changes in the level of economic activity, and misallocations arising from ignorance about relative prices.

We will start with the income and wealth redistributions. The direction of the income redistribution associated with unanticipated inflation will depend on the details of the contract structure of the economy. It has

---

[1] Preliminary evidence by Modigliani and Cohn [1979] seems to show that the capital markets do, at least in aggregate, correctly adjust for inappropriate inventory and depreciation accounting, but do not adjust for capital gains accruing to equity owners as inflation reduces the real value of outstanding debt.

typically been believed that wages lag behind in inflation, and that inflation therefore implies a shift away from wage-earners, and towards profits. It is presumably on the same grounds that the claim is often made that inflation hurts the poor relatively more than the rich.

There seems to be no way *a priori* of predicting the direction of the income redistributions, by function (wage, rent, etc.) or size, associated with unanticipated inflation; the direction may well depend on the source of the unanticipated inflation. For instance, an exogenous wage push would have different implications for the redistribution of income associated with the induced inflation than would a change in the price of oil. Empirical evidence for the post War United States economy is that inflation has, if anything, redistributed income to the lower quintiles of the income distribution [Blinder and Esaki, 1978], and towards labor income [Bach and Stephenson, 1974]. However, examination of the cited empirical results will show that the effects are indeed very small; inflation does not appear to have major effects on the functional or size distributions of income[1].

The wealth redistributions arising from unanticipated inflation are more substantial. The redistribution is obviously from nominal creditors to nominal debtors. The emphasis in discussing these redistributions is usually along sectoral lines, an approach we shall follow for expositional purposes. From the viewpoint of the private sector as a whole, the unanticipated change in the price level reduces the real value of their outstanding claims on the government. But that is not the end of the story. The reduction in the real value of the debt reduces the real value of future tax payments required to service or retire the debt.

The increased disposable income of the younger generation, whose taxes have been reduced, leads them to save more, thus increasing the capital stock, while the corresponding reduction in consumption comes from the retired, whose real wealth has been reduced. There is thus a redistribution from the older generation to younger and future generations. The transfer should be thought of as chiefly intergenerational within the household sector rather than between the private and public sectors; its extent is reduced insofar as retired consumption is financed through indexed social security.

Within the private sector, the shift between the corporate and household sectors is frequently singled out for special discussion as an effect of an unanticipated increase in the price level. The unanticipated increase in the price level reduces the real value of outstanding corporate debt,

---

[1] Preliminary empirical work shows that the results of Blinder and Esaki and Bach and Stephenson are not fundamentally changed when the effects of anticipated and unanticipated inflation on the income distribution are distinguished.

apparently benefitting corporations at the expense of households. The redistribution is ultimately, however, between different households; the reduction in the value of the outstanding debt should be reflected in an increase in the value of corporate equity, leaving the net wealth of the private sector unaffected. The redistribution is fundamentally from the more risk averse to the less risk averse — this perhaps corresponding to the popular notions of suckers and sharpies.

However, the assumption that the value of corporate equity rises with unanticipated inflation is not borne out by United States data [Bodie, 1976; Nelson, 1976]. Part of the explanation for this consistent empirical finding may be the increased real tax burden caused by an increase in the price level. Other explanations for this characteristic of the United States capital market are examined in Lintner [1975] and Modigliani and Cohn [1979].

The extent of the wealth redistributions associated with unanticipated inflation is examined in some detail in the article of Modigliani and Papademos in this volume (pp. 736sqq.) and will be only summarized here. It is shown to depend on the maturity structure of existing debt and on the path of unanticipated inflation over the life of the assets. Specifically, for an asset of a given (remaining) maturity the redistribution is roughly proportional to the unanticipated change in the price level over the life of the asset (or the cumulated unanticipated rate of inflation). It follows in particular that a one percent unanticipated inflation in the current period followed by no unanticipated inflation in later periods would produce a transfer of one percent of the value of outstanding debt.

Table 2 — *Outstanding Volume of Nominal Assets in U.S. Economy,*
December 31, 1975 (billion $)

Demand deposits and currency		290.3
Time and saving accounts		884.6
Life insurance and pension reserves, plus interbank		
claims		591.8
Credit market instruments		2,626.7
Federal government	558.1	
State and local government	230.5	
Corporate and foreign bonds	317.2	
Mortages	803.3	
Other	717.6	
Trade credit		308.9
		4,702.3

Source: Flow of Funds Accounts [1976, p. 90].

Now, how large are the wealth redistributions associated with un-anticipated inflation in the United States? The total value of nominal assets in the United States economy on December 31, 1975 was about $ 4.7 trillion, composed of the assets shown in Table 2. This does not mean that an unanticipated change in the price level of one percent redistributes $ 47 billion of wealth, since individuals and institutions hold both nominal assets and nominal liabilities, and because there is some pyramiding of the asset structure.

It is more relevant to the question of redistributions to look at the household sector's balance sheet for nominal assets and liabilities[1]. Table 3 shows that the household sector had in 1975 about $ 1.8 trillion in nominal assets, and just under $ 800 billion in nominal liabilities. The net out-standing value of nominal assets held by the private sector was over $ 1 trillion, so that an unanticipated change in the price level by one percent would have reduced the real value of household sector net holdings of nominal assets by about $ 10 billion. However, this $ 10 billion figure probably understates the total real losses of those who on balance lost from inflation since the balance sheets of different individuals no doubt differ in proportions from those of the sector as a whole. Assuming no major changes in asset positions since 1975, a number like $ 15 billion would be in the ball park as a measure of the loss of real wealth suffered on nominal asset account by all those in the private sector who on balance lose on nominal asset account from the inflation.

Table 3 — *Balance Sheet for Nominal Assets and Liabilities Held by House-hold Sector in the U.S., December* 31, 1975 (billion $)

Assets			*Liabilities*		
Demand deposits and currency		165.6	Credit market instruments . .		753.5
Time and savings accounts . .		776.2	Mortgages	508.2	
Credit market instruments . .		346.8	Consumer credit	197.3	
Federal government	123.4		Other	48.0	
State and local government .	74.2		Other		29.3
Corporate and foreign bonds	65.9				
Mortgages	72.7		Total liabilities		782.8
Other	10.5		Net		1,039.8
Life insurance reserves		164.6			
Pension fund reserves		368.6			
Total assets		1,821.8			

Source: *Flow of Funds Accounts* [1976, p. 100].

Of course, $ 15 billion does not reflect the total effects of the inflation on distribution, since it does not adjust for the effects of a change in the price level on the real value on non-nominal assets and liabilities, par-

---

[1] The household sector in these tables is actually "Households, Personal Trusts, and Nonprofit Organizations."

ticularly equity and housing. For equity, existing evidence is that an increase in the price level reduces real value; for housing there is little evidence, but a belief that the real value of housing rises with inflation[1]. We must, therefore, acknowledge a great deal of uncertainty as to the net effect of inflation on the real value of real assets in the United States.

One very important aspect of wealth redistribution is from the young to the old, but unfortunately the relevant evidence is skimpy. The only systematic information we have is taken from Bach and Stephenson [1974]. (Table 4 reproduces part of the relevant table from Bach and Stephenson.) Using a 1969 survey[2], they find that the ratio of net nominal to real assets rises with the age of the head of household, and, in particular, that it is only after the age of 55 that households become net creditors in nominal terms. If this evidence stands up, then the indication is that the redistributions which occur when the price level rises chiefly reduce the real wealth of the old, while increasing the real wealth of the young. As noted above, such redistributions tend to be mitigated by the existence of indexed social security in the United States.

Table 4 — *Assets and Debts of Households*, Early 1969

Age of head of household	Percent of all households (1)	Total assets (billion $) (2)	Percent of total assets			(2)/(1)
			monetary assets	variable price assets	debts	
18—24	10	27	14	86	49	2.7
25—34	21	189	8	92	48	9.0
35—44	18	335	9	91	37	18.6
45—54	17	366	13	87	22	21.5
55—64	15	301	21	79	9	20.1
65—	19	404	23	77	3	21.2
By 1968 money income before taxes ($):						
Under 3,000	17	92	20	80	8	5.4
3,000—4,999	14	119	20	80	15	8.5
5,000—9,999	33	350	18	82	23	10.6
10,000—14,999	24	420	14	86	29	17.5
15,000—24,999	9	359	12	88	21	39.9
25,000—49,999	2	177	14	86	18	88.5
50,000 and over	0.4	105	18	82	10	262.5

Source: Bach and Stephenson [1974, p. 6], based on data from Survey of Consumer Finances [1969].

We can also use Table 4 to look at the net nominal creditor position by income class. It turns out that those with very high and very low

---

[1] Budd and Seiders [1971] in their study of the effects of inflation on distribution argue that real estate maintains but does not increase its real value in the face of inflation. They do claim that real equity values rise with inflation.

[2] The Michigan Survey Research Center stopped its surveys of consumer finances after 1970; they are in the process of being reinstated in 1978.

incomes are net nominal creditors, while the middle of the income distribution is occupied by nominal debtors. Thus we can think of the redistribution as being from those with high and low current incomes to those with intermediate incomes, but we should emphasize that such statements cannot be made meaningful without standardizing for the stage of the life cycle, something we are not able to do with the data we have.

We have so far been discussing the extent of redistribution caused by an unanticipated one percent change in the price level. We noted, however, that the redistribution caused by a change in the inflation rate depends on the maturity of the outstanding stock of nominal obligations. Of the assets and liabilities of the households shown in Table 3, about $ 900 billion of assets and over $ 500 billion of liabilities are of a term longer than one year. On the assets side, life insurance and pension fund reserves are of long maturity, as are mortgages on the liability side. The effects of a change in the inflation rate might roughly cancel out for these classes of assets and liabilities. That still leaves over $ 400 billion of other longer-term nominal assets. The maturity of these assets is not known, though that of federal obligations is close to three years[1]. Accordingly, a one percent change in the inflation rate would reduce the current value of these assets by substantially more than $ 4 billion.

It is clear that the wealth redistributions arising from unanticipated inflation are large, of the order of one percent of GNP per one percent unanticipated increase in the price level. While these effects are large, it is difficult to attach a social cost to them. For every loser there is a gainer; to calculate the social costs of the redistributions it would be necessary to have a Bergsonian social welfare function that appropriately weights the welfare of every individual. Unfortunately, there are no data on individual redistributions, and we do not have an accepted welfare function at hand.

We have devoted considerable attention to the wealth redistributions associated with unanticipated inflation. This is partly because the redistributions have received a good deal of attention in the literature, and in part because there are some relevant data; but it is also because the extent of the redistributions is substantial.

We turn next to the other real effects that occur through the use of nominal contracts. The fixity of some prices might give unanticipated inflation real effects on the level of economic activity. One of the main theories underlying the Phillips curve [Lucas, 1973] argues that unanticipated inflation increases labor supply and therefore output, and Keynesian

---

[1] *Economic Report of the President* [1977, Table 77].

sticky wage theories would also suggest that unanticipated inflation increases output.

The fixity of nominal prices may also lead to misallocations of resources in the face of unanticipated inflation, as relative prices change — because of the differential costs of changing prices in different markets, and because of imperfect information about relative prices among consumers. It is reasonably well established that relative price variability increases with the inflation rate [Jaffee and Kleiman, 1975; Vining and Elwertowski, 1976]; such increased variability leads to misallocations of resources, and to the absorption of resources in search and information gathering activities.

V. Real Effects of Uncertainty of Future Inflation

Practical men tend to emphasize that inflation makes it difficult to plan in the absence of knowledge of future prices. This argument clearly implies that uncertainty about future price levels is increased at high inflation rates. We know that in principle there is no necessary link between the rate of inflation and the variability of the inflation rate. In fact, it appears that the variability of the rate of inflation (which is not quite the same as uncertainty about the rate) increases with the level of inflation. Flemming [1976] suggests the reason may be that governments typically announce unrealistic stabilization programs as the inflation rate rises, thus increasing uncertainty about what the actual path of prices will be.

If we accept the link between the level of inflation and uncertainty about future price levels, we can ascribe to inflation the effects that arise from the need to make decisions with decreased certainty of future price levels. The first effect is a change in the pattern of asset accumulation. If there is no indexed asset, increased uncertainty about future prices reduces the safety of nominal assets, and increases the relative attractiveness of real assets as inflation hedges. Residential structures occupy a prominent position among such assets, especially when the performance of the equity values is as disappointing as it has been in the recent inflation all over the world. Other assets the public may turn to include non-reproducible tangible wealth such as land, gold, art work, etc. Given the fixity of the supply, the prices of such assets will tend to be bid up faster than the general price level. It is entirely conceivable that the resulting "capital gains" increase in real wealth will result in a decline in saving and, finally, in physical investment.

A second effect of uncertainty about the rate of inflation is the shortening of contracts. Uncertainty about the real value of the quid for which the quo is being exchanged is likely to reduce the use of long-term contracts. Uncertainty about the rate of inflation should lead also towards the use of indexed contracts. There seems to be some evidence of this in labor markets, but very little in capital markets, except through the use of floating rate notes, which are equivalent to shortening the effective maturity of the contracts. This reduces uncertainty about the real value of the payments over the lifetime of the note, but also implies sacrificing the possibility of hedging against future movements of the real rate.

Both the changes discussed in the previous two paragraphs — shifts in the demand for assets, towards inflation hedges, and the shortening, of contracts — would tend to reduce the rate of investment by firms, and lead to investment in shorter lived assets.

VI. Real Effects of Government Attempts to Suppress Symptoms of Inflation

Governments frequently attempt to suppress inflation using wage and price controls. Such controls are likely to produce serious distortions and inequities, particularly when they are introduced at times of excess demand. Measures of the extent of the distortions for particular cases have apparently not been undertaken, though anecdotal evidence on shortages induced by wage and price controls abound.

Governments also intervene in attempts to control rising interest rates, or the consequences of potential increases in interest rates. Attempts to keep interest rates from rising in inflationary situations may result from the desire of the government to avoid the imposition of capital losses on bond holders, in part under the fear that large capital losses would tend to destroy the capital markets. Attempts to keep interest rates low by monetary policy are ultimately destabilizing; attempts to keep them low through controls lead also to credit rationing and also to disintermediation and misallocation of funds.

In the United States, Regulation Q, which controls the interest rates paid by financial intermediaries, has been responsible for episodes of disintermediation in credit crunches in 1966, 1970, and 1974. The disintermediation resulted in sharp reductions in construction activity. However, the control over interest rates imposed by Regulation Q may well have been desired by the financial intermediaries, since competitive rises in interest rates would have led to large losses for them, as the rates they would have had to pay on their liabilities would have exceeded receipts from their assets [Modigliani and Lessard, 1975]. The ultimate cause of Regulation Q and the credit crunches may be thought of as the extreme imbalance in the maturity structure of the balance sheets of financial intermediaries — borrowing very short, lending very long —

53*

rather than government concern with interest rates as such. The effects we attribute here to government intervention are certainly partly to be ascribed also to the existence of nominal institutions in the private sector. It is worth noting that the financial intermediaries in the United States have innovated significantly in recent years, both by introducing new debt instruments (roll over mortgages, variable rate mortgages, etc.) and by inventing new liabilities (generally of longer term, some with variable interest rates, tied to the treasury bill rate).

It should be recognized that the cost of government intervention must be set against the possible reduction in cost that may arise from success in suppressing some symptoms or concomitants of inflation. For instance, if it succeeded in keeping the price level permanently lower, then it might avoid the cost of redistribution. On the other hand artificially holding down long-term interest rates reduces the cost to the initial holders of long-term debt, but it increases the cost to those investing in money fixed assets, thereby perpetuating the transfer from creditors to debtors. A full cost-benefit analysis of government intervention is actually a complex task. The prevailing conviction among economists today seems to be that the costs resulting from attempts to suppress or reduce inflation through government interferences with the market mechanism — some of which costs are outlined above — are likely on balance to outweigh the benefits even when, if initially, they may appear to produce small gains. Though this view could no doubt stand some closer scrutiny, particularly in terms of redistribution effects, the task is clearly beyond the scope of this survey.

VII. Concluding Comments

Perhaps the only surprising feature of this paper is the length of the list of the real effects of inflation. Conventional analysis of the welfare costs of inflation emphasizes the area under the demand curve for money as the cost of anticipated inflation and redistributions as the cost of unanticipated inflation. However, in economies that have not fully adapted to inflation — and that means all economies — potential real effects are far more pervasive. Some of these real effects are very hard to pin down — for instance, the extent of misallocations caused by variability of relative prices and uncertainty of future price levels — but they may well be as important as the costs that are conventionally emphasized.

We should also repeat that measurement of these costs of the real effects that we have listed is obviously a task of importance. Our hope is that systemization of the list of real effects will assist in organizing attempts to measure the costs (and benefits) of inflation.

References

Aaron, Henry J. (Ed.), *Inflation and the Income Tax*, The Brookings Institution, Studies of Government Finance, Series 2, Washington, D.C., 1976.

Bach, G. L., and James B. Stephenson, "Inflation and the Redistribution of Wealth", *The Review of Economics and Statistics*, Vol. 56, Cambridge, Mass., 1974, pp. 1—13.

Blinder, Alan S., and Howard Y. Esaki, "Macroeconomic Activity and Income Distribution in the Postwar United States", *The Review of Economics and Statistics*, Vol. 60, Cambridge, Mass., forthcoming 1978.

Bodie, Zvi, "Common Stocks as a Hedge against Inflation", *The Journal of Finance*, Vol. 31, New York, N.Y., 1976, pp. 459—470.

Budd, Edward C., and David F. Seiders, "The Impact of Inflation on the Distribution of Income and Wealth", *The American Economic Review*, Vol. 61, Menasha, Wisc., 1971, *Papers and Proceedings*, pp. 128—138.

Davidson, Sidney, and Roman L. Weil, "Inflation Accounting: Implications of the FASB Proposal", in: Henry J. Aaron (Ed.), *Inflation and the Income Tax*, The Brookings Institution, Studies of Government Finance, Series 2, Washington, D.C., 1976, pp. 81—120.

The Economic Report of the President to the Congress, 1977, Washington, D.C.

Feldstein, Martin, *The Welfare Cost of Permanent Inflation and Optimal Short-Run Economic Policy*, Harvard University, Cambridge, Mass., 1977, unpubl.

—, Laurence Summers, "Inflation, Tax Rules, and the Long-Term Interest Rate", *Brookings Papers on Economic Activity*, Washington, D.C., 1978, pp. 61—99.

Fellner, William, Kenneth W. Clarkson and John H. Moore (Eds.), *Correcting Taxes for Inflation*, American Enterprise Institute for Public Policy Research, Domestic Affairs Study, 34, Washington, D.C., 1975.

Fischer, Stanley, "Capital Accumulation on the Transition Path in a Monetary Optimizing Mode", *Econometrica*, New Haven, Conn., forthcoming 1979.

Flemming, J. S., *Inflation*, London, 1976.

Flow of Funds Accounts, 1946—1975, Board of Governors of the Federal Reserve System, Washington, D.C., 1976.

Foster, Edward, *Costs and Benefits of Inflation*, Federal Reserve Bank of Minneapolis, Studies in Monetary Economics, 1, Minneapolis, 1972.

Jaffee, Dwight M., and Ephraim Kleiman, *The Welfare Implications of Uneven Inflation*, University of Stockholm, Institute for International Economic Studies, Seminar Paper, No. 56, Stockholm 1975.

Laidler, David E. W., *On the Costs of Anticipated Inflation*, University of Western Ontario, London, Ont., 1975, unpubl.

—, and Michael Parkin, "Inflation: A Survey", *The Economic Journal*, Vol. 85, Cambridge, 1975, pp. 741—809.

Lintner, John, "Inflation and Security Returns", *The Journal of Finance*, Vol. 30, New York, N.Y., 1975, pp. 259—280.

Lucas, Jr., Robert E., "Some International Evidence on Output-Inflation Trade-offs", *The American Economic Review*, Vol. 63, Menasha, Wisc., 1973, pp. 326—334.

Modigliani, Franco, and Richard Cohn, *Inflation and the Stock Market*, forthcoming 1979.

Modigliani, Franco, and **Donald Lessard,** *New Mortgage Designs for Stable Housing in an Inflationary Environment,* Federal Reserve Bank of Boston, Conference Series, No. 14, Boston, Mass., 1975.

Nelson, Charles R., "Inflation and Rates of Return on Common Stocks", *The Journal of Finance,* Vol. 31, New York, N.Y., 1976, pp. 471—482.

Okun, Arthur M., "Inflation: Its Mechanics and Welfare Costs", *Brookings Papers on Economic Activity,* Washington, D.C., 1975, pp. 351—390.

Phelps, Edmund S., *Inflation Policy and Unemployment Theory, The Cost-Benefit Approach to Monetary Planning,* New York, 1972.

—, "Inflation in the Theory of Public Finance", *The Swedish Journal of Economics,* Vol. 75, Stockholm, 1973, pp. 67—82.

Shoven, John B., and **Jeremy I. Bulow,** "Inflation Accounting and Nonfinancial Corporate Profits: Physical Assets", *Brookings Papers on Economic Activity,* Washington, D.C., 1975, pp. 557—598.

—, and —, "Inflation Accounting and Nonfinancial Corporate Profits: Financial Assets and Liabilities", *ibid.,* 1976, pp. 15—57.

Sidrauski, Miguel, "Rational Choice and Patterns of Growth in a Monetary Economy", *The American Economic Review,* Vol. 57, Menasha, Wisc., 1967, *Papers and Proceedings,* pp. 534—544.

Solow, Robert M., "The Intelligent Citizen's Guide to Inflation", *The Public Interest,* New York, N.Y., 1975, No. 38, pp. 30—66.

Sunley, Jr., Emil M., and **Joseph A. Pechman,** "Inflation Adjustment for the Individual Income Tax", in: Henry J. Aaron (Ed.), *Inflation and the Income Tax,* The Brookings Institution, Studies of Government Finance, Series 2, Washington, D.C., 1976, pp. 153—171.

Survey of Consumer Finances, 1969, The University of Michigan, Institute for Social Research, Ann Arbor.

Tobin, James, *Inflation Control as Social Priority,* Yale University, New Haven, Conn., 1976, unpubl.

Vining, Jr., Daniel R., and **Thomas C. Elwertowski,** "The Relationship between Relative Prices and the General Price Level", *The American Economic Review,* Vol. 66, Menasha, Wisc., 1976, pp. 698—708.

*   *   *

Zusammenfassung: Zum Verständnis der realen Wirkungen und Kosten der Inflation. — Die traditionelle Ansicht, daß eine Inflation, weil Geld neutral ist, keine nennenswerten realen Wirkungen hervorbringt, erweist sich nur für eine Volkswirtschaft als annähernd richtig, deren Regelungen vollständig inflationssicher sind, d. h. für eine vollindexierte Wirtschaft. Die Realwirkungen erweisen sich aber als um so verbreiteter und schwererwiegend, je mehr bei wirtschaftlichen Regelungen Nominalwerte verwendet werden. Der Aufsatz untersucht nacheinander die Folgen von amtlichen Regelungen auf Nominalbasis (Steuersystem, Definition des steuerpflichtigen Einkommens, Buchführungsmethoden), von privaten Einrichtungen und Übereinkünften auf Nominalbasis (Hypotheken, Rentenverträge, Einkommensberechnungen), selbst für den Fall, daß die Inflation vollständig antizipiert wird bzw. wurde. Anschließend werden die Wirkungen einer nicht antizipierten Inflation geprüft, die in den bestehenden nominalen langfristigen Verträgen nicht berücksichtigt worden ist, und die Wirkungen einer ungewissen zukünftigen Inflation. Soweit es möglich ist, wird versucht, die sozialen Kosten von verschiedenen Realwirkungen abzuschätzen, obwohl es zur Zeit nicht möglich ist, die allgemeinen sozialen Kosten der Inflation zu ermitteln.

*

Résumé: Vers une compréhension des effets réels et des coût d'inflation. — Nous démontrons que la vue traditionelle d'après laquelle l'inflation ne produit pas des effets réels appréciables à cause de la neutralité d'argent est valide pour une économie seulement dont les institutions sont complètement étanche à l'inflation, c'est-à-dire il s'agit d'une économie indexée. Mais nous démontrons que les effets réels deviennent plus et plus diffusés et sérieux comme les institutions de l'économie deviennent presque plus nominales. L'article examine succédamment les conséquences des institutions nominales de gouvernement (le système fiscal, la définition de revenu taxable, la procédure comptable); des institutions privées nominales et des conventions comptables (les contrats de hypothèque et d'annuité, le mesurage de revenu), même si l'inflation est, et a été complètement anticipée. En plus l'article examine les effets de l'inflation pas anticipée et pas incorporée dans les contrats nominaux existants à long terme, et de l'inflation future incertaine. S'il est possible, nous entreprenons l'effort de fixer les coût sociaux des effets réels différents même bien qu'il ne soit pas possible au moment présent de fixer tous les coût sociaux de l'inflation.

*

Resumen: Hacia el entendimiento de los verdaderos efectos y costos de la inflación. — La visión tradicional que la inflación no produce efectos reales apreciables debido a que el dinero es neutral, es solamente válida en forma aproximada para una economía cuyas instituciones están completamente a prueba de inflación, p.ej. una economía completamente indexada. Pero se muestra que los verdaderos efectos se generalizarán más y más y serán más serios en la medida que las instituciones de la economía sean más cercanamente nominales. El artículo examina en forma sucesiva las consecuencias de instituciones gubernamentales nominales (sistema de impuestos, definición del ingreso imponible, procedimientos contables); de instituciones privadas nominales y convenciones contables (hipotecas y contratos de renta anuales, medición del ingreso), incluso cuando la inflación es y ha sido totalmente anticipada. Examina en seguida los efectos de inflación no anticipados, que no han sido incorporados dentro de los contratos de largo plazo existentes, y de inflación futura incierta. En los casos que fue posible, se hizo un esfuerzo por determinar el costo social de varios efectos reales, aunque en este momento no es posible apreciar los costos sociales totales de la inflación.

Errata

Page 816, third paragraph, fourth line: "purpose" should read "purposes."
Page 826, first line of second paragraph: "from the young to the old" should read "from the old to the young."
Page 829, second paragraph, second line: delete the commas that follow "assets" and "shortening."

by Franco Modigliani and Richard A. Cohn

Inflation, Rational Valuation and the Market

▶ The ratio of market value to profits began a decline in the late 1960s that has continued fairly steadily ever since. The reason is inflation, which causes investors to commit two major errors in evaluating common stocks. First, in inflationary periods, investors capitalize equity earnings at a rate that parallels the nominal interest rate, rather than the economically correct real rate—the nominal rate less the inflation premium. In the presence of inflation, one properly compares the cash return on stocks, not with the nominal return on bonds, but with the real return on bonds.

Second, investors fail to allow for the gain to shareholders accruing from depreciation in the real value of nominal corporate liabilities. The portion of the corporation's interest bill that compensates creditors for the reduction in the real value of their claims represents repayment of capital, rather than an expense to the corporation. Because corporations are not taxed on that part of their return, the share of pretax operating income paid in taxes declines as the rate of inflation rises. For the corporate sector as a whole, this effect tends to offset any distortions resulting from basing taxable income on historical cost.

If a firm is levered, inflation can exert a permanently depressing effect on reported earnings—even to the point of turning real profits into growing losses. On the other hand, a firm that wishes to maintain the same level of real debt despite inflation must increase its nominal

debt at the inflation rate; the funds obtained from the issues of debt needed to maintain leverage will precisely equal the funds necessary to pay interest on the debt and maintain the firm's dividend and reinvestment policies.

Rationally valued, the level of the S&P 500 at the end of 1977 should have been 200. Its actual value at that time was 100. Because of inflation-induced errors, investors have systematically undervalued the stock market by 50 per cent. ▶

UNTIL their poor performance in recent years, equities had traditionally been regarded as an ideal hedge against inflation. Equities are claims against physical assets, whose real returns should remain unaffected by inflation. Furthermore, many equities represent claims against levered assets, and inflation is supposed to benefit debtors.[1]

Today, the level of the Standard & Poor's 500 stock index, when measured in nominal terms, is approximately the same as it was in the second half of the 1960s. In real terms, the S&P has fallen to around 60 per cent of its 1965-66 level, or 55 per cent of its 1968 peak. Figure I provides another indication of the magnitude of the debacle. Curve 1 plots an estimate of the market value (debt plus equity) of all U.S. nonfinancial corporations in relation to an estimate of the replacement cost of their assets.[2] By 1977, the market value of all firms represented less than two-thirds of the replacement cost of their assets, having fallen from a ratio somewhat above one in 1964-65.

This article analyzes three possibilities that, singly or in combination, could account for this extraordinary performance. First, we examine the possibility that, contrary to expectations, inflation has been accompanied by a significant deterioration of profits. Second, we consider the possibility that the application of economically sound valuation methods decrees that the warranted price-earnings ratio (or, equivalently, the

Franco Modigliani is Institute Professor of Economics and Finance at the Alfred P. Sloan School of Management, Massachusetts Institute of Technology. Richard Cohn is Associate Professor of Finance at the University of Illinois at Chicago Circle.

The authors wish to express their gratitude to their colleagues, Benjamin Friedman, John Lintner, Stewart Myers and Paul Samuelson, and to William Hicks of Wellington Management and Glenn Strehle, Treasurer of M.I.T., for their valuable suggestions. They also wish to thank David Modest for his help in carrying out the computations and Judith Mason for seeing the manuscript through. The Sloan School of Management provided financial support for the computations.

1. Footnotes appear at end of article.

capitalization factor to be applied to earnings) should systematically decrease with the rate of inflation. This would imply that even when earnings are keeping up with inflation, market values should decline in real terms—clearly a challenge to the traditional view that equities' growth in nominal terms fully reflects the rate of inflation. Third, we examine the possibility that investors, at least in the presence of unaccustomed and fluctuating inflation, are unable to free themselves from certain forms of "money illusion" and, as a result, price equities in a way that fails to reflect their true economic value.

The startling conclusion of our research is that, while neither the first nor second explanation finds support in the facts or in the theory of rational valuation, the third explanation is surprisingly consistent with the evidence and can largely account for the puzzling behavior of U.S.equities in the last decade. Our analysis provides evidence that investors do in fact tend to commit two major, inflation-induced errors in evaluating corporate assets:

(1) They fail to correct reported accounting profits for the gain accruing to stockholders as a result of the real depreciation in nominal corporate liabilities. Because inflation (especially in the U.S.) has tended to produce a commensurate rise in nominal interest rates, it has also tended to reduce accounting profits, even if correctly measured profits have in fact kept up with inflation.

(2) They tend to capitalize equity earnings at a rate that follows the nominal rate, whereas (as has long been known to students of finance) the economically sound procedure is to capitalize them at the real rate—that is, at the nominal rate less that portion of it representing the inflation premium or, alternatively, the compensation due to creditors for the expected real devaluation of their debt claims.

The Real Profitability of Corporate Capital

Series 3 in Figure II plots for U.S. nonfinancial corporations from 1950 to 1977 the fraction of value added represented by returns to lenders and shareholders.[3] Here total return is defined as adjusted operating income (OI)—the sum of interest plus after-tax profits adjusted to eliminate the effect of paper gains on inventories and to reflect depreciation on a replacement, rather than a historical, cost basis. Except for a distinctive bulge in the middle 1960s, this series can best be characterized as trendless. Indeed, from 1975 on, this ratio remained at a level not significantly different from, and certainly not lower than, that prevailing from the beginning of the 1950s through the first half of the 1960s.

A similar picture emerges from Series 2 in Figure I, which shows the rate of return on capital computed as the ratio of adjusted OI to the estimated replacement cost of capital.[4] Again, the series shows a line that is roughly flat, with a bulge in the mid-1960s. The results

of other researchers consistently show that, although both measures of return to capital—share of value added and return on replacement cost—respond to cyclical forces, neither exhibits a significant trend over the postwar period.[5]

How can we reconcile these results with the popular view that profits have been declining steadily over the last decade?[6] In the first place, both series demonstrate that the mid-1960s represented a time of unprecedented return to capital, whether measured as a share of value added or as a rate of return. In the perspective of the entire postwar period, the last decade is highly misleading. In the second place, those who stress the declining profits viewpoint typically measure return to capital by using stockholder profits (frequently before taxes) adjusted for inventory valuation and for depreciation at replacement cost. Series 1 in Figure II graphs the share of that measure of profits: It does show a clearly negative trend that begins accelerating in 1965, and it hits its lowest point by 1975. Series 2 shows what happens if taxes are deducted; the decline is less dramatic, but still clear.

Profit series based on stockholder returns have acquired particular popularity because of their availability; they are regularly computed by the Department of Commerce and published in the National Income Accounts. But they underestimate true corporate profits, and by an amount that grows larger as the rate of inflation increases. They do so because, as the inflation premium needed to compensate lenders for the erosion of real principal rises, interest expense grows larger. A six per cent inflation that caused interest rates to rise from three to nine per cent, for example, would cause interest expense to treble.

Thus, even though total return to capital (Series 3, Figure II) remains unaffected by inflation, adjusted profits (Series 2) decline as interest bills increase. But those adjusted profits are not the correct measure of stockholders' return. That part of the interest bill corresponding to the inflation premium is actually repayment of real principal, which compensates creditors for the reduction in the purchasing power of their claims. It therefore represents a use of profits, rather than an expense.

As long as total return to capital as measured by operating income does not decline, returns to shareholders as properly measured cannot decline either, unless the real interest rate rises—something that surely has not happened in recent years. Indeed, to claim that inflation has raised the real rate of interest is tantamount to claiming that creditors have in the long run benefited from inflation—a view hardly anyone would seriously propound. The fact that creditors are not better off despite the higher interest they receive—together with the finding that total return to capital has remained stable—confirms the conclusion

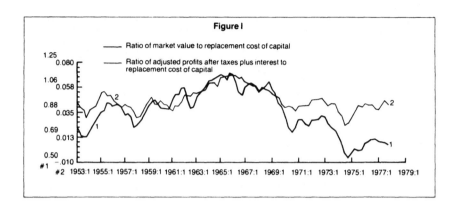

Figure I

—— Ratio of market value to replacement cost of capital

—— Ratio of adjusted profits after taxes plus interest to replacement cost of capital

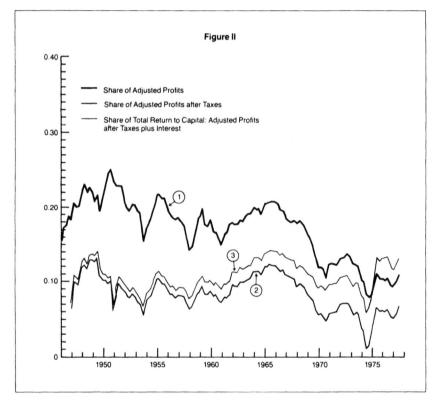

Figure II

—— Share of Adjusted Profits

—— Share of Adjusted Profits after Taxes

—— Share of Total Return to Capital: Adjusted Profits after Taxes plus Interest

that stockholders are not worse off, despite the higher nominal interest they are paying.

Inflation and Taxation

It has been claimed that inflation has seriously depressed stockholders' returns because of its effect on corporate taxation.[7] The ostensible explanation is that corporations are taxed on reported, rather than adjusted, profits. As taxes rise with inflating reported profits, the effective tax rate on real profits also rises.

This explanation fails to recognize, however, that stockholders are not taxed on that part of their return that consists of depreciation of debt. In other words, they are allowed to deduct their entire interest expense even though the portion of it corresponding to the inflation premium is really a return of capital. Because of this, the share of pre-tax operating income paid in taxes declines with the rate of inflation.

The tax system in effect taxes what should not be taxed and does not tax what should be taxed. By and large, the results tend to cancel out for the U.S. corporate sector as a whole (although not necessarily for individual firms). This conclusion can be verified by examining the three series in Figure II. The difference between Series 1 and Series 2—profits before and after taxes, respectively—is the corporate tax liability. The tax burden can be inferred from the magnitude of this gap relative to Series 3. There is no systematic evidence of a change in the tax burden in recent years; there is evidence of a substantial decline relative to the 1950s and early 1960s.

The evidence rejects the first of our three possible explanations for the stagnation of nominal equity values and the great decline in real values—namely, that recent equity performance reflects a significant decline in after-tax return to capital and to equityholders in particular. This conclusion receives striking support from a comparison of the two series in Figure I: The dramatic decline in market value to replacement cost shown in Series 1 cannot be accounted for by a decline in the rate of return on capital (denoted as Series 2). Instead, what these series show is a remarkable decline in market value relative to profits—a decline that began in the late 1960s, shortly after inflation began to rise, and grew fairly steadily thereafter. We therefore proceed to the second possible explanation—namely, that rational valuation procedures imply that the capitalization factor applicable to profits should fall as the rate of inflation increases.

Valuing Stocks Under Conditions of Inflation

For convenience of exposition, we concentrate first on the case of a no-growth firm—one expected to generate a constant stream of real profits over time—with no net debt in its capital structure. (No *net* debt means essentially that interest expense is offset by interest income,

if any.) For now, we exclude from consideration the potential distortions caused by inflation's effect on taxes.[8]

If there is no inflation and none expected, then the value of the firm generally at any date t, V(t), is the present value of the perpetual stream of profits, or operating income, X. That is, we can arrive at V(t) by capitalizing X at the discount rate for firms in the appropriate risk class (ρ). Thus:

$$V(t) = X/\rho . \tag{1}$$

Now suppose that inflation sets in at date 0, and that it is expected to continue indefinitely (and does) at the constant rate p. Since it is fully anticipated, we may reasonably posit the standard assumption that it will have no effect in real terms. With the real stream of earnings unchanged, the nominal stream will rise at the rate p so that:

$$X(t) = X(0)e^{pt} , \tag{2}$$

where X(t) and X(0) represent operating income on a replacement cost basis (hereafter referred to as "adjusted").[9] The behavior of the income stream according to Equation 2 is depicted by the curve in Figure IIIA, which is constant up to date 0 and rises exponentially thereafter at the rate of inflation (assumed to be 20 per cent per year).

The process of inflation will also affect market (nominal) interest rates. Since, by assumption, the real interest rate on riskless securities remains unchanged, the nominal rate must rise by the rate of inflation, p. This serves to compensate lenders for the erosion at that rate of the real purchasing power of their claims.[10] If r(0) represents the interest rate just prior to the introduction of inflation, then R(t), the nominal interest rate at date t, equals r(0) plus p for any time after 0^+—the point when inflation begins.

There are two equivalent rational ways to determine at any point in time the nominal value of the firm in this world of inflation—(a) capitalize current adjusted profits at any time t at the real capitalization rate or (b) discount the stream of nominal adjusted profits from t on at the appropriate nominal rate. Pursuing the first approach, consider the value of the firm at 0^+, the instant inflation begins. Since the stream of adjusted profits is unaffected, the value of the firm is still given by Equation 1. For any later date t, we find, using Equation 2, that current adjusted profits will be $X(0)e^{pt}$. Therefore:

$$V(t) = \frac{X(0)e^{pt}}{\rho} = V(0)e^{pt} , \tag{3}$$

which implies in particular

$$V(0^+) = \frac{X(0)}{\rho} = V(0) . \tag{3A}$$

The behavior of the value of the firm is shown in

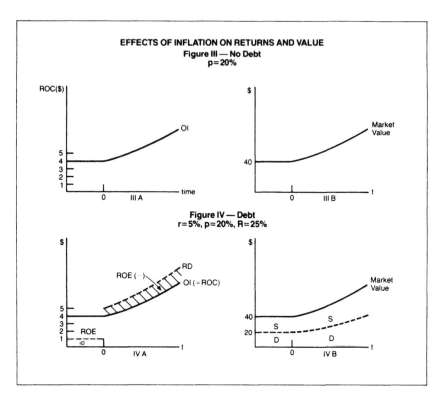

EFFECTS OF INFLATION ON RETURNS AND VALUE
Figure III — No Debt
p=20%

Figure IV — Debt
r=5%, p=20%, R=25%

Figure IIIB. It is worth noting that the graph is valid even if the inflation that begins at date 0 had been anticipated at any time during the preceding period of price stability. The value of the firm will start to rise when, and only when, the anticipated inflation begins. In other words, current market values should not be affected by fully anticipated future inflation; expected values for any future date will of course reflect the anticipated inflation.

In discounting the stream of nominal adjusted profits—the alternative approach b—the rate of nominal adjusted profits at any date following t (say, t + τ) is given by $X(0)e^{p(t+\tau)}$. This is discounted at the appropriate nominal rate (in this case, ρ + p—the real equity discount rate, ρ, corrected for the rate of inflation, p) to arrive at the present value of profits as of t:

$$[X(0)e^{p(t+\tau)}] [e^{-(\rho+p)\tau}] = [X(0)e^{pt}] e^{-\rho\tau} .$$

The sum (integral) of these elements for all values of τ from zero to infinity reduces by a well known formula to yield the present value of the firm:

$$V(t) = \frac{X(0)e^{pt}}{\rho} = V(0)e^{pt} , \qquad (4)$$

which is the result given by Equation 3.

This analysis of the unlevered firm has three important implications. First, inflation should not affect the *real* value of the firm. At any date t, it will be V(t) divided by the price index at date t (e^{pt}) or, according to Equation 4, V(0). Thus an unlevered stream of corporate profits should provide a hedge against inflation. Second, to obtain a correct valuation of the firm under inflation, one should capitalize the current level of adjusted profits at the very same real rate that prevailed before the inflation, even though nominal interest rates will have increased.

Third, Equations 3 and 4 imply that the real rate of return to stockholders is not affected by inflation. It is X(0)/V(0), or ρ, both before and at any time during the inflationary process. This implication is consistent with inflation being neutral. On the other hand, if we let the time rate of change of the nominal value V(t) be dV(t)/dt, the *nominal* rate of return to stockholders is given by [X(t) + dV(t)/dt]/V(t), which reduces to ρ + p. In other words, in addition to the current cash return of ρ, the stockholder earns a nominal capital gain equal to the change in the current value of the firm's assets, which change in turn equals the rate of inflation.

It follows that, in comparing stock returns with debt returns, one cannot merely compare the cash return on stocks, X(t)/V(t)=ρ, with the nominal return on bonds, R. That procedure is valid only in the absence of significant inflation. With inflation, the cash return can be compared meaningfully only with the real return on bonds, r(0) ($\equiv$ R-p); conversely, the nominal return on bonds, R, can be compared only with the nominal total return on stocks, ρ + p.

This result can be generalized to incorporate variations in the real income stream over time. To value the firm correctly, one must either (1) discount the deflated value of future nominal profits at the real rate or (2) discount future nominal profits at the nominal rate. If either valuation is done correctly, the real value of the firm will be found to be unaffected by inflation. To illustrate, suppose that the stream of real cash payments grows at a constant rate, g. Applying the first method:

$$V(0) = \frac{X(0)}{\rho\text{-}g} \ .$$

$$V(t) = \frac{X(t)}{\rho\text{-}g} = [X(0)/(\rho\text{-}g)] \ e^{(p+g)t} \ . \tag{5}$$

The real value of the firm at any date t is given by V(t)e^{-pt} = [X(0)/(ρ-g)] e^{gt}, which coincides with the standard result for the case of no inflation.

The frequently held view that inflation should affect the real value of the firm stems from one of two valuation errors. One is the belief that the correct way of valuing shares is to capitalize current cash profits at the nominal rate, ρ + p. This implies a value for the no-growth firm of:

$$V(0) = \frac{X(0)}{\rho\text{+}p} \ , \tag{6}$$

which means that, for any given level of profits, the greater the rate of inflation (whether anticipated or not), the lower stock prices should be. This error, if widely held, could contribute to explaining the current depressed level of the stock market.

But why do Equations 3 and 3A represent rational valuation formulas, while Equation 6 does not? The answer is simple. In Equation 3, the stockholder's expected return coincides with the remuneration he intends to receive as reflected in the capitalization rate he used. Bonds have a nominal return, R = r + p, and a real return, r. Using Equation 3, the stockholder prices

the stock so as to receive ρ in real terms and ρ + p in nominal terms. His nominal return is:

$$\frac{X(0) + \dfrac{dV(0)}{dt}}{V(0)} = \rho + p,$$

as intended, and his real return is ρ. On the other hand, the investor using Equation 6 with the intention of receiving the same nominal return, ρ + p, has actually priced the stock so that he will receive a nominal return of:

$$\frac{X(0) + \dfrac{dV(0)}{dt}}{V(0)} = \rho + 2p,$$

which exceeds his required rate of return by the capital gain component p. (Whether this disappointment of expectation leads at least gradually toward the correct valuation procedure is addressed later.)

The other, and diametrically opposite, error in valuation is to discount the *nominal* profit stream at the real rate ρ—a practice applicable only in the absence of inflation. This error implies that:

$$V(0) = \frac{X(0)}{\rho\text{-}p} \ . \tag{7}$$

This view may be implicit in the notion that real share values benefit from inflation. Using this valuation formula, the investor can expect to receive a nominal rate of return equal to ρ, instead of to the intended ρ + p.

The Effect of Leverage

In the absence of inflation, the value of the equity of a firm with debt outstanding in the amount D and with neutral taxes is given by:[11]

$$S(0) = V(0) - D(0) = \frac{X(0)}{\rho} - D(0)$$

$$= \frac{X(0) - rD(0)}{\rho\text{+}d(\rho\text{-}r)} \ . \tag{8}$$

where d = D(0)/S(0). The numerator, X(0) - rD(0), is the income stream accruing to the stockholder, while the denominator, ρ + d(ρ-r), is the capitalization rate appropriate to that levered stream.

Now suppose that a fully anticipated steady state inflation begins at date 0. For convenience, assume that all debt is repayable on demand, or is otherwise structured so that it always provides the current interest rate. In this case, the nominal interest rate will rise from r(0) to R (= r(0) + p), and measured adjusted profits, $\Pi(0^+)$, become:

$$\Pi(0^+) = X(0) - RD(0) = X(0) - (r+p)D(0). \tag{9}$$

V(0), D(0) and S(0) represent, respectively, the value of the firm, its debt and its equity at the time fully anticipated steady state inflation first begins. From previous analysis of the no-leverage case, and from Miller and Modigliani's proposition that the market value of the firm is independent of leverage, it follows that $V(0^+)$ equals $V(0)$—that is, that the market value of the firm will not change discontinuously as a result of the inception of inflation. Since debt is payable on demand, its market value will also not change; so $D(0^+)$ equals $D(0)$. Thus the value of equity under inflation, $S(0^+)$, will equal $S(0)$.

The same conclusion can be reached by capitalizing flows, if one knows the firm's debt policy. Assuming that inflation does not change the firm's leverage policy—i.e., that debt remains constant in real terms while rising in nominal terms at the rate of inflation—then $D(t)$ equals $D(0)e^{pt}$. Figure IVB graphs the behavior of $D(t)$.

Figure IVB also depicts the behavior of the total market value of the firm—debt plus equity; the curve here is the same as the one shown in Figure IIIB. The difference between the market value curve and the debt curve represents, accordingly, the market value of the firm's equity (S). The figure illustrates the conclusion, previously reached, that at the time inflation begins, the value of equity is unchanged.

Knowing the behavior of the firm's debt, one can infer the behavior of total interest expense—$RD(t) = RD(0)e^{pt}$—and the behavior of conventional adjusted accounting profits:

$$\Pi(t) = X(t) - RD(t) = [X(0) - (r+p)D(0)]e^{pt}$$
$$= \Pi(0^+)e^{pt} = \Pi(0)e^{pt} - pD(0)e^{pt}. \quad (10)$$

Equation 10 has two implications. First, at time 0, as inflation begins, adjusted profits exhibit a discontinuous reduction equal to $pD(0)$. Second, and perhaps more surprising, at some rate of inflation, the accounting profits of a highly levered firm will suddenly turn *negative* at the time inflation begins and will *grow more negative* with time. The condition for this result to hold is: $X(0) - (r+p)D(0)<0$, which can be restated in either of the following forms:

$$p > \frac{X(0)}{D(0)} - r = \frac{V(0)}{D(0)} \rho - r . \quad (11)$$

or

$$\frac{D(0)}{V(0)} > \frac{\rho}{r+p} = \frac{\rho}{R} .$$

Thus if the unlevered discount rate (ρ) equals 0.1, the real interest rate equals 0.5 and the ratio of the firm's debt to the firm's value equals 0.5, conventionally measured adjusted profits will turn negative if the rate of inflation (p) is greater than 0.15.

These results are illustrated in Figure IVA. The solid curve—operating income—coincides by assumption with the curve in Figure IIIA. The dashed curve shows the behavior of interest expense assuming that leverage is 50 per cent of market value (or 20 initially) and the

real rate is 0.05. As inflation begins at time 0 at the rate of 20 per cent, the nominal interest rate, R, jumps by a factor of five, from 0.05 to 0.25. As a result, interest expense also increases by a factor of five (from one to five in the graph)—and exceeds profits by $(5-4)/4$, or by 25 per cent. As the debt rises exponentially thereafter, the dashed curve also rises exponentially; thus the firm's accounting loss, represented by the shaded area between the two curves, keeps rising over time at the rate of inflation, although it remains a constant 25 per cent of operating income.

We conclude that, for given operating income, inflation does exert a permanently depressing effect on stockholders' reported earnings—and may even turn profits into growing losses, especially if leverage is high. Yet, as we have just demonstrated, the market value of the levered firm's stock, if correctly priced, should remain unaffected by inflation, regardless of leverage. Inflation can reduce adjusted profits while leaving equity values unchanged because, in the presence of significant inflation, adjusted accounting profits are a seriously misleading measure of true returns to the stockholders of a levered firm.[12] The reason, as we have argued, is that the component $pD(t)$ of interest "expense" is a payment to the creditor in compensation for the reduction in the real value of his claim; it represents, not an expense, but a portion of profits utilized to repay a corresponding amount of real debt principal.

It follows that the true flow of profits received by shareholders, $\Pi^*(t)$, is:

$$\Pi^*(t) = \Pi(t) + pD(t) = X(0)e^{pt} + (p-R)D(t)$$
$$= e^{pt}[X(0) - rD(0)] = \Pi(0)e^{pt} . \quad (12)$$

Equation 12 confirms that, although inflation reduces accounting profits, it does not affect "true" profits.

Equation 12 also confirms our previous conclusion that inflation does not initially affect the market value of the stock. Indeed, the market value of equity, being the present value of the stream $\Pi^*(t)$, must equal the market value of the stream $X(t) = X(0)e^{pt}$ minus the value of the stream $rD(0)e^{pt}$. But the present value of the nominal stream $X(0)e^{pt}$, or operating income, is of course $V(0)$, as shown above. Similarly, the present value of "real" interest expense, $rD(0)e^{pt}$, when discounted at the nominal rate, R, is simply $D(0)$. Thus:

$$S(0^+) = V(0) - D(0) = S(0) . \quad (13)$$

More generally:

$$S(t) = [V(0) - D(0)]e^{pt} = S(0)e^{pt} . \quad (14)$$

From Equations 12 and 14, and taking into account Equation 8, we can infer that:

Saving, Deficits, Inflation, and Financial Theory

$$\frac{\Pi(t) + pD(t)}{S(t)} = \frac{X(0) - rD(0)}{S(0)}$$

$$= \rho + (\rho - r)d , \tag{15}$$

which can be rewritten as:

$$S(t) = \frac{\Pi(t) + pD(t)}{\rho + (\rho - r)d} = \frac{\Pi^*(t)}{\rho + (\rho - r)d} \tag{16}$$

Equation 16 shows that one possible way to value the firm's equity under inflation is to capitalize "true" profits at the capitalization rate that applies in the absence of inflation. True profits—the numerator of the right-hand side of Equation 16—are adjusted accounting profits corrected by adding pD to reflect the reduction of the real value of the debt or, equivalently, the repayment of principal component of the nominal interest paid to creditors. Equations 15 and 16, which were derived for the case of constant leverage, will hold independent of leverage policy (as long as the firm does not have special growth opportunities), even though S(t), D(t) and, therefore, $\Pi(t)$ will clearly depend on that policy.

It follows from Equation 16 that:

$$\frac{\Pi(t)}{S(t)} = \rho + (\rho - r)d - pd \tag{17}$$

This implies that, when levered equities are rationally priced, the earnings-price ratio—the ratio of adjusted profit to market value—should decrease with an increasing rate of inflation. Another way of stating this result is to rewrite Equation 17 as:

$$S(t) = \frac{\Pi(t)}{\rho + (\rho - r)d - pd} = \frac{\Pi(t)}{K}, \tag{18}$$

with K being the rate appropriate for capitalizing adjusted earnings.

Unlike the rate used to capitalize true earnings (given by Equation 16), K is not a real rate independent of p; it declines with the rate of inflation and, indeed, becomes negative when $d/1+d$ exceeds ρ/R (corresponding to the case, noted above, in which adjusted profits actually become negative). This result confirms that, under inflation, a levered firm reporting negative profits should not necessarily be liquidated.[13] The reason is, of course, that $\Pi(t)$ is not the complete return to the shareholders, omitting as it does the repayment of real principal term pD(t).

Equations 16 and 18 correspond to the first approach (a) used to analyze the no-leverage firm—i.e., capitalizing the appropriate measure of current profits by the appropriate rate. But the second approach (b) can also be utilized and is, in fact, the only operational one when operating income or leverage policy varies over time. In this approach, either the stream of "true"

nominal profits is discounted at the rate appearing in the denominator of Equation 16, but with the real rates ρ and r replaced by the nominal rates $\rho + p$ and $r + p$, respectively; or the stream of adjusted profits is discounted at the rate given in the denominator of Equation 18 with, again, the real rates replaced by nominal ones.

Inflation and Profits

So far we have shown how a firm and a firm's equity should be valued under conditions of steady state inflation, and how using proper valuation leaves the real value of the firm and its equity unchanged by inflation. At the same time, we have shown that inflation will tend to reduce adjusted profits for a levered firm and that, in fact, the reduction may go so far as to turn profits into losses.

The reader may ask himself how these two propositions can possibly be reconciled: How can a firm whose profits have fallen sharply or even turned into losses continue to pay dividends, or even the interest on its debt? If it can't, how can its valuation be unaffected?

For an answer to these puzzles, first consider the case in which the leverage policy of the firm is unaffected by inflation. This case may well be regarded as the norm, since there is no reason why leverage policy should depend on inflation, at least in a world of no money illusion, in which creditors are aware of the nature of the effect of inflation on adjusted profits. In the case of a no-growth firm, the assumption of unchanged leverage policy means that the firm's real debt will remain constant and its nominal debt therefore grow at the rate of inflation.

In the case of a firm growing through reinvestment of retained earnings (or even new stock issues), the assumption means that the firm's nominal debt will grow in time relative to what it would have been without inflation at a rate equal to the rate of inflation. Under these circumstances, the funds obtained from the increase in debt needed to maintain the same real debt will be found to equal precisely the funds needed to pay interest on the debt and maintain unchanged the firm's dividend and reinvestment policy.

If its adjusted profits actually turn negative, the firm will appear to be paying, not only dividends, but even the interest on its debt from fresh borrowings. This procedure may seem unorthodox and outright imprudent. The truth of the matter is that the firm should be seen as borrowing in order to maintain its original financial structure—the share of its assets financed by outside sources—and as using its unchanged "true" profits as before. Indeed, the rate at which debt has to increase to maintain leverage, namely pD(t), precisely equals the repayment component of the firm's nominal interest payments.

The situation will, of course, be different in the case

of a firm that changes its leverage policy because of inflation. In the absence of inflation, a firm could not decide at some point to reduce its debt and at the same time continue to pay the same dividends and retain and invest the same amount from earnings. Under inflation, a firm that allows its debt to grow at less than the rate of inflation is repaying (real) debt at the expense of dividends or reinvestment. But even such a change in leverage policy (recalling our assumption that taxes are neutral) should not affect the firm's market value initially, or at any later date so long as investment policy remains unaffected.

To be sure, this analysis presumes a world of rational people and institutions without money or inflation illusion. It may not apply in the real world. In particular, lenders may refuse a firm that apparently uses loans to pay dividends or, even worse, to pay interest; they may even insist on a reduction of the initial debt if the firm appears to be making losses. We are well aware that inflation may have not only these, but also many other, mostly unfavorable, real consequences. The remainder of this article analyzes one limited aspect of inflation's real effect—its impact on market valuation.

Market Valuation and Inflation

Equations 16 and 18 above define the rational valuation formulas appropriate under inflation. But have real-world investors used these models (or even approximations of them) to value equities in the postwar period? To answer this question, we focused on the market's valuation of a portfolio of shares deemed to constitute a fairly representative sample of large U.S. corporations—namely, the portfolio corresponding to the Standard & Poor's index of 500 stocks (S&P 500).[14] We were particularly concerned with the behavior of share prices as reflected in this valuation over the 25 years, or 100 quarters, from 1953 to 1977. (By beginning in 1953, we avoided the distortions that might have resulted from the Korean War and the period before the Treasury Accord, while we still had at our disposal a large number of observations covering periods of both relative price stability and relatively high and volatile inflation.)

For testing purposes, we recast Equation 18 in logarithmic form:

$$s = \pi^e - \ln[\rho + (\rho-r)d - pd - g] \,, \quad (19)$$

where s and π^e denote the logarithms of S (the market value of equity) and Π (the flow of expected profits). The appendix explains how we approximated the variables in the right-hand side of this equation in terms of observable variables. (Table A in the appendix details the subsidiary variables involved and how they were measured. In the case of the capitalization rate, the basic observable variables on which we relied were the

long-term interest rate and the rate of inflation. The logarithmic form of Equation 18, with all subsidiary relationships spelled out explicitly, appears in the appendix as Equation H.1.)

For present purposes, the results of our estimation of Equation 19 can be summarized by the following equations:

$$s = \pi^e + 3.24 - 0.06r - 0.08p, \text{ or} \quad (19A)$$
$$s = \pi^e + 3.42 - 0.08r - 0.115p, \quad (19B)$$

where 19A refers to estimates based on levels and 19B to estimates based on first differences (as explained in the appendix). The coefficients of r and p (which are measured as percentages) indicate the estimated percentage change in market value resulting from a one percentage point (100 basis points) change in the real interest rate r and the inflation rate p, respectively.

Figure V compares the actual course of the S&P 500 with the value as computed by our level-form estimates for the quarter century beginning in 1953. To encompass the wide movements of the S&P, Figure V uses a semi-logarithmic scale, so that the distance between the actual and computed values represents the percentage error of our equation.[15]

It is clear that Equation 19A adequately captures all the major movements of the S&P index over the last 25 years. Furthermore, some of the most visible errors—such as those corresponding to the Kennedy setback of the second half of 1962—are not entirely surprising. That particular dip, which was in any event short-lived, has been widely recognized as a confidence crisis, which our model was not designed to capture.[16]

Implications for Valuation Errors

Using Equations 19A and 19B, we can draw inferences as to whether equity values have been significantly affected by valuation errors traceable to inflation and, if so, the extent of this effect. For the sake of conciseness, we will refer only to the estimates of Part A of Table A in the appendix, summarized in Equation 19A.[17]

As we have already shown, correct market valuation implies that inflation will not affect market value, given adjusted profits and the real rate. It also implies that the coefficient of p in Equation 19A should be zero for unlevered firms. For a levered firm with debt D equal to a fraction d of equity, the coefficient of p in Equation 19A should be d/K, where K is the capitalization rate for adjusted earnings measured as a percentage (because we measured p as a percentage). We can thus infer that the coefficient of p in the market valuation Equation 19A is $+0.08 + d/K$ smaller than it should be (i.e., it is -0.08 instead of $+d/K$). Thus the fractional change in market value S for a one percentage point change in the inflation rate is:

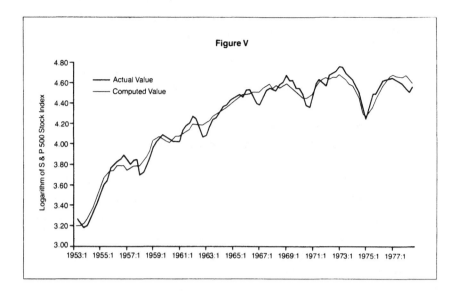

Figure V

Logarithm of S & P 500 Stock Index

— Actual Value
— Computed Value

1953:1 1955:1 1957:1 1959:1 1961:1 1963:1 1965:1 1967:1 1969:1 1971:1 1973:1 1975:1 1977:1

$$\frac{ds}{dp} = \frac{1}{S}\frac{dS}{dp} = -(0.08+d/K) \qquad (20)$$

This implies that, for a given real rate r and expected adjusted profits Π, inflation reduces market value at the rate $0.08 + d/K$ per cent per percentage point of inflation. In this formula, the term d/K can be thought of as measuring the percentage reduction in adjusted profits resulting from subtracting inflation-swollen nominal interest expenses without crediting back the repayment of principal component pD. Indeed (since from Equation 12, $\Pi = \Pi^* - pD$, where Π^* is true profits), we have for the fractional change in adjusted profits for a one percentage point change in inflation rate p:[18]

$$\frac{1}{\Pi}\frac{d\Pi}{dp} = \frac{-\dfrac{D}{\Pi}}{100} = \frac{D/S}{(\Pi/S)100} = -\frac{d}{K} . \qquad (21)$$

Thus the term d/K in Equations 18 and 20 serves to correct for the inflation-induced decline in Π.

The value of d/K or D/Π can in principle vary over time for many reasons. In particular, it varies because inflation systematically affects Π and S. D/A, the ratio of debt to total assets, for the U.S. has tended to be around 0.25 in the absence of inflation, at least since the early 1960s. Hence D/(A-D), the ratio of debt to equity measured at replacement cost, is around one-third. Since K has averaged around six per cent, the

"normal" value of d/K can be put at about 0.05 (0.33/6).

Substituting back in Equation 20, we have for the fractional change in market value S for a one percentage point change in inflation rate p:

$$\frac{1}{S}\frac{dS}{dp} = -(0.08 + 0.05) = -0.13 .$$

Our empirical results imply that each percentage point of inflation typically reduces market value by a staggering 13 per cent relative to what it would be if valued rationally! As of year-end 1977, early 1978, the rate of inflation expected by the market, and built into the 8.5 per cent per annum long-term interest rate, can be placed at around six per cent. If so, our analysis implies that, at that time, actual market value was only 46 per cent ($e^{-0.13 \times 6}$) of its correct value. In other words, we estimate the warranted market value to be more than twice (specifically, 2.2 times) current market value—implying a "rational" value for the S&P index of somewhat over 200.[19]

If Inflation Subsides

What does our analysis have to say about the conditions under which market undervaluation would disappear? Clearly, one way to eliminate undervaluation completely would be for investors to recognize the two valuation errors they have been committing—faulty measurement of profits and use of a nominal capitali-

FINANCIAL ANALYSTS JOURNAL / MARCH-APRIL 1979 ☐ 33

zation rate. But undervaluation would also disappear if the current and anticipated rate of inflation decreased. In particular, if inflation were miraculously to end, and be replaced by an era of price stability and lowered interest rates, market undervaluation would totally disappear.

This possibility may be too unrealistic to deserve much consideration; but it may be worthwhile to examine what would happen if inflation returned to the level of roughly two per cent (or a bit less), which prevailed during the period preceding the Viet Nam War. In other words, how much higher would market value have been at the end of 1977, had inflation been, say, four percentage points lower (i.e., around two per cent, instead of six) and had the corresponding long-term nominal interest rate been 400 basis points lower, or around 4.5 per cent?

If we apply Equation 20, using for d/K our estimate of 0.05, the answer is that the market would have been higher by a factor of about two-thirds ($e^{0.13 \times 4} = 1.68$). However, we must qualify this by noting that, at the end of 1977, the value of d/K was in fact appreciably larger than the "normal" value of 0.05—a result of the fact that Π was severely depressed by inflation, raising the value of D/Π in Equation 21. (Equivalently, d (=D/S) was unusually high, more than offsetting the unusually high value of K.) According to one estimate, for instance, aggregate debt of nonfinancial corporations in 1977 totaled around \$550 billion, while (according to the Department of Commerce), adjusted profits were at about \$55 billion, implying a (D/Π)/100 of 0.10.[20] Hence a reduction in inflation from six to two per cent would increase profits by at least 40 per cent.

This figure will be somewhat too high if the estimated value of debt is too high—as compared, for example, with prevailing interest rates and net interest payments, which the NIA estimates at \$34 billion. An alternative estimate of the effect on profits of a reduction in inflation to two per cent might be obtained by assuming that the reduction in inflation and interest rates would reduce net interest paid by nonfinancial corporations by one-half, or \$17 billion. This would increase profits by about one-third—from \$55 billion to \$72 billion. One further check can be obtained by relying on the assumption (set forth earlier) that the Department of Commerce's downward correction of profits to compute adjusted profits is roughly equal to the upward correction required by the pD term. Since, for 1977, that correction amounts to just about \$30 billion, adding back two-thirds of that correction would raise profits by 20/55, or a bit over one-third. All this suggests that the effect on profits we are interested in can be conservatively placed at 35 per cent.

The effect of a return to two per cent inflation can be estimated as follows:

(1) Effect on capitalization rate

(a) four percentage point reduction in nominal rate: $e^{-0.06 \times (-4)} = e^{+0.24}$

(b) reduced direct negative impact of inflation: $e^{-0.02 \times (-4)} = e^{+0.08}$

(2) Effect on adjusted profits: + 45 per cent

Total Effect: $e^{+0.32} \times 1.35 = 1.9$.

Our analysis implies that, if inflation in 1977 had been around the traditional level of two per cent, the S&P index would have been very nearly twice as high as it was (or, more precisely, twice as high as the value projected by our equation for that period, which is just over 100, or a little higher than the actual).

This undervaluation may at first appear too huge to be explained by a mere four per cent differential in inflation. Yet several indications support this estimate. First, in 1965 the S&P quarterly average fluctuated between 86.6 and 91.7, averaging about 88. Our analysis implies that, between 1969 and 1977, the S&P should have increased by some 110 per cent, in contrast to an actual increase of less than 10 per cent. Is this growth unreasonably high? Surely not when one considers that, over that span of years, GNP increased 170 per cent and adjusted operating income of nonfinancial corporations doubled.

What is even more relevant, quarterly earnings per share of the S&P index rose from 1.30 to 2.73, or 110 per cent—a figure that would be even larger if one compared the average of current and past profits adjusted for unemployment, which in our empirical analysis was found to provide the best indication of expected profits. It is true that these earnings are unadjusted but, as we have indicated repeatedly, they can be taken as a reasonable approximation of fully corrected earnings.

One last suggestive bit of evidence is that, if the market value of equity had been roughly twice as high as it actually was, then the market values of firms would have kept up with their replacement costs, instead of falling way below them, as they did. Indeed, at the end of 1977, replacement costs totaled \$2,150 billion, and market values only \$1,380 billion (of which equity accounted for \$740 billion).[21] Had the value of equity been roughly twice as large, total market value in 1977 would have approximated replacement cost.

So far, in assessing the effect of a reduction in inflation from six to two per cent, we have used an estimate of d/K for 1977 of roughly 0.10. In assessing the extent of absolute undervaluation, we used a value of 0.05. If a four percentage point reduction in inflation should increase adjusted profits by some 35 per cent, then total disappearance of inflation should increase adjusted profits by one and one-half as much, or by a bit over 50 per cent. In that case, the overall underestimate would work out like this:

(1) Effect on capitalization rate
  (a) nominal interest rate
     = real rate: $e^{-0.06 \times (-6)} = e^{+0.36}$
  (b) elimination of direct
     negative effect of
     inflation: $e^{-0.02 \times (-6)} = e^{+0.12}$
(2) Effect on adjusted
   profits: $+ 1.5 \times 35$ per cent
        Total effect: $e^{+0.48} \times 1.35$
                        $\times 1.5 = 2.5$.

In other words, rational valuation would imply a value of around 250 for the S&P index at the end of 1977—not 100, which was its actual value, and not 200, which we initially suggested. The reason we chose to rely on a lower estimate of d/K is twofold. First, we acknowledge, we did not want to shock the reader at the outset and close his mind. Second, and more important, we believe the relation between the intrinsic economic value and the market value of the S&P is closer to two than to 2.5.

This view is prompted by the consideration that, in estimating the effects of the market shedding money illusion, or of inflation abating, we assumed that the real rate would be unchanged. In particular, an unchanging real rate implies that a reduction in inflation would be reflected entirely in lower nominal rates (a not unreasonable assumption as long as we deal with variations within the realm of past experience, and one that implies a ratio of market value to replacement cost not much above unity). But a zero rate of inflation is outside our experience, and an increase of the S&P to 250 would imply an estimated ratio of market value to replacement cost of nearly 1.2—well above the normal relation of one to one and above values experienced in the postwar period. We suspect, therefore, that if inflation did come down to zero—or if investors learned to value equities correctly—the real rate of interest would rise enough to keep the ratio of market values to replacement costs from rising much above unity. But, as we have already shown, as of 1977 a value of unity for that ratio would have required roughly a doubling of equity values.

Are These Conclusions Reasonable?

The reader may ask: "Is it credible that investors have systematically undervalued equity values for at least a decade, and are still undervaluing them by as much as 50 per cent, solely as the result of the mistakes suggested by your analysis?" "Is there any other explanation for the abnormal performance of the stock market in recent years?" "If the market is truly under-valued, are there any forces that would tend to push it back toward equilibrium, and if so, how fast?"

As to the first question, we readily admit that our conclusion is indeed hard to swallow—and especially hard for those of us who have been preaching the gospel of efficient markets. It is hard to accept the hypothesis of a long-lasting, systematic mistake in a well organized market manned by a large force of alert and knowledgeable people. In fact, it can be reported as a contribution to intellectual history that, when the hypothesis first crossed the mind of the senior author some four years ago, it was lightly dismissed as too preposterous to be entertained seriously. But over the ensuing three years that hypothesis continued to provide the only seemingly useful clue to market performance, and we finally succumbed to the temptation of undertaking the systematic tests reported in this article.

Several other considerations pushed us in that direction. One was the finding that many people, clearly knowledgeable in finance, found several aspects of our valuation formulas surprising and counterintuitive—e.g., the fact that the appropriate capitalization rate may become negative with enough inflation. In addition, the financial press kept asserting that earnings-price ratios had to be compared with nominal interest rates, while not even mentioning the fact that profits of firms with large debts should be adjusted for the inflation premium.

To be sure, the financial press may not be the best source of information about how investors value equities. We therefore endeavored to secure recent memoranda from large brokerage firms providing advice to institutional investors; in virtually every case, it was clear that analysts did not add back to earnings the gain on debt, and that they also relied at least partly on the capitalization of earnings at a nominal rate. In fact, one memorandum on valuing the S&P explicitly noted that interest was an expense that had to be deducted in order to estimate long-run earnings and also emphasized the need to include the expected rate of inflation in the capitalization rate.

Another memorandum advised estimating stock prices 10 years from now as expected earnings 10 years from now capitalized at today's nominal required rate of return. Such procedure makes the future price-earnings ratio, even assuming no error in measuring earnings, a declining function of today's anticipated rate of inflation. And a lower P/E ratio 10 years from now implies a lower price, hence a lower P/E, today. But the price-earnings ratio should be unaffected by changes in inflation expectations (other than in response to the effect, if any, of such changes on the required real rate of return).

Another valuation model implied that P/E should be equal to $(1/i)(1 + g/i)$, where i is the current nominal equity discount rate and g the long-run real growth rate of earnings per share. Clearly, once again, P/E is supposed to decline if i rises in response to increased inflation.

Confronted with overwhelming statistical evidence consistent with our error hypothesis, and with no direct evidence inconsistent with it, our original skepticism turned into a degree of confidence approaching belief—and certainly high enough to justify placing our findings before the public. But one might still ask, ''Are there other plausible explanations for our finding of a highly significant and large negative association between capitalization rates and inflation?''

Is it possible that our measure of inflation is simply proxying for some other relevant variable, or variables? Or that inflation might perversely affect market values even though the market commits no serious valuation error? Of course, these possibilities cannot be ruled out, for the well known reason that one can never prove a hypothesis, only establish its consistence with the evidence. Acceptance of our explanation is, in the final analysis, a subjective matter.

Some of those with whom we discussed our results suggested that inflation affects value because it affects the risk premium. If this hypothesis has to be entertained as a serious challenge to ours, its proponents will have to come forth with a credible and, one hopes, testable, explanation as to why the risk premium should be a monotonic and roughly linear function of the *level* of inflation, and with a huge coefficient on the order of 0.15. One can well imagine that a rise in inflation would have some effect on the risk premium, in part because it might foreshadow restrictive economic measures on the part of the Federal Reserve and the government. (This may in fact explain why the coefficient of inflation is found to be somewhat larger than that of the nominal interest rate.) But it is hard to believe that profits are appreciably more risky with a steady six per cent inflation than with a steady two per cent inflation.

If, on the other hand, one argues, *ad hoc*, that changes in inflation change equity values *because* they change the risk premium, then there is no way we can reject this alternative explanation, since its observable implications are indistinguishable from ours. The only possible difference is that, under our explanation, inflation could conceivably cease to depress market values if investors learned to value equities correctly. In that case, proponents of the alternative explanation would no doubt claim that inflation had ceased to affect the risk premium!

It must be recognized that, once one accepts the novel hypothesis that investors are unable to see through the veil of inflation, and thus suffer from a variety of inflation illusions, one must also be prepared to entertain the likelihood that lending institutions and business managers are subject to similar illusions, with

real consequences for the behavior of firms and adverse effects on their profitability.[22] Such phenomena could provide a partial explanation for the depressing effect of inflation on market values, through their effects on profits. However, our analysis has been concerned with the existence of, and explanation for, the huge undervaluation of equities, *given* the profit experience. We feel justified in concluding that, at the moment, we cannot see a reasonable explanation for this undervaluation that is genuinely different from the one we have advanced, although we can confidently predict that someone will attempt to provide one.

It remains for us to tackle the last question: ''Can today's severe undervaluation be expected to disappear, even if inflation persists, and under what conditions?'' We have already indicated that one possible circumstance that would result in the elimination of undervaluation is for a substantial portion of investors to become aware, directly or through their advisers, of past valuation errors. The resulting switch from money-fixed securities to undervalued equities could rapidly generate the momentum needed to return the market to reasonable levels.

However, this is not the only scenario under which market value might tend to move toward, even if not all the way to, rational valuation. As we have shown, when investors capitalize earnings at the *nominal* rate and neglect the pD correction of profits, the yields they receive will turn out to be larger than they had bargained for, *provided* inflation is constant. Specifically, in the case of unlevered streams, investors will tend to receive an earnings yield equal to the nominal rate, plus a capital gain equal to the rate of inflation. If sustained, this excess return should lead investors to reassess the relative attractiveness of stocks versus bonds. In principle, stock prices should be bid up to rational valuation, since only at that valuation will the unanticipated excess yield disappear.

Unfortunately, this mechanism is weak in practice because extra returns will materialize only if inflation is constant (or declining) and if there are no other significant random factors disturbing market value. In reality, such disturbances are large, and extra returns tend to be swamped by unanticipated capital gains and losses. In particular, if inflation fluctuates on an overall rising trend—as it has in the U.S. over recent years—then the tendency for stocks to get progressively more undervalued will mean that investors may never notice the extra returns (which would anyway take the form of capital gains) and may never even receive them. If and when inflation stabilizes, or begins to decline, there will be a better chance that undervaluation will be noted, although even in these circumstances it might take a considerable time. (There were, in fact, some recent indications that investors were beginning to recognize the undervaluation of the market, but it appears that recognition has been interrupted by the renewed rise of inflation and interest rates.)

These considerations help to explain why only those investors who followed the market in pricing securities incorrectly had a chance of coming through this recent period unscathed while holding a well diversified portfolio (a conclusion that, incidentally, may vindicate the advisers' valuation formulas reviewed earlier). On the other hand, those experts of rational valuation who could correctly assess the extent of the undervaluation of equities, had they acted on their assessment in the hope of acquiring riches, would have more than likely ended up with substantial losses. In view of our results, we have a bit of advice to offer to those experts: The next time someone chides you for your poor performance, you should reply: "If you know so much about finance, why aren't you poor?" ■

APPENDIX

Do Investors Use Equation 18 to Value Stocks?

In principle, we could have used either Equation 16 or Equation 18 to test our hypothesis. Since we did not have an estimate of the average debt per share in the S&P portfolio, required to compute the "true" profits appearing in the numerator of Equation 16, we based our test on Equation 18, which relies on adjusted profits and requires only an estimate of d, which may be thought of as "target leverage."

Since the right-hand side of Equation 18 takes the form of a ratio, it was convenient for the purpose of our tests to recast it in logarithmic form. This form also has advantages from the point of view of estimation because it reduces heteroscedasticity. Letting small letters denote the logarithms of capital letters, Equation 18 becomes:

$$s = \pi^e - k . \tag{A1}$$

with k the logarithm of the capitalization rate, K, and equal to:

$$k = \ln[\rho + (\rho - r)d - pd - g] . \tag{A1A}$$

The expression in brackets is simply the denominator of Equation 18, generalized to allow for expected long-run growth of real profits at the rate g. It must be remembered, however, that g does not relate to that part of growth in per share profits that reflects only the utilization of retained earnings, and it therefore tends to be small for the average of all firms. In Equation A1, π^e is the logarithm of adjusted profits; the superscript e has been added as a reminder that the numerator in Equation 18 should be thought of as measuring, not current profits but, rather, noise-free or long-run average expected profits.

Modeling the Numerator of Equation 18

Our first problem was deriving an estimate of adjusted profits. What in fact is available is a measure of reported earnings and dividends for the portfolio of shares that constitute the S&P index, but the reported earnings are not "adjusted." [23] We relied on the NIA estimate of adjusted profits for the corporate nonfinancial sector and assumed that the ratio of adjusted to unadjusted profits for the S&P firms was approximately the same, at least up to a proportionality factor. This did not seem unreasonable, considering the importance of the firms included in the S&P index. In fact, in a recent study Davidson and Weil compared adjusted and reported profits for a sample of companies from the Fortune 500 for the year 1973. They reported that the median ratio of adjusted to unadjusted profits was roughly two-thirds; according to the NIA, the ratio for that year was 0.68. [24]

Deriving an estimate of long-run expected profits presented a difficult problem. We hypothesized that rational investors would tend to base their projection of expected profits on an estimate of noise-free operating income reduced by the expected future cost of borrowed capital. In other words:

$$\pi^e = \ln[OI^e - RD^*] \approx \ln OI^e [1 - \left(\frac{D}{OI^e}\right)*R]$$
$$\approx oi^e - \left(\frac{D}{OI^e}\right)*R . \tag{A2}$$

Here $(D/OI^e)^*$ may be thought of as a measure of target leverage. From an examination of the actual behavior of the ratio of debt to operating income (as estimated respectively by von Furstenberg and the NIA), making allowance for transient cyclical effects, one can infer that over the period of our analysis this target has remained reasonably stable (at the level of five or so). The approximation in the last step of Equation A2 is justified by the consideration that DR/OI has been generally small compared with unity—below 0.3—although it must be acknowledged that our approximation becomes less satisfactory in periods when interest rates reach two digit level.

To estimate expected OI, we made use of the standard assumption that a major source of information on which the market must rely to form profit expectations is the past history of profits itself. This hypothesis led to:

$$oi^e = \mathcal{J}[oi(t-\tau)] . \tag{A3}$$

where $\mathcal{J}$ is a distributed lag operator to be estimated from the data.

Unfortunately, information on OI is not available for the S&P. However, we relied on the fact that $OI(t) = \Pi(t) + R(t)D(t) = \Pi(t)[1 + R(t)D(t)/\Pi(t)]$. Substituting in Equation A3 and using the approximation in the last step of Equation A2, we obtained:

$$oi^c = \mathscr{S}[\pi(t-\tau)] + \mathscr{S}\left[\frac{RD}{\Pi}(t-\tau)\right] . \qquad (A4)$$

Finally, substituting Equation A4 back into Equation A2 yielded:

$$\pi^c(t) = \mathscr{S}[\pi(t - \tau)] + \mathscr{S}\left[\frac{RD}{\Pi}(t - \tau)\right] - \left(\frac{D}{OI^c}\right)*R . \qquad (A5)$$

Each of the RD$(t-\tau)$ terms in Equation A5 reflects interest payment on the debt contracted at a particular time in the past at then-prevailing market interest rates. If we invoke the relative stability of the ratios D/Π and (D/OI^c)*, the last two terms on the right-hand side of Equation A5 can be approximated by a long distributed lag of past interest rates, terminating with the current one:

$$\pi^c = \mathscr{S}[\pi(t - \tau)] + \sum_{\tau=-t}^{0} w_\tau R(t - \tau) . \qquad (A6)$$

As can be inferred from Equation A5, the weight w_τ should be negative for $\tau=0$ and positive for all other τ, although declining toward zero as τ grows.

This hypothesized structure of the weights reflects the fact that, for a particular history of past adjusted profits, expected profits and, therefore, market value should tend to respond positively when past interest rates exceed the current rate, since this implies that the future interest bill to be deducted from OI will be lower than in the past. However, this direct effect on profit expectation should be partially offset by the fact that, when past rates are on average higher than the current rate, the firm's debt will sell at a premium; this transient effect should tend to reduce the market value of shares for a given OI^c. As a result, we expected the distributed lag to contribute only modestly to the explanation of market value, except possibly during times of wide movements in interest rates. This conclusion is reinforced by the consideration that the sum of the weights should be close to zero because, when interest rates have been stable over the relevant past, they should have no effect on profit expectations, given past profits.

We introduced two further modifications into the basic Equation A6 to enhance its ability to capture investor expectations. First, we dealt with the problem arising from the fact that, in a growing economy, past profits provide downward biased information about expectations because of the intervening growth of the firm. We updated each term $\pi(t - \tau)$ in the distributed lag by means of the ratio of the capital stock of all nonfinancial corporations at time t to the same measure at time $t - \tau$.[25] Since all data were in current dollars, this updating served to correct, not only for real growth, but also for growth of monetary values as a result of inflation. Note that this procedure is equivalent to postulating that expected profits equal an average of past rates of return multiplied by the current capital stock.

Second, we hypothesized that investors, in forming expectations from past profits, would be likely to adjust reported profits upward during cyclically depressed periods of relatively low capacity utilization and downward during periods of exceptionally high activity. We therefore multiplied profits by an exponential function of labor force to employment.

Finally, we added to the right-hand side of Equation A6 a distributed lag of past and current dividends to allow for the so-called "information content" of dividends—an issue that is discussed later in the appendix.

Modeling the Denominator

Since our test revolves around the question of whether the market uses the correct capitalization rate, the most sensitive part of our formulation related to the denominator of Equation 18. It is generally agreed that the required rate of return on unlevered equity streams should depend on the real interest rate, r, though exceeding it by a risk premium. We further allowed for the possibility that the risk premium might vary systematically with r, which led us to express the required rate as:

$$\rho_t = a_t + br_t . \qquad (A7)$$

which implied a risk premium of:

$$\rho_t - r_t = a_t - (1-b)r_t , \qquad a > 0 \; 0 < b < 1 .$$

The first term is written as a_t in recognition of the fact that the risk premium can, in principle, change over time for reasons other than changes in the real rate of interest. Whether such changes are important, and what might cause them, is one of the classical issues in valuation theory and practice. The problem is one of disentangling what proportions of changes in value are to be attributed to changes in the numerator—expected profits—and what proportion to changes in the denominator—the capitalization rate.

For our purposes, we allowed for one measure of systematic change in the risk premium, which was developed in connection with the stock market sector of the MPS model. The measure used, labeled DVF, is a moving 15-year average deviation of the unemployment rate from four per cent, and is meant to reflect variations in undiversifiable risk over time arising from the instability of the economy. This series declines steadily until 1970 and rises steadily thereafter.

We also used the relation:

$$r(t) = R(t) - p^e(t) . \qquad (A8)$$

where R(t) is the nominal long-term interest rate and p^e can be thought of as the expected rate of inflation over

Saving, Deficits, Inflation, and Financial Theory

the life of long-term instruments. Accordingly, r is the perceived real rate implied by those expectations. Substituting in Equations A7 and A1A, we obtained:

$$k = \ln[A + Br - dp^e] , \qquad (A9)$$

where A equals $(1 + d)a - g$ and B equals $b(1 + d) - d$, and where one should expect A and B to exceed zero.

For purposes of testing, we approximated Equation A9 as:

$$k \simeq \alpha + \beta r - \delta p^e . \qquad (A9A)$$

This linear approximation is justified, provided that $Br-dp$ is small in absolute value relative to A, a condition that seems *a priori* reasonable, but that will be subject to empirical verification.

By equating the derivatives of Equations A9 and A9A, respectively, with respect to r and p^e, it is apparent that the following relationships hold between the parameters of these equations:

$$\beta = \frac{B}{K} ,$$

$$\delta = \frac{d}{K} . \qquad (A9B)$$

In Equation A9A, the real rate r is not directly observable. It was therefore convenient to express it in terms of the nominal rate, through Equation A8. This substitution is appropriate in that the variable R already appears in Equation A1 as a component of π^e (and in that the variables R, r and p^e cannot be used simultaneously as independent variables because they are collinear). Equation A9A then becomes:

$$k \simeq \alpha + \beta R + \gamma p^e, \qquad (A10)$$

where:

$$\gamma = -(\beta+\delta) = -(\beta+ \frac{d}{K}) . \qquad (A10A)$$

Since the term p^e is not observable, we had to fall back on the traditional method of estimating it as a distributed lag of past prices.

Equation A10A is of crucial importance for our test. It shows that, if the market uses the appropriate capitalization rate, taking into account the effect of inflation on adjusted profits, as called for by Equation 18, then the coefficient γ of the estimated inflation rate p^e should have a sign opposite to that of R. Furthermore, it should exceed it in absolute value, and the excess should be on the order of d/K, where d and K are numbers that can be estimated reasonably well from available data.

If this rationality condition holds—and only if it holds—inflation will have no real effects on equity values (except insofar as it affects directly adjusted

operating income). If, on the other hand, the coefficient γ is algebraically larger than indicated by the above condition, then inflation will systematically depress equity values—unless it happens to increase operating income sufficiently.

Equation A10A can fail under two conditions. If investors do not correct adjusted profits for the effect of inflation, but capitalize these profits at the real rate appropriate to true profits given by the denominator of Equation 16, then γ should be close in absolute value to β, the coefficient of R. In this case, inflation depresses levered equity values because it causes adjusted profits of levered firms to fall short of true profits. If, in addition, the market commits the error of capitalizing adjusted profits at a nominal rate, then γ should be much smaller than β in absolute value, and possibly not very different from zero. In this case, the effect of inflation on market values may well be drastic.

Arriving at a Valuation Model

Using the valuation Equation A1, we substituted for π^e from Equation A6 and for k from Equation A10, and combined like terms. The result was the following valuation formula (labeled H.1 for Hypothesis One), which provides the basis for our tests:

$$
\begin{aligned}
s_t = a_0 &+ \Sigma w_\tau^{(1)} \pi(t-\tau) \\
&+ \Sigma w_\tau^{(2)} \text{div}(t-\tau) \\
&+ a_3 \Sigma w_\tau^{(3)} \frac{LF}{E} (t-\tau) \\
&+ a_4 DVF(t) - \beta\Sigma w_\tau^{(4)} R (t-\tau) \\
&+ \gamma\Sigma w_\tau^{(5)} p(t - \tau) + u(t) ,
\end{aligned}
\qquad (H.1)
$$

where

s = the logarithm of the Standard & Poor's 500 stock price index,

$\pi(t-\tau)$ = the logarithm of (earnings per share of the S&P lagged τ periods times the ratio of adjusted to reported profits for all nonfinancial corporations times the ratio of current capital stock at replacement cost to capital stock lagged τ periods),

div = the logarithm of (dividends per share of the S&P times the ratio of current to lagged capital stock),

$\frac{LF}{E}$ = the ratio of labor force to employment,

DVF = a moving 15-year average deviation in the unemployment rate from four per cent,

R = the new issue interest rate on AA corporate bonds,

P = the rate of change in the Consumer Price Index and

u = the residual.

We expected the weights of the profit terms to add up to unity, since a proportional change in all past profits should imply an equiproportional change in expected profits, hence in market values, for a given capitalization rate. Accordingly, we estimated the weights $w^{(1)}$ subject to that constraint.

Our hypothesis with respect to dividends was that their role in valuation is basically one of providing clues about future profits. This implies that, for a given value of expected profits, variations in the overall level of dividends, indicating changes in pay-out policy, should have no permanent effect on market value. If so, the sum of the weights $w^{(2)}$ should be zero. More precisely, we expected the early weights to be positive, but to be offset by the weights of terms sufficiently lagged, implying that a rising trend of dividends for given past profits provides an indication of a forthcoming rise in profits (and dividends). In our estimation procedure, we initially imposed the zero-sum constraint, but since we realized that this view of the role of dividends is not uncontroversial, we also tested the constraint to see whether it was supported by the evidence; the results are given later in the appendix. The weights $w^{(3)}$, on the other hand, should all be positive, and they were estimated without any constraint.

The weights $w^{(4)}$ of the interest rate term should reflect both the distributed lag in Equation A6 and the role of R as a component of the capitalization rate. But since we expected the weights in Equation A6 to add to zero, the sum of the $w^{(4)}$ weights can be taken as an estimate of β, which should of course be negative. Accordingly, the $w^{(4)}$ should at first be negative, reflecting the unfavorable effect on market value of a current rise in interest rates, through its effect both on profits and on the capitalization rate, given price expectations. On the other hand, lagged rates should have a positive weight because, as noted earlier, they imply that past profits represent an underestimate of current investor expectations of long-run profits.

Finally, with respect to the error term u, it can be shown that, if the change in market value is a martingale, as many tests have suggested, and if hypothesis H.1 provides an explanation of market value that is consistent with this martingale property, the error term must itself be a martingale—that is, of the form $u = u_{-1} + \epsilon$, where ϵ is white noise.[26]

Empirical Results

Table A reports the results of estimating the basic valuation formula H.1. The first three columns, under Part A, present the results obtained when the serial correlation of the error term is estimated from the data themselves. Part B shows the results obtained from estimating H.1 in first-difference form—a procedure that enforces the constraint suggested by the martingale hypothesis of a unit autoregressive coefficient.

As can be verified from the statistic reported in Row 10, the serial correlation estimated from the data is very high—0.74—conforming to our expectations if our hypothesis is a valid approximation of market behavior. In fact, an F-test based on the residual errors of the two alternative estimates shown in Row 11 indicated that the serial correlation is barely smaller than random samples from a world in which the first-order autoregressive coefficient is unity would generate one time in 20, but larger than such samples would generate one time in 100.[27]

In view of this result, it is not surprising that the estimates of the coefficients under the two alternative procedures are generally close, especially in terms of point estimates. Accordingly, in the following analysis of the results, we concentrate on the level estimates (Part A) and refer to the first-difference results (Part B) only when they differ appreciably.

Interpreting Table A

The estimates reported in the first three rows of Table A relate to the determinants of profit expectations—the numerator of Equation 18. As Row 1 shows, we found that the best estimate of expected adjusted profits is provided by a five-year average of current and past adjusted profits "updated." This result is somewhat surprising. Even though we had expected that a rational forecast for a series as volatile as profits would take into account past experience over a long horizon, we had also anticipated that recent experience would matter more than more remote experience. Various tests based on adding to the equation distributed lags of the deviation of updated profits from the mean (to preserve the homogeneity constraint) not only contributed very little to the explanation but, in addition, implied that profits further removed in time mattered more than more recent ones. Because this finding was *a priori* highly improbable and was not very significant statistically, we rejected it.

The results of Row 2 are consistent with our hypothesis that, in forming expectations, the market adjusts at least the more recent profits for cyclical underutilization of capacity—a factor we captured by the convenient measure of the ratio of labor force to employment. This is evidenced by the graph pictured in Column 3. The solid line graphs the point estimates of the coefficients of LF/E lagged τ periods (estimated by a second-degree Almon polynomial); the two dotted curves are drawn one standard error above and below the point estimates, and the area between them thus represents a band of two standard errors centering on the coefficient. It is also seen from Column 1 that the total effect of this variable—the sum of current and lagged coefficients—is highly significant.

In the case of dividends, the coefficients graphed in Column 3, Row 3 can be interpreted as follows: In

TABLE A: Dependent Variable-log of S & P

Independent Variable	A Level Estimate		Weighting Function and 1 Standard Error Band	B First Difference Estimate		Weighting Function
	Long-Run Effect (sum of weights)			Long-Run Effect		
	Point Estimate	Standard Error		Point Estimate	Standard Error	
1) π	1	Constrained	Equal weights (constrained)	Same as level form		
2) $\dfrac{LF}{E}$	6.47	1.55		8.71	2.96	Same basic shape as level estimate
3) div	0	Constrained		Same basic shape		
4) $\dfrac{R}{\text{(per cent)}}$	−0.059	0.028		−0.089	0.044	Same basic shape
5) $\dfrac{p}{\text{(per cent)}}$	−0.021	0.017		−0.025	0.019	Same basic shape
6) DVF	−0.048	0.013		−0.050	0.038	
7) Constant	3.35	0.13		0	Constrained	
8) Period of observation (100 quarters) 1953:1 to 1977:4				Same		
9) Degrees of freedom		85		87		
10) Autoregressive coefficient (RHO)		0.74				
11) Standard Error with error feedback		0.042		0.0437		
12) S.E. without error feedback		0.063		not applicable		
13) DW		1.54		1.73		

forming profit expectations, the average of past profits is multiplied by the ratio of average (updated) dividends over the more recent past to an average of dividends over the previous five years with declining weights. In the figure, the weight (elasticity) of more recent dividends is represented by the height of the horizontal line (0.28). The weights of past dividends are represented by the curve beginning in the negative quadrant; they are negative because what matters is the *difference* (the logarithm of the ratio) between recent dividends and the five-year average.[28]

We imposed a zero constraint that, in essence, formalizes the notion that, for given profits, dividend (pay-out) policy has no effect on market value. We made several tests of this constraint and can report that every test in which it was removed (while retaining the homogeneity constraint on profits) showed that the unconstrained sum was not significantly different from zero. In fact, we regard this evidence as one of the significant results of our study.

The next three rows of the table pertain to the capitalization rate, the denominator of Equation 18. Row 4 reports the results for the interest rate: The coefficients of the distributed lag (approximated by a second-degree Almon polynomial) clearly conform to our expectations. They start significantly negative (the first two coefficients have t-ratios on the order of three) but soon turn modestly positive.

On the other hand, the coefficients of inflation reported in Column 3 of Row 5 are in striking disagreement with the implications of rational valuation. They should be consistently positive—more than offsetting the coefficients of R—so that the sum of these two sets of coefficients should add up to the positive number d/K (a number that, as we show in the text, is on the order of 0.05).[29] Instead, the coefficients of p are consistently negative, even if marginally significant; as a result, the sum of the coefficients of R and p, instead of being around 0.05, is −0.08 with a standard error of 0.015!

Finally, the variable DVF is seen to be highly significant, even if numerically small.

Estimation in first-difference form (Part B of Table A) yields substantially similar results, as can be seen from comparing Columns 4 and 6 with 1 and 3. The estimated long-run effect of the interest rate (Row 4) is somewhat higher, and the surprising negative effect of inflation is also moderately higher.

Two further tests are important from the standpoint of the degree of confidence one can ascribe to any conclusions. First, in the tests reported in Table A, we have assumed that the relevant measure of profits is adjusted profits. This is a strong assumption, for it implies that investors are able to perceive the generally recognized pitfalls that plague reported profits in a period of inflation, properly deducting paper gains on

inventories and taking into account the implications of inadequate depreciation. Is it not more credible that they would base valuation on reported profits uncorrected, or corrected only partially?

The evidence strongly rejects this hypothesis: If adjusted profits are replaced with S&P profits as reported, the fit deteriorates dramatically—the sum of squared residuals goes up by nearly one-quarter. Extensive tests of the hypothesis that reported profits might be corrected only partially were found to be equally inconsistent with the data in that, for every positive fraction tested, the fit was found to be uniformly worse, or at least no better than with full adjustment.

Our second test addressed the question of the intertemporal stability of the coefficients. The 25 years spanning the interval from 1953 to 1977 constitute a long period, one varied in experiences in many respects and particularly with respect to inflation, with reasonable price stability prevailing during the first half of the period and growing, although variable, inflation in the second half.

We broke the full period into two roughly equal parts—one period corresponding to price stability and terminating in the fourth quarter of 1964 (12 years) and one period from the first quarter of 1965 on (13 years). Tests of the hypothesis that the coefficients were the same in the two periods indicated that this hypothesis could not be rejected at the five per cent significance level (or, for that matter, a much lower one), at least as long as one maintains the hypothesis of an autoregressive coefficient close to one.

It is also worth noting that the sum of the coefficients of the nominal interest rate and of inflation—which should, as noted above, be positive under rational expectations—is negative in each subperiod and of the same magnitude as for the period as a whole. For instance, in the first-difference form that sum, which is −0.114 for the entire period, with a standard error of 0.015, turns out to be −0.124 for both the first and second subperiods (and highly significant for both).

Plugging in Numerical Estimates

From the results reported in Table A, we can now infer numerical estimates for the parameters of Equation A10. From Table A, Part A:

$$k = -3.24 + 0.06R + 0.02p , \qquad \text{(A11)}$$

where k is the logarithm of the capitalization rate and the constant term is derived from the estimate in Row 7.[30] The coefficients of R and p are those reported in Rows 4 and 5 of Column 1, on the grounds that, for present purposes, we are interested in the response of the capitalization rate to "permanent" changes in the respective variables, and not in the dynamics of short-run adjustments. Note that, in Equation A11, the coefficients of Column 1 appear with their signs inverted because the estimated coefficients are those of the logarithm of the reciprocal of the capitalization rate.

For present purposes, it is convenient to recast Equation A10 in the form of Equation A9A, or:

$$k = -3.24 + 0.06r + 0.08p , \qquad (A12A)$$

where we assume that changes in p^c correspond to permanent changes in p. This leads to the following estimate of the capitalization rate itself:

$$K = 0.0392 \exp (0.06r + 0.08p) , \qquad (A13A)$$
$$\simeq 0.0392 (1 + 0.06r + 0.08p) .$$

If the value of the coefficient is derived from the estimates reported in Part B of Table A, Equation A12A becomes:[31]

$$k = -3.424 + 0.089r + 0.115p , \qquad (A12B)$$

and Equation A13A becomes:[32]

$$K = 0.0325 \exp (0.089r + 0.115p) \qquad (A13B)$$
$$\simeq 0.0325 (1 + 0.089r + 0.115p) .$$

Footnotes

1. There is extensive empirical literature on whether common stocks are inflation hedges, but the evidence is mixed to say the least. Reuben A. Kessel found (as reported in "Inflation-Caused Wealth Redistribution: A Test of a Hypothesis," *American Economic Review*, March 1956, pp. 128-141) that shares of net debtor firms rose in price as a result of inflation, while those of net creditors declined. Phillip Cagan indicated (in "Common Stock Values and Inflation—The Historical Record of Many Countries," *National Bureau Report Supplement* (New York: 1974)) that while stock prices sometimes reflected inflation over long periods of time, they often failed to keep up with inflation over short periods. Zvi Bodie found that real rates of return on common stocks were negatively correlated with both anticipated and unanticipated inflation, at least in the short run; his results appear in "Common Stocks as a Hedge Against Inflation," *Journal of Finance*, May 1976, pp. 459-470. His findings are consistent with those of John Lintner, reported in "Inflation and Common Stock Prices in a Cyclical Context," *NBER Annual Report* (New York: 1973), pp. 23-36.
2. The estimate of replacement cost of assets and of market value of debt and of preferred stock is taken from George M. von Furstenberg, "Corporate Investment: Does Market Valuation Matter in the Aggregate?" *Brookings Papers on Economic Activity* No. 2, 1977, Table 1, p. 351ff., columns 3, 5 and 6. 1977 values were kindly supplied by Professor von Furstenberg.
   We have replaced von Furstenberg's estimate of the market value of common stock (column 7) with an estimate, developed by us as part of the research presented in this paper, to be documented in a forthcoming article. The two estimates are generally close beginning with the middle 1960s. In the earlier period, our estimate

is appreciably higher, though the difference diminishes over time.
3. This graph is based on data employed by Michael Lovell in "The Profit Picture: Trends and Cycles," *Brookings Papers on Economic Activity* No. 3, 1978, pp. 769-788, and described in the appendix on data sources in that paper.
4. Series 2 is computed as the ratio of National Income Accounts (NIA) adjusted operating income to the replacement cost of capital as computed by von Furstenberg, "Corporate Investment."
5. The results shown graphically in Series 2, Figure 1 and Series 3, Figure II have been confirmed by a number of regressions run by other investigators who have tested for evidence of time trends in the share of capital in value added or in the rate of return on capital. Rudiger Dornbusch and Stanley Fischer of M.I.T. have not yet published the results of their research in this area. See Daniel Holland and Stewart Myers, "Trends in Corporate Profitability and Capital Costs" (Working Paper, Sloan School of Management, M.I.T., October 1977); Michael Lovell, "The Profit Picture"; and von Furstenberg, "Corporate Investment."
6. This conclusion first acquired currency on the basis of William D. Nordhaus' "The Falling Share of Profits," *Brookings Papers on Economic Activity* No. 1, 1974, pp. 169-208. It is still widely held and often quoted in the press.
7. See Martin Feldstein, "Inflation and the Stock Market" (Working Paper No. 276, National Bureau of Economic Research, August 1978). See also Charles Nelson, "Inflation and Capital Budgeting," *Journal of Finance*, June 1976, pp. 923-931.
8. One possible distortion is that resulting from the taxation of nominal accounting income rather than true income. We already have shown, at least for the United States, that this effect is not major because of offsetting "inequities." There is a more complex issue arising from the interaction of personal and corporate income taxes and capital gains taxes. We are currently investigating this problem and the results will be reported in a forthcoming paper. Our preliminary analysis suggests that taxes would not change our conclusions qualitatively.
9. Equation 2 presents a nominal measure of income that corresponds to conventionally reported operating income adjusted for the effects of inflation on the cost of goods sold stemming from historical cost accounting for depreciation and inventories. See, for example, Lawrence Revsine, *Replacement Cost Accounting* (New York: Prentice-Hall, 1973).
10. This formula is an approximation. The exact increase would be p + rp, but rp is likely to be so small that it can be dropped.
11. Franco Modigliani and Merton H. Miller, "The Cost of Capital, Corporation Finance and the Theory of Investment," *American Economic Review*, June 1958, pp. 261-297.
12. Accountants have long been aware of the bias in conventional accounts stemming from the treatment of interest in a period of inflation. (See, for example, Sidney Davidson and Roman L. Weil, "Inflation Accounting: What Will General Price Level Adjusted In-

come Statements Show?'' *Financial Analysts Journal,* January/February 1975, pp. 27-31 and 70-84.) General price level adjusted accounting is a proposed technique that in effect explicitly adjusts reported income for the part of stated interest that represents a real payment of principal.

13. See Giorgio Ragazzi, ''Inflation Accounting and the 'Real' Earnings of Italian Industrial Firms,'' *Revista de Politica Economica* No. 10, 1976, pp. 77-100.

14. Similar tests were performed on a measure of the aggregate value of the equity of all U.S. nonfinancial corporations, and similar results were obtained.

15. These computed values were obtained without making use of the information provided by the previous error. If that information were utilized, the fit would, of course, be much closer. (As can be seen from Rows 11 and 12 of Table A in the appendix, the standard deviation of the differences between actual and computed values in Figure V can be cut down by one-third.) The computed values shown for the first two quarters of 1978 represent an extrapolation of our equation based on data that are partly preliminary (and partly guesswork), hence should be regarded as no more than indicative.

16. Although Figure V indicates that our level-form equation explains the level of the stock market remarkably well, one should not be tempted to infer that the equation can be profitably employed to forecast future stock prices. If the error term is a martingale, one's ability to forecast the level of the market would depend on how well one could forecast the relevant future values of the independent variables.

17. We chose 19A for a number of reasons (some of which will become apparent later in the article). We regard these estimates as more reliable than those of Equation 19B for the purpose of estimating the long-term effect of the relevant variables. However, the interested reader can readily work out the implications of the alternative estimates by substituting the parameters of Equation 19B for those of Equation 19A in the various expressions given below.

18. The division by 100 in the first and second right-hand side expressions reflects the fact that p is measured as a percentage (see footnote 29).

19. If one relies on the alternative estimate given by Equation 19B, the undervaluation resulting from a one per cent change in inflation will rise to some 16 per cent (implying that, at the end of 1977, market value was not quite 40 per cent of the warranted value).

20. Estimate of aggregate debt from von Furstenberg. See Footnote 2.

21. *Ibid.*

22. See on this point the considerations set forth at the end of the section ''Valuing Stocks Under Conditions of Inflation.'' John Lintner, in his Presidential Address (''Inflation and Security Prices,'' *Journal of Finance,* May 1975, pp. 272-276) has suggested two mechanisms by which inflation would tend to reduce profits systematically, forcing also a greater dependence on outside sources of financing. First, inflation reduces the real return on one of the firm's assets—cash, insofar as non-interest-bearing. This effect is well known from the literature on inflation, but is generally regarded to be of a very small order of magnitude. Second, Lintner

hypothesizes a similar effect on account receivables, on the grounds that firms suffering from inflation illusion fail to adjust their credit terms even as nominal interest rates change. If Lintner is right in this conjecture, inflation illusion is more gross than we thought likely. However, even in this case it should be recognized that the magnitude of the effect depends on the size of *net* receivables (the difference between receivables and payables), which is likely to be small relative to total assets of a large and diversified sample of firms, such as we are using.

23. Quarterly dividends for the S&P are not regularly published as a series. We obtained the data directly from Standard & Poor's Corporation.

The S&P index is computed at frequent intervals, but our analysis relies on a number of variables obtainable only from quarterly U.S. National Income Accounts. Therefore all the variables we use, including the value of stocks, are quarterly averages or quarterly flows, unless otherwise specified.

24. Davidson and Weil, ''Inflation Accounting.'' It is true, of course, that the reported profits published by Standard & Poor's index and examined by Davidson and Weil are taken from shareholder reports, while those published in the National Income Accounts are taken from tax reports. This difference is unlikely to damage the validity of the approximation.

25. Ratios estimated from Holland and Myers, ''Trends in Corporate Profitability.'' Since their series only goes to the first two quarters of 1977, the last two quarters were estimated by extrapolation based on investment data.

26. This proof will be presented by the authors in a forthcoming paper. But see Franco Modigliani's comment on Frederic S. Mishkin, ''Efficient-Market Theory: Implications for Monetary Policy,'' *Brookings Papers on Economic Activity* No. 3, 1978, pp. 757-762.

27. The F-statistic for the test was 3.9, with two and 85 degrees of freedom. The critical 0.01 and 0.05 levels are, respectively, 4.9 and 3.1.

28. The last three coefficients turn somewhat positive, a result that is not consistent with our hypothesis, but which can be dismissed because none of these coefficients is significantly different from zero.

29. Because we measure R and p as percentages, K, the earnings-price ratio, must also be measured as a percentage.

30. The constant -3.24 of Equation A11 was obtained from the figure in Row 7, Column 1, 3.35, by adjusting it for the mean value of DVF (-0.048 times $2.3 = -0.11$) and then changing its sign for the reason discussed in the appendix.

31. The constant term is estimated from the condition that the capitalization rate implied by Equation A12B at the mean of r and p coincides with the (geometric) mean capitalization rate.

32. These results broadly agree with those reported by John Lintner in ''Inflation and Common Stock Prices.'' Those results rely on annual observations for the much longer period from 1900 to 1971 (and thus exclude the most recent period of high inflation). His coefficient estimates imply a somewhat smaller responsiveness of equity values to the interest rate, but a similar response to inflation, given the real rate.

Erratum

Page 29, second column, fourth line after equation (7): delete ''to'' before ''the.''

Financial Markets

Franco Modigliani

The decade of the 1970s has confronted us with many problems, brought about by unforeseen and unusual developments. I concentrate on developments that we may expect to see in the 1980s, in an effort to find solutions to the problems. To make my life simple, however, I am primarily concerned with those changes that *should* come about rather than those that *will* occur. I have two good excuses for taking this course. First, if I can persuade you of the soundness of the solutions I discuss, it may perhaps make it easier for those solutions to be realized. Second, by sliding over the distinction between "should" and "will," I can avoid the risk of being criticized in ten years because my forecasts were not very good. Of course if they should not turn out to be very good, I can always blame you for inadequate support and the politicians for failing to take advantage of good advice!

If we look at the financial markets, I think that the dominant problems we face that need solutions are related to the current high rate of inflation and to the fact that this inflation can be expected to be with us for quite a while. In other words I see inflation as the dominant problem-producing and adjustment-requiring issue of the 1980s. The reason why inflation strikes me as such an important problem is not necessarily that I believe that the rate of inflation will be very high, but rather that I do believe and forecast with great confidence that it is going to be extremely hard to forecast with any confidence the future of inflation. In other words we have to contend with a world in which inflation is necessarily quite uncertain. What is relevant here is not just the momentum-type of inflation from which we are suffering—for by its own nature that process is persistent, but does not create volatility. The uncertainty comes in the first place from random shocks—such as the oil shocks that have hit us in the past and may quite possibly strike in the future. In addition we have the kind of political cycle in which we fight inflation hard, but then, as the costs get larger and larger, we give up and reverse our course and inflation rises again. It is very hard to decide if you are more tired of inflation or more tired of the cost of fighting it.

Now looking at the problems that inflation is imposing on capital markets, I would like to make a distinction between the liquidation of problems that have arisen because of the unanticipated inflation due to previous oil and other shocks and problems that arise from adjusting to living with inflation, even if anticipated, because we cannot get rid of it quickly (and probably should not even try), unless luck intervenes. If so much oil were suddenly found that the price of oil went to zero, then I think things might look different. But for the moment it does not look like we need to worry about that much luck!

Regarding the effects of past unanticipated inflation, there are of course many that by now are bygones, and there is nothing to do. Some people have been made a lot richer, and some have been made a lot poorer. Homeowners who borrowed before the onset of inflation find themselves paying very substantially negative interest rates if one allows for inflation. And of course the poor guys who put money in savings deposits so far have been getting 5 percent or 6 percent. They are getting negative returns. In other words the principal has shrunk badly in purchasing power without compensation from higher interest rates. But those, I am afraid, are bygones; there is not much we can do.

But there is one major problem we have inherited for which I think we most probably have to do something,—that is, the plight of the thrift institutions, particularly savings and loan institutions. These institutions, like many others in this country, were designed for a world of stable prices, no inflation, or at any rate of very little and stable inflation and therefore very stable interest rates. In this world, which I think regulators quite foolishly assumed would exist forever, these institutions, which were supposed to be bastions of financial solidity, were told to engage in the highly speculative and risky activity of borrowing short and lending long.

For decades they have engaged in financing 20- or 30-year loans on the basis of demand liabilities (even though formally they may not have done so). That is equivalent to making a forward sale for each of the next 30 years at a price fixed now, intending to honor that contract by purchasing the commodity in the spot market at the uncertain price ruling over the next 30 years. If the market moves against you, if the spot price moves appreciably above what you sold for, you are in pretty hot soup. This is just what happened as inflation drove up market interest rates, and these institutions would probably by now be out of commission had it not been for efforts to save them by imposing ceilings on the "price" they could pay on the spot market—that is, ceilings on the maximum rate they can pay their depositors. This operation has had some limited success in preventing a catastrophe, thanks to the monopolistic character of the industry. Because there is not too much substitution between the assets they offer and other assets, you could persuade people to continue to lend to them even under very unfavorable conditions. Remember that these savings deposits are, by and large, the assets of the poor, and there was nothing much else for the poor to invest in. We have been systematically taking advantage of the poor over this period, even though the rich complain bitterly, as you all know. At every spurt of inflation and interest rates, however, the S & Ls have lost the ability of attracting or even keeping the more sophisticated money, with dramatic effects on the housing industry.

The situation has somewhat improved recently in terms of new commitments. On the one hand there has been a tendency to encourage these institutions to significantly lengthen their liabilities, thus covering, as it were, their forward sales with forward purchases, and, at the same time, some innovations are being introduced to ensure that the return on their investment—the price of their forward sales—is not fixed once and forever, but can be adjusted, in response to the spot price. The way this is being achieved, through the so-called variable rate mortgages, is actually very unsatisfactory from the borrower's point of view, as I will indicate later, but it does improve matters for the lenders. The problem is that this device applies only to new loans, and there still is a very large block of loans much below the current market rates. Under these circumstances if we proceed to deregulate this industry, as we have intended for a while and have begun to accomplish with recent legislation, there is a very real risk that this industry may not be in the position to pay the current market rates on the totality of the liabilities needed to support their assets.

My view is that we should definitely continue to deregulate, but that we should also be prepared to take care of the past mistakes, at public expense—for example, by appropriate intervention by the Treasury to make up a share of the difference between the face value and the market value of the assets. But why, you might ask, should the public pay for the mistakes of these institutions? The answer is that those institutions, especially the S & Ls, got into their current problem because of public regulation. They were required to invest all in long-term instruments. They were never warned against relying on short-term liabilities—in fact they were encouraged to borrow short. So if they got into the recent predicament, I do not think it is entirely their fault, although they may have contributed to their plight a little. But although I favor providing some relief, I also feel that we must require of them that in the future there be a matching of the maturity of assets and of liabilities. Funds lent at a fixed rate for, say, ten years, should be covered by borrowing for ten years at a fixed rate. Short-term liabilities should be used only to make short-term loans or long-term loans at a floating rate anchored to a short-term rate.

Note that this requirement of matching maturities is pretty universal in other countries. It is a particular feature of the United States, which otherwise boasts a pretty sound financial structure, that it has tolerated and encouraged the thrift institutions to engage in the unsound, highly risky practice of borrowing very short and lending very long. This practice has had me worried for the last two decades, though it was not until the late sixties that the gamble turned sour.

So that is how one of the most serious current financial problems, that of the thrift institutions, should find a solution in the 1980s: fix the consequences of past errors—if necessary with some recourse to public funds—but then make sure that they do not occur again. We do not need to regulate the interest rate that thrift institutions can pay or the number of windows they can open—let them be free to decide, let them compete. But because their deposits must be safe, require them to match maturities and to stop speculating with the depositors' money. This, I believe, is the appropriate kind of regulation.

I next move on to a second set of adjustments for the 1980s, which may be labeled Adjusting and Learning to Live with Inflation. This process has two quite different aspects. The first adjustment revolves around learning not to be fooled by inflation, that is, seeing through the many and treacherous distortions that inflation introduces in the calculations, which we have learned to carry out in nominal terms.

A well-known illustration is represented by the calculations of the true return from financial assets fixed in nominal terms. If inflation is 10 percent, and I own a nominal asset that pays me, say, 12 percent after personal taxes, then the true or real income from that asset is only 2 percent—all that I can afford to consume if I do not intend to consume my capital, that is, to have negative saving. The remaining 10 percent must be recognized not as income, but rather as the equivalent of reimbursement of principal. That reimbursement must be reinvested to preserve the purchasing power of my capital. The reverse is true if you are a borrower. Though you pay 12 percent, only 2 percent of this should be regarded as the true cost of the money you use; the remaining 10 percent should be added back to your income as representing a reduction or repayment of principal.

These are simple examples. But the calculations required to make sound investment decisions, whether in financial or in physical assets, are typically far more complex, and I have become convinced that inflation is producing many serious distortions in our economy because of the difficulties of making warranted, rational calculations in a world of high and variable inflation.

As some of you may know, I have suggested that one area where such distortions are both large and produce serious consequences is in the valuation of equities. I have concluded that because of inflation-induced valuation errors, the value of stocks may be on the average as much as one-half below what it should be.

What are the mistakes that investors make? Very briefly the first one arises because reported profits tend to decline with high inflation because interest paid rises by a large factor. If, for example, 10 percent inflation drives interest rates from 3 percent to 13 percent, the interest bill will more than quadruple. This decline in reported profits, however, is a fictitious inflation illusion; it would disappear if investors added back to profits that part of the rise in interest that offsets inflation. This is the appropriate procedure, as the example illustrates.

I believe that, by and large, investors fail to make an adequate correction on this account (even though they seem to have learned to make some correction for other distortions related to depreciation and inventory profits). It is significant that even the National Income accounts do not up to now make the appropriate correction in reporting corporate profits. Failure to make this correction can make a huge difference, depending on the rate of inflation and on a firm's debt equity ratio. I have estimated that for the United States, this error in computing profits may account for perhaps one-third of the market undervaluation.

The second important error that is depressing the market, in my view, is that the market tends to discount profits at the nominal interest rate. To put it another way, earning-price ratios have tended to move up and down with interest rates, something you can readily verify for yourself. Because, on balance, interest rates have risen a great deal, earning-price ratios have risen a great deal even though the rise in interest rates is more than accounted for by rising inflation. Now, as any "expert" will tell you, and a little thought will confirm, the earning-price ratio should *not* change with inflation. The earning-price ratio is a "real" rate because, unlike bond holders, stockholders need not be compensated for the erosion of the principal due to inflation. The value of their asset, like profits, should move with the price level. So if the stock market behaved the way it should, then the earning-price ratio should not have risen with inflation. It should be the same today as it was 10 to 15 years ago. The fact that it is much higher—or the price-earning ratio much lower—accounts for the remaining two-thirds of the undervaluation.

Can we expect this undervaluation to disappear in the 1980s? How and why should it disappear? The answer is that there are two ways in which this undervaluation can come to an end. The first way is for people to become convinced that I am right in asserting that the market is undervalued. This of course is something that should happen instantaneously as I speak; that is why I usually make sure when I speak about the subject that everybody has telephones by their chairs so that they can immediately call their brokers. In a more serious tone, what is required is that people learn to see through the veil of inflation. As people come to understand this process, they will be led to change the valuation assigned to stocks.

A second circumstance that would end this undervaluation, however, would be if inflation merely stopped growing. The reason this would work is that if inflation stops growing, interest rates will also tend to stay put, and if I am right, the price-earning ratio will stop falling. That means, however, that prices will rise at the same rate as earnings—namely, at the rate of inflation. But the realized return will then become the earning-price ratio plus the rate of inflation, which is far greater than the return from bonds (especially after taxes). Indeed this is precisely the sense in which I claim stocks are undervalued. To illustrate, in 1980 with the earning-price ratio around 15 percent and inflation around 10 percent, the average return from stock would be around 25 percent before taxes and above 20 percent after 40 percent taxes on dividends, implying a real return of around 10 percent. This return compares with after-tax (or tax exempt) bond returns of 8 percent to 9 percent, or a negative real return of around −2 percent.

Of course once investors see these extraordinary differential returns from stocks, they will rush to buy them, driving up their prices toward the correct valuation. In the process of course there will be additional capital gains that will make stocks even more attractive. In other words the great current undervaluation offers two alluring promises to the holder—a large yield and a large capital gain—sometimes. But once the process of correction gets going, it is likely to keep on going. In the ensuing bull market we may well end up overshooting the mark.

We have already seen a situation in this country in which the market responded to inflation in this fascinating way. I am referring to what happened during and just after the First World War. A severe inflation began in 1916, of a bigger dimension than what we are now experiencing, which drove prices up not far from double the initial level by 1920. What happened to the stock market in that period? It was absolutely flat. Just as in the recent experience, the nominal value did not move and the real value of stocks declined.

Then in 1920, after a final big spurt, inflation came down with a bang, in a way that is no longer to be seen in the world. In 1921 prices actually declined, by something like 40 pecent in one year. Then amazingly the inflation was over. From that point on inflation fluctuated narrowly around zero. Then the market began to catch up with the higher price level; by the mid-twenties it had done so. To do so it had to rise pretty fast, and this quick rise may well have contributed to fueling the boom that culminated in 1929. Now I would not be surprised if the 1980s should see something like that, because once we begin to catch up with the warranted valuation, the capital gains earned in the catching-up process produce large returns that make stocks appear more attractive than they really are. So you can very easily generate a speculative boom. If that should happen in the 1980s, I hope that I will be around to warn you that stocks are overpriced!

INFLATION AND THE STOCK MARKET

by Franco Modigliani
and Richard A. Cohn

This paper discusses the authors' recent research into the effect of inflation on the value of corporate equity. This work stemmed from an attempt to understand the causes of the substantial decline in price-earnings ratios in the United States over the period from the mid-1960s to the present, a period characterized by volatile and rising inflation.

Our research grew out of a broader study concerned with understanding the impact of high and variable inflation on the economy in general and on the financial markets in particular. In the course of that study we came to realize that one of the serious problems which inflation creates in an economy not accustomed to deal with it arises from the very real difficulties inflation introduces into the making of valid, rational economic and financial calculations. These considerations alerted us to the possibility that the puzzling dismal performance of the stock market might have arisen from errors of valuation produced by inflation. We were led to conjecture that the market might be making two distinct errors, both of which would result in a serious undervaluation of equity values. One would cause an undervaluation of profits, and the other would cause a serious upward bias in the rate at which those earnings were capitalized. Both of these errors could be traced to the effect of inflation in increasing nominal interest rates.

In the course of 1978 we designed a set of tests of this hypothesis based on a time-series or intertemporal analysis of the behavior of the Standard & Poor's 500 Stock Index in relation to inflation and other relevant variables. These tests are discussed in more detail below. Their results, which were

99

published in spring 1979, appeared to support fully our hypothesis and to account for the observed behavior of the market in the course of recent inflation.[1] The results also suggested that, had equity values been rationally appraised, they would have been not far from twice as high as they then were.

Since that time we have been engaged in a second study, designed in part to respond to a variety of criticisms which were provoked by our original study. The second study is based on a comparative analysis of the behavior of stocks of individual companies. This approach has permitted us to deal with issues which could not be adequately resolved by the method of our first study. The results of the second study, which are also reported below, appear to lend further credence to our hypothesis.

The undervaluation hypothesis

In the past 12 to 15 years, U.S. stock prices, as measured by broad-based market indexes, have been roughly stagnant in nominal terms, while the general price level has more than doubled. This relationship is shown in Figure 6-1. Series 1 depicts stock prices, as measured by Standard & Poor's Industrials, and series 2 portrays general prices, as measured by the gross domestic product deflator for the 1968-79 period.

This phenomenon is not accounted for by a decline in aftertax profitability. This can be seen by comparing series 2 with the behavior of an estimate of aggregate profits for the nonfinancial corporate sector, fully corrected for the measurement biases induced by inflation, which is shown by series 3 in Figure 6-1. Generally speaking, profits have kept up with inflation, at least in recent years.

The profit series reported in Figure 6-1 is obtained by adjusting reported profits for three types of inflation dis-

---

[1] Franco Modigliani and Richard A. Cohn, "Inflation, Rational Valuation, and the Market," *Financial Analysts Journal*, March-April 1979.

100

Figure 6-1

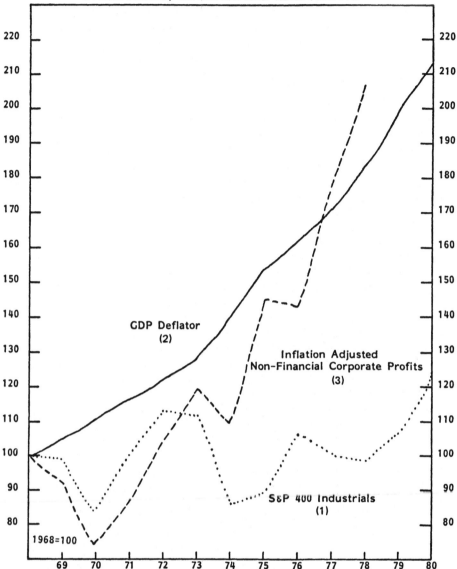

STOCK PRICES, INFLATION AND REAL PROFITS

In all cases, 1968 = 100.
Series 1: Standard & Poor's 400 Industrial Index.
Series 2: Gross domestic product deflator.
Series 3: Inflation-adjusted nonfinancial corporate profits.

101

tortions. The first has to do with depreciation, the second with inventory profits, and the third with interest on debt. Since depreciation is based on the historical acquisition cost of fixed assets, inflation causes reported depreciation expense to be an understatement of actual capital consumption. Firms that use first-in, first-out (FIFO) inventory accounting show paper profits during periods of inflation because their cost of goods sold understates the cost of replacing inventory. The third distortion results from a failure to add back to profits the gain from the real depreciation of monetary liabilities.

While the first two distortions serve to make reported profits an overstatement of true profits, the third has the opposite effect. It turns out that for the U.S. nonfinancial corporate sector as a whole, these effects offset each other to a considerable extent. As a result, reported earnings represent a reasonable approximation to fully adjusted earnings.[2] This conclusion is of some interest because it suggests that there is little foundation to the argument that inflation raises the corporate tax burden because taxes are based on reported income which exceeds true profits.

The conclusion that inflation-adjusted profitability has not been noticeably hurt by inflation is confirmed by other measures. In particular, total aftertax return to capital—the sum of profits adjusted for depreciation and inventory valuation plus interest—in relation to the reproduction cost of capital or corporate value added, can best be described as trendless over the post-World War II period. Even though inflation is currently high by U.S. historical standards, profitability is no worse now than it was during the bull market of the 1950s and early 1960s.

Because of the gradual erosion of real stock prices in the face of largely unchanged real profits, the rise in inflation has

---

[2] The net effect of the three distortions will, of course, vary substantially among firms.

102

been accompanied by a remarkable decline in the average price-earnings ratio, so that it is now less than half as large as it was in the late 1960s. A similar phenomenon has been observed in many other countries during this period of world-wide inflation.

This observation, which runs conspicuously counter to the traditional view that equities are hedges against inflation, raised in our minds the question of whether there might be a causal connection between the rise in inflation and the decline in price-earnings ratios (or, equivalently, the rise in earnings-price ratios).

One may first ask whether the observed positive association between earnings-price ratios and inflation can be attributed to rational investors' behavior. After all, it is a well-known and widely observed phenomenon that interest rates do rise roughly in step with inflation. The reason is that debt instruments have a value fixed in nominal terms whose purchasing power is eroded by inflation. Hence, interest rates tend to incorporate an inflation premium which maintains unchanged the "real interest rate," that is, the difference between the nominal interest rate and the rate of inflation. But it is a well-known proposition in the theory of rational equity valuation that the capitalization rate for earnings (the earnings-price ratio) should behave like the real rate of interest, that is, it should not change with inflation—except insofar as inflation changes the real interest rate itself (or the risk premium required by investors). The reason why the earnings-price ratio should behave like the real rate of interest instead of responding to inflation in the same way as nominal interest rates, is that equities, in contrast to debt, represent a claim on real assets and on the resulting real profit stream, which is, presumably, not significantly affected by inflation. Therefore, the earnings-price ratio can be viewed as the investor's real rate of return—analogous to the real rate of interest on debt. His nominal return will consist of the earnings-price ratio plus the rise in the price of stock in re-

103

sponse to the inflation-induced rise in nominal profits. This nominal appreciation of the asset performs the same function as the inflation premium component of interest rates.

These considerations led us to conjecture that the behavior of the market could reflect the mistaken view that a stock should be priced so as to produce an earnings-price ratio commensurate with the nominal rate of interest. Our suspicion was reinforced by a number of considerations, including the following: (1) Casual observation of the negative association between market action and interest rate movements, (2) The consideration that the association of earnings-price ratios and interest rates is consistent with rational behavior in the absence of inflation, for then changes in the nominal rate are in fact changes in the real rate. We thought it plausible that the market could be carrying over into an unaccustomed inflationary environment a behavior which had been appropriate for a long time, but was no longer so, (3) Perusal of the financial press, including brokerage house memorandums, and conversations with portfolio managers, which pointed in the direction of our conjecture.

We also hypothesized that there might be a further reason why inflation affected stock prices adversely—namely, a failure to properly correct profits for the gains from the inflation-induced depreciation of monetary liabilities. This failure means that the rise in interest rates due to inflation premiums results in a fictitious decline in observed profits. In this area too we observed a good deal of erroneous thinking as to whether a correction to profits was called for. It was argued, for example, that this gain from depreciation of debt should not be included in profits because it was a windfall gain rather than income, or because it did not represent a cash inflow.

To be sure, the correction for the depreciation of the debt, as indicated earlier, is but one of three corrections to reported earnings which should be made in the presence of inflation to obtain a true measurement. But we became convinced that the need for the adjustment for depreciation and

104

inventories was on the whole broadly appreciated by investors. Thus we concluded that the failure to make the monetary liabilities adjustment was not compensated by errors in the opposite direction but was likely instead to result in a significant net downward bias. We were struck in this connection by the fact that even the prestigious national income accounts of the United States (and not only the United States) conscientiously make the two downward adjustments but fail to make the upward correction for the depreciation of monetary liabilities.

Time-series tests

In an effort to test our twin hypotheses, we related (by regression analysis) the behavior of a measure of the price-earnings ratio to the behavior of a measure of interest rates and inflation for the period 1953-77. The measure of price was the Standard & Poor's 500 Stock Index. The measure of earnings was earnings per share of the index, with an estimated adjustment for the depreciation and inventory valuation biases. Further auxiliary variables were utilized to correct current earnings for cyclical and other biases so as to approximate "noise-free" earnings.

Our review of the principles of rational valuation implies that the price-earnings ratio should respond inversely to the real rate of interest, that is, to the *difference* between the nominal rate of interest and the rate of inflation. This means that increases in the nominal interest rate and in inflation should both affect the price-earnings ratio significantly, but in a largely offsetting fashion—the first reducing it, the second increasing it. Thus, if in a given period the nominal rate should increase, say, 10 percent, but inflation increases as much, then the P/E should not change. Actually, because our measure of profits was not adjusted for the gains from depreciation of the debt, the positive effect of inflation should more than offset the negative effect of interest rates. Put differently, with an unchanged real rate inflation should

105

increase the ratio of price to a measure of earnings which is understated by not incorporating the gain from the depreciation of the debt.

On the other hand, if there are valuation errors of the type we hypothesize, the effect of inflation should be less positive than under rational valuation. In the limit, if P/Es were controlled exclusively by nominal interest rates and profits were not corrected for the gain from debt, then the effect of inflation would be zero.

The results of our test were striking. The model was successful in accounting, quite closely, for the behavior of the price-earnings ratio throughout the period. The coefficient of inflation was close to zero; in fact, it was modestly *negative*. These findings are inconsistent with rational valuation and strongly supportive of both our hypotheses.

The results also provide a basis for assessing the quantitative effect of the valuation error on prices. We find that every percentage point increase in the steady-state inflation rate causes expected profits to fall by 5 percent and the capitalization rate to rise by 8 percent. Thus, every 1 percent increase in the long-run expected rate of inflation causes stock prices to fall by 13 percent in relation to true profits. Assuming that a permanent rate of inflation of 6-7 percent was anticipated at the end of 1977, stock prices at that time were undervalued on the order of 50 percent. We suspect that the level of undervaluation is not very different at present.

Criticism

Our hypothesis that market participants are making systematic errors in valuation has, not surprisingly, provoked a good deal of uneasiness on the part of our academic colleagues and the investment community and has elicited a fair amount of criticism.

One criticism is that it is not appropriate to treat the inflation premium component of interest as part of profit because it is not part of cash flow and is therefore not available for

106

distribution to shareholders. Two responses are in order. First, leverage measured as the ratio of net debt to the reproduction cost of corporate assets appears to be stable for the nonfinancial corporate sector. Such stability implies that corporations have tended to refinance the repayment of principal induced by the inflation premium, thereby restoring the cash which they would otherwise have lost because of that premium. Second, since cash flow is conventionally defined as profit after taxes plus noncash charges, this component of interest payments is part of cash flow because it is properly part of aftertax profits. It is a repayment of real principal and should no more be treated as a deduction from cash flow than any other principal repayment.

Another criticism we have received is that, at most, only part of the inflation premium component of interest should be added to conventionally measured profits because the inflation gain that accrues to the debtor corporation is offset by a corresponding loss to the corporate pension plan. This loss in the final analysis falls on the corporation as the de facto guarantor of the promises made by its pension plan to beneficiaries.

Here we must distinguish between the effect of anticipated inflation fully reflected in interest rates and the effect of unanticipated inflation. With respect to the former, inflation does not benefit debtors, for the debt devaluation precisely offsets the higher interest they pay. Thus the corporate debtor does not gain. By the same token, the creditor pension plan does not lose. In this case, therefore, there is only a downward bias in reported corporate income if one fails to add the inflation premium to profits. And, it might be noted, there is a corresponding upward bias in the pension plan's income if it treats interest entirely as current income rather than as partly a compensation for loss of real principal.

Unanticipated inflation, by contrast, is a source of real gain to the debtor insofar as it results in his paying a rate of interest below the current market rate and possibly negative in real terms. This gain is, to some extent, offset for the

107

entire corporate sector by the loss accruing to the creditor pension plans, though the extent of this offset would vary from firm to firm. However, these windfall gains and losses have nothing to do with the correction of profits for gains on monetary liabilities which we have advocated. To be sure, to the extent that fully corrected profits reflect some windfall gains but fail to reflect the corresponding windfall losses of corporate pension plans, there would be some ground for expected profits to be below actual profits, justifying some decline in the ratio of price to adjusted earnings. But this effect could explain no more than a small portion of the observed decline in the overall price-earnings ratios.

Yet another criticism has dealt with our model of equity valuation, which employs an earnings capitalization approach. We have been told that investors actually use a dividend discounting approach, and since dividends are simply dividends, an error in measuring profits can have no effect on valuation. But earnings capitalization and dividend discounting approaches to valuation should be consistent. Therefore, there must be something wrong with this argument. The difficulty is that expected future dividends must relate to expectations concerning the amount of earnings retained and reinvested; since retained earnings are the difference between total earnings and dividends, an underestimate of earnings leads to an underestimate of expected future dividends.

Perhaps the most challenging criticisms we have received are those which argue that inflation has produced a systematic, rationally warranted change in the price-earnings ratio. One of these criticisms argues that inflation has somehow reduced expected earnings relative to current earnings, specifically by reducing the anticipated real growth rate of corporate profits. Another holds that the rise in inflation has coincided with a rise in the risk premium that stock market investors require, perhaps because of oil price shocks, perhaps because of a climate unfavorable to business, perhaps because inflation itself has produced a new element of uncertainty in the economy, even if irrationally. The validity of these two

108

criticisms cannot easily be ruled out by means of time-series analysis because, while inflation can be directly measured, our critics have not offered an explicit measure of profit expectations or risk. However, some tests can be made by means of a comparative analysis of the values of individual stocks during the inflationary experience since the mid-1960s. Our attempt to apply this method is described below.

Cross-sectional analysis

The hypothesis of a rising market risk premium, which can be referred to as the Risk Premium Explanation (RPE), can be usefully illustrated by means of the graph in Figure 6-2. The vertical axis represents the required real rate of return as measured by the earnings-price ratio. Along the horizontal axis we measure the risk of individual stocks in terms of the well-known beta coefficient of the capital asset market model, as developed by Sharpe and others.[3] The lower upward-sloping solid line depicts the mid-1960s relationship between beta and the earnings-price ratio.

The intercept of this market line corresponds to the real (aftertax) interest rate, and the line rises since the required return increases with risk. The height of the line corresponding to a beta of one represents the average earnings-price ratio prevailing in the mid-1960s. Between the mid-1960s and the present the average earnings-price ratio roughly doubled, as shown by the upper horizontal dashed line, which represents the current level.

Any explanation of this current market earnings-price ratio must produce a market line which goes through the intersection of the higher dashed horizontal line and the vertical dashed line corresponding to a beta equal to unity. According to the MCH, the new market line can be approximated by the upper rising solid line. This is because the MCH

---

[3] W. F. Sharpe, "Capital Asset Price: The Theory of Market Equilibrium under Conditions of Risk," *Journal of Finance,* September 1964.

109

Figure 6-2: Alternative explanations of the collapse in price-earnings ratios since the mid-1960s

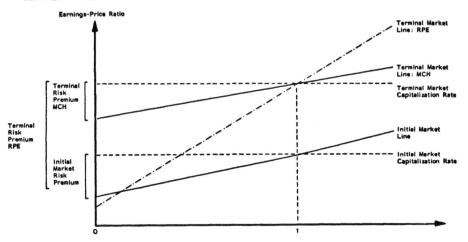

RPE: Risk premium explanation.
MCH: Modigliani-Cohn hypothesis.

attributes the change in the average earnings-price ratio to the fact that the inflation-induced rise in interest rates has produced an across-the-board rise in the required rate of return quite independently of the initial beta. If so, the market line must have shifted roughly parallel to its original position and the change in the average earnings-price ratio must be roughly the same as the rise in the intercept.

By contrast, according to the RPE, the new market line can be represented by something like the dotted dashed line. Indeed, according to this view, the intercept was initially and still remains the real aftertax rate of interest as called for by rational valuation. As that rate has actually fallen since the mid-1960s, the new intercept is somewhat lower than that of the original market line. The position of the market line is now fixed by that point and by the fact that it must go through the average earnings-price ratio at a beta of one. Thus, while earnings-price ratios for low-beta stocks should have been largely unchanged, those for high-beta stocks

110

should have increased substantially, enough to account for the increase in the average earnings-price ratio.

These alternative hypotheses have very different implications as to what should account for the change in the P/Es of individual stocks in the course of each period. The RPE suggests that there should have been little change in P/E for low-risk stocks and larger and larger declines for stocks characterized by high-beta risk. In other words, it is the high-beta stocks that are responsible for the decline in the average. We should thus observe a strong negative correlation between the change in price-earnings ratio and the beta of the stock.

According to the MCH, by contrast, there should be a clear negative association between the proportional change in the price-earnings ratio of a stock and its initial price-earnings ratio. The reason for this proposition is that the lower the initial earnings-price ratio, the larger the proportional increase that an increment to earnings-price ratios of a given amount represents and therefore the larger the proportional decline in P/E. To illustrate this point, suppose stock A had initially a P/E of 5, or an earnings-price ratio of 0.2, and stock B had a P/E of 20, or an earnings-price ratio of 0.05. Suppose further that because of inflation, interest rates rose by 500 basis points. According to the MCH, this would tend to increase all earnings-price ratios by that amount. For stock A, the earnings-price ratio would rise by one quarter, to 0.25, and the P/E would fall by 20 percent, to 4. For stock B, on the other hand, the earnings-price ratio would double, to 0.1, and the P/E would fall by 50 percent, a much greater decline than in the case of stock A. On the other hand, under the MCH one would not expect a significant relation between the change in the P/E and the initial beta.

In order to test these alternative hypotheses, we examined by means of regression analysis changes in price-earnings ratios in relation to the initial price-earnings ratio and beta for a sample of some 200 U.S. industrial corporations over the period from the end of 1968 to 1973, 1973 to 1978, and the entire decade 1968-78. These firms were selected with

111

the help of E. F. Hutton & Company securities analysts from those which they actively followed. The performance of these samples roughly matched that of the S&P Industrials. We included as independent variables information on earnings growth expectations and the change in the dividend payout ratio in order to control for changes in expected real growth that should have affected price-earnings ratios. We also employed a leverage measure as an independent variable in order to test our hypothesis that the market fails to correct profits for the inflation premium component of interest.[4]

The results of our study are strikingly supportive of the MCH and counter to the implications of the RPE.[5] It is, indeed, stocks that started out with a high P/E that suffered the largest relative decline; the estimated increase in the intercept of the market line over the 1968-78 period is on the order of the increase in inflation and interest rates. At the same time, there is no evidence that the high-beta stocks experienced above-average declines, as suggested by the RPE. If anything, high-beta stocks tended to perform relatively better. Thus our results imply that there is absolutely no evidence that the decline in the market was due to a rise in the risk premium as related to beta. If anything, the market risk premium appears to have declined during the 1968-78 period.

Our test also throws some light on the view that the market decline can be attributed to a decline in anticipated profits or in their growth rate. To test this notion, we secured estimates of five-year expected growth in earnings per share for each firm at the beginning of each interval. Our sources were the Value Line Investment Survey and E. F. Hutton securities analysts. We find that there was only a modest decline in the anticipated real growth rate of earnings be-

---

[4] The authors are deeply grateful to E. F. Hutton & Company, and particularly to Peter N. Smith of that firm, for providing us with much of the data that we required.

[5] The results are summarized in the appendix at the end of this chapter.

112

tween the beginning and end of the full period. In particular, there was essentially no change from the end of 1973 to the end of 1978, a period during which the average price-earnings ratio for the firms in our sample declined 36 percent.

Given rational valuation, one would have expected a noticeably positive relationship between leverage and the change in our measure of P/E, which was based on *reported* earnings not corrected for the effects of inflation. This is because the inflation premium component of interest increases with inflation, thus lowering reported earnings in relation to true earnings. But the observed relationship is actually negative, suggesting, as we had hypothesized on the basis of our time-series results, that leveraged firms are penalized by the market when interest rates rise in response to increases in expectations of inflation.

Conclusion

In summary, both our time-series and our cross-sectional results suggest that inflation, through its effect on nominal interest rates, has caused systematic valuation errors as a result of which stocks are at present seriously undervalued. The most undervalued shares appear to be those of firms characterized by relatively high price-earnings ratios, low betas, and high leverage.

What do our findings imply about the future course of stock prices? If the current historically low level of stock prices in relation to earnings is the result of a serious inflation-induced valuation error, as we have hypothesized and have endeavored to document, then this level cannot last indefinitely. Indeed, this is precisely what we mean by saying that equities are "undervalued." We mean that, provided earnings continue to keep up with inflation, as it seems only reasonable to expect, then current P/Es cannot endure. The reason is that a continuation of the current P/Es implies a return from equities so disproportionally high in relation to

113

the return from bonds and other fixed-rate instruments that investors could not fail to recognize that the market was seriously undervalued and to respond accordingly.

To illustrate this point, even after the rise in stock prices in 1980 the average earnings-price ratio for the S&P 500 was around 12 percent. With the rate of inflation running around 10 percent, a constant P/E implies a 10 percent rise in stock prices on this account alone, and thus a total nominal rate of return of 22 percent. This compares with a return on corporate bonds of about 14-15 percent in late 1980.

But the differential is even more dramatic on an aftertax basis, which is the relevant one. For equities, the only portion of the 22 percent return subject to income tax is the dividend, which amounts to some 5 percent. Assuming a representative marginal tax rate of 40 percent, the aftertax real return of equities would come to 10 percent. One must also allow for the effect of the capital gains tax, which is harder to estimate because of its deferrability. A reasonable guess of its present value might be perhaps 150 basis points, leaving a net real return of roughly 8½ percent. For corporate bonds, on the other hand, a similar calculation yields a real aftertax return of minus 2 percent. An alternative calculation based on tax-exempt bonds yields a slightly higher return of plus 1 percent. A differential of this magnitude between stocks and bonds, if maintained, cannot fail to induce investors to shift the composition of their portfolios in the direction of equities, thus bidding up equity prices until P/Es have moved back (or possibly snapped back) to a level consistent with rational valuation.

Even though P/Es could not stabilize without setting the stage for significant recovery, one can conceive of an alternative scenario in which, as in recent years, P/Es tend to sag. For when P/Es decline, the undervaluation implicit in unduly large earnings-price ratios is hidden from investors as the high return from earnings is offset, possibly more than offset, by the capital loss resulting from the sinking price.

How likely is this alternative scenario? In terms of our

114

hypothesis of irrational behavior, this could only happen if the rate of inflation continued to increase steadily over the coming years. While it is not our purpose here to evaluate the probability of such a trend, we would like to note that even if nominal interest rates should continue to rise under the spur of rising inflation, a further decline in P/Es is not inevitable. We have shown that such a decline is the result of irrational inflation illusion. We believe it entirely possible that the market may gradually learn to see through inflation fallacies—even without the benefit of reading our papers. Indeed, one might interpret recent market action as supporting this hopeful belief. To conclude, one can see many reasons why—before too long—the market should stage a healthy recovery toward the much higher level called for by rational valuation. But anyone who pursues an investment policy based on rational valuation in a world in which lapses from rationality seem to have a way of persisting does so at his peril.

APPENDIX

In the equations reported below (in Exhibit A-1), which are representative of those we obtained in our cross-sectional study, the dependent variable is the change in the logarithm of the price-earnings ratio.

The sample size represents the number of firms for which all of the relevant information was available.

The critical coefficients from the standpoint of our hypothesis are those of P/x and D_0. The absolute values of the coefficients of P/x represent estimates of the increase, measured as a decimal, in the intercept of the market line referred to in the text. The reported estimates of the coefficients for the two time periods are somewhat larger than the corresponding increases in interest rates, but these estimates are probably upward-biased, primarily because of the general tendency of price-earnings ratios to regress toward the mean. After correcting for this bias, we estimate the increase in the

115

Exhibit A-1

Time period	Number of observations	Independent variable	Estimated coefficient	$t =$ statistic	Mean value
1968-73	177	a_0	-.066	-0.54	
		P/x	-.032	-2.41	20.67
		D_0	-.027	-2.32	2.74
		$\beta \cdot P/x$	.012	1.21	21.59
		$\dot{d} - \dot{\pi}$	.543	4.02	-0.28
		$\dot{x} \cdot P/x$	.025	5.00	9.32
		$(g_1 - g_0)P/x$	.001	1.90	-2.73
1973-78	175	a_0	.158	3.56	
		P/x	-.043	-7.12	17.86
		D_0	-.020	-3.02	2.62
		$\beta \cdot P/x$	.010	2.13	18.82
		$\dot{d} - \dot{\pi}$	.286	4.93	0.01
		$(g_1 - g_0)P/x$	.0004	1.93	33.66

Where

a_0 = Constant term
P = Initial price per share
x = Weighted average of initial earnings and dividend per share
D_0 = Initial ratio of net debt to earnings
β = Equity beta
$\dot{d} - \dot{\pi}$ = Change in logarithm of dividend payout ratio over the period
$\dot{x}$ = Change in logarithm of x over the period
$g_1 - g_0$ = Change in expected percentage growth in x over the period

intercept of the market line to be .025 and .033 over the 1968-73 and 1973-78 periods, respectively.

The other coefficients of interest, those of the leverage variable, D_0, should be positive according to rational valuation. As indicated in the text, however, and as shown, their estimated values are negative.

Errata

Page 110, Figure 6-2: the x-axis should be labeled "B."

Page 111, third paragraph: the last sentence is incorrect because B is one determinant of P/E. However, one can readily establish that the relation between ΔP/E and B implied by MCH has sign opposite to that implied by RPE. This is what the data actually show—see the report on empirical results that follows.

117

THE INFLATION-PROOF MORTGAGE: THE MORTGAGE FOR THE YOUNG

Franco Modigliani

The inflation of the past fifteen years has produced devastating effects on the housing industry all over the world. The rise in mortgage rates that has accompanied, and roughly matched, the rise in inflation has placed home ownership out of the reach of major portions of the population, notably the young and the first-time owners. Simultaneously the rapid rise and increase in volatility of interest rates has nearly wrecked the major suppliers of funds for home financing and in particular that sector of the financial system that has traditionally provided mortgage funds, financing them with relatively short-term liabilities. Even where the acquisition of houses has been financed by mortgage bonds issued by specialized mortgage banks, the loss of value and the price variability of these instruments has profoundly disrupted their market.

Both of these problems can be largely traced to a common cause, namely, the overwhelming reliance for home financing on the conventional, fully amortized, level-payment, long-term mortgage. To be sure, this instrument, which became popular in the aftermath of the great depression, represented a vast improvement over methods prevailing in earlier days and has proved of great value—but only as long as inflation has been of very modest proportions. But that same financing vehicle has turned out to be conspicuously unsuitable and outright harmful for a world of high and fluctuating inflation and interest rates. The reasons for this failure can be summarized as follows:

1. As financial analysis suggests, and recent experience broadly confirms, the long-term rate is highly responsive to inflation; to a good approximation an increase in inflation by one percentage point tends to be accompanied by a one-percentage-point rise in market interest rates. At first glance one might think that this adjustment of interest rate to inflation would ensure that the monthly payments required to finance a house with a conventional mortgage would rise in line with inflation—for example, an increase of inflation from 0 to 5 percent would increase payment by 5 percent. But in fact this inference is totally wrong—the change in payments required is far greater than that. To illustrate, suppose we take as a base the interest rate

that used to prevail in the pre-inflationary decades of the 1950s and 1960s, around 5 percent; it then turns out that for every *1-percent* increase in the interest rate above this base the monthly payment on a long-term mortgage (25 years or longer) rises by some *10 percent* and more.

It follows that inflation, even of moderate size, has a dramatic effect in increasing the share of income that a family must earmark to meet its monthly payments. To illustrate, suppose that a family bought a house worth the traditional 2½-times income. With zero inflation and a 5-percent interest rate, it would take 20 percent of the family income to finance the house on a 20-year mortgage. If instead inflation were to rise to 5 percent, and hence the mortgage rate to 10 percent, the monthly mortgage payment would become *50 percent larger* (10 times the rise in interest rate of 5 percentage points); the share of initial income needed to meet the monthly payment would thus rise from 20 to 30 percent. Similarly with a 10-percent inflation the initial share could be expected to rise further to 40 percent, or twice the zero-inflation figure, and so on. It is no surprise then that with widespread double-digit inflation, so many young people can no longer afford the house they could aspire to only a few years back.

2. When there is large uncertainty over the future of inflation, the conventional mortgage exposes the borrower and lender to a very high risk as to the real cost of acquiring a house and as to the real return from the investment. Until recently, because inflation has tended to rise above expectation and government policy has endeavored to hold down nominal rates relative to inflation, the risk has resolved itself into an actual outcome favorable to the borrower and unfavorable to the long-term lender. But, especially with the recent large rise in the nominal rate, and evidence that inflation is finally coming under control, it is entirely possible that over the next 20 or 30 years of a contract, inflation will turn out appreciably larger or smaller than the expectation reflected in nominal rates. This added uncertainty, to the extent that it falls on the borrower, tends to further increase the subjective cost of buying a house on credit. To be sure, the risk to the borrower from lower inflation will be reduced to the extent that the law, or contractual arrangements, give him the right to repay the loan at little or no penalty (call option). But in this case the risk is merely shifted to the supplier of funds, who will endeavor to recoup through higher rates or by charging "points" or both.

3. The increase in the long-term rates that has accompanied rising inflation has hurt all creditors that have lent long-term at a fixed interest rate. These include institutions that have supplied mortgages, which is one of the longest-term instruments presently in use. But it has hurt particularly severely those institutions that have financed mortgages with short-term funds, such as short-term deposits. A case in point is that of the saving and loan industry in the United States, and similar institutions in many other

parts of the world. These financial institutions have seen their profits dwindle since the second half of the 1960s or early 1970s and even turn negative, because they had to pay much higher rates to secure the funds needed to finance their outstanding mortgages than they were obtaining from the "older" portion of their portfolio. Equivalently the value of their assets has tended to fall short of that of their liabilities.

In recent years there have been many attempts at eliminating, or at least mitigating, the shortcomings of the traditional mortgage—high initial payment for borrowers and the risk of fluctuations in future interest rates and inflation for borrowers and lenders. These attempts have taken the form of variants of the conventional mortgage, such as variable interest rate, graduated-payment, roll-over, shared-appreciation mortgages, and the indexed mortgage, just to mention the major types. But in my view none of these proposals provides a satisfactory solution to the distortions caused by inflation. They generally address but one of the problem areas, at the cost of aggravating other shortcomings. To understand why these remedies have failed to provide the answer, one must consider just how and why inflation destroys the usefulness of the conventional mortgage.

As has been demonstrated in the literature, the problem described under 1—the prohibitively high initial monthly payment—cannot be attributed merely to the fact that inflation increases interest rates. For the rise in interest rates is only intended to compensate the lender (and recapture from the borrower) the inflation-induced erosion in the purchasing power of the outstanding principal, thus preventing inflation from reducing the overall return to the lender and cost to the borrower. Why then does inflation have such a disruptive effect on the monthly payment of a house financed by a conventional mortgage? The reason is that with a conventional mortgage inflation produces a drastic distortion in the way in which the unchanged cost is distributed over the life of the mortgage. It does so because the conventional mortgage calls for a monthly payment that is level in nominal terms. But in the face of inflation this implies a "real" payment (that is, measured in dollars of constant purchasing power), which declines steadily as the debt approaches maturity. The resulting "tilt" in the path of the real monthly payment means that a conventional mortgage calls for an initial real payment that is much higher than would be required in the absence of inflation—for example, 100 percent higher, for a rate of inflation no more than 10 percent—to make up for the fact that eventually inflation will cause the payment to become much too small in real terms.

In short with the conventional mortgage inflation has the effect of redistributing the total cost of financing, placing a growing portion of that cost up front, where a large class of would-be home buyers can afford it least, if at all. This class includes in particular younger households at the beginning of their careers and hence with income below life expectation, having little accumulated equity, and frequently carrying an above-normal family load.

Clearly what is needed to eliminate this shortcoming of the conventional mortgage is an alternative instrument that eliminates that redistribution and gives rise to a *real* (rather than nominal) *payment stream*, which, independent of the size, variability, and predictability of inflation and nominal interest rates, is roughly as stable, predictable, and low-start as *that generated by the conventional mortgage when there is no inflation.*

On the other hand the problems described under 2 and 3—the uncertainty of future nominal and real interest rates resulting from a long-term nominal contract—need to be handled by appropriately extending to home financing the device that has long been adopted in other loan markets to deal with the uncertainty of future interest rates, namely, replacing the fixed long-term interest rate with a floating rate, anchored to some suitably chosen, short-term market rate.

The Inflation-proof Mortgage (IPM)[*] is designed to eliminate the major shortcomings of existing methods of financing by satisfying simultaneously the two requirements. The basic principles underlying this type of mortgage were developed at the Massachusetts Institute of Technology by a research team, including members of the Economics and Finance Department, headed by myself[†], with a special view of relieving the serious problems created by inflation for first-time buyers in general and the young in particular.

A Brief Description of the IPM and How it Works

In a nutshell the IPM endeavors to insulate borrowers from the effects of inflation by offering them an initial monthly payment which, relative to their income, is roughly equal to what they would have to pay at the low interest rates that would prevail in the absence of significant inflation. For the United States at present, with the prevailing market mortgage rate in the 12-to 14-percent range, this means, for the typical 20- to 30-year mortgage, a payment at least one-third lower than with a conventional mortgage. The payment would thereafter tend to rise over the life of the mortgage, as in a "graduated payment" mortgage, but the rise would occur only insofar as and to the extent that high inflation and high interest rates were to continue to prevail. Most important the rise from year to year would occur in moderate steps, *designed to remain below the rise in the price level*, and

---

[*]The loan instrument described in this paper has also been or may be referred to in other papers by several other names, in particular, the Flexible Graduated Payment Mortgage (FGPM), the MIT Dual Rate Mortgage, the Affordable Variable Rate Mortgage (AVRM).

[†]For a fuller description, see Franco Modigliani and Donald Lessard (eds.), "New Mortgage Design for a Stable Housing in an Inflationary Environment," Federal Reserve Bank of Boston, Conference Series No. 14. (Reprinted in this volume.)

therefore also below the growth in the typical or average income of families qualifying for a mortgage loan. In other words even though the nominal payment might rise, the payment, measured in real terms, or as a fraction of family income, would tend to decline over the life of the contract.

At the same time the IPM is designed to eliminate the risks that arise for lenders or borrowers or both, in the presence of high and unpredictable inflation, from unforeseeable changes in nominal and real interest rates and from financing long-term fixed interest loans with short-term funds. Offering the lender a *yield that floats* with a chosen reference market rate, such as the U.S. Treasury Bill rate, ensures the lender a return that at all times keeps up with the return available in the market and therefore also protects the market value of the principal by maintaining it close to par. In particular it would enable saving institutions to finance 20- or 30-year mortgages from short-term deposits or other short-term funds, while eliminating the risk inherent in the mismatching of maturities, for it ensures them at all times a return that keeps up with the cost of acquiring and retaining short-term funds.

These results are achieved by making use of two distinct interest rates—a floating "effective rate," which controls what the borrower and lender effectively pay and receive, and a fixed "payment rate," whose only purpose is to ensure a desirable, affordable path of monthly payments:

1. *The "Effective Rate"*: The *borrower pays* (and hence the lender receives), on the *balance outstanding* at any point of time, *an interest rate*, called *the effective rate*, that is *adjusted periodically*—say annually—*on the basis of an agreed-upon reference short-term rate*. As indicated, such a short-term rate could be the U.S. Treasury Bill rate or the commercial paper rate for some stated term, for example, one year.

2. *The "Payment Rate" and the calculation of the monthly payment*: In the conventional mortgage the monthly payment is computed for the duration of the loan by applying to the initial debt a factor that converts the amount borrowed into a sequence of equal monthly installments. This conversion factor is called hereafter the "payment factor." Its value depends on the agreed-upon mortgage rate, but exceeds it by an amount that reflects the smooth amortization of the principal and that is larger the shorter the duration of the loan.

In the IPM the monthly payment is also based on an interest rate that is fixed for the duration of the contract—the *payment rate*. But the computation of the monthly payment differs from the conventional mortgage in three fundamental respects:

1. The fixed payment rate has no bearing on the interest rate actually earned by the lender and paid by the borrower, which depends only on the effective rate. It is merely a device for scheduling the monthly payments in such a way as to ensure that the repayment of principal and interest over the life of

the mortgage will occur in a conveniently smooth and affordable fashion, without jeopardizing the security of the lender.

2. The monthly payments are recomputed at regular intervals—say, once a year. The payments for the next twelve months are set at the rate that is required to repay the principal that is outstanding at that time plus interest in equal installments over the remaining life of the mortgage, at an interest rate equal to the "payment interest rate" (which is fixed by the contract and is completely independent of the variable effective rate). Equivalently the monthly payment for the year is computed by applying, to the beginning-of-the-year balance, the "payment factor" that would apply to a new mortgage with a maturity equal to the *remaining* life of the IPM and carrying an interest rate equal to the payment interest rate. The payment factor—the payment scheduled for the current year as a percentage of the balance due at the beginning of the year—will of course grow toward 100 percent as the mortgage approaches maturity—in the last year it actually exceeds 100 percent per year (by the effective rate), so as to ensure full repayment of the debt.

3. *The principal at the beginning of each year* of the contract is the balance at the beginning of the previous year adjusted by the difference between the amount credited to borrowers, on account of their scheduled monthly payment and the amount debited to them, on account of the interest effectively due for that year, as determined by the debit balance and the effective rate.

3. *The choice of payment rate*: Because both the payment factor and the opening balance to which it is applied vary from year to year, depending on the actual course of the effective rate, the monthly payment will change in time as with an adjusted rate mortgage (ARM) or graduated payment mortgage (GPM). But with these types of mortgages, the path of the monthly payments has harmful, undesirable properties for the borrower or the lender, or both. In the case of the IPM, on the other hand, a desirable path can be achieved by an appropriate choice of the payment rate. This rate should be chosen as to roughly equal the average real short-term rate expected to prevail during the life of the contract, plus a moderate "safety" margin (say, around 2 percentage points). Under present circumstances, and including an intermediation margin of the order of 200 basis points, the prospective real rate that the borrower can expect to pay can be placed at 3 to 5 percent. Allowing further for the safety margin finally suggests a possible range for the "payment rate" of some 7 percent, plus or minus 1 percentage point.

Some Illustrative Examples Based on Recent American Experience

The mechanics of the computation of the monthly payment and of the outstanding balance for the IPM is illustrated in table 1. (To conserve space

Table 1 Performance of a 20-Year IPM beginning in 1972 with a Payment Rate of 7 percent

	(1)	(2)	(3)	(4)	(5)	(6)	(7)	(8)	(9)	(10)	(11)	(12)	(13)
Year	Outstanding Principal	Payment Factor	Total Annual Payment	Effective Interest Rate	Interest Charged	Amortization (3) − (5)	Principal Year End (1) − (6)	Deflator	Inflation Rate	Payment Over Deflator (3)/(8)×100	Payment Over Per Capita Disposable Income 1972=100	Principal Over Deflator (7)/(8)	Payment Over Residential Rent Index 1972=100
1972	100000.00	0.09439	9439.00	0.0628	6280.00	3159.00	96841.00	100.00	—	9439.00	100	96841.00	100
1973	96841.00	0.09675	9369.37	0.0789	7640.75	1728.61	95112.39	105.70	0.06	8864.11	89	89983.34	95
1974	95112.39	0.09941	9455.12	0.0942	8959.59	495.54	94616.85	116.40	0.10	8123.20	81	81288.40	91
1975	94616.85	0.10243	9691.60	0.0883	8354.67	1336.94	93279.92	125.30	0.08	7734.68	78	74444.87	89
1976	93279.92	0.10586	9874.61	0.0781	7285.16	2589.45	90690.47	131.70	0.05	7497.67	74	68860.15	86
1977	90690.47	0.10979	9956.91	0.0729	6611.33	3345.57	87344.89	139.30	0.06	7147.85	68	62703.03	82
1978	87344.89	0.11434	9987.02	0.0928	8105.61	1881.41	85463.49	149.10	0.07	6698.21	62	57319.62	77
1979	85463.49	0.11965	10225.71	0.1241	10606.02	−380.31	85843.80	162.50	0.09	6292.71	57	52826.65	73
1980	85843.80	0.1259	10807.73	0.1406	12069.64	−1261.90	87105.70	179.00	0.10	6037.84	55	48662.40	71
1981	87105.70	0.13336	11616.42	0.1608	14006.60	−2390.18	89495.88	194.10	0.08	5984.76	53	46108.13	70
1982	89495.88	0.14238	12742.42	0.1632	14605.73	−1863.30	91359.19	205.30	0.06	6206.73	56	44500.33	72
1983	91359.19	0.15349	14022.72	0.1078	9848.52	4174.20	87184.99	214.00	0.04	6552.67	56	40740.65	77
1984	87184.99	0.16747	14600.87	0.10	8718.50	5882.37	81302.61	226.84	0.06	6436.64	54	35841.39	75
1985	81302.61	0.18555	15085.70	0.10	8130.26	6955.44	74347.18	240.45	0.06	6273.93	52	30919.96	74
1986	74347.18	0.2098	15598.04	0.10	7434.72	8163.32	66183.86	254.88	0.06	6119.82	50	25966.94	73
1987	66183.86	0.24389	16141.58	0.10	6618.39	9523.20	56660.66	270.17	0.06	5974.60	49	20972.22	72
1988	56660.66	0.29523	16727.93	0.10	5666.07	11061.86	45598.80	286.38	0.06	5841.16	47	15922.47	71
1989	45598.80	0.38105	17375.42	0.10	4559.88	12815.54	32783.26	303.56	0.06	5723.83	46	10799.49	70
1990	32783.26	0.55309	18132.09	0.10	3278.33	14853.77	17929.49	321.78	0.06	5634.99	45	5572.03	70
1991	17929.49	1.10	19722.44	0.10	1792.95	17929.49	0.00	341.08	0.06	5782.29	46	0.00	72
Totals			260572.70		160572.70	100000.00							

Column 1: *Principal year start* is the loan balance remaining to be paid at the start of a year.

Column 2: *Payment factor* is the amount that must be paid, per dollar of outstanding principal, on a 7 percent mortgage with a life equal to the remaining term to maturity. It is taken from a standard mortgage table and includes both interest and amortization of principal.

Column 3: *Annual payment* is the amount the borrower pays, that is, principal times annuity factor.

Column 4: *Effective rate* is for one-year U.S. Treasury Bill yield for the first week of each year, plus a 2-percent premium. From 1984 on the rate is assumed to be 10 percent.

Column 5: *Interest charges* are principal at year's start (Column 1) times effective rate (column 4).

Column 6: *Amortization* is the amount by which the outstanding principal changes in given year. It is the borrower payment of column 3 minus the interest due of column 5. Amortization will be a variable amount. When it is positive, the outstanding principal (column 7) declines. Under certain conditions it may be negative (1979–1982), in which case the principal rises.

Column 7: *Principal year end* is the beginning principal (column 1) less amortization (column 6).

Column 8: *Personal consumption deflator* is the index of prices of consumers' goods and services as measured by the Department of Commerce, Bureau of Economic Analysis. From 1984 on it is assumed to rise at constant rate of 6 percent per year.

Column 10: *Real payment* is the borrower's payment divided by the personal consumption deflator (column 8 divided by 100). It translates the borrower payment from current dollars into dollars of the year the loan began.

Column 11: This is the ratio of annual payment (column 3) to average (per capita) disposable income (that is, income inclusive of Social Security, unemployment compensation, and other transfers, less personal taxes). Index: 1972 = 100. From 1984 on it is assumed that per capita income rises 7 percent per year (implying a conservative 1 percent per year growth of real per capita income).

Column 12: This is the year-end principal of column 7 divided by the consumption deflator (column 8 divided by 100). It expresses the debt outstanding at each year's end in dollars of constant purchasing power of the year the loan began.

Column 13: Index of the ratio of the annual payment (column 3) to an index of residential rental rates, as measured by the Residential Rent component of the Bureau of Labor Statistics' Cost of Living Index. Index: 1972 = 100. From 1984 on, in line with historical experience, the rent index is assumed to grow 1 percent per year less than the overall cost of living (that is, at 5 percent per year).

---

in the tables, we assume the borrower makes a single payment per year.) Table 1 also provides a picture of how creditors and debtors would have fared if they had entered into a $100,000, 20-year IPM at the beginning of 1972, choosing 7 percent as the payment rate, and the one-year Treasury Bill rate plus a spread of 2 percent as the effective rate. For the years from 1984 to maturity in 1991, the effective rate is assumed at 10 percent and the inflation rate at 6 percent. The meaning and operational definition of the entries in each of the columns is explained in the notes of table 1.

Table 2 shows a similar calculation, but on the assumption that the IPM was entered on at beginning of 1976 instead of 1972, thus much closer to the time of the unprecedented escalation of interest rates that began in 1978 and culminated in early 1982.

Tables 3A and 3B cover the same experience as tables 1 and 2, except that it reports the monthly payments, recomputed each year, rather than the annual payments for each calendar year, and the reference rate used to compute the effective rate for each year is the average value of the Treasury Bill rate for November and December of the year before, whereas tables 1 and 2 are based on the more erratic value for a single week—the first of the given year.

Figure 1 shows the time path of the annual payment of table 2 both in nominal terms—column 3—and in real terms—column 10—comparing it with the corresponding payment path for a conventional level payment mortgage.*

Basic Properties of the IPM—Determinants of the Time Profile of the Annual Payment and Debt Balance, and the Choice of the "Payment Interest Rate."

The preceding examples also serve to illustrate the essential properties of the IPM that make it uniquely suitable for financing long-term mortgages in the presence of high and variable inflation.

1. The borrower's payment begins basically at the same level that prevails in the absence of inflation. Thus the payment is unaffected by the escalation of nominal rates accompanying inflation, in contrast to the conventional mortgage or the ARM for which the initial payment increases with inflation by something on the order of 10 percent and over (relative to the no-inflation payment) per 1-percent rise in inflation.

2. In the ensuing years the payment may rise or fall depending on the relation between the variable effective rate and the fixed payment rate. The next year's payment will exceed the current payment if and when the current year's effective rate exceeds the payment rate; it will fall in the opposite case. And in either case the percentage change from the year before is approximately equal to—though somewhat larger than—the spread between the two rates. (The exact relation between the percentage change in monthly payment and the spread varies somewhat over the life of the contract). This relation can be readily verified in table 1. For instance, in 1974 the effective rate—column 4—was 9.4 percent or 2.4 percent above the 7 percent payment rate. It is seen from column 3 that the 1975 annual payment is 2.5 percent larger than in 1974. On the other hand in 1973 the payment falls slight-

---

*The small difference between the graph and the figures of columns 3 and 10 arises from the fact that the figure includes an extra charge of ¼ of 1 percent, for insurance.

Table 2 Performance of a 20-Year IPM beginning in 1976 with a Payment Rate of 7 percent

Year	(1) Outstanding Principal	(2) Payment Factor	(3) Total Annual Payment	(4) Effective Interest Rate	(5) Interest Charged	(6) Amortization (3) − (5)	(7) Principal Year End (1) − (6)	(8) Deflator	(9) Inflation Rate	(10) Payment Over Deflator (3)/(8) × 100	(11) Payment Over Per Capita Disposable Income 1976 = 100	(12) Principal Over Deflator (7)/(8)	(13) Payment Over Residential Rent Index 1976 = 100
1976	100000.00	0.09439	9439.00	0.0781	7810.00	1629.00	98371.00	100.00	—	9439.00	100	98371.00	100
1977	98371.00	0.09675	9517.39	0.0729	7171.25	2346.15	96024.85	105.77	0.06	8998.14	93	90785.88	95
1978	96024.85	0.09941	9545.83	0.0928	8911.11	634.72	95390.13	113.21	0.07	8431.83	84	84258.08	89
1979	95390.13	0.10243	9770.81	0.1241	11837.91	−2067.10	97457.23	123.39	0.09	7918.87	78	78985.34	85
1980	97457.23	0.10586	10316.82	0.1406	13702.49	−3385.66	100842.90	135.91	0.10	7590.65	75	74195.58	83
1981	100842.90	0.10979	11071.54	0.1608	16215.54	−5144.00	105986.89	147.38	0.08	7512.22	72	71913.83	82
1982	105986.89	0.11434	12118.54	0.1632	17297.06	−5178.52	111165.41	155.88	0.06	7774.05	75	71312.64	83
1983	111165.41	0.11965	13300.94	0.1073	11983.63	1317.31	109848.10	162.49	0.04	8185.67	75	67602.78	88
1984	109848.10	0.1259	13829.88	0.10	10984.81	2845.07	107003.04	172.24	0.06	8029.42	73	62124.40	87
1985	107003.04	0.13336	14269.92	0.10	10700.30	3569.62	103433.41	182.57	0.06	7815.95	70	56652.77	85
1986	103433.41	0.14238	14726.85	0.10	10343.34	4383.51	99049.91	193.53	0.06	7609.64	67	51180.97	84
1987	99049.91	0.15349	15203.17	0.10	9904.99	5298.18	93751.73	205.14	0.06	7411.10	65	45701.22	82
1988	93751.73	0.16747	15700.60	0.10	9375.17	6325.43	87426.30	217.45	0.06	7220.36	63	40205.43	81
1989	87426.30	0.18555	16221.95	0.10	8742.63	7479.32	79946.98	230.50	0.06	7037.85	61	34684.77	80
1990	79946.98	0.2098	16772.88	0.10	7994.70	8778.18	71168.80	244.33	0.06	6864.97	59	29128.67	79
1991	71168.80	0.24389	17357.36	0.10	7116.88	10240.48	60928.32	258.99	0.06	6702.07	57	23525.79	78
1992	60928.32	0.29523	17987.87	0.10	6092.83	11895.04	49033.28	274.52	0.06	6552.38	55	17861.18	77
1993	49033.28	0.38105	18684.13	0.10	4903.33	13780.80	35252.48	291.00	0.06	6420.76	53	12114.43	76
1994	35252.48	0.55309	19497.79	0.10	3525.25	15972.55	19279.93	308.46	0.06	6321.10	52	6250.48	75
1995	19279.93	1.10	21207.93	0.10	1927.99	19279.93	0.00	326.96	0.06	6486.34	50	0.00	78
Totals			286541.21		186541.21	100000.00							

For definitions, see notes to table 1.

Table 3 A   MIT Inflation-proof Mortgage, Payment Rate of 7.0 Percent

Year	March Balance	Repayment Factor	Monthly Payment	T-Note Rate + 2.0%	Interest Charges	Inflation	Real Balance	Real Payment
1972	10000.00	0.007753	77.53	0.0644	52.95	0.0000	10000.00	77.53
1973	9705.04	0.007942	77.08	0.0734	58.75	0.0405	9327.41	74.08
1974	9485.13	0.008155	77.35	0.0952	75.16	0.0905	8359.78	68.17
1975	9458.79	0.008397	79.43	0.0950	74.68	0.0928	7628.80	64.06
1976	9401.78	0.008672	81.53	0.0846	65.68	0.0563	7178.48	62.25
1977	9211.56	0.008988	82.79	0.0710	53.56	0.0549	6667.42	59.92
1978	8860.83	0.009354	82.88	0.0896	65.46	0.0579	6062.67	56.71
1979	8651.77	0.009781	84.62	0.1216	87.85	0.0873	5444.55	53.25
1980	8690.48	0.010284	89.37	0.1418	103.59	0.1000	4971.74	51.13
1981	8861.16	0.010884	96.44	0.1652	124.01	0.0950	4629.73	50.39
1982	9192.05	0.011611	106.73	0.1463	112.44	0.0666	4502.60	52.28
1983	9260.56	0.012506	115.81	0.1104	83.60	0.0416	4354.80	54.46
1984	8874.03	0.013634	120.99	0.1200	86.91	0.0500	3974.41	54.19
1985	8465.03	0.015093	127.76	0.1000	67.84	0.0600	3576.63	53.98
1986	7746.04	0.017049	132.06	0.1000	61.37	0.0600	3087.59	52.64
1987	6897.75	0.019801	136.58	0.1000	53.75	0.0600	2593.83	51.36
1988	5903.83	0.023946	141.37	0.1000	44.86	0.0600	2094.41	50.15
1989	4745.65	0.030877	146.53	0.1000	34.51	0.0600	1588.25	49.04
1990	3401.36	0.044772	152.29	0.1000	22.50	0.0600	1073.91	48.08
1991	1843.91	0.087916	162.11	0.1000	8.45	0.0600	549.22	48.29
Totals			26055.00		16055.00		−0.01	13583.50

Nov./Dec. 1-year T-Note rate, March 1st change date, first quarter PCE deflator.

Saving, Deficits, Inflation, and Financial Theory

Table 3 B MIT Inflation-proof Mortgage. Payment Rate of 7.0 Percent

Year	March Balance	Repayment Factor	Monthly Payment	T-Note Rate + 2.0%	Interest Charges	Inflation	Real Balance	Real Payment
1976	10000.00	0.007753	77.53	0.0846	70.22	0.0000	10000.00	77.53
1977	9912.30	0.007942	78.72	0.0710	57.98	0.0549	9396.71	74.63
1978	9663.44	0.008155	78.81	0.0896	71.87	0.0579	8659.62	70.62
1979	9580.19	0.008397	80.44	0.1216	98.04	0.0873	7896.03	66.30
1980	9791.38	0.008672	84.91	0.1418	117.78	0.1000	7336.45	63.62
1981	10185.87	0.008988	91.55	0.1652	144.09	0.0950	6970.13	62.65
1982	10816.31	0.009354	101.18	0.1463	134.01	0.0666	6939.17	64.91
1983	11210.29	0.009781	109.65	0.1104	102.79	0.0416	6904.39	67.53
1984	11128.00	0.010284	114.44	0.1200	111.10	0.0500	6527.48	67.13
1985	11087.92	0.010884	120.68	0.1000	91.07	0.0600	6135.82	66.78
1986	10732.57	0.011611	124.62	0.1000	87.78	0.0600	5603.00	65.06
1987	10290.48	0.012506	128.69	0.1000	83.73	0.0600	5068.12	63.38
1988	9750.96	0.013634	132.94	0.1000	78.82	0.0600	4530.57	61.77
1989	9101.56	0.105093	137.37	0.1000	72.95	0.0600	3989.47	60.21
1990	8328.50	0.017049	141.99	0.1000	65.98	0.0600	3443.98	58.72
1991	7416.41	0.019801	146.85	0.1000	57.79	0.0600	2893.22	57.29
1992	6347.74	0.023946	152.00	0.1000	48.23	0.0600	2336.15	55.94
1993	5102.47	0.030877	157.55	0.1000	37.10	0.0600	1771.56	54.70
1994	3657.07	0.044772	163.73	0.1000	24.20	0.0600	1197.85	53.63
1995	1982.68	0.087916	174.31	0.1000	9.09	0.0600	612.66	53.86
Totals	−0.01		28775.50		18775.50			15195.10

Nov./Dec. 1-year T-Note rate, March 1st change date, first quarter PCE deflator.

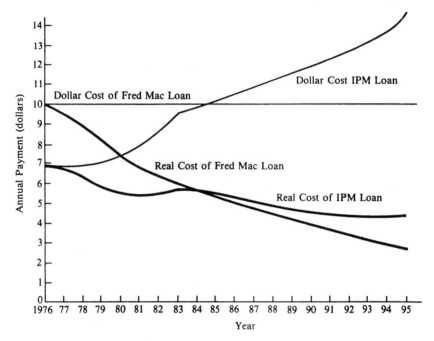

Figure 1. Comparison of nominal and real payments for an IPM and a 13.25-percent interest rate level payment mortgage loan of $70,000, if made in January 1976. Assumptions: (1) IPM 7-percent payment rate, 10-percent effective rate after 1983. (2) Inflation rate is GNP deflator to 1982; 6 percent per annum thereafter.

ly below the 1972 level because the effective rate in 1972 was below 7 percent.

The relation between the effective rate, the payment rate, and the change in the annual payment constitutes the very essence of the IPM and the key for an understanding of its desirable properties. For we know from well-established historical experience that in the absence of significant inflation, it is highly unlikely that our reference rate, the Treasury Bill rate, could rise above 5 percent and hence that the effective rate—Treasury Bill plus 2 percent—could rise above 7 percent, the rate we recommend for the payment interest rate. Put differently, whenever the effective rate has exceeded 7 percent, the rate of inflation has typically been positive and in fact 2 to 4 percentage points larger than the difference between the two rates. This relation holds with but few exceptions, generally related to episodes of extreme stringency in monetary policy. But this means that if and when a rise in the market rate above the 7-percent payment rate faces the borrower with a larger payment, all other prices and incomes will be rising too, and typically even faster, by some 2 to 4 percent. Thus the larger dollar outlay will actually tend to represent a fall in the payment, measured in "real terms" or in terms of dollars of constant purchasing power.

Saving, Deficits, Inflation, and Financial Theory

This conclusion is clearly supported by the historical experience summed up in column 10 of tables 1 and 2. Despite the high interest rates and the resulting sizable increases in the annual payment—column 3—that occurred since the first oil shock in 1974, the "real" payment—column 10—has tended to decline year after year, with but a few modest exceptions. Similarly column 11 shows that even in years when the *annual payment* has risen, it *tended to increase less fast than average after-tax income* as measured by per capita disposable income—again with few and modest exception. Finally, column 13 offers an alternative perspective on the affordability of the IPM. It shows that over the period from 1972 to 1983 *the rise in payment remained fairly consistently below the rise in the monthly rental rate confronting a typical renter* (as measured by the index of residential rents embodied in the CPI cost-of-living index).

3. From the considerations developed in 2, one can readily establish the relation between the IPM and the "fully indexed mortgage—the other mortgage design that has been strongly recommended for some time by economists concerned with the destructive effects of high inflation on housing. In this instrument, which has been successfully tried out in countries with extremely high inflation (Israel, Brazil, Chile), the principal is indexed and hence revalued periodically, according to a chosen price index, and the debtor pays on the principal a "real" interest rate. It should be apparent that an IP-type mortgage will behave like (some variant of) the indexed mortgage under the following two conditions: (1) Fisher's Law (the market rate equals a constant "real" rate plus inflation) holds exactly, and (2) the payment rate is chosen to be the real rate. Indeed if Fisher's Law holds, the effective rate is the constant real rate plus the rate of inflation; and if the payment rate is the real rate, the difference between the effective rate and the payment rate is precisely the rate of inflation. Hence as in the fully indexed mortgage, the payment will rise from year to year at a rate close to that of inflation. But the equivalence is limited to this very special set of conditions. When these conditions do not hold, there are many reasons to believe that the IPM has a number of advantages, in principle as well as in practice.

4. It was shown under 2 why, for the borrower as well as the lender, what should be most relevant is the behavior of the *payment in real terms* , as in column 11. Clearly regardless of whether the actual payment rises or falls in any year, the real payment will *decline* as long as the percentage rise in the actual payment of column 3 is less than the increase in the price level—that is, less than the rate of inflation of column 9. Now the change in nominal payment is roughly equal to the difference between the nominal rate and the payment rate. Hence the real payment will tend to decline when the nominal rate less the payment rate is smaller than the rate of inflation or, equivalently, when the nominal rate less the rate of inflation—the so-called real rate—is less than the payment rate.

It follows that if one chooses for the payment rate a value that exceeds, by some suitable margin, the expected average real rate over the life of the contract, one can expect the real payment to tend to decline gradually on the average up to maturity, even though the nominal payment might increase. The percentage decline will clearly tend to be faster the larger the spread between the payment rate and the real rate, and in fact it will be of the same size as the spread, (though its actual value will also be somewhat affected by other circumstances such as the remaining life of the contract and the rate of inflation). This implies in particular that with a prudent choice of the payment rate, one can eliminate the possibility of a terminal real payment substantially larger than in the earlier years of the contract, and possibly beyond the borrower's means.

These properties of the IPM can be verified from table 1. During the 50 years of their existence, Treasury Bills have had an average real yield of 1 percent to 2 percent, very seldom exceeding 4 percent and then only for very short periods, with the possible exception of the very recent period of extreme monetary stringency. Allowing for a 2-percent intermediation and risk spread over the Treasury Bill rate, as in the tables, this means that the average effective real rate can be placed at 3 percent to 4 percent, seldom exceeding 6 percent. The choice of 7 percent as the annuity rate, as illustrated in the tables, is thus designed to ensure with high confidence a declining trend in the real payment until maturity. It can be seen from tables 1 and 2 that this purpose is in fact achieved: The real annual payment reported in column 10 decreases steadily, at an average rate of about 2 to 2.5 percent per year. The only exceptions occur in 1982 and 1983, which reflect the unusual financial turmoil of 1981 and 1982, and resulting exceptionally high real rates.

Column 11 shows that the monthly payments have declined even faster relative to per capita disposable income (income including unemployment benefits and other transfers, less direct taxes and contributions). The reason of course is that per capita (or per family) disposable incomes have, almost without exception, kept up or more than kept up with inflation. In both tables 1 and 2 the annual payment falls steadily relative to income (with the minor exception of 1982 and 1983) and by the last year is half the initial value or even less. A similar calculation based on gross average weekly (private) nonagricultural earnings shows a broadly similar picture, though the decline is somewhat less pronounced—about one-third instead of half. Considering that families with limited equity qualifying for a mortgage, an IPM in particular, should exhibit income growth prospects not appreciably below average, we can conclude that the IPM is an unusually safe loan as long as it is made under the same standards that apply to conventional mortgages with little inflation.

5. Looking at the debt outstanding rather than the annual payment, one can readily see that the nominal debt will fall from year to year as long as

the effective rate, at which borrowers are debited, is below the payment factor, which determines their payment. But the nominal debt may also rise—so-called negative amortization—in the opposite case. Considering that the effective rate will tend to move with inflation, and that the payment factor rises with the age of the contract (compare column 2 of tables), we should expect negative nominal amortization only if inflation and the effective rate are high—close to the two-digit range—and then only in the early years of the contract. It is seen that in table 1, negative amortization does occur in the years of high inflation and correspondingly exceptionally high interest rates—1980 to 1983. But is is only when this occurs close to the beginning of the contract, as in table 2, that the debt actually rises above the initial amount, the excess reaching 11 percent in my example.

But again what matters is the behavior of the real debt, that is, expressed in terms of purchasing power. As can be seen from column 12, the real debt decreases steadily, even when amortization is negative. In fact it can be readily established that as long as the payment rate remains above the effective *real* rate, and thus the real payment declines, the real debt will decline *faster* than it would with a conventional mortgage, in the absence of inflation. Thus in both tables the real balance due declines faster than under the conventional mortgage with stable prices in every year, except 1981 and 1982, and its level is universally appreciably lower. In this sense the IPM is less risky for the lender than the traditional mortgage, under a stable price level, though it does not match the unintended additional safety margin that lenders have been enjoying as a result of the high inflation.

6. Despite the fact that the instrument relies on two distinct rates, one used to compute the monthly payment and the other to compute the effective interest charged to borrowers, the computation of the monthly payment is simple and transparent in comparison with other variable rates or inflation indexed instruments.

7. Finally, the mechanics of the computations make it possible to inform the borrower about the rate of his monthly payment a full year before it goes into effect, a significant advantage over all other common kinds of variable-rate mortgages.

The IPM versus Other Major Alternatives to the Conventional Mortgage

It has been repeatedly stated that the IPM offers decided improvements over the other major alternatives that have been proposed in recent years. The basis for this claim can be summarized as follows:

1. *Adjustable rate mortgage (ARM)* With respect to this widely used instrument, the superior performance of the IPM comes from two factors. First, the IPM offers an initial annual payment that is roughly at the same low level as in the absence of inflation, whereas the ARM initial payment is computed at the current long-term market rate and therefore will rise very rapidly with inflation. Second, whenever the rate is adjusted in the ARM,

the annual payment makes a sudden jump because the new higher rate is used to recompute a new level payment until the maturity of the instrument, whereas in the IPM one uses the unchanged payment rate. For instance, if the floating rate were to rise 2 percent, the annual payment under the ARM would increase by something on the order of 20 percent of the cost of a no-inflation mortgage; by contrast under the IPM the payment would become only some 2 percent higher.

2. *Graduated payment mortgage (GPM)* The GPM, like the IPM, has the desirable property of starting low. In principle it could be made to start at the same level as the IPM. The problem, however, is that under the usual graduated payment scheme, the payment increases year after year, and the increase is prescheduled and independent of what actually happens to inflation. Thus although the payment in nominal terms is foreseeable, the payment in *real terms*, which is what matters, is completely unforeseeable and therefore also very risky. With the IPM, on the other hand, the payments will generally tend to increase in time, but only to the extent that there is inflation and generally by less than inflation or the change in family income.

3. *Rollover mortgage* This instrument is basically the same as the ARM, except that the change in interest rates occurs at longer intervals. This means that the payment starts high, then presumably declines in real terms until the time comes for the rollover to make a large jump of unforeseeable magnitude.

4. *Indexed mortgage* This is in many ways the instrument that comes closest to the IPM. There are two reasons why it is less desirable, except possibly when inflation gets really wild. First, it is not particularly suitable for use by conventional financial intermediaries, such as savings banks or the like, because in our system these intermediaries are financed by nominal instruments, such as deposits or certificates of various kinds. By making indexed loans, the intermediary will be exposed to the risk of mismatch between what they earn and what they have to pay on their deposits. This problem could of course be solved if the intermediaries were in turn allowed to issue indexed deposits. This might well be a good idea, but there is very little likelihood that such a development will occur in the United States, at least in the near future. Thus indexed mortgages could be used only if financed by institutions like insurance companies and pension funds or if financed by the issue of indexed bonds.

A second likely drawback to the indexed mortgage compared with the IPM is that the (real) rate on such a mortgage would most likely exceed significantly the average real rate that the borrower would pay under the IPM. This is at least what is suggested by past experience. The reason for this difference can be traced in part to the fact that the IPM effective rate is a short-term real rate, which is probably lower than the long-term real rate—though the borrower is also taking the risk of the future short-term real rate. But more important it arises from the risk premium that must be awarded to the lenders for accepting the unusual and unknown indexed instrument. Finally, the index mortgage runs into a number of tax and legal problems (which cannot be detailed here), which the IPM avoids.

5. *Shared appreciation mortgage* With this instrument the borrower repays the loan in two parts: (1) by a conventional mortgage at below market rate, and (2) by yielding to the lender a share of the house appreciation at the sale of the house or at some other stated time. The only good feature of this instrument is that, as for the IPM as well as the GP and the indexed mortgage, in the presence of significant inflation, the monthly payments start below the level corresponding to the standard mortgage. But this positive result is acquired at the cost of many serious shortcomings. In the first place the lender must take an equity position, shared with the owner, which seriously limits the class of possible lenders. In addition the instrument involves a high risk for lenders, because the level nominal payment on the mortgage component means that after a while the portion of their real debt repaid by the borrower falls below what it would be with a conventional mortgage with no inflation and hence a fortiori below what it would be with an IPM mortgage. All told, this instrument is one of the least rational variants of the traditional mortgage, and this explains its very limited acceptance.

Further Comments

The basic approach underlining the inflation-proof mortgage lends itself to many variations that can be used to accommodate the condition of the borrower or the lender or both and to fit a changing economic environment in regard to interest rates, inflation, and the degree of uncertainty concerning the future of both.

To begin with, the annuity factor rate can be lower than 7 percent (by as much as one percentage point). This would have the effect of lowering the initial payment by about 8 percent. This result is obtained, however, at the cost to the borrower of a more rapid rise in the later monthly payments and a growing (though still small) risk of a rising real payment; similarly lenders would face a lower build-up of equity in the home, making their position somewhat riskier.

Conversely a rate above 7 percent makes the initial payment higher, but reduces later payments and speeds the equity build-up. Accordingly a good case for a lower annuity factor can be made if and when inflation and nominal interest rates begin to move clearly below the two-digit range and are expected to stop there for some time; alternatively a new burst of inflation and uncertainty might suggest a rate above 7 percent. And of course if the IPM were financed from tax-exempt issues of bonds, as other, less desirable forms of financing have been in the past, the payment factor could be reduced substantially, probably to as low as 4 percent, without impinging on its risk.

Another variation in design would consist of lender and borrower agreeing on a reference rate of longer term, perhaps a three-year rate, to be renegotiated every three years. In this case both borrower and lender know in advance the effective rate for the coming three years, and the borrower knows for sure the rate at which the mortgage payments will grow—simply the difference between the chosen payment rate and the reference effective rate. Such a mortgage contract would look very much like a three-year rollover mortgage, but with the advantage that at the end of each three-year period, there would be a smooth change in monthly payments in response to the new effective rate, avoiding the sudden sharp increases or decreases that sometimes occur with standard rollover instruments.

PART IV

Further Contributions to the Theory of Finance

COUPON AND TAX EFFECTS ON NEW AND SEASONED BOND YIELDS AND THE MEASUREMENT OF THE COST OF DEBT CAPITAL*

Robert J. SHILLER

University of Pennsylvania, Philadelphia, PA 19104, USA

National Bureau of Economic Research, Cambridge, MA 02138, USA

Franco MODIGLIANI

Massachusetts Institute of Technology, Cambridge, MA 02139, USA

Received June 1978, revised version received August 1979

A model of the tax structure of interest rates is developed and simple approximate expressions relating yield to coupon are derived. The effect on these simple expressions of alternative assumptions about holding period length, expectations of future interest rates, and other factors, is evaluated. It is shown that with recent U.S. yield averages the new-seasoned yield spread varies with the new-seasoned coupon spread as the theory prescribes. It is concluded that new issue yield averages should provide a more reliable measure of the cost of debt capital than is provided by seasoned yield averages.

1. Introduction and summary

The cost of debt capital has traditionally been assessed both by market analysts and by econometricians by means of yield averages of seasoned bond issues of stated quality such as Moody's Aaa series. An alternative possible measure is represented by a yield average on new issues of comparable quality. It has become apparent over the years that these two measures differ from each other in ways which are both quantitatively significant and cyclically systematic. This is evident from fig. 1 below, in which we have plotted a seasoned average R_s (Moody's Aaa utility yield average) and a new issue yield average R_n (the Federal Reserve new issue yield average for Aaa utility bonds) and the spread between the two $R_n - R_s$.[1]

*Research was supported by the National Bureau of Economic Research and National Science Foundation under Grant #SOC 77-26798. Research assistance was provided by Edward Hendricks. Benjamin Friedman and Walter Torous made helpful comments.

[1]The Federal Reserve (1972) series, which begins in 1960, was developed by Kichline, Laub and Stevens (1973). It is a carefully constructed series which purports to measure yield on new utility issues which are rated Aaa by Moody's. Both series are averages for the first month of the quarter.

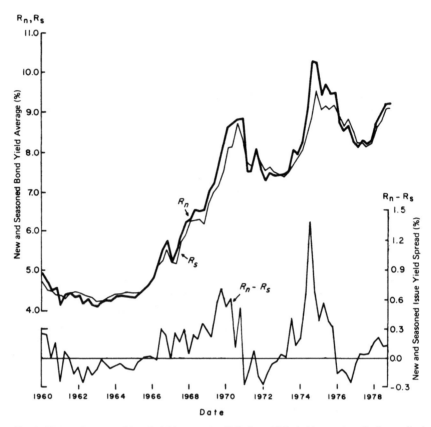

Fig. 1. New and seasoned bond yield averages; 1960–1 to 1978–4. Upper plot: R_n (heavy line) Federal Reserve Aaa utility new issue yield average and R_s (light line) Moody's Aaa utility yield average; scale for upper plot is at left. Data are averages for first month of quarter. Lower plot: $R_n - R_s$, new issue seasoned yield spread; scale for lower plot is at right.

The new issues yields rise substantially above those of seasoned bonds as interest rates approach cyclical peaks, and accordingly, the spread tends to reach a peak in coincidence with cyclical peaks of interest rates. At the most recent peak, in the third quarter of 1974, the spread reached 137 basis points. On the other hand, in other periods the yield spread is small or even negative, falling as low as -27 basis points.

The usual explanation for this phenomenon relies on the favorable differential tax treatment in U.S. tax law accorded to capital gains on bonds as against the cash income generated by the coupon. This treatment, which was instituted by the Revenue Act of 1934, creates an incentive for holding low coupon – discount issues (as are generally included in seasoned bond yield averages) rather than par issues (as in the new issue yield average) thus tending to lower the yield on such discount issues relative to that on par issues. This effect of tax laws has been noted and some measures of its quantitative significance put forth by Pye (1969), Robichek and Niebuhr (1970), McCallum (1973), McCulloch (1975), and Caks (1977).

We develop here a complete model of the tax structure of interest rates based on after-tax return equalization with the purpose of assessing how well such a model can account for phenomena of the sort observed in fig. 1. The model enables us to gauge the quantitative importance of a number of issues, which were not fully discussed in the studies cited above. These issues include: (1) How can we characterize in a simple way the relationship implied by after-tax return equalization between the spread $R_n - R_s$ and the new issue yield-seasoned coupon spread $R_n - C$? (2) How does this relation depend on the time to maturity, and assumed tax bracket? (3) How sensitive is the relation to variations in the assumed holding period of the investment? (4) Could the phenomenon be attributed to a non-level pattern of expected future interest rates in the absence of taxes?

In the final section of the paper we will see that the data shown in fig. 1 are roughly consistent with a model which attributes much of the new-seasoned yield spread to the differential taxation of income versus capital gains. In addition, some tendency for seasoned yields to lag behind new issue yields was found, which is due to the inclusion in the seasoned bond yield average of nominal yields of bonds not currently traded.

The empirical study here cannot be considered definitive, since it does not entirely control for such things as the effects of non-level expectations of future interest rates, or call provisions. Nonetheless, it does suggest that our interpretation of the phenomenon is a reasonable one. We conclude that the new issue yield is probably a better measure of the cost to firms of debt capital and should probably be used for this purpose in econometric models in place of the seasoned yield. The appreciation (according to the revenue act of 1954) of original issue discount bonds is treated as income, so the lower yield that seasoned bonds sometimes carry is not available to would-be borrowers.[2] Moreover, if seasoned bond yields averages lag behind new issue

---

[2]Before 1954 (as in Canada today), no distinction was made in tax law between original issue discount bonds and other discount bonds, and hence firms *could* issue discount bonds and expect a lower yield due to the tax advantage. Firms could elect accrual basis and deduct the amortization of original issue discount from corporate profits, and would thus be relatively indifferent on corporate profits tax considerations between discount and par issues of the same yield, while bond holders would prefer discount issues. Kaitz (1954) analyzed this tax advantage, and could find no reason why firms issued deep discount bonds so infrequently besides 'lack of information, lack of courage or both'. The puzzle is analogous to that posed by firms' failure to retain all earnings to postpone shareholders' tax liability. It is possible that firms concluded the tax law regarding original issue discount might be changed if they tried to take advantage of it. Since the 1954 tax code specified (shortly after Kaitz wrote) that original issue discount should be taxed as income when sold or redeemed, the obvious

yields then they do not reflect current market conditions, and once again seasoned bond yield averages are poor measures of the cost of debt capital.

2. Determinants of the yield spread: Taxes, coupons and other factors

2.1. Effects of taxation

We will develop here a model of the pricing of bonds on the assumption that after-tax returns on all bonds are equalized for a single 'representative tax bracket'. In reality, of course, it is unlikely that after-tax returns should be equalized for any single tax bracket. We would in fact expect, if individuals in a variety of tax brackets hold bonds, that high coupon taxable bonds should be held by persons in relatively low tax brackets, low coupon taxable bonds and low coupon tax exempts by persons in higher tax brackets, and high coupon tax exempts by persons in the highest tax brackets [Shiller (1972)].[3] For simplicity and in consideration of the use we intend for the model, however, the single tax bracket assumption will suffice. It should be emphasized that the representative tax bracket is not necessarily the average tax bracket of all bond holders. Rather it is the tax bracket of the bond holders who are more or less indifferent between deep discount bonds and par bonds. The fact that tax exempt institutions are very important in the bond market does not mean the representative tax bracket is zero. We shall also assume that tax rates and tax laws relating to capital gains are, and are expected to be, unchanging. In reality, these tax laws have changed somewhat over our sample period, and we imagine there are non-level expected changes in tax laws that arose from time to time. If we wished to model such expectations for our purposes, we would need to model the public expectations at each point of time of the time paths of future applicable tax rates until the maturity of the bond in question. Because of the difficulty of doing this, we assume merely that relevant tax rates are taken to be roughly constant. We shall also assume, at the outset, that the short term interest rate r_t at time t is expected to continue indefinitely at its current level. This assumption would be reasonable if short term interest

---

advantage to such bonds was in fact eliminated. A tax advantage for original issue discount remained after 1954, for firms on an accrual basis when bondholders are on cash basis, since bondholders may thus postpone tax liability until bonds are sold. Even this advantage was eliminated by the Tax Reform Act of 1969, which specified that individuals must declare amortized original issue discount as income. The present U.S. tax system is still not quite neutral because of the difference between linear amortization and exponential interest, as analyzed by Livingston (1979) and Racette and Lewellen (1976).

[3]Barriers to arbitrage must play a role in such models, otherwise, persons in the highest tax bracket would buy up all discount bonds by issuing par bonds. Such arbitrage opportunities, if eliminated, would imply that after-tax returns are equalized for the highest tax bracket [Shiller (1972)]. Our results below do suggest equalization of holding period returns for high tax brackets.

rates described a 'martingale'. We shall disregard considerations of risk by assuming that bonds are priced as if short rates are known with certainty to continue at their present level. These assumption will imply, in our model, that $R_{n_t} = r_t$, i.e., the term structure for par bonds is always flat. We will discuss the possibility of a non-level pattern of expected short rates below.

We denote the price of a bond at time t by P_t and normalize the bond so that it has a price of $1.00 at maturity at time m, $P_m = 1$. The bond is assumed to carry a coupon of $C < 1$ dollars per period, and was issued at par.

We will denote the marginal income tax rate by i and the effective rate of taxation on capital gains by g. For most of our sample period and most tax brackets it is useful to regard g as about one-half of i, since (until 1979) only half of capital gains are taxable as income. We may define a 'differential tax rate factor' $H = (1 - i)/(1 - g)$ for the representative tax bracket. Any taxable income is worth, on an after-tax basis, H times as much as a capital gain of the same amount for someone in this tax bracket. The upper possible limit of H is 1.00 for the 0% tax bracket. We intend, as noted above, to assume H is constant through time. However, we note that over the years the possible range of H for a single tax year varies due to changes in the tax law. From 1960 to 1963, the lowest possible value of H occurred with the highest marginal income tax bracket $i = 0.91$ and alternative capital gains tax of $g = 0.25$ making $H = 0.12$. In 1964, when the highest tax bracket fell to $i = 0.77$ the lowest possible value of H rose to 0.32. From 1965 to 1978 the highest income tax bracket was $i = 0.70$ and so the lowest possible value of H was 0.40. In 1978, tax law changes pushed the lowest possible value of H to $(1 - 0.7)/(1 - 0.28) = 0.42$. Other tax law changes had the effect of altering certain individuals' applicable effective capital gains tax rates but not the possible range of H.[4]

The basic idea which underlies our analysis can be seen most readily by considering first seasoned discount bonds which are close to maturity and hence are selling near par. We can approximate their price by the price at maturity, which we have assumed is 1.00. If such bonds are held for one time

---

[4]Notable changes in the tax treatment of capital gains occurred in 1969, 1976 and 1978. The Tax Reform Act of 1969 limited the 25% alternative capital gains tax to the first $50,000 of capital gains and enacted a stepwise elimination of the alternative tax for amounts in excess of $50,000. The Act also created a minimum tax of 10% on tax preference items, which include the untaxed 50% of capital gains, above a $30,000 exemption, and a maximum tax of 50% on earned income adjusted for tax preference items above the exemption. The Tax Reform Act of 1976 changed the minimum tax rate from 10% to 15% and the exemption from $30,000 to $10,000. The Act also increased the minimum holding period for long term capital gains in a stepwise fashion from six months to one year. None of the above changes affect our calculations in the text of the minimum possible H, since not all individuals are affected by the changes. The Revenue Act of 1978 repealed the 25% alternative tax, excluded the untaxed portion of capital gains from tax preference items relevant to the minimum and maximum tax, and increased the capital gains deduction percentage from 50% to 60%.

period (which we assume is an interval long enough that long-term capital gains rates apply) then equalization of after tax returns implies

$$\Delta P_{t+1} + HC = Hr_t. \tag{1}$$

The left-hand side of this expression is the return for holding the seasoned bond from period t to period $t+1$ corrected by the differential tax rate factor H. The right-hand side of the expression represents the return on an alternative investment in taxable short instruments, corrected by the differential tax rate factor.

The current yield (which we may also regard as yield to maturity) R_{s_t} on the seasoned bond is computed without the differential tax rate correction,

$$R_{s_t} = \Delta P_{t+1} + C. \tag{2}$$

Now, solving (1) for ΔP_{t+1}, substituting the result in place of ΔP_{t+1} in (2), rearranging and using the fact that $R_{n_t} = r_t$, we find

$$(R_{n_t} - R_{s_t}) = (1 - H)(R_{n_t} - C), \tag{3}$$

and, thus, the new-seasoned yield spread is proportional to the spread between the new issue yield and the coupon on the seasoned bond, with the factor of proportionality equal to one minus the tax rate differential. This suggests that the observed spread in fig. 1 can be explained in terms of the spread between the new issue series and the average coupon in the seasoned series.

The result (3) will form, with some modification, the basic conclusion of the empirical section of this paper. The above analysis, while suggestive, however, is generally accurate only for relatively short term bonds or more precisely, when time to maturity $T = m - t$ times the interest rate is small so that returns as a percent of price today are close to returns as a percent of price at maturity. Once we allow compounding of interest rates, the length of the assumed holding period (whether one year or the life of the bond) over which after tax returns are equalized also may become important for an explanation of the yield spread.

In the appendix (section A.1) we derive the relationship between the yield of a seasoned bond selling at a discount to its coupon under the assumption that the left-hand side of (1) is replaced by the correct expression, i.e., an expression divided by P_t. In the appendix the model is cast in continuous time, for convenience. This achieves some mathematical simplification, since the model involves compounding. The model assumes that there is no minimum holding period for long-term capital gains rates to apply, while in fact the minimum holding period ranged from 6 to 12 months over our sample period. The model may be regarded as a continuous approximation to a discrete model with a six to twelve month time interval. Using this assumption and the assumption of a flat expectation of future interest rates, it is shown in the appendix that, if after tax returns are equalized at each point of time, then the price of a taxable bond is given by

$$P_t = C/R_{n_t} + [1 - C/R_{n_t}] \exp(-HR_{n_t}(m-t)), \tag{4}$$

and that of a tax exempt by

$$P_t = C/((1-i)R_{n_t}) + [1 - C/((1-i)R_{n_t})] \exp(-HR_{n_t}(m-t)). \tag{5}$$

Panel (a) of fig. 2 shows the relation between P_t and C implied for bonds below par value in (4) – lower curve – and (5) – upper curve – under the following fairly 'realistic' assumptions: $R_{n_t} = 0.06$, $i = 0.5$, $g = 0.25$ (implying $H = 2/3$), and $T = m - t = 25$. Fig. 2, panel (b) shows with the solid curves the relation between coupon and yield implied under the same assumptions for taxables (upper curve) and for non-taxables (lower curve). Both curves intersect at the vertical axis at HR_{n_t}. Although such zero coupon long-term bonds taxed as we have described do not exist, it is useful to recognize that in theory the corporates and municipals schedules intersect here. At this point, the tax exemption of coupon is of no value and both municipals and corporates are taxed at the capital gains rate. Also included in this figure is a dotted 'par value line', or 45° line. Any bond whose yield and coupon lie on this line has a price of 1. If H is changed and R_{n_t} held constant, then both curves will shift on the left of this line. In particular, we note that the intercept with the vertical axis is also affected by tax changes. Since our model applies only to bonds selling at a discount, we have discussed the curves only below the par value line in panel (a) and to the left of the par value line in panel (b). Considering that the amortized premium on premium corporates may be counted against income, we would (disregarding the difference between linear amortization and actual decline in price) expect the corporates to yield 6% regardless of coupon when coupon exceeds 6% and hence in panel (b) the corporates line to be horizontal at 6% to the right of the par value line. For municipals no deduction is allowed for the amortized premium which means that the municipals whose coupon exceeds 3% will yield 3% regardless of coupon and hence in panel (b) the municipals line is also horizontal to the right of the par value line.

Also shown in fig. 2(b) is the line for corporate bonds predicted by eq. (3). This line is a dash-dot line intersecting the curve for corporate bonds both at par and $C = 0$. Eq. (3) thus approximates fairly well the theoretical relationship between yield and coupon. However, for bonds fairly near par we can get a better approximation to the curve by deriving a linear function

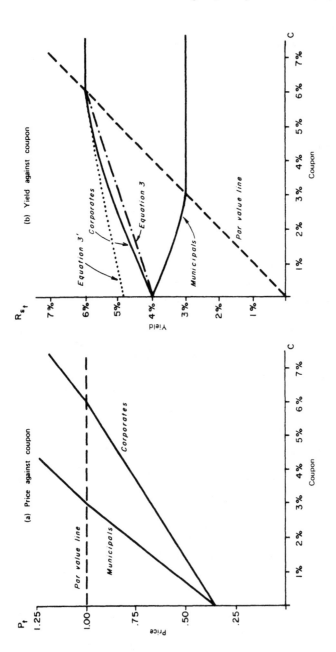

Fig. 2. Illustrative example showing (with the solid lines) the theoretical relationship of seasoned bond price and yield to coupon under continuous after-tax holding period return equalization. It is assumed here that the fully taxable short-term interest rate is constant at 6% so that new issues and par seasoned corporate bonds have 6% yield to maturity. The income tax rate i is assumed to be 0.5 and the capital gains tax rate g is 0.25 so that the differential tax rate factor H is 2/3. Time to maturity is 25 years. Curves are kinked at par because of the asymmetrical tax treatment of discount and premium bonds. Solid lines below par in panel (a) are given by expressions (4) and (5) for corporates and municipals, respectively, and above par are prices reflecting yields of 6% and 3%, respectively. Solid lines in panel (b) show yields to maturity corresponding to prices shown in panel (a). The approximations (3) and (3') to the solid line below par are shown by the dot-dashed and dotted lines, respectively.

which is tangent to the curve at par [shown in fig. 2(b) as the dotted line]. This linear function and the function (3) will then bracket the true curve, to the left of the par value line.

The slope of the linearized function will, of course, depend on relevant parameters such as taxes and maturity. Taking a Taylor expansion of (4) to linear terms around the point where the coupon equals the long term rate, or $C = R_{s_t} = R_{n_t} = \rho$, we find

$$(R_{n_t} - R_{s_t}) \cong \frac{e^{-H\rho T} - e^{-\rho T}}{1 - e^{-\rho T}} (R_{n_t} - C), \tag{3'}$$

which replaces expression (3) above which we have noted relies on an unsatisfactory approximation when time to maturity T is large. One may easily verify that the limit of the coefficient of $R_{n_t} - C$ in this expression as $T \to 0$ or $\rho \to 0$ is $1 - H$ as in expression (3). For large ρT, on the other hand, the effect of compounding interest is to substantially reduce the coefficient and in the limit, as ρT goes to infinity, the coefficient goes to zero. For the dotted line example shown in fig. 2 for which $1 - H$ is 0.333 and $T = 25$, the coefficient in (3') is 0.186. A more complete picture of the effects of compounding on this coefficient for various values of i, ρ and T and $g = i/2$ can be seen in table 1.

The intuitive reason for the smaller effect of differential taxation on yields among longer term bonds is that coupon bonds selling at a discount with a great deal of time to maturity appreciate slowly, since coupon over price is high, and large capital gains per period of time are not required to offset low coupon returns. Since capital gains are small, the tax advantage is reduced. As is well known, as long as the coupon rate is greater than zero there is a tendency for the rate of appreciation to increase as the bond approaches maturity so that capital gains then become more important.

The downward concavity of the upper curve in fig. 2(b) can thus be interpreted. The corporate bond yield is higher than predicted by (3) whenever the rate of capital gain is non-constant, i.e., increases through time, which is everywhere except at par and at $C = 0$. The differential taxation of income versus capital gains influences the time path of capital gains in a manner our model has taken into account, but which our intuitive explanation cannot consider. In the extreme case, however, as T approaches infinity, the matter becomes very simple. The bond becomes a perpetuity or 'consol' and capital gains and hence the tax advantage go to zero.

A different analysis is called for if we wish to assume that after tax returns are equalized over a longer holding period, because the deferral of payment of capital gains tax becomes an additional advantage to discount bonds even if $g = i$ so that the differential tax rate factor H equals one. The existence of this additional advantage suggests that the coefficient of $R_{n_t} - C$ in an expression explaining the yield spread will be larger than is the case in expression (3').

To explore this possibility we consider the opposite extreme, in which bonds are assumed held to maturity, and after tax returns when the bond matures are equalized. We assume that coupons are reinvested at the taxable short rate r_t though it should be noted that there is nothing restrictive about this assumption. If our model holds for bonds of all maturities, then clearly it would make no difference if coupons were reinvested in other bonds selling at a discount and maturing on the same date, since these bonds will also

Table 1

Theoretical yield spread relationship coefficients: The table gives theoretical values for the coefficient b in the relation $(R_n - R_s) = b(R_n - C)$ where $R_n - R_s$ is the new-seasoned yield spread and $R_n - C$ is the spread between the new issue yield and the coupon of the seasoned bond. Upper figure assumes instantaneous equalization of after-tax returns [coefficient is from expression (3')] and lower figure (in parentheses) assumes equalization of after-tax returns to maturity [coefficient is from expression (3")]. It is assumed that capital gains are taxed at half the income tax rate, $g = i/2$.

Tax bracket	Years to maturity	Assumed rate of compounding			
		$\rho_0 = 0.00$	$\rho_0 = 0.04$	$\rho_0 = 0.06$	$\rho_0 = 0.08$
$i = 0.00$ ($H = 1.00$)	25	0.000 (0.000)	0.000 (0.000)	0.000 (0.000)	0.000 (0.000)
	30	0.000 (0.000)	0.000 (0.000)	0.000 (0.000)	0.000 (0.000)
$i = 0.14$ ($H = 0.925$)	25	0.075 (0.075)	0.045 (0.060)	0.034 (0.049)	0.025 (0.039)
	30	0.075 (0.075)	0.041 (0.055)	0.029 (0.043)	0.020 (0.031)
$i = 0.32$ ($H = 0.810$)	25	0.190 (0.190)	0.122 (0.151)	0.095 (0.127)	0.073 (0.103)
	30	0.190 (0.190)	0.111 (0.141)	0.081 (0.112)	0.058 (0.088)
$i = 0.50$ ($H = 0.667$)	25	0.333 (0.333)	0.230 (0.266)	0.186 (0.230)	0.148 (0.195)
	30	0.333 (0.333)	0.212 (0.252)	0.163 (0.210)	0.122 (0.169)
$i = 0.70$ ($H = 0.462$)	25	0.538 (0.538)	0.415 (0.446)	0.357 (0.400)	0.303 (0.354)
	30	0.538 (0.538)	0.391 (0.428)	0.324 (0.372)	0.264 (0.320)
$i = 1.00$ ($H = 0.00$)	25	1.00 (1.00)	1.00 (1.00)	1.00 (1.00)	1.00 (1.00)
	30	1.00 (1.00)	1.00 (1.00)	1.00 (1.00)	1.00 (1.00)

show the same after tax returns as the short instrument. It is shown in the appendix (section A.2) that under this assumption the linearized relation between $R_{n_t} - R_{s_t}$ and $R_{n_t} - C$ is not (3) or (3′) but

$$(R_{n_t} - R_{s_t}) \cong \frac{(1 - e^{-i\rho T}) - g(1 - e^{-\rho T})}{(1 - e^{-\rho T})(e^{(1-i)\rho T} - g)} (R_{n_t} - C). \tag{3″}$$

The coefficient of $R_{n_t} - C$ in (3″) is zero for $i = g = 0$, and approaches 1 as i approaches 1, so that it has the same value at those extremes as the coefficient of $(R_{n_t} - C)$ in (3) or (3′). As either ρ or T goes to zero, the coefficient of (3″) approaches $1 - H$, or the coefficient in (3). In table 1, the coefficients from (3″) are shown for various values of the marginal tax bracket ($g = i/2$), time to maturity T and compounding rate ρ. The coefficient (in parentheses) is always fairly close to and slightly higher than the figure above it, which is the coefficient from expression (3′). It may surprise some readers that the assumption that capital gains taxes are deferred to maturity makes so little difference to the coefficient, since it is commonly claimed that the effect on total returns of deferral to maturity of the tax payment on capital gains is much more important than the effect of the lower tax on capital gains. One must bear in mind, however, that even though deferral of payment of taxes on capital gains makes a great impact on the final value of the portfolio at maturity, that date is quite distant in time and so it is not inconsistent to say that there is relatively limited impact on the yield today.

Eq. (3″) was omitted from fig. 2(b) for simplicity. It would intersect at par with the lines representing eqs. (3) and (3′) and would lie between them, with a slope of 0.230, close to the line for eq. (3′), to the left of par.

2.2. Coupon effects in the absence of taxes – Implications for the new-issue seasoned yield spread

In general, the yield to maturity of a bond will be affected by its coupon even in the absence of taxes, so long as the time pattern of future interest rates is not level. The size of the coupon, relative to the principal due at maturity, affects the 'weighting' given to expectation of future interest rates in determining today's yield. In the appendix (section A.3) we derive the general principle that if interest rates are expected to decrease on average through time, then higher coupon bonds will tend to have a higher yield than do lower coupon bonds. Conversely, if t is expected to increase 'on the average' with time, yield will fall with coupon. Intuitively, bonds with low C and thus selling at a discount, produce a stream that is more tilted toward the future than those selling at par. Hence, they will be more valuable if interest rates have a declining trend, and thus will have a lower yield. Conversely, with interest rates expected to rise, low coupon bonds will tend to have a higher yield. Moreover, as Weingartner (1966) has pointed out, there is only one limiting case in which, in the absence of taxes, yield is independent of coupon, namely the case already considered in which the future short term interest rate is expected to remain constant until maturity or $r_t = \rho$ for all $t < m$.

This result has some interesting implications when it is combined with the empirical observation to which Keynes first called attention, namely that expectations (and interest rates themselves) are regressive; that is, when short term interest rates are high relative to past experience, they are expected to decline whereas, when they are relatively low they are expected to rise.[5] The combination of regressive expectations with the coupon effect just established implies a systematic tendency for new issues to have a higher yield than seasoned issues. Thus, suppose that interest rates are high relative to past experience; this means clearly that seasoned issues will tend to carry on the average a lower coupon than current new issues. At the same time the regressiveness of expectations implies that interest rates will be expected to decline, which in turn means that seasoned low coupon bonds will tend to have a lower yield. Conversely, if interest rates are low relative to past experience, then seasoned issues will tend to carry higher coupon than new issues; but because interest rates will be expected to rise, seasoned issues will (given their higher coupon) again tend to have a lower yield. Thus, new issues will, in both circumstances, tend to have a higher yield than seasoned issues of comparable maturity. This result might then provide part of the explanation of the phenomenon observed over the past 25 years that new issues tend in general to have higher yields than do seasoned bonds (except when there is no clear trend in yields, at which time they are about equal), even without recourse to tax effects.

A numerical example will illustrate the importance of the coupon on yields in a world with no taxes. Suppose that r_t is expected to change linearly with time: $r_t = 0.04 + (0.04/25)t$ and suppose $m = 25$ so that at time $t = 0$ the short rates are expected to double over the life of the bond. In the appendix (section A.4) it is shown how such an example may be conveniently evaluated using tables for the cumulative normal density. Under these assumptions, the yield of a par bond is 5.53%, so that we have a substantial upward slope in the yield curve. The spread between long and short rates is over 150 basis points. The price at time zero of a bond with a three percent

---

[5]Such regressive expectations must be rational if we assume interest rates are stationary stochastic processes. A number of recent papers have claimed that interest rates can be described as random walks, which are unstationary. While it is true that changes in long term interest rates over short differencing intervals show low serial correlation, over most historical sample periods interest rates do show tendencies to regress toward the mean [Shiller (1979)]. Short rates show an especially clear tendency to return to the mean over most time periods.

coupon is, however, 0.645 which implies a yield of 5.65%. Even though short rates are expected to double and the yield curve is thus quite non-level, the yield spread between seasoned and new issues is only 12 basis points. The ratio $(R_n - R_s)/(R_n - C)$ is only 0.047, which is smaller than the value of b in table 1 for any but the lowest tax brackets. The reason for the relatively small effect on yield today is that the difference caused by different coupons in the effective weight given to near term versus future interest rates in arriving at todays' yield is relatively subtle.

3. Behavior of new and seasoned bond yield averages

Is it reasonable to attribute the actual behavior of new and seasoned bond yield averages as observed in fig. 1 to the effects of the differential taxation of capital gains versus income? We will provide some evidence on this by estimating a linear relation between $R_n - R_s$ (shown in fig. 1) and $R_n - C$ where C is the average coupon of the bonds in the sample used by Moody's to construct the R_s series. An ordinary least squares estimate appears as regression one of table 2. A constant term has been included to reflect possible market imperfections or underwriting practices which might cause a temporary premium on new issues.[6] Because of the low Durbin–Watson statistic, the equation was re-estimated using the Cochrane–Orcutt technique (regression 2 of table 2).

The coefficient of 0.300 on $R_n - C$ in table 2, regression 2, can be interpreted in terms of eqs. (3') or (3''). The average time to maturity of the bonds in the sample used by Moody's to construct this R_s series averaged, over the sample period 1960-2 to 1978-4, 27.2 years with a standard deviation through time of 2.89 years. Using for ρ the average value over the sample of R_n of 6.71%, and for T the figure 27.2, we find that the coefficient 0.300 corresponds by (3') to $H = 0.485$, and if $g = i/2$ to $i = 0.680$, or if $g = 0.25$ to $i = 0.636$. In contrast, (3'') gives us, if $g = i/2$, that $H = 0.544$ and $i = 0.626$.[7] Thus, the data suggest that after tax returns are equalized for persons in high tax brackets, and thus that there are no major opportunities for arbitrage by borrowing at the new issue rate and investing in discount issues.

Further examination of the results suggests, however, that we cannot conclude that the tax theory alone can explain most of the spread. The R^2 in

[6]Conard and Frankena (1969) noted that new issue yields tend to fall a few basis points on average relative to seasoned yields immediately after the termination of the underwriting syndicate. This suggests that new issue yields are temporarily elevated, so that investors can expect a quick capital gain, contradicting the expectations theory. West (1965) and Ibbotson (1975) suggest that underwriters may be able, in effect, to extract some hidden 'side payment' from investors in oversubscribed new issues, thus offsetting the expected capital gain. The estimated intercept is, however, negative in our regressions.

[7]Expression (3) would give us $H = 0.716$ and if $g = i/2$, $i = 0.442$. However, if time to maturity is large, expression (3) gives a good approximation for the slope only for bonds whose coupons are close to zero, as we have noted.

Table 2

Explanation of yield spread between new issue and seasoned rates.[a]

Regression no. / Period	Period of fit	Method of estimation	Estimated coefficients of[b]					R^2	S_ε	D.W.	Dependent variable
			Const.	$R_N - C$	ΔR_n	S	λ				
(1) Quarterly	1960-2 to 1978-4	O.L.S.	-0.087 (0.035)	0.239 (0.030)	—	—	—	0.471	0.206	0.860	$R_n - R_s$
(2) Quarterly	1960-3 to 1978-4	Cochrane-Orcutt	-0.134 (0.062)	0.300 (0.043)	—	—	0.615	0.650	0.168	2.51	$R_n - R_s$
(3) Quarterly	1960-3 to 1978-4	Cochrane-Orcutt	-0.047 (0.058)	0.173 (0.045)	0.265 (0.052)	—	0.629	0.743	0.145	2.47	$R_n - R_s$
(4) Annual	1961 to 1978	Cochrane-Orcutt	-0.102 (0.116)	0.209 (0.085)	0.424 (0.146)	—	0.472	0.675	0.213	2.03	$R_n - R_s$
(5) Annual	1961 to 1978	Cochrane-Orcutt	-0.089 (0.165)	0.239 (0.072)	0.174 (0.119)	—	0.679	0.577	0.210	1.46	$R_n - R_s^*$
(6) Quarterly	1960-3 to 1971-1	Cochrane-Orcutt	-0.232 (0.036)	0.235 (0.058)	0.118 (0.080)	0.003 (0.004)	-0.221	0.810	0.108	1.85	$R_n - R_s$

[a]Standard errors are shown in parentheses beneath coefficient estimates. Quarterly data are for first month of the quarter. Annual data are for July. λ is the coefficient of the lagged residual estimated with the Cochrane–Orcutt technique.

[b]In eq. (5), C^* is used in place of C.

R_n : Federal Reserve Aaa utility new issue yield average.
R_s : Moody's Aaa utility yield average.
R_s^* : Yield average of those bonds from the sample used by Moody's to compute its Aaa utility average which were traded in the middle week of July on the New York Stock Exchange.
C : Average coupon of the sample used to compute R_s.
C^* : Average coupon of the sample used to compute R_s^*.
ΔR_n : R_n minus R_n lagged three months (both for quarterly and annual).
S : Salomon Brothers yield spread between callable new issues and new issues with deferred call

the untransformed regressions is only about one half. Moreover, when a ΔR_{n_t} term was added to the regression, it was found to be highly significant (regression 3 of table 2). The coefficient of $R_n - C$ then drops to 0.173 which corresponds by (3′) to $H = 0.649$ and if $g = i/2$ to $i = 0.520$, or by (3″) to $H = 0.715$ and $i = 0.444$.

A possible explanation for the presence of the ΔR_n in the regressions might be suggested by the observation that the market for seasoned bonds is relatively 'thin' and hence seasoned bond yields may not reflect current market conditions. Conard and Frankena (1969) and Lindvall (1977) have offered reasons why small trades in seasoned bonds may take place at somewhat outdated prices. Their reasons hinge in part on 'inflexible conventions and procedures' (Conard and Frankena) of bond buyers who may continue to purchase seasoned bonds they are familiar with even when (in the case of a falling market) they have a lower yield, and on dealers' 'attempts to maintain the price of their inventory' (Lindvall).

A simpler possible explanation, which does not rely on the assumption of 'inflexible procedures' is that seasoned bond yield averages lag behind new issue yield averages because the seasoned bond yield averages include lagging quotations of bonds not currently traded. Some bonds in the Moody's sample will go untraded for months. Suppose the *true* new issue yield average on currently traded seasoned bond is $R_{s_t}^*$ and that, because of lagging quotations on bonds not currently traded, the *observed* R_{s_t} is a moving average of $R_{s_t}^*$,

$$R_{s_t} = (1 - h)R_{s_t}^* + hR_{s_{t-1}}^* = R_{s_t}^* - h\Delta R_{s_t}^* \quad \text{where} \quad 0 < h < 1.$$

Then

$$R_{n_t} - R_{s_t} = R_{n_t} - R_{s_t}^* + h\Delta R_{s_t}^*.$$

By this interpretation, if ΔR_{n_t} proxies for the unobserved $\Delta R_{s_t}^*$, then the coefficient of ΔR_{n_t} in the regressions is an estimate of h.

To establish that this is a reasonable explanation for the ΔR_{n_t} term, we collected an annual $R_{s_t}^*$ and associated C_t^* series consisting of one observation per year, namely for July of the year. These series are average yield and coupon series for those bonds among the bonds in the sample used by Moody's to compute their Aaa utility yield average which were actually traded on the New York Stock Exchange in the middle week of July. When $R_{s_t}^* - R_{s_t}$ was regressed on a constant and ΔR_{n_t} (R_{n_t} for July minus R_{n_t} for April) the constant was insignificant and the coefficient of ΔR_{n_t} was 0.260, roughly in accordance with our estimated coefficient of ΔR_{n_t} in table 2, regression 3.

Regression 4 in table 2 consists of the same regression as that of regression 3 with annual data consisting of the third quarter, i.e., July data of the series

R_n, ΔR_n, R_s and C. Regression 4, like its quarterly counterpart regression 3, shows a highly significant ΔR_n term. Regression 5 is the same as regression 4 but with R_s^* substituted for R_s and C^* for C. Regression 5 shows the coefficient on ΔR_n substantially smaller and insignificant. These results show that it is indeed the lagging quotations which are responsible for the significance of the ΔR_n term. Moreover, the coefficient of $R_n - C^*$ is, in regression 5, within the range observed in the quarterly regressions.

One important problem remains in our interpretation of the regression results. Both White (1962) and Conard and Frankena (1969) suggested that the relation of coupon to yield might have something to do with coupon related differences in call protection. It is indeed possible that such a consideration can be important to our results. New issues are, as a general rule, less likely than seasoned bonds to be vulnerable to call since their call protection will have a longer life. However, during most of our sample period, bond yields were rising, so that seasoned bonds were selling at a discount. When a substantial discount prevails, seasoned bonds are probably more safe from ultimate call than new issues. Since the prospect that a bond will be called serves to raise its yield [see e.g., Pye (1969)], the yield on new issues will tend to be higher than that on deep discount seasoned bonds, even in the absence of taxes. When $R_n - C$ becomes smaller, however, the advantage that seasoned bonds enjoy will tend to disappear. Ultimately, as C becomes closer to R_n, it will happen that it will be the seasoned bonds which have the higher yields. Indeed, when seasoned bonds are selling near par, they differ from new issues mainly in that the temporary call protection they have had will usually be expired or shorter lived. As a result, we would expect that even in the absence of taxes, the usual call provisions that bonds carry will cause a positive correlation between $R_n - R_s$ and $R_n - C$. In our estimates, the coefficient of $R_n - C$ reflects the sum of the effect of tax laws and the effect of call provisions.

The effect of call provisions on yield can be differentiated from the effect of taxes since the former is related to market expectations relating to the probability of call. One measure of this probability is afforded by a series prepared by Salomon Brothers, which is the yield spread between callable new issues and new issues with deferred call. This spread (which we will here call S) is always positive or zero, for the 1960–71 time period, and it is large when the probability of call within the period of call protection (and hence most likely also the probability of call after the period of call protection) is considered by the market to be high. In our sample period, when seasoned bonds generally sold at substantial discounts, we would then expect that $R_n - R_s$ would be positively correlated with S.

Unfortunately, the series is available only through 1971–1, and accordingly, the test of this variable in regression 6 is based on a sample terminating in that quarter. The coefficient of this variable is positive as we expected, but it is insignificant. We thus find no direct evidence that such call considerations are important. We would not, however, rule out the possibility that the coefficient of $R_n - C$ in the regressions is due partly to this factor.

The estimates of the marginal tax bracket for corporate bond holders that are implicit in the coefficient estimates might well be improved upon with more refined techniques. We feel, though, that our main purpose has been fulfilled, namely to show that our model is well supported by the data and is capable of accounting fairly well for the behavior of the spread between the yield of new issues and the yield of seasoned issues as measured by the conventional Moody Aaa series.

4. Conclusion

The theory and empirical tests presented here suggest that in the presence of differential taxation of cash and capital gains returns, the coupon rate can be of major importance in explaining the behavior of the average yield of seasoned bonds. In particular, when market rates rise rapidly, the seasoned yield will tend to underestimate systematically the true long term rate which borrowers must pay to raise funds. In addition, under these conditions, the widely used Aaa bond yield series is further distorted in a downward direction by its use of a lagging quotation for non-traded issues. For both of these reasons it would appear that the new issue rate is a more reliable measure of the true cost of long term debt funds and should be used in any model purporting to explain behavior which depends effectively on this cost. The fact that the existing measure of the new issue yield is possibly subject to a somewhat larger error of measurement may be a drawback, especially at time when few new issues are coming to market, but still does not justify continuing use of a measure which we have shown to be subject to serious systematic biases.

Appendix

A.1. Instantaneous equalization of after-tax returns

Under the assumptions described in the text, expression (1) should be replaced by

$$(\dot{P}_t + HC)/P_t = Hr_t, \tag{A.1}$$

where the dot above the P denotes time derivative. We are assuming here that coupons are paid continuously and as noted in the text that there is no minimum period for which capital gains rates apply. To find the relationship between the yield spread $R_{n_t} - R_{s_t}$ and the spread $R_{n_t} - C$ implied by this model, under the assumption that all future interest rates are known and that all after tax returns are equalized, we will solve the differential eq. (A.1) to get an expression for price in terms of tax rates, coupons, and expected future short rates. We can then use the definition of yield of a bond to find the relationship of yield to these variables. The implicit definition of yield R_{s_t} is

$$P_t = C/R_{s_t} + [1 - C/R_{s_t}] \exp(-R_{s_t}(m - t)). \tag{A.2}$$

Standard bond tables do not assume continuous compounding or continuous coupon payments. Yet, even at the highest yield levels, R_{s_t}, computed from (A.2) from P_t, C and $m - t$ differ by less than 10 basis points from yields given in the tables.

For the purpose of writing the solution to (A.1) it is convenient to adopt notation for the present discounted value function. We define

$$\delta(s, t) = \exp\left(-\int_t^s r_w \, dw\right),$$

which gives the present discounted value at time t of a dollar at time s, and so $\delta(s, t) = \delta(t, s)^{-1}$. It follows that

$$r_t = -(\partial \delta(t, s)/\partial t)/\delta(t, s). \tag{A.3}$$

Substituting this expression using $s = m$ into (A.1) and rearranging yields a differential equation in the form

$$\dot{P}_t \delta(t, m) + H(\partial \delta(t, m)/\partial t)P_t = -HC\delta(t, m). \tag{A.4}$$

The solution to this differential equation is easily found when one notes that if one multiplies both sides of this equation by $\delta(t, m)^{H-1}$, then one is left on the left-hand side with the derivative with respect to time of the expression $P_t \delta(t, m)^H$. Then one can integrate both sides of the equation and set the constant of integration so that the terminal condition $P_m = 1$ is satisfied. This yields the solution to the differential equation

$$P_t = \delta(m, t)^H \left\{ 1 + CH \int_t^m \delta(w, m)^H \, dw \right\}. \tag{A.5}$$

For discount municipal bonds, for which coupons are untaxed but capital gains are taxed at the capital gains rate, expression (A.1) is replaced by

$$((1-g)\dot{P}_t + C)/P_t = (1-i)r_t,$$

with solution

$$P_t = \delta(m,t)^H \left\{ 1 + (CH/(1-i)) \int_t^m \delta(w,m)^H \, dw \right\}. \tag{A.6}$$

Our purpose is to explain the relation of yield R_{s_t} to C, H, i and the expectations of future $r(t)$. An implicit expression for R_{s_t} is found by replacing P_t in the above solutions (A.5) and (A.6) with the implicit expression for yield (A.2). For the case of taxable securities, this gives

$$C/R_{s_t} + (1 - C/R_{s_t}) \exp(-R_{s_t}(m-t)) = \delta(m,t)^H \left\{ 1 + CH \int_t^m \delta(w,m)^H dw \right\}, \tag{A.7}$$

this equation can be considered as the basic equation for our analysis: it expresses the relation between yield to maturity, R_{s_t} and its determinants which are seen to be (i) the life of the instrument, $m-t$ – denoted also by T; (ii) the path of the short term rate over the life, expressed by $\delta(w,m)$; (iii) the tax parameter H (depending in turn on i and g); and (iv) the coupon rate C. Unfortunately, since expression (A.7) cannot be solved for R_{s_t} it is not easy to describe the relation of R_{s_t} to the variables listed above. We can, however, tell whether an expression of the form (4) is reasonably accurate as a gauge of the importance of tax effects. To do this, we will assume short term interest rates are expected to be constant, equal to R_{n_t}. Then $\delta(m,t) = \exp(-R_{n_t}(m-t))$ and substituting this into (A.5) and (A.6) and simplifying yields expressions (4) and (5) in the text.

A.2. Equalization of after tax returns to maturity

The $T = m-t$ period return Z on a dollar invested in a discount bond with coupon C at time t and held until time m reinvesting coupon at rate r_t is[8]

$$Z = (1-g)((1-P_t)/P_t) + (1-i)(C/P_t) \int_t^m \delta(w,m)^{(1-i)} dw.$$

If T period yields are equalized, Z must equal $\delta(t,m)^{(1-i)} - 1$. Thus, price and

[8]If one sets this expression equal to $\delta(t,m)^{(1-i)} - 1$ and rearranges, one gets an expression which closely resembles expression (2) in McCulloch (1975). The apparent difference is due to the fact that McCulloch's discount function uses the after tax rate.

yield are then given by

$$\frac{(1-g)+(1-i)C\int_t^m \delta(w,m)^{(1-i)}dw}{\delta(t,m)^{(1-i)}-g}$$

$$=P_t=C/R_{s_t}+(1-C/R_{s_t})\exp(-R_{s_t}(m-t))$$

If we then assume $r_t=\rho$, we can again derive a Taylor expansion of $R_{\bar{s}_t}$ as a-function of C, and R_{n_t} around $C=R_{s_t}=R_{n_t}=\rho$. As before, $\partial R_{s_t}/\partial C + \partial R_{s_t}/\partial R_{n_t}=1$, so that truncating after the first term as before, we derive the approximation (3″) in the text.

A.3. Coupon effects in the absence of taxes

If there are no taxes, then the relationship between yield and coupon is given by (A.7) with $H=1$. As has been noted before, we cannot solve this expression for R_{s_t}. We can, however, find an expression for the derivative dR_{s_t}/dC by total differentiation of (A.7). We find

$$\frac{dR_{s_t}}{dC}=\frac{(1/R_{s_t})(1-\exp(-R_{s_t}T))-\delta(m,t)\int_t^m\delta(w,m)dw}{(C/R_{s_t}^2)(1-\exp(-R_{s_t}T))+T(1-C/R_{s_t})\exp(-R_{s_t}T)}.$$

Now, at $C=0$, $\delta(m,t)=\exp(-R_{s_t}T)$ so that $R_{s_t}=-\ln(\delta(m,t))/T$ and

$$\frac{dR_{s_t}}{dC}=\frac{-T(1-\delta(m,t))/\ln(\delta(m,t))-\delta(m,t)\int_t^m\delta(w,m)dw}{T\delta(m,t)},$$

and thus

$$\frac{dR_{s_t}}{dC}\gtreqless 0 \quad \text{as} \quad \frac{\delta(t,m)-1}{\ln(\delta(t,m))}\gtreqless\frac{\int_t^m\delta(w,m)dw}{m-t}.$$

It can be shown, furthermore, that this relation holds as well for all $C\geqq 0$. Khang (1975), drawing on earlier work by Buse (1970), showed that for $C>0$, $dR_{s_t}/dC\gtreqless 0$ as $\delta(m,t)\gtreqless\exp(-R_{s_t}T)$, that is, as the yield on a pure discount bond $\gtreqless$ the yield on a bond with $C>0$. This condition says that the slope dR_{s_t}/dC has the same sign as the slope of a line between $R_{s_t}(C)$ and $R_{s_t}(0)$. Khang's result implies, then, that R_{s_t} as a function C is monotonic for $C>0$ which tells us that the inequalities above hold for all $C>0$.

This condition of the sign of dR_{s_t}/dC can be given a simple interpretation. The right-hand side of the second inequality is the average value of $\delta(w,m)$ over $t\leqq w\leqq m$, while the left-hand side is an increasing function of $\delta(t,m)$ since $t<m$. Thus, $dR_{s_t}/dC>0$ if $\delta(t,m)$ is large for a given average value. Noting that the equality holds if r_t is a constant, $r_t=\rho$, so that $\delta(w,m)=$

$\exp(\rho(m-w))$, the condition under which $dR_{s_t}/dC > 0$ can be interpreted to mean that $\delta(t, m)$ is larger than the value at time t of a constant r_t discount function with the same average value. Or, loosely speaking, $dR_{s_t}/dC > 0$ if r_t decreases 'on average'.

A.4. Numerical example

If $r_t = a + bt$, then $\delta(m, t)$ is $\exp(-a(m-t) - (b/2)(m^2 - t^2))$ and the price at $t = 0$ of a bond maturing at time m is, from expression (7),

$$P_0 = \exp(-am - (b/2)m^2)$$
$$\times \left\{ 1 + C \int_0^m \exp(-a(w-m) - (b/2)(w^2 - m^2))dw \right\}.$$

The integral can conveniently be evaluated by completing the square in the exponent and using tables of the cumulative normal distribution function $F(x)$. That is

$$P_0 = \exp(-am - (b/2)m^2)$$
$$+ C\sqrt{(2\pi/b)}\exp(a^2/2b)\{F(m\sqrt{b} + a/\sqrt{b}) - F(a/\sqrt{b})\}.$$

References

Buse, A., 1970, Expectations, prices, coupons and yields, Journal of Finance 25, 809–818.

Caks, John, 1977, The coupon effect on yield to maturity, Journal of Finance 32, 103–115.

Conard, Joseph W. and Mark W. Frankena, 1969, The yield spread between new and seasoned corporate bonds, in: Guttentag and Cagan, eds., Essays on interest rates, Vol. 1 (Columbia University Press and NBER, New York) 143–222.

Federal Reserve Board, 1972, Yields on newly issued corporate bonds, Federal Reserve Bulletin 58, 783–784.

Ibbotson, Roger C., 1975, Price performance of common stock new issues, Journal of Financial Economics 2, 235–272.

Kaitz, Haskell A., 1954, Tax advantages of discount bonds in corporate financing, Taxes: The Tax Magazine 32, 453 ff.

Khang, Chulsoon, 1975, Expectations, prices, coupons and yields: Comment, Journal of Finance 30, 1137–1140.

Kichline, James L., P. Michael Laub and Guy V.C. Stevens, 1973, Obtaining the yield on a standard bond from a sample of bonds with heterogeneous characteristics (Federal Reserve Board Staff Economic Study, Washington, DC).

Lindvall, John R., 1977, New issue corporate bonds, seasoned market efficiency and yield spreads, Journal of Finance 32, 1057–1067.

Livingston, Miles, 1979, A note on the issuance of long-term pure discount bonds, Journal of Finance 34, 241–246.

McCallum, John S., 1973, The impact of the capital gains tax on bond yields, National Tax Journal 26, 575–583.

McCulloch, J. Huston, 1975, The tax adjusted yield curve, Journal of Finance 30, 811–830.

Pye, Gordon, 1966, The value of call deferment on a bond, Journal of Political Economy 74, 200–205.

Pye, Gordon, 1969, On the tax structure of interest rates, Quarterly Journal of Economics 83, 562–579.

Racette, George A. and Wilbur G. Lewellen, 1976, Corporate debt coupon rate strategies, National Tax Journal 29, 165–177.

Robichek, Alexander A. and W. David Neibuhr, 1970, Tax induced bias in reported treasury yields, Journal of Finance 25, 1081–1090.

Shiller, Robert J., 1972, Rational expectations and the structure of interest rates, Unpublished dissertation (M.I.T., Cambridge, MA).

Shiller, Robert J., 1979, The volatility of long-term interest rates and expectations models of the term structure, Journal of Political Economy, Dec.

Weingartner, H. Martin, 1966, The generalized rate of return, Journal of Finance and Quantitative Analysis 1, 1–29.

West, Richard, 1965, New issue concessions in municipal bonds: A case of monopsony pricing, Journal of Business, 134–148.

White, William, 1962, The structure of the bond market and the cyclical variability of interest rates, International Monetary Fund Staff Papers, 107–146.

Errata

Page 298, first line: "issues" should read "issues'."

Page 299, last line: "yields" should read "yields'."

Page 301, line 3: "assumption" should read "assumptions."

Page 308, second paragraph, line 15: insert "a" in front of "higher."

Debt, Dividend Policy, Taxes, Inflation and Market Valuation

FRANCO MODIGLIANI*

I. Introduction

IN THIS CONTRIBUTION, I propose to go once more over two "core issues" of corporate finance—how do leverage and dividend policy affect market valuation? These are issues that were supposed to have been settled in the two contributions that students often refer to as MoMi (Modigliani and Miller [1958]) and MiMo (Miller and Modigliani [1961]). The basic message in these papers, was that with rational investors, well functioning markets, and no taxes (or at most, only of a certain type), financial policy does not matter!

But that conclusion did not carry over to a world with taxes, which have been, and still are, a continuing source of trouble. After a false start in MoMi, the MM "Correction" [1963], on the assumption that (i) all corporate returns are taxed equally at the personal level, and (ii) the tax saving from the use of debt can be regarded as a perpetual riskless flow, concluded that each dollar of debt in the capital structure should add to the market value of the firm at a rate equal to the corporate income tax.

The gain from leverage results, derived from the demand-side analysis, in turn created immediate problems. If debt is valuable, why should firms not be financed as nearly as possible by debt alone, with the optimum leverage representing a corner solution? This implication was disturbing because it was both counterfactual and against common sense. Accordingly, it has given rise to a good deal of work focussing on the supply side. This analysis has uncovered and analyzed four major ways in which leverage could unfavorably affect the market value of the firm: (i) the most obvious and traditional is through bankruptcy costs which reduce the expected flow to all concerned (numerous references, beginning with 1967, are provided in Williamson [1981], p. 18); (ii) a second is through agency costs, resulting from the arrangements needed to protect the creditors (Jensen

* Massachusetts Institute of Technology. The material for this paper is based upon work supported in part by the National Science Foundation under Grant SES 7926733. The author wishes to express his appreciation to Terry Marsh, Lucas Papademos, Julio Rotemberg and Robert Shiller for reading an earlier draft of the manuscript and making valuable suggestions. I have also benefited from the advice of Fischer Black, Robert Merton and Stewart Myers.

255

and Meckling [1976]; Chen and Kim [1979]); (iii) the third, and most sophisticated way, is what might be called moral hazard or foregone valuable opportunities (Myers [1977]) which would be particularly relevant for firms with true growth opportunities. A fourth and most recent argument for an interior solution relies on the consideration, first developed by Brennan and Schwartz [1978], that debt is valuable in so far as it serves to shelter income from taxes, though at a cost. As debt rises, there is a growing probability of income falling below a threshold level where the shelter can not be used. This argument has since been generalized by taking into account the availability of shelters other than debt and, in particular, tax credits (DeAngelo and Masulis [1980]; Cordes and Sheffrin [1981]).

In the midst of the efforts to explain why the supply of debt would be limited, even if leverage commanded a positive price, Miller [1977] took a radical turn on the demand side. He relies on the consideration that, contrary to the MM assumption, the personal taxation of equity returns is typically lower than that of interest—and the differential is larger the higher the tax bracket. As first shown by Farrar and Selwyn [1967], this implies that the *personal* value of leverage to any investor is a decreasing function of his income tax rate, becoming negative once that rate exceeds the corporate income tax rate by a factor depending on the capital gain rate. Now, Miller argues, the *market* valuation of leverage must reflect the personal tax of the *marginal* holder of corporate debt, and, given the availability of tax exempt securities, that marginal rate must rise continuously as the quantity of corporate debt outstanding rises. If the supply of debt is infinitely elastic and the top personal tax rate exceeds the corporate rate, as he assumes, then, in equilibrium the market value of leverage must be zero.

Ever since the appearance of Miller's 1977 paper, I have been skeptical of his conclusions. First, I found unconvincing his off-hand dismissal of factors limiting the supply of debt; if the supply of debt has costs, then the intersection of demand and supply can only come at a point where debt is valuable at the margin, and therefore leverage is a serious issue of financial policy. Second, I felt uneasy that his argument rested on tax exempt securities whose rate was taken as exogenously given, an approach that has generally been accepted by those who have since made use of his model, favorably or critically, (Lewellen, Stanley, Lease and Schlarbaum [1978]; Taggart [1980]). I suspected that the validity of his argument could not depend on the existence of tax exempt debt. Furthermore, his model implied a counterfactual coincidence between the ratio of tax exempt to fully taxed interest on the one hand, and the corporate tax rate on the other (Gordon and Malkiel [1981]; Skelton [1980]). But, in the process of validating these suspicions—a task which has since been at least partly accomplished by others (e.g., DeAngelo and Masulis [1980])-I discovered serious difficulties with Miller's framework, because of its tendency to lead to unstable corner solutions.

It soon became apparent that these counterfactual implications came from failure to properly take into account the role of diversification in a world of uncertainty and risk aversion. I was, thus, led to pursue the problem in the mean-variance framework, along lines first successfully considered in the pioneering contribution of Brennan [1970], and later extended to the analysis of individual portfolios by Elton and Gruber [1978] and Auerbach and King [1981].

In what follows, I propose to show that this framework can provide clear answers to a good number of long standing issues on the effect of alternative financial policies on market valuation and portfolio composition in the presence of various taxes and of (steady) inflation. Furthermore, the results, which coincide with MM in limiting cases, are intuitively appealing, and appear broadly consistent with empirical evidence, though with one important exception to be discussed presently, pertaining to the effects of inflation.

Because of space limitations, this paper concentrates on the demand side, taking the supply as largely given, though the concluding section outlines the integration of the demand with the supply side.

Some of the major conclusions can be summarized as follows:

1) We can expect, with great confidence, leverage to be valuable, but the value could be modest if, as one might expect, the market regards the tax saving flow as subject to risk, like the underlying profit stream, rather than as a sure perpetuity, as assumed in MM.

2) Inflation should increase the value of leverage and, through that route as well as others, also increase the *price-earnings ratio* (though not necessarily the *level* of stock prices).

3) The payment of dividends should, unequivocally, tend to reduce market value, but the effect could, again, be modest if the tax consequences are capitalized at a risky rather than at the sure rate.

4) Differential rates of taxation between investors as well as between sources of return, will result in clientele effects. That is, people having the same risk tolerance will have different portfolio compositions. Moving from the lowest brackets to the highest, one should find a steady rise in the share of the portfolio invested in stocks with low dividend yield (which generally accompany high true growth) and with relatively low betas, due in particular, to low leverage. However, the differences to be expected in the portfolio composition of a high versus a low tax bracket appear to be modest in contrast to Miller's corner type solutions.

5) Inflation can be expected to increase this polarization of portfolios.

II. Derivation of Market Equilibrium

1. *Individual demand*

In the spirit of the mean-variance model, we confine our attention largely to the market for equities and debt. We begin by deriving the demand for stocks and debt by individual investors from the maximization of the utility function, whose only arguments are portfolio mean and variance. We rely on the following notation: τ_c = corporate tax rate; τ_g = capital gain rate; τ_p = personal income tax rate; $\theta_x = 1 - \tau_x$; $x = c, g, p$; μ = cash flow (EBIT), $\mu^* = \theta_c\mu$; $[M]$ = variance-covariance matrix of tax adjusted cash flows, μ^*; S = market value of equity; D = net corporate debt; $V = S + D$ = market value of firm; Δ = dividend payment; R = nominal rate of interest; p = rate of inflation; $r = R - p$ = real rate of interest; $r_p = \theta_p R - p$ = real interest rate after personal taxes; $r_c = \theta_c R - p$. Finally, a letter superscript will characterize an investor, a subscript, a firm; the superscript $\sim$ denotes a random variable; and a bold letter stands for a column vector.

The expected return to the mth investor, y_i^m, from holding a fraction, n_i^m, of the equity of firm i, net of all corporate and personal taxes, and allowing for a fully anticipated, constant rate of inflation, p, can now be written as:

$$y_i^m = n_i^m \{ [\mu_i - \tau_c(\mu_i - RD_i) - RD_i + pD_i - \Delta_i]\theta_g^m + \Delta_i \theta_p^m \}$$
$$= n_i^m [(\mu_i^* - r_c D_i)\theta_g^m + \Delta_i(\theta_p^m - \theta_g^m)] \qquad \text{II.1}$$

Making use of II.1 and the standard budget equation, we can express the total expected portfolio return to the mth individual, having wealth w^m, as:

$$y^m = (w^m - \sum_i n_i^m S_i)r_p^m + \sum_i n_i^m[(\mu_i^* - r_c D_i)\theta_g^m + \Delta_i(\theta_p^m - \theta_g^m)] \qquad \text{II.2}$$

where r_p^m is the after-personal-tax real rate, $\theta_p^m R - p$.

We will pursue first the implications of the "traditional" MM assumption that the flows associated with debt are both permanent and riskless. If we extend this assumption also to dividends, the only stochastic component of returns in II.2 is μ_i^*, and the variance of the portfolio return for the mth individual takes the form:

$$(\sigma_y m)^2 = E(\tilde{y}^m - y^m)^2 = (\theta_g^m)^2 \sum_i \sum_j n_i^m \mu_{ij}^* n_j^m \qquad \text{II.3}$$

where μ_{ij}^* is the covariance of $\tilde{\mu}_i^*$ with $\tilde{\mu}_j^*$.

Maximization of a utility function of the form:

$$u^m = u^m[y^m, (\sigma_y m)^2], \quad u_1^m > 0, \ u_2^m < 0, \quad \text{and} \quad u_2^m/u_1^m = -\gamma^m/2$$

with respect to n_i^m, $i = 1, 2, \cdots, N$, subject to the budget constraint, leads to a system of first order conditions that can be expressed in vector notation as:

$$(\mu^* - r_c D)\theta_g^m - S r_p^m - (\theta_g^m - \theta_p^m)\Delta = \gamma^m(\theta_g^m)^2[M]n^m \qquad \text{II.4}$$

where μ^* is a column vector of the μ_i^*'s, and similarly for D, S, etc., and $[M]$ is the variance-covariance matrix of the μ_i^*'s.

2. Market equilibrium

As shown by Brennan [1970], one can, from these conditions, obtain a general equilibrium solution for the price of all "firms" (or risk classes). To this end, multiply both sides of II.4 by:

$$\frac{\Lambda}{\gamma^m(\theta_g^m)^2}, \quad \text{where} \quad \Lambda = 1/\sum_m \frac{1}{\gamma^m(\theta_g^m)^2}$$

and then sum over all individuals. Taking into account the fact that:

$$\sum_m n_i^m = 1, \ \forall \ i$$

the result of this summation can be written as:

$$(\mu^* - r_c D)\theta_g - S r_p - \Delta(\theta_g - \theta_p) = \Lambda[M]1 \qquad \text{II.5}$$

Here:

$$\theta_g = \sum_m \theta_g^m \times \frac{\Lambda}{\gamma^m(\theta_g^m)^2} \qquad \text{II.5A}$$

is an average of the θ_g^m, weighted by $\dfrac{1}{\gamma^m(\theta_g^m)^2}$, Λ being the inverse of the sum of the weights [and also $1/M$ the harmonic average of the quantities $\gamma^m(\theta_g^m)^2$]. Similarly, $r_p = \theta_p R - p$, with θ_p the same weighted average of the θ_p^m.

The market value of each firm's equity is obtained by solving II.5 for S. To obtain the market value of the firm as a whole, $V_i = S_i + D_i$, we can add and subtract Dr_p on the left hand side of II.5, rearrange terms, and solve for V to obtain:

$$V = \frac{1}{r_p}[\mu^*\theta_g - \Delta(\theta_g - \theta_p) - \Lambda[M]1] + lD \qquad \text{II.6}$$

where the ith row of $[M]1$ is $\text{cov}(\mu_i\mu)$, and:

$$l = \left(1 - \frac{r_c}{r_p}\theta_g\right) \qquad \text{II.7}$$

is the "value of leverage" to be discussed presently.

Equations II.5 and II.6 can also be usefully restated in terms of risk premia and CAPM β's. To this end we sum the equations II.6 over all firms to obtain:

$$V - lD + \frac{\theta_g - \theta_p}{r_p}\Delta \equiv V^* = \frac{\mu^*\theta_g - \Lambda\,\text{var}(\tilde{\mu}^*)}{r_p} \qquad \text{II.8}$$

Here, μ^*, Δ and V are the aggregate cash flow, dividend and total value respectively, $\text{var}(\tilde{\mu}^*)$ is the variance of overall market returns, while V^* denotes that part of market value that is due to the risky return, and excludes the portion, if any, due to the capitalization of the government contribution through tax shields and treatment of dividends. Thus, V^* corresponds to the MM notion of the "value of an unlevered stream". II.8 implies:

$$\frac{\Lambda\,\text{var}(\tilde{\mu}^*)}{V^*} = \frac{\mu^*\theta_g}{V^*} - r_p \equiv \pi \qquad \text{II.9}$$

and $(\mu^*/V^*)\theta_g$ is the after (average) tax rate of return on the unlevered market, in the absence of dividends. The expression after the first equality in II.9 can therefore be labeled the "tax adjusted excess return"—the difference between the market return and the interest rate, after both are adjusted by the weighted average tax rate defined by II.5A. II.9 tells us that this difference, or risk premium, which is denoted by π, is proportional to the variance of market returns adjusted for taxes (implicit in Λ), a generalization of the familiar CAPM result.

Using the above definition of π, one can express total market value as:

$$V = \frac{\mu^*\theta_g}{r_p + \pi} + lD - \frac{\theta_g - \theta_p}{r_p}\Delta \qquad \text{II.10}$$

Expressions analogous to II.10 can also be derived for individual stocks by defining:

$$V_i^* = V_i - lD_i + \Delta_i(\theta_g - \theta_p)/r_p \qquad \text{II.11a}$$

$$\beta_i = \text{cov}\left(\frac{\mu_i^*}{V_i^*}, \frac{\mu^*}{V^*}\right) \qquad \text{II.11b}$$

Using II.11b and II.9, $\Lambda[M]1$ in the right hand side of II.6 can be replaced by $(\mathbf{V}\boldsymbol{\beta})\pi$, and the equation can then be solved for V. For the ith firm, one obtains:

$$V_i = \frac{\mu_i^* \theta_g}{r_p + \beta_i \pi} + lD_i - \Delta_i \frac{\theta_g - \theta_p}{r_p} \qquad \text{II.12}$$

Subtracting the debt from both sides of II.12 yields an expression for the value of equity:

$$
\begin{aligned}
S_i &= \frac{\mu_i^* \theta_g}{r_p + \beta_i \pi} - (1 - l)D_i - \Delta_i \frac{\theta_g - \theta_p}{r_p} \\
&= \frac{(\mu_i^* - r_c D_i)\theta_g}{r_p + \beta_i^* \pi} - \Delta_i \frac{\theta_g - \theta_p}{r_p}
\end{aligned}
\qquad \text{II.13}
$$

where

$$\beta_i^* = \beta_i\left[1 + d_i' \frac{r_c \theta_g}{r_p}\right] \quad \text{and} \quad d_i' = D_i \Big/ \left[S_i + \Delta_i \frac{\theta_g - \theta_p}{r_p}\right]. \qquad \text{II.13a}$$

The second equality is a rearrangement of the first for the purpose of expressing S in terms of stockholders' profits.

II.12 and II.13 are seen to be consistent with well known MM "Correction" formulae for the special case $\theta_g^m = \theta_p^m$ and no inflation (Modigliani and Miller [1963], equations (3) and (6) respectively), but they enable us to analyze the effect of financial policies under more general conditions, including inflation.

3. The effect of financial policies in the absence of inflation

i) The value of leverage

Remembering the definition of r_c and r_p, the value of leverage l, given in II.7, can be written in the following form, which separates out the effect of inflation:

$$l = q + (q - \tau_g)\frac{p}{r_p}; \quad q = 1 - \theta_c \theta_g / \theta_p \qquad \text{II.14}$$

For $p = 0$, l is seen to reduce to q, an expression made familiar by Farrar and Selwyn [1967]. It is consistent with the *MM* formulae and also with Miller's $l = 0$, if $\theta_g \theta_c = \theta_p$. But, according to our analysis, there is no reason why this equality should hold (at least for the U.S.). Indeed, with θ_c around 0.5, the value of $\theta_c \theta_g$ can not be appreciably in excess of 0.45, while the value of θ_p must, assuredly, be significantly higher, most likely around ⅔. This assessment of θ_p is supported by two considerations.

First, according to Miller, what insures the equality of θ_p and $\theta_c \theta_g$ is that θ_p represents the tax factor of the marginal holder of levered stock (i.e., the holder for whom leverage is least advantageous). Accordingly, θ_p decreases with the supply of leverage. An infinitely elastic supply together with sufficiently high tax brackets then insures that, in equilibrium, q must be zero. But once we take into account the benefits of diversification, the value of leverage, l, is *independent* of its supply and depends instead on the (weighted) *average* tax factors θ_p, and θ_g, and on θ_c.

The average value of τ_p^m, the personal tax rate, can probably be put at somewhat less than 0.4 (for some empirical evidence see, e.g. Lewellen, Stanley, Lease and Schlarbaum [1978]; Feldstein and Summers [1979]; Kim, Lewellen and McConnell [1979]). But the value of τ_p relevant in II.14 should be appreciably less than this average. In the first place, one should allow for tax exempt investors. Secondly, as long as there is a substantial market for tax exempt securities, the "effective" rate for any investor should be either his actual rate or $(1 - i/R)$, where i is the (nominal) rate on tax exempt securities, whichever is lower. For, clearly, regardless of his income, an investor always has the opportunity to invest in tax exempt securities yielding i, which is equivalent to investing in conventional debt at an "effective" rate, $\tau_p = 1 - (i/R)$. Thus, as long as i/R is larger than $\theta_c \theta_g$, corporate leverage is valuable to all investors, regardless of income. Now, at least for long maturities, i/R has consistently been well above one half. It has, in fact, tended to stay around 0.7 and uniformly above 0.6 (Mussa and Kormendi [1973]; Skelton [1980]). This suggests, therefore, that the average of the effective values of θ_p^m can be safely placed at no less than ⅔. If so, in the absence of inflation, l could be expected to be positive with a value around ⅓, compared with MM's τ_c or 0.5. Furthermore (as can be verified from II.12), if one can suppose that an expansion of interest payments is necessary and sufficient to enable the firm to cut dividends by an equal amount, then the (marginal) value of leverage is the full MM's τ_c (Brennan [1970]; Litzenberger [1980]).

An alternative way of assessing the value of leverage is to ask how much it can contribute to market value in relative terms. We find:

$$\frac{dV_i}{V_i} = \frac{q}{\theta_g}\,(r_p + \beta_i \pi)\,dd \qquad \text{II.15}$$

where $d = D_i/\mu_i^*$ and the derivative is evaluated at $D_i, \Delta_i = 0$. With q/θ_g estimated at below .4, the value of this expression for the "average" β of 1 can be put at between .02 and .03. Thus, a rise in d from 0 to as much as 10, and even neglecting any "cost" of leverage, would generate a rise in value of around 25 per cent—not negligible but not very large either.[1]

ii) *Valuation and dividend policy*

Since θ_g can be taken as larger than θ_p, at least for the U.S., from II.12 we can infer that the payment of dividends must unequivocally reduce the market value of the firm, at least within the set of cost-benefits explicitly modeled. This conclusion agrees with Brennan's result [1970] and with a widely held view, though it is hard to reconcile with prevailing payout policies.

If the market regarded the flow of extra taxes associated with dividends as fixed and perpetual as assumed in II.10, then the unfavorable effect of dividends on value would appear to be hefty. For instance, with the usual assumptions about the tax parameters, and assuming further that r_p is of the order of ½ π, one finds that an increase in the payout from zero to 10 percent would have the effect of reducing market value by some 8 percent, or even more for a high β stock. But

---

[1] II.15 suggests that the effect could be substantially larger, for high β stocks. But this implication is questionable—see section II.5 below.

this estimate is surrounded by considerable uncertainty. On the one hand, it might be argued that the value of τ_p applicable to dividends might be higher than that relevant to the leverage effect. But, on the other hand, Miller and Scholes [1981] have attempted to show (even if not entirely convincingly) that the relevant $\tau_p - \tau_K$ might be small or negative! Finally, the estimate would also be reduced if, as seems plausible, the market takes as given the payout policy rather than the dividend itself (see 5 below).

4. The impact of inflation on valuation

As is apparent from II.12, 13, and 14, inflation has an effect on valuation through, and only through, the real after tax rates r_p and r_c. Hence its impact depends critically on how these rates, particularly r_p, respond to inflation.

i) *Effect on interest rates*

Unfortunately, as is well known, the interest rate cannot be derived from the CAPM framework alone. We propose to handle this difficulty by relying on an approach which is appealing, at least if we are concerned with long run implications. It consists in adding an equation expressing the requirement that, in long run equilibrium, the market value of corporate capital must coincide with the reproduction cost of that capital (or, that Tobin's q should be one). Thus:

$$V = K$$

where K is the reproduction cost.[2]

Substituting K for V in II.8, we can solve that equation for the real rate, r. For present purposes, however, it turns out to be more convenient to solve for the real after tax rate, r_p. This yields:

$$r_p = \theta_p r - \tau_p p = \left[p\theta_K \frac{\theta_p - \theta_c}{\theta_p} d^* + \rho\theta_c\theta_K - \delta^*(\theta_K - \theta_p) \right.$$
$$\left. - \Lambda\theta_c^2 \operatorname{Var}(\rho)K \right]/(1 - qd^*) \quad \text{II.16}$$

where $\rho = \mu/K$, $d^* = D/K$ and $\delta^* = \Delta/K$.

As one should expect, r_p rises with the net-of-tax return from assets and declines with the risk premium (the last term in the numerator). But, the effect of lowering θ_c or θ_K (raising taxes) is uncertain since it lowers the after tax return but it also lowers its variance (provided losses can be fully recouped).

The effects of inflation are captured primarily through the first term. Because θ_p exceeds θ_c, inflation should have a positive effect on r_p (through leverage). But, on the basis of our estimate of the tax coefficient, this effect is moderate: the tax factor comes to just over 0.2, so that with, say, a 25 percent average ratio of debt to total capital, 10 percent inflation would raise r_p by some 50 basis points.

The remaining terms do not involve p explicitly, but could nonetheless be systematically affected by inflation. In particular, even supposing that p is neutral

---

[2] As a result of tax effects, the market value may be taken as proportional rather than equal to reproduction cost.

with respect to K, the after tax return, $\rho\theta_c$, is likely to be systematically reduced through the taxation of paper profits from inflation. Suppose, for the moment, that the leverage and $\rho\theta_c$ effects roughly cancel. Then, II.16 says that inflation should leave unchanged the *after* (average) *tax, real* personal *rate* of return ($R\theta_p - p$). Thus it confirms the conclusion already reached by others (e.g., Feldstein [1976]; Summers [1981a]) that the nominal rate should *not rise* by p as stated by Fisher's Law, but rather p/θ_p (or, for the U.S., some one-and-a-half times as much as inflation), a proposition that may be labelled "Super Fisher's Law." Of course, even if r_p is inflation invariant, the after tax real rate will fall for those in above-average brackets, including corporations, and rise for low ones. In addition, the leverage and $\rho\theta_c$ effect need not offset each other precisely and, accordingly, the nominal and real rates might rise somewhat more or less than called for by the Super Fisher's Law. However, with significant inflation, one should definitely expect a nonnegligible rise in the (before-tax) real rate.

ii) Inflation and the value of leverage

To see what these results imply for the impact of inflation on the value of leverage, one can turn to II.14. Suppose inflation left roughly unchanged the after tax rate, r_p, as suggested by the result of the previous section. In this case, l can be seen to be a linear function of p. Furthermore, the coefficient of p/r_p is close to that of q, since τ_g is 0.1 or even less. Now, r_p is presumably a rather small number, say 2 to 3 percent. That implies a quite large response of l to inflation— a rise in p from zero to no more than 4 percent would be sufficient to double l! These results reflect the fact that, even if inflation does not increase the advantage of personal borrowing (r_p is constant), it will reduce r_c increasing the gains from corporate debt, and the gain is capitalized at a low rate. Even more dramatic effects should result if r_p declines—for example, because the *real* rate is constant.

iii) *Inflation and the stock market*

III.13 shows that the response of equity values to a (permanent) rise in the anticipated rate of inflation should reflect the effect of that rise on three components of S: (i) μ^*; (ii) l; and (iii) r_p. The effect on the first component unequivocally tends to lower S. But it might be more than offset by the effect on the remaining two components, which we have shown to push in an upward direction. This is true even if the higher tax burden, through the taxation of paper profits, has exceeded the lower burden due to the treatment of interest, and other effects, as has been maintained, e.g. by Feldstein and Summers [1979] (though the issue is by no means settled; see, e.g. Briden [1981]). For this development should have been offset by the fall in r_p, at least through the 70s, whether or not this fall is related to the higher tax burden claimed by Feldstein and Summers.

But whether S should have risen or not, one inference that can be clearly drawn from II.13 is that the price-earnings ratio (P/E) should have risen, and very substantially, during the rising inflation—for this effect depends only on components (ii) and (iii), both of which push unequivocally and strongly in an upward direction. Furthermore, the rise in P/E should be greater the higher the leverage.

To conclude, the model clearly implies that inflation should exert a pronounced upward thrust on the value of leverage and on P/E. However, there are grounds for discounting the implied large quantitative effects, especially those associated with possible near zero or even negative values of r_p, as a result of inflation. Actually, such values must be ruled out if r_p is to be interpreted as the "consol" rate. To be sure, a negative real rate is perfectly possible, but *not* if there exist *perpetual* positive real streams of returns (e.g., via tax saving).

This observation points to one important limitation of our analysis of the value of leverage and dividends, namely that the results are strictly applicable only when the relevant variables are expected to be *indefinitely* maintained and *certain*. This limitation must be kept in mind in interpreting all results, but particularly those associated with nominal quantities, such as R and p. There is no basis for the expectation that a high level of p and R would be preserved forever. Furthermore, if inflation is not neutral (notably because of nominal institutions or illusions), it is very doubtful that investors would, or should, act as though any given constellation of R, p, and institutions would last forever, especially if it gives rise to unusual advantages.

Another factor that could be counted on to reduce the magnitude of the response to inflation is the stochastic rather than deterministic nature of tax saving flows associated with alternative financial policies, to which we now turn.

5. *The implications of uncertain tax savings and dividends*

The implications of the market regarding the future stream of interest and dividend payments and the associated tax consequences as stochastic, rather than as certain, perpetual streams, depend on the stochastic properties of the expected streams. For the sake of illustration, we shall pursue the implications of the market taking as given, and nonstochastic, the debt-equity and payout policy, d_i and δ_i, rather than the interest and dividend flows. (This formulation has been suggested, with particular reference to debt and capital budgeting, by Miles and Ezzell [1980].)

The total return from firm i can now be written as:

$$\tilde{y}_i^m = \tilde{\mu}_i^*[\theta_R^m + (r_p^m - r_c\theta_R^m)d_i - \delta_i(\theta_R^m - \theta_p^m)]$$

where $d = D/\mu^*$, $\delta = \Delta/\mu^*$. Since equity holders are presumed to absorb all the risk, the variance associated with the equity must be var($\tilde{y}_i$).

By repeating the steps leading from II.4 to II.12, one obtains the following reformulation of equation II.12:

$$V_i = \mu_i^*[\theta_R + d_i(r_p - r_c\theta_R) - \delta_i(\theta_R - \theta_p)]/(r_p + \bar{\beta}_i\pi) \qquad \text{II.17}$$

Here the tax parameters are again averages of the individual investor's rates weighted by his shares of the market, $\bar{\beta}_i$ is a similarly weighted average of the β_i's of the individual portfolios, and π is the spread between the overall after tax rate of return on equity and the average after tax interest rate.[3]

---

[3] This proposition holds on the plausible assumption that $n_i^m\beta_i^m$ is not appreciably correlated with π^m across investors.

From II.17, the value of leverage becomes:

$$l^* = \frac{dV_l}{dD_l} = \frac{lr_p}{\beta_i\pi + r_p} \quad \text{or} \quad \frac{1}{V}\frac{dV}{dd^*} = \frac{qr_p}{\theta_g}$$

This suggests l^* can be put at roughly one-third the value of l implied by II.14, or at a bit above .10, and similarly for the relative change in value. The effect of dividend policy on value is also reduced by a factor of $\frac{2}{3}$, to a fairly modest effect, suggesting that in setting dividend policy, tax considerations could well be swamped by other factors.

In summary, there can be little doubt that the estimate of l of $\frac{1}{3}$ obtained under the assumption of perpetual, sure consequences suffers from serious upward bias, but there is little basis for pinpointing its magnitude. Even .10 need not provide a lower bound. It is interesting nonetheless, that the latter figure is not inconsistent with the recent estimates by Masulis [1981] relying on the ingenious technique of measuring the impact of various types of exchange offers on the price of common stock.[4]

It is much harder to assess the consistency with the evidence of our results for dividends, mainly because at present the evidence itself is so controversial. Some authors find no evidence in support of the hypothesis that dividends are valued significantly below other corporate returns,[5] while others report strong evidence consistent with that hypothesis, especially when allowing for the valuation to vary with the size of dividend yield, as implied by tax clientele effects.[6] In the latest application of the latter approach, Auerbach [1981] has estimated the effect of dividends on returns over a 15 year period for each of a large sample of firms. His average coefficient, .22, compared favorably with the value implied by II.17, $(\theta_g - \theta_p)/\theta_g$, or around .25.

At the same time, the implications of the model about the effects of inflation seem to be grossly inconsistent with the empirical evidence: (i) the after tax real rate has declined markedly, and even the real rate has hardly kept up during most of the last 15 years (for an analysis of earlier experiences, see Summers [1981a]); (ii) equity values, and most particularly price-earnings ratios, have declined dramatically, whereas they should have risen appreciably, especially in light of the decline in r_p; (iii) levered firms, instead of appreciating, have tended to lose value, at least according to one recent study;[7] and (iv) there is little

---

[4] While his "preferred" estimate is below .10, it should be remembered that it reflects also effects associated with the "cost of leverage" (see conclusions). In fact, if there is an interior optimum debt and the exchange were aimed at that optimum, the effect of the exchange on value would be appreciably smaller than l.

[5] See, e.g., Black and Scholes [1974], Gordon and Bradford [1980], and Miller and Scholes [1981].

[6] Elton and Gruber [1970]; Litzenberger and Ramaswamy [1980]. The Elton and Gruber results have been severely criticized and called in question by Kalay [1977], but it is not clear that his criticism applies to the other studies. It may be noted in this connection that even the results of Miller and Scholes, when they classify firms by dividend yield, are strikingly supportive of the hypothesis of a dividend effect, despite the authors' attempt at discrediting them by calling attention to outliers in one of the nine cells of the table.

[7] The study, carried out by myself and Richard Cohn, is still unpublished, but a short description is provided in Modigliani and Cohn [1982]. However, quite different results have been reported recently by Summers [1981b], using a somewhat different approach.

evidence of any significant increase in leverage, even though its profitability should have gone up.[8]

We suspect that this total failure can be attributed to the assumption of rational behavior, whereas in the presence of inflation, at least of a moderate size, the market may suffer from inflation illusion of the type hypothesized by Modigliani and Cohn [1979]. It can be verified that dropping the term p from II.1, and replacing R_p for r_p in equations like II.10 and II.12, as suggested by that hypothesis, would go a long way toward explaining the contradictions highlighted above.

III. Individual Portfolio Composition

1. *Taxes and portfolio allocation—basic characteristics*

It is well known that, in the absence of taxes, and with uniform assessments, the mean-variance approach implies that the optimum portfolio of every investor will hold the same fraction of every firm's equity.

As has been shown by a number of authors (Black [1971, 1973], Elton and Gruber [1978], Gordon and Malkiel [1981], Auerbach and King [1981]) this proposition no longer holds when investors are differently taxed. This conclusion can be verified by solving the equilibrium condition II.5 for S and substituting in the first order condition II.4. This yields, after some rearrangement:

$$(\mu^* - r_c \mathbf{D})\left(\theta_g^m - \frac{r_p^m}{r_p}\theta_g\right) - \Delta\left[(\theta_g^m - \theta_p^m) - \frac{r_p^m}{r_p}(\theta_g - \theta_p)\right] + \frac{r_p^m}{r_p}\Lambda[M]\mathbf{1}$$
$$= \gamma^m(\theta_g^m)^2[M]\mathbf{n}^m \quad \text{III.1}$$

The system can be solved for $\mathbf{n}^m$ (assuming $[M]$ nonsingular) and the solution can be cast in the form:

$$\mathbf{n}^m = \frac{\Lambda}{\gamma^m}\left\{T_1^m\mathbf{1} + \frac{1}{\Lambda}[M]^{-1}[(\mu^* - r_c\mathbf{D})T_2^m - T_3^m\Delta]\right\} \quad \text{III.2}$$

where

$$T_1^m = \frac{r_p^m/r_p}{(\theta_g^m)^2} \quad \text{III.2a}$$

$$T_2^m = \frac{\theta_g^m - (r_p^m/r_p)\theta_g}{(\theta_g^m)^2} \quad \text{III.2b}$$

$$T_3^m = [(\theta_g^m - \theta_p^m) - r_p^m/r_p(\theta_g - \theta_p)]/(\theta_g^m)^2 \quad \text{III.2c}$$

---

[8] The evidence occasionally offered to support the proposition that leverage has increased dramatically, is uniformly based on measures which are irrelevant in the presence of inflation, such as using book value in the denominator or relying on market value, whose relevance is, at least, questionable in view of its dramatic decline (cf., for instance, Gordon and Malkiel [1981, Table 1]. If one relies on more suitable measures of the denominator, such as reproduction costs of assets, the association with inflation disappears (Gordon and Malkiel, ibid.), and the same tends to happen using a variable like *EBIT*.

In the absence of personal taxes, or, more generally, when everybody is taxed equally, III.2 implies the standard result, $n_i^m = \Lambda/\gamma^m$ for all i; every investor holds a share of the market, inversely related to the investor's risk aversion γ^m.

Next, if individuals were taxed differently, but (i) all property income was taxed at the *same* rate, or $\theta_g^m = \theta_p^m$ (as assumed implicitly in the MM "Correction" [1963]), and (ii) there was no inflation (or only real interest was taxed), then, since under those conditions $\theta_g = \theta_p$, and $r_p^m/r_p = \theta_p^m/\theta_p$, we find $T_2 = T_3 = 0$, and

$$n_i^m = \frac{\Lambda}{\gamma^m(\theta^m)^2} \; \forall \; i$$

Thus, each portfolio consists again of a share of the market, but that share now depends also on the investor's tax bracket, θ^m, relative to the average θ (implicit in Λ). Since θ^m is a decreasing function of the tax rate, for given risk preference, n^m is an increasing function of the investor's tax bracket. The reason, basically, is that a higher tax rate implies an equal decline in the (expected) return from equity and from debt, but it also implies a decline in the variance of the after tax outcome from equity, which makes equity relatively more attractive.

Finally, if, and only if, both individuals and sources of income are taxed differently, investors will hold different shares of any given firm depending on both their tax rates and their risk aversion. However, if any two investors, say, m and m', are subject to identical tax rates, then T_1, T_2, T_3 of III.2 will have the same value, and therefore: $n_i^m/n_i^{m'} = \gamma^{m'}/\gamma^m$, $\forall \; i$. Thus, it remains true that every investor could, in principle, secure his optimum portfolio by combining positive or negative debt with a share of a single appropriate "tax fund," which held shares in the relative quantities appropriate to his tax bracket, as given by III.2.

2. *Firms' characteristics and portfolio composition*

To examine how the portfolio composition of funds suited for different tax brackets should be expected to respond to various characteristics of the firm, it is convenient to consider first the special case where $[M]$ is diagonal. In this case, from III.2, the equation prescribing the holdings of the ith stock for a fund catering to investors with any given set of rates, say $\hat{\theta}_g, \hat{\theta}_p$, can be written as:

$$n_i = k[T_1 + x_i(T_2 - \delta_i T_3)] \qquad \text{III.3}$$

Here, T_1, T_2, and T_3, are the same as defined in III.2, but with θ_p^m, θ_g^m, r_p^m, replaced by $\hat{\theta}_p, \hat{\theta}_g, \hat{r}_p$; δ is the payout ratio and k is a proportionality factor that depends on the size of the fund. Finally:

$$x_i = \frac{(\mu_i^* - r_c D_i)}{\Lambda \mu_{ii}} = \frac{(\mu_i^* - r_c D_i)}{(\beta_i^* \pi S_i)} = \left(1 \, pl \, \frac{r_p}{\beta_i^* \pi}\right)(\theta_g)^{-1} \qquad \text{III.3a}$$

where β_i^* is the β of the rate of return to equity, defined in II.13a. The second equality in III.3a follows from II.9 and the fact that, with a diagonal matrix, $\text{var}(\tilde{\mu}_i) = \text{cov}(\tilde{\mu}_i\tilde{\mu})$, while the last follows from II.13.

It is apparent from III.2 that both T_2 and T_3 are zero for the "average" tax fund which, therefore, holds the market, and that they are increasing functions of the tax rate, τ_p, as long as $d\tau_R/d\tau_p$ is well below unity, as is the case for the U.S. It then follows from III.3 that for a fund that caters to higher tax brackets, the relative share held of any stock will be higher the higher that stock's x (cf. Auerbach and King [1981]), and the lower its payout ratio (Elton and Gruber [1978])[9]. The converse is true for a below-average tax fund. Furthermore, the *variation* in the *relative* shares held of different equities will be larger the larger (in absolute value) the slope coefficient T_2, that is, the more the fund's target tax rates deviate from the average, in either direction.

It should be noted that though a high bracket portfolio will hold a *relatively* smaller share of low x firms, nonetheless, higher taxes will lead to holding a larger *absolute* share of every stock, including those with low x,[10] (provided their dividend rate is sufficiently low). This behavior reflects, in addition to the variance effect noted earlier, the favorable tax treatment of corporate returns, other than dividends, relative to interest.

3. *Extent of variation in optimum portfolios*

With the help of III.3, one can endeavor to go beyond these qualitative results and get some idea of just how sensitive portfolio composition might be to both taxes and firms' characteristics. One way to measure this sensitivity is to ask how much difference one should expect to find between the largest and smallest relative shares of firms held in the portfolio of funds for which the differences tend to be largest, namely those aimed at extreme tax brackets.

Ignoring inflation at first, and focussing on the role of x, from equation III.3, we obtain:

$$\frac{1}{\bar{n}} dn_i = \frac{k(T_2 - \delta_i T_3)}{\bar{n}} dx_i = \frac{kT_2(1 - \delta_i)}{\bar{n}} dx_i \qquad \text{III.4}$$

since, without inflation, $T_2 = T_3$ as can be seen from III.2b and c.

Thus, the range of variation of n_i depends on the range of x and on the "slope", $T_2(1 - \delta_i)$, which will be largest (in absolute value) when the payout is zero. Consider, then, the lowest possible tax class, $\theta_p = \theta_R = 1$. Relying on the earlier estimate of ⅔ for θ_p, and 0.9 for θ_R, one can put $kT_2/\bar{n}$ at just below 0.3.[11] For a very high tax fund, say, $\theta_p = .5$, $\theta_R = .85$, the slope is even lower, about .25. To estimate the relevant range of x, we can rely on III.3a. If, as seems reasonable, the bulk of the β's can be presumed to fall within the range of 0.5 to 2.0, the range of x is 1.4 to 2.2, or less than one. This implies that the variations in the relative shares of different stocks within one fund, or of the same stock between funds, arising from differences in x, would fall within a quite modest range of about 25 percent.

A second set of questions we can examine with the help of III.3 concerns the impact of leverage on the tax clientele of the firm. First, suppose we classify firms

---

[9] Elton and Gruber's result is actually stated in terms of the dividend yield, Δ_i/S_i.

[10] From III.2, for the smallest possible value of x which, from III.3a, is θ_R^{-1}, one finds:

$$n_i^m = \frac{\Lambda}{\gamma^m} \left[T_1 + \frac{T_2}{\theta_R} - \frac{T_3}{\theta_R} \delta_i \right] = \frac{\Lambda}{\gamma^m \theta_R} [(\theta_R^m)^{-1} - T_3\delta_i]$$

which is an increasing function of the tax rate for sufficiently small values of δ_i.

[11] n/k is estimated from II.3 putting $x = 1.5$ (i.e., $\beta = 1$), and $\delta = .5$.

by debt-equity ratios and compute the average tax rate for each leverage class—how should the average tax rate change as leverage increases? In a well known contribution, Kim, Lewellen and McConnell [1979], have provided empirical evidence on this question, based on a large sample of portfolios. They find, as expected, that the estimated average tax rate of stockholders declines systematically as the debt-equity ratio rises from zero to roughly 2 in the highest class, but that the fall—roughly from 41 percent to 37 percent—is modest relative to the implications of Miller's model.

The implication of our model can be deduced from III.3 by examining how the relative share of firms characterized by different leverage differs in the portfolios of funds aimed at different tax brackets. It is apparent from III.2, III.3, and II.13a that leverage affects n_i through, and only through, β^*, and hence x. One can deduce from II.13a that, if leverage were uncorrelated with the asset's β, a rise in d' from zero to 2 would decrease x on the average from 1.5 to 1.2.[12] In light of III.4, this implies a very modest effect of leverage on relative shares. Even for the zero tax fund ($T_2 \simeq .3$) the difference between the relative holdings of unlevered and highly levered firms would be within 10 percent. In reality, there is substantial evidence that leverage is negatively correlated with risk and hence with β. Accordingly, the change in x, and hence n_i, between leverage classes should be even smaller. Clearly, these implications of the model can be easily reconciled with the results of Kim et al., cited above.

A related question concerns the effect that a change in debt policy could be expected to have on the tax clientele of a firm. Here, again, it is found that even for a relatively low β firm, and for a zero tax fund—the combination most sensitive to changes in leverage—the maximum swing in portfolio's relative shares might be within 20 percent, implying that changes in debt policy would not be a source of major shifts in clientele.

Turning finally to the effect of dividend policy, one can readily establish along the lines used above that its effect on portfolio composition should not be very large. But a comparison of the model's implications with empirical evidence is again complicated by the contradictory nature of this evidence. Our model seems to be broadly consistent with the systematic, though modest, association between dividend yield and average tax reported by Lewellen, Stanley, Lease, and Schlarbaum [1978][13] and by Blume, Crockett, and Friend [1974], but not with the rather large differentials that are implied by the results of Elton and Gruber [1970] and Auerbach [1981].[14]

4. The effect of inflation on portfolio allocation

How are these various conclusions affected by the presence of inflation? From III.3, one can see that inflation has an effect on n_i through the real after tax rates,

[12] This estimate is obtained by assigning to β in II.13a, the representative value of 1, and noting that the coefficient of d' in II.13a can be put at around $2/3$.

[13] At least for tax 1, and dollar weighted positions, as reported in Table 5.

[14] One may suspect that the results of these authors, and others using a similar methodology, may be biassed by the fact that, the higher the dividend yield, the more likely it becomes that institutions that are tax exempt, or not taxed more heavily on dividends then on capital gains, will find it worth while to arbitrage the gains resulting from failure of the ex dividend price to fall commensurately with the dividend.

r_p^m, r_p, and r_c, which appear in T_1, T_2, and T_3, and also through the leverage component of x. The effect through the T coefficients is found to be:

$$\frac{d(n_i/\bar{n})}{dp} = \{-(x_i - \bar{x})[\hat{\theta}_g + (\delta\bar{x})(\hat{\theta}_p\theta_g - \hat{\theta}_g\theta_p)] + [\delta_ix_i - \delta\bar{x})]$$

$$\cdot[\hat{\theta}_g - \hat{\theta}_p + \bar{x}(\hat{\theta}_p\theta_g - \hat{\theta}_g\theta_p)]\}\frac{1}{\bar{n}^2}\frac{d}{dp}(\hat{r}_p/r_p) \quad \text{III.5}$$

where $\bar{x}$ and $(\delta\bar{x})$ are values x and δx that correspond to $n = \bar{n}$ and:

$$\frac{d}{dp}(\hat{r}_p/r_p) = \left(\frac{\hat{\theta}_p\tau_p - \theta_p\hat{\tau}_p}{r_p^2}\right)\left(1 - \frac{p}{r}\frac{dr}{dp}\right) \gtreqless 0, \quad \text{as} \quad \hat{\theta}_p \gtreqless \theta_p \quad \text{III.6}$$

Conditions III.5 and III.6 are somewhat involved but their broad implications can be readily brought out. First, note that the coefficients of $(x_i - \bar{x})$ and $(\delta_ix_i - \delta\bar{x})$ can, both, be taken to be positive for all investors (or funds). We can then infer that for an *above average tax bracket*, for whom, according to III.6, $\hat{r}_p/r_p$ declines with p, there will be a tendency for inflation to increase the relative share of stock i if x_i is above average and the dividend, δ_ix_i, is below average. Conversely, for a below-average tax bracket, will increase if x_i is below and δ_ix_i above average. But this means that inflation tends to increase n_i in portfolios where it was above average to begin with, and to reduce it when below average. In short, inflation has the effect of magnifying the difference between the portfolio composition of high and low tax funds.

If one tries to quantify the above effects, one runs again into the difficulty that the value of leverage appears unrealistically sensitive to the rate of inflation, especially if inflation is accompanied by a fall in the after tax real rate, r_p.

Inflation also tends to raise x through the leverage effect, but this increase does not seem to have systematic consequences for portfolio diversity (except through some increase in the range of x).

From these results one can infer that inflation should have an appreciable effect in increasing portfolio diversity between tax brackets. At the same time, the considerations stated in II.5 suggest that the numerical implications of III.3 and III.6 should be heavily discounted on the ground that nonneutral inflation effects should not, and will not, be taken as permanent by investors. As for empirical evidence, none seems presently available on this issue.

5. Implications of a non-diagonal variance-covariance matrix

In general, the variance-covariance matrix, $[M]$, will not be diagonal, and equation III.3 has to be replaced by:

$$n_i = k\left[T_1 + \frac{1}{\Lambda}\sum_{j=1}^{N}M_{ij}^{-1}(\mu_j^* - r_cD_j)(T_2 - \delta_jT_3)\right] \quad \text{III.7}$$

where M_{ij}^{-1} denotes the elements of the inverse.

Thus, n_i now depends not only on characteristics of stock i, but in principle, on those of all other stocks as well. The meaning of the additional terms in III.7 is readily understood. The first order condition requires that, at the margin, the risk premium for every stock held be equal to that stock's contribution to portfolio variance. But, except when $[M]$ is diagonal, raising n_i^m will contribute to variance (positively or negatively) through the covariance with every other stock in the portfolio, as shown by the last term of II.4; $[M]\mathbf{n}^m = n_i \mu_{ii} + \sum_{j \neq 1} n_j \mu_{ij}^*$. The summation in III.7 corresponds precisely to the summation term above, but with n_j expressed in terms of its ultimate determinants, and thus allows for the dependence of each n on every other one.

To see the implications of this generalization, we note that III.7 requires no change in our conclusions about how a stock's own characteristics interact with tax rates in contributing to the attractiveness of that stock for a given tax bracket. As for the effect of all other stocks, we can think of them as falling into two classes: those which have a net positive correlation with, and may be thought of as substitutes for, stock i, and those, more rare, with a negative net correlation, which behave like complements of stock i. The demand for i declines with the attractiveness of its substitutes and rises with that of its complements.

Despite these indirect influences, one would normally expect n_i to be largely determined by the characteristics of stock i. But one cannot reach any definite conclusion unless one imposes restrictions on the variance-covariance matrix, as was done by Elton and Gruber [1978].

The same difficulty arises in analyzing the implications of the generalization III.7 for portfolio diversity. There is, nonetheless, one broad generalization that may be put forward in this case, suggesting a downward bias in our estimates of section III.3, namely that the prevalence of high substitution is likely to increase the extent of portfolio diversity and specialization until, in the limit, perfect correlation leads to the prevalence of corner solutions.[15]

Concluding Remarks and Agenda

In closing, attention must first be called to certain limitations of the current analysis of the demand side, mainly the failure to impose appropriate constraints on portfolios, such as limitations on short sales and on personal debt. This omission may be particularly serious in the case of debt, since it would appropriately give a greater role to wealth in portfolio composition. As one might expect, with such a constraint, it is no longer true that every portfolio includes every stock (in positive or negative amounts). Firms then have a clientele including only a subset of investors and the parameters of equations like II.12 or II.15 might differ between firms reflecting that clientele.

A second limitation is the failure to model explicitly the market for tax exempt securities, but this task is really trivial and the gap has no appreciable effect on the results.

Finally, closure of the model would require combining the demand analysis with an analysis of the forces limiting the supply of corporate debt. This has actually been done in good measure elsewhere (e.g., DeAngelo and Masulis [1980];

[15] This conclusion is illustrated by the result of Elton and Gruber [1978] for the case of equal correlation, equation (B.4); as ρ tends to unity, the fraction invested in stock j tends to plus or minus infinity.

Williamson [1981]). From the point of view of integration with the demand side, we note that the various supply limiting mechanisms which have been analyzed basically imply that an expansion of debt—total assets constant—must eventually either reduce the expected value of the flow, μ, produced by the firm, and/or cause lD to rise at a decreasing rate, because of decreasing probability of utilizing the costly tax shield. If II.12 is modified along the above lines, it turns into a nonlinear function of D_i with negative second derivative, and V will, in general, be maximized for some interior value of D_i, say $\hat{D}_i$. This maximization will fix the individual and aggregate supply of debt.

REFERENCES

Auerbach, Alan J., "Stockholder Tax Rates and Firm Attributes," forthcoming in *Journal of Public Economics*.
—— and Mervyn A. King, "Taxation, Portfolio Choice and Debt-Equity Ratios: A General Equilibrium Model," forthcoming in *Quarterly Journal of Economics*.
Black, Fischer, "Taxes and Capital Market Equilibrium," Working Paper 21A, Sloan School of Management, M.I.T., April 1971.
——, "Taxes and Capital Market Equilibrium Under Uncertainty," Working Paper 21B, Sloan School of Management, M.I.T., May 1973.
—— and Myron Scholes, "The Effects of Dividend Yield and Dividend Policy on Common Stock Prices and Returns," *Journal of Financial Economics*, Vol. 1, pp. 1-22, 1974.
Blume, Marshall E., Jean Crockett, and Irwin Friend, "Stockownership in the United States: Characteristics and Trends," *Survey of Current Business*, November 1974, pp. 16-40.
Brennan, M. J., "Taxes, Market Valuation and Corporate Financial Policy," *National Tax Journal*, Vol. XXIII, No. 4, 1970, pp. 417-427.
—— and E. Schwartz, "Corporate Income Taxes, Valuation, and the Problem of Optimal Capital Structure," *Journal of Business*, January 1978.
Briden, George, "The Effect of Inflation on Corporate Taxes," unpublished paper, Brown University, 1981.
Chen, A. H. and E. H. Kim, "Theories of Corporate Debt Policy: A Synthesis," *Journal of Finance*, June 1979.
Cordes, Joseph J. and Steven M. Sheffrin, "Taxation and the Sectoral Allocation of Capital in the U.S.," forthcoming in *National Tax Journal*, December 1981.
DeAngelo, H. and R. W. Masulis, "Optimal Capital Structure Under Corporate and Personal Taxation," *Journal of Financial Economics*, March 1980.
Elton, Edwin J. and M. Gruber, "Marginal Stockholder Tax Rates and the Clientele Effect," *Review of Economics and Statistics*, Vol. 52, 1970, pp. 68-74.
—— and ——, "Taxes and Portfolio Composition, *Journal of Financial Economics*, Vol. 6, 1978, pp. 399-410.
Farrar, Donald E. and Lee L. Selwyn, "Taxes, Corporate Financial Policy, and Returns to Investors," *National Tax Journal*, December 1967, pp. 444-454.
Feldstein, Martin, "Inflation and Income Taxes and the Rate of Interest: A Theoretical Analysis," *American Economic Review*, Vol. 66, December 1976, pp. 809-820.
—— and Lawrence Summers, "Inflation and the Taxation of Capital Income in the Corporate Sector," *National Tax Journal*, Vol. XXXII, No. 4, December 1979, pp. 445-470.
Gordon, R. H. and D. F. Bradford, "Taxation and the Stock Market Valuation of Capital Gains and Dividends," *Journal of Public Economics*, October 1980, pp. 109-136.
—— and B. G. Malkiel, "Corporation Finance," in H. J. Aaron and J. A. Pechman, eds. *How Taxes Affect Economic Behavior*, Washington, D.C.: The Brookings Institution, 1981.
Jensen, M. C. and W. H. Meckling, "Theory of the Firm: Managerial Behavior, Agency Costs, and Ownership Structure," *Journal of Financial Economics*, October 1976.
Kalay, A., "The Behavior of the Stock Price on the Ex-Dividend Day—A Reexamination of the

Clientele Effect," unpublished Ph.D. Dissertation, Graduate School of Management, University of Rochester, 1977.

Kim, E. Han, W. G. Lewellen and J. J. McConnell, "Financial Leverage Clienteles, Theory and Evidence," *Journal of Financial Economics*, Vol. 7, 1979, pp. 83–109.

Lewellen, Wilbur G., K. L. Stanley, R. C. Lease and G. G. Schlarbaum, "Some Direct Evidence on the Dividend Clientele Phenomenon," *The Journal of Finance*, Vol. XXXIII, No. 5, December 1978, pp. 1385–1399.

Litzenberger, Robert H., "Debt, Taxes and Incompleteness: A Survey," mimeo, 1980.

——— and K. Ramaswamy, "Dividends, Short Selling Restrictions, Tax-Induced Investor Clienteles and Market Equilibrium," *The Journal of Finance*, Vol. 35, 1980, pp. 469–482.

Miles, James A. and J. R. Ezzell, "The Weighted Average Cost of Capital, Perfect Markets, and Project Life: A Clarification," *Journal of Financial and Quantitative Analysis*, Vol. XV, No. 3, September 1980, pp. 719–730.

Miller, Merton H., "Debt and Taxes," *The Journal of Finance*, May 1977.

——— and Franco Modigliani, "Dividend Policy, Growth, and the Valuation of Shares," *Journal of Business*, Vol. 34, October 1961, pp. 411–433.

——— and Myron S. Scholes, "Dividends and Taxes: Some Empirical Evidence," Working Paper #55, University of Chicago, May 1981.

Modigliani, Franco and Richard Cohn, "Inflation and the Stock Market," *The Stock Market and Inflation*, eds., Anthony Boeckh and Richard T. Coghlan, Homewood, Il: Dow Jones-Irwin, 1982.

——— and ———, "Inflation, Rational Valuation and the Market," *Financial Analysts Journal*, March/April, 1979, pp. 24–44.

——— and Merton H. Miller, "The Cost of Capital, Corporation Finance and the Theory of Investment," *American Economic Review*, Vol. 48, June 1958, pp. 261–297.

——— and ———, "Corporate Income Taxes and the Cost of Capital: A Correction," *American Economic Review*, June 1963, pp. 433–443.

Myers, Stewart C., "Taxes, Corporate Financial Policy, and the Return to Investors: Comment," *National Tax Journal*, December 1967, pp. 455–462.

———, "Determinants of Corporate Borrowing," *Journal of Financial Economics*, November 1977.

Mussa, M., and R. Kormendi, *The Taxation of Municipal Bonds*, Washington, D.C.: American Enterprise Institute, 1973.

Skelton, Jeffrey L., "Bank Arbitrage and the Relative Pricing of Tax-Exempt and Taxable Bonds," mimeo, July 1981.

———, "The Relative Pricing of Tax-Exempt and Taxable Debt," mimeo, April 1980.

Summers, Lawrence H., "The Non-Adjustment of Nominal Interest Rates: A study of the Fisherian Effect," forthcoming in *Symposium in Honor of Arthur Okun*, eds., Peckman and Tobin, 1981a.

———, "Inflation and the Valuation of Corporate Equities," Working Paper No. 824, National Bureau of Economic Research, 1981b.

Taggart, Robert A., "Taxes and Corporate Capital Structure in an Incomplete Market," *The Journal of Finance*, June 1980.

Williamson, Scott H., "The Moral Hazard Theory of Corporate Financial Structure: Empirical Tests," Ph.D. Thesis, Massachusetts Institute of Technology, November 1981.

Errata

Page 257, line 6 of section II: "EBIT" stands for earnings before interest and taxes.

Page 263, first line of part iii: "III.13" should read "II.13."

Page 269, footnote 14, line 3: "then" should read "than."

Debt, Dividend Policy, Taxes, Inflation, and Market Valuation: Erratum

FRANCO MODIGLIANI*

THE FOLLOWING IS A correction to The Presidential Address published in the *Journal of Finance* 37 (May 1982). It first arises in Equation II.1 (p. 258) and results from the fact that, in computing the (real) return from the ith share, I failed to subtract the tax on the nominal capital gain accruing to that share as a result of inflation, namely: $\tau_g^m p S_i$. Accordingly, this quantity should be added with a negative sign in the curly bracket in the first equality of II.1, and in the square bracket in the second equality in II.1 as well as in II.2.

Unfortunately this error turns out to affect a good many of the equations, though its magnitude seems small enough so as not to require significant revisions of any major conclusions. Accordingly, and to save space, I will report specific corrections for some basic formulae and only indicate the nature of required changes in most others.

In Equation II.4, r_p^m should be replaced by $(r_p^m + p\tau_g^m)$, and, similarly, in Equations II.5 to 13a, 15, and 17, whenever r_p appears, it should be replaced by $(r_p + p\tau_g)$. Note in particular that the value of leverage given by II.7 and II.14, now becomes

$$l = 1 - \frac{r_c}{r_p + p\tau_g}\theta_g = q + \frac{q\theta_g}{r_p + p\tau_g}p$$

from which one can infer that the increase in l with inflation is somewhat larger than implied by II.7. In fact, since τ_g is presumably small, less than .1, the coefficient of p in the second equality above is close to q/r_p. Hence, with r_p of the order of 2 to 3 percent, and assuming it is inflation invariant, a rise in inflation from zero to no more than 2 to 3 percent, would be sufficient to double l. The corresponding expression for l^*, the value of leverage when tax savings are uncertain, given at the top of page 265, becomes

$$l^* = \frac{r_p + p\tau_g}{\beta_i \pi + r_p + p\tau_g}l$$

Thus, l^* can still be put at about ⅓ of l when p is zero, but tends to rise relative to l with inflation.

On the right-hand side of II.16, the first term in square brackets is to be replaced by $p(d^*q - \tau_g)$, which implies a somewhat smaller effect on r_p from inflation for given leverage, but a larger impact from leverage, for given p. In

---

* Sloan School of Management, Cambridge, Massachusetts. I am thankful to Lucas Papademos for bringing this error to my attention.

1041

Equations III.1 to III.2c wherever r_p^m/r_p appears, it must be replaced by $(r_p^m + p\tau_g^m)/(r_p + p\tau_g)$ which affects also Equations III.5, III.6. Note that, if capital gains taxes are proportional to income taxes, then the difference between the correct ratio and the original ratio, r_p^m/r_p, is proportional to $p(\tau_p^m - \tau_p)$, from which one can infer the effect of the correction on T_1, T_2, T_3. The right-hand side of III.3a, which needs to be corrected also for another misprint, should be substituted by:

$$\left(1 + \frac{r_p + p\tau_g}{\beta_i^* \pi}\right)\theta_g^{-1}$$

Finally, I am glad for this opportunity to correct a serious omission in the list of acknowledgements in the first footnote of the paper, namely that of Richard Cohn, whose painstaking review of the manuscript was invaluable.

Inflation and Corporate
Financial Management

Richard A. Cohn
University of Illinois at Chicago

Franco Modigliani
Massachusetts Institute of Technology
Cambridge, Massachusetts

In discounting cash flows for capital budgeting purposes, one can, in principle, use either anticipated nominal flows and the appropriate nominal discount rate or the corresponding real flows and rate. But inflation has real effects, especially as a result of taxes, that need to be considered in implementing proper investment and financing decisions. Furthermore, a divergence between the firm's own forecast of inflation and the financial market's can have important implications.

Some recent studies of the effects of inflation on stock valuation suggest that the level of E/P ratios is, surprisingly, directly related to the rate of inflation. If this seemingly irrational relationship is transitory (and there is reason to believe that it is), inflation provides corporate financial managers with intriguing investment and financing opportunities.

Another important aspect of inflation is its implications for final-average pension plans. Because such plans' liabilities are basically real, they should be valued as such for accounting and planning purposes.

341

Inflation and Corporate
Financial Management

INTRODUCTION

In this paper we discuss the principal implications of inflation for corporate financial management. We seek to acquaint practitioners of corporate finance with the lessons of the large though disparate body of academic literature dealing with the interactions between inflation, valuation, and corporate finance.

Our initial concern is: How does inflation change standard financial decisions? We concentrate on the principal corporate financial decisions: investment and financing. We also investigate the implications of inflation for corporate pension plans, an area of some controversy. To limit the scope of the paper to manageable proportions, issues involving inflation and working capital management, including inventory management, and the specialized problems of regulated firms are not addressed. Also, we will gloss over issues which are by now broadly agreed, to focus on those which are less well understood or controversial.

Tools developed in a world of stable prices can provide poor service when applied in a world of inflation if they are not properly reinterpreted and adapted. Inflation raises important questions of proper measurement. Inflation appears to be a potential source of mismeasurement by management and even by the securities markets, a potential mismeasurement which has, in turn, important feedbacks for corporate decisions.

The second section examines issues of investment and financing in a world of rational financial managers and markets. The following section investigates the possibility that inflation has produced distortions in market valuation and considers the implications of distortions for corporate financial decisions. Then, the nexus between inflation and corporate pension plans is addressed and, finally, the paper is summarized.

343

INFLATION AND CORPORATE INVESTMENT
AND FINANCING

Although finance textbooks are often not explicit as to how inflation considerations should be incorporated in capital budgeting decisions, the academic literature is in general agreement with respect to the principal modifications that, due to inflation, must be made in investment analyses. There is reason to believe, however, that corporate financial managers have frequently failed to take inflation considerations properly into account. In a master's thesis at MIT, Naugle (1980) conducted a questionnaire survey of the top 100 companies in the Fortune 500, aimed at ascertaining whether their capital budgeting procedures were rational in the face of increasing inflation. Thirty one, or 47 percent, of the 66 firms from which he obtained valid responses appeared to fail to pass the test of rationality. A thorough discussion of the lessons of the academic literature in this area would therefore seem warranted.

Textbooks almost invariably argue that potential investments should be selected on the basis of net present value (*NPV*). The interesting question, however, is how inflation affects the net present value calculation.

Any present value reflects a future value and a discount rate or set of discount rates. The net present value of an investment opportunity represents the aggregate present value of all the relevant cash inflows and outflows, discounted at a rate usually referred to as the cost of capital.

In the presence of inflation, one must keep clearly in mind the distinction between nominal future net returns (or cash flows) and nominal discount rates (or cost of capital) on the one hand and real flows and discount rates on the other. Nominal future flows are, of course, simply the realized future cash flows. Real cash flows are returns expressed in terms of constant prices, or equivalently, deflated by a "general price index" (that is, by the price index of an appropriately defined broad basket of commodities). Similarly, the one-period *nominal* discount factor (one plus the discount rate) measures the number of *dollars* the investors require next period for giving up $1 this period, while the *real* discount factor measures the number of dollars *of current purchasing power* that investors demand next period per dollar invested now; put differently, it is the number of commodity baskets next period that investors require per initial commodity basket. The relation between the (short-term) nominal rate, say R, and the real rate, say r, is given by the well-known formula $(1 + R) = (1 + r)(1 + p)$, where p is the rate of inflation over the period of the loan. This relation is commonly simplified to $R = r + p$ by dropping the term rp which, for limited inflation, is very small compared to $r + p$.

A basic proposition about capital budgeting, and, more generally, about valuation, in the presence of anticipated inflation is that there are two alternative warranted ways of proceeding. One way is to discount future *nominal flows* at the *nominal discount rate* (the nominal-nominal approach); the other is to discount future *real flows* at the *real discount rate* (the real-real method). (See, e.g., Brealey and Myers (1981), pp. 86–88). It can be readily verified that these two procedures will give the same answer if applied consistently—that is, provided the inflation rate implied by the relation between the nominal and real forecasted future flows is the same as the inflation rate implied by the relation between the nominal and the real rate.[1] The net present values thus obtained will be the same because, while the expected nominal flows (the "numerators") are raised in the nominal calculation, as a result of rising prices, this increase is precisely undone in the present value calculation when the inflation is reflected in the nominal discount rate (the denominator).

Inconsistencies in the estimate of inflation, explicitly or implicitly built into the numerator and denominator, on the other hand, will, generally, lead to wrong decisions. In particular, deflating nominal flows by real discount factors will overstate the true net PV (if inflation is positive), while discounting real flows by nominal discount factors will lead to the opposite bias.

The fact that the two approaches consistently applied will give the same answer does not necessarily imply that one should be indifferent between the two methods. On the contrary, given the extreme unreliability of long-term inflation forecasts, strikingly confirmed by recent experience, there is much to be said in favor of approaches that can dispense from, or depend less critically on, forecasts of forthcoming inflation. We suggest that, because generally effective planning requires, in any event, the development of forecasts of outputs, inputs, and earnings in constant prices, one can make a good prima facie case for the real-real approach as the basic procedure. At the same time, in some instances the nominal-nominal approach may prove more effective. These propositions can be illustrated by some examples.

The case of pure equity financing

Consider the case where a firm is entirely equity-financed. In the absence of inflation (and assuming further that the firm has no significant true growth opportunity), it is well known that the required rate of (equity) return, say ρ, can be inferred from the earnings-price ratio (E/P). The appropriate measure of earnings for this purpose is sustainable, cyclically "noise-free" earnings, not simply the latest 12 months' earnings per share.[2]

The same conclusion continues to hold under inflation except that E/P must now be recognized as the required *real* rate of return. This rate must be distinguished from the nominal rate of return from holding the security, say ρ_n, which includes, in addition to the earnings, also any capital appreciation. Since earnings may be expected to rise at the rate of inflation (at least when inflation is neutral—see below), as long as E/P is constant, the price must also rise at the rate of inflation, producing a capital gain per dollar equal to the rate of inflation, p. Thus, the nominal equity rate is $\rho_n = \rho + p$.

Suppose, first, that after-tax profits can be taken as inflation-neutral, that is, (roughly) proportional to the price level. (Note that this neutrality requires the absence of assets depreciable for tax purposes.) In this case, it should be apparent that the NPV can be conveniently computed through the real-real approach by combining the forecast of the real cash flows, presumably already needed for other purposes, with the estimate of the required real rate of return, inferred from E/P. This approach eliminates altogether the need for a forecast of future inflation. Not only does this save costs, but it also avoids the danger, inherent in the nominal-nominal calculation, that different, and hence inconsistent, forecasts of inflation may be embedded in the estimation of flows and in that of the nominal required rate. This danger is particularly serious when those responsible for cash flow estimates differ from those responsible for choosing the required rate of return.

Consider next the case where inflation is not neutral in that future real flows depend on the future price level (or on the rate of inflation). Even in this case, it may be possible, through a variant of the real-real approach, to eliminate the need for an explicit forecast of inflation, notably where the nonneutrality derives from some component of the net nominal flow being fixed in nominal terms. An important illustration of this problem is provided by the depreciation tax shield, arising when net corporate income is taxed after deducting depreciation. In this case, since tax depreciation is based on historical acquisition cost, the depreciation deduction is fixed in nominal terms once the depreciable asset is acquired and placed in service. Accordingly, to compute the contribution to NPV from the present value of the depreciation tax shield, one should discount these flows at the *nominal rate*. (Note that this implies that inflation, by raising the nominal rate, reduces the value of the tax shield.) This would suggest the need for a forecast of inflation in order to estimate the p term of the nominal discount factor, $\rho_n = E/P + p$. In reality, a good case has been made in the finance literature that the depreciation flow should be discounted at the nominal "riskless" interest rate rather than at the equity rate, which generally includes a risk premium. This conclusion rests on the consideration of the relatively low level of uncertainty surrounding the realization of the depreciation tax shields, compared with other operating cash flows, especially given the opportunity to carry losses back three years for tax purposes. Opportunities to carry losses forward and to enter into sale and leaseback arrangements also serve to mitigate uncertainty associated with the eventual realization of these tax shields.

Now, an estimate of the nominal rate, and in fact of the whole term structure of nominal rates, can be conveniently derived from the yields in the markets for short-term nominal instruments and for bonds of various maturities. They reflect the market consensus about the future of nominal rates, and hence they can be used directly to discount fixed nominal flows like the depreciation tax shield. Thus, even when some flows, such as the depreciation deduction, are fixed in nominal terms, the NPV calculation can be carried out without relying on an explicit forecast of inflation. To this end, one would discount at the equity rate the (inflation-neutral) real cash flow before interest and taxes ($EBIT$), adjusted for taxes (by multiplying by one minus the tax rate), and then add on the depreciation tax shield discounted at the market interest rate.

To be sure, an internal forecast of future prices might reveal an apparent inconsistency with the implicit market forecast of the real rate and of inflation implicit in R. It is important to remember that even in this case rational behavior calls for basing calculations on the market rate, rather than on that implied by the internal forecast. In other words, even if there is sufficient confidence in the internal forecast to conclude that the market will prove wrong, this information is most effectively used not for calculating NPV but, if anything, to "speculate" against the market. Thus, if the market appears to understate future inflation and future rates, the firm could capitalize on this information by borrowing long and lending short.

Nonneutral inflation and debt financing

Of course, the real value of future flows may depend on the rate of inflation (or, equivalently, the nominal value of future flows may not be proportional to the price level) for reasons other than the nominal fixity of the flows. Similarly, the required rate of return may be systematically related to the rate of inflation. This dependence may spring from many causes, such as regulation, features of tax laws, long-term contracts, "fixity" of exchange rates, etc. In such cases, it will generally not be possible to avoid a forecast of inflation, whether one uses the real-real or the nominal-nominal approach.

This same conclusion holds, in principle, when a firm is financed by a combination of equity and debt capital because the real cost of debt capital to a firm depends not only on the market nominal rate but also directly on the rate of inflation. Specifically, in the presence of corporate income taxes of the U.S. description, the real cost per dollar of debt, r_c, can be expressed as:

$$r_c = (1 - \tau)R - p = (1 - \tau)r - \tau p \tag{1}$$

where τ is the corporate income tax rate.

It will be seen from equation (1) that inflation should tend to reduce the cost of debt but for reasons entirely different from the traditional—and largely erroneous—view that it redistributes wealth from creditors to debtors. That redistributional gain can occur only when inflation is, at least partially, unanticipated. But when the inflation is fully anticipated, the nominal rate will tend to rise enough to compensate for the loss of real value of the principal, leaving the real rate unchanged (or possibly even raising it to maintain the real rate after personal taxes). But equation (1) shows that, in the presence of corporate income taxes, inflation reduces r_c even if the real rate is unchanged, the reason being that the income tax allows the deduction of all interest, including that part which compensates the creditor for inflation and is therefore in the nature of a repayment of principal.

Of course, what is relevant for capital budgeting is not the cost of debt funds but the overall real cost of capital, defined as the required tax-adjusted *EBIT* per dollar of capital. The relation between r_c and the overall real cost, say ρ, is conventionally expressed in terms of the so-called weighted average cost of capital:

$$\rho = i\frac{S}{V} + r_c\frac{D}{V} \tag{2}$$

Here, i represents the required rate of return on equity capital;

$$i = \frac{(EBIT - RD)(1 - \tau) + pD}{S} = \frac{(EBIT)(1 - \tau) - r_c D}{S} \tag{3}$$

while the "weights" S/V and D/V represent the shares of equity and debt, respectively, in the overall capital structure. These weights,

S/V and D/V, should be interpreted as representing the target shares for the firm as a whole rather than the share existing at the moment, or contemplated for the particular investment.

It is readily apparent from the above formulas that, with a levered capital structure, consistent capital budgeting will unavoidably require a forecast of inflation. Indeed, in the real-real approach, one needs an estimate of the real required return given by equation (2). Although an estimate of the equity component i given by equation (3) might, in principle, be derived directly from current and historical market data, measuring the real cost of debt capital involves not only the observable long-term rate R but also an explicit forecast of inflation. Nor can this requirement be avoided by relying on the nominal-nominal approach. Indeed, in this case, one needs to measure the nominal required rate of return, which is obtained from equation (2) by adding the rate of inflation, p, to both sides. Using equation (1), this yields:

$$\rho_n = \rho + p = i\frac{S}{V} + [(1 - \tau)R - p]\frac{D}{V} + p$$
$$= (i + p)\frac{S}{V} + (1 - \tau)R\frac{D}{V} \qquad (4)$$

In equation (4) the nominal cost of debt component, R, can be read from the market, but the (nominal) cost of equity requires a forecast of p. Furthermore, as already pointed out, that forecast should be the very same one that underlies the estimate of nominal flows.

However, the conclusion derived from equations (1) and (2), that even the real cost of capital depends on inflation, needs to be properly qualified in that it assumes that r_c can change independently of i. But this independence cannot be taken for granted. Indeed, according to the so-called Modigliani-Miller (1958) proposition, at least under certain conditions (absence of taxes and rational investor behavior), the relation between i and $r_c D/V$ will be such that the overall cost of capital will be independent of leverage, and need not vary when r_c varies.

Recently, Miller, in a well-known contribution (1977) argued that this conclusion is valid, even allowing for taxes. Furthermore, his model would seem to imply that the conclusion would hold as well in the presence of inflation (see Hochman and Palmon (1983)). If he were right, the overall cost of capital would be unaffected by leverage or by the rate of inflation, and could be inferred from the relation between market value and *EBIT* cash flow.

This conclusion, however, has been widely criticized. In particular, Modigliani (1982), (1983), taking into account the role of portfolio diversification neglected by Miller, has confirmed that, in the presence of taxes, (1) some leverage is valuable, tending to reduce the cost of capital, and that, (2) for given leverage, the cost of capital is further reduced by inflation.[3] This result is consistent with the conclusion based on equations (1) and (2), although it should be recognized that the market expectation of inflation also has some indirect effects on the cost of capital through i, depending on the extent to which inflation affects the real rate.

How, then, should one arrive at a forecast of (average) inflation over the life of the project? If one accepts the market long-term rate, R, as the best available estimate of the future of nominal interest rates, the problem is that of decomposing R into the expected real rate and expected inflation implicit in it. Under normal circumstances, a practical way to do that is that of estimating the real rate component. Such an estimate might be derived, without an explicit forecast of inflation, from the history of realized short-term real interest rates. While these rates have not remained constant, they have tended to fluctuate within a fairly narrow spread, resulting in a relatively stable moving average—at least until the last two or three years. One may therefore be able to put together an estimate of the prospective average real rate over the life of the project from past data, with proper adjustment for unusual developments, like the persistent large government deficits currently in prospect.

The estimate of the short real rate so derived might have to be further adjusted for term premium, i.e., systematic differences in yields between short and long maturities. (These premiums, which can be, in principle, of either sign, would again have to be inferred from historical behavior and other considerations.) Subtracting the resulting estimate of the real long rate from the nominal rate yields the implied market forecast of average inflation. Of course, the validity of this method now depends closely on the method followed by the market in projecting real rates resembling that described above. In any event, the resulting price forecast would have to be examined for reasonableness and consistency with explicit inflation forecasts spread through the financial press.

Alternatively, the firm may be in a position to elaborate its own independent forecast from other methods and sources. If available, such a forecast can be used to advantage to improve investment decisions both in terms of measuring the cost of capital or hurdle rate, and in terms of choosing the financing package. The choices in this respect go from financing at a fixed long-term rate with no or minimal call provisions to financing through a sequence of short-term loans, or more realistically, through a longer-term loan, but with interest floating with a short-term rate.

Once we recognize that inflation over the life of the project is uncertain, it appears that the real cost of debt funds is itself uncertain and dependent on the form of financing chosen, as well as on the realization of inflation. We can illustrate this proposition in terms of the real cost of the two limiting types of borrowing mentioned earlier, long-term noncallable L, and floating short-rate loans S. From equation (1) we deduce:

$$\tilde{L} = (1 - \tau)RL - \tilde{p} \tag{5a}$$
$$\tilde{S} = (1 - \tau)\tilde{R}S - \tilde{p} = (1 - \tau)\tilde{r} - \tau\tilde{p} \tag{5b}$$

where the tilde denotes a stochastic (uncertain) variable. Capital budgeting must rely on a measure of expected cost. It is apparent from equations $(5a)$ and $(5b)$ that that measure depends both on the financial package adopted and on what forecast of inflation one is prepared to rely, the market's (implicit) expectations or the firm's own forecast.

We can throw light on the considerations relevant to a choice by considering alternative circumstances. Suppose, first, that the internal forecast is lower than the implicit market forecast (and the difference is not compensated by a higher forecast of the real rate). Then, the internal forecast implies that, over the relevant period, the average value of the short-term rate, RS, will be lower than the current long-term rate (adjusted for term premium). In this case, a very good case can be made, insofar as a project is to be financed, for choosing a short-term type of instrument. One can readily establish that this choice will reduce the expected real interest cost, r_c, by $(1 - \tau)$ $(p_m - p_f)$, where p_m is the implicit market forecast, and p_f the firm's forecast. Furthermore, if the uncertainty of future inflation is substantially larger than that of the real rate, as experience suggests, that choice will also reduce the uncertainty of the r_c outcome. Note, however, that because inflation reduces the cost of capital, the lower inflation expectation will also imply a larger value of r_c than implied by the market expectation, by an amount $\tau(p_m - p_f)$. The cost of capital should be based on this higher cost rather than on the lower implicit market estimate.

Suppose, on the other hand, that the firm's forecast of inflation exceeds the market's. In this case, the minimization of expected r_c will call for long-term financing, especially if it can be made more flexible through call protection (although, as long as the difference in expectations is not large, a case can still be made for short-term financing in order to minimize risk). Supposing long-term financing is adopted, then the firm's higher expectation of inflation will imply a value of r_c lower than that corresponding to the market forecast. In this case, however, it is advisable to maintain the cut-off at the higher level of r_c implied by the market expectation. In other words, any project not having positive net present value for r_c based on market expectations should be rejected even if it has positive *NPV* at the lower r_c implied by the firm's expectation. The reason is that any funds borrowed could be expected to produce a higher return through financial speculation, i.e., investing them in short loans than by investing them in the project.

To summarize, we have shown that capital budgeting can be based indifferently on the real-real or nominal-nominal approach as long as they are applied consistently. We have suggested that, in view of the great difficulties in arriving at reliable projections of long-run inflation, one should give preference to approaches that do not require forecasts of inflation or do not lean heavily on such a forecast. We have illustrated a number of cases where some variant of the real-real approach appears to offer that advantage, though admittedly these are cases of limited practical relevance. We have further shown that the fact that inflation is typically more uncertain than real rates makes a good prima facie case for preferring short- to long-term financing, although the choice should be influenced by the internal expectation of inflation relative to the market's as well as by the availability and cost of call clause and related arrangements.

The discussion of this section has been concerned with identifying rational managerial behavior in a world of rational investors and financial institutions. However, before one finds fault with firms that appear to behave irrationally with respect to inflation, such as those identified by Naugle, one must consider the possibility that the world is not one of rational investors and institutions. We examine the evidence on this question and its implications for corporate decisions in the following section. There are strong reasons to suppose that inflation may produce serious distortions in the value of the market as a basis for the calculation of required returns.

INFLATION-INDUCED DISTORTIONS IN MARKET VALUATION AND IMPLICATIONS FOR INVESTMENT

Inflation and the valuation of common stock

The economics of corporate finance has long been grounded in the normative view that the goal of firms' management should be the maximization of the firm's stock price. In this section we investigate the relationship between inflation and the value of corporate equity.

Common stocks have traditionally been thought of as a sound asset to hold in the presence of inflation, in contrast to assets fixed in nominal terms whose real value is eroded by inflation. This assessment rests on the consideration that stocks of nonfinancial corporations represent levered claims against real assets. If real assets' values tend to keep up with the price level under inflationary conditions, and creditors lose as a result of unanticipated inflation, then stockholders should gain in real terms to the extent that creditors lose. Actually, this popular view needs to be greatly qualified since, as indicated earlier, its validity is limited to the case when inflation is totally, or at least partially, unexpected. When it is fully anticipated, one may expect the nominal interest rate to rise in step with the inflation, leaving no special advantage for the borrower to reap. However, as was also indicated, despite Miller's contrary conclusion, there is reason to believe that inflation should benefit levered corporate enterprises, because of the corporate income tax which allows the deduction of all interest, including the inflation premium component (see Modigliani (1982), (1983)).[4]

The traditional, as well as the tax angle view that inflation is good for corporate stock, has all but been shattered by the experience of the last three decades, particularly the last decade and a half. Numerous researchers have documented a negative relationship between stock prices, or rates of return, and inflation (Lintner (1973), Bodie (1976), Jaffe and Mandelker (1976), Nelson (1976), Modigliani and Cohn (1979)).

The clearest way to view the association between stock prices and inflation is to examine the relationship between earnings-price (E/P) ratios and inflation. Because earnings are inherently a real variable, as was argued above, the E/P ratio is in principle a real rate. But Figure 1 shows an unmistakable positive correlation between the E/P ratio of the Standard & Poor's 500 stock index, based on reported earnings, and the inflation rate. Since the relationship between E/P ratios and inflation is a direct one, the relationship between the price-earnings (P/E) ratio and inflation is inverse.

Of course the question of earnings measurement must be raised in any discussion of the nexus between inflation and E/P ratios. Many are wary, and properly so, of errors induced by inflation in reported earnings as measures of true economic earnings in a period of inflation. There are three types.

Two of these measurement errors are well known, while one of them continues to be poorly understood. The two that are generally

FIGURE 1

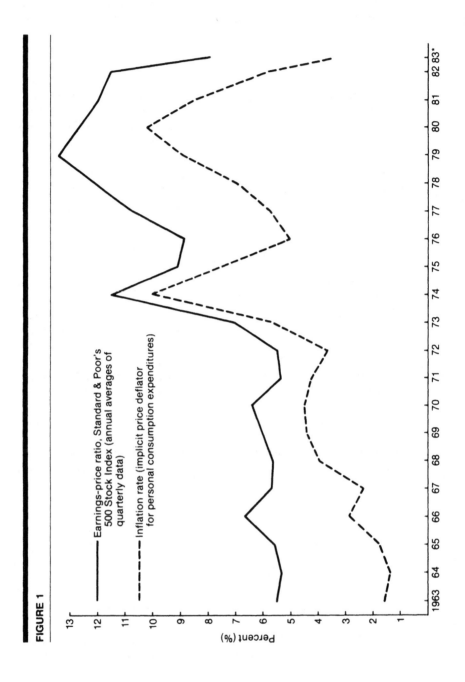

Earnings-price ratio, Standard & Poor's 500 Stock Index (annual averages of quarterly data)

Inflation rate (implicit price deflator for personal consumption expenditures)

understood have to do with measuring the cost of goods sold for nonfinancial firms. First, firms that employ FIFO accounting for inventories tend, in a period of inflation, to expense a cost of goods sold that reflects less than the economically relevant replacement cost of inventories, which is essentially what would be reflected in the use of LIFO accounting. Another way of putting it is that the reported income of FIFO firms includes "paper" gains on inventories. Second, since depreciation is based on the historical acquisition cost of assets, reported depreciation tends to understate depreciation appropriately calculated on a replacement cost basis when there has been a significant increase in the general price level since a substantial fraction of the firm's depreciable assets was acquired. The effect of both these errors is to cause reported income to exceed income adjusted for both biases, to which we will refer hereafter as adjusted income.

The third measurement error, the one that seems not to be generally understood, is important because it works in the opposite direction. Reported income per period is net of *nominal* interest; however, during the period inflation reduces the real value of the principal by pD, where p is the inflation rate. The pD component of interest, as implied previously, is, in real terms, a repayment of principal. True income should therefore be measured net of real interest, not nominal interest. Consequently, in fully adjusting reported income for the effects of inflation so as to produce a true figure, pD must be added back to adjusted income.

Interestingly, Modigliani and Cohn, hereafter referred to as M-C, and Pearce (1982) find that, in recent years, for the nonfinancial corporate sector taken as a whole, year by year, the overestimate of true income due to the first two reasons tends to offset the underestimate due to interest, so that reported income approximates true income fairly closely. While this result applies to the typical firm or to the firms in the stock market as a whole, and thus validates the E/P ratios presented in Figure 1, it need not obtain for any particular firm.

Another way in which to observe the real stock market debacle that has occurred since the onset of inflation in the mid-1960s is to examine what has happened to the ratio of the market value of net corporate debt and equity to the replacement cost of the underlying real assets. This ratio is usually referred to as Tobin's q. The q ratio has fallen from a level somewhat above one in 1964–65 to a level substantially below one, at least until the recent drastic reduction in inflation.

One question raised by the increased E/P ratio in recent years is why corporate investment has not been depressed as a result of the corresponding rise in the cost of equity capital. One possibility is that corporate managers, in implementing the nominal-nominal approach discussed earlier, employ a downward-biased estimate of the weighted-average nominal cost of capital, one based on nominal interest rates on debt but E/P ratios for equity, rather than the correct nominal cost of equity. Naugle (1980) finds some support for this notion.

Why has the E/P ratio risen?

The academic literature contains a number of potential explanations for the observed increase in E/P ratios. One such explanation is taxes. This culprit is cited by Feldstein and Summers (1979) and Feldstein (1980). They point out that FIFO accounting produces paper gains for tax as well as financial reporting purposes. They also point out that tax-deductible depreciation understates true depreciation. As a result of both the inventory and the depreciation effects, the effective tax burden on corporate income rises as a result of inflation,[5] causing a fall in the market value of stock relative to true before-tax earnings, even if the true capitalization rate is unchanged.

This argument could also explain why E/P ratios seem to have risen as a result of inflation. For, at the same time as inflation lowers the value of stock, it also raises reported, relative to true, earnings, through the inclusion of paper profits on inventories and underdepreciation of capital assets, thus raising E/P.

There seems to be little empirical support for this argument. The reason is that the adverse tax effects of FIFO and underdepreciation are virtually completely undone by the offsetting effect of nontaxation of the pD component of earnings, which is deductible for tax purposes in computing corporate income. M-C, Gonedes (1981), R. Gordon (1981), Pearce (1982), and M. Gordon (1983) all find little evidence to support the hypothesis that tax effects account for the real decline in the market value of stock.

Some argue theoretically (see, for example, Carr and Halpern (1981)) that there should be no offsetting tax gain from debt. The reason they give is that interest rates should rise in response to increases in expectations of inflation so as to preserve after-tax real costs of borrowing. They argue that with a corporate tax rate t, the pretax nominal interest rate, R, should be equal to $(r' + p)/(1 - t)$, where r' is the after-tax real interest rate. Thus an increase of one percentage point in p would imply an increase in R of $1/(1 - t)$ percentage points. But Summers (1983) provides ample evidence that interest rates have risen, at most, point for point with inflation, at least until recently.

Feldstein offers another tax-related reason to explain the observed direct relationship between E/P and inflation. He correctly points out that investors are taxed at the personal level on paper capital gains stemming from inflation. He then argues that investors in stock demand higher E/P ratios under inflationary conditions so as to preserve their after-tax real rates of return. However, if this effect on E/P ratios exists, it is likely to be of an inconsequential magnitude. The reason is that the effective tax rate on capital gains at the personal level is extremely modest because of the ability of investors to defer this tax, to determine the timing of the realization of gains, and to escape the tax at death.

Another argument explaining the observed relationship between E/P ratios and inflation is the risk-premium hypothesis of Malkiel (1979); see also his article in Boeckh and Coghlan (1982) and Friend and Hasbrouck (1982). They argue that the risk premium required by investors has been directly related to the rate of inflation, and therefore the equilibrium E/P ratio has also been related to inflation. Risk and inflation may go together because they are both related to such real shocks as the various oil crises. Historically, high and variable inflation may also give rise to uncertainty, though such nonneutrality is not necessarily rational. Of course, if inflation and risk go together, they are impossible to distinguish.

Both Fama (1981) and Geske and Roll (1983) explain the observed negative relationship between inflation and stock rates of return on the basis of real shocks and their effects on corporate profitability. But neither approach serves to explain the rise in E/P ratios.

While Fama does not really explain the link between shocks and inflation, his results can be interpreted in one of two ways. Perhaps diminished rates of return have resulted from decreased profitability, measuring assets at replacement cost with the q ratio unchanged. But then the E/P ratio would have fallen, not risen, and the real value of stock would not have fallen. Or perhaps shocks have reduced profits while the E/P ratio has remained unchanged. But this interpretation is not consistent with a rise in the E/P ratio either.

Geske and Roll tell a rather unconvincing story in an attempt to explain the linkage between shocks and inflation. They see real shocks leading to a fall in government revenue and therefore a rise in the deficit, which is in turn monetized, thus producing inflation. A particularly weak link in this story is that dealing with the monetization of the deficit. In recent years Federal Reserve purchases of

Treasury debt have fluctuated little around a rising trend. While the deficit has increased over this period from a negligible to a modest fraction of GNP, Federal Reserve purchases as a fraction of Treasury new issues have fallen from as much as 50 percent in 1964, for example, when the new issues were small, to 4–9 percent in the last few years (Sinai and Rathjens (1983)). While Geske and Roll might have an explanation for a decline in real profits, the empirical evidence does not support such a claim when profits are measured properly, and their argument does not explain a rise in the E/P ratio.

Another argument explaining the observed rise in the E/P ratio is inherently untestable. This argument suggests that, because of real shocks, E is transitorily high and the true E/P ratio has not actually increased.

On the basis of a set of time-series tests, M-C concluded that inflation illusion largely accounted for the observed relationship between E/P ratios and inflation. They found that investors make two errors in valuing corporate stock as a result of inflation causing nominal interest rates to exceed real rates. First, investors capitalize earnings at a rate that follows the nominal rate rather than the appropriate real rate. Second, investors capitalize adjusted earnings rather than true earnings. This second error applies, of course, only to levered firms. Both errors have the effect of driving stock prices below their rationally warranted level.

The M-C hypothesis implies that E/P ratios are positively related to nominal interest rates even though changes in nominal rates are largely explained by changes in the expected rate of inflation over the period M-C studied, 1953–77. The graph in Figure 2 pictures the relationship between E/P ratios and nominal interest rates since 1963.

The aggregate stock market experience since 1977 would seem to accord quite well with the M-C hypothesis that nominal interest rates move the market. In particular, the rise in P/E ratios that began in August 1982 with the onset of the current bull market and which continued through the first half of 1983 would seem largely related to the concurrent fall in nominal interest rates. There is no prima facie evidence that real interest rates fell during this period. The decline in the rate of inflation over the period was approximately the same as the decline in nominal interest rates. In fact, while nominal interest rates were fairly stable during the first half of 1983, inflation continued to fall.

M-C (1982) performed an extensive set of cross-sectional tests of Malkiel's and Friend and Hasbrouck's risk-premium hypothesis. M-C reasoned that, if the decline in the stock market as a whole

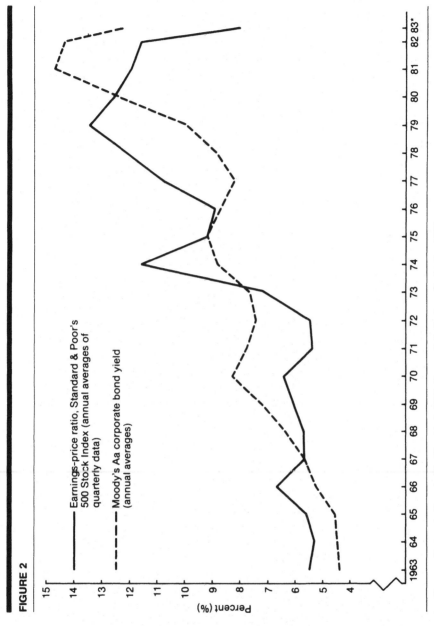

FIGURE 2

Earnings-price ratio, Standard & Poor's
500 Stock Index (annual averages of
quarterly data)

Moody's Aa corporate bond yield
(annual averages)

Percent (%)

15
14
13
12
11
10
9
8
7
6
5
4

1963 64 65 66 67 68 69 70 71 72 73 74 75 76 77 78 79 80 81 82 83*

Sources: *Economic Report of the President*, 1983; *Economic Indicators*, September 1983.

resulted from a rise in the average required risk premium, then stocks with above-average risk premiums (as captured by beta) would experience a greater than average decline in their P/E ratios. What they found, however, was that high-beta stocks experienced below-average declines in their P/E ratios over the 1968–78 period, one characterized by increasing inflation and nominal interest rates. This result is inconsistent with the hypothesis of rising risk premiums for stocks unless the increases in risk premiums are unrelated to beta.

Implications for investment and financing

If one accepts the view that E/P ratios are only transitorily high and that the true E/P ratio has not risen, then inflation has had no real effect on the cost of equity capital. However, if one accepts the strong evidence for a substantial increase in the E/P ratio, then the real cost of equity capital has increased substantially. Investments that do not meet this new high criterion should, on the basis of traditional considerations, not be undertaken.

If the M-C hypothesis is correct, the effect of inflation is to raise the real cost of debt as well as equity. The reason is that the valuation of levered firms is penalized as a result of investors capitalizing adjusted earnings. M-C found direct evidence for this penalty in their cross-sectional study (1982). While Summers (1981) finds empirically that levered firms benefit from inflation, his results conflict not only with those of M-C but also with the difficulties researchers in recent years have experienced in trying to support the "debtor-creditor" or "nominal contracting" hypothesis, the argument that net-debtor firms benefit from unanticipated inflation and unanticipated changes in expected inflation as a result of losses inflicted on creditors of firms (see Bloom et al. (1980) and French, Ruback, and Schwert (1983)).

If inflation causes the valuation of levered firms to suffer as a result of the inflation illusion cited by M-C, then corporate financial managers face a dilemma insofar as retained earnings are not sufficient: They can finance externally only by issuing undervalued equity or by increasing leverage, thereby threatening to make their equity even more undervalued.

But the M-C hypothesis is an inherently unstable view of the valuation process. The undervaluation implied by the hypothesis will tend to disappear over time as inflation and interest rates stabilize. The reason is that if inflation and interest rates cease rising, E/P ratios will stop falling. If then earnings continue to keep up with the price level, which, history indicates, is a reasonable expectation, then investors will find themselves earning an unexpectedly high nominal rate of return equal to the E/P ratio (in the case of the "no true growth" firm) plus the rate of inflation. This return is in excess of expectations as, according to the hypothesis, shares were priced to yield an expected nominal rate of return equal to the E/P ratio. The excess return in turn should make the undervaluation apparent and cause it to disappear. If inflation and interest rates actually fall, this process will be speeded up, for the E/P ratios will also fall.

This scenario of eventual revision implies that firms may wish to consider investments based on their values in the event of such a revision. If the M-C hypothesis is correct, real asset values as reflected in the values of claims in the financial markets are irrationally depressed as a result of investors capitalizing income at nominal rates. Managers can then make real investments which will eventually be vindicated when the undervaluation comes to an end.[6] The capital gains will accrue to the firm's shareholders over the period during which the undervaluation diminishes.

To be sure, this argument favors firms obtaining financing for new investment from their internal cash flow rather than new equity issues. New issues would dilute eventual per share gains. For the same reason, debt financing is to be preferred to new equity financing.

One way to raise the amount of cash flow available internally would be to decide not to increase dividends over time as earnings per share, properly measured, increase. Shareholders should further gain from a reduction in the target payout ratio owing to the adverse tax implications of dividends (Modigliani (1982)).

If a firm perceives that it does not have worthwhile real investment opportunities, even based on an elimination of undervaluation, it may wish to consider purchasing shares of other firms. It may also want to consider a repurchase of its own stock.

INFLATION AND CORPORATE PENSIONS

Inflation has profound but widely misunderstood implications for corporate pension plans. Today the typical corporate pension plan is a single-employer, trusteed, noncontributory, final-average defined benefit plan. Munnell (1982, pp. 173–74) cites a Bankers Trust Company study showing that 76 percent of conventional defined benefit plans, those that base benefit promises on compensation as well as length of service, determined benefits solely on the basis of final-average pay during the period 1975–79. By 1979, 83 percent of these plans calculated average pay on the basis of the last five years of employment.

Participants in such plans probably view their claims as at least partially hedged against inflation. Workers presumably anticipate that the compensation on which their pensions will be based will tend to keep up with the general price level.

If employees' expectations are rational, then one would anticipate that at least part of the pension plan assets would be invested so as to produce a stable real rate of return over time. One would anticipate that the managers of pension plans would seek inflation hedges as investments, at least to the extent such investments could be deemed prudent.

It is probably the failure of stocks and bonds to serve as inflation hedges in recent years that has caused corporate pension plans to become increasingly interested in real estate equities as investments. But this route is not the only one that should be considered.

Values of short-term debt securities are affected adversely by unanticipated increases in expected inflation, but not very much. If a one percentage point increase in the expected rate of inflation causes the nominal rate to rise, say from 10 percent to 11 percent, the fall in the value of a 3-month security would be approximately one quarter of 1 percent. The corresponding fall in the value of a 20-year 10 percent bond whose yield to maturity rose to 11 percent would be approximately 8 percent. Short-term debt instruments by their very nature provide much more stable (inflation-invariant) real rates of return, even under conditions of variable inflation, than long-term bonds.

The market for short-term debt instruments may be such, however, that lenders are willing to pay a premium for liquidity and for inflation hedging, resulting in somewhat lower interest rates (although in the recent inflation the premium has actually been negative). Most pension plans today probably have little need for liquidity. Not only do they enjoy highly predictable short-term cash flows, but many of them also anticipate that they will experience net cash inflows for several years to come. On this account, they may find short-term instruments unattractive.

These considerations suggest that long-term but variable- or floating-rate debt instruments should prove to be an appealing investment for pension plans. Such a demand would probably elicit a corresponding supply.

One can fairly easily imagine a good bit of the demand for mortgage credit being met by pension plans using floating-rate instruments. What would seem to be needed for this purpose, however, is not the standard variable-rate mortage, which has proved to be fairly unpopular among borrowers, but a mortgage which provides a more attractive stream of payments for the borrower.[7]

A particularly appealing candidate for this purpose is what has come to be known as the MIT flexible graduated payment mortgage. This instrument provides the lender with a rate of interest tied to a short-term reference market interest rate, but offers the borrower a relatively low monthly payment at the start. The reason is that the payment is determined on the basis of a fixed annuity factor, based on the real short-term interest rate, applied to the remaining balance. For a fuller discussion of this type of mortgage instrument, see Modigliani and Lessard (1975). Such an instrument, when properly understood, is likely to be appealing to both lenders and borrowers.

Another issue we propose to review is the controversial one about the appropriate way of computing pension plan liabilities in the presence of inflation. Accounting disclosure for corporate pension plans in the United States is governed by the Financial Accounting Standards Board's Statements of Financial Accounting Standards Nos. 35 and 36. These statements require disclosure of the present value of accrued benefits together with the assumed rate of return on investment. It is this rate which is used as the discount rate in determining the present value of accrued benefits. The interesting issue is whether accrued liabilities should be discounted to the present using basically a nominal or a real rate. Economic common sense suggests that the second answer is the broadly correct one. The reason is that under a final-average pay plan, the pension actually paid will depend on terminal wages, and it seems reasonable, for both accounting and planning purposes, to expect wages and salaries to tend to keep up with the price level. The effect of such an assumption on projected pension benefits is profound. If, for example, inflation is no more than 5 percent per year, then, even if real wages are merely constant, the pension actually paid to someone retiring 30 years from now would exceed the current liability to him by something like four and one half times. In essence, the pension fund liability is a real liability that keeps up with the price level. Accordingly, to compute the present value of the liability, one should either take the *future nominal* value and discount it at the *nominal rate*, or take the future *real* liability (i. e., in today's prices) and discount it at the *real rate*; but the future real liability is simply today's accrued liability. The only course that would seem patently wrong is to discount today's accrued liability at the nominal rate; the result would be a serious underestimation of the reserves needed to fund liabilities already incurred.

This seemingly obvious conclusion has, in fact, been challenged recently, notably by Bulow (1981). He argues that final-average plan liabilities are, at any point in time, strictly nominal in nature because the employer can discharge the employee or terminate the pension plan at any time and that such liabilities should therefore be discounted at the nominal rate. He points out that the employer pension liability to any employee participating in a final-average plan at the end of any period is, in effect, a pension based on his past final-average salary. Therefore, the present value of what is owed at retirement is the present value of what is owed currently upon retirement. It follows that to measure reserves needed against liabilities incurred by a fund, the currently accrued liabilities should be discounted at the nominal rate. His view has obtained a good bit of support among financial economists; see, for example, Bodie and Shoven (1983).

Bulow is aware that the promised pension will rise if the employee's final-average salary increases in nominal terms as a result of continued employment. Because pensions in a final-average scheme are based on years of service as well as final-average pay, inflation induces an increase from year to year in the pension promised at retirement that is larger than the inflation rate. Specifically, the linkage to final-average pay causes continued employment to raise the real value of employees' benefits, by preventing inflation from downgrading it. The linkage, in effect, revalues past compensation to the most recent average level.

This analysis seems to imply that, in the presence of inflation, under the typical pension contract, the real compensation provided to the worker in the form of an increment in matured real pension rights increases with the number of years of service. Bulow focuses on this particular and peculiar aspect of the impact of inflation on pension arrangements. He suggests that, if the employer does not fire the worker in order to save himself the growing cost of updating the pension, associated with longer tenure, then one must conclude that that cost should be regarded as incurred in future years as the employee is retained. Therefore, it should not be included in the currently outstanding liabilities, a conclusion justifying the discounting of accrued liabilities at the nominal rather than at the real rate.

But Bulow's approach fails to recognize the multiperiod nature of implicit labor contracts. Employees expect to be rewarded for loyal continuing service, and employers expect to reward them for their loyalty. One of the often-stated and widely recognized goals of pension plans is to reward and encourage employee loyalty. Employees presumably do consider the cost in terms of the ultimate pension reduction before they voluntarily resign to seek employment elsewhere.

But once the employment relationship is viewed in terms of implicit contracts, it is not the case that older workers generally cost the employer more, as Bulow's view would suggest. We suggest, therefore, that Bulow's view is legalistic and swayed by the form rather than the substance of pension arrangements. What matters for the issue at hand is not whether employers have the power to fire workers and thereby freeze their nominal obligation, but whether inflation leads them to significantly greater use of this power. This conclusion is supported by the following considerations. Assume, first, a world without inflation: Then all would presumably agree that a firm's obligation should be measured by discounting currently accrued liabilities at the nominal rate, which, of course, is the same as the real rate. Next, suppose there is steady (neutral) inflation but that the pension rules are such that all pensions are fully indexed: to wages for those who remain employed and to the general price level for those who quit or are fired before retirement. It is apparent that, under these conditions, the liability of the fund must be basically the same as in the absence of inflation. But this clearly means that currently accrued liabilities must be discounted at the same rate as before, namely the real rate.

Next, suppose that the pensions of those who are fired or separated for other reasons are not indexed, but suppose, at the same time, that, in fact, nobody is separated. In this case the cash flows confronting the pension fund are identical to those of the previous two cases. It would, therefore, seem appropriate again to discount the accrued liabilities at the real rate and to reject Bulow's prescription of discounting them at the nominal rate, with a drastic decline in the assessed liabilities of the fund. Of course, in reality there will be some separations. However, in the absence of evidence that inflation has brought about a radical increase in the dismissal of older workers or in the relation between wage rate and age, the best way to handle the problem is to apply nominal discounting only to the liabilities accrued for those who have left. But for those who are working, accrued liabilities would be discounted at the same real rate as without inflation, although some allowance should also be made for the prospective rate of attrition. In addition, of course, allowance should also be made for the fact that the pension, once it begins, tends to remain fixed in nominal terms. Note that because of the two "nonneutralities" just mentioned, inflation does tend somewhat to reduce pension liabilities resulting from a given contract, but nowhere as severely as implied by Bulow's recommended approach.

To conclude, although Bulow's argument is ingenious and stimulating, his conclusion that pensions, based on past service, should be discounted at the nominal rate must be rejected on factual and practical grounds. To a first approximation, and abstracting from changes in real wages, the nominal liabilities at any point in time of a final-average plan are in the nature of real liabilities and therefore should be discounted at the real rate.

SUMMARY

In a world of rational investors and financial institutions, corporate managers should analyze investment opportunities either by discounting the relevant nominal flows at an appropriate nominal rate or by discounting the corresponding real flows at the corresponding real rate. Capital budgeting analyses are complicated by inflation because of the following sources of real effects: taxes, debt, and other long-term contracts. An estimate of the securities markets' expectation of inflation is usually needed in order to implement either the real-real or the nominal-nominal approach. A comparison of the manager's expectation of inflation with the markets' can provide important implications for investment and the desired maturity structure of debt financing.

An examination of the effects of inflation on earnings-price (E/P) ratios provides impressive evidence that the world is not one of rational investors. Inflation appears, through its effects on nominal interest rates, to increase irrationally E/P ratios, with the resulting effect of raising the real cost of equity capital, as well as perhaps the real cost of debt. There is reason to suspect, however, that these effects will prove to be transitory, and managers may want to consider investment and financing decisions that would benefit their shareholders in the event of a decline in E/P ratios.

Inflation has important implications for final-average pension plans. To a first approximation, the liabilities of such plans are real in nature, rather than nominal. They should be valued as such, and managers of assets of such plans should, accordingly, consider investing, to some extent, in an inflation-hedged fashion.

Notes

1. Let x be the nominal and x the real forecasted flow for next period: then, consistency requires $x = \$x/(1 + p)$. Using the nominal-nominal approach, the PV is:

$$\frac{\$x}{1 + R} = \frac{\$x}{(1 + r)(1 + p)} = \frac{x}{1 + r}$$

and the last expression corresponds to the real-real calculation.

2. Earnings should be measured on a fully inflation-adjusted basis, a concept discussed at length in the next section.

3. Specifically, it is shown in Modigliani (1982), (1983) that, abstracting from the effect of dividend policy and assuming that the present value of the capital gain tax is not appreciably different from zero, the cost of capital to a levered firm can be expressed as:

$$\rho = \rho^* \left(1 - l\frac{D}{V}\right), \ l = \frac{R}{\rho^*}(\tau_c - \tau_p)$$

Here, ρ^* measures the required return for an unlevered firm with the same risk characteristics, and τ_p is the average "marginal" personal tax rate, which may be taken as appreciably smaller than τ_c.

4. The tax advantage would exist even if the real rate rose with inflation enough to maintain unchanged the after-personal-tax real rate.

5. Why many corporations, in effect, voluntarily pay taxes on inventory profits must be accounted a great mystery. The usual argument is that corporate managers are reluctant to report lower profits using LIFO than would be shown using FIFO or average cost. But strong evidence exists that investors are not fooled by this reported earnings effect (Sunder (1975)).

6. Much recent merger activity involving acquisitions financed by cash has been based on the idea that the stock market has been under-valuing assets.

7. Black (1980) discusses tax reasons favoring pension plan investments in debt rather than equity securities.

REFERENCES

Bierman, H. Jr. *Financial Management and Inflation.* New York: The Free Press, 1981.

Black, F. "The Tax Consequences of Long Run Pension Policy." *Financial Analysts Journal* (July-August 1980), pp. 21–28.

Bloom, R., P. T. Elgers, J. R. Haltiner, and W. H. Hawthorne. "Inflation Gains and Losses on Monetary Items: An Empirical Test." *Journal of Business Finance and Accounting* (Winter 1980), pp. 603–18.

Bodie, Z. "Common Stocks as a Hedge Against Inflation." *Journal of Finance* (May 1976), pp. 459–70.

――――― and J. B. Shoven. "Introduction to Financial Aspects of the U.S. Pension System." In *Financial Aspects of the United States Pension System.* ed. Z. Bodie and J. B. Shoven. Chicago: University of Chicago Press, 1983.

Boeckh, J. A. and R. T. Coghlan, eds. *The Stock Market and Inflation*. Homewood, Ill.: Dow Jones-Irwin, 1982.

Brealey, R. and S. Myers. *Principles of Corporate Finance*. New York: McGraw-Hill, 1981.

Bulow, J. "The Effect of Inflation on the Private Pension System." National Bureau of Economic Research Working Paper No. C103, March 1981.

Carr, J. L. and P. J. Halpern. "Interest Rate Deductibility and Effective Tax Rates." *Financial Analysts Journal* (May-June 1981), pp. 71-72.

Chen, A. "Uncertain Inflation and Optimal Corporate Investment Decisions." In *Handbook of Financial Economics*. ed. J. L. Bicksler. Amsterdam: North-Holland Publishing Company, 1979, pp. 243-56.

———— and J. A. Boness. "Effects of Uncertain Inflation on the Investment and Financing Decisions of a Firm." *Journal of Finance* (May 1975), pp. 469-83.

Cooley, P. L., R. L. Roenfeldt, and It-K. Chew. "Capital Budgeting Procedures Under Inflation." *Financial Management* (Winter 1975), pp. 18-27.

Fama, E. F. "Stock Returns, Real Activity, Inflation, and Money." *American Economic Review* (September 1981), pp. 545-65.

Feldstein, M. "Inflation and the Stock Market." *American Economic Review* (December 1980), pp. 839-47.

———— and L. H. Summers. "Inflation and the Taxation of Capital Income in the Corporate Sector." *National Tax Journal* (December 1979), pp. 445-70.

French, K. R., R. S. Ruback, and G. W. Schwert. "Effects of Nominal Contracting on Stock Returns." *Journal of Political Economy* (February 1983), pp. 70-96.

Friedman, B. M. "Price Inflation, Portfolio Choice, and Nominal Interest Rates." *American Economic Review* (March 1980), pp. 32-48.

Friend, I. and J. Hasbrouck. "The Effect of Inflation of the Profitability and Valuation of U.S. Corporations." In *Saving, Investment, and Capital Markets in an Inflationary Economy*. ed. M. Sarnat and G. P. Szego. Cambridge, Mass.: Ballinger, 1982, pp. 37-119.

Geske, R. and R. Roll. "The Fiscal and Monetary Linkage Between Stock Returns and Inflation." *Journal of Finance* (March 1983), pp. 1-33.

Gonedes, N. J. "Evidence on the 'Tax Effects' of Inflation under Historical Cost Accounting Methods." *Journal of Business* (April 1981), pp. 227-70.

Gordon, M. J. "The Impact of Real Factors and Inflation on the Performance of the U.S. Stock Market From 1960 to 1980." *Journal of Finance* (May 1983), pp. 553-69.

Gordon, R. H. "Inflation, Taxation and Corporate Behavior." Paper presented at National Bureau of Economic Research Conference on Inflation and Financial Markets, May 1981.

Hochman, S. and O. Palmon. "The Irrelevance of Capital Structure for the Impact of Inflation on Investment." *Journal of Finance* (June 1983), pp. 785–94.

Jaffe, J. F. and G. Mandelker. "The 'Fisher Effect' for Risky Assets: An Empirical Investigation." *Journal of Finance* (May 1976), pp. 447–58.

Lintner, J. "Inflation and Common Stock Prices in a Cyclical Context." *Annual Report*, National Bureau of Economic Research, 1973, pp. 23–36.

Malkiel, B. G. "The Capital Formation Problem in the United States." *Journal of Finance* (May 1979), pp. 291–306.

Miller, M. H. "Debt and Taxes." *Journal of Finance* (May 1977), pp. 261–75.

Modigliani, F. "Debt, Dividend Policy, Taxes, Inflation and Market Valuation." *Journal of Finance* (May 1982), pp. 255–73.

———. "Debt, Dividend Policy, Taxes, Inflation, and Market Valuation: Erratum." *Journal of Finance* (June 1983), pp. 1041–42.

——— and R. A. Cohn. "Inflation, Rational Valuation and the Market." *Financial Analysts Journal* (March-April 1979), pp. 24–44.

———. "Inflation and the Stock Market." In *The Stock Market and Inflation*. ed. J. A. Boeckh and R. T. Coghlan. Homewood, Ill.: Dow Jones-Irwin, 1982, pp. 97–117.

——— and D. R. Lessard, eds. *New Mortgage Designs for Stable Housing in an Inflationary Environment*. Conference Series No. 14, Federal Reserve Bank of Boston, 1975.

——— and M. Miller. "The Cost of Capital, Corporation Finance and the Theory of Investment." *American Economic Review* (June 1958), pp. 261–97.

Munnell, A. H. *The Economics of Private Pensions*. Washington, D.C.: The Brookings Institution, 1982.

Myers, S. C. and N. S. Majluf. "Stock Issues and Investment Policy When Firms Have Information That Investors Do Not Have." Alfred P. Sloan School of Management Working Paper No. 1258–82, Massachusetts Institute of Technology, July 1982.

Naugle, D. G. "Accounting for Inflation in Capital Decisions." Unpublished S.M. thesis, Massachusetts Institute of Technology, 1980.

Nelson, C. R. "Inflation and Rates of Return on Common Stocks." *Journal of Finance* (May 1976), pp. 471–83.

Nichols, W. D. and M. H. Morris. "The Rate of Return Assumption: Insights from the New FASB Statement No. 36 Disclosures." *Financial Analysts Journal* (September-October 1982), pp. 10–15.

Pearce, D. K. "The Impact of Inflation on Stock Prices." *Economic Review* Federal Reserve Bank of Kansas City, March 1982, pp. 3–18.

Rappaport, A. and R. A. Taggart, Jr. "Evaluation of Capital Expenditure Proposals Under Inflation." *Financial Management* (Spring 1982), pp. 5–13.

Sinai, A. and P. Rathjens. "Deficits, Interest Rates, and the Economy." Data Resources Economic Studies Series, No. 113, June 1983.

Summers, L. H. "Inflation and the Valuation of Corporate Equities." National Bureau of Economic Research Working Paper No. 824, December 1981.

_____. "The Nonadjustment of Nominal Interest Rates: A Study of the Fisher Effect." In *Macroeconomics, Prices, and Quantities: Essays in Memory of Arthur M. Okun.* ed. J. Tobin. Washington, D.C.: The Brookings Institution, 1983.

Sunder, S. "Accounting Changes in Inventory Valuation." *Accounting Review* (April 1975), pp. 305–15.

von Furstenberg, G. M. "Corporate Investment: Does Market Valuation Matter in the Aggregate?" *Brookings Papers on Economic Activity* No. 2 (1977), pp. 347–97.

Weston, J. F. and M. B. Goudzwaard. "Financial Policies in an Inflationary Environment." In *Treasurer's Handbook.* ed. J. F. Weston and M. B. Goudzwaard. Homewood, Ill.: Dow Jones-Irwin, 1976, pp. 20–42.

Errata

Page 344, first paragraph, third line from end: delete "to pass."

Page 352, first paragraph, second to last line: insert "rather" before "than." In the last line delete "by."

Page 352, second paragraph, last line: "clause" should read "clauses."

Page 357, third paragraph, third line: replace the semicolon with a comma and insert a comma after "(1982)."

Page 367, endnote 3, third line: "gain" should read "gains."

Page 367, endnote 3, last line: insert "the corporate tax rate," before "τ_c."

MM—Past, Present, Future

Franco Modigliani

Before getting serious about the MM theorem's past and future, I would like to
say a few words about its more intimate aspects—MM *chez-soi* as it were.

Past—Some Reminiscences

One of the most productive days in my life was the day in 1956 when it was
agreed that Merton Miller—then a shy and retiring young man (would you believe
it!)—would sit in my graduate course in "Money and Macroeconomics" at Carnegie
Institute of Technology. It was an exciting course with excellent students. It took a
broad view of the subject. One issue that was covered was the cost of capital as a
determinant of the rate of investment. I had been intrigued by the subject ever since
attending a National Bureau conference on Business Finance at which I gave a (fairly
conventional) paper (Modigliani and Ziman, 1952). But mostly I listened to a paper
by David Durand (1952) in which the possibility that financial structure would not
affect the market valuation or the cost of capital was suggested, only to be rejected as
not relevant to the actual capital markets.

In preparing my lecture dealing with the cost of capital, I was able to provide
(for a world of no taxes) a sort of proof of Proposition I, based on arbitrage. I reported
the result to my class the next day, adding that I didn't really believe my result and
there probably was something wrong. But Miller was instantly captured by the result
because, he said, he knew of a recent paper (Allen, 1954) which provided empirical
support for the result, even though it lacked a convincing rationale. We thus formed,

■ *Franco Modigliani is Institute Professor and Professor of Economics and Finance, Sloan School
of Management, Massachusetts Institute of Technology, Cambridge, Massachusetts.*

there and then, the MM alliance, pledged to go to the bottom of the issue. Except for the fortuitous presence of Miller in this class and his immediate appreciation for the importance of this issue, the MM proposition (Modigliani and Miller, 1958) might never have seen the light. As explained by Miller, the second paper on dividend policy (Miller and Modigliani, 1961) was a derivative of the first, initially spurred by the intention of completing and refining our proof.

The MM paper is unquestionably the most popular of my writings, primarily because it has been, and continues to be, required reading for many graduate business schools. The way it is used in master's programs, as far as I can ascertain, is as a whipping boy—the instructor assigns the paper for reading and then has a feast tearing it to shreds. Wherever I have gone I have found former MBA students recognizing my name and quickly relating it to their MM days. But I have discovered that MM is particularly popular among Washington's young taxi drivers, since an extraordinarily large portion of them seem to be African students going to graduate business schools. Whenever I take a taxi in Washington and find that it is driven by a young man with an accent, I try to bring the subject around to MM and the almost universal result is instant kinship, together with a complaint—one that is actually fairly universal among former MBA students—that the article is much too difficult, though I suspect that they enjoy talking about the article just because it was so difficult (cognitive dissonance!). I am told its essence could have been restated in a more comprehensible fashion.

I have always been ready to apologize for causing trouble, and have offered explanations in our defense. Surely now that the MM theorem seems almost trivial, one could easily present a proof in a more readily intelligible fashion. But not then, when colleagues (academic and practitioner) took it as self-evident that there was a unique, value-maximizing debt ratio and regarded our propositions as plainly preposterous. There was therefore a need for rigorous and varied arguments to show the formal proof of the result and provide the "new" intuition as to why it made sense. Thus the article had never been meant as an expository paper for master's students in business. It was addressed to finance specialists and it was written tongue-in-cheek, not really to demonstrate that leverage could not possibly affect market values in the actual world but to shock those who accepted the then-current naive view that some debt in the capital structure had to reduce the cost of capital even in the absence of taxes simply because the interest rate was lower than the earnings-price ratio on equity.

Present and Future

Miller has reviewed, in his usual masterly fashion, the validity and working of the MM theorem under conditions of perfect market and no taxes. There seems little to add to that subject, especially since, by now, countless alternative proofs of the theorem have been provided.

So I would like to come back to some issues that are still with us—and probably will be for a long time. How should the MM propositions be modified in the presence of taxes and how well do they perform in accounting for observed behavior? For convenience I shall refer to the original Modigliani-Miller paper (1958) as MM; to the correction paper (1963) as MMC; to Miller's "Debt and Taxes" paper (1977) as MI; and finally to my own paper on the subject (Modigliani, 1982) as MO.

The Tax Effect of Leverage

In the MMC paper, after rejecting our conclusions in MM about the effect of taxes as a false start, we proceeded to present a corrected set of conclusions, confident that they represented the final word. According to the new conclusions, the value of leverage increased a great deal: a dollar of debt was supposed to increase value by τ_c, the marginal corporate profit tax rate (labeled τ in MMC, equation 3). By constrast, in MM the increase in value was put at $(r/\rho)\tau_c$ (see MMC, equation 4), where r is the riskless interest rate and ρ the capitalization rate for the relevant "risk class." For the postwar period r/ρ seems to have been on the order of $1/3$.

As I have tried to establish in MO (1982), there are at least two things that are wrong in MMC: (1) we made an unjustifiable assumption concerning the appropriate rate for discounting the flow of tax saving produced by the debt; and (2) we proceeded as though firms were to be valued on the basis of the total stream of net of tax income they generated (dividends plus retained earnings plus interest). This is clearly wrong when there are personal taxes, for then what matters is the total return net of personal as well as corporate taxes and in general, the personal taxes paid depend on the composition of the income generated by the corporation.

Consider first the question of the appropriate capitalization rate for the tax saving from leverage. In MM, after establishing the MM theorem—the independence of market value from leverage in the absence of taxes—we went on to assert (p. 14), "it can be shown that the market value of firms ... must be proportional in equilibrium to their expected return net of taxes"—though proof of this proposition was not actually offered.

The anticipated return net of taxes, X^τ, is the sum of stockholders return net of taxes and interest paid. It can be written as (cf. MM, equation 1)

(1) $$X^\tau = (1 - \tau_c)(\bar{X}Z - rD) + rD = (1 - \tau_c)\bar{X}Z + \tau_c rD;$$

here $\bar{X}$ is the expected return before taxes and interest, and Z is a drawing from a distribution having unit expectation. MM asserted that the value of the firm should be proportional to be expected return, with the proportionality factor given by the capitalization rate ρ appropriate to a risky stream in the given risk class. Thus, the value of an unlevered firm V_u and of a levered firm V_L(cf. MM, equation 4) can be expressed as

(2) $$V_u = [(1 - \tau_c)\bar{X}]/\rho$$

(3) $$V_L = [(1 - \tau_c)\bar{X}]/\rho + (\tau_c rD)/\rho = V_u + \tau_c r/\rho D.$$

Thus a dollar of debt would increase the value of the firm by $\tau_c(r/\rho)$.

In MMC we rejected this result on the ground that the stream of annual tax saving $\tau_c rD$, in contrast to the profit stream $(1 - \tau_c)\overline{X}Z$ was "a sure stream" (MMC, p. 435); therefore it should be capitalized not at ρ but at the sure rate r. In that case, the last term of (3) becomes $(\tau_c rD)/r = \tau_c D$, (cf. MMC equation 3) which is the basic contribution of MMC. With the corporate rate nearly 50 percent at the time of our writing, a dollar of debt would raise the market value of the firm by roughly 50 cents. But this result rests on the assumption that the tax saving stream $\tau_c rD$ is constant, perpetual, and absolutely certain like the coupon of a government bond. In MMC we did mention some limitations to the validity of the assumption, on account of the possibility of changes in the tax code as well as of profits falling below contractual interest. But the much more fundamental objection relates to the assumption that leverage policy can be modeled as the choice of an amount of debt in the capital structure, fixed once and for all. This assumption seems untenable in a world in which the movement of expected profit and size of the firm is widely supposed to follow something like a random walk (or a martingale). It seems much more reasonable to suppose that the leverage policy of the representative firm can be described as aiming at maintaining the debt in a stable relation to the scale of the firm as seen at any given date. If, for example, the appropriate scale variable is approximated by the net of tax cash flow of the (unlevered) firm (or equivalently by market value of the firm V_u), we can write

$$(4) \qquad\qquad \tilde{D} = d(1 - \tau_c)\overline{X}Z$$

where d embodies the firm's debt policy, and the superscript $\sim$ on D is to remind us that future debt, like future profit, is a random variable. Under these conditions total after-tax return of the levered firm X^τ, given by (1), can be restated as:

$$(5) \qquad X^\tau = (1 - \tau_c)\overline{X}Z + \tau_c rd(1 - \tau_c)\overline{X}Z = (1 - \tau_c)\overline{X}Z(1 + \tau_c rd).$$

The essential difference with equation (1) above is that according to (5), the return of the levered firm can be seen as proportional to that of the unlevered firm, $(1 - \tau_c)\overline{X}Z$, the proportionality factor being $(1 + \tau_c rd)$. This proportionality of returns in turn implies that the market value of the levered firm V_L must also be proportional to that of the unlevered firm, V_u, given by equation (2), with the same proportionality factor. Thus

$$(6) \qquad\qquad V_L = V_u(1 + \tau_c rd) = V_u + \tau_c rdV_u$$

$$= V_u + \tau_c rd\left[(1 - \tau_c)\overline{X}Z/\rho\right];$$

or using (4),

$$(7) \qquad\qquad V_L = V_u + \tau_c rD/\rho$$

According to (7) the value of tax saving comes to $(r/\rho)\tau_c D$ which is much smaller than MMC's $\tau_c D$. In fact, for the postwar period, it is only about $1/3$ as large.

One particularly intriguing implication of (7) is that the value of leverage it implies is the same as that implied by the original MM (see equation (3) above). In other words, if one accepts the reasonable notion that the appropriate discount rate for $\tau_c rD$ is ρ rather than r, then the correction paper and its "definitive" corrections need never have been written: Personal taxation aside, the definitive truth was all in MM (though the original way of establishing the result was defective). Of course this is somewhat of an exaggeration since it would be foolhardy to claim that ρ is the appropriate way to discount the tax saving under all circumstances and tax regimes (for example, independently of loss carryover and loss salability provisions). In particular, a number of considerations suggest that the tax saving might be even riskier than the basic cash flow, because of possible changes in interest rates, leverage policy, taxation, and so on. Perhaps if we had been very wise we should have presented the basic valuation formula in a form more general than either MMC or the proposed alternative given by (7) (and the original MM), namely as

$$(8) \qquad V_L = V_u + \chi \tau_c rD$$

Here χ denotes the reciprocal of the discount rate to be applied to $\tau_c rD$, which could range from r to ρ or even higher. Note that (8) retains the MM assumption that the gain from leverage is proportional to D. This may not be strictly true when we take account of bankruptcy cost, and the probability that taxable profits (as reduced by investment tax credit and other factors) may fall short of interest. As a result, V_L might increase with D but at a decreasing rate, at least beyond some point.

But even if MM was more nearly correct than MMC in the treatment of tax saving, it did contain a second error as suggested earlier—namely, neglecting the role of differential personal taxation of the different sources of return produced by a corporation. Clearly, the value of leverage to investors must depend on the amount of additional taxes, corporate and personal, that could be avoided by paying out an additional dollar of corporate returns in the form of interest (which is subject to the personal income tax) while reducing by a dollar stockholders profits (which are subject to the corporate plus the appropriate personal income taxes).

There is presumably broad agreement ever since the Farrar, Selwyn contribution (1967) that under the U.S. system of taxation, what leverage adds to the investor's stream of returns net of both corporate and personal taxes can be written as the second term of (8) but with the corporate tax rate, τ_c, replaced by a different coefficient, say

$$(9) \qquad l = 1 - (1 - \tau_c)(1 - \tau_g)/(1 - \tau_p)$$

where τ_p and τ_g are respectively the personal income and capital gain tax rate. This expression coincides with the coefficient of BL in Miller's equation for the gains from leverage in this volume (except for notational differences).

The common sense of (9) is that if a dollar of profit is received as return on equity, and assuming that none is paid out in the form of dividends, then the tax that will be paid is first the corporate tax τ_c and then the capital gains tax τ_g leaving $(1 - \tau_c)(1 - \tau_g)$. On the other hand, a dollar of interest will be taxed only at the personal level, leaving $(1 - \tau_p)$. In the limiting case when there are no personal taxes or, more generally, capital gains are taxed like all other personal income, that is, $\tau_g = \tau_p$, it can be seen that l reduces to MM's τ_c because it makes no difference in what form corporate earnings are paid out—leverage is valuable only because it saves corporate income taxes. Thus we are back to the MM results. However, if $\tau_g < \tau_p$, then $l < \tau_c$ and could even be zero if, for example, τ_g were zero and $\tau_p = \tau_c$.

However, despite the agreement about l, there is room for disagreement as to what it implies for the market valuation of levered stock. Miller (and others) interpret his above-mentioned equation as indicating what a particular investor would stand to gain or lose from corporate versus personal leverage, given his specific marginal tax rates. He then relies on the notion that the equilibrium market valuation must be determined by the marginal holder and on the existence of tax-exempt securities to conclude that the marginal holders, who determine the market value of l, may (and will tend to) be characterized by a set of individual marginal tax parameters such that $\tau_p = \tau_c$. Combined with the assumption that τ_g is small, this condition, as we have just shown, implies that the market value of leverage, l, is close to zero. In equilibrium leverage is, taxwise, basically worthless.

In my own analysis, inspired by a number of earlier contributions (Brennan, 1970; Elton and Gruber, 1974; Auerbach and King, 1982) I have relied on the mean-variance framework and shown that, because of the benefits of portfolio diversification, it implies that every investor will, in principle, be led to hold a position (possibly negative) in a wide variety of stocks (in principle all), albeit the stocks will be held in different combinations reflecting tax parameters as well as risk preferences. Under these conditions, it turns out that in (8) above, τ_c is still replaced by l, but l is evaluated using not the parameters of the marginal holders as in Miller, but rather an average of all relevant marginal tax rates (since basically everyone is holding all the stocks) but weighted by both tax parameters and risk aversion, which contribute to determine individual holdings.

Since up to the latest tax reform the average capital gain tax was much smaller than the average personal tax rate, my approach implies that l is substantially positive, though well below τ_c. In MO it was estimated that, for the postwar years up to 1988, the coefficient l—computed from estimated average tax rates—could be placed around 0.33. Accordingly, the value of tax saving could be estimated at 0.33 if the saving were capitalized at the sure rate, but only at 0.11 if capitalized at the more relevant risky rate. This last estimate implies that a 10 percent rise in leverage would increase market valuation by just over one percent (instead of some 4 percent if tax savings are capitalized at the sure rate). Obviously this effect is small enough to suggest that, up to the Tax Reform Act (TRA), leverage policy decisions must have been largely swayed by considerations other than tax saving. Note that this conclusion is not very different from that reached by Miller in MI, but it is based on an entirely different reasoning which has quite different implications with respect to the effect of changes in tax laws, such as the most recent one.

One salient nature of this revision is that all sources of income from the corporation—capital gains, interest, dividends—are taxed basically in the same way. Only the capital gains tax remains marginally lower because of the possibility of postponing realization (and the postponement may be quite long under the so-called death loophole). Therefore, to a first approximation, we are back in the regime implicitly assumed in both MM and MMC for which l is approximately τ_c. Note that this conclusion holds whether one accepts Miller's formulation relying on marginal taxes or ours, based on average tax rate, since $l = \tau_c$ for every individual (including tax exempt institutions), and τ_c is of course the same for all, namely 0.34, under the new law.

Miller seems to view this feature of new tax law with alarm for it changes his value of l very significantly: from zero, or close to, in the old regime, to τ_c or 0.34, under the new tax system. He thinks that corporations might engage in an extensive search for types of organizations other than the standard corporate form in response to the loss of favorable tax treatment of capital gains due to retained earnings. He further suggests that they might respond to the opportunity to reduce taxes through leverage, by "gut[ting] the corporate tax with high leverage capital structure." He even suggests that the Tax Reform Act may provide a unique opportunity to test these expectations.

However, according to my analysis, the effects of TRA on leverage should be negligible. The reason is that though Miller and I agree that under the new regime $l = \tau_c = 0.34$, it happens that in the old regime, my estimate of l is very nearly the same number, namely, 1/3 (see above). This is the result of the fact that, although τ_c was close to 0.5, my estimate of l, based on average tax rates, was appreciably lower than l. If the tax gains are capitalized at the risky rate, then both the above figures should be divided by 3. Clearly, there is essentially no change in the value of leverage on account of TRA, and therefore, according to my analysis, no reason to expect any changes in leverage policy. There continues to be an advantage to leverage, though rather small.

With such sharp differences in implications, perhaps the next few years may serve as a crucial experiment. But I don't really expect that we will be so lucky as to witness the experiment. No doubt there will be numerous interferences from exogenous shocks, such as further changes in tax laws, or changes in incentives to leverage other than income taxes, not to mention the possibility of inconclusive results.

The Tax Effects of Dividend Policy

We can readily establish that, at least under the MM (1961) assumption that investment policy is independent of dividend policy, a company paying Δ dollars of dividends will increase the flow of taxes and reduce the net of tax stream received by the public by $(\tau_p - \tau_g)\Delta$—at least as long as the alternative to paying dividends is to buy back equity. The effect on the value of a corporation can then be assessed by capitalizing the stream of tax losses. If we are prepared to assume that the current dividend Δ will be paid forever and with complete certainty, then it would be appropriate to capitalize the tax loss at the sure rate r, following the procedure used by MM in capitalizing the stream of tax saving $\tau_c rD$. The contribution to value from dividends would then come to $(\tau_g - \tau_p)\Delta/r$, implying a very large negative effect—something like a reduction in market value of $8.00 per dollar of dividend, or a decline in value of the order of 8 percent for a 10 percent increase in payout ratio.

But again, there seems to be absolutely no justification for the assumption that incremental tax dollars due to the current dividend will continue forever and with as much certainty as if they represented the interest on a government bond—barring limiting cases where the income itself is certain. How can the dividends be more certain than the stochastic income out of which they are generated? This suggests as one possible reasonable alternative that what the market should value is dividend policy, defined, say, as the long run pay-out ratio or as the proportion δ of (long run) tax corrected expected profits to be paid out in dividends. (It may be argued that many companies have a short-run policy of stabilizing dividends rather than the payout rate. But this is because payout policies typically call for dividends proportional to smoothed income which is, clearly, not inconsistent with our hypothesis of long-run proportionality of dividends and income.) Under the above hypothesis, the expected flow of dividend induced by the policy becomes a stochastic variable:

$$(10) \qquad \tilde{\Delta} = \delta \bar{X}(1 - \tau_c)Z$$

which presumably should be capitalized at the risky rate ρ just like the tax saving from leverage. Accordingly, the loss in value becomes $[(\tau_p - \tau_g)\delta\bar{X}(1 - \tau_c)]/\rho$. This implies that a 10 percent change in the payout δ would reduce market value by less than 3 percent. Needless to say, using ρ as the discount rate seems plausible (a lot more than using r), but alternative formulations could no doubt be defended. Thus, the risk in the tax stream arising from dividends might be greater than for profits because of possible changes in dividend policies (which our analysis suggests should therefore be avoided) or in the tax treatment of capital gains versus ordinary income, of which we have just had a conspicuous example.

If our formulation is reasonably close to truth, then it would suggest that the impact of dividend policy on value by way of tax effect could again easily be swamped by other factors, such as the lack of investment opportunities plus restraint in buying back one's own share because of IRS disapproval or convention, or perhaps even signalling (despite some skepticism on my part).

These considerations bring us back once more to the implication of the grand experiment represented by the TRA. Under the new law, $\tau_p - \tau_g$ will be zero except for the postponability of the tax on capital gains. Thus, the tax cost of paying dividends will have been whittled down to a negligible level, even if not actually to zero. Anyone taking the view that dividends, though quite costly under the old tax law, were nonetheless being extensively paid out (on the average not far from 50 percent of profits) must conclude that with the great reduction in the tax cost of dividends, brought about by the new tax law, there must be a substantial increase in dividend payout. In addition, one should expect other observables, like a rise in the price of firms which were paying large dividends in relation to low-paying firms.

On the other hand, if I am right in holding that the cost of paying dividends was reasonably small under the old tax, then the effect of the new regime should be small at best. For the same reason there should be no significant realignment in the value of firms with different payouts. Here, too, in principle the TRA should provide an opportunity for a crucial experiment, though again I have doubts that the opportunity will be realized. The tax regime may not stay put long enough, and even if it does it may not be easy to interpret observed behavior of boards of directors and markets as unequivocally supporting one model or the other. For instance, little change, which in principle should be interpreted as support of my model, could simply reflect noise in the data, unobservable expectations, or even plain inertia.

And I must recognize in this connection that, ever since my work in analyzing the effects of inflation on market valuation (Modigliani and Cohn, 1979), I have become a bit disenchanted with the indiscriminate use of superrationality as the foundation for models of financial behavior. In particular, I have come to the conclusion that the effects of inflation on valuation derive primarily from the market's failure to understand how to value equities in the presence of significant inflation, which results in systematic, predictable error. I have supported this contention with evidence that this hypothesis can account for the depressed market of the late 1970s and early 1980s, the recovery until 1986, the bubble of 1986–87, and its recent unavoidable bursting (Modigliani 1979, 1980).

I must finally acknowledge that there is one further reason for little short-run changes in dividends (or even leverage policy) which is consistent with alternative valuation models and rational behavior, namely a widely held belief by the public that equal taxation of capital gains and other personal income will just not last. In an era which, in a matter of a very few years, has witnessed the most remarkable sequence of "permanent" changes in business and personal income taxation, there is certainly ample rational grounds for not responding to the changes implied by the latest tax bill as though they were as perennial as the Rock of Gibraltar!

■ *I wish to express my thanks to Robert Merton, Enrico Perrotti and Robert Taggart for reading an earlier version of this manuscript and making many valuable suggestions.*

References

Allen, F. B. "Does Going into Debt Lower the 'Cost of Capital'?," *Analysts Journal*, August 1954, *10*, August, 57–61.

Auerbach, Alan J., and Mervyn A. King, "Taxation, Portfolio Choice and Debt-Equity Ratios: A General Equilibrium Model," 1983, *Quarterly Journal of Economics*, *98*, 4, 587–609.

Brennan, M. J., "Taxes, Market Valuation and Corporate Financial Policy," *National Tax Journal*, 1970, *23*, 4, 417–427.

Durand, David, "Cost of Debt and Equity Funds for Business: Trends and Problems of Measurement." In *Conference on Research in Business Finance*, New York: National Bureau of Economic Research, 1952, pp. 215–147.

Elton, Edwin J., and M. Gruber, "Marginal

Stockholder Tax Rates and the Clientele Effect," *Review of Economics and Statistics*, 1970, *52*, 68–74.

Farrar, Donald E., and Lee L. Selwyn, "Taxes, Corporate Financial Policy, and Returns to Investors," *National Tax Journal*, December 1967, *20*, 4, 444–54.

Miller, Merton H., "Debt and Taxes," *The Journal of Finance*, May 1977, *32*, 2, 261–75.

Modigliani, Franco, "Financial Markets," lecture presented for the Industrial Liaison Program, Massachusetts Institute of Technology, Cambridge, MA, 1980, unpublished.

Modigliani, Franco, "Debt, Dividend Policy Taxes, Inflation and Market Valuation," *The Journal Of Finance*, May 1982, *XXXVII*, 2, 255–73.

Modigliani, Franco, and Richard A. Cohn, "Inflation and the Stock Market." In Boeckh, Anthony, and Richard T. Coghlan, eds., *The Stock Market and Inflation*. Homewood, IL: Dow Jones-Irwin 1979, pp. 3–23.

Modigliani, Franco, and Richard A. Cohn,

"Inflation, Rational Expectation, and the Market," *Financial Analyst Journal*, March/April 1979, *35*, 2, 24–44.

Modigliani, Franco, and Merton H. Miller, "The Cost of Capital, Corporation Finance and the Theory of Investment," *The American Economic Review*, June 1958, *XLVIII*, 3, 261–97.

Modigliani, Franco, and Merton H. Miller, "Dividend Policy, Growth, and the Valuation of Shares," *Journal Of Business*, October 1961, *34*, 411–33.

Modigliani, Franco, and Merton H. Miller, "Corporate Income Taxes and the Cost of Capital: A Correction," *American Economic Review*, June 1963, *53*, 3, 433–43.

Modigliani, Franco, and M. Ziman, "The Effect of Availability of Funds and the Terms Thereof, on Business Investment." In *Conference on Research in Business Finance*. New York: National Bureau of Economic Research, 1952.

Erratum

Page 157, second paragraph, last line: delete "1979."

CONTENTS

Volume I   Essays in Macroeconomics

Part II. The Demand and Supply of Money and Other Deposits

Part III. The Term Structure of Interest Rates

Part IV. The Determinants of Investment

Part V. The Determinants of Wages and Prices

Contents of Volumes 2 and 3

Acknowledgments

Name Index

CONTENTS

Volume 2   The Life Cycle Hypothesis of Saving

CONTENTS

Volume 3   The Theory of Finance and Other Essays

CONTENTS

Volume 4 Monetary Theory and Stabilization Policies

ACKNOWLEDGMENTS

The author, editor, and the MIT Press thank the publishers of the following essays for permission to reprint them here. The selections are arranged chronologically, with chapter numbers in brackets.

"Inflation and the Housing Market: Problems and Potential Solutions" (with Donald Lessard), *Sloan Management Review* 17 (Fall 1975):19–35. Cambridge, MA: Massachusetts Institute of Technology. [10]

"Some Currently Suggested Explanations and Cures for Inflation: A Comment," *Institutional Arrangements and the Inflation Problem*, edited by Karl Brunner and Allan H. Meltzer, Carnegie-Rochester Conference Series on Public Policy, vol. 3, pp. 179–184. Copyright 1976 by the North-Holland Publishing Co. [11]

"Towards an Understanding of the Real Effects and Costs of Inflation" (with Stanley Fischer), *Weltwirtschaftliches Archiv [Review of World Economics: Journal of the Kiel Institute of World Economics]* 114 (1978): 810–833. Tübingen: J. C. B. Mohr (Paul Siebeck). [12]

"Inflation, Rational Valuation and the Market" (with Richard A. Cohn), *Financial Analysts Journal* (March/April 1979):24–44. Copyright 1979 by The Financial Analysts Federation. [13]

"Coupon and Tax Effects on New and Seasoned Bond Yields and the Measurement of the Cost of Debt Capital" (with Robert J. Shiller), *Journal of Financial Economics* 7 (1979):297–318. Copyright 1979 by the North-Holland Publishing Co. [17]

"Inflation and the Stock Market" (with Richard A. Cohn), *The Stock Market and Inflation*, edited by J. Anthony Boeckh and Richard T.

Coghlan, pp. 99-117. Homewood, IL: Dow Jones-Irwin, 1982. Copyright 1982 by BCA Publications Ltd. [15]

"Debt, Dividend Policy, Taxes, Inflation and Market Valuation," *The Journal of Finance* 37 (May 1982):255-273. Copyright 1982 by The American Finance Association. [18]

"Debt, Dividend Policy, Taxes, Inflation, and Market Valuation: Erratum," *The Journal of Finance* 38 (June 1983):1041-1042. Copyright 1983 by The American Finance Association. [19]

"Determinants of Private Saving with Special Reference to the Role of Social Security—Cross-country Tests" (with Arlie Sterling), *The Determinants of National Saving and Wealth*, edited by Franco Modigliani and Richard Hemming, pp. 24-55. London: The Macmillan Press, Ltd., 1983. Copyright 1983 by the International Economic Association. [1]

"Government Deficits, Inflation, and Future Generations," *Deficits: How Big and How Bad?* edited by David W. Conklin and Thomas J. Courchene, pp. 55-71. Copyright 1983 by the Ontario Economic Council. Reprinted by permission of University of Toronto Press. [4]

"Inflation and Corporate Financial Management" (with Richard A. Cohn), *Recent Advances in Corporate Finance*, edited by Edward I. Altman and Marti G. Subrahmanyam, pp. 341-370. Copyright 1985 by Richard D. Irwin. [20]

"Life Cycle, Individual Thrift and the Wealth of Nations," Nobel Prize lecture, pp. 260-281. Copyright 1986 by The Nobel Foundation. [2]

"Government Debt, Government Spending and Private Sector Behavior: Comment" (with Arlie Sterling), *The American Economic Review* 76 (December 1986):1168-1179. Copyright 1986 by the American Economic Association. [6]

"The Economics of Public Deficits," *Economic Policy in Theory and Practice*, edited by Assaf Razin and Efraim Sadka, pp. 3-44. London: The Macmillan Press, Ltd., 1987. Copyright 1987 by Assaf Razin and Efraim Sadka. [5]

"The Growth of the Federal Deficit and the Role of Public Attitudes" (with Andre Modigliani), *Public Opinion Quarterly* 51 (Winter 1987): 459-480. Copyright 1987 by the American Association for Public Opinion Research. [7]

"Fiscal Policy and Saving in Italy since 1860" (with Tullio Jappelli), *Private Saving and Public Debt*, edited by Michael J. Boskin, John S. Flemming, and Stefano Gorini, pp. 126-170. Copyright 1987 by Basil Blackwell. [8]

"The Determinants of Interest Rates in the Italian Economy" (with Tullio Jappelli), *Review of Economic Conditions in Italy*, no. 1 (1988): 9-34. Rome, Italy: Banco di Roma. Copyright 1988 by Banco di Roma. [9]

"The Role of Intergenerational Transfers and Life Cycle Saving in the Accumulation of Wealth," *Journal of Economic Perspectives* 2 (Spring 1988):15–40. Copyright 1988 by the American Economic Association. [3]

"MM—Past, Present, Future," *Journal of Economic Perspectives* 2 (Fall 1988): 149–158. Copyright 1988 by the American Economic Association. [21]

NAME INDEX

Kormendi, R., 130, 143, 147, 150–154, 156–158, 183, 224n, 226, 230n, 253, 399, 411
Kotlikoff, L. J., xv, 46, 48, 49, 55, 60–64, 67–79, 81, 82, 144
Kravis, I. B., 25, 34
Kuh, E., 19, 33
Kuznets, S., 37

Ladd, Everett, 173n, 176
Laidler, David E. W., 283n, 301
Lasch, Christopher, 166, 176
La Terza, S., 144
Laub, P. Michael, 371n, 391
Lease, R. C., 394, 399, 407, 411
Lecaldano, E., 144
Leff, N., 10, 33, 43, 55, 144
Lessard, Donald, xvii, 291, 299, 302, 353n, 435, 441
Lewellen, Wilbur G., 374, 392, 394, 399, 407, 411
Lindvall, John R., 385, 391
Lininger, Charles A., 175
Lintner, John, 294, 301, 323n, 324n, 425, 441
Lipsey, R. E., 103
Litzenberger, Robert H., 399, 403n, 411
Livingston, Miles, 374, 391
Long, Clarence D., 83
Lovell, Michael, 323n
Lucas, Robert E., Jr., 297, 301
Lydall, H., 46, 55, 66, 83

McCallum, John S., 373, 391
McConnell, J. J., 399, 407, 411
McCulloch, J. Huston, 373, 389n, 391
MacDonald, G. M., 29n, 33, 34n
Majiluf, N. S., 441
Malkiel, B. G., 394, 404, 404n, 429, 430, 441
Mandelker, G., 425, 441
Mariano, Roberto, 147, 158, 183, 207, 226
Marotta, G., 144
Masera, R. S., 144
Mason, A., 55, 135, 144
Masson, Andre, 49, 55, 80, 83
Masulis, R. W., 394, 403, 409, 410
Mayer, T., 51, 55
Meckling, W. H., 394, 410
Menchik, P. L., 47, 51, 52, 55, 59, 62, 63, 64, 66, 81, 82, 83
Meyer, L. H., 129, 145
Miles, James A., 402, 411
Miller, Merton, xx, xxi, 310, 323n, 393, 394, 395, 398, 399, 400, 403n, 405, 407, 411, 421, 422, 425, 441, 443, 444, 445, 447, 448, 449, 452
Mirer, T. W., 46, 55, 66, 83
Mishkin, Frederic S., 324n
Modigliani, Franco, xxi, 4, 5, 6, 8, 10, 13, 33, 37, 39, 40n, 43, 45, 50, 52, 53, 55, 56, 59, 60, 61, 68, 69, 69n, 83, 103, 114, 120,

121, 123, 130, 135, 140, 144, 147, 149, 153, 154n, 155, 158, 183, 184, 186, 187, 189, 195, 209, 222, 223, 224n, 226, 231, 234, 235, 248, 252, 253, 273, 291, 292, 292n, 294, 299, 301, 302, 310, 323n, 324n, 332n, 342, 353n, 393, 395, 398, 399, 403n, 404, 405, 411, 421, 425, 427, 433, 435, 439n, 441, 443–445, 451, 452
Moore, John H., 301
Morcaldo, G., 226, 253
Morgan, J. N., 54, 61, 62, 82, 83
Morris, M. H., 441
Mortensen, J., 110, 143
Mueller, Eva, 175
Munnell, A. H., xiv, 34, 45, 56, 433, 441
Mussa, M., 399, 411
Myers, Stewart C., 323n, 324n, 394, 411, 417, 440, 441

Naugle, D. G., 416, 424, 428, 441
Neisser, H. P., 42, 56
Nelson, Charles R., 294, 302, 323n, 425, 441
Nichols, W. D., 441
Niebuhr, W. David, 373, 392
Nordhaus, William D., 323n

Okun, Arthur M., 283n, 285n, 302

Pagano, Marco, 144, 153, 158, 226, 231, 252, 253
Palmon, O., 421, 441
Papademos, Lucas, viii, x, 294
Parkin, Michael, 283n, 301
Pearce, D. K., 427, 428, 441
Pechman, Aaron, 26, 34
Pechman, Joseph A., 287, 302
Peterson, Paul E., 175n, 176
Phelps, Edmund S., 283n, 284n, 302
Pieper, Paul, 126, 143
Plosser, C., 232, 253
Poole, W., 258n, 273
Projector, D., 45, 51, 56, 61, 62, 63, 73, 81, 83
Protopapadakis, A., 110, 144
Pye, Gordon, 373, 386, 392

Racette, George A., 374, 392
Ragazzi, Giorgio, 324n
Ramaswamy, K., 403n, 411
Rappaport, A., 441
Rasche, R., 253
Rathjens, P., 430, 442
Reagan, Ronald, 87, 89, 102, 160, 161, 169, 180
Reid, Margaret, 37, 56
Reimers, C., 12, 34
Repaci, F. A., 189, 223, 224, 226
Ricci, U., 38, 56
Robichek, Alexander A., 373, 392
Roenfeldt, R. L., 440
Roll, R., 429, 430, 440

Printed in the United States
by Baker & Taylor Publisher Services